WOMEN'S STUDIES IN THE ACADEMY
Origins and Impact

Edited by

ROBYN L. ROSEN

PEARSON

Prentice
Hall

Upper Saddle River, New Jersey

Library of Congress Cataloging-in-Publication Data

Women's studies in the academy : origins and impact/edited by Robyn L. Rosen.
    p. cm.
  ISBN 0-13-092928-X
    1. Women's studies—United States—History. I. Rosen, Robyn L.

HQ1181.U5W6553 2004
305.4'07'073—dc21

2003048277

Publisher: Nancy Roberts
Administrative Assistant: Lee Peterson
Production Liaison: Frances Russello
Marketing Manager: Marissa Feliberty
Marketing Assistant: Adam Laitman
Manufacturing Buyer: Mary Ann Gloriande
Cover Art Director: Jayne Conte
Cover Design: Suzanne Behnke
Cover Art: Kathy Warinner/SIS, Inc.
Cover Image Specialist: Karen Sanatar
Composition/Full-Service Project Management: Terry Routley/Carlisle Communications
Printer/Binder: Hamilton Printing Company
Cover Printer: The Lehigh Press, Inc.

Pearson Education LTD. London
Pearson Education Singapore, Pte. Ltd
Pearson Education, Canada, Ltd
Pearson Education-Japan
Pearson Education Australia PTY, Limited

Pearson Education North Asia Ltd
Pearson Education de Mexico, S.A. de C.V.
Pearson Education Malaysia, Pte. Ltd
Pearson Education, Upper Saddle River,
  New Jersey

10 9 8 7 6 5 4 3 2 1

ISBN 0-13-092928-X

Contents

PART II
Women's Studies in Action
107

HISTORY 109

SCIENCE 147

SOCIOLOGY 183

COMMUNICATION 234

ENGLISH/LITERARY STUDIES 269

Preface

This book was born out of a simple, yet ambitious goal: to create text that would introduce undergraduates to Women's Studies. It has been a labor of love. Twenty years ago I took my first undergraduate Women's Studies class at Brandeis University. This class quite literally changed the course of my life. It introduced me to the politics of knowledge, the problem of bias, and the promise of feminism to make things at least better, if not right. Declaring a minor in Women's Studies, I pursued my education with a renewed intellectual vigor that emanated from the dynamism I now saw all around me in the academy. In the academy that I was now operating debates raged, ideas were challenged, theories revised, and new questions asked. This was an intellectual ferment into which that I could sink my teeth, and it was made manifest to me through Women's Studies. The attraction of being part of this ferment led me to graduate school where I studied women's history and began to lend my own voice to the great conversations I had been introduced to as an undergraduate.

Twelve years ago I taught my first undergraduate class. It was an Introduction to Women's Studies class, and I was free to shape it in any way I saw fit. As I developed the course, I gave a lot of thought to the question: How can I introduce something as big and complex as Women's Studies in a sixteen-week semester and make it coherent, accessible, and exciting? There seemed so much to cover. I decided that the class had to accomplish two purposes: to place the development of Women's Studies in a historical perspective and to show its impact on the academy. First, I wanted my students to know where Women's Studies had come from—a long struggle for access to and then reform of higher education. This struggle for women's education emanated from the larger struggle for political and legal rights for women. Simply put, there would be no Women's Studies without social movements dedicated to women's equality. In fact, Women's Studies has been described the "academic arm" of feminism. Furthermore, as the first section of this text will show, there would be no movements dedicated to women's equality without other movements for racial and social justice. It is vital to show today's undergraduates how their present experience of the academy has been influenced by the struggles of the nineteenth and twentieth centuries. Specifically, cultural notions of womanhood, ethnicity, class, and race shaped both access to and the curricular contents of higher education. In other words, the historical factors that help to explain why women and minorities either weren't educated or were educated differently than white males also help to explain what the curriculum looked like in past eras and why its content has been challenged by "outsiders."

Placed in this context, the emergence of Women's Studies in the late 1960s is properly recognized as an accomplishment of great historical significance. Historicizing the development of Women's Studies encourages recognition of the rich and varied contributions made by women's movements. Furthermore, this context makes clear the integral connections between Women's Studies and other struggles for inclusion and social justice. It highlights the political nature of education—who has access to it, what it looks like, and what its purposes are—and reminds today's students that these issues still require their attention. The omission of this history does a disservice to our students. It is my hope that beginning this class and this text with this history will provide students with the perspective necessary to both appreciate and think critically about their education. I encourage all students to use their experience with Women's Studies to evaluate what and how they are taught, what purpose their education serves, and how critical perspectives enhance the dynamism and relevance of the academy.

Once the historical dimensions have been established, the next objective of this text is to show students exactly what Women's Studies has accomplished. All scholars ask and answer questions in a manner particular to their disciplinary training. For example, historians might ask about the causes and origins of events and then collect and analyze certain kinds of evidence to ascertain answers, while literary critics might ask about the themes or symbolism in a text and apply theoretical and analytical strategies to explore these questions. Feminist scholars have altered the questions scholars ask and the strategies and methods used for answering those questions. In 1995, feminist scholar Peggy McIntosh of the Wellesley College Center for Research on Women encapsulated the power of Women's Studies in the following manner: "Once you've been given permission to connect the dots in a different way, you see new constellations in the sky." This astute and poetic observation captures the essence of my dedication to Women's Studies as a crucial aspect of education. Feminist scholars have literally changed the face of the curriculum: they have connected the dots in different ways and uncovered new constellations. These new constellations are represented by the wide array of readings in this text. It presents a sample of the most innovative and exciting work by feminist scholars over the past thirty years to show students exactly how Women's Studies has transformed the academy. Students will be introduced to research that has been shaped by a feminist consciousness and commitment and can decide for themselves whether this perspective improves or detracts from accuracy or a quest for the "truth."

Feminist scholarship is wide ranging. Just as feminism is not monolithic, neither do feminist academics always (or even often) agree on research agendas, methodologies, or institutional frameworks. Despite these differences, certain important themes and tensions emerge from this collection, which helps to characterize and capture the impact of Women's Studies in the academy.

First, feminist scholars have participated in lively debates regarding the value of objectivity/neutrality traditionally associated with scholarly inquiry versus the value of engagement traditionally associated with political consciousness and activism. Feminists find themselves trying to resolve this tension or defy its existence. This text provides examples of scholars arguing that feminist perspectives make scholarship stronger and more accurate, and others who flout objectivity as a false construct perpetuated precisely to exclude women's voices.

Second, students will be introduced to the tension in feminist research between the pull of the disciplines and the notion that studying women is an intrinsically interdisciplinary project. Some of the readings reveal the aim of ridding a discipline of masculinist bias and using feminist perspectives to enhance theory building and research methods. Others decry the artificial boundaries among disciplines and search for more holistic ways to investigate and solve problems.

Third, feminist scholars have confronted the problem of what to do about sexism in the academy. They ask, "Can we work within existing frameworks to clean things up, or do we need to 'throw out the master's tools'?" This collection contains examples of feminists who find value, despite flaws in their disciplinary tradition, and seek to correct flaws while adhering to conventional criteria and standards. Others can be labeled "rejectionists" as they attempt to create bold, new theories, methods, and standards.

Fourth, many feminist scholars seek ways to recognize and include more women in their theory, research, and teaching so as not to replicate the exclusionary practices that Women's Studies was created to combat. This text presents varying approaches to grappling with this tension of inclusion/exclusion. Some scholars particularly see feminist perspectives as a window into oppression of all kinds, sensitizing them to the ways that the academy has ignored or distorted the experience of marginalized people.

This text is designed not to proselytize or promote a certain perspective, but to present the very idea of perspective to undergraduates who are new to both the academy and encountering Women's Studies and feminism for the first time. It is built on the premise that the academy is a rich and dynamic arena where people dedicated to a search for answers to profound questions engage in lively debates that require disciplined thinking and credible research. This is the academy that this book seeks to introduce to undergraduates. This is also the academy that may get lost in pursuit of major field requirements, professional training, or simply classes that emphasize acquiring information over the assessment of that information. Put simply, the most significant thing Women's Studies can do is help students to think critically. Even more fundamentally, it can serve to introduce the whole concept of critical thought as it offers examples of how scholars have mounted challenges to hegemonic concepts across the disciplines and altered the very nature of those disciplines. In this sense, the introduction to Women's Studies presented in this text is offered in service to all students pursuing any discipline.

I sincerely appreciate the suggestions from the following reviewers: Suzanne J. Cherrin, University of Delaware; Valerie Burks, Florida Atlantic University; Eden Torres, University of Minnesota; and Garlena Bauer, Otterbein College.

Robyn L. Rosen

PART I
Historical Background

This section, divided into three parts, offers a historical perspective to help students understand the field of Women's Studies. Unlike many other disciplines that have been part of the academy for centuries, Women's Studies is a relatively recent addition. Its programmatic birth can be traced directly to the political and cultural upheavals of the 1960s and 1970s. However, the story of Women's Studies begins much earlier when the first generation of education reformers demanded access to higher education for women. The historical record shows that access to and the content of education has been shaped by cultural norms and values. Women and people of color have been stigmatized as intellectually inferior and pushed outside of the academy and toward domesticity or vocational training. Courageous individuals learned to make arguments for education that alternatively incorporated and defied these norms. In the first part, *Women and Education*, the documents show the obstacles women faced in seeking an education and how these obstacles differed among women of different races and ethnicities.

The next part, *The Politics of Education and the Birth of Women's Studies,* provides insight into the political context out of which this new field was created. Movements dedicated to racial justice, peace, free speech on college campuses, student involvement in administrative and curricular matters, and women's liberation all contributed to the development of Women's Studies. The student movement, the civil rights movement, the anti-war movement, and the women's movement shared the conviction that education was fundamental for advancing social justice. Their critiques of the educational system ranged from attacks on a biased curriculum to condemnation of institutional policies and regulations, and even incorporated a discussion of pedagogy and the power relations between teacher and student. One key accusation that ran through all these criticisms was the political nature of education. Reformers and activists insisted on evaluating the educational system on the grounds that it either contributed to or undermined unequal power relations among whites and people of color, the poor and the rich, women and men, teachers and students. Once the politics of education was uncovered, curricular, institutional, and pedagogical changes followed. Women's Studies can be better understood as being one component of those changes.

The last part, *Visions of Women's Studies,* offers examples of how feminists have interpreted and decided to confront the politics of education. One writer advances the notion that students should seek personal empowerment through education. This line of thought has been one of the most controversial and perhaps also most popular aspects of the Women's Studies agenda. Another scholar presents a challenging argument for the existence of conceptual barriers that hinder both educational reform and gender equality. She contends that curricular transformation is needed and explains the difference between radical and liberal feminist perspectives, which will be explored thoroughly in Part Two. Students will also be introduced to a pragmatic and broad vision for curricular reform that posits the importance of faculty development and reminds us of the full meaning of inclusiveness.

Women and Education: A Historical Perspective

This section contains both primary documents and secondary sources that shed light on the historical development of Women's Studies in the United States. We begin with Florence Howe's "Feminism and the Education of Women" to provide an introduction to the connections between the history of women's struggle for education and the emergence of Women's Studies in the late 1960s. She shows that notions of womanhood shaped the kind of education women received throughout the nineteenth and into the twentieth centuries; education reformers had to grapple with these cultural norms in designing their schools and curriculums. A document by education reformer Catharine Beecher illustrates this dynamic. The next three documents complicate this history by drawing attention to the ways that ethnicity and race compounded gender conventions to further frame the parameters of education in the nineteenth century. Elizabeth Ihle provides an overview of black women's education after emancipation. She shows that African-American women faced some of the same obstacles to education as white women, but also many others that were particular to their race. Anna Julia Cooper's speech from 1893 offers an example of an African-American woman presenting a cogent argument for women's education in the face of rampant racism in American culture. Next, in Devon A. Mihesuah's examination of a seminary for Native American girls, we see the ways that race, class, and color add new dimensions to Howe's three stages.

Critical Thinking Questions

1. Do you agree with Howe's characterization of the curriculum as "male-centered"? What might account for this bias, and what are the justifications for and problems associated with it?
2. Howe claims that the ideology behind the first phases of women's fight for education still exists today. To what extent do you agree with this? What evidence exists to support this claim?

3. What is Beecher trying to prove about women in this excerpt? To what extent do her ideas sound conservative and to what extent radical in the context of the time period?
4. Compare the different perspectives of white southerners, white northerners, and African-Americans on educating black women after emancipation.
5. Based on the Beecher and Cooper documents, how did cultural attitudes and norms shape the kinds of arguments women made for educational access?
6. What conclusions can be drawn about perceptions of gender, class, and race among students at the Cherokee Female Seminary from their own writings in the school newspaper?
7. In what ways did African-American and Native American women's educational opportunities and experiences differ than those of white women? In what ways were they similar?

1

Feminism and the Education of Women

(1975)

Florence Howe

In 1974–1975, I held a Ford Fellowship for the Study of Women in Society. This essay grew out of an attempt to discover, through a search in the archives of nine colleges and universities, whether curriculum could be found that was not male-centered and male-biased. Although the search for curriculum that included women's history and achievements proved nearly fruitless, the research illuminated controlling feminist assumptions behind three phases of women's education; the seminary movement that established secondary education for women; the movement that established eastern women's colleges and coeducation; and the current women's studies movement.

I wrote this essay during a visit to the University of Utah in the spring of 1975, when I worked in the archives following a week's teaching to faculty and administrators of an intense introductory seminar in women's studies. The program, organized by Shauna Adix, director of the Women's Resource Center, included a comfortable residence in which I was able to write. Once written, the essay became a lecture for the 1975 series organized by Judith Stiehm of the University of Southern California, and was eventually published by that university's press as part of a volume called The Frontiers of Knowledge.

In the summer of 1976, when I was invited to guest edit an issue of Boston University's Journal of Education, *called "Toward a History of Women's Higher Education," I revised the essay. The special issue appeared in August 1977, and that version appears here.*

WHEN I WAS A STUDENT my least favorite course was history. I had not learned to ask two or three questions which might have made a difference: *why? who made that decision? and what were women doing?* Indeed, I accepted history as given—a bland series of causes and results of wars. Even revolutions were uninteresting, the Civil War without human content, and the terms of U.S. presidents undistinguishable except for Washington, Lincoln, and the current (second) Roosevelt. I am not exaggerating. Although history repeated itself several times in the course of my education in New York City's public schools and Hunter College, I went off to graduate school without the slightest interest either in U.S.

Howe, Florence. *The Myths of Coeducation.* Indianapolis: Indiana University Press, 1984. By permission of author.

history or literature, and for the next four years, I read British literature and as little British history as I could manage. It never occurred to me that *people* wrote history, ordinary people. It never occurred to me that women were part of history and might write the story of their lives.

During my first year in graduate school, at Smith College, I chose to study Chaucer and Shakespeare, and to write my master's thesis on Jonathan Swift's poetry, especially those poems addressed to or about women. Twenty-five years ago when I made that choice I was not a feminist, nor could I ask any questions of history. Although I chose to write about Swift's poems *on women*, my thesis projected one message only: Swift was an underestimated poet; indeed, I urged that he was a fine poet. Somehow, I had become his admirer and defender. My thesis explicated his poems, pointing to their well-constructed rhymes and rhythms, and urging the cleverness of their content, even on occasion the appropriate wisdom of their views as expressed formally (aesthetically) by the poem. Never did I question the status of women in the eighteenth century, or seek information about the comparative privileges allotted to women and men, nor did I attempt to evaluate Swift's views of women as compared with those of other men. And while I had read other eighteenth century *men* of letters on women—it would have been difficult to avoid the Spectator and Tatler papers or Pope's Belinda or Dr. Johnson's view of a woman preacher—never did I consider searching for actual writings of *women*.

Feminist scholars today are saying that women's history, achievement, and future are important enough to be studied, described, analyzed, reported, worked for. A philosophical feminist says "I care about women and I believe that their history and ideas are important to all of us." When I call myself an ideological feminist, I am adding something to the philosopher's position: I am saying that I will put my research at the service of changing the status and conceptions of women. Indeed, my research project exists because I have very real questions to ask about where women's education is going, where it should go, and how it should get there. I am interested in history because I hope that it will shed some light on the present and into the future. I want to understand not only how we got into some of our current predicament but how we are to proceed from here.

The questions I began my research with have grown out of a decade of discovering that the curriculum I had been taught from, and the very one I was passing on to my students, was male-centered and male-biased. White middle-class, male-centered and male-biased. Countless studies and other kinds of analysis now exist to demonstrate the cultural sexist bias of the curriculum. But I should like to make clear that when I was in college or graduate school, I never once heard the names of Elizabeth Cady Stanton or Susan B. Anthony, much less studied their writings and achievements. I had not read Simone de Beauvoir until 1965, when I was also reading Betty Friedan and Doris Lessing. For me, and for other feminists of my generation and for those younger as well, Kate Millett's *Sexual Politics* was the ultimate "awakening." For people like me who need information as well as experience, Millett was, like de Beauvoir and Friedan, compelling.

LOST MASTERPIECES REGAINED

Because of those books and others that I was reading even as I was trying to teach women students about their histories and to move them to talk about their lives, hopes, and desires, I began to realize that if we were to change the education of women, to provide them with the history and role models they needed, we would have to write new materials or republish those that had been lost. The Feminist Press was born during this period and at the end of its first year, Tillie Olsen offered our first lost treasure, *Life in the Iron Mills* published anonymously by Rebecca Harding Davis. I mention this work because it is an admitted masterpiece, lost to us from its first date of publication in 1861, and hence until this time never part of the curriculum. If Davis had been lost, we speculated, how many others were there? That question began to haunt me, as The Feminist Press began to publish other lost American women writers: Charlotte Perkins Gilman, Agnes Smedley, Kate Chopin, and Mary Wilkins Freeman. Why had they been lost? Who had "lost" them?

I began to wonder, what if I had read these writers when I was young? How might I have turned out? And then again, other possibilities occurred; perhaps they had not been lost originally at all? Perhaps it is the history of these writers that has been lost? Perhaps young people, at some moment in time, had read these lost women writers? Perhaps, I speculated, young women in college late in the nineteenth century had read feminist fiction writers and other feminist prose writers as well. Perhaps they had also studied, as part of their history courses, the history of efforts to gain suffrage?

And perhaps you are beginning to see how I got from my dissatisfaction with the male-centered curriculum and my desire for a more balanced and inclusive curriculum to wanting to know whether there had ever been anything different. I need to add to this process one other factor. Since the women's movement touched the campus, an entire educational phenomenon known as women's studies had developed. I added to my list of questions about the history of the curriculum, others about the future of women's studies. Should women's studies courses and programs be developed into separate departments with their own faculties, budgets, majors, etc.? What *is* the future of women's studies? What is the best way to design a curriculum that reflects and is immediately responsive to the explosion of knowledge created by the academic arm of the women's movement?

What have I found? My research has made clear to me three phases of feminism—we are now in the third— each of which has involved a battle over the function of women's education and the content of the curriculum. They each involve separatism and considerations of vocational purpose as well as the ideas of marriage and motherhood. The first phase, in part because it's the earliest, is the most persistent and the most acceptable to men. For these reasons, it is still a force with us today.

The women who fought the first series of battles for women's higher education in the early nineteenth century were all interested in training teachers. They thought women ought to be educated separately from men, and for one specific vocational purpose: teaching. Three-quarters of the history of women's education in the nineteenth century—whether at single-sex or at allegedly coeducational institutions—is also the story of teacher education. We should all know these names: Mary Lyon, the founder in 1837 of Mt. Holyoke, Emma Willard, the founder in 1821 of Troy Seminary, Catharine Beecher, the founder of Hartford Seminary, and later of other schools for women in the midwest—they and others worked through the early decades of the nineteenth century to persuade men of the value of educating their daughters, and to raise funds for the establishment of permanent institutions for women. Abbott Female Academy, for example, was founded in Andover in 1829 for "young ladies who may wish to qualify themselves to teach." According to A. C. Cole, Mary Lyon's "original and primary objective," as she worked through the 1830's to raise funds for opening Mt. Holyoke Seminary, "was the preparation of teachers for the millions crying for education, especially in the great valley of the west." Mary Lyon's scheme was the education of very young women—admission to Mt. Holyoke at 14 was not unusual—who would teach two to four years "and then marry and become firm pillars to hold up their successors." This "circulatory system" (we would use the term "revolving door") she thought "would accomplish more for education than a smaller number of teachers who, by not marrying, could devote 20 or 30 years to the profession." So teaching was not only an appropriate profession for women; it was also work that might also prepare them for marriage, child-rearing,

and the community support of education. In my archival research, I have found person after person, female and male, commenting or arguing that the education of women would not be wasteful, since even if women married and therefore had to resign from their teaching jobs, their preparation was also useful for their expected work as mothers. Such statements, appearing either in catalogues themselves, or in presidents' reports, justify to a board of regents or to a legislature or to parents the expense involved in educating women who, it was expected, could only work for a short period before marriage and motherhood. It is important to understand also that early feminists regarded teaching as the prime means of earning a modest livelihood in dignified and socially useful work—for women who could not or would not marry.

DEVELOPING A DIFFERENTNESS: FEMINISM'S FIRST PHASE

The feminist ideology behind such views of women's education emphasizes women's separate and subordinate social role. Women *are* different from men, such feminists proclaimed, but women ought to be allowed to develop that differentness for the greater good of society. As Emma Willard, founder of Troy Seminary in 1821 put it, schools for women ought to be "as different from those appropriated for the other sex, as the female character and duties are from the male." Cole writes that the purpose of such education is twofold: "implanting proper ideas and ideals in future mothers" and "furnishing properly trained teachers." The ultimate purpose is gloriously ideal: "to elevate the standards of morality and of public education." The ideological portrait is incomplete, however, until we add Catharine Beecher's belief in the value of self-sacrifice. All of these women were devout Christians. For them, teaching was an appropriate female activity, since it was the obverse, secular version of clerical ministerial work. Women teachers were the secular arm of the church. Teachers were missionaries, moral emissaries, shapers of young minds and destinies. The purpose of women's education, according to Catharine Beecher, was to enable women not to *shine*, but to *act*." And to *act*, of course, in a moral manner for its own sake, to act as well as a natural role model for others and also as a deliberate moulder of others' morality. Catharine Beecher believed that women were especially suited for the role of moral teacher, since women were a) "continually striving after purity" and b) "consistently" self-sacrificial in their own homes (as contrasted with man's domestic selfishness and generosity outside the home). The key ideas for this entire generation of feminist educators were sacrifice and service: women, they argued were better equipped than men for sacrifice and service. Mary Lyon described for her students the opportunity for sacrificial service by "going to destitute places in the West to labor" (meaning to teach in Ohio and Kansas). As to pecuniary rewards, she said, "Ladies should not expect more than a mediocrity—less than $100 a year usually."

Not surprisingly, a significant number of men including some in charge of education decided that it was in their interest to heed the pleas of these feminists. All the members of the boards of trustees and many of the financial supporters of early seminaries and later women's colleges and normal schools were men. And why not: these feminists were not challenging the status quo; they were simply saying we can do the child-rearing job better than men and even, on a massive scale, more economically. Not only are we women naturally more moral and thus more ready to maintain law and order; we are also self-sacrificing and thus we will do all this for the benefit of society and not our own pocketbooks. What has been called by Michael Katz "the feminization of the teaching force" satisfied both the nineteenth century's social need for an economical and efficient system of public education and the early feminists' need for work that could be rationalized without social offense.

Later in the century, with the extension of secondary education, and the growth of public education into large systems, once again the twin needs for "economy and improvement" continued the demand for women teachers. As Katz describes the process, a school committee in Quincy, Massachusetts., in 1874, called for the establishment of large schools of 500 students, in which "one *man* [italics added] could be placed in charge. . . . Under his direction could be placed a number of female assistants." "Females," the *male* committee explained in 1874, "are not only adapted, but carefully trained, to fill such positions, as well [as] or better than men, excepting the master's place, which sometimes requires a man's force. . . . " And as if that were not enough reason—and of course idealogically from a male point of view it is not—the committee added, "and the competition is so great [among women for these jobs and between women and men] that . . . [women's] services command less than one-half the wages of male teachers."

On reflection, perhaps none of this history is surprising. How then does a subservient population convince its masters to allow it an increment of social progress? Obviously, by convincing the masters of its usefulness for *them*. Thus women teachers offered both an economical means to accomplish public education and the willingness as well to do so within the terms of the society's patriarchy. Women were to be taught how to teach the moral code that kept them enthralled in the first place. As Catharine Beecher surmised, as early as 1829, therefore, "the most important object of education" is not the acquisition of knowledge, but rather, "the formation of personal habits and manners, the correction of the disposition, the regulation of the social feelings, the formation of the conscience, and the direction of the moral character and habits." These, she said, "united, [are] objects of much greater consequence than the mere communication of knowledge and the discipline of the intellectual powers."

If the function of such teaching was ultimately moral uplift for the nation, the curriculum had to reflect this goal. Teachers were the secular arm of the church; women as teachers could accomplish the moral reformation of character, a duty that the church allowed only to males. The curriculum that followed from such educational principles and goals supported patriarchy, and taught women that the home or, temporarily, the classroom

was their appropriate domain. Catharine Beecher proposed a department of moral philosophy, one that would teach such principles to future teachers, as the center of her school.

The curriculum differed in kind and degree from the classical education offered to their brothers through most of the nineteenth century; it simply verified women's distinct, traditional roles as nurturant servers of domestic life, propagators, child-rearers, and teachers. Women had to learn enough mathematics, and later science, as well as other skills to enable them to be adequate teachers of young children and older adolescents, but their education was not meant to develop in them the capacity either to question knowledge or to investigate its outer reefs. They learned enough to teach rudiments to others, not to shape knowledge anew.

But education, as we know, is not entirely predictable, or controllable. We often do not teach students what we want to or what we think we are teaching. The relationship between the early feminist educators I have described and the later ones connected to the founding of women's colleges after 1870 has not yet been traced in detail. The differences between the two groups concern us here, since we are the inheritors of their battle, the second major educational battle for women's education in the nineteenth century. That battle was initiated by the feminists we know as suffragists.

THE DRIVE FOR EQUALITY: FEMINISM'S SECOND PHASE

Both Elizabeth Cady Stanton (who went to Emma Willard's Troy Seminary) and Susan B. Anthony (who was of course a teacher) believed that there were *no intellectual differences* between men and women and that therefore their education ought to be identical, just as their social, economic, and political rights ought to be identical. Their ideology insisted on equality, not on distinct and separate spheres. And the founders of such colleges as Smith and Wellesley, as well as the second president of Bryn Mawr, M. Carey Thomas, put this theory into practice by adopting for women's colleges a curriculum identical to that proscribed for the men of Harvard and Yale. Women, such educators announced, could and should do all that men do. So long as Latin and Greek were staples of that curriculum, women at Bryn Mawr or Smith did Latin and Greek. As the curriculum broadened at Harvard and much later at Yale, so did it at the elite women's colleges.

Here is M. Carey Thomas in 1901, arguing that the education of women must be no different from the education of men. "The burden of proof, is with those who believe that the college education of men and women should differ." She too focuses on vocation, but it is that of the professions themselves. Her argument rests on the assumption that "women are to compete with men" in these professions. "There is no reason to believe that typhoid or scarlet fever or phthsis can be successfully treated by a woman physician in one way and by a man physician in another way. There is indeed every reason to believe that unless treated in the best way the patient may die, the sex of the doctor affecting the result less even than the sex of the patient." She argues similarly for bridge-building. And for cooking. And she concludes on a high note of warm optimism: "This college education should be the same as

men's, not only because there is, I believe, but one best education, but because men and women are to live and work together as comrades and dear friends and married friends and lovers, and because their effectiveness and happiness and the welfare of the generation to come after them will be vastly increased if their college education has given them the same intellectual training and the same scholarly and moral ideals."

But what of the coeducational colleges and universities, the Oberlin of 1837 and the land grant colleges after the Morrill Act of 1862? At Oberlin, the story is not an heroic one. Jill Conway, Smith College's president, tells it in an essay in *Daedalus:* Oberlin was a "manual-work school" aimed to fill "an ever-expanding need [in the west] for trained clergy":

In its early informal manifestations young men would undertake to work the land of a minister with sound theological knowledge if he would instruct them in return for their labor. Oberlin was a formal institutionalization of such an arrangement since the college was linked to a five hundred-acre farm where it was hoped that the students would produce enough in crops to reduce the cost of their education considerably. No sooner was the experiment launched, however, than it became clear that another element of cost could be eliminated if there were women students who could carry out the domestic chores in return for instruction. Once admitted to the college, they duplicated there all the existing service roles of women within the domestic economy. Classes were not held on Mondays so that the women students could launder and repair the men's clothes. Cooking and cleaning were done on a careful schedule outside classroom hours, and the women students always waited on table. Thus, the effect of the experiment was hardly consciousness-raising, and those few feminists, like Lucy Stone, who were early Oberlin graduates were radicals on such questions before they entered college.

Women were offered a secondary curriculum, called "literary," and when one young woman wanted to study theology, she was not encouraged. Antoinette Brown, a close friend of Lucy Stone, attended classes in theology for an extra three years, though she was ignored, indeed was not ordained or graduated.

Kansas State Agricultural College, now KSU, one of the first of the land-grant colleges to be founded one year after the Morrill Act was passed, was a pioneer in practical education for an increasingly broad base of U. S. citizenry. Thus, in 1874, President John A. Anderson issued a *Hand-book* arguing the uselessness of a classical education in Latin, Greek, and Mathematics—a very daring departure—and calling for the establishment of three curricula: 1) agricultural; 2) mechanics [engineering]; and 3) women's. The women's curriculum, an early version of home economics, provided for classes in "Special Hygiene" appropriate to women, "Gardening" (mainly ornamental without the "manual labor that should be done by men"); "Household Economy" (including "Lectures upon household chemistry. . . . embracing cooking, domestic management, and kindred topics"); "Sewing"; and "Farm Economy" (including those operations which usually come under the supervision of the farmer's wife or daughter, and which are not included in "Gardening" or "Household Economy," such as butter and cheese mak-

ing, etc.) as well as literature and other subjects appropriate to women. Kansas also pioneered courses in industrial arts, but these were also carefully sex-typed: printing, for example, in its English origins a woman's industry, was in the 1874 curriculum, labeled as being only for men. (It was delightful to find it open to both sexes by the president who followed in 1884.) At other co-educational universities, it is clear that women were channelled into the Normal course—teacher education—and not into mining and metallurgy or chemistry or other areas of hard science, law, or medicine.

And so there were two possibilities for women at coeducational institutions—and these are still possible today: first, women could and did study alongside men in such courses as United States history or the literature of Great Britain or introduction to psychology; in each case, the curriculum is designed for and geared to the interests and achievements of men—it is male-centered and male-biased. Second, they might "elect" to study in almost totally female "professional" ghettoes—elementary education, for example, or home economics, or nursing. In these courses, the curriculum is for the most part still either male-centered, or male-biased. That is, women studying home economics assume that the traditional patriarchal forms of marriage and family organization are desirable, inevitable and unchangeable.

CHALLENGING MALE HEGEMONY: FEMINISM'S THIRD PHASE

Through the early twentieth century, the education of women in women's colleges or in coeducational institutions continues to alternate between two poles: 1) that women need a separate, special education, for vocations especially suited to them—teaching, nursing, or social work, for example; and 2) that women are men's intellectual equals and may therefore study appropriately all that men do. In both cases women had to accept the traditional view of themselves as entering acceptable female-typed activities or professions; or taking the more daring position of M. Carey Thomas— that women were as good as men and therefore could do *men's* work. In neither case, however, had there been a challenge to male hegemony *over the curriculum or knowledge in general*. In neither case had women said, *no, we are going to redefine the terms of the work world. We are going to look closely at the history of work and reassess job classifications in the rational light of social needs today*. That is the crux for us today. In the past women either carved out for themselves an area that men did not want anyway—domestic science, for example,—or they studied within the purview of patriarchal knowledge, that is, history as males have seen it or known it, or science, with priorities established by males.

David Reisman, writing an introduction to Jessie Bernard's *Academic Women*, in 1964 conveniently summarizes the state of higher education for women with particular relevance for teacher education: "Women," he says, "prefer to be *teachers, passing on a received heritage* and responsively concerning themselves with their students while men of equivalent or even lesser ability prefer to be *men-of-knowledge, breaking the accustomed mold* and remaining responsive not to students but to the structure of the discipline and their colleagues in the invisible university" (italics added).

Just one decade later, this sentence sharply divides the past from the present. Yes, that was the way it was for 150 years. Now it is different. Women will no longer be content to pass on "a received heritage"; rather, women have become, are becoming—in Riesman's terms women-of-knowledge, "breaking the accustomed mold."

I am of course referring to women's studies which is truly a new third feminist development: for the first time, feminists in an organized manner are querying education's ultimate—the curriculum and the sources of that curriculum, knowledge itself. Unlike the work of earlier feminists like Catharine Beecher, moreover, the queries are not confined to women's domestic sphere, but encompass many of the traditional male bastions, especially history, economics, sociology, psychology, anthropology, law, even medicine, as well as literature and the arts. Indeed, without the perspective provided by what we call women's studies, I could not have traced the preceding historical patterns.

The new feminism is profoundly different from both forms of the old. We are not saying today simply allow us a piece of the turf (Beecher, Lyon, and others of the first wave), or let us into your castle (second wave: equality), but rather, let us reexamine the whole question, all the questions. Let us take nothing for granted. Most definitely, let us refuse to pass on that "received heritage" without examining its cultural bias. And since women are half the population, they are black as well as white, poor as well as rich;

they include all religions, all national and ethnic origins; since one can not talk about women as a monolith, examining cultural bias becomes a complex task far reaching in its potential for education.

Let me give you one immediate and practical example of current feminist thought about the curriculum. The study of American literature is not as old as the history I have been describing. The formal study of both English and U.S. literature hearkens back less than one hundred years. A staple of such reading has been Benjamin Franklin's *Autobiography*. Why? Why have millions of us, female and male, members of minorities and whites, rich and poor, been handed Franklin and not Frederick Douglass, for example, or Elizabeth Cady Stanton? (I will not detour into questions of literary style, but both Douglass and Stanton are at least as interesting on that count as Franklin.) New feminists are not saying that Franklin ought to be dismissed, but they question his value as a single representative of *all* Americans. They are saying that the life of one white male is inadequate to represent us all. His life needs to be viewed in the company of at least one woman's life; moreover, white lives are, alone, inadequate: they ought to be viewed in the company of at least the lives of some members of minorities.

This is a very different kind of feminism from Beecher's or Thomas's. Beecher might have wished her students to study women's lives, but not Stanton's, for she was a rebel. Beecher thought that women teachers should learn their subordinate role exceedingly well. She did not think women ought to get into politics; their domain was the household and, temporarily, the classroom. M. Carey Thomas, president of Bryn Mawr shortly after its founding about a hundred years ago, would also not have argued for reading Stanton's life. She wanted her students to be prepared exactly as men were: that meant follow the leader; read whatever men decided should be read.

New feminists like me are saying, let us look closely at this polyglot. Let us review the hierarchy. Let us study not one life as an example of how we were or how we ought to be. Let us study many lives—and what is equally important—how these lives related each to each. Why could Elizabeth Cady Stanton in 1830 not follow her brother to Union College? What college could a black person, male or female, attend in 1830? And how did educational deprivation affect her/his life opportunities? More significant, read in the company of Franklin's life, Stanton's tells us that bearing and rearing seven children did not prevent her from accomplishments that can be matched by few males in any century.

Today we inherit both sets of ideas about the education of women. Many of us still see women as more honest, virtuous, self-sacrificing, and hence more willing to serve—meaning teach—than men. Others see women as potentially as capable as men in all their spheres. Those who hold this view will usually adopt males as models for female accomplishment. You have heard women say, we can do anything men can do. Feminists today may be found in both those camps still, though I believe that the central thrust of today's feminists needs to be different. Especially for those engaged in education, feminism in all its forms is once again of central importance. On the one hand, we live in a sex-role defined job world. The ghettoes of nursing, elementary education, office work, and social work are realities. On the other hand, we are urging students to enter "nontraditional"—meaning male—fields.

And now I would like to return to my original questions. Have I learned—am I learning—anything of immediate use for those of us engaged in women's studies? The answer is yes and no. Yes, it seems to me that for the first time I can see the logic of our feminist history and I can appreciate and understand those women who struggled for their modest goals. Without them, we could not now be insisting that we too have a history to study and learn from. Their achievements as well as their strategies and tactics are not inconsiderable and we have much to learn from them.

On the other hand, there is no clear model for the current development of women's studies. That is not difficult to understand. It means that we have not been, before today, convinced of our own hegemony over knowledge, our own power to decide about the curriculum. That is an awesome responsibility. We do not want Harvard as a model. We know its severe limitations. We do not have elder brothers, male patrons to establish institutions and guidelines for us. Remember, it was Henry Durant, the intrepid founder of Wellesley who not only said, "Women can do the work. I give them the chance"—but who made it possible. Today *we* are making it possible, and the revision of the curriculum, the explosion of knowledge in all fields, will effect men as well as women. Ultimately—perhaps I am describing still another century of struggle—we will live in a very different educational world.

So, you have heard my optimism, and I am sometimes attacked for it, especially by academics who are "naturally" cynical. Reading history has made me more, rather than less, optimistic. In 1938, when Virginia Woolf wrote a militant feminist and pacifist book called *Three Guineas*, she asked the key question that new feminists have been asking these past ten years. She looked at "our brothers who have been educated at public schools and universities" and asked other women, "do we wish to join that procession or don't we? On what terms shall we join that procession? Above all, where is it leading us, the procession of educated men?" Woolf concluded that the procession was leading us downhill to war and to the degeneration of the human race. Yet she saw no way out but to join the procession, even on its own terms, for women then were powerless—without education, jobs, professions, money. If I am optimistic today, it is because I think that a sizeable number of us with and without jobs, professions, money, are prepared, have begun, to turn the procession at least half an inch off course. Another way to put it is to say that because of the history I have outlined, because of the positions and concessions of earlier feminists, we are more numerous and more powerful today. I am optimistic that we will use that power ultimately and well.

2

Educational Reminiscences

(1874)

Catharine Beecher

INTRODUCTION

It is over half a century, that the author of this volume has devoted her time and chief attention to the higher education of woman, and has had a wide field both of observation and experience. Owing to this fact, frequent requests have been made for some records which will avail for the guidance of others who are commencing similar efforts. There are special reasons, at this time, for directing public attention to the topics in this work. The subject of "Woman's Rights and Wrongs" is now agitating communities all over the nation, sustained by wide spread organizations of energetic, intelligent, and conscientious men and women, many of them in high positions of influence.

The question of woman's admission to men's colleges and professional schools is exciting much discussion. The subject of woman's health, as connected with methods of education, is involving many questions of difficulty and delicacy.

The question as to how far the supervision and control of public schools and higher institutions of her own sex should be committed to women *equally* with men is another

topic that is increasing in public interest and attention. This is especially a matter of more than ordinary interest, as very large benefactions for establishing institutions for women have recently been given exclusively to the control of business and professional men, who have had little or no experience in regard to female education, and who are seeking counsel from those who have had more.

The personal history of the writer and her family, friends, and colaborers, will serve to illustrate some important principles of mind which have been too little regarded in family and school education.

This contribution of past experience and observation includes a narrative of serious mistakes as well as of successes, which may serve both as needed warning and cheering encouragement. Especially will it illustrate the beneficent power committed to cultivated and benevolent American women, which it is hoped ere long will be more effectively *organized*, so as greatly to promote the safety and prosperity of our country. As it has become so common for authors and public characters to publish their own autobiography, and as much of the family history of the author is already before the public, what follows of that nature will be allowed without need of apology.

CHAPTER II.

Woman's Domestic Duties Cultivate the Intellect.

A large portion of housekeepers are neither wives nor mothers, and yet have the control and education of the young, who are either orphans, or servants, or children of friends. The aged and the sick also are dependent on their counsel and ministries; while often a family of boarders brings to their care and sympathy persons of all ages, characters and conditions. Thus many housekeepers have more difficult and complex duties than usually rest on most wives and mothers.

These multiform duties call into constant exercise all the mental faculties, especially those popularly called the intellectual powers. Philosophers place among the intellectual powers what in common parlance are called sometimes *Reason* and sometimes *Common Sense*. These are dependent on that feature of our mental organization which leads every sane mind to the feeling and belief that "whatever is *best* for all concerned is *right* as fitted to secure the *end* for which all things are made." For, without any metaphysical or theological training, all men say that whatever secures the most good with least evil to all concerned is *right*. Thus the words *best* and *right* in practical questions express the same idea to the mass of mankind.

This feature of our mental constitution is that which especially distinguishes man from the lower animals; for the beasts have no power to compare, to judge and reason as to what is *best* for all concerned, even for life, much less for the life to come.

This distinctive feature of a rational being is constantly called into exercise by woman's domestic duties. For a housekeeper must attend, contrive, reason and judge every hour of the day.

She must compare, imagine, calculate and reason as to the best kind of house to seek; the best way of furnishing and ornamenting it; the best way of warming and ventilating it; the best heating apparatus and the way of managing it; the best cooking apparatus for economy, convenience and comfort; the best kinds of fuel for economy, health and convenience; the best way of storing and using it. She must arrange and provide the best kind of food for the young, the aged and the invalid; the best modes of purchasing, storing and preserving it; and the best modes of cooking, for health, economy and enjoyment. She must decide as to the best stuffs for clothes and furniture, the best way to cut, fit and mend; the best mode of washing and ironing, and the best way to secure the neat and cleanly ways of comfort.

A housekeeper is responsible for the health of all the inmates of her family; especially of children and servants who have not the needful knowledge and discretion. She must seek the best modes of preserving health and of treating common illness so as to keep a doctor away or send for him when needed; she needs to know the best way of managing a new born infant and its mother; the best way to manage young children; the best way of training and controlling servants; the best way of giving religious instruction, and the best school for the children. All these topics of transcendent interest for both time and eternity are demanding the exercise of every intellectual power for almost every woman who is a housekeeper.

To these add the distinctive duties of the wife and mother, and there is another long list of questions to be considered, compared, reasoned upon, and judged in settling what is the *best* and so the *right* course.

It is true that in many of these duties a husband and father shares both care and responsibility. But many housekeepers have neither father nor husband. Moreover that vast majority of men who toil all day in the field, the shop, the mill, the store and the office, are at home but little during the day, and often are too wearied to bear any more burdens. The woman must, in such cases, do much of the contriving, executing and governing in the family state, and in almost every department; while the husband or father listens to her results with the veto power which in most sensible families is seldom used.

In a family of children in humble or even moderate circumstances, the eldest daughter, almost in infancy, begins to share the duties and cares of the mother. She learns to help wash and dress the younger ones, to guard and regulate the impulses of an infant, and to contrive methods of safety and amusement. She aids in teaching language, learns herself, and then teaches the younger to sew, knit, and perform many other domestic operations which demand intellectual effort and perseverance, as much so as any school study or exercise.

3

Black Women's Education in the South

The Dual Burden of Sex and Race

(1990)

Elizabeth L. Ihle

Often laboring under the dual burden of sexism and racism, black women have been expected to live up to cultural stereotypes both of what it means to be black and what is means to be female. Since few scholars have realized that not all blacks share the same experiences and that not all women are exposed to the same expectations, black women have tended to get lost in analyses of sex and race. Researchers have frequently assumed, for instance, that education of all women developed in similar patterns and that most blacks, regardless of their sex, were exposed to approximately the same education. These assumptions have made it possible to lose sight of black women's educational development. This essay attempts to look at these dual variables of sex and race as it reviews the pedagogy that developed to educate southern black women between 1865 and 1940.

During this period, black women's education in the South developed in ways that supposedly fit their schooling to prevailing sexual and racial stereotypes. The education which developed was based upon society's concept of black women as potentially promiscuous and naturally suitable for work outside the home. Its results predictably preserved some traditional female and black roles but also inadvertently helped take black women beyond the pale of sexual and economic dominance of whites.

The decades after the Civil War witnessed the establishment of several forms of schooling for blacks. Among the first were the Freedman's Bureau schools and private black schools, some of which were started by the ex-slaves themselves. Schools begun by various northern missionary societies followed shortly afterwards. Some of these eventually closed, and others became the foundation for the

South's black colleges. In the 1880s, under the provisions of the Morrill Act, Virginia, Mississippi, and South Carolina each founded some kind of public secondary, technical, or collegiate institution for blacks. The 1890 Morrill Act forced the rest of the southern states to do the same. Public elementary schooling for blacks was unenthusiastically supported from the 1870s onward and varied in quality, with urban areas providing much more fully for black citizens than did rural areas. Public high schools for blacks generally did not develop until the twentieth century.

The post-war impulse to establish black schools came not from the southern white community, which feared that education would lead to a restive and unhappy laboring class, but from northerners and blacks themselves. Blacks viewed access to schooling quite positively because they thought schooling safe-guarded them from being defrauded and manipulated by their former owners, and possibly because it was the fruit forbidden to them during years of slavery. Blacks' enthusiasm for acquiring an education after the war has been amply documented. As Harriet Beecher Stowe wrote in 1879, "They rushed not to the grog-shop but to the schoolroom—they cried for the spelling-book as bread, and pleaded for teachers as a necessity of life." This remark describes the importance of education to blacks as a symbol; attending school signified blacks' capability as human beings to learn, and repudiated their historical image as unintelligent brutes. Additionally, blacks shared with many other Americans a faith in education as a tool for getting ahead;

through the receipt of schooling, a field worker could aspire to less demanding physical labor and more remunerative work. Aspirations for better employment eventually led to aspirations for equal rights. In these senses, education met blacks' psychic needs, held out the hope of material progress, and inspired the movement toward full citizenship and equality under the law.

Northerners, too, shared blacks' faith in education, but for different reasons. Many viewed it as a way of correcting the faults they perceived in the black race and/or as preparation for citizenship and responsibility. Martha Schofield, a teacher serving with a missionary society, told ex-slaves in South Carolina in 1866:

> You must *prove* yourselves worthy of freedom, you are free men & free women, responsible for every one of your acts, *you* men must be educated, so that if the ballot is placed in your hands, you will know how to use your power, & you women must strive to elevate yourselves so that you may be fit to train your children for noble men & women—.

Many white southerners were hostile or indifferent to black education until the turn of the century. Then, as they realized that their community and economic health was dependent upon the education of all their citizenry, they began to promote an appropriate black education that would result in community improvements and a more skilled work force. Southern community leaders began to cooperate actively with various northern philanthropies in developing an education appropriate to blacks' perceived place in society—an education that would produce loyal, responsible, and docile citizens and works but which would not threaten the social, economic, or legal status of the white community.

In the earliest years of black schooling after the Civil War, teachers focused upon moral training as well as literacy. Nineteenth-century morality dictated differing roles to each sex, and northern missionary teachers were careful to make those distinctions in teaching ex-slaves. Schofield's address clearly stated that while men were to be prepared for citizenship, women were to be "elevated." This idea—that black women needed elevation of some sort in order to be proper parents—was shared by a majority of the white shapers of black women's education and served as a major stimulus to its development.

The kind of elevation implied was moral improvement, a goal partially grounded in the assumption that black women were sexually promiscuous and needed education in order to change their ways. White men's sexual activity with often unwilling black girls and women had not died away with slavery, and black women had little hope of legal redress. Instead of punishing the perpetrators, reformers sought instead to educate the victims—a circuitous and not very effective solution to the problem, but certainly an impetus to black women's education. The result, often unanticipated by whites, was to train black women for positions where their contacts with white men were minimal.

Another reason behind the emphasis on morality in black women's education was that black women shared with their white sisters throughout the nation the burden of being considered responsible for the morality of both their family and community. Often this morality was closely associated with religion. In this sense, black women's education resembled that of their white sisters more than it did that of their black brothers. One writer who surveyed black womanhood for the Slater Fund, which gave large amounts of money to support black industrial education, maintained in 1896 that "it is impossible to look for a moral community where the women have never been taught by example and precept that Christian virtue which raises the human being above the animal." With sentiments like that one, it is not surprising that schooling lay great emphasis on inculcating morality. Teachers were supposed to provide the example of morality, while texts helped inculcate the precepts.

There is some evidence that middle-class black women internalized this drive toward morality and proper behavior. Septima Poinsett Clark recalled that during her childhood around the turn of the century her mother insisted that Clark act like a lady when she shopped. That meant no eating or yelling, wearing gloves, and not telling anyone who asked what she was doing; the penalty for breaking these rules was a whipping. The Daytona Normal & Industrial Institute for Girls (later Bethune-Cookman College), founded in 1904 by Mary McLeod Bethune, offered as one of its objective "to develop Christian character, to send forth women who will be rounded homemakers, Christian educators and moral leaders." A graduate of the school in 1918 recalled an emphasis on character training, especially the idea that her education was designed to help her fellow human beings. This emphasis was apparent on the college level as well. Fisk, one of the most prestigious black colleges in the nation, noted in its 1928–29 *Handbook* that

> the college girl of today starts [*sic*] for a high standard of womanliness which includes scholarship, good health, justice and fair play, self-control, a love of beauty, courtesy toward all, and an essential goodness of heart. These standards are foremost in the ideals long held by Fisk women.

Early post-war southern black schools thus taught sex-typing and moral training as well as elementary literacy. One avenue of this special pedagogy was the textbook. All nineteenth-century girls read textbooks that stereotyped girls and women to one degree or another as docile, fearful, and domestic creatures best supervised by the male sex; black girls also had to read about their race in terms of being happy but not intelligent. In the few texts published specifically for ex-slaves, women are praised for their exemplary behavior, not their accomplishments. The poet Phillis Wheatley, for instance, is cited for her modesty and character rather than for her skill as a poet.

School practices and extracurricular activities also reinforced the importance of specific forms of feminine morality. On special days girls did "readings" of someone else's work, while boys were allowed to make speeches. This type of practice limited girls' initiative to think for themselves and to stand up for their ideas. Records from a number of countywide school fairs in Arkansas in 1915 demonstrate expectations for girls who competed for prizes for the daintiest dress, the best kitchen apron, and the best doll dress, clearly implying that being ladylike, domestic, and motherly were valued characteristics.

Black girls and women frequently labored under rules more stringent than those for black males or white females, particularly in secondary and college settings. They were often required to wear uniforms and were chaperoned when visiting or shopping off campus. For example, Fisk required college women to wear uniforms until the mid-1920s, decades after that practice had been abandoned at white schools. At the turn of the century, Atlanta University required female students but not male ones to have chaperones off-campus. Many campus clubs were sex-segregated, and interaction with men was carefully regulated and scrutinized. Tennessee State had two literary societies for each sex in 1918 and announced in its 1926 *Bulletin* that "no young man is allowed to call on a young lady or be in her company except on regular calling days as announced by the President and Matron."

Nearly all black schools were coeducational, a fact that suggests the true priorities of the shapers of black education. While heated debates regarding the propriety of coeducation for white women slowed their admission into men's private and public institutions throughout the nation but particularly in the South, this discussion is virtually absent in the development of black women's education. Considering that coeducation's effect upon student morality was the most controversial facet of the debate and that blacks' morality (and particularly that of black women) was frequently suspect, it is paradoxical that few educators presumed a need to educate the black sexes apart from each other. The explanation lies both in economics and the value system of the time. Operating a coeducational school was less expensive than two single-sex ones, and money for black education was scarce. It could be hypothesized that despite their rhetoric about black morality, few philanthropists, or the public, cared sufficiently about blacks to insist upon single-sex schools to protect blacks' moral health. In black education, schooling as many as possible took precedence over preserving the sexual integrity of black women. In white education the converse was argued—it was better to have women uneducated than to have their virtue possibly polluted by contact with men.

Although northern and southern whites alike wanted to use moral education to produce a better community, they did not anticipate that black families would come to regard schooling as a tool for the sexual liberation of black women from white men. Without schooling, black women were often destined to become domestic workers in homes and offices in positions which sometimes risked their integrity. By getting an education, a black woman could possibly receive employment that would put her beyond the reaches of most white men. Consequently many black families who were unable to educate all their children sent their sons into the work force after elementary school while keeping their daughters in school.

A 1923 survey of county training schools for blacks, first established in 1911–12 in rural areas of Louisiana, Arkansas, Virginia, and Mississippi, showed that although substantially more girls than boys attended county training schools at every level, the difference grew wider in the upper grades. Nearly ten percent more girls attended than boys overall, but in the upper grades—nine through twelve—the difference grew to forty-two percent. At the time, few considered it amiss to assume that six or seven years of elementary schooling was sufficient academic background for teaching in a black rural elementary school. Consequently, for prospective teachers, the county training school, the precursor of black rural high schools, generally provided enough pedagogical training to meet the requirements for teaching in a black school.

Black women were also more likely to attend college than men, a pattern that did not emerge among white women until the 1970s. However, they enrolled more frequently than men in normal programs, and their number of baccalaureate degrees did not outnumber men's until 1940. The 1915 *Catalog* from Fisk reported that its alumni included 370 male and 136 female college graduates and 39 male and 377 female normal graduates. Trends at other schools were similar. Women attended college but did not get degrees.

Blacks and whites perceived the goals of educating black women differently, but the actual education met each group's needs at least to a degree. Whites perceived that the emphasis upon morality was a means of counteracting traditional stereotypes of promiscuity among black women, while blacks viewed it as a means of protection from white men. Both groups agreed upon maintaining the traditional pattern of educating all women as the moral leaders of their families and communities.

A second major theme of black women's education was preparation for work. Black women shared this emphasis with black men but not with most white women. While white women's education was generally designed to produce cultured and learned graduates with appropriate moral standards, black women's education was supposed to fill that purpose and simultaneously to produce workers. For example, the charter for the institution that eventually became Spelman College, the premier black women's college, proposed in 1888 "the establishment and maintenance of an Institution of learning for young colored women in which special attention is to be given to the formation of industrial habits and of Christian character."

Few observers saw any paradox in preparing black women, but not white ones, for the work force. Since black women had worked throughout slavery, the assumption that they would continue to do so was "natural," and because of the economic circumstances of most black families, it was correct. In many black families education served as insurance for economic security. Black women's employment was often more stable and secure than black men's. In 1917, Fisk reported that nineteen percent of its graduates were homemakers. This statistic reflects the more comfortable economic status of educated blacks (when compared with uneducated black women) which allowed a larger portion of married women to stay at home. Compared to the college-educated white community, however, where a married woman working outside the home was exceptional, the percentage of black homemakers was quite low.

Training black women for work, particularly in the domestic area, began in the elementary years. The skills girls learned were predictable ones—simple cooking, sewing, and housekeeping. Sometimes they tended school gardens and prepared produce from them; older girls sometimes learned to can. The advent of Jeanes teachers in the 1910s further encouraged the acquisition of these skills. Anna T. Jeanes, a wealthy Quaker woman, established a fund in 1907 to supply black teachers who would travel from one rural black school to the next offering more training in practical skills than the regular teacher could provide. Although Jeanes teachers enriched the manual skills of children of both sexes until the 1940s, the nature of their work made them prime instruments of sex-typed education. The Jeanes teachers passed domestic training on to an older generation by frequently organizing mothers' clubs and community meetings. Since mothers were perceived as the foundation of a domestic household, Jeanes teachers naturally targeted them as a means of improving both morality and living standards.

Black women's education, particularly on the secondary and college levels, was designed more for practical work in the black community than for competence in traditional academic studies. While black males with baccalaureate degrees sometimes taught, they were more likely to enter the ministry, law, or medicine and take their place as leaders within the segregated black community. In keeping with their roles as ladies, black women were not to aspire to leadership but to serve the community in supporting roles as mothers, teachers, and lay church leaders. In nearly every college through the 1940s, they were required to take at least one home economics course regardless of their majors.

Although normal training was a particularly popular educational specialty for both black and white women, black women who could not afford to attend college, or chose not to, could pursue other specialities not open to white women because of their different status in society. This training was largely available in the various state and private industrial institutes, which specialized in developing blacks' working skills and which received far more popular support from southern whites than did the academically oriented black colleges. For instance, in 1906 the mayor of Daytona, Florida, suggested that the Daytona Educational and Industrial School for black girls "should be endorsed by every southern man and woman as a feasible means of effecting reform in social evils existing today and of producing an efficient and courteous class of servants much needed in the South if not in every state in the Union."

Predictably, much of the training available to black women was geared to their perceived vocational roles. One official at the black Arkansas-Haygood Industrial College in Pine Bluff, Arkansas, appealed to a philanthropy for funds to improve its home economics facilities, emphasizing that

> the need of better training for domestic duties among the people of the Colored Race in the South particularly is an urgent one. Whether the young women are to find occupation in their own homes as homebuilders or whether they are to be employed as domestics in the homes of others, we regard the study and practice of home economics as vital.

In 1906, Tuskegee, one of the most sophisticated of all the industrial schools, offered girls courses in plain sewing, dressmaking, millinery, cooking, laundering, soapmaking, domestic training, mattress making, broom making, and basketry. In 1916 Hampton offered its women students three home economics programs. One was to "train young women to make good homes and to enable them to teach others to make good homes"; the second trained special teachers of cooking and sewing who could also supervise industrial work in rural schools, and the final one specialized in large-scale domestic service in kitchens, laundries, dormitories, and hospitals. Both Hampton and Tuskegee were well-funded private institutions, and at most schools, especially the public ones, the curriculum for women was not so diverse. Alcorn Agricultural and Mechanical College in Mississippi offered women cooking, sewing, and nursing in 1915, while the State Colored Normal, Industrial, Agricultural, and Mechanical College at Orangeburg, South Carolina, had only cooking and sewing for women. In all these cases, black men were given more training options than women.

Another form of girls' industrial education took place in the county training schools. Approximately three-fifths of school time in these institutions was spent on academics and the remaining on industrial education, which was predictably sex-typed. Boys typically studied agriculture and did shop work, while girls concentrated on home arts and sciences and "housewifery." In the early 1930s the Montgomery County Training School in Waugh, Alabama, was teaching girls how to make colored cotton dresses while boys learned to slaughter hogs. Boys learned how to cut and dress hogs, while girls learned how to make sausages. The unspoken message was that performance expectations differed according to sex, and the resulting reality was unequal wages in the labor market.

As did moral training, the emphasis on educating black women to be workers extended past the formal curriculum into other aspects of institutional life. Combining extracurricular work and classroom activities was very common, and the work usually took the form of caring for the school facilities. Girls at Hampton, for instance, were in charge of washing, ironing, and housework. Working in the teachers' residence hall, cleaning rooms and cooking and serving meals, was considered a privilege, awarded only to the most diligent. At the Okolona Industrial School in Mississippi, girls could earn extra funds by doing the laundry of teachers and young men in addition to their regular chores. Many schools had daily room inspections and more rigorous ones on Sundays to reinforce the importance of the girls' domestic responsibilities.

The fact that black women were expected to work more than white women is demonstrated at the college level by a 1930 study that indicated that 28% of black women worked while they attended college, while only 0.64% of white women attending private women's colleges and 7% in public coeducational ones did so. Black women's high rate of employment also reflected the limited financial resources of many black families.

The result of this emphasis on work in black girls' and women's education was that black families took very seriously the impact of schooling on a daughter's working life. Many ambitious families who could afford it transferred their daughters out of public schools, which frequently emphasized only domestic skills, into private schools, which they believed could provide a more academic education which would lead to teaching certification. Others moved to a different location in order to provide better educational possibilities.

Educating black women for lives working outside the home met the needs of both races. Whites gained a larger and better trained work force, while blacks used the education offered them to win more economic independence, and eventually, the rights of full citizenship. Few black families were entirely successful in reaching these goals by the 1950s, for few positions were entirely dependent only on the black community. Teaching, the profession to which a large number of black women aspired, was dependent upon the goodwill of white school boards which were generally not reluctant to fire personnel whose words or actions had offended them. Still, teaching was about the best-paying position to which a woman could aspire, and brought prestige to herself and to her family. Because teachers became increasingly well educated and recognized the injustice of a pay scale based on race, they developed aspirations to change the inequities of the system, a consequence definitely not intended by whites.

The practice of training black, but not white, women for the work force gave the black community a tradition of women working outside the home far sooner than it did whites. Today's discussions about the effects of the "new" phenomenon of women working outside the home almost always ignores a sizeable portion of black women who have traditionally done just that.

Between 1865 and 1940 the dual burden of sexual and racial stereotypes helped shape black women's education in the South in ways both predictable and unforeseen. Unsurprisingly, they ensured an emphasis on morality and domestic skills in their education and followed white women's patterns of educating women to play a subordinate role to men. Their race alone necessitated in many cases the preparation for paid work outside their own homes. However, black women's education also often prompted a liberation from the sexual predations of white men as more black women developed skills that moved their employment away from white homes and offices.

Furthermore, their education sometimes allowed them to assume teaching positions from which they more clearly viewed racial injustices. By the early 1940s they were ready to challenge the system of unequal pay and move into more central controversies of civil rights, a consequence of their education unintended by the white South. Thus, variables of both race and sex have stimulated the growth of black women's education in unique ways shared by neither black males nor white females.

4

Discussion of the Same Subject

The Intellectual Progress of Colored Women of the U.S. Since the Emancipation

(1893)

Anna Julia Cooper

The higher fruits of civilization can not be extemporized, neither can they be developed normally, in the brief space of thirty years. It requires the long and painful growth of generations. Yet all through the darkest period of the colored women's oppression in this country her yet unwritten history is full of heroic struggle, a struggle against fearful and overwhelming odds, that often ended in a horrible death, to maintain and protect that which woman holds dearer than life. The painful, patient, and silent toil of mothers to gain a fee simple title to the bodies of their daughters, the despairing fight, as of an entrapped tigress, to keep hallowed their own persons, would furnish material for epics. That more went down under the flood than stemmed the current is not extraordinary. The majority of our women are not heroines—but I do not know that a majority of any race of women are heroines. It is enough for me to know that while in the eyes of the highest tribunal in America she was deemed no more than a chattel, an irresponsible thing, a dull block, to be drawn hither or thither at the volition of an owner, the Afro-American woman maintained ideals of womanhood unshamed by any ever conceived. Resting or fermenting in untutored minds, such ideals could not claim a hearing at the bar of the nation. The white woman could at least plead for her own emancipation; the black woman, doubly enslaved, could but suffer and struggle and be silent. I speak for the colored women of the South, because it is there that the millions of blacks in this country have watered the soil with blood and tears, and it is there too that the colored woman of America has made her characteristic history, and there her destiny is evolving. Since emancipation the movement has been at times confused and stormy, so that we could not always tell whether we were going forward or groping in a circle. We hardly knew what we ought to emphasize, whether education or wealth, or civil freedom and recognition. We were utterly destitute. Possessing no homes nor the knowledge of how to make them, no money nor the habit of acquiring it, no education, no political status, no influence, what could we do? But as Frederick Douglass had said in darker days than those, "One with God is a majority," and our ignorance had hedged us in from the fine-spun theories of agnostics. We had remaining at least a simple faith that a just God is on the throne of the universe, and that somehow—we could not see, nor did we bother our heads to try to tell how—he would in his own good time make all right that seemed wrong.

Schools were established, not merely public day-schools, but home training and industrial schools, at Hampton, at Fiske, Atlanta, Raleigh, and other central stations, and later, through the energy of the colored people themselves, such schools as the Wilberforce; the Livingstone, the Allen, and the Paul Quinn were opened. These schools were almost without exception co-educational. Funds were too limited to be divided on sex lines, even had it been ideally desirable; but our girls as well as our boys flocked in and battled for an education. Not even then was that patient, untrumpeted heroine, the slave-mother, released from self-sacrifice, and many an unbuttered crust was eaten in silent content that she might eke out enough from her poverty to send her young folks off to school. She "never had the chance," she would tell you, with tears on her withered cheek, so she wanted them to get all they could. The work in these schools, and in such as these, has been like the little leaven hid in the measure of meal, permeating life throughout the length and breadth of the Southland, lifting up ideals of home and womanhood; diffusing a contagious longing for higher living and purer thinking, inspiring woman herself with a new sense of her dignity in the eternal purposes of nature. Today there are twenty-five thousand five hundred and thirty colored schools in the United States with one million three hundred and fifty-three thousand three hundred and fifty-two pupils of both sexes. This is not quite the thirtieth year since their emancipation, and the colored people hold in landed property for churches and schools twenty-five million dollars. Two and one-half million colored children have learned to read and write, and twenty-two thousand nine hundred and fifty-six colored men and women (mostly women) are teaching in these schools. According to Doctor Rankin, President of Howard University, there are two hundred and forty-seven colored students (a large percentage of whom are women) now preparing themselves in the universities of Europe. Of other colleges which give the B.A. course to women, and are broad enough not to erect barriers against colored applicants, Oberlin, the first to open its doors to both woman and the negro, has given classical degrees to six colored women, one of whom, the first and most eminent, Fannie Jackson Coppin, we shall listen to tonight. Ann Arbor and Wellesley have each graduated three of our women; Cornell University one, who is now professor of sciences in a Washington high school. A former pupil of my own from the Washington High School, who was snubbed by Vassar, has since carried off honors in a competitive examination in Chicago University. The medical and law colleges of the country are likewise bombarded by colored women, and every year some sister of the darker race claims their professional award of "well done." Eminent in their professions are Doctor Dillon and Doctor Jones, and there sailed to Africa last month a demure little brown woman who had just outstripped a whole class of men in a medical college in Tennessee. In organized efforts for self-help and benevolence also our women have been active. The Colored Women's League, of which I am at present corresponding secretary, has active, energetic branches in the South and West. The branch in Kansas City, with a membership of upward of one hundred and fifty, already has begun under their vigorous president, Mrs. Yates, the erection of a building for friendless girls. Mrs. Coppin will, I hope, herself tell you something of her own magnificent creation of an industrial society in Philadelphia. The women of the Washington branch of the league have subscribed to a fund of about five thousand dollars to erect a woman's building for educational and industrial work, which is also to serve as headquarters for gathering and disseminating general information relating to the efforts of our women. This is just a glimpse of what we are doing.

Now, I think if I could crystallize the sentiment of my constituency, and deliver it as a message to this congress of women, it would be something like this: Let woman's claim to be as broad in the concrete as in the abstract. We take our stand on the solidarity of humanity, the oneness of life, and the unnaturalness and injustice of all special favoritisms, whether of sex, race, country, or condition. If one link of the chain be broken, the chain is broken. A bridge is no stronger than its weakest part, and a cause is not worthier than its weakest element. Least of all can woman's cause afford to decry the weak. We want, then, as toilers for the universal triumph of justice and human rights, to go to our homes from this Congress, demanding an entrance not through a gateway for ourselves, our race, our sex, or our sect, but a grand highway for humanity. The colored woman feels that woman's cause is one and universal; and that not till the image of God, whether in parian or ebony, is sacred and inviolable; not till race, color, sex, and condition are seen as the accidents, and not the substance of life; not till the universal title of humanity to life, liberty, and the pursuit of happiness is conceded to be inalienable to all; not till then is woman's lesson taught and woman's cause won—not the white woman's, nor the black woman's, nor the red woman's, but the cause of every man and of every woman who has writhed silently under a mighty wrong. Woman's wrongs are thus indissolubly linked with all undefended woe, and the acquirement of her "rights" will mean the final triumph of all right over might, the supremacy of the moral forces of reason, and justice, and love in the government of the nations of earth.

5

Cultivating the Rosebuds

The Education of Women at the Cherokee Female Seminary, 1851–1909

(1995)

Devon A. Mihesuah

Teachers and prospective students began arriving in Park Hill in November 1850. Both the male and female seminaries were to have begun instruction the previous month, but the openings were postponed because of delays in construction and in the delivery of furniture. Many faculty members and students returned home, but others waited in Tahlequah until the schools finally opened seven months later.

The Female Seminary was built to accommodate one hundred students, but to assure the school's successful operation, the National Council allowed only twenty-five pupils to enroll the first year. Each year thereafter, twenty-five more applicants would be admitted, until the enrollment reached one hundred. In theory, a quarter of the students would graduate by the end of the fourth year, and so the number of new pupils and graduates would remain constant thereafter. Both schools were to provide

pupils with lodging, food, textbooks, lighting fuel, and laundry services, but students had to furnish their own linens, clothes, toiletries, and "comforts." In addition to money allotted for basic expenses, the National Council allocated eight hundred dollars to each seminary for books, paper, and miscellaneous "school apparatus."

Applicants to the seminaries were required to be members of the Cherokee tribe (possessing any degree of Cherokee blood), to be proficient in the skills taught in the common schools, and to be prepared to remain for the entire four years of study unless they had attended other high schools and wanted to enter as students in the upper classes. To assess prospective students' abilities, school officials administered English-language admissions tests, requiring applicants to demonstrate proficiency in reading, spelling, arithmetic, grammar, and geography. The first of these tests took place on 1 May 1851 and the "Flowers of the Cherokees" who passed the examinations were notified the next day.

The National Council claimed that family wealth was not a factor in admittance because there was no tuition. But of the seventy-five enrollees in the 1850s, at least fifty were daughters of district sheriffs, councilors, senators, or judges, or of National clerks and treasurers. In addition, many of the girls were members of affluent mixed-blood families such as the Bushyheads, Rosses, Adairs, Candys, McNairs, and Mayeses. The majority of students who passed the tests were mixed-bloods with English-speaking, educated parents who could afford private tutors. These students contrasted sharply with many pupils in the public schools—predominantly fullbloods—who spoke no English and whose teachers could not speak Cherokee. Many of those children had no chance to learn even the rudiments of reading, writing, and arithmetic. The two fullbloods who were admitted to the seminary the first year had received thorough instruction at the mission schools, and they eventually graduated from the seminary.

On 6 May 1851, the Male Seminary finally opened, and the next morning the female school began its classes with much fanfare. The military band from Fort Gibson played to the sizable crowd—many citizens of the Cherokee Nation had eagerly awaited the opening of their seminaries—and Chief John Ross spoke of the importance of education, recalling the days when instruction was not readily available to the Cherokee people. He correctly predicted that the day would be remembered by Cherokee youths who "should be so fortunate as to enter the temples of education."

Following the advice of Mary Chapin, the principal of Mount Holyoke who, at the request of Chief John Ross, had designed the Female Seminary's curriculum after her own school's four-year course of study, the National Council divided the school year into two sessions of twenty weeks each, with classes five days a week, six hours a day. However, the ambitious plan was not immediately realized. Because of the oppressive humidity in August during the first year, the school closed after only thirteen weeks, seven weeks ahead of schedule.

The female students were divided into four classes, and the curriculum was essentially the same as at the Male Seminary. First-year students studied geometry, Greek history, intellectual theology, and a course based on Paley's *Natural Theology*—the same work Mary Lyon used to impress the importance of Christianity upon her Mount Holyoke pupils. The second-year class studied algebra, physiology, Latin, and Watts's *Improvement of the Mind*. Third- and fourth-year students studied geography, Latin, and advanced arithmetic. The board also required seminary teachers to instruct students in vocal music. This course of study—which never included any courses on Cherokee culture—remained unchanged through the school's first five years. Unlike some schools, the seminary did not include any "home management" courses, following instead the Mount Holyoke philosophy that "home is the proper place for the daughters of our country to be taught [domestic science] and the mother is the appropriate teacher." Pupils did not cook any meals, nor did they wash their own clothes or linens. It is not known if Cherokee citizens were paid to allow their black slaves to work at the school.

One of the newly recruited teachers, Ellen Rebecca Whitmore of Marlborough, Massachusetts, became the first principal of the Female Seminary, serving from 1851 to late 1852, even though she was still a year away from graduation at Mount Holyoke. Sarah Worcester, the tall, handsome daughter of Samuel and Ann Orr Worcester, acted as her assistant. Worcester had undoubtedly helped to convince Whitmore and the other new teachers, Oswald Woodford and Thomas Van Horne, of the safety and opportunities offered by the Park Hill area and had probably assured them of the level of acculturation among the Cherokees living there. Worcester had grown up with the Boudinot children before and after removal, and was well aware of the political rivalries within the Cherokee Nation. Eager to begin teaching the Cherokees, Worcester was dedicated to instructing her students in the "social graces" and "meticulous refinements of good breeding" as well as in academic disciplines. The women arrived in Park Hill on 13 November 1851, but since the construction of the seminary was unfinished, Whitmore spent the winter with the Worcester family. During those months she oversaw the completion of the building and prepared for the institution's opening in the spring.

Another authority figure present at the seminary was the steward, a position that would always be filled by a male, possibly to offset the female teachers. The first steward, Dr. Elizur Butler, was a missionary of the American Board. He had worked from 1821 to 1824 at Brainerd Mission, had been a medical missionary in the Eastern Cherokee Nation, and had served as a physician with one of the removal parties that went west during 1838 and 1839. After reaching Indian Territory, Butler worked at Fairfield Mission, where Chief Ross appointed him the Cherokee National Physician. Butler accepted the position of Female Seminary steward in 1851, and he and his wife, Lucy, moved into the school the following May. They had the considerable responsibility of providing meals, maintaining seminary property, and overseeing the washing, ironing, and mending of clothing and bedding. Dr. Butler preached at the seminary each Sunday and also cared for sick students, but when any pupils became seriously ill, Dr. E. Poe Harris of Tahlequah assisted in treating them. Although the stewards' wives were always present and were known as "co-stewards," the women were not paid.

Although Whitmore and Worcester had arrived at Park Hill determined upon careers as teachers among the Cherokees and had immersed themselves in their work, their terms at the seminary were brief. After only one year as principal, Whitmore resigned, and on 17 June 1852 she married Warren Goodale, a missionary, at John Ross's Rose Cottage. Shortly afterward the newlyweds moved to Hawaii to continue their missionary work. Worcester also married a missionary, Dr. Daniel Dwight Hitchcock, a graduate of Amherst and of Bowdoin Medical College. They wed on 15 February 1853 in the Female Seminary parlor. After Sarah's death at Park Hill just four years later, Hitchcock married her sister, Hannah.

Although Whitmore's tenure at the seminary was short-lived, she evidently enjoyed her work. Before resigning on 16 March 1852, she wrote to Mary Chapin at Mount Holyoke, remarking on the "superior order" of the "society of the neighborhood" at Park Hill. She described the country as "delightful," the salary as "large . . . $800.00 a year." Although she alluded to being homesick, her said her seminary work was "the pleasantest field in which I have ever been called to labor. . . . I have found warm friends here whose unremitting kindness I can never repay." Whitmore seems to have socialized only with members of the Ross and Worcester families and the teachers at the Male Seminary, not with the fullbloods who lived in the vicinity of Park Hill.

Whitmore urged Chapin to send a replacement who was a "dedicated, active Christian, one lovely and pleasing in her manners." She advised that the new principal should expect to stay at least three or four years, for if her health was good and she was as "happy as I have been," she would "not want to leave." Yet Whitmore warned that the candidate should not be too young since the position was not "free from trials." Indeed, as the first principal of a new institution, Whitmore had found herself under extreme pressure to make the seminary successful. Caring for twenty-five homesick adolescent girls was a demanding job. During the winter and spring months, cases of pneumonia and chills were common, and in the summer the heat was almost unbearable. Many girls who presented discipline problems were evidently agitated by the rigorous regimen. One student, Na-Li, complained, "I can't sit here all day and study; I want some running about to do." Other students behaved erratically, apparently because of the regular doses of morphine they took to counteract boredom.

After Whitmore's resignation, Harriet Johnson of Sturbridge, Massachu-setts, became principal. She was an experienced educator, having taught from 1848 to 1852 at Roxbury, Boston, and Mount Holyoke. But Johnson stayed in the Cherokee Nation only one year. She married the Reverend Robert McGill Loughridge in October 1853 and the couple moved to a mission in the Creek Nation.

The principal's job was filled in late 1853 by Pauline Avery, an 1850 graduate of Mount Holyoke. Pauline's older sister, Mary, had taught in Tuscaloosa, Alabama, and in the Cherokee public schools in the 1840s. Their father, Deacon Joseph Avery, was a Mount Holyoke trustee from 1836 to 1855. Assisting Pauline Avery were Charlotte "Lotta" E. Raymond, a native of Philadelphia, and Eliza Jane Ross, the niece of Chief John Ross and the sister of the future chief, William Potter Ross. Eliza Ross had attended school at Cane Hill in Arkansas and had been enrolled in the Bethlehem Female Seminary in Pennsylvania for four years. Avery remained at the Female Seminary until 1856, when she wed Rev. Oswald Langdon Woodford, one of the original teachers at the Male Seminary, who taught there from 1851 to 1855. Pauline Avery Woodford died in 1858 in Grasshopper Falls, Kansas, after the birth of a daughter.

Seminary principals were paid an annual salary of eight hundred dollars; the first assistants, six hundred dollars; and the second assistants, five hundred dollars. In addition to salaries, all faculty members were provided with room and board. Reflecting the importance placed on female education in the Cherokee Nation, Chief John Ross reported in 1855 that the instructors at the Male Seminary had complained about being paid the same as the women at the Female Seminary, but Ross dryly noted that the women had "never interposed any objection."

Teachers and administrators conducted yearly public examinations at both schools, and all classes were periodically open to the public for observation. At such times, a representative from each class recited the events that had occurred during the year. Chief Ross reported with "unmingled pleasure" that the first evaluation was a success and that the "deportment" of the students was "in a high degree gratifying and satisfactory." At the 1852 evaluation, George Butler, an Indian agent, found that the seminary students showed vast improvement in "letters and morals" since the school's opening. Their conduct "fully met, or even exceeded the anticipations of the public," he said, and they had made "commendable progress" in all courses of study. This had been accomplished with relatively "little restraint" on those at the female school, but twenty students at the male school had been expelled for misbehaving. The Reverend William

Schenk Robertson from Tullahassee Mission (the largest of the Creek Nation schools, which was located on the Arkansas River a few miles northwest of Muskogee) also attended the 1852 evaluation and wrote to his parents that "quite a number of teachers are here," and the forty-six girls present "appeared well, very well—all dressed in white with pink belts." Impressed by their recitations, he commented that they were "a credit to their teachers and their Nation may well be proud of them."

No problems arose during the next two years, except for a ten-month delay in obtaining textbooks because low water levels in the Arkansas River prohibited boats from delivering supplies. The schools continued to prosper, and Principal Avery reported a "marked improvement, both in deportment and application to study." The following list (which shows some overlap in class periods) was prepared for the 1855 "Examination Day" and illustrates the regimentation of the seminary's class schedule at that time.

Subject	Time	Supervising Teacher
Devotions	7:1/4 to 7:1/2	
Geography	7:1/2 to 7:50	Raymond
Latin	7:50 to 8:1/4	Avery
Arithmetic	8:1/4 to 9:00	Ross
Rhetoric	9:00 to 9:1/2	Raymond
Geometry and Star of Twilight Abou Ben Adem [sic]	9:1/2 to 10:1/4	Avery
Physiology	10:00 to 11:1/4	Ross
Recess	11:1/2	
Algebra	11:00 to 12:20	Raymond
Intellectual Philosophy	12:20 to 1:00	Ross
Dinner	1:00 to 1:1/2	
Natural Theology and "Merry Goes the Time"	1:1/2 to 2:1/4	Raymond
Evidences of Christianity	2:1/4 to 3:00	Avery
Music—"We Plough the Fertile Meadow"	3:00 to 3:15	Avery
Paper and Marks; Singing— "I'm Going Home"	3:15 to 3:3/4	

Not long after its opening, the Female Seminary became the center for social events. In 1854, when the Methodist congregation of the Sehon Chapel lacked sufficient funds to complete its building near Park Hill, the seminary students gave concerts and donated the proceeds to the church building fund. Seminary students often visited Tahlequah to attend lectures, to dine, and to shop, and on New Year's Eve, boys from the Male Seminary attended celebrations at the girls' school. Teachers from both seminaries occasionally mingled for tea at the female school and took carriage rides together.

The girls eagerly anticipated the Friday mail delivery (the parcels were left by the side of the road leading to the seminary to be delivered by anyone en route to the school)[19] and the weekly visit of Chief John Ross for Sunday services at the seminary. Maintaining his lifestyle as a wealthy Southern planter, Ross and his new wife, Mary Stapler, the daughter of a wealthy Philadelphia merchant, arrived at the seminary entrance in their elegant coach driven by their liveried black coachman.

Religion played a primary role in shaping the values of the seminarians. The seminary was not associated with any religious denomination, but in accordance with the emphasis placed on piety among the Cherokees and at Mount Holyoke, the students' "Christian spirituality" was a prime concern of the National Council. In 1852, several tribal members formed the Cherokee Educational Association, an organization for promulgating a "wholesome Christian influence on the public schools." The board required students to attend church services of "their choice" on Sunday, although the selection was limited to Presbyterian, Baptist, Methodist, Moravian, or Congregational churches. Over half the fifty girls enrolled at the seminary in 1853 had attended Dwight Mission, but there is scant documentation as to which churches the seminary students actually did attend. An excerpt from a letter that Sarah Worcester wrote to her brother John (as noted, their father, Samuel, was a missionary for the American Board of Commissioners for Foreign Missions [ABCFM]) in 1856 suggests that not many took part in Methodist or Baptist services: "John, the Methodists are growing worse and worse. The last Sabbath of last term they 'opened the doors of the church' to the scholars of the F. Seminary, saying they wanted to 'have their share.' They preach Methodism, instead of Christ.—I think that I can receive Baptists as cordially as I can Methodists, for the former do not reject any of the great truths of the Bible." All the seminary teachers and administrators in the early years were members of the Presbyterian, Moravian, or Baptist churches.

Teachers and ministers were careful not to preach against slavery, even if they were abolitionists, in order to avoid being expelled from the Cherokee Nation. They were well aware that many of the students were from slave-holding families and that even Chief Ross owned at least forty slaves. Because of the clergymen's cautious approach, it is doubtful that most students had to go through a "crisis conversion" (pro-slavery to anti-slavery) in order to join the churches. The teachers and missionaries from the North were apparently more frustrated about the issue than were the students.

In October 1854, George Butler indicated that the religious fervor among the Cherokees continued unabated. He wrote to his superiors that "the influence of the Bible [permeates] our common schools, our high schools, our temperance societies, and even our form of government." Samuel Worcester reported that several of the pupils at the seminaries had joined the Park Hill church, and others were expected to join the nearby Sehon Chapel upon its completion in 1856.

Besides their interest in religion, the seminary students found an alternative to class work in publishing a school newspaper. The official newspaper at the Female Seminary in the 1850s was the *Cherokee Rose Buds*, which was published by the girls and sold for ten cents per copy. Making its first appearance on 2 August 1854, the paper was edited by seminary students ("co-editresses," they called themselves) and was devoted to "the Good, the Beautiful, and the True." Measuring ten by twelve inches, each page consisted of three columns, with some editorials written in English and in Cherokee so all the tribe's citizens could read them. The paper contained notices of forthcoming events, editorials, engagement and wedding announcements of prominent persons, short stories, and poetry. In 1855, the name of the newspaper was changed to *A Wreath of Cherokee Rose Buds*.

There is not enough evidence to reconstruct what the students were taught regarding their gender role and "Indianness," but the editorials and stories in the *Rose Buds* reveal that the race-conscious and ethnocentric students were attempting to define their roles as women and as Cherokees. The females who have been the focus of studies of domesticity and Protestant evangelism have usually been white, but like them, the Cherokee students of the Female Seminary were advocates of the "true woman" ideal. The seminarians were confident about the influence women could have on humanity, and the stories they incorporated in the *Rose Buds* declared their belief that women's responsibilities were important and distinctive. In the commentary "Female Influence," for example, student Qua-Tay asserted that "the destiny of the world depends on woman . . . [as] the appointed agent of morality . . . the inspirer of those feelings and dispositions which form the moral nature of man." A student named Alice further elaborated on the grace of women, in her essay entitled "Beauty": "But man, himself, in physical beauty, excels in the works of God. What more admirable than the noble form, erect in God-like majesty, or the more perfect gracefulness of woman? Like flowers, the more they are cultivated the more beautiful they become."

The seminarians adopted the names "Rose Buds" and described rosebuds (and, indirectly, themselves) as "beautiful," "fresh," "flourishing," and potentially "blossoming" into roses. The reference to roses was used by Indian agents, parents, and chiefs to refer to the girls, and it permeated the students' poetry:

> The Seminary our garden fair
> And we, the flowers planted there . . .
> Like roses bright we hope to grow,
> And o'er our home such beauty throw
> In future years—that all may see
> Loveliest of lands,—the Cherokee.

Editorials and poetry in the Male Seminary's newspaper, *The Sequoyah Memorial* (dedicated to "Truth, Justice,

Freedom of Speech and Cherokee Improvement"), praised women, reiterating the theme of roses:

> Though far away 'neath orient skies
> Where clouds come not, nor sweeps
> the storm,
> The maid may blush in roseate eyes
> Like hues upon the angel's form;
> The flashing light of jeweled fire
> That wealth may shower o'er neck
> and arm,
> Though soft, voluptuous, gay attire
> May heighten every dazzling
> charm,—
> Still, wanton Nature's dark-eyed child,
> Is far more dear to me—
> The sweetest flower that gems the
> wild,
> Is the Rose of Cherokee.

Issues of the *Rose Buds* are filled with religious overtones. Music, for example, "is surely a gift sent from Heaven," stars are "holes in the floor of heaven, to let the glory through," and wind is "like the spirit of God omnipresent." One issue focused on Catharine Brown, a mixed-blood who, almost thirty years earlier, had joined Brainerd Mission and was baptized. She remained devout the rest of her life, despite the missionaries' fears that she would be unable to adapt to the role of domestic female. She made a strong impression on the missionaries, and later, on the female seminarians, who immortalized her in a poem (although they misspelled her name):

> Ah Cherokee! Where is the daughter
> of Brown?
> She is resting beneath the tall tree;
> But her spirit, so spotless, has
> silently flown
> Far away to Guh-lul-Inhdi-a-hi!
> Death marked her his prey in the
> blossom of youth,
> From his grasp no kind angel could
> save;

> And innocence, meekness, religion
> and truth
> All slumber in CATHARINE'S GRAVE.

As with women in other parts of the United States, the religious female seminarians were understandably concerned about the flow of liquor into their communities and the effect of alcohol on their families. They never tired of attending the Sons of Temperance meetings or of discussing ways that they could better their society. According to student comments in the *Rose Buds*, the subject of intemperance "cannot be worn out. . . . Dissipation or intemperance is one of the greatest evils in our [Cherokee] Nation. . . . Ought we not all try to lend our aid in putting down this great evil? If we are young, we have an influence so let us one and all give our utmost influence for this noble cause." The female seminarians may have been repressed by males in some parts of their lives, but by banding together and touting temperance, they were able to rebel against male dominance at least a little. Many of the male seminarians (some of whom were brothers of female seminarians) did in fact break their pledge of abstinence and were expelled from the school for being intoxicated. The female students felt that by attending weekly church services, the seminary's daily chapel services, and temperance meetings, in addition to using the *Rose Buds* to express their opinions, they were fulfilling their roles as "true women" and doing something worthwhile for society.

The seminaries were established fifty years before W. E. B. Du Bois espoused his philosophy of the "Talented Tenth," that is, the belief that "the Talented Tenth of the Negro race must be made leaders of thought and missionaries of culture among their people. No others can do this work and Negro colleges must train men for it. The Negro race, like all other races, is going to be saved by its exceptional men." But the seminarians already subscribed to the philosophy that they had a duty to save their nation, and the *Rose Buds* reveals that the students were convinced of their superiority over the "unenlightened" members of their tribe. These attitudes reflected the growing class system within the tribe, based not only on differing cultural ideals between the progressives and the traditionals, but also between those who looked "Indian" (i.e., had darker skin) and the generation of mixed-blood children, who had lighter skin and hair. As time passed and more Cherokees intermarried with whites, the offspring appeared even more Caucasian. In 1899, the preponderance of mixed-blood Cherokees in Tahlequah was noted by Ora Eddleman, a writer for *Twin Territories*, who expressed dismay over the wealthy Cherokees and the "blond Cherokee women."

Rose Buds editorials reflected the seminarians' deep-seated belief in their duty to "uplift" the Cherokee Nation and their inclination to monitor one another's behavior. One writer urged, "Let us begin now in new energy that we may gain that intellectual knowledge which will reward the hopes of our Nation, fitting us for doing much good among our people." Another warned, "Young people—do not forget a remark made at the [recent] temperance meeting . . . that your character is weighed by those around you." Other writings and poems addressed themes such as the "Power of Kindness," "Tardiness,"

"Patience," "Angry Words," and "Conscience" (who, "with her small voice, gives no rest for the wicked"). Another student writer, perhaps reflecting the girls' affluent backgrounds, espoused the idea that "however beautiful or wealthy we may be, it is but for a moment. . . . Beauty of the soul will, if properly cultivated, flourish long after the Earth with all it contains, has passed away."

There are no records indicating that the Female Seminary subscribed to one of the premier women's magazines of that day, *Godey's Lady's Book*, but the students and teachers certainly adhered to the publication's philosophy that women were subordinate to men. The *Lady's Book* editors did take notice of the Female Seminary in 1857, however, calling the school "quite imposing" in a "Nation of red men."

During the 1850s, there were only two fullblood Cherokee girls enrolled, prompting citizens of the Cherokee Nation to charge that there was elitism and prejudice against the fullbloods at the seminary. But in 1854, a progressive fullblood student named Na-Li staunchly defended her seminary by stating in the *Rose Buds* that "it is sometimes said that our Seminaries were made only for the rich and those who were not full Cherokee; but it is a mistake. . . . Our Chief and directors would like very much that they [full Cherokees] should come and enjoy these same privileges as those that are here present." Na-Li, however, had been adopted by a mission at an early age, had a thorough primary education, and could easily pass the seminary entrance examination.

In further defense of her heritage and her skin color, Na-Li asserted that although her parents were "full

Cherokees . . . belonging to the common class," she felt it "no disgrace to be a full Cherokee. My complexion does not prevent me from acquiring knowledge and being useful hereafter. . . . [I will] endeavor to be useful, although I sometimes think that I cannot be." Apparently, the more Cherokee blood a seminary girl had, or the more "Indian" she looked, the more she felt she had to prove herself as a scholar and as a "useful" member of a society that she believed valued only those women who were white in appearance and attitude.

The early seminarians were indeed defensive about the color of their hair and skin. A popular theme of the anecdotes and stories published in the Cherokee seminary's paper was physical appearance, particularly blue eyes. For example, one story told of the consequences that young "Kate M." faced after plagiarizing a poem for literature class. "Fun and abundance," a student named Lusette wrote, "peeped from her blue eyes . . . and the crimson blush stole upon her cheeks." In the same issue, an author named Inez wrote about what her schoolmates might be doing in four years. One was described as a "fair, gay, blue-eyed girl" and another was a "fairy-like creature with auburn hair." Still another story by a student, Icy, was entitled "Two Companions" and paired Hope ("the very personification of loveliness") with a "tiny blue-eyed child" named Faith. In an 1855 issue of *A Wreath of Cherokee Rose Buds*, offended seminarians complained in an editorial about the Townsend (Massachusetts) Female Seminary's paper, the *Lesbian Wreath*, which referred to the Cherokee girls as their "dusky sisters." Evidently, seminary students believed that blue eyes

were the epitome of enlightenment and civilization.

Students took pleasure in comparing the old Cherokee ways with the new-and-improved lifestyles of the tribe to show that many tribe members had progressed past savagery and were on their way to equality with whites. In an 1854 issue of *Rose Buds*, a student named Edith championed the virtues of nineteenth-century white society and boasted of the progress the Cherokees had made. "Instead of the rudely constructed wigwams of our forefathers which stood there [the Park Hill area] not more than half-a-century ago," she wrote, "elegant white buildings are seen. Everything around denotes taste, refinement, and progress of civilization among our people."

The prolific Na-Li collaborated with another student in 1855 to illustrate their uneducated ancestors' backwardness, and more important, to emphasize the vast improvements the tribe had made. In "Scene One" of the essay "Two Scenes in Indian Land," Na-Li described a "wild and desolate estate of a Cherokee family" comprised of "whooping, swarthy-looking boys" and plaited-haired women, all of whom, she wrote, "bear a striking resemblance to their rude and uncivilized hut." She concluded that the poor imbeciles "pass the days of their wild, passive, uninteresting life without any intellectual pleasure or enjoyment," except, she added, to attend the green corn dance, a "kind of religious festival."

"Scene Two," by a girl named Fanny, painted a completely different picture of Cherokee life. In her commentary, even the environment around the family's home has magically blossomed from the influence of the missionaries. "Civilization and nature are here united," she declared. "Flowers, music, and even better, the *Holy Word of God* is here to study, showing that religion has shed its pure light over all." The Indian lad, "in place of his bow and arrow, is now taught to use the pen and wield the powers of eloquence. The girl, instead of keeping time with the rattling of the terrapin shells [around her ankles] now keeps time with the chalk as her fingers fly nimbly over the blackboard." Fanny then professed her hope that "we may advance, never faltering until all the clouds of ignorance and superstition and wickedness flee from before the rays of the Suns of Knowledge and Righteousness."

In these tales, then, there was the promise that the "wild Cherokee Indian" could be changed and become a new person. The seminarians were not shy in verbalizing their hope that their unsophisticated tribes-people would make the transition.

The attitude that the Cherokees needed a moral change was also illustrated in the *Sequoyah Memorial,* the newspaper of the Cherokee Male Seminary. One student wrote that "the bow and arrow have been laid aside," and until the Cherokees reached the "summit of civilization and refinement," they could never be "happy and contented." A female student named Estelle exclaimed, "O! that all, especially among the Cherokees, could but learn the vast importance of a good education. This and only this will place us on equality with other enlightened and cultivated Nations . . . if we love our country, if we would have the name of a Cherokee an honor, let us strive earnestly to value education aright."

The seminarians were convinced of their superiority over members of other tribes. After a group of Osage men visited the seminary in 1855, a student named Irene wrote a romantic essay—not unlike those of white authors of the day—about the "lofty, symmetrical forms, and proud, free step of these sons of nature just from their wild hunting ground." She found their war dance amusing ("those tall, dusky forms stomping and stooping around . . . making a wailing sound"). In comparing her tribe and theirs, she pointed out that the Osages listened to the seminarians sing "Over There" so attentively because, she assumed, at least the "wild and untutored Savage had an ear for music as well as the cultivated and refined."

Other articles in the *Rose Buds* include anecdotes about "hostile Indians" out in the "wild and unknown regions" attacking peaceful Cherokees on their way to the California gold fields, and about "barbarous Camanches [*sic*]" living in their "wild wilderness." A student named Cherokee described a Seneca Dog Dance in which the drum "made a very disagreeable noise," and she observed, "what there was in such music to exite the Seneca belles is more than I can imagine." Although she judged the dancers to be graceful, she believed they "ought to have been at something better."

No reference to blacks or slavery is made in any of the *Rose Buds* or *Sequoyah Memorial* issues, or in the memoirs of the early female teachers. The students' exact ideas on the subject are unknown, although most students' families did own slaves and dozens of male seminarians fought (and died) for the Confederacy. In regard to the slavery issue, life at the seminary was much calmer than in the rest of the Cherokee Nation. While the students were occupied with studies, the debates over slavery were much in evidence outside the seminaries. For example, late in 1860, Dr. Torry, supervisor of the ABCFM missions, was denied access to the Fairfield missions because of his alleged antislavery remarks, and John B. Jones, a Baptist missionary, was expelled from the Nation for promoting abolitionism. In 1859, the anti-slavery Keetoowah Society was organized within the Nation (its members were also known as "Pin Indians"), with the goal of preserving traditional Cherokee customs and traditions, but none of the seminarians at that time joined the group. After 1860, numerous male seminarians did become members of the Knights of the Golden Circle, an organization dedicated to the preservation of slavery. However, beginning in the early 1870s, many young people whose fathers were Keetoowahs did enroll in both seminaries.

While a faction of the seminarians and faculty believed themselves superior to the unenlightened members of their tribe, to other tribes as a whole, and to blacks, these same girls and teachers felt somewhat inferior to whites, despite the fact that many of seminarians had far more "white blood" than Cherokee (especially those who were enrolled after 1870). The same *Rose Buds* issue that discussed the "elegance and civilization" of the Cherokee Nation also compared it unfavorably with Eastern states, noting that the new bride of Chief John Ross, Mary Stapler, admirably left her more civilized surroundings in Philadelphia in order to "dwell with him in his *wild* prairie home" (the editors' emphasis). Another editorial, commenting on the completed 1855 spring term, said, "We present you again with a collection of Rosebuds, gathered from our seminary garden. If, on examining them, you chance to find a withered or dwarfish bud, please pass it by . . . we hope for lenient judgment, when our efforts are compared with those of our white sisters." The article "Exchanges" acknowledged the newspapers received from girls' schools in New England. But the Cherokee seminarians did not send copies of the *Rose Buds* in return because, as an editor explained, "we feel ourselves entirely too feeble to make any adequate recompense. . . . we are simply Cherokee school girls." These students appear to have been much like the individuals E. Franklin Frazier later described as the "Black Bourgeoisie," those blacks who develop feelings of inferiority because they judge themselves by white standards.

But the students can hardly be blamed for focusing upon skin color and the acculturative achievements of their tribe. Many had a parent who was white or at least of mixed blood. Even fullblood students still attempted to emulate whites who deemed themselves superior to blacks and other races. In addition, the works of Charles Caldwell, Samuel George Morton, and Josiah C. Nott, physicians who believed in the inherent superiority of the Caucasian race, were available in the seminary library for the students to read and fret over. Considering the seminary's philosophy ("white is best"), the students' skin coloring (usually dark), and the "backwardness" of many Cherokees, it is little wonder that the seminarians berated themselves for falling short of the white ideal.

In February 1855, the Female Seminary graduated less than half of its first class. Of the twelve graduates, eleven were mixed-bloods. The other, Catherine Hastings, was a fullblood Cherokee whose English name had been given her by missionaries at the Dwight Mission. In comparison, because of unruly behavior and consequent expulsion, only five pupils graduated from the Male Seminary that year.

The year 1855 marked a high point in the early history of the seminary, for in the next year the school's fortunes waned. Not only was the tribe facing financial difficulties, but arguments flared over the need for two high schools that served a small minority of the tribe. Critics of the schools charged that the seminaries were elitist and were racist toward fullbloods and traditional Cherokees. Because the seminaries' newspapers were sold not only to seminarians but also to the Nation's citizens, the viewpoints of the male and female students—who believed that those Cherokees who possessed lighter hair and skin were superior to the darker girls, and especially, to those who were traditionalists— were widely known and not always appreciated.

The Politics of Education and the Birth of Women's Studies

These documents show how the politics of the 1960s played a crucial role in shaping the goals of Women's Studies. Specifically, the civil rights and student movements provided a model for women to follow in their own struggle for justice and helped to uncover the ways that the educational system perpetuated injustice. The first piece describes the transformative experience of the Mississippi Freedom Schools. Created in 1964 during a voter registration campaign known as Freedom Summer, these alternative educational institutions were staffed by young black and white civil rights workers who came to Mississippi to challenge the system of segregation, disenfranchisement, and injustice. As a Freedom Summer volunteer, Florence Howe first began to recognize the ways in which education could either support or subvert social conventions, oppress or liberate human potential. The next document, written five years after Freedom Summer, illustrates the development of a radical perspective on education within the civil rights movement. Compare the insights described by Howe with the demands made by the Black Student Unions. Do they share a common or compatible perspective or set of goals? The next primary document provides a description of a strike launched by white student radicals at Columbia University whose opposition to the Vietnam War led them to concerns closer to home. In particular, they posed questions regarding the proper role of the university in terms of its responsibilities to students and the larger community. A feminist who was significantly influenced by both the civil rights and student movements wrote the last document. In one of the earliest imaginings of what Women's Studies might be, Robin Morgan presents a holistic portrait of the changes that must take place in the academy to accommodate women's needs and include feminist perspectives.

Critical Thinking Questions

1. What insights about the politics of education did Howe learn by participating in the Mississippi Freedom Schools?

2. In your opinion, what were the most significant innovations and accomplishments of the Mississippi Freedom Schools? Were they in the area of curriculum or pedagogy?
3. How and to what extent do you think education played an important role in the civil rights and anti-war movements?
4. Evaluate the Ten-Point Program of the Black Student Unions. Written over 30 years ago, have these demands been met?
5. In what ways did the Ten-Point Program and Columbia strikers link education with social and political concerns in innovative ways? To what degree do these links sound reasonable and compelling today? How do you think they were received in 1969?
6. In what ways does Robin Morgan's wish list for Women's Studies reflect the earlier demands of civil rights and student activists?
7. Compare curricular, pedagogical, and institutional changes that were demanded, created, or imagined by the reformers of the 1960s. Which vision sounds most appealing, most radical, most realistic? Which has come the closest to fruition?

6

Mississippi's Freedom Schools
The Politics of Education
(1964)

Florence Howe

ALL EDUCATION IS POLITICAL. In Mississippi, at least, it is impossible to find this trite. There, it is inescapable that the educational system furthers the political, that the kind of learning the individual gets depends completely upon the role he* is supposed to live.

A thirteen year old Jackson, Mississippi girl, sitting within a Freedom School circle this summer, described the events of the last day, the previous year, in her public (segregated) junior high school. Students in a high school nearby had asked the students in "Shirley's" school to join them in a protest-demonstration against local school conditions and procedures. "Shirley's" (Negro) teacher had threatened the class with failure for the year, should they walk out to join the demonstrators. Most of the class was intimidated, but not "Shirley" and several of her friends. She left, she said, because she knew that she had not failed for the year, she knew she had earned good grades, and she knew that it was right to join the demonstrators. As she and her friends reached the downstairs floor, they met, head on, the (Negro) principal "who was coming at us with a board." They turned, fled, back-tracked through the cafeteria and out the back way to join the demonstrators.

The Negro school child in Mississippi, like "Shirley," associates the school he attends, in spite of the color of his teachers and principal, with the white world outside him—the police, the White Citizens' Council, the mayor or sheriff, the governor of his state. And the school child's instinctive vision is perfectly correct. His teachers are either timid and quiescently part of the system or they are actively extra-punitive, dictatorial, hostile, vengeful, or worse. Sometimes his teachers are badly-trained, misinformed, but even when they know just that, they remain fearfully bound to the system that made them. The teacher with the ruler or iron chain or whip is himself caught

---

*Each time I have reread this essay in preparation for this book's publication, I have been tempted to change the pronouns throughout. After all, I wrote the essay as a woman writing about the experience of teaching students, most of whom were women. Temptation admitted, I leave the ringing male pronouns as a reminder of the history we share with those who have gone before us.

Howe, Florence. *The Myths of Coeducation*. Indianapolis: Indiana University Press, 1984. By permission of author.

in a power structure that allows him to teach only by rote to rote-learners. You learn this, he says, and you too can learn to get along. Get used to the violence, get used to being struck, get used to taking orders, for that is the way life is on the outside. You too can learn to follow the rules and get to sit up here, ruler in hand, ready to strike out at anything out of line.

It is possible to sympathize with the middle-class Negro teacher caught between his own desire to rise from the poverty around him and his fear of the white power structure that controls his ability to rise. For the Negro teacher and his Negro principal are directed by white school superintendents, themselves under the direction of other white political forces. In Negro schools, the intercom is used by the principal to intimidate and harass the teacher. The principal, in turn, is harassed by others. And only the "Shirley," finally, is able to stand up and sing, with her friends and associates in Freedom Schools:

> Before I'll be a slave
> I'll be buried in my grave
> And go home to my Lord and be free.

If the official public school system of Mississippi is geared and oiled to operate efficiently for the status quo, it is no wonder, then, that the civil rights movement should have conceived of the Freedom School. But would children for whom a school was an unpleasant training ground for a repressive society come, voluntarily, even to a "Freedom" school? Of course, voluntarily was the first clue. No one had to come, and once there, no "attendance" was taken. You came if you wanted to and you stayed if you were interested and you left if you felt like leaving. Your teacher, moreover, was "Tom" or "Leo" or "Gene," who shook your hand, called you by your first name, and said how glad he was to meet you. In your "class," your teacher sat with you in a circle, and soon you got the idea that you could say what you thought and that no one, least of all the teacher, would laugh at you or strike you. Soon, too, you got the idea that you might disagree with your teacher, white or black, and get a respectful hearing, that your teacher was really interested in what *you* thought or felt. Soon you were forgetting about skin colors altogether and thinking about ideas or feelings, about people and events.

As educators, we live in a fool's paradise, or worse in a knave's, if we are unaware that when we are teaching *something* to anyone we are also teaching *everything* to that same anyone. When we say we are teaching mathematics to Freddy, we also must admit that we are teaching Freddy what kind of person we are, how we live in the kind of world we control (or the kind of world that controls us), and how he can grow up to be one of the controllers or controlled. Teaching, we become, as so many people have said, a model for Freddy to learn from, quite apart from the mathematics or French or history we may be teaching him. And sometimes we are very "good" models. Sometimes, like "good" parents or "good" political leaders, we teach Freddy to love his neighbors, to honor honesty and integrity, to value the means as well as the ends, to abstain from using and controlling and killing human life. But sometimes we are not so inclined. Sometimes, at our worst, we educators resemble tyrants.

The idea of the Freedom School turns upside down particularly effectively the conventions of many public school systems that have to do with the role of the teacher. The teacher is not to be an omnipotent, aristocratic dictator, a substitute for the domineering parent or the paternalistic state. He is not to stand before rows of students, simply pouring pre-digested, pre-censored information into their brains. The Freedom School teacher is, in fact, to be present not simply to teach, but rather *to learn with* the students. In the democratic and creative sense that Wordsworth understood when he described the poet as "a man among men," the Freedom School teacher is a student among students. He does not have all the answers; his creativity is his ability to communicate with his students, to listen to them as much as they listen to him. The vitality of the teacher, as Freedom Schools would have it, lies in the student's and the teacher's mutual apprehension of life. A Freedom School teacher knows that education is the *drawing out* not of blood from stones, but rather of experience and observation from human beings. He knows that a thirteen year old who has survived his years in Mississippi understands, however fearfully or inarticulately, a great deal about the world he has survived in. The Freedom School teacher is there not as professional manipulator, but as concerned questioner—who really wants to hear what his companions will say, who really wants, himself, to be led by it. And thus he can turn the key to help the student break through the door that confines him—and all without recourse to the same means, authoritarianism, repression, violence, that have kept him locked in.

For much of the month of August, I coordinated and taught in one of Jackson, Mississippi's nine Freedom Schools. Opened on the fifth of August, these were in addition to the more than forty others that functioned through the summer in more than twenty different towns. Like most of the schools around the state, mine was located in the basement of a church. The basement room was acoustically difficult for a single voice and yet many voices together filled it uncomfortably. How to get attention, even briefly for announcements or for the start of some activity, perhaps the breaking up of the group into small discussion units? On the second day, when my voice had begun to hurt and when clapping my hands had begun to seem ineffectual, I hit accidentally upon the Quakerly method of raising your right hand. The children saw me standing before them, my right hand raised, and for communication's sake, my left index finger against my lips. They began to nudge one another, to raise their own hands, and to place their own fingers on their lips. And very quickly, the room grew quiet. I said, "All hands down," and delighted that the method had worked, added, "Isn't this a lovely way to get silence?" Of course the children responded all together to me and to each other, and we had to begin all over again, right hands raised. But the method did work.

Also on one of the very first days, in the hot afternoon, with the teachers uncomfortable because they had had no lunch, and the children restless because we had not yet solved the problem of outdoor play space, two little boys began to fight. They were small enough so that I could forcibly separate them, but even in the midst of my hot, hungry exasperation, I had a vision of other fights and bigger boys whom I would be unable to pull apart. And from somewhere came the words: "Now, look here, we have few rules in this school, but we do have one important one and that is we do not hit each other— we talk. Understand? We talk here. This is a school for talking. Whenever you feel like hitting someone, remember to talk instead." The children looked puzzled and I said it all again. And then I sat down—in the midst of chaos—to talk with the two little boys about their fight. There were more fights in the next several days, but my words had begun to spread so that some of the older children were repeating them to the younger ones. And while we were never entirely free from an occasional blow—it was virtually impossible, for example, to keep older brothers from "punishing" their younger siblings—there were few or no fights after the first week.

The Greater Blair Street AME Zion Church, under the direction of Reverend R. M. Richmond, gave us not only shelter and equipment but most of all moral support and friendly protection. We drew our students, regardless of church membership, from the neighborhood. The families in a six to ten block radius ranged from lower-middle class to very poor (incomes from close to nothing to four thousand). The people in the neighborhood, like most of Jackson, were nervous about the arriving Freedom School teachers and were especially loathe to give us housing, for that would signify open support. Reverend Richmond convinced the people next door to give their empty

room to the two male teachers. They, Gene Gogol and Tom Timberg, in the company of friendly students-to-be, had been canvassing the neighborhood during the time I was spending getting acquainted with the minister. When they reported back that they had had several offers of spare cots that could be moved elsewhere as well as of food—signs, of course, of a desire to help but without the attendant danger of housing a summer volunteer—we were able to make arrangements to move the beds into the empty room in the house next door to the church.

Our first impressions of the community were not incorrect: the parents continued to be cautious. With few exceptions, we had no contact with parents. But the children, of course, were different. They turned up, they turned out, they were willing to do anything, to go anywhere with us.

As Staughton Lynd, professor of history at Yale and summer director of all Freedom Schools in Mississippi, said, it was "a political decision for any parent to let his child come to a Freedom School." And many parents, in Jackson at least, avoided making that decision. I had assumed that parents knew that their children were attending Freedom School—until the day when I took up the question of sending a representative from our school to the state-wide Freedom School convention in Meridian. Expenses would be paid and the weekend program would be entertaining; I felt certain, that morning, that it would be difficult choosing the one delegate we were allowed to represent us. But to my surprise no one was willing to make a nomination—it was as if they all understood something I did not. I asked for volunteers and got no response again. Then I asked a thirteen year old girl, who had been particularly articulate the day before in a discussion, whether she would like to go. She said, first, only an abrupt "No," but when questioned in disbelieving tones, she admitted to, "Yes, but I can't."

"But why not, then? All your expenses would be paid, and you know you'd enjoy it."

She finally said that her father would not allow her to go, that he disapproved of her association with "the movement" in general, and that he did not approve even of her attending Freedom School. She was deliberately vague about whether or not he knew she was attending. When I asked whether it would help if I went to see him, she first laughed and then urged me most seriously not to. The story repeated itself, with certain variations, around the room.

Two young mothers, both of them relatively new to the neighborhood, were sympathetic enough to the movement and interested enough to issue invitations to us. The mother of a six year old, who sent her daughter to Freedom School, sent word also that she would like to see "the teachers" after school, at which point she invited all of us to a hot dinner the following afternoon at three. Later, she asked to be included in our evening activities. Another mother of a teen-ager, whose own family disapproved of the student's attending Freedom School, also sent for the teachers, whom she then invited to accompany her to a jazz concert. Later, this mother held a party for the departing teachers and announced her willingness to be of service to Freedom Schools in the future.

Freedom Schools were planned originally with high school students in mind. In most places around the state, when Freedom School opened, *all* children turned up, regardless of publicity about high school students. Eventually, around the state, community centers were founded, first to take care of the younger children, later to function in ways that Freedom School could not or would not. When we opened our Blair Street doors on Wednesday, August 5, at eight a.m., "children," ages three to twenty-three, began to arrive. And of course we turned no one away. They came in twos and threes, sometimes several from a family, the teen-agers holding the hands of their younger brothers and sisters. Fifty-one students arrived throughout that first day and fifty more during the next several days. Some stayed a while and left, never to appear again. Others stayed that day and came every day thereafter. Some came and disappeared, and then came again to stay to the end.

Nearly half of any total number of children present at the Blair Street School were under the age of ten. For these children we ran a combined school and community center in one of the two basement rooms of the church. Luckily, on the day before school had opened, I had met Leo Reese, a magically personable reading specialist from Gary, Indiana, the father of eleven children, who had volunteered to spend one week in Jackson. Leo, a native Mississippian and a Negro, had been born and raised in Paseagoula, on the Gulf. In the few days that Leo was present, he organized a program for the younger children, and because of his skills, freed three of the four assigned teachers for work with the older students.

Later, after Leo had gone, two young women, Shirley Logan, a Jacksonian and a recent college graduate, and her cousin from Chicago, Superior Walker, came to the Blair Street School for a visit and stayed for two weeks to carry on the program with the younger children.

Mornings at Freedom School began slowly without opening bells. On some days we sang freedom songs until the group collected. On one day, August 6, Hiroshima Day, I told the students about what had happened nineteen years ago. On another day, I read from Langston Hughes' poems and then listened to reactions from the students. By nine-thirty, we were usually numerous enough to break into smaller discussion groups. Those children under ten went off to their room, generally for the rest of the day, unless there was to be a special activity in the afternoon. The older students separated sometimes into several age groups for a discussion that occupied most of the morning. The Citizenship Curriculum, about which I shall have more to say later, is the core of the program shared by all Freedom Schools in Mississippi. There was usually time, an hour before lunch and one after, for two hours of "electives." Negro history, chemistry, biology, English, French, and typing were the subjects settled on by the groups' desires and their teachers' abilities.

The afternoons were particularly hot, and more and more frequent were the noisy visits to the drinking fountain and the lavatories at the back of the church. There was no outdoor play space, but, eventually, teachers began to take groups of students to the playground of a nearby Catholic school that the sisters allowed us to use. One of the older boys organized a softball team and both boys and girls were eager to play ball regardless of the heat. Late in the afternoon (called "evening" in Mississippi) some of the teachers and students joined the regular COFO precinct workers for voter registration work.

The best afternoons at Blair Street were those filled with special events. On opening day, for example, Pete Seeger, arrived at one-thirty in the afternoon to give us a private concert. With the whole school present, the very littlest ones asleep in any arms that would hold them, Pete talked first of his recent visit to twenty-seven countries around the world. He told us that all children were the same the world over and that music was a language that flew easily over even the highest walls. He demonstrated his statements by playing and singing Indian, African, Chinese, and Polynesian songs, in each instance allowing the rhythms to illustrate the emotion before offering a translation of the words. "Isn't this a happy song," he said, after singing, in African dialect, "Everybody Loves Saturday Night." He taught the children to sing the foreign words of several songs, and though we didn't know it then, that was the high moment for them. The Blair Street students had no idea that Pete was a famous man, but they wanted to hear more of him and happily turned up that evening to be transported across town to Anderson Chapel where Pete Seeger sang for a packed and overflowing house until his voice gave out.

Films were also a good afternoon activity. On the day we showed the full-length *Oliver Twist* to an audience of more than one hundred, I heard one boy of ten mutter to himself about Oliver, "He sho' is white, but he's a slave just the same." The film ran too late in the afternoon for discussion, but the following morning was filled with questions and talk about child labor. Another group of films were part of a special, state-wide program arranged by Paul Lauter, a professor of English at Smith College. All bearing upon the connections among the struggle for civil rights, nonviolence, and the need for world peace, the four films were used by Paul to spark discussions. Two of these films were documentaries, one about Gandhi, the other about the Montgomery, Alabama, bus strike. The students were more interested in talking, however, about the other pair of films. One was a recent Polish film, *The Magician*. The other, an animated cartoon, *The Hat*, consisted of a dialogue between two soldiers (Dizzie Gillespie—whose music also filled the film—and the British comedian, Dudley Moore) who guard either side of a line, the hat of one falling onto the side of the other as they march. The students were quick to compare lines that divided nations with lines that divided people within nations. They remembered, during the discussion that followed, relevant details through which the film attempted to show that talking, in human terms, helps to erase lines.

Evening activities provided still other kinds of experience for the Freedom School student. Apart from concerts, there were mass meetings, at one of which, for example, A. Philip Randolph spoke along with leading Jackson ministers. Best of all was the Free Southern Theatre's production of *In White America*, which toured the state as part of a continuing program of special entertainment for Freedom Schools. Most of these students had never seen live theatre, and certainly not a play about themselves in history. Their response as audience was continuously energetic, especially since, as they reported the next day, they enjoyed recognizing incidents they had been reading of or discussing. One student, Kaaren Robinson, age fifteen, wrote the following as part of a review published in the *Blair Street Freedom Bugle:*

> It portrayed the brutal transportation of the Negro from his native Africa to a new country, the inhuman treatment upon his arrival, the confusing position of the political-minded white man with regard to his stand on the slave question and the continuous struggle of the Negro against over-whelming odds.
>
> . . . Because of his up-bringing, the new freedom put the Negro in a confusing state which naturally led him back into another kind of slavery. This slavery has lasted until now.
>
> The author achieved these points through narration and conversation.
>
> Through this medium the Negro of today can better understand why the white man feels as he does toward him. However, this does not justify his feelings nor his actions. In *White America* is a great and moving drama which should be seen by black and white alike.

Though questioned, Kaaren resisted any attempt to enlarge upon the play's effect. From her point of view, the play allowed her to understand the white man's confusion; it told her nothing about the Negro she did not already know.

Charles Cobb, a student at Howard University before he joined the SNCC staff, was responsible late in 1963 for suggesting the idea of Freedom Schools. He has written cogently of their *raison d'être,* in a piece called "This is the Situation":

> Repression is the law; oppression, a way of life—regimented by the judicial and executive branches of the state government, rigidly enforced by state police machinery, with veering from the path of "our way of life" not tolerated at all. Here, an idea of your own is a subversion that must be squelched; for each bit of intellectual initiative represents the threat of a probe into the why of denial. Learning here means only learning to stay in your place. Your place is to be satisfied—a "good nigger."
>
> They have learned the learning necessary for immediate survival: that silence is safest, so volunteer nothing; that the teacher is the state, and tell them only what they want to hear; that the law and learning are white man's law and learning.
>
> There is hope and there is dissatisfaction—feebly articulated—both born out of the desperation of needed alternatives not given. This is the generation that has silently made the vow of no more raped mothers—no more castrated fathers; that looks for an alternative to a lifetime of bent, burnt, and broken backs, minds, and souls. Their creativity must be molded from the rhythm of a muttered "white son-of-a-bitch"; from the roar of a hunger bloated belly; and from the stench of rain and mud washed shacks. There is the waiting, not to be taught, but to be, to reach out and meet and join together, and to change. The tiredness of being told it must be, "cause that's white folks' business," must be met with the insistence that it's their business. They know that anyway. It's because their parents didn't make it their business that they're being so systematically destroyed. What they must see is the link between a rotting shack and a rotting America.

The Citizenship Curriculum, the discussion of which filled most of our mornings, is frankly a response to the repressive society Charles Cobb has described. It is aimed at meeting two basic needs of students: first, a need for information; second, a need for identity and hence activity. The "facts" of history: in terms of dates, people's names, places, events, as well as the interpretations of history—all this has been denied to them, and denied particularly in relation to their own situation as American Negroes. Not only is Negro history unknown to them, but even the history of the current Negro revolution is known only in bits and pieces, largely through television, since their newspapers are notoriously uninformative. The second need, the need for identity and activity, is organically one with the need for facts. It has to do with what happens when an individual begins to know himself as part of history, with a past and a potential future as well as a present. What happens when an individual begins to assess himself as a human being? The aim of the Citizenship Curriculum here is to assist the growth of self-respect, through self-awareness, both of which lead to self-help. In this way, the curriculum at the center of the Freedom Schools is frankly and avowedly a program for leadership development.

In many different ways, the mimeographed curriculum makes clear the Freedom Schools' purpose: "to provide an educational experience for students which will make it possible for them to challenge the myths of our society, to perceive more clearly its realities, and to find alternatives, and ultimately, new directions for action." Or more briefly, "to train people to be active agents in bringing about social change." The curriculum itself, however, declares that "It is not our purpose to impose a particular set of conclusions. Our purpose is to encourage the asking of questions, and hope that society can be improved."

Because the chief tool is the question, the curriculum is hopefully "developmental," that is, one that "begins on the level of the students' everyday lives and those things in their environment that they have either already experienced or can readily perceive, and builds up to a more realistic perception of American society, themselves, the conditions of their oppression, and alternatives offered by the Freedom Movement." The seven units are as follows:

1. Comparison of students' reality with others (the way the students live and the way others live)
2. North to Freedom? (The Negro in the north)
3. Examining the apparent reality (the "better lives" that whites live)
4. Introducing the power structure
5. The poor Negro and the poor white
6. Material things versus soul things
7. The Movement

In addition, two sets of questions are to be constantly in the minds of the teachers and frequently introduced to the students:

The Basic Set of Questions:

1. Why are we (teachers and students) in Freedom Schools?
2. What is the Freedom Movement?
3. What alternatives does the Freedom Movement offer us?

The Secondary Set of Questions:

1. What does the majority culture have that we want?
2. What does the majority culture have that we don't want?
3. What do we have that we want to keep?

Some of my own experience was with a relatively young group—eleven to fourteen-year-olds. After describing their own houses, they went on to describe the houses of whites in Jackson that they had seen, either because they had themselves worked as domestics, or because their mothers did. When asked what changes they would like made in their own houses, while their answers varied from additional rooms to more yard space, no one thought in terms as grandiose as the "white" houses they had described, and most of them thought of their houses as "comfortable." On the other hand, they were certain that their (segregated) schools were inferior, even when they admitted that the buildings were new. They resented their hand-me-down textbooks, they suspected the inadequacy of their teachers, and they complained particularly bitterly about the repressive atmosphere. In their schools, they reported that no questioning or discussion was allowed, except in rare instances when they and a particular teacher knew they were "taking a chance." Of course, they knew little or nothing of conditions in white schools, either in Mississippi or elsewhere, beyond their impression that these, somehow, were "better."

High school juniors and seniors were especially interested in the subject of going north to freedom. On the one hand, many of them expressed a wish to go north to college, in part because they suspected that Negro colleges in Mississippi were as inadequate as their public schools, but also because they wanted the experience of learning in an integrated group. They were articulate about the need for communication between black and white. The freedom songs they sang each day—"Black and white together/ We shall overcome," for example—were not simply words to be mouthed. On the other hand, some of them had been reading with us from the works of Richard Wright and James Baldwin* of the Negro in Chicago or Harlem; and they knew they were living through a summer that had brought riots to northern cities, though not to Jackson, Mississippi. They questioned the condition of Negroes everywhere, and many of them concluded that it was probably better to stay in Mississippi and work to improve things there than to imagine that things were better in another place.

The Freedom School curriculum's most substantial statement about values, "Material Things and Soul Things," takes as its central idea the society that is "humane" because it is "nonviolent." Negroes, of course, are no more naturally violent or nonviolent than any other group. But these students, brought up on the edge of a volcano, named as their heroes Martin Luther King and Medgar Evers, and, when they knew of him, Gandhi as well. At Blair Street, I asked the question about heroes because Paul Lauter had reported that when he asked the question at Freedom Schools throughout the state, those very three names occurred. It was also Paul's impression that as SNCC people became veterans at their jobs, nonviolence for them became not strategic manner but genuine convic-

tion. For the veteran SNCC worker, Matt Suarez, who dropped in one afternoon at Blair Street for a visit and stayed for a discussion, nonviolence had become essential to life. Some of the students who listened to him had also experienced organized demonstrations within the discipline of the nonviolent movement. But their minds were far from decided. They questioned the theory; they suspected themselves of "violent feelings"; they talked about "strategy"; they asked for a "speaker"—and got more discussion!

Because the student needs to learn not only about the world he lives in, but also how to be free enough to live in it, the chief tool of Freedom Schools always was discussion. Ideally, discussion began with the question, "How do you feel about . . . ?" or "How would you feel if . . . ?" and moved on to questions about motivation ("Why do you feel this way?" or "Why would anyone feel this way?"). Once the discussion had begun, the questions could move on to students' reactions to each other's ideas. At first, of course, students were distrustful of the situation generally. Some were also shy before their peers as well as frightened of their teacher. But of course they all had feelings and they all had some words with which to describe them. And eventually the moment came, unnoticed and passed over, when a student could say easily to his (white) teacher or to a fellow student, "I disagree," and explain why.

The teacher's main problem was to learn to keep quiet, to learn how to listen and to question creatively rather than to talk at the students. He had to discard whatever formal classroom procedures he had ever learned and respond with feeling and imagination

*In 1964, I had not heard of Zora Neale Hurston, and the poets and prose writers I was prepared to discuss were all males. The literary curriculum I offered included e. e. cummings, William Carlos Williams, Langston Hughes, Richard Wright, and James Baldwin.

as well as with intelligence and good humor to the moods and needs of the group. Above all, the students challenged his honesty: he could not sidestep unpleasantness; he could not afford to miss any opportunity for discussing differences.*

I have no crystal ball, but I can submit two aspects of my own experience that suggest that the Freedom Schools of '64 spread more than transitory ripples in a huge Mississippi sea. The first was a discussion that led directly to social action independently instigated by the students themselves. The second was an experiment that led directly to the students writing poetry.

The third week of Freedom Schools in Jackson was also the week of school registration for those Negro first-graders who were to attend previously white schools. Registration was scheduled for early Thursday morning; a mass meeting for interested parents had been called by thirty-six Negro ministers of Jackson for Tuesday night. This was Monday morning, and the group at the Blair Street School had begun, for some reason, to talk about the "myth" of Negro inferiority. At one point, when there was silence, I asked how many of the twenty students present (ages fourteen to twenty) knew some first-grader who was about to start school. Everyone did. Did anyone know any who were going to a white school? No one did. When I asked why, I got many different responses:

My sister thinks her son would be unhappy with white children.
My brother hasn't gone to kindergarten.

*So strong was the power of the male-centered universe that, although I am describing my own experience, I use the pronoun "he."

The white school is too far away.
My mother wants my brother to be with his friends.
My father says he doesn't like the idea.

None of the students had mentioned the word fear. They all looked uncomfortable and I felt my anger rise: "What am I going to say to my friends back North when they ask me why Negro mothers haven't registered their children in white schools? That they like things the way they are?" I could see the consternation on the face of Gene Gogol, my fellow teacher, who began, "I disagree, Florence, you just don't understand the situation." I felt that his rebuke was probably a just one, but then the students began to smile wryly and, one by one, they began to talk of the various fears that "perhaps" these parents were feeling. Personal safety. Economic security—the loss of jobs because they weren't being "good niggers." Failure in the white school—either because of social ostracism or because of poor training and possibly the alleged intellectual inferiority. But then suddenly, I do not know exactly what shifted the discussion, perhaps something about the white faces that Gene and I wore in the midst of the black ones, suddenly the students were talking about *positive* reasons for sending children into integrated schools. Then one of the sixteen-year-old girls sugge sted that perhaps we—meaning those of us in the discussion group—ought to go out into the neighborhood and talk with parents who were reluctant to send their children to white schools, that perhaps we were most suited for this job since we knew the value of good education and we knew there was really nothing to fear. When I suggested that we try one of the school's favorite procedures, role-playing, there were volunteers immediately for mother, father, child, and for two visitors from the Freedom School. The players were evenly matched so that the play-discussion rehearsed all the arguments we had heard. The role-playing father remained essentially unconvinced, but his wife assured the visitors that she had really changed her mind and that, after they had gone, she would "work on" her husband.

Gene and a crew of student volunteers worked all the rest of Monday, Monday night, and all of Tuesday. They talked to more than seventy families and received from twenty-seven of these assurances that at least the mother would attend Tuesday night's mass meeting, perhaps would take advantage of the transportation we would provide. Disappointingly, only one mother kept her promise. But on Wednesday morning, Gene and some students began their visits again, and by Thursday noon, all of Blair Street's Freedom School were boasting that eleven of the forty-three Negro children in Jackson who actually registered to attend previously white schools had done so as a direct result of Gene's and the students' talks with parents.

Thus the students had direct evidence that their school experience had led them to create something that was lasting and profound. Additional evidence—this of a more personal nature—followed their reading and discussion of poetry.

We had begun with poems by Langston Hughes. They knew immediately that when Hughes, in a poem called "As I Grew Older," mentioned a "thick wall" and a "shadow" growing between him and his childhood "dream," he was talking about walls and shadows they knew every day in Jackson: the barbed wire around the parks, for example, or the hate in white men's faces when they tried to go to a movie downtown. I did not need to be a teacher showing the difference between literal meaning and what was "symbolized." There *was* curiosity about forms. Do all poems rhyme? What is rhyme, anyway? Can poets use any words they like? The students, who had never heard of Langston Hughes, were surprised by his slang, by his use of jazz expressions. They listened to the occasional irregularity that made rhythms interesting, especially in a Hughes song-poem like "The Weary Blues"—which they never tired of.

One day, when discussion had flagged, I suggested a "game." Let's divide into four groups of five and try writing a "group" poem. I even offered a subject: try writing about yourselves and Jackson—we had just been reading about Hughes and Harlem. When I returned, half an hour later, cries of "Listen to this" greeted me. With one exception, the poems were not group products—the groups had stayed to watch individual members create. The best poem came from a sixteen year old girl, a visitor to Jackson from Pascagoula, who had just come for the first time to Freedom School, and who was to continue attending thenceforth. This is Alice Jackson's poem called "Mine":

> I want to walk the streets of a town,
> Turn into any restaurant and sit down,
> And be served the food of my choice,
> And not be met by a hostile voice.
> I want to live in the best hotel for a week,
> Or go for a swim at a public beach.
> I want to go to the best university

And not be met with violence or
uncertainty.
I want the things my ancestors
Thought we'd never have.
They are mine as a Negro, an
American;
I shall have them or be dead.

In the days that followed, we read poems by Sandburg and Frost, two poets the students had heard of, but the greatest excitement came from their introduction to e e cummings, especially to the poem "Anyone Lived in a Pretty How Town." One day, after two hours of a discussion of cummings' poems, I asked the eight or nine students present—ages fourteen to seventeen—whether they wanted to try writing again. When I asked whether they wanted a suggested subject, I heard an overwhelming series of no's. No subject . . . let us write what we feel like writing.

Within twenty minutes, Shirley Ballard, age seventeen, was reading aloud to me a poem called "Time." She read it slowly, emphasizing the individuality of certain words and phrases. Its feeling was clearly fragmentary. But then she showed me the page on which she had written the poem: four long lines, resembling her reading not at all. She had read it in a manner that suggested something else, and I showed her cummings' page. She caught on instantly, took her page, and returned in several minutes with the following version:

Time goes by so slowly
my mind reacts so lowly
    how faint
how moody
    I feel,
        I love not
    I care not.
Don't love me.

Let me live.
  Die
  Cry
  Sigh
All alone
    Maybe someday I'll go home.

Another seventeen year old, Sandra Ann Harris, quickly produced a cummings-like poem—even to the elimination of all capitalization:

why did i my don'ts
why did i my dids
what's my didn'ts' purpose
is it to fulfill my dids

what isn'ts have i proclaimed
what ises have i pronounced
why can't i do my doings
my couldn'ts do renounce

my wouldn'ts are excuses
my couldn'ts couldn't be helped
my weren'ts were all willful
my words of little help

the haven'ts were just there
my didn'ts did believe
that all my won'ts are daring
my wills to receive

If it is startling to consider how much these students learned so quickly, it is also instructive to consider that in Freedom Schools all over Mississippi this summer students were becoming both social activists and poets. An impressive volume of poetry (which may soon be published) appeared in Freedom School newspapers. And a Mississippi Student Union has been formed. The connection between poetry and politics should surprise no one who has read the Romantics or, more recently, the poets of the Irish Renaissance. What is surprising is that, in some ways, it took *so little* to accomplish so much in the Mississippi Freedom Schools.

Consider the discussion circle, the union of teachers and students in a status-free ring. Consider too the position of these students—blacks in a white culture—as outsiders who were now, in 1964, *conscious* outsiders, youngsters seeing new possibilities ahead of them and, at the same time, young adults with the wisdom to see what Negro slavery has been. Under these special new conditions, one could talk and think about what it was like to be a slave and what it might be like to be free. One could even try *being* free. Under these special conditions—the consciousness of being suppressed combined with the proffered opportunity to base education on that consciousness—creativity was the natural response.

What have we to learn from Freedom Schools? The politics of education. That our schools are political grounds in which our students begin to learn about society's rules. That, therefore, if we wish to alter our students and our society, we must alter our schools. That if we would have strong and creative minds we must remove chains both from bodies and spirits. That we as adults and educators have to listen and respond rather than preach. That we need to share with our students a sense of being open to what each uniquely experienced companion can reveal. That this perspective of equality is itself a revolution that goes far beyond the surface movement of Negroes into white society. And that if Freedom School teachers in Mississippi society know themselves as unwelcome and harassed outsiders, not unlike the Negro students, then authentic teachers anywhere must face a similar knowledge.

The Freedom School students and teachers who heard Langston Hughes' "As I Grew Older" understood that Hughes' prayer was theirs too—for strength and wisdom to break through all spiritual prisons of self and society and so to reach freedom:

> My hands!
> My dark hands!
> Break through the wall!
> Find my dream!
> Help me to shatter this darkness,
> To smash this night,
> To break this shadow
> Into a thousand lights of sun,
> Into a thousand whirling dreams
> Of sun!

7

Ten-Point Program

(1969)

Black Student Unions

We want an education for our people that exposes the true nature of this decadent American Society. We want an education that teaches us our true history and role in the present day society. We believe in an educational system that will give our people a knowledge of self. If a man does not have knowledge of himself and his position in society and the world, then he has little chance to relate to anything else.

1. *We want freedom. We want power to determine the destiny of our school.*

   We believe that we will not be free within the schools to get a decent education unless we are able to have a say and determine the type of education that will affect and determine the destiny of our people.

2. *We want full enrollment in the schools for our people.*

   We believe that the city and federal government is responsible and obligated to give every man a decent education.

3. *We want an end to the robbery by the white man of our black community.*

   We believe that this racist government has robbed us of an education. We believe that this racist capitalist government has robbed the Black Community of its money by forcing us to pay higher taxes for less quality.

4. *We want decent educational facilities, fit for the use of students.*

   We believe that if these businessmen will not give decent facilities to our community schools, then the schools and their facilities should be taken out of the hands of these few individual racists and placed into the hands of the community, with government aid, so the community can develop a decent and suitable educational system.

5. *We want an education for our people that teaches us how to survive in the present day society.*

   We believe that if the educational system does not teach us how to survive in society and the world it loses its meaning for existence.

6. *We want all racist teachers to be excluded and restricted from all public schools.*

   We believe that if the teacher in a school is acting in racist fashion then the teacher is not interested in the welfare or development of the students but only in their destruction.

7. *We want an immediate end to police brutality and murder of black people. We want all police and special agents to be excluded and restricted from school premises.*

60

We believe that there should be an end to harassment by the police department of Black people. We believe that if all of the police were pulled out of the schools, the schools would become more functional.

8. *We want all students that have been exempt, expelled, or suspended from school to be reinstated.*

We believe all students should be reinstated because they haven't received fair and impartial judgment or have been put out because of incidents or situations that have occurred outside of the school's authority.

9. *We want all students when brought to trial to be tried in student court by a jury of their peer group or students of their school.*

We believe that the student courts should follow the United States Constitution so that students can receive a fair trial. The 14th Amendment of the U.S. Constitution gives a man a right to be tried by a jury of his peer group. A peer is a person from a similar economical, social, religious, geographical, environmental, historical and racial background. To do this the court would be forced to select a jury of students from the community from which the defendant came. We have been and are being tried by a white principal, vice-principal, and white students that have no understanding of the "average reasoning man" of the Black Community.

10. *We want power, enrollment, equipment, education, teachers, justice, and peace.*

As our major political objective, an assembly for the student body, in which only the students will be allowed to participate, for the purpose of determining the will of the students as to the school's destiny.

We hold these truths as being self-evident, that all men are created equal, that they are endowed by their creator with certain inalienable rights, that among these are life, liberty, and the pursuit of happiness. To secure these rights within the schools, governments are instituted among the students, deriving their just powers from the consent of the governed, that whenever any form of student government becomes destructive to these ends, it is the right of the students to alter or abolish it and to institute new government, laying its foundation on such principles and organizing its power in such form as to them shall seem most likely to effect their safety and happiness.

Prudence, indeed, will dictate that governments long established should not be changed for light and transient causes, and accordingly all experiences have shown, that mankind are more liable to suffer, while evils are sufferable, than to right themselves by abolishing the forms to which they are accustomed. But when a long train of abuses and force, pursuing invariably the same object, reveals a design to reduce them to absolute destruction, it is their right, it is their duty, to throw off such government and to provide new guards for their future security.

February, 1969

8

Columbia Liberated

(1968)

The Columbia Strike Coordinating Committee

Something is happening here but you don't know what it is, do
you, Mr. Jones?

R. Dylan

"Up against the wall, motherfuckers!"

*Entire Math Commune to Several
Hundred Members of the
New York City Police Dept.'s
Tactical Patrol Force, April 30, 1968.*

THE STRIKE IN CONTEXT

The most important fact about the Columbia strike is that Columbia exists within American society. This statement may appear to be a truism, yet it is a fact too often forgotten by observers, reporters, administrators, faculty members, and even some students. These people attempt to explain the "disturbances" as reaction to an unresponsive and archaic administrative structure, youthful outbursts of unrest much like panty raids, the product of a conspiracy by communist agents in national **SDS** or a handful of hard-core nihilists ("destroyers") on the campus, or just general student unrest due to the war in Vietnam.

But in reality, striking students are responding to the totality of the conditions of our society, not just one small part of it, the university. We are disgusted with the war, with racism, with being a part of a system over which we have no control, a system which demands gross inequalities of wealth and power, a system which denies personal and social freedom and potential, a system which has to manipulate and repress us in order to exist. The university can only be seen as a cog in this machine; or, more accurately, a factory whose product is knowledge and personnel (us) useful to the functioning of the system. The specific problems of university life, its boredom and meaninglessness, help prepare us for boring and meaningless work in the "real" world. And the policies of the university—expansion into the community, exploitation of blacks and Puerto Ricans, support for imperialist wars—also serve the interests of banks, corporations, government, and military represented on the Columbia Board of Trustees and the ruling class of our society. In every way, the university is "society's child." Our attack upon the university is really an attack upon this society and its effects upon us. We have never said otherwise.

The development of the New Left at Columbia represents an organized political response to the society. We see our task, first as identifying for ourselves and for others the nature of our society—who controls it and for what ends—and secondly, developing ways in which to transform it. We understand that only through struggle can we create a free, human society, since the present one is dominated by a small ruling class which exploits, manipulates, and distorts for its own ends—and has shown in countless ways its determination to maintain its position. The Movement at Columbia began years ago agitating and organizing students around issues such as students' power in the university (Action), support of the civil rights movement (CORE), the war in Vietnam (the Independent Committee on Vietnam). Finally, Columbia chapter Students for a Democratic Society initiated actions against many of the above issues as they manifest themselves on campus. Politically speaking, SDS, from its inception on campus in November, 1966, sought to unite issues, "to draw connections," to view this society as a totality. SDS united the two main themes of the movement—opposition to racial oppression and to the impe-

rialist war in Vietnam—with our own sense of frustration, disappointment, and oppression at the quality of our lives in capitalist society.

One of the most important questions raised by the strike was who controls Columbia, and for what ends? SDS pointed to the Board of Trustees as the intersection of various corporate, financial, real-estate, and government interests outside the university which need the products of the university—personnel and knowledge—in order to exist. It is this power which we are fighting when we fight particular policies of the university such as expansion at the expense of poor people or institutional ties to the war-machine. We can hope for and possibly win certain reforms within the university, but the ultimate reforms we need—the elimination of war and exploitation—can only be gained after we overthrow the control of our country by the class of people on Columbia's Board of Trustees. In a sense, Columbia is the place where we received our education—our revolutionary education.

President Emeritus Grayson Kirk, in his 5,000 word "Message to Alumni, Parents, and Other Friends of Columbia," concludes

the leaders of the SDS—as distinct from an unknown number of their supporters—are concerned with local parochial university issues only as they serve as a means to a larger end.

Though Kirk perceives that we are interested in more than Columbia University, he ignores the fact that the issues we raise are not at all "local parochial university issues," but indeed transcend the physical and class boundary of the university to unite us, the students, with neighborhood people, blacks and Puerto Ricans, and even the Vietnamese, with all the people oppressed by this society.

But why do students, predominantly of the "middle-class," in effect, reject the university designed to integrate them into the system and instead identify with the most oppressed of this country and the world? Why did the gymnasium in Morningside Park become an issue over which Columbia was shut down for seven weeks? Why pictures of Che Guevara, Malcolm X, and red flags in the liberated buildings?

Basically, the sit-ins and strike of April and May gave us a chance to express the extreme dissatisfaction we feel at being *caught in this "system."* We rejected the gap between potential and realization in this society. We rejected our present lives in the university and our future lives in business, government or other universities like this one. In a word, we saw ourselves as oppressed, and began to understand the forces at work which make for our oppression. In turn, we saw those same forces responsible for the oppression and colonization of blacks and Puerto Ricans in ghettos, and Vietnamese and the people of the third world. By initiating a struggle in support of black and third world liberation, we create the conditions for our own freedom—by building a movement which will someday take power over our society, we will free ourselves.

As the strike and the struggle for our demands progressed, we learned more about the nature of our enemy and his unwillingness to grant any of our demands or concede any of his power. Illusions disappeared: the moral authority of the educator gave way to police violence, the faculty appeared in all its impotent glory. On the other hand, tremendous support came in from community residents, black and white alike, from university employees, from high school students, from people across the country and around the world. Inevitably, we began to re-evaluate our goals and strategy. Chief among the lessons were (1) We cannot possibly win our demands alone: we must unite with other groups in the population; (2) The 6 demands cannot possibly be our ultimate ends: even winning all of them certainly would not go far enough toward the basic reforms we need to live as human beings in this society; (3) "Restructuring" the university, the goal of faculty groups, various "moderate" students, and even the trustees, cannot possibly create a "free" or "democratic" university out of this institution. (First, how can anyone expect any meaningful reforms when even our initial demands have not been met?) Secondly, we realize that the university is entirely synchronized with the society: how can you have a "free," human university in a society such as this? Hence the SDS slogan "A free university in a free society." The converse is equally true.

The basic problem in understanding our strike—our demands, tactics, and history—consists of keeping in mind the social context of the university and of our movement. If you understand that we are the political response to an oppressive and exploitative social and economic system, you will have no difficulty putting together the pieces that follow.

THE ISSUES

From the first afternoon of the demonstrations, back on April 23 the striking students put forward essentially six demands. A joint steering committee of members of **SDS**, the Students' Afro-American Society, and unattached liberals created what were to become a cause and an entity unto themselves, the famous "six demands" later ratified by every striking group—from Hamilton Hall through the six thousand eventually represented on the Strike Coordinating Committee.

The six demands:

1. That the administration grant amnesty for the original "IDA 6" and for all those participating in these demonstrations.
2. That construction of the gymnasium in Morningside Park be terminated immediately.
3. That the university sever all ties with the Institute for Defense Analysis and that President Kirk and Trustee Burden resign their positions on the Executive Committee of that institution immediately.
4. That President Kirk's ban on indoor demonstrations be dropped.
5. That all future judicial decisions be made by a student-faculty committee.
6. That the university use its good offices to drop charges against all people arrested in demonstrations at the gym site and on campus.

The first was the precondition for negotiations over the other demands.

As the strike progressed, three main demands emerged: those concerning amnesty, the gymnasium, and IDA. This development was natural and inevitable, due to the fact that these demands represented the three issues uppermost in our minds, namely, racism in our society, the war in Vietnam and the United States' imperialist policies throughout the world, and the attempt for us to take power over the conditions of our lives—at the university and elsewhere.

On an intermediate level, these demands were representative of our opposition to a whole series of university policies in support of racism, U.S. imperialism, as well as its own autocratic power for exploiting community residents and employees, and manipulating and controlling students.

After the first bust (April 30), a great cry went up in almost all quarters for "restructuring" of the university. Accordingly, a second precondition was added to the first: recognition of the right of students to participate in restructuring the university (May 3). But since this had already, in fact, been granted, and since "restructuring" seemed to the radical majority of the Strike Coordinating Committee to be merely procedural and empty without the granting of our substantive demands, the original demands and what they stand for continue in the forefront of our attention.

***

APRIL 23

Three strains united in the explosive April 23 demonstration: the heightened anti-racist feeling, the almost unanimous hatred for the war in Vietnam, and for the whole imperialist American foreign policy, and opposition to the administration's attempt to repress the Left.

Monday, April 22, the IDA 6 were placed on disciplinary probation. The demonstration organized for the next day drew approximately six hundred supporters around three demands: (1) End all university ties with the Institute for Defense Analyses, (2) End construction of the gym on land stolen from the people of Harlem, and (3) An open hearing, with full rights of due process, for the IDA 6. The intention of the demonstration was to defy the president's ban again with a demonstration in Low Library, but the demonstrators found their way to Low blocked by several hundred counter-demonstrators, and, more important, locked entrances. A proposal from David Truman to sit down with him in McMillan theater to "discuss" the whole matter having been rejected outright, approximately 300 of the demonstrators moved on the gym site in Morningside Park and tore the fence down. One student was busted there. On returning to the campus, the demonstrators decided to take Hamilton Hall as a hostage for the brother busted at the gym; upon taking Hamilton, they discovered that they had not only the building, but also Acting Dean of the College Henry Coleman as hostage.

Immediately, a steering committee for the building was organized, consisting of 3 members of SDS, 4 members of Students' Afro-American Society, and 2 "unaffiliated liberals." This committee's first task was drawing up the original six demands listed above, demands approved by the body of demonstrators later ratified time and again by other groups throughout the campus, as well as community and high school groups throughout the city. Besides solving problems of food, defense, entertainment, and certain political questions, the steering committee also invited community people and other university students to join the occupation of Hamilton Hall, to join the fight against Columbia, in which many had already been involved. Community support was swift and impressive: high school kids, older people from Morningside Heights and Harlem,

and from all over the city, were immediately on the scene with food, money, and manpower. It was this moral and material support, continuing throughout the occupation of the buildings and the strike, which was crucial to the strength and growth of the movement.

The feeling of unity in Hamilton Hall began to evaporate as the separate political identities of the black and white demonstrators emerged in a dispute over tactics. The black students, seeing themselves as representatives of the Harlem community and black people everywhere, had as their goal the stopping of gym construction. In order to exercise the rights of black people over this racist institution, they realized that they had to barricade and hold Hamilton Hall— nothing less would force the administration to capitulate. A majority of the white students, on the other hand, saw their task as one of building the radical movement, convincing more and more white students of the relevance of their radical analysis. Accordingly, they believed that to barricade Hamilton would result in confrontation with other students wanting to go to class, rather than with the real enemy, the administration. Also at present in this decision was an element of timidity and lack of understanding of the effects of militancy on "radicalizing" people. In a joint steering committee meeting in the early morning of April 24, the black students asked the whites to leave the building, because they had decided that the only possible tactic was to barricade and hold Hamilton, while the whites were split, disunited, lacked discipline and militancy. It was agreed that the whites would create "diversionary action."

TAKING MORE BUILDINGS

After leaving Hamilton, about 200 white students forced their way into Low Library and President Kirk's office. As police began arriving on campus, rumors that 40 had been busted in Low Library (though not in Kirk's office) induced all but about 25 in Low to leave, believing that busts would make no sense toward gaining more support.

The 25 or so who stayed were at that time presented by a professor with the first in a long series of proposals for joint disciplinary boards which were supposed to pacify the strikers and get them to leave the building. This one, like all the others, was rejected.

Many of those who left Low, as well as many who did not enter in the first place, stood in pouring rain as a buffer in front of Hamilton, pledging to pose themselves between the blacks inside and the police. This barrier was maintained throughout the liberation of the buildings, right to the bust of April 30.

In a sense, the flight from Low Library, on Wednesday morning, was the low point of the strike. From there, the students began to learn from their mistakes: they saw that their power was in holding the buildings, that a bust would not mean defeat, that the barricades were a symbol of defiance and a statement of the militancy of those inside, that it was this militancy which won people over. More and more people reentered Low, expanding the number of rooms held. Wednesday evening, the students of the School of Architecture seized Avery Hall. Later that morning, graduate students seized Fayerweather. A meeting of several hundred on Wednesday evening called for a university-wide strike, and, accordingly, pickets went up at all classroom buildings on Thursday.

IN THE COMMUNES

Life within the communes, as the liberated buildings were called, was a totally liberating experience for those inside, the core of the strike. Politics and life were integrated as the communards spent hour after hour discussing policy decisions of the strike, questions of defense, and questions of organization of the commune itself. For many, the communal life within the building represented a break with their individualistic, isolated, fragmented lives as Columbia students: many talked of this as the most important experience of their lives, a new, beautiful high.

The goal of the action was kept in mind at all times—students were not only fighting for significant social (non-student) issues, they were not only uniting with those in the buildings, but with the oppressed of the world.

The best way to understand the sense of common struggle, the awareness of the significance of this struggle, and the sense of liberation gained by those in the buildings is to let the communards speak for themselves. The following are excerpts from a leaflet to "The Brothers and Sisters of Math Commune" by members of Up Against the Wall, Motherfucker chapter of SDS (from the Lower East Side) who were in Math:

> The experience of rebellion has given us five new senses. . . . We have a sense of brotherhood and love for each other. We have a sense of the enemy.

We have a sense of the ongoing struggle created in our own society and isolated territory. And we have a sense of our needs for the future.

We all feel the loss of Math Hall and the life that it provided. But we don't need Math Hall to live. . . . Wherever we are together is the place. We have lost Math Hall, but we have gained our own environments. Liberated people liberate the air they breathe and the ground they walk upon. . . . We want it all.

OUTSIDE

While the strikers in the five liberated buildings were forming their communes, the campus outside was a sea of ferment and turbulence with waves of support gradually spreading out from the centers of agitation. People were talking to each other for perhaps the first time in the history of Columbia University; everyone searched his soul to see where he stood. Some joined those in the buildings. Some pledged themselves to support them. Others attempted, futilely, to stand in the middle, while some were so threatened that they found it necessary to oppose the strikers (this last group, however, was the smallest).

A group demanding amnesty for the demonstrators and a peaceful solution to the "troubles" on campus came into being. This was the "green arm-bands," hundreds of whom kept a vigil at the sundial and pledged themselves to protecting the demonstrators in the buildings from the cops. When the bust did come, many were seriously injured.

A group of liberal faculty members met and pledged that they would interpose themselves between the students and the police if the administration called for a bust. Further, they declared that the problem should be settled peacefully, without the use of police. The Ad Hoc Faculty Group began meeting almost around the clock, formulating compromise proposals which would return the university to normalcy. Their position was that of mediator between two sides. Though they for the most part acted conscientiously and in good faith, they were politically naive in not understanding that they had to take a position for or against the strike, that their position "in the middle" supported the administration since they agreed with the administration that amnesty was an "impossible" demand.

The temporary strike committee which had been functioning since Wednesday decided that they should engage in talks with the faculty to clarify the strikers' position and to attempt to win the faculty over to the strike. These talks, however, had two results: first, they convinced the faculty that "progress" was being made and that they should retain their mediator position, not move toward the students, and second, the illusion of progress forestalled a bust.

These forestalling talks were significant the morning of April 26. The first threat of a bust came at 1 A.M., that Friday morning, when Kirk and Truman panicked after Mathematics Hall was liberated by about 30 strikers. Faculty members convinced Kirk and Truman to close school and wait over the weekend while "talks" went on between the occupants of the buildings and the faculty. By then, however, the cop invasion had already resulted in one casualty, French instructor Dick Greeman, who was guarding Low Library.

An organization of right-wing students, calling itself the Majority Coalition, a deliberate misnomer, formed over the weekend. Its main activity was a blockade of Low Library which attempted to keep food and medical supplies from the strikers in Kirk's office. Backing them up was a faculty line which stopped any food going through the "jock" line, claiming they were separating the "jocks" from the strikers inside. Several plainclothesmen were spotted among the faculty cops.

On Friday, the first Strike Coordinating Committee was formed, consisting mostly of representatives from each building except Hamilton. Since each building had to agree before a major policy decision could be made, constant discussion went on in each building, and constant communication ties were set up. The SCC was responsible for policy statements, negotiations, physical arrangements and coordinating activities. A central staff in Ferris Booth Hall kept a flow of press releases, leaflets, information going. It also was responsible for feeding 1,000 people per day. This latter task was accomplished completely through private donations and the help of a few student councils from other schools.

THE BUST

The bust came in the early morning of Tuesday, April 30, 1,500 uniformed and plainclothes cops removed approximately 1,000 people from the five buildings. 720 were arrested on charges ranging from criminal trespass and resisting arrest to incitement to riot. Several hundred people, including numerous faculty, were beaten. Since no demonstrators in any of the buildings resisted arrest or attacked the cops, the violence against the demonstrators was entirely gratuitous and unprovoked. Many people, including certain professors, have reported evidence that the cops also broke furniture, threw ink on walls, and stole and destroyed much property in an effort to discredit the demonstrators as hoodlums.

THE NEW STRIKE COMMITTEE—MASS STRIKE

After the bust, numerous groups rallied to the support of the students—hundreds from other high schools and universities, thousands from the Morningside Heights and Harlem communities, many faculty members, as well as previously uncommitted students. The police attack vindicated the strikers, proving that the administration was more willing to have students arrested and beat-up and to disrupt the university than to stop its policies of exploitation, racism, and support for imperialism, and sacrifice some of its arbitrary power. According to university propaganda, which administrators themselves began to believe, the demonstrations were the work of a handful of hard-core nihilists, not the result of thousands of peoples' opposition to Columbia's policies. To have forced thousands of people to act against their wills, SDS leaders would have had to be, according to Kirk and Truman's view, the most fantastic hypnotists ever to have lived.

But thousands of people, including a large portion of the faculty, were now quite rationally calling for a strike against the administration. At a meeting of over 1,200 people in Wollman auditorium, the six demands were re-ratified, and a new Strike Coordinating Committee was established on the basis of one vote for every 70 members of a constituent group which pledged to support the strike. Any group in or out of the university could send delegates—students, faculty, employees, community residents, and high school students.

Many of the 6,000 people who eventually sent delegates to the Strike Coordinating Committee were moderates who had been shocked by the police brutality and who also sincerely wanted a reformed university. The majority, however, accepted the view of the radicals that the strike must keep pushing primarily for the original demands—for the content of reform, not the empty formalities. A proposal to demand the resignation of President Grayson Kirk and Vice President David Truman, as well as the Trustees responsible for the bust, was rejected because it emphasized personalities as responsible, not the structure of the system which students oppose.

Later in the strike, approximately 25 of the moderate delegates broke away from the Strike Coordinating Committee, choosing to form a new group, Students for a Restructured University, to concentrate on the work of reforming Columbia. In leaving, however, they pledged to support the original six demands of the strike.

The first day of classes after the bust proved to be almost no classes at all. The College had asked classes to meet, very few, in fact, took place, since most students and faculty respected the picket lines. The strike was approximately 80% effective on the Morningside campus.

The mass meeting which originally established the coalition Strike Coordinating Committee in addition passed a proposal mandating the committee to serve as the provisional government for the university, to get it started again under the people's auspices. One of its primary tasks was the establishment of Liberation Courses, classes in all fields taught by students, faculty, and people from outside Columbia. These classes were designed to experiment in content and teaching form—to break out of the stultification of hierarchical and bourgeois learning traditional at Columbia and other schools. New types of courses appeared—everything from "Alienation from Hegel to Columbia" and "What a university will look like in a liberated society" to "Urban blues" and "Motorcycle mechanics." This was a time of tremendous intellectual excitement, a time in which every traditional concept was re-evaluated. The function of the teacher, the content of courses, people's relationships to each other were all questioned in relation to the struggle in which all were engaged.

COMMUNITY SEIZES A BUILDING

Although various tenant groups on Morningside Heights had for years been fighting Columbia's expansion into the community, the strike gave new impetus to this struggle. A new group of activist Morningside residents, the Community Action Committee, sending delegates to the SCC, was dedicated to organizing the community for its self-preservation. Columbia's' plans call for the eviction of 11,000 more residents (7,500 having already been thrown out), in order to turn Morningside Heights into an upper-middle class institutional enclave with apartments for a few respectable white people. On May 17, approximately 50 members of the Community Action Committee seized two apartments in a partially emptied building owned by Columbia to demand that Columbia's expansion plans be halted as well as the rehabilitation of vacant housing for people's use. Over 1,000 students gathered outside the tenement in support of the comrades inside. That night, as on April 30, the Columbia administration responded in the only way it could—with police power. Forty demonstrators were arrested in the building, along with 100 students and others who had been outside in support of the community people.

THE REPRESSION—
HAMILTON II

The administration, determined to punish further those involved in the demonstrations, demanded that four of the original IDA 6, people they considered leaders of the strike, report to Dean Platt's office by Tuesday, May 21. When the four did not appear, but sent 300 supporters instead into Hamilton Hall, they were immediately suspended. While deliberating on the next move, the demonstrators in Hamilton were told by the administration that the police had been called and that any student arrested would also be suspended by the University. After many hours of debate, approximately 120 of those present decided to stay. Seventy of these were students, approximately

20 were faculty members, and the rest were parents, community people, or students from other schools. Their thinking was that they had to show unity with the suspended leaders, that this was the only way the movement could survive.

The administration's reason for using police a third time was given by President Grayson Kirk in a telephone interview with WKCR, the campus radio station: the nihilist-anarchist hard-core inside Hamilton was "exploiting the presence" of "community children" (code name for black kids) for some unstated, dark purpose.

Equally ludicrous was the administration's decision to use 1,000 TPF cops to "clear the campus" after the bust in Hamilton. Students had set up barricades at both ends of college walk to defend the campus, and when the cops attacked, some students defended themselves with bricks. But the police charge was not repulsed and dozens of students were beaten by uniformed and plainclothes cops, including many *inside* dormitory lobbies and corridors. . . .

The felony charges, the beatings, the mass arrests, and the discipline all represent various attempts to repress and kill the student strike. The administration uses the New York City Police Dept. and the courts to stop a political movement under the theory that if you punish people enough, they will be intimidated into submission. . . . Though the physical power of the administration is strong, they cannot possibly stop the movement at Columbia or the movement for revolutionary change in this society.

June 4, 1968, commencement day at Columbia, saw over 400 graduates walk out of the commencement held in the Cathedral of St. John the Divine, a commencement guarded by close to 1,000 police, including numerous plainclothes cops dressed in academic robes (also used as ringers to fill up the empty seats). The graduates, along with several thousand guests, attended the real commencement of Columbia University, held at the traditional site, Low Plaza, by Students for a Restructured University, and the Strike Coordinating Committee. Following various speeches, approximately 1,000 people attended a rally and picnic at the gym site in Morningside Park. This was as Erich Fromm noted, a movement for life; the commencement was the festival of life which marked the close of one phase of the struggle.

As the fall begins, it is clear that Columbia will be the scene of much more radical political action. No demands have yet been met. The university is prosecuting in criminal court close to 1,100 people, most of whom are students. At least 79 students have been suspended, hundreds more placed on probation. Columbia's exploitation of the community and her support for the Government's imperialist policies continue. Most important, people now know that they are fighting the forces behind Columbia, the power of the ruling class in this society, not just the institution. And they have the commitment to keep fighting. The Democratic National Convention killed electoral politics for young people in this country and the Chicago Police Dept. provided an alternative—to fight. So did Columbia in the spring. So does it now, along with every other university in this country. The struggle goes on. Create two, three, many Columbias, that is the watchword!

9

The Proper Study of Womankind

On Women's Studies

(1973)

Robin Morgan

We must be careful not to contract contagious patriarchal thought. Sometimes it wears the face of pedantry; sometimes it masquerades as anti-intellectualism. The "anti-articulate line," for example: you should not be able to phrase anything in words over one syllable. My response is that a serious revolutionary would no more wield in effective language than she would carry a clogged gun. Because language is a weapon like anything else, and I for one want us to use it as best and movingly and efficiently as we can. I want us to seize that tool like any other. I want to have everything, in fact: feminist colleges, feminist universities, a feminist world.

In the meantime, though, I must admit that mere survival is a priority. So let's examine the temporary solution—the women's studies program. I shall share with you my fantasy of the ideal program, if we all keep in mind that settling for less than everything is absurd—and eventually unnecessary.

I know, as I'm sure you do, most of the arguments for and against a program's being interdisciplinary or au-tonomous; obviously the approach taken would depend largely on the school, the support for such a program, and other local "tactical" elements. Personally, I favor the autonomous program, where the university gets to write the funding check and thereafter is permitted to maintain a respectful silence. My ideal program would be run collectively by that aforementioned coalition of women: student/faculty/staff/faculty wife. Other features would include:

—a "floating credit": I don't think that's an official academic phrase, but by it I mean that any woman could take a course for credit and then apply it anywhere she wished, to another school or program.

—a minor, a major, *and* a graduate-studies program.

—courses in every discipline, all taught by women.

—an emphasis on history because, politically, if we do not know our own past we are, cliché or not, doomed to repeat it. (History not only to cover the suffrage struggles, of course, but also to explore the ancient gynocratic societies, tying in with anthropological and archeological studies in these areas.)

—self-defense for *credit;* this is *not* an extracurricular activity, as most schools today regard it. For women, it is a basic survival need.

—classes in legal rights and consumer rights.

—paramedical and midwifery training, in addition to pre-med courses.

—free child-care facilities controlled by the people (adults *and* children) who use them, but funded by the university.

—a generous athletic budget, emphasizing noncompetitive sports.

—a strong emphasis on outreach—to grammar schools, high schools, adult education, and community women—to keep the program from becoming an incestuous campus-based clique.

—new and exploratory disciplines: mythography, medical ethics, etc.

—new approaches to old disciplines: I, for one, want to know less who won which battle as the boys played war games, and more about women's history; not only about which remarkable women entered the male history as exceptions but about the women who were never permitted entrance at all or only invisibly. And what about the trends made invisible? For example, when was the tampon invented and what effect, socially, did it have on women? When, did the pressure begin, in modern times, for women to start shaving legs and armpits? Was it with the invention of the modern razor blade; was it with the marketing of silk stockings? What did that *mean* in a socioeconomic context? I think this is part of history. I think we must transform the subjects we study as well as be willing to be transformed by them. There must be an emphasis on the hard and soft sciences. We need to know about inovulation, or as men call it, cloning. We need to know about the technology. You cannot rant about seizing power and then turn around and say all education is bourgeois.

There are people at this conference who came with the admitted purpose of "turning women off" to women's studies. Why? Why are women the only oppressed group who should be ashamed of going to school? You don't hear the black community saying that it's bourgeois to go to school. On the contrary. The black community wants *open admission* to get those educational tools. Yes, it's odious to have to go to the Man for them, but we must take them and use them in a new way. Not to move up the ladder: to destroy the ladder. *That* is the revolutionary approach.

Meanwhile, back to the harsh realities of ivory-tower academia. Survival measures for women currently struggling day by day in a co-educational institution might include some of the following demands:

—a grievance board to deal with complaints about the sexist comments made in class by male instructors, the emotional and/or physical rape of women students, the offensive material on the reading list, the contempt with which feminist papers are met by so many male professors.

—a lesbian counselor chosen by the lesbian feminists on the campus; this, in addition to a heterosexual feminist counselor. No male counselor should presume to counsel women, whatever their sexual proclivities.

—an emphasis on the issues of rape and abortion; abortion referral and contraception available *on* the campus, as well as childbirth and post-partum care and advice;

—maternity *and* paternity leave—he should be home dealing with the baby, too, if he's around. And he should *be* around if she wants him around and *not* if she doesn't.

The demands could go on and on. Women's work is truly never done. But there are many ways and means. Study the curricula, organizing suggestions, and advice in the literature from the Feminist Press and KNOW, Inc., in Pittsburgh. The work they have done in creating the Clearing House for Women's Studies and the *Women's Studies Newsletter* is invaluable. Read the journals coming out on this whole new area. In addition, read the *Penn Women's Studies Planners Pamphlet*. (This began as a summer project required of Penn women by the university. The women felt that as long as it was an obligatory task they would do a really comprehensive study to be of service to other women elsewhere. I highly recommend it for its wit as well as its expert counsel.) Investigate the plans for a National Women's Studies Association.

One more hint about winning. There is something that all of the following have in common: New College, Florida; University of Kansas at Lawrence; Boston State College; American University; Penn at Philadelphia campus; Berkeley; University of New Mexico at Albuquerque; Harvard; Barnard College. Within the past two years feminists on these campuses, after going all the proper routes and channels, have become fed up and have seized property. And I offer this to you in case, at some point, everything else fails. I say it obliquely so as to avoid getting in trouble again for crossing another state line to incite another you-know-what.

Visions of Women's Studies

The documents in this section offer three visions of what women's studies might do or mean for individuals seeking an education, the academy as an institution, and the larger world of which the academy is a part. Together, they provide a glimpse into the broad and bold agenda of Women's Studies, which ranges from making women students more comfortable in the classroom to rethinking what, why, and how we teach and learn. Adrienne Rich's speech to women college students presents a picture of education as an empowering force for women, reminding us of the important gains for which generations of women fought. She implores women to take themselves seriously as learners and to demand that their education be relevant to their own lives. Next, Elizabeth Minnich and Elizabeth Higginbotham explore the mission of women's studies as a movement for curricular reform or transformation. They both present ideas about what might stand in the way of achieving the aims of women's studies. Minnich's essay focuses on different strategies employed by feminists in the academy and provides a framework for distinguishing between liberal and radical perspectives and goals. She argues that true transformation of the curriculum would require more than new courses and new faculty; it would necessitate fundamental changes in our thinking patterns and the ways we construct knowledge. Higginbotham seeks to bring marginalized peoples into the curriculum and to find practical ways to ensure that these voices are included by instructors and heard by students.

Critical Thinking Questions

1. Rich, Minnich, and Higginbotham all expect feminism to have a significant impact on education. Compare and contrast their perspectives.
2. What does women's studies or feminism have to do with "claiming" your education? How can you or how are you currently claiming your education?
3. Why is it important to Minnich to understand that women were excluded, not omitted, from the curriculum? What difference does this understanding make?

4. Explain the difference between curriculum transformation and the "add women and stir" strategy. Do you agree with Minnich that the former is better than the latter?
5. According to Higginbotham, what are the main obstacles to true curriculum transformation? To what extent do the obstacles she identifies differ from Minnich's?
6. How has your own education—your experience as a student and the curriculum you have been exposed to—reflected the exclusions and flaws discussed by these authors?

10

Claiming an Education

(1977)

Adrienne Rich

For this convocation, I planned to separate my remarks into two parts: some thoughts about you, the women students here, and some thoughts about us who teach in a women's college. But ultimately, those two parts are indivisible. If university education means anything beyond the processing of human beings into expected roles, through credit hours, tests, and grades (and I believe that in a women's college especially it *might* mean much more), it implies an ethical and intellectual contract between teacher and student. This contract must remain intuitive, dynamic, unwritten; but we must turn to it again and again if learning is to be reclaimed from the depersonalizing and cheapening pressures of the present-day academic scene.

The first thing I want to say to you who are students, is that you cannot afford to think of being here to *receive* an education; you will do much better to think of yourselves as being here to *claim* one. One of the dictionary definitions of the verb "to claim" is: to *take as the rightful owner; to assert in the face of possible contradiction.* "To receive" is *to come into Possession of; to act as receptacle or container for; to accept as authoritative or true.* The difference is that between acting and being acted-upon, and, for women it can literally mean the difference between life and death.

One of the devastating weaknesses of university learning, of the store of knowledge and opinion that has been handed down through academic training, has been its almost total erasure of women's experience and thought from the curriculum, and its exclusion of women as members of the academic community. Today, with increasing numbers of women students in nearly every branch of higher learning, we still see very few women in the upper levels of faculty and administration in most institutions. Douglass College itself is a women's college in a university administered overwhelmingly by men, who in turn are answerable to the state legislature, again composed predominantly of men. But the most significant fact for you is that what you learn here, the very texts you read, the lectures you hear, the way your studies are divided into categories and fragmented one from the other—all this reflects, to a very large degree, neither objective reality, nor an accurate picture of the past, nor a group of rigorously tested observations about human behavior. What you can learn here (and I mean not only at Douglass but any college in any university) is how *men* have perceived and organized their experience, their history, their ideas of social relationships, good and evil, sickness and health, etc. When you read or hear about "great issues," "major texts," "the mainstream of Western thought," you are hearing about what men, above all white men, in their male subjectivity, have decided is important.

Black and other minority peoples have for some time recognized that their racial and ethnic experience was not accounted for in the studies broadly labeled human; and that even the sciences can be racist. For many reasons, it has been more difficult for women to comprehend our exclusion, and to realize that even the sciences can be sexist. For one thing, it is only within the last hundred years that higher education has grudgingly been opened up to women at all, even to white, middle-class women. And many of us have found ourselves poring eagerly over books with titles like: *The Descent of Man; Man and His Symbols; Irrational Man; The Phenomenon of Man; The Future of Man; Man and the Machine; From Man to Man; May Man Prevail?; Man, Science and Society;* or *One Dimensional Man*—books pretending to describe a "human" reality that does not include over one-half the human species.

Less than a decade ago, with the rebirth of a feminist movement in this country, women students and teachers in a number of universities began to demand and set up women's studies courses—to claim a woman-directed education. And, despite the inevitable accusations of "unscholarly," "group therapy," "faddism," etc., despite backlash and budget cuts, women's studies are still growing, offering to more and more women a new intellectual grasp on their lives, new understanding of our history, a fresh vision of the human experience, and also a critical basis for evaluating what they hear and read in other courses, and in the society at large.

But my talk is not really about women's studies, much as I believe in their scholarly, scientific, and human necessity. While I think that any Douglass student has everything to gain by investigating and enrolling in women's studies courses, I want to suggest that there is a more essential experience that you owe yourselves, one which courses in women's studies can greatly enrich, but which finally depends on you, in all your interactions with yourself and your world. This is the experience of *taking responsibility toward* yourselves. Our upbringing as women has so often told us that this should come second to our relationships and responsibilities to other people. We have been offered ethical models of the self-denying wife and mother; intellectual models of the brilliant but slapdash dilettante who never commits herself to anything the whole way, or the intelligent woman who denies her intelligence in order to seem more "feminine," or who sits in passive silence even when she disagrees inwardly with everything that is being said around her.

Responsibility to yourself means refusing to let others do your thinking, talking, and naming for you; it means learning to respect and use your own brains and instincts; hence, grappling with hard work. It means that you do not treat your body as a commodity with which to purchase superficial intimacy or economic security; for our bodies and minds are inseparable in this life, and when we allow our bodies to be treated as objects, our minds are in mortal danger. It means insisting that those to whom you give your friendship and love are able to respect your mind. It means being able to say, with Charlotte Brontë's Jane Eyre: "I have an inward treasure born with me, which can keep me alive if all the extraneous delights should be withheld or offered only at a price I cannot afford to give."

Responsibility to yourself means that you don't fall for shallow and easy solutions—predigested books and ideas, weekend encounters guaranteed to change your life, taking "gut" courses instead of ones you know will challenge you, bluffing at school and life instead of doing solid work, marrying early as an escape from real decisions, getting pregnant as an evasion of already existing problems. It means that you refuse to sell your talents and aspirations short, simply to avoid conflict and confrontation. And this, in turn, means resisting the forces in society which say that women should be nice, play safe, have low professional expectations, drown in love and forget about work, live through others, and stay in the places assigned to us. It means that we insist on a life of meaningful work, insist that work be as meaningful as love and friendship in our lives. It means, therefore, the courage to be "different"; not to be continuously available to others when we need time for ourselves and our work; to be able to demand of others—parents, friends, roommates, teachers, lovers, husbands, children—that they respect our sense of purpose and our integrity as persons. Women everywhere are finding the courage to do this, more and more, and we are finding that courage both in our study of women in the past who possessed it, and in each other as we look to other women for comradeship, community, and challenge. The difference between a life lived actively, and a life of passive drifting and dispersal of energies, is an immense difference. Once we begin to feel committed to our lives, responsible to ourselves, we can never again be satisfied with the old, passive way.

Now comes the second part of the contract. I believe that in a women's college you have the right to expect your faculty to take you seriously. The education of women has been a matter of debate for centuries, and old, negative attitudes about women's role, women's ability to think and take leadership, are still rife both in and outside the university. Many male professors (and I don't mean only at Douglass) still feel that teaching in a women's college is a second-rate career. Many tend to eroticize their women students—to treat them as sexual objects—instead of demanding the best of their minds. (At Yale a legal suit *[Alexander v. Yale]* has been brought against the university by a group of women students demanding a stated policy against sexual advances toward female students by male professors.) Many teachers, both men and women, trained in the male-centered tradition, are still handing the ideas and texts of that tradition on to students without teaching them to criticize its anti-woman attitudes, its omission of women as part of the species. Too often, all of us fail to teach the most important thing, which is that clear thinking, active discussion, and excellent writing are all necessary for intellectual freedom, and that these require *hard work*. Sometimes, perhaps in discouragement with a culture which is both anti intellectual and anti-woman, we may resign ourselves to low expectations for our students before we have given them half a chance to become more thoughtful, expressive human beings. We need to take to heart the words of Elizabeth Barrett Browning, a poet, a thinking woman, and a feminist, who wrote in 1845 of her impatience with studies which cultivate a "passive recipiency" in the mind, and asserted that "women want to be made to *think actively*: their apprehension is quicker than that of men, but their defect lies for the most part in the logical faculty and in the higher mental activities." Note that she implies a defect which can be remedied by intellectual training; *not* an inborn lack of ability.

I have said that the contract on the student's part involves that you demand to be taken seriously so that you can also go on taking yourself seriously. This means seeking out criticism, recognizing that the most affirming thing anyone can do for you is demand that you push yourself further, show you the range of what you *can* do. It means rejecting attitudes of "take-it-easy," "why-be-so-serious,""why worry—you'll-probably-get-married-anyway." It means assuming your share of responsibility for what happens in the classroom, because that affects the quality of your daily life here. It means that the student sees herself engaged *with* her teachers in an active, ongoing struggle for a real education. But for her to do this, her teachers must be committed to the belief that women's minds and experience are intrinsically valuable and indispensable to any civilization worthy the name; that there is no more exhilarating and intellectually fertile place in the academic world today than a women's college—of both students and teachers in large enough numbers are trying to fulfill this contract. The contract is really a pledge of mutual seriousness about women, about language, ideas, methods, and values. It is our shared commitment toward a world in which the inborn potentialities of so many women's minds will no longer be wasted, raveled-away, paralyzed, or denied.

11

Transforming Knowledge

(1990)

Elizabeth Kamarck Minnich

I believe that unless feminist scholarship is accompanied by ongoing work on why and how the dominant liberal arts curriculum in all its varied expressions is not and, without fundamental reconception, *cannot* be receptive to the study of the majority of humankind, it remains at risk of disappearing as it has through the centuries before this wave of the Women's Movement. As we produce "the new knowledge of women," we must continue to work to understand why it is recurrently "new," rather than a further unfolding of all that has gone before. What is it, I ask through this book, that functions so effectively in the dominant meaning system to hold women and so knowledge of, by, and about women outside that which has been and is passed on, developed, taught?

This is a curricular matter. It is also more than that. The conceptual blocks to the comprehension and full inclusion of women that we find in familiar scholarly theories and arguments, as in their institutional expressions in organizations and systems, political

and economic and legal, are at root the same blocks that are to be found within the curriculum. And if we do not remove them from the curriculum, much if not all that we achieve elsewhere may prove to be, once again, a passing moment. It is, after all, to a significant extent through what we teach to new generations that we bridge past, present, and future. That which is actively excluded from—or never makes it into—the curriculum is very likely to be forgotten and is almost certain to continue being devalued, seen as deviant and marginal at best.

Our educational institutions—those inspiring, impossible, frustrating, appealing, appalling systems within which we usually try simply to find the space and time to do our work of teaching and learning—are, not alone but preeminently, the shapers and guardians of cultural memory and hence of cultural meanings. Here too, then, we must do our work of critique, remembering, creation.

As we do so, we also accept a number of risks. I am not referring only to the obvious risks of losing the privileges of participation in the Academy. As Linda Gordon puts it, "Existing in between a social movement and the academy, women's scholarship has a mistress and a master, and guess which one pays wages." That these risks are complex and personally troubling does indeed need to be recognized. It is terribly difficult to work against the grain of what, after all, stands in our culture for "the life of the mind," particularly when one has had to struggle to achieve access to the institutions that have claimed to define it, and have, indeed, succeeded all too well in professionalizing it, marking it as their own. I do not mean to trivialize even for a moment the struggle for access, the continuing difficulty of 'getting in.' But I want to point out here the risks that feminist scholars have warned one another about since the beginning of the curriculum change movement.

The dangers of such projects are indicated by the difference between the term "mainstreaming" and the phrase that, I am glad to say, has superseded it, "curriculum transformation projects." "Mainstreaming" implies that there is one main stream and what we want is to join it, that we are a tributary at best, and that our goal is to achieve the 'normalcy' of becoming invisible in the big river. "Transformation," on the other hand, puts the emphasis not on joining what is but on changing it.

Teresa de Lauretis characterizes the problem, the risk, of "mainstreaming" as "the appropriation of feminist strategies and conceptual frameworks within 'legitimate' discourses or by other critical theories" in a way that "deflect[s] radical resistance and . . . recuperate[s] it as liberal opposition," which is "not just

accommodated but in fact anticipated and so effectively neutralized." That, indeed, would be the result of "mainstreaming." But it is something else again to work on transforming the curriculum with the full realization that women cannot be added to the present construction of knowledge because knowledge of, by, and for women is not simply more of the same; is not only knowledge of a subset of "mankind" that is conceptually compatible with that of which it is a subset; is not a category of exotica that can be tacked onto courses without implications for that which remains safely 'normal'; is not, indeed, neatly separable in any way from any knowledge that is adequate to human-kind.

The belief that knowledge about women is simply additive to, or a subset of, or a complement to, knowledge about men has been and is held both by nonfeminist scholars and educators and by some feminists involved with Women's Studies and curriculum-change projects. I understand those beliefs and know that some good work can indeed be done by those who hold them (just as valuable work is done in Women's Studies to find the women who did what women were not allowed to do so as to "prove that we can do it," that we "have been there"). But I do not believe such work is, by itself, adequate, because it remains within a system built on principles of exclusion and characterized by the conceptual errors those principles necessitate and perpetuate.

It is precisely to continue work on transforming the curriculum, not simply achieving access to it or joining its 'mainstream' or providing it with an oppositional perspective that it can accommodate in the sense de Lauretis rightly fears, that this book is being written. Let me repeat here what I first wrote in 1979: what we are doing is as radical as undoing geocentrism, the notion that the earth is the center of the cosmos. If the earth—if Man—is not the center, then everything predicated on taking it/him to be so no longer stands as it has been formulated. This is not to say that there are no schools of thought with which we can join, or that there is nothing in the existing tradition we can draw on, use, and ourselves choose to perpetuate. It is not even to say that all feminist scholarship is or ought to be that radical, that it ought to work on that fundamental level. It is to say that as we do our work, we need to hold on to the radical critique, the effort to go to the root (*râdix*) of the tradition that is premised on our exclusion, or we will watch helplessly as the tree of knowledge continues to grow exactly as it did before.

But making the case for that position is what this book is about, so I will leave the point now with the statement that refusal to engage in, or at least support, work on transforming the curriculum leaves us not pure but vulnerable to being, once again, excluded, rendered marginal, or brought into and utterly lost within the mainstream that has through the ages flooded and washed away the recurrent spring growth of feminist scholarship and thought.

EARLY—AND CONTINUING—QUESTIONS

There is also another way to move into the subject of transforming knowledge, and the ways we think. We can change our perspective from the dramatic, stirring, inspiring, and troubling history of the times in which this commitment re-emerged, and focus on the unfolding thinking itself. To do so, it may be helpful to return to some of the early questions. We could start with the conclusions reached after much thought, making them as clear and accessible as possible, but some may find it more helpful to start where the thinking started, to move into the thinking as it actually developed rather than, or in addition to, focusing on its historical or its purely conceptual contexts. There are always lots of ways to begin, different contexts within which to locate that which we wish to understand, many perspectives on what we are trying to see.

Scholarship vs. Politics?

From the beginning, the commitments of feminist scholars have been complex and often in creative, demanding tension with each other. For example, an early conference in a continuing series run by the Barnard College Women's Center took on the question of the relation of scholarship to politics (the conferences, led by Jane Gould as director of the center, were in the late 1980s still called "The Scholar and the Feminist"). Were we, as many of those opposed to Women's Studies held, threatening to 'politicize' scholarship and the Academy in some new and dangerous way? Is it true that formal scholarship as traditionally conceived and practiced is disinterested, objective, removed from the interested, subjectively grounded advocacy efforts of the political realm? Are knowledge and action two separate human activities, and ought they to be so? Can one serve both equity and excellence, or does commitment to one threaten to undermine the other? To respond to such questions, we were faced with the need to rethink what scholarship has meant and should mean, and that effort led us to undertake an analysis and critique of the construction of knowledge.

The Disciplines

Among the most evident characteristics of the prevailing construction of knowledge is its disciplinary nature, a characteristic that is given power by the discipline-based departments that are at the heart of academic institutions. Hence, we were faced with an obvious intellectual and institutional problem. Women's Studies put the study of women at the center of concern as no then-existing discipline did. In what discipline-department were we to work? Women as authors-scholars and as subject matter were largely or wholly invisible in all of them. Furthermore, the search for any *one* disciplinary-departmental 'home' quickly came to seem peculiar, since it is quite obvious that women cannot be studied adequately in only one discipline any more than men can. That is in part why Florence Howe issued her well-known call to "break the disciplines," and why we early claimed that Women's Studies must be "interdisciplinary."

But then we had also to ask whether even interdisciplinary work would suffice. Were *any* of the standing disciplines adequate to the study of women? Obviously not. How, then, could an amalgam of fields, none of which had proved open or adequate

to the subject, transcend its component parts? It seemed clear that we would have to create a new field, not a pastiche of old ones, in order to be free to locate and when necessary create the theoretical frameworks, the methods and techniques of research and of teaching, that we might need to illuminate our complex subject.

A new debate arose. Should the goal of Women's Studies be the creation of a new discipline, and a new department, rather than the transformation of all the other standing disciplines? But the scholars who worked on Women's Studies were themselves trained in those disciplines, and the students who might take Women's Studies would also take other courses that would continue to exclude and/or devalue women. Our task seemed to require us not 'only' to create a whole new field, but also to rethink each discipline and all disciplines—separately, in relation to each other, and as they reflected and perpetuated this culture's understanding of knowledge. We realized that scholarship that refuses old exclusions and invidious hierarchies not only does not fit into any of the old fields, but, for that very reason, potentially transforms them all.

Therefore, we have worked to establish a new discipline, Women's Studies, and, simultaneously, to support that work with efforts to spread "the new scholarship on women" (as Catharine Stimpson early named it) to all fields through curriculum-transformation work. Despite the concern of some feminist activists and scholars that woman-focused work would be lessened by curriculum-transformation work, both undertakings have flourished side by side, one often leading to the other. The

Academy has been changed by the burgeoning of feminist scholarship in general, its fostering in Women's Studies programs in particular, and its effects on all disciplines. The decision as to which kind of work to undertake has in fact usually been the result of realistic assessments of what is most possible and likely to succeed in a particular institutional setting at a particular time.

"Lost Women"

Both projects—the creation of Women's Studies programs and work toward the transformation of courses in and across all disciplines—depend, of course, on the availability of works by and about women. At first it seemed that, whatever anyone's intentions, it might be impossible to include knowledge of women in any courses at all until generations of dedicated scholars had produced enough sound new knowledge. Across the country some women and a very few men (notably, William Chafe and Joseph Pleck), while teaching what they had been hired to teach and struggling to continue the research on which jobs, promotions, and tenure depended, turned to finding the "lost women" whose lives, works, and perspectives could be brought into the curriculum. There was a sense that we had to prove that women and women's works really did exist, but—more important—there was an urgent desire to find our history. Stunning works of retrieval emerged with equally stunning speed: for example, Ann Sutherland Harris and Linda Nochlin's work locating, documenting, and studying women artists resulted in the ground-breaking show of women artists at the Brooklyn

Museum of Art. The catalogue, later *Women Artists: 1550—1950*, was immediately picked up and used as a text. Also enriching our sense of continuity, culture, and complexity in women's lives were (and are) Gerda Lerner's anthology, *Black Women in White America*, and Rayna Rapp Reiter's anthology, *Toward an Anthropology of Women*, among many others, as well as Dorothy B. Porter's monumentally inspiring long-term work collecting, commenting on, and making available the story of Black women and men through the Moorland Spingarn Research Center at Howard University.

As such work appeared, it allowed us to deepen the critique of the construction of knowledge, to question more concretely the notion that what had been taught was the product of disinterested, nonpolitical, objective scholars. Nochlin's early essay, "Why Are There No Great Women Artists?" that uncovered and analyzed the historical realities of discrimination faced by women began questioning of the very definitions of art that reflected and appeared to legitimize that discrimination.

The search for 'lost' women again pushed our quest for knowledge about women deeper than some had expected. We began to realize the full, complex implications of the obvious statement, "Women have always been here." We refined our understanding of the intellectual problems we faced when we realized that we have always been here *and* that we have been largely invisible in the body of knowledge passed on by the educational and research institutions whose purview is supposed to be the preservation, transmission, and enrichment of humankind's knowledge.

"Add Women and Stir"

In a now-famous line, Charlotte Bunch characterized the problem: "You can't," she said, "just add women and stir." It was an apt observation, crystallizing what many had learned in their own efforts to find 'lost' women and add them to their courses. The women could, in fact, be found. There have been women mathematicians, women physicists, women philosophers, women writers, women musicians. There have been women in history, in classical Greece and Rome, and women in politics. But, once found, they often didn't *fit*, couldn't just be dropped into standing courses. Why not? In looking for individual women who had done what men had done, we had not, after all, shifted anything very radically (as we would, and by now have). The problem was that although the now-found 'lost' women seemed to prove something that needed proving yet again—that women are by no means and in no ways inferior to men—we had not, in fact, learned much about *women*. In fact, we had not even proved anything about female abilities: exceptions, as we know, can easily be used simply to prove the rule. If some women were mathematicians, why were not more mathematicians women? There must be something about most if not absolutely all females that disqualifies us. That was not, of course, a reasonable conclusion. In finding the 'lost' women, we had also found more about why and how they were 'lost.' We began to know more about the practices of exclusion exercised against our sex.

But was the point of all our efforts to document that women had not performed as well as men in all the 'important' areas of life because we were discriminated against and actively excluded? Yes, of course that needed, and needs, to be acknowledged, studied, comprehended. But it leaves untouched some other critically important questions. What were women who led the lives prescribed for women doing in the past? What were *those* lives like? What do we all, women and men, need to learn from as well as about them? Those were the questions we could not ask within the constraints of the familiar courses and fields on our campuses. We realized that we did not need only to find the few women who did what men did, but to ask, Where were the women? What can we know about *women?* We needed to undo the established centrality of men.

What was required was a complete rethinking, first of the basic models of reality, truth, and meaning in the dominant tradition, and then of all the knowledge predicted on them. If *it is an intellectual, moral, and political error to think that Man has been, is, and should be the center of the human system, then we must rethink not only the basic models but all knowledge that reflects and perpetuates them.*

To be additive, knowledge must rest on the same basic premises, be of the same basic sort, as that to which it is to be added. But, in the language most often used in the earlier days of Women's Studies work, knowledge about women cannot be added to knowledge about men, because the center of the system has shifted radically when women are moved from "margin to center" (to use the phrase adopted by bell hooks for her second book).

That apprehension is sound, but it was not yet adequate to explain, or at least help us begin to explore fruitfully, the challenge of Women's Studies to the old male-centered curriculum. The basic errors that put some men (in their falsely universalized, singular representation as Man) at the center needed to be explored directly and in depth along with at least some of their conceptual consequences. Those errors began to appear as we realized that problems in each field were by no means unique, that there were striking commonalities on a deep level across all fields and outside the Academy as well.

There were many more issues debated and questions raised as we moved further into the effort to rethink a tradition that had excluded so many for so long, but perhaps those I have discussed will suffice to introduce that effort for now. What is important is to think through for oneself, as well as with others, how scholarship and politics are related, why the new scholarship on women did not become simply a subspecialty within the standing disciplines, why finding things that women had done that were as similar as possible to men's achievements did not tell us anything about the lives of *women*, and why, then, it would not suffice—was not even possible—just to add women on to scholarship that was premised on our devaluation and exclusion.

Clearly, we had to consider not just what was already known and how women could be added to it, but how knowledge was constructed, and what kind of thinking the dominant tradition has privileged. We need not give up all that has come to be known, or all the ways and forms and techniques of thinking that have been developed. Quite the contrary: we need to make use of whatever can

help us think not only within but also about the dominant tradition. There is no articulable, communicable stance *utterly* outside the tradition for us to take. Should we try to find such a position, we risk falling back into silence just as surely as we do if we speak only within and in the established terms of the dominant culture.

Fortunately, humans are creatures of translation, transitive creatures able to understand more than one language and to move between languages without losing either what is unique to each or what is common enough to make translation possible. We are able to apprehend more than can be spoken in any one language, and can stretch that language in ways that change and enrich it. There are many ways to be both within and without our own cultures.

CRITIQUE AND REFLEXIVE THINKING

In addition to the personal, historical, political, and intellectual contexts within which efforts to change the curriculum developed, there is also what must, I suppose, be called a philosophical context. No one undertakes an effort to understand anything without bringing to that effort some more or less formulated, more or less conscious, philosophical assumptions, tools, frameworks, values. Certainly I do not; in fact, as I have said, some of the primary conversations that have informed my work have been with philosophers. *Furthermore, even more now than when I began, I believe that the effort to find out why and how our thinking carries the past within it is part of an on-going philosophical critique essen-*

tial to freedom, and to democracy. As we work on the curriculum, and so on understanding the dominant tradition, maintaining a critical stance will allow us to avoid tripping ourselves up precisely when we most need to think creatively and, often, in radically new ways.

Thinking With and Without the Tradition

I found my thinking in this book on a commitment to critique in a generally Kantian sense, asking, What is *behind* this knowledge, this mode of thought? What were and are the conditions of its possibility? What makes, and keeps, it what, and as, it is? And I take the ground for the possibility of critique to be the human gift of reflexive thought, which is, I believe, not only a given possibility for us all but one of the primary bases of both the idea and the personal experience of freedom. Neither critique nor reflexive thinking is enough to give us freedom, but they help us comprehend and experience it in ways that help us know and value it as a necessity for full human being.

Still, I must note that I am well aware that there is some irony in the project of thinking ourselves free, of transforming knowledge. The tradition to be critiqued is being used against itself. I count on some familiarity with the dominant tradition as part of the common ground we share as we communicate with each other about what needs to be changed, and I draw, to a large extent, on established forms and methods and rules of thought to try to speak with and persuade people. However, I believe in the liberatory quality of reflexive thinking. In thinking about thinking,

we are not simply running around in circles like a squirrel in a cage, trapped despite all its frantic activity. We are working to see the thought displayed in particular ways of thinking from a standpoint that is relatively, not absolutely, outside them. I claim no 'higher' or more privileged—let alone absolute or definitive or 'pure'—perspective. I simply claim that it is possible for humans to think as and about ourselves, to think reflexively, self-consciously as we do when we observe ourselves becoming angry, or notice how we see something, or pay attention to how we learn and make discoveries. In what follows, I will discuss patterns of thought and of knowledge I have found in all disciplines as well as in the broader culture in the belief and hope that, having seen them, we may choose to use, vary, or discard them more freely.

That is, I do not believe that we are trapped by the fact that we learned to think in particular ways in this particular culture and in the Academy, nor do I believe that we can simply decide to be free of our formal and informal education. There is no either/or here, no "We are free *or* we are determined." Such dilemmas, created by abstracting two possible positions from all that grounds them in real experience and placing them artificially in opposition to each other, are part of a pattern of thought by which we may refuse to be coerced. In fact, we all know perfectly well that while we can and too often do think in ways that reflect a trap, we can also think about any specific trap and how it works to limit our thought in such a way that the problems it seemed to pose simply dissolve. We can think about our thinking as well as that of others and, in so doing, actualize a specific mode of human freedom that never suffices unto itself to effect genuine liberation but, as I have said, underlines and supports all other efforts—except, of course, those that are animated by a desire to replace one hegemonic system and ideology with another that is equally absolutized; and I, at least, do not consider those to be genuinely liberatory even if the new system seems in many ways better than the old.

Effects of Exclusion

Analyzing the conceptual errors that lock the dominant meaning system shaping liberal arts curricula into exclusive, invidiously hierarchical sets of structures, values, principles, beliefs, and feelings is the basic task and challenge of this book. More, much more, will be said about the errors I introduced earlier. Here, I will simply summarize a major problem in including women and the excluded groups of men in the dominant meaning system by repeating that some conceptual errors are so fundamental to the dominant Western tradition that an additive approach to change simply cannot work. For example, work by and about women is not just missing from the academic curriculum; it is to a remarkable extent incompatible with it. That is, *knowledge that is claimed to be inclusive—claimed to be both about and significant for all humankind—but that is in fact exclusive must be transformed, not just corrected or supplemented.* Discoveries indicating that the world is round do not merely supplement knowledge shaped by and supportive of the theory that the world is flat. Similarly, feminist work by and about women is not just missing from the academic canon: it is incompatible with some of the canon's basic, founding assumptions. And that means *not* that feminist scholarship is 'out of order' but that whatever makes noninclusive knowledge unable to open to the subjects and perspectives so long devalued and/or excluded must itself be changed.

I had the notion behind this idea for quite some time, but, as with many such flashes of understanding, it illuminated my thought only fitfully. I had not allowed it to stay, had not let myself think it through. But one day, after I had given my talk at a conference opening a curriculum-transformation project, it came to me. I was listening to other speakers on changes taking place in specific disciplines when suddenly I found myself whispering to the sociologist Margaret Anderson, who was sitting next to me, "We weren't *omitted*. We were *excluded*."

As I have said, that is obvious. But it remains hard to say. It sounds as if constant evil intent, was involved, and so it threatens to move the attention of both speaker and audience from the *effects* of the intent to exclude that remain in the curriculum to the *motivation* of the excluders. And that shift is almost certain to make those who have not changed their courses, or their way of thinking about their work, suddenly feel attacked rather than included in an exciting effort to think about our thinking. But if I and others do not say, "We/women were excluded," we cannot get to the critical observation that *the reasons why it was considered right and proper to exclude the majority of humankind were and are built into the very foundations of what was established as knowledge.*

That is, women were not overlooked through a prolonged fit of the famous academic absentmindedness (much like that attributed to the British to 'explain' how they ended up with an empire), as the use of the word "omitted" tends to imply. Women were excluded from lives of scholarship, as from 'significant' subject matter, as from positions of authority and power, when the basic ideas, definitions, principles, and facts of the dominant tradition were being formulated. But does that mean that *all* the creators and guardians and transmitters of the dominant tradition were and are personally animated by a consistent, purposeful intent to think consciously about excluding women, and many men, every moment? No, it does not (although it does not preclude the observation that some, indeed, were and, I fear, still are so animated). It reminds us that *the principles that require and justify the exclusion of women, and the results of those principles appearing throughout the complex artifices of knowledge and culture, are so locked into the dominant meaning system that it has for a very long time been utterly irrelevant whether or not any particular person intended to exclude women.* The exclusion was and is effected by the forms and structures within which we *all* try to live, work, and find meaning.

Thus, although it at first sounds as if using the strong term "excluded" might divide us radically from each other, such that all who are not part of the solution are seen as actively, consciously, and willfully part of the problem, in fact it reminds us of something quite different. We are all, albeit to varying degrees that matter a great deal, a part of the problem. Insofar as we speak and think and act in ways that make sense to other people within the dominant meaning system, we cannot avoid participating (again to varying degrees) in precisely that which we wish to change. We have all at times thought, said, and done things that, as our consciousness grew through the use of our ability to think reflexively, we wish we could disavow or at least hope we have outgrown. And that "we" includes (again in critically different ways, and with critically different results) not only those who benefit but also those who suffer from the dominant system. One of the struggles of the oppressed, excluded, and colonized is always to break free of internalized oppression—which does *not* mean that "women are their own worst enemies," a ridiculous exaggeration of the reasonable insight that we tend to learn what the dominant culture teaches us, and reteaches us, sometimes harshly, when we begin to struggle free.

This is, of course, only another way of saying that prejudices such as sexism and the deeply related homophobia, racism, and classism are not just personal problems, sets of peculiar and troubling beliefs. Exclusions and devaluations of whole groups of people on the scale and of the range, tenacity, and depth of racism and sexism and classism are systemic and shape the world within which we all struggle to live and find meaning. I and other white women benefit to varying degrees from the system of racism, however strongly we oppose it, just as all men benefit to varying degrees from the sex/gender system. And those of us who work in various ways within and with the Academy benefit from it, too, however much our work is designed to change it. That all these systems also, and profoundly, damage in some ways those who benefit from them can be recognized without thereby excusing them/us from responsibility for their perpetuation.

Men and women sometimes say to me, "But men suffer, too. They aren't allowed to cry or be nurturant, and they die younger than women on the average because they carry an inordinate amount of responsibility." I recognize the problem and am very pleased to see men join in dismantling the systems that give them burdens related to their privileges. However, it must be noted that while some of the privileged of all groups understand and feel the harm done to them, most seem to want to get rid of the harm without giving up the privilege. The movements of many, many people we have come to associate with Mahatma Gandhi, Martin Luther King, and Susan B. Anthony provide striking examples of how the harm done to those in power as a result of their holding that power can indeed be brought to consciousness, and that consciousness can be enlisted in support of a collective (if by no means inclusively egalitarian) political movement. Each of these movements developed important methods of persuasion as well as coercion, of what we might call consciousness-raising, not only among movement activists but among those against whom they were protesting. They did not simply take up guns and try to force agreement; they used what Gandhi called *satyagraha*, soul-force, to convert others to the view that a *system* must be changed, a system that was unjust and so harmful for all.

But by itself consciousness of the costs of systems that also give privileges often does no more than make those in power a bit guilty and grumpy—harder, not easier, to live with.

The questions of 'harm' and 'benefit,' of 'consciousness' and 'false consciousness,' of 'oppression' and 'internalized oppression' are extraordinarily complex. Such complexities are important. They serve to hold us to the level of systemic analysis without allowing us to forget that it is individuals who participate in and rebel against systems. We can critique these systems from within, often using their own abstract principles against them. In the case of the Academy, it is clear that knowledge that is claimed to be objective and inclusive yet reflects and perpetuates societal discrimination and prejudices fails even on its own terms. Knowledge that was created and has been passed on within a culture that, until very recently indeed, excluded the majority of humankind from the activities, positions, and thinking that were considered most important can hardly be disinterested and politically neutral, as it is claimed to be. It replicates in what it covers, how it treats its subjects, how it explains and judges, the most basic assumptions of the dominant culture—not entirely, not absolutely, but consistently enough so that it remains related to the culture from which it arose. Such knowledge is almost certainly blind to some of its own basic assumptions and methods, but they are there to be found.

Consider the example of geocentrism. Copernicus's move to put the sun at the center of the cosmos was greeted as what it indeed was, a challenge to many of the most deeply held beliefs of his culture, and more—a challenge to a remarkable range of systems of explanation, of knowledge, even of mores and morals. Darwin's theory of evolution had, and for some still has, the same devastating effects. It dethrones Man, suggesting that he is *not* the center, is not a unique creation that is discontinuous with and superior in kind to all else. Shifting from an invidiously hierarchical view of humankind entailed then, and entails now, a concomitant shift in all areas of knowledge, of ethics, of politics. Consider, too, the deep differences between the knowledge of the English and Europeans who colonized this country and the knowledge of the Native Americans. One set of cultures saw the land as given to Man to tame, to use, to make his own so that thinking about the earth tended to be instrumental. The other saw the land as sacred; thinking about it tended to be descriptive, celebratory, mythic, with the instrumental entering in the mode of propitiation, not mastery.

Centering attention on women rather than on a particular group of men involves a shift in focus, a reconfiguration of the whole, that is just as profound and suggestive. To take only one example for now, we can return to one of the initial insights of the Women's Movement, the realization that the personal is political. The full implications of that simple statement are still unfolding, but from the start it reminds us that everything that appears in public needs to be seen in relation to the private, and vice versa, so the terms "public" and "private" themselves cease to be firmly distinct. Thus, among other effects, the whole panoply of 'women's virtues' is released from containment within the functions relegated to women to reveal its significance and value in and for everyone, rather than being shunned by the 'Real Man' who must, above all, display no 'effeminate' qualities, whether 'virtuous' or not. Heroism can then cease to be a singular individual quality expressed in highly visible deeds and become a quality of character developed in a whole life, a life led in relation to many others that expresses care, honesty, integrity, intimacy, constancy, as well as (even instead of) the ability to 'win' through dramatic confrontations and adventures. And leadership can then be understood not in terms of dominance but as an ability to empower others.

Consider the 'conquest' of the West in the United States. Was it really the work of single scouts, of brave men 'penetrating' the wilderness, of lone individuals developing a culture based primarily on an individualistic notion of self-reliance? What about women struggling to establish homes, to care for families, to find and build the community that was essential to efforts to survive? What about the sexual and physical abuse of women, which, while it remains an untold story, makes all other frontier stories not just incomplete but dangerously falsifying? What about the terrible dangers of childbirth in situations where little or no care was available?

When we remember women, the story and its interpretation change, become much more complex; context and community reenter; the exigencies and heroism of everyday life, of reproducing and caring for life itself, take on the importance they really have.

Most basically, perhaps, we can say that when we focus on women the peculiarly abstract versions of the dominant Story of Mankind are undone so that the logics of connection, concreteness, context, and community can emerge. Such modes of relation cannot simply be added to a logic of externally related monads, of abstract individualism, of singular Great Deeds, of public life apparently ungrounded in and distinct from 'private' life. The coherence in many of the stories we have inherited was manufactured after the fact to make sense of characters, events, and motivations that had been removed from their real contexts. To uncover what women were doing and undergoing is to locate and ground a different and more truthful coherence, and that means, again, that we are not merely adding information but fundamentally reconceiving what we thought we knew.

Examples could be multiplied, but let us just note here the basic point: the shaping assumptions on which influential knowledge—which is always knowledge-accepted-as-such by a particular group in a particular culture—continues to be based are influential not *despite* but *because of* the fact that most people are unaware of them.

Thus knowledge and the whole culture and accepted process of knowledge-making need to be changed in their congruent basic claims and assumptions before that which has been defined as out of order, as rightly to be excluded, can be heard, seen, studied—comprehended. Old knots and tangles that are in all our minds and practices must be located and untied if there are to be threads available with which to weave the new into anything like a whole cloth, a coherent but by no means homogeneous pattern.

12

Designing an Inclusive Curriculum
Bringing All Women Into the Core
(1990)

Elizabeth Higginbotham

To be successful, transforming the curriculum involves three interrelated tasks. The first is to gain information about the diversity of the female experience. The second task is to decide how to teach this new material, a process that typically involves reconceptualizing one's discipline in light of a race, class, and gender-based analysis. Often this means learning to move typically marginal groups into the core of the curriculum. Furthermore, efforts can be made to present issues on people of color in their complexity, rather than in stereotypic ways. The third task is to structure classroom dynamics that ensure a safe atmosphere to support learning for *all* the students. This paper will discuss each of these tasks. It begins with a critique of the traditional curriculum in light of its treatment of people of color.

MARGINAL IN THE TRADITIONAL CURRICULUM

When I consistently see many bright and respected scholars failing to take steps to bring women of color into their teaching and research, I look for social, structural explanations. A sociological perspective can help us to understand the roots of racist thinking and the many forms it takes in traditional disciplines and women's studies. This approach is more productive than blaming these scholars—or simply attacking them as racists. The search for the social, structural roots of the marginalization of people of color in scholarship and education takes me back to my early schooling.

As a black person in a society dominated by whites, I was always an outsider—a status—that Patricia Hill Collins argues has advantages and costs. I was cognizant even as a young child that the experiences of black people were missing in what I was taught in elementary school. This pattern was later replicated in junior high and high school, then in college, and later in graduate school. But while I had been critical all along, not until I entered graduate school could I debate with others about the content of courses.

Reprinted from *Women's Studies Quarterly* 18, nos 1 & 2 (spring/summer 1990): 7–23. Copyright © 1990 by the Feminist Press.

Throughout my whole educational career, agents of the dominant group attempted to teach me the "place" of black people in the world. What was actively communicated to me was that black people and other people of color are on the periphery of society. They are marginal. I learned that what happens to people of color has little relevance for members of the dominant group and for mainstream thinking.

Early in school, when we were studying the original thirteen North American colonies, I was exposed to the myths about who we were and are as a nation. One of the first lessons was that America is a land that people entered in search of freedom—religious freedom, the freedom to work as independent farmers, freedom from the privileged nobility and the hierarchical stratification of Europe, and freedom from the rapid industrialization of Europe. Colonists, and later white immigrants, wanted change in their lives, and they took the risk to begin life anew in this budding but already glorious nation. The fact that they were seeking their "freedom" while enslaving others (principally Native Americans and Africans) was not viewed as a contradictory activity, but just "one of those things" the United States had to do to build a great and prosperous nation.

New York, where I grew up and received much of my education, prided itself on being a progressive state, and required schools to devote time to the Negro experience (as it was called). We discussed slavery in the South, and during Negro History Week we learned about Harriet Tubman, Booker T. Washington, Frederick Douglass, and George Washington Carver. We were explicitly taught that black people did not share the same history as whites. African people had been forced to come to North America against their will, and instead of finding freedom, they had had to work as slaves.

The experiences of Afro-Americans never informed the standard characterizations of the society: even the slave experience of Africans and Afro-Americans did not alter the image that America was a land in which people found freedom. As a student, I had to master the myths and accept them as part of my socialization into the political system. I also learned that the information I accumulated about black people—and later other people of color—was nice to know for "cultural enrichment." Exposure to the experiences of Afro-Americans, Puerto Ricans, and others was useful to develop tolerance for difference and make us better citizens, but this information was never meant to identify concepts, to develop perspectives, or to generate images or theories about the society as a whole.

I was in school to learn the experiences of the dominant group which was also very male, as well as white and affluent—and that would be the basis for an understanding of the system. If I learned that, I could go to college and perhaps do more interesting work than my parents did.

In spite of the intended message, it was hard for me to understand why the experiences of black people were not incorporated into our images of who we are as a nation. At the time there was no mention of Asian Americans, Chicanos, or Native Americans. But I came to understand the practice. Whatever happened to black people was an exception to the rule—we were a deviant case—just like using "i" before "e" except after "c." Since the experiences of black people did not have to be included in our search for the truth, they were not the material from which theories and frameworks were derived.

As I reflect on my early educational experiences, I see that the messages I received as a child, an adolescent, and an adult blamed the victim. For example, we were taught that the African people who "came" to America were not civilized; therefore, they could not pursue the American dream as initial settlers and white immigrants had been able to do. The lack of black participation in mainstream American society was attributed to lesser abilities, defective cultures, lack of motivation, and so forth. To make a "victim-blaming" attribution, teachers did not actually have to say that black Americans were lazy, ignorant, or savage—although that would surely do the trick. Instead, victim-blaming was subtly encouraged in classes where images of America as the land of freedom and opportunity were juxtaposed with the black experience, without any reconciling of the contradictions through a structural explanation. Students then relied on prevailing myths and stereotypes to explain the black "anomaly."

As a young black girl, I found these messages problematic, and throughout my life I have sought answers to questions about the experiences of black people at different historic moments. As a scholar, I still struggle with how best to use the knowledge I have gained. Thus, I approach the issue of curriculum integration with a fundamental critique of the traditional curriculum. I did not begin by discovering that women were missing from the curriculum—instead I have always perceived schools as foreign institutions. The information taught in schools was alien to me, to my family, to my neighborhood, and in a certain respect to the city, New York, in which I lived. Yet, in order to move to the next educational level and succeed in society, I had to master this information and pass tests. In my view, you were smart if you could pass the tests, but you had to look elsewhere for information to help you survive in the real world.

Today's wave of curriculum reforms presents an opportunity to restructure education, to alter the environment that was alien to me and many others. Such a remedy would include in the curriculum all the people in the classroom and the nation. Instead of focusing solely on the experiences of dominant group members, faculty members would teach students to use and value many different experiences in order to develop conceptions of life in this country and around the world.

I began by discussing my early experiences, because these experiences are common to many. Although we learn these lessons as members of either privileged or oppressed groups, they are similar lessons. If we are clear about the origins of practices that exclude people of color, we can dispense with blaming ourselves and each other for the difficulties we face in trying to change the curriculum. We are swimming upstream against the intellectual racism that flows through American ideology. The *disregard* for the experiences of black people and other people of color is part of the American creed. To create a multicultural curriculum we must "unlearn" the ideology that marginalizes all but a tiny elite of American citizens.

Curriculum transformation has the potential for changing our traditional visions of education in American society. Yet, it can also replicate old biases. This is especially likely to occur in situations where the integration process is envisioned as a minor tune-up to an educational system that is fundamentally solid. From my perspective, however, our curriculum needs a major overhaul. It needs much more than the addition of women. It must incorporate the men who are omitted—especially working-class men and men of color. Elizabeth Minnich reminds us that fundamental change is not possible unless we first understand why these groups were excluded. Enlightened by such a critique, we can decide how we want to change and what we will teach. We can then select the path that leads to a restructuring of the curriculum toward inclusiveness across many dimensions of human experience.

CURRICULUM CHANGE STARTS WITH FACULTY DEVELOPMENT

Integrating the diversity among women into the curriculum is difficult. Most faculty members are just learning about women through recent exposure to feminist scholarship; few of them are knowledgeable about and at ease with material on women of color. This is understandable. No one mentioned women of color when most contemporary college faculty pursued their degrees, yet the lack of correct information is a major contributor to the limited and inadequate treatment of women of color in courses and in research projects.

As the products of educational experiences that relegated people of color and women to the margins of their fields, faculty members need to compensate for the institutionalized biases in the educational system. They can work to eliminate this bias by gaining familiarity with the historical and contemporary experiences of racial-ethnic groups, the working class, middle-class women, and other groups traditionally restricted to the margins. The first step is to acknowledge one's lack of exposure to these histories.

Structural difficulties make learning new information about women and people of color problematic. It is often hard for faculty members to compensate for the gaps in their knowledge when they are faced with heavy teaching responsibilities and the pressure to publish. College administrators can encourage efforts with release time, financial support for workshops and institutes, and the like. Even without such resources, faculty members can develop long- and short-term strategies—for example, by organizing seminars to explore the new scholarship. All that is needed is a commitment and a shared reading list.

Another difficulty is the interdisciplinary nature of women's studies. Most faculty members are trained to research a specific discipline. Fortunately, over the years, more resources and tools have become available to help navigate this interdisciplinary field. The Center for Research on Women at Memphis State University has been a pioneer in this area; other research centers and curriculum projects have produced bibliographies, collections of syllabi, essays, and resources to assist with curriculum change. Some resources specifically include race, class, and gender as dimensions of analysis.

Institutionalized racism and sexism are structured into both the commercial and academic publishing markets, thus making it more difficult for scholars studying women and people of color to publish their work. Women's studies centers have initiated projects to help faculty identify relevant citations and locate new research, and the development of women's studies and racial-ethnic studies journals has helped a great deal, but structural barriers persist that impede access to research on certain populations, particularly women of color, working-class women, and women in the southern and western regions of this nation. Thus, the very resources college faculty need about women of color are difficult to locate.

Learning to identify myth and misinformation about people of color is a critical task in course and curriculum revision. It is a process that alters teaching content and classroom dynamics. For example, with new knowledge faculty members can teach students in ways that appreciate human diversity. Faculty members will also be better prepared to interrupt and challenge racist, sexist, class-bias, and homophobic remarks made in the classroom.

My own areas of specialization have given me information on the experiences of different racial and ethnic groups in this society. I often forget that everyone is not familiar with how most of the Southwest became part of the United States; with the Chinese Exclusion Act of 1882; with the implications of the Immigration Act of 1924 for people of color; with the internment of Japanese American citizens during World War II; and with the fact that Puerto Ricans are citizens, not immigrants, and cannot be considered undocumented workers. One has to remember that most dominant-group faculty and students are not nearly as familiar with these histories as are students who belong to specific ethnic and racial-ethnic groups. This history of oppression is part of the oral traditions in ethnic and racial-ethnic communities as well as religious groups. Afro-American, Latino, Asian American, and Native American students enter our classrooms with at least a partial awareness of the historic struggles of their people. They frequently feel alienated in educational settings where their teachers and other students relate to them without any awareness of their group's history. For example, a faculty member or a student who talks about how Japanese Americans have *always* done well in this country denies the reality that racism has severely marred the lives of both Japanese immigrants and Japanese Americans. For much of this century Japanese aliens were denied the opportunity to become citizens. During World War II they were removed from the West Coast and placed in internment camps, primarily because Anglos resented their economic success. Non-Japanese American faculty and students may be unaware of this history. The lack of correct information on the part of faculty members has consequences for what happens in the classroom: to the Japanese American student, Anglo ignorance of these issues is symptomatic of the persistent denial that racism is an issue for this group.

With new information, faculty can challenge myths and begin to interrupt racism in the classroom. The mastering of new information is a key ingredient in combatting the feelings of powerlessness many faculty members experience in the face of the racist and sexist attitudes of their students. Once we acknowledge our lack of information, we can use the many resources available to learn about the experiences of women, people of color, working-class people, and other traditionally marginalized groups.

WHAT DO I DO WITH NEW INFORMATION?

A key issue faced by faculty is finding a "place" for working-class women, black women, and other women of color in the curriculum. How do we challenge established practices of marginalizing these populations and truly develop a different educational process? How do we weave this new information on women and specifically women of color into a course on the family, the labor market, the sociology of education, the introduction to political science, and so forth? This is where many faculty learn by trial and error.

Revising the content of one's course requires the clarification of personal goals and educational aims. This is not an issue that faculty approach lightly. One cannot introduce a reading or a lecture where minority women are covered and then merely assume that the goal has been achieved. Curriculum transformation requires much more. Yet, as we move toward that goal, our individual educational philosophy and commitment to our discipline will play a key role in how we resolve these issues.

It is common practice to begin initial integration efforts with one or two lectures on women of color. Faculty who stop at that level of inclusion find that their course is not transformed

and that this addition has little impact on students. In fact, this approach can generate new problems. An instructor who performs the obligatory lecture often encounters opposition from students. For example, a black woman colleague of mine taught a traditional course on the family and included a unit on the black family. A few vocal students were quick to remind her that they had signed up for a course on the family, not the "black family." Had she incorporated material on the black family in every unit throughout the course, the "black family" would not have appeared to be anomalous, but an integral part of the study of the family.

Yet, this additive approach is problematic. If faculty introduce material on black women or women of color as interesting variations on womanhood, such actions indicate that readings and lecture materials on these populations are not part of the "core" knowledge covered in the class. Students can tolerate a certain amount of cultural enrichment, but if this material exceeds more than one or two lectures, they lose their patience because they think the instructor is deviating from the core. This reaction can be avoided if material on white working-class women, black women, and other women of color (as well as men of color and working-class people) is integrated throughout the course. The diversity of experiences should be presented as knowledge that students are responsible for learning and will be evaluated for covering.

Approaches that keep women of color on the margins or peripheral to the course materials fail to address critical issues of racism, sexism, and classism. Faculty who use such approaches tend to introduce material on white middle-class people as the norm, and then later ask for a discussion on the variations found among working-class whites and people of color. This approach does a great deal to foster ideas that blame the victim. Students may even use such discussions as opportunities to verbalize the racism they have learned from the media and other sources. Such interactions tend to polarize a class, and then the faculty member has an additional battle to wage.

In sociology, where attention is given to norms, ideal types, and the like, women of color are often incorporated as deviant cases. Peripheral treatments of groups are obvious to students; furthermore, these approaches complement students' previous learning about racial-ethic groups. Often when an instructor is about to begin the one obligatory lecture on the black family, the black woman, Latinas, working-class women in the labor market or whomever, a student will ask the question all the students want answered, "Are we going to be tested on this?" This also tends to happen when a guest speaker who is a racial minority or a female is invited to class. Students may listen politely but not feel compelled to write anything down or remember what was said.

Students carry old lessons into the classroom. They have already learned that what happens to people of color (or to women) does not count. This has been evident in their learning prior to college and continues in most college courses. Learning about different groups is treated as cultural enrichment, not as a part of the basic scholarship of a field. These are essentially correct impressions on the part of students. The core material is still about affluent white men: the

historical experiences, social conditions, and scholarly contributions of people of color and women are marginal to the disciplines.

Beyond a Universal Model of Gender

In many curriculum integration efforts in social science teaching, the marginalization of women of color takes two forms. Women of color are addressed either as tangents to the "generic" woman or as the "exceptional" woman of color. In the first case, African American, Asian American, and Native American women and Latinas are present, but their experiences are not critical to the development of theory or paradigms. This teaching strategy is often linked with the view that gender relations are the foundation for universal experiences. Within this framework, other sources of inequality, particularly race and class, might be acknowledged, but they are clearly less important than gender. As a result, scholarship on women of color in both women's studies and curriculum integration efforts is marginalized. Faculty tend to rely upon the experiences of white, middle-class, heterosexual Americans as the norm and view all others are merely exceptions to the rule.

Sandra Morgen is very critical of this universalist stance. She identifies how looking at the experiences of women of color expands our understanding of critical issues for women and gives a feminist perspective greater depth. Morgen examines how we can develop deeper appreciations of motherhood, the feminization of poverty, and women and resistance by examining the historical and current situations of women of color.

With regard to motherhood, Morgen identifies the way that most white, middle-class feminist scholars see the nuclear family as normative. In a discussion of Dinnerstein's *Mermaid and the Minotaur* (1976), Adrienne Rich's *Of Woman Born* (1976), and Nancy Chodorow's (1978) *The Reproduction of Mothering*, Morgen argues that much feminist scholarship about "the" family

> presumes that working women are a relatively recent phenomenon, and that working mothers are even newer, and that the normative family is mom, dad, and the kids, and that mothers live with their children and are the primary, if not near exclusive, force in their socialization. These assumptions are problematic when explaining the historical and contemporary experiences of many poor and working-class women, and of many women of color. These women have as a group been in the labor force for a much longer period of time, and in situations like slavery, sharecropping, domestic work, or unregulated industrial production that did not allow for the kind of full-time motherhood, or the specific mother-child relations which are presumed in Chodorow, Dinnerstein, and Rich.

The impact of racial oppression on the mothering behavior of women of color in the nineteenth century is a theme in the work of Bonnie Thornton Dill. She describes how racial oppression not only shaped the productive roles of African American, Latina, and Asian immigrant women, but also influenced the reproductive labor of these women. Dill's and Morgen's works demonstrate that much can be gained by using the experiences of women of color to develop new theo-

ries about women's experiences. Such approaches sharply contrast with those that fit the experiences of women of different classes and races into a universal model.

Morgen also describes how an analysis of the feminization of poverty can be informed by looking at the circumstances of women who are not new to poverty. She is joined by other scholars who have discovered that not all women are a husband away from poverty. While many middle-class white women experience a significant decline in their social status when they sever their attachment to a middle-class white male, many working-class women and women of color find themselves attached to men and still poor. Their poverty is not only a gender issue but is related to a legacy of class and racial discrimination.

We can also see beyond approaches that focus on women as victims by learning how working-class women and women of color resist class and racial oppression. Rather than a continuum from accommodation to rebellion, Morgen sees diverse personal and protracted struggles against oppression. These women actively resist the limitations placed on their lives by gender, class, and racial oppression. Denied access to many public spheres, they do not protest by voting or writing letters to congressmen; instead, they are involved in grass-roots organizing, efforts to improve public schools and other neighborhood institutions, jobs actions, and the like. Morgen's book (coedited with Ann Bookman) *Women and the Politics of Empowerment* incorporates much of the new research on women and resistance, research that is primarily on working-class women.

Rich examples of resistance are also found in the new scholarship on women in domestic work.

If we abandon the practice of keeping working-class women and women of color on the margins in our teaching and our research, and seek ways to incorporate the diversity of women's experiences, we are more likely to involve students and challenge their racist assumptions. We can also move students beyond seeing women of color and working-class women as victims.

Addressing the Lives of Ordinary Women of Color

A second way that women of color are introduced into the curriculum is by a brief look at a few "exceptional" examples. This method is very common in history and the social sciences, where "exceptional" black women such as Sojourner Truth, Harriet Tubman, Ida B. Wells, and Mary McLeod Bethune are discussed. In contrast to marginal treatments of women of color, described above, where the population of women of color is seen as an undifferentiated mass, this approach holds up a few models—nonvictims—for admiration. In the case of black women, this is often done under the guise that racism has not been terribly difficult for them. The subtle message to students is that if successful black women could achieve in the face of obstacles, other black women failed to attain the same heights because of faulty culture, lack of motivation, and other individual deficits. A faculty member might not intend to reinforce the individualistic les-

sons of the American ideology, but students interpret the material in this way because it is a common theme in our history. The "exceptions" approach fails to depict the larger social system in which the struggles of women of color, whether successful or not, take place.

In "The Politics of Black Women's Studies," by Barbara Smith and Gloria Hull, which is the introductory essay in *But Some of Us Are Brave: Black Women's Studies*, the authors warn of this practice:

> A descriptive approach to the lives of black women, a "great black women" in history or literature approach, or any traditional male-identified approach will not result in intellectually groundbreaking or politically transforming work. We cannot change our lives by teaching solely about "exceptions" to the ravages of white-male oppression. Only through exploring the experiences of supposedly "ordinary" black women whose "unexceptional" actions enabled us and the race to survive, will we be able to begin to develop an overview and analytic framework for understanding the lives of Afro-American women.

To do otherwise is to deceive ourselves. The experiences of a few exceptional black women, as typically portrayed in the classroom, serve to deny the reality of oppressive structures. This approach does not help students develop an appreciation for the role of race, class, and gender in people's lives. As we attempt to bring women of color out of the margins, we must be prepared to challenge students' tendency to romanticize a few heroines.

These two practices, teaching about women of color as tangents to the "generic" woman and examining the lives of exceptional women of color, work to justify and perpetuate the marginalization of women of color in women's studies scholarship. Approaches such as these retard the field of women's studies and complicate the task of integrating women into the high school and college curricula. While these approaches might represent a step or phase in the process of changing the curriculum, we must also remain clear on the larger goals and objectives of curriculum transformation. As pointed out earlier, each step in transformation brings its own set of problems and contradictions into the classroom. If we are not clear about our ultimate goal, we may become discouraged and retreat before new problems. In the end, we seek a curriculum that teaches an awareness and appreciation of the diversity of human experiences as well as the commonality of the human condition.

If a course is structured around the dominant-group experience and people of color are marginalized, faculty members lose the opportunity to critically address social structure—that is, the ways in which the institutions of society shape our options and influence our behavior. Transforming the curriculum requires explicit discussions of the roles of gender, race, and class in shaping the lives of everybody. This is accomplished by exploring the diversity of the experiences of men and women in the United States and around the world. For example, being female means privileges and the accompanying restrictions of dependency for some women, while for others it means poverty and the burden of supporting themselves and dependents.

Within this framework, no norm or modal case is taken for granted. If one teaches the sociology of the American family, it is with an eye on examining the diversity of family forms and lives. In family studies, only a minority of today's families fit the supposed norm of the 1950s and 1960s, of a full-time-employed father and a mother at home with the children. Therefore, it is easier and more accurate to look at the variations of family forms and discuss which factors obstruct or support specific types of family structures. Faculty members might even find that students, who are well aware of the variety of families, might be motivated to explore the factors behind this diversity. This perspective is the core of a recent textbook about the sociology of the family, *Diversity in American Families,* by Maxine Baca Zinn and D. Stanley Eitzen. The book, which elaborates how race and class, major structures of inequality, affect specific family forms, is well received by students because it does not hold up any single type as the norm by which all other families are judged.

RACISM, DIVERSITY, AND CLASSROOM DYNAMICS

Racism is a pervasive classroom problem that has to be addressed. One approach is to inform students that racism often takes the form of misinformation about racial-ethnic groups. Discussions of how misinformation is systematically taught in the schools and the media, and in informal ways from friends, parents, and the like, may relieve individual students from feeling guilty for holding racist notions. Students should be encouraged to think critically about the information they get regarding their own group and others' groups, so that they will learn to question broad generalizations like "All whites are middle class" and "All blacks are poor." Information that sheds light on the diversity within a group is more likely to be correct.

Students should be encouraged to think critically about information that devalues or dehumanizes members of specific groups. For example, any idea that some people (usually blacks, Latinos, or Native Americans) are more comfortable with hunger, poverty, and the like than other groups (usually white Americans) implies that the former are "less than human." Any information that students received that has the effect of dehumanizing a group can be identified as racist and therefore not a fact of the social world.

These are just a few ideas to help faculty think about combatting racism in the classroom. Correct information and changing teaching methods will do a great deal to challenge the racism embedded in our educational system—where there are a limited number of legitimate lines of inquiry and where "inquirers are only allowed to ask certain questions." . . .

The routes individual faculty members take to enhance classroom dynamics will vary widely, but there can be some goals we all share. Part of the task of the college instructor is to create an environment where there can be an honest and open exchange about the material and where students can do what they are rarely asked to do—learn from each other.

CONCLUSION

Curriculum transformation is a challenge in which all faculty can participate. As we pursue short- and long-term goals, it is important to be mindful of the several tasks involved in the process: securing information, integrating material into our teaching, and establishing a supportive classroom. Do not become discouraged by the slow progress. Establishing support for faculty can be critical in the success of projects. Join with other colleagues in learning new materials and experimenting in the classroom. The presence of support groups can help faculty members reflect on their progress and motivate them to take new risks. Faculty who accept this new challenge may find a rejuvenated interest in teaching their students.

PART II
Women's Studies in Action

Since the 1970s, every discipline has been confronted with and had to absorb or deflect feminist criticism to some degree. Feminists have identified biases, expanded and altered the scope and methods of research, challenged cherished concepts, and staked out new territory. Part Two of this text is designed to provide a representative sample of Women's Studies scholarship across the disciplines. Within each chapter, students will read three contributions by feminists. Some pieces present overviews of feminist work within a particular discipline, outlining major trends and debates. These essays are meant to introduce students to the ways in which feminist scholarship has engaged with traditional scholarship to provoke change and growth. They also offer insight into the variety of goals and strategies employed by women's studies scholars over the past forty years. Other pieces were chosen because they represent decisive and influential contributions that have altered the direction of a field of scholarship.

Foremost among my goals is to show the variety of ways that feminism has contributed to the dynamism of the academy: posing new questions, finding new sources, and offering new interpretations. Furthermore, this collection seeks to celebrate a wide spectrum of feminist scholarship. Students will be confronted with radicals and liberals, those committed to the academy and their own disciplinary training, and those who work to break down barriers between activism and scholarship and among the disciplines. Brief introductions to each section will provide a foundation and context for the three essays. Questions are designed to promote critical thinking and suggest connections among the works of scholarship and with students' own lives and educational experiences.

History

History can never be the written record of all that happened in the past. Certain questions get asked, sources consulted, and stories told while others do not, depending on the historian's sense of what is significant. Not surprisingly then, the field has been thoroughly altered by feminist scholarship. Initially focused on restoring forgotten (or excluded) women to accounts of the past, feminist historians then moved on to show how the new knowledge about women required a rewriting of history. In the first piece, Joan Scott offers an overview of the important work historians of women have done and argues for the strategies she finds most productive. Note the distinction she makes between studying women in history and using gender to study history. In the next two readings, we see examples of how attention to women alters conventional historical narratives—in the case of slave rebellion and Victorian sexual culture. In both Darlene Clark Hine's and Carroll Smith-Rosenberg's essays, new questions and new sources force a reconsideration of events, institutions, and culture. When reading these essays, consider the extent to which and the reasons why history as a discipline has been open to the contributions of feminists.

Critical Thinking Questions:

1. How have historians of women gone beyond the "add women and stir" strategy and forced paradigm shifts in the field?
2. According to Scott, how does the study of women differ from the study of gender in history?
3. What examples does Scott offer of significant contributions made by historians of women that illustrate "the ways in which politics constructs gender and gender constructs politics"?
4. What aspects of the slave experience are uncovered by attention to females?
5. How were the intimate or "private" choices made by enslaved women connected to the political and economic institution of slavery?
6. How did asking new questions and seeking new sources help Smith-Rosenberg discover an entire "world" that previous generations of historians overlooked?
7. To what extent does Smith-Rosenberg's article illustrate what women have gained since the Victorian era, and to what extent does it illustrate what women have lost? Which insight is most compelling to you and why?

13

Women's History

(1999)

Joan Scott

> What one wants, I thought—and why does not some brilliant
> student at Newnham or Girton supply it?— is a mass of
> information; at what age did she marry; how many children
> had she as a rule; what was her house like; had she a room to
> herself; did she do the cooking; would she be likely to have a
> servant? All these facts lie somewhere, presumably, in parish
> registers and account books; the life of the average Elizabethan
> woman must be scattered about somewhere, could one collect
> it and make a book of it. It would be ambitious beyond my
> daring, I thought, looking about the shelves for books that
> were not there, to suggest to the students of those famous
> colleges that they should rewrite history, though I own that it
> often seems a little queer as it is, unreal, lop-sided; but why
> should they not add a supplement to history? calling it, of
> course, by some inconspicious name so that women might
> figure there without impropriety?
>
> Virginia Woolf, *A Room of One's Own*

During the last decade, Virginia Woolf's call for a history of women— written more than fifty years ago—has been answered. Inspired directly or indirectly by the political agenda of the women's movement, historians have not only documented the lives of average women in various historical periods but they have charted as well changes in the economic, educational, and political positions of women of various classes in city and country and in nation-states. Bookshelves are being filled with biographies of forgotten women, chronicles of feminist movements, and the collected letters of female authors; the book titles treat subjects as disparate as suffrage and

Scott, Joan. "Women's History." In *Gender and the Politics of History,* New York: Columbia University Press, 1999.

birth control. Journals have appeared that are devoted exclusively to women's studies and to the even more specialized area of women's history. And, at least in the United States, there are major conferences devoted entirely to the presentation of scholarly papers on the history of women. All of this adds up to what is justifiably termed "the new knowledge about women."

The production of this knowledge is marked by remarkable diversity in topic, method, and interpretation, so much so that it is impossible to reduce the field to a single interpretive or theoretical stance. Not only is a vast array of topics studied, but in addition, on the one hand, many case studies, and, on the other hand, large interpretive overviews, which neither address one another nor a similar set of questions. Moreover, women's history does not have a long-standing and definable historiographic tradition within which interpretations can be debated and revised. Instead, the subject of women has been either grafted on to other traditions or studied in isolation from them. While some histories of women's work, for example, address contemporary feminist questions about the relationship between wage-earning and status, others frame their studies within the context of debates among Marxists and between Marxists and modernization theorists about the impact of industrial capitalism. Reproduction covers a vast terrain in which fertility and contraception are variously studied. Sometimes they are treated within the confines of historical demography as aspects of the "demographic transition." Alternatively they are viewed within the context of discussions about conflicting political analyses by Malthusian political economists and socialist labor leaders, or within the very different framework of evaluations of the impact of nineteenth-century "ideology of domesticity" on the power of women in their families. Yet another approach stresses feminist debates about sexuality and the history of women's demands for the right to control their own bodies. Additionally, some Marxist-feminists have redefined reproduction as the functional equivalent of production in an effort to incorporate women into the corpus of Marxist theory. In the area of politics, investigations have sought to demonstrate simply that women were to be found "in public," or to illustrate the historical incompatibility between feminist claims, on the one hand, and the structure and ideology of organized trade unions and political parties, on the other hand (the "failure" of socialism, for example, to accommodate feminism). Another quite different approach to politics examines the interior organization of women's political movements as a way of documenting the existence of a distinctively female culture.

More than in many other areas of historical inquiry, women's history is characterized by extraordinary tensions: between practical politics and academic scholarship; between received disciplinary standards and interdisciplinary influences; between history's atheoretical stance and feminism's need for theory. Feminist historians feel these tensions in many ways, perhaps most acutely as they try to identify the presumed audiences for their work. The disparate nature of these audiences can lead to uneven and confusing arguments in individual books and essays and it makes impossible the usual kind of synthetic essay on the state of the field.

What is possible, instead, is an attempt to tease out from this vast accumulation of writings some insight into the problems historians face as they produce new knowledge about women. For whatever the topical range and variety, there is a common dimension to the enterprise of these scholars of different schools. It is to make women a focus of inquiry, a subject of the story, an agent of the narrative—whether that narrative is a chronicle of political events (the French Revolution, the Swing riots, World War I or II) and political movements (Chartism, utopian socialism, feminism, women's suffrage), or a more analytically cast account of the workings or unfoldings of large-scale processes of social change (industrialization, capitalism, modernization, urbanization, the building of nation-states). The titles of some of the books that launched the women's history movement in the early 1970s explicitly conveyed their authors' intentions: those who had been "Hidden from History" were "Becoming Visible." Although recent book titles announce many new themes, the mission of their authors remains to construct women as historical subjects. That effort goes far beyond the naïve search for the heroic ancestors of the contemporary women's movement to a reevaluation of established standards of historical significance. It culminates in the set of questions raised so tellingly by Woolf: can a focus on women "add a supplement to history" without also "rewriting history"? Beyond that, what does the feminist rewriting of history entail?

These questions have established the framework for debate and discussion among historians of women during the past fifteen years. Although there are clear lines of difference discernible, they are better understood as matters of strategy than as fundamental divides. Each has particular strengths and limits, each addresses the difficulty of writing women into history in a somewhat different way. The cumulative effect of these strategies has been the creation of a new field of knowledge marked not only by tensions and contradictions but also by an increasingly complex understanding of what the project of "rewriting history" entails.

Not only has that understanding emerged from debates internal to the field of women's history; it has also been shaped in relation to the discipline of history itself. As feminists have documented the lives of women in the past, provided information that challenged received interpretations of particular periods or events, and analyzed the specific conditions of women's subordination, they have encountered the powerful resistance of history—as a disciplined body of knowledge and as a professional institution. Meeting this resistance has been an occasion variously for anger, retreat, and the formulation of new strategies. It has also provoked analyses of the deeply gendered nature of history itself. The entire process has generated a search for terms of criticism, conceptual reorientations, and theory that are the preconditions for feminist rewritings of history.

Much of the search has revolved around the issue of woman as a subject, that is as an active agent of history. How could women achieve the status of subjects in a field that subsumed or ignored them? Would making women visible suffice to rectify past neglect? How could women be added to a history presented as a universal human story exemplified by the lives of men? Since the specificity or particularity of women already made them unfit representatives of humankind, how could attention to women undercut, rather than reinforce, that notion? The history of women's history during the last decade and a half illustrates the difficulty of finding easy answers to these questions.

In this essay I will examine that history as a way of exploring the philosophical and political problems encountered by the producers of the new knowledge about women. I will draw most heavily on North American scholarship that focuses on the nineteenth and twentieth centuries because I am most familiar with it, and because in the United States there has been the fullest elaboration of theoretical debates about women's history.

One approach—the first chronologically—to the problem of constituting women as historical subjects was to gather information about them and write (what some feminists dubbed) "her-story." As the play on the word "history" implied, the point was to give value to an experience that had been ignored (hence devalued) and to insist on female agency in the making of history. Men were but one group of actors; whether their experiences were similar or different, women had to be taken explicitly into account by historians.

"Her-story" has had many different uses. Some historians gather evidence about women to demonstrate their essential likeness as historical subjects to men. Whether they uncover women participating in major political events or write about women's political action on their own behalf, these historians attempt to fit a new subject—women—into received historical categories, interpreting their actions in terms recognizable to political and social historians. One example of this approach looks at a women's political movement from the perspective of its rank-and-file members rather than its leaders. In the best traditions of the social histories of labor (which were inspired by the work of E. P. Thompson), Jill Liddington and Jill Norris offer a sensitive and illuminating account of working-class women's participation in the English suffrage campaign. Their material, drawn largely from Manchester records and from oral histories they collected, documents the involvement of working-class women in the struggle to win the vote (previous histories described it as almost entirely a middle-class movement) and links demands by these women for suffrage to their work and family lives and to the activities of trade union and Labor Party organizers. The predominance and wisdom of the Pankhurst wing of the movement is called into question for its elitism and its insistence on female separatism (a position rejected by the majority of suffragettes). A book on the history of the French women's suffrage movement by Steven Hause offers another illustration. The author interprets the weakness and small size of the movement (in comparison with its English and American counterparts) as the product of the ideologies and institutions of French Catholicism, the legacy of Roman law, the conservatism of French society, and the peculiar political history of French republicanism, especially the Radical Party during the Third Republic.

Another strategy associated with "her-story" takes evidence about women and uses it to challenge received interpretations of progress and regress. In this regard an impressive mass of evidence has been compiled to show that the Renaissance was not a renaissance for women, that technology did not lead to women's liberation either in the workplace or at home, that the "Age of Democratic Revolutions" excluded women from political participation, that the "affective nuclear family" constrained women's emotional and personal development, and that the rise of medical science deprived women of autonomy and a sense of feminine community.

A different sort of investigation, still within the "her-story" position, departs from the framework of conventional history and offers a new narrative, different periodization, and different causes. It seeks to illuminate the structures of ordinary women's lives as well as those of notable women, and to discover the nature of the feminist or female consciousness that motivated their behavior. Patriarchy and class are usually assumed to be the contexts within which nineteenth- and twentieth-century women defined their experience, and moments of cross-class collaboration among women directly addressed to women's oppression are stressed. The central aspect of this approach is the exclusive focus on female agency, on the causal role played by women in their history, and on the qualities of women's experience that sharply distinguish it from men's experience. Evidence consists of women's expressions, ideas, and actions. Explanation and interpretation are framed within the terms of the female sphere: by examinations of personal experience, familial and domestic structures, collective (female) reinterpretations of social definitions of women's role, and networks of female friendship that provided emotional as well as physical sustenance.

The exploration of women's culture has led to the brilliant insights of Carroll Smith-Rosenberg about the "female world of love and ritual" in nineteenth-century America, to an insistence on the positive aspects of the domestic ideology of the same period, to a dialectical reading of the relationship between middle-class women's political action and the ideas of womanhood that confined them to domestic realms, and to an analysis of the "reproductive ideology" that constructed the world of the bourgeoises of northern France in the mid-nineteenth century. It has also led Carl Degler to argue that American women themselves created the ideology of their separate sphere in order to enhance their autonomy and status. In his rendering of the story, women created a world neither within nor in opposition to oppressive structures or ideas that others imposed, but to further a set of group interests, defined and articulated from within the group itself.

The "her-story" approach has had important effects on historical scholarship. By piling up the evidence about women in the past it refutes the claims of those who insist that women had no history, no significant place in stories of the past. It goes further, by altering some of the standards of historical significance, asserting that "personal, subjective experience" matters as much as "public and political activities," indeed that the former influence the latter.

And it demonstrates that sex and gender need to be conceptualized in historical terms, at least if some of the motives for women's actions are to be understood. It establishes not only the legitimacy of narratives about women but the general importance of gender difference in the conceptualization and organization of social life. At the same time, however, it runs several risks. First, it sometimes conflates two separate operations: the valuation of women's experience (considering it worthy of study) and the positive assessment of everything women said or did. Second, it tends to isolate women as a special and separate topic of history, whether different questions are asked, different categories of analysis offered, or only different documents examined. For those interested there is now a growing and important history of women to supplement and enrich conventional histories, but it can too easily be consigned to the "separate sphere" that has long been associated exclusively with the female sex.

"Her-story" developed in tandem with social history; indeed, it often took its lead from the methods and conceptions developed by social historians. Social history offered important support for women's history in several ways. First, it provided methodologies in quantification, in the use of details from everyday life, and in interdisciplinary borrowings from sociology, demography, and ethnography. Second, it conceptualized as historical phenomena family relationships, fertility, and sexuality. Third, social history challenged the narrative line of political history ("white men make history") by taking as its subject large-scale social processes as they were realized in many

dimensions of human experience. This led to the fourth influence, the legitimation of a focus on groups customarily excluded from political history. Social history's story is ultimately about processes or systems (such as capitalism or modernization, depending on the theoretical stance of the historian), but it is told through the lives of particular groups of people who are the ostensible, though not always the actual, subjects of the narrative. Since human relationships of all kinds constitute society, one can study a variety of groups and topics to assess the impact of processes of change and it is relatively easy to extend the list from workers, peasants, slaves, elites, and diverse occupational or social groups to include women. Thus, for example, studies of women's work were undertaken, much as studies of workers had been, to assess capitalism's impact or to understand its operations.

These studies have led to a proliferation of that "mass of information" Virginia Woolf asked for. They have documented the extraordinary range of jobs women held and drawn patterns of female labor force participation according to age, marital status, and household income—belying the notion that one could generalize categorically about women and work. The studies have shown that women formed labor unions and went on strike, albeit at different rates from men; they have examined wage-scales and charted changes in employment opportunities, suggesting the greater importance of demand than supply in structuring female job markets.

There is as well a rich interpretive debate. Some historians insist that wage-earning enhanced women's status; others that women were exploited as a cheap labor supply and that, as a result, men perceived women as a threat to the value of their own labor. While some historians point out that family divisions of labor attributed economic value to a wife's domestic role, others have argued that family conflict centered on control of wages. Those who maintain that sex-segregation undermined women's job control and hence their ability to organize and strike are challenged by those who suggest that when women command sufficient resources they engage in collective action identical to men. All of this indicates a need not only to look at women but to analyze their situation in relation to men, to introduce into general studies of labor history questions about family organization and sex-segregated labor markets.

At the same time that it has enabled documentation of topics like the history of women's work, social history has also raised problems for feminist historians. On the one hand, social history made room for the study of women by particularizing and pluralizing the subjects of historical narratives—no single universal figure could possibly represent the diversity of humankind. On the other hand, it reduced human agency to a function of economic forces and made gender one of its many by-products. Women are just one of the groups mobilizing resources, being modernized or exploited, contending for power, or being excluded from a polity. Feminist questions about the distinctiveness of women and the centrality of social relations between the sexes tend to be displaced by or subsumed within economist and behaviorist models.

Both "her-story" and social history establish women as historical subjects; indeed, they are often overlapping or intersecting approaches in the work of historians of women. They differ, however, in their ultimate implications because each is associated with a somewhat different analytic perspective. Social history assumes that gender difference can be explained within its existing frame of (economic) explanation; gender is not an issue requiring study in itself. As a result, social history's treatment of women tends to be too integrationist. "Her-story," in contrast, assumes that gender explains the different histories of women and men, but it does not theorize about how gender operates historically. For that reason, its stories seem to be uniquely about women and can be read in too separatist a manner.

Attempts to conceptualize gender are, of course, also part of the history of women's history, and they have run through the discussions and debates from the beginning. The late Joan Kelly set as the goal for women's history the making of sex "as fundamental to our analysis of the social order as other classifications such as class and race." For Natalie Zemon Davis the aim was "to understand the significance of the sexes, of gender groups in the historical past." This could be accomplished by examining social definitions of gender as they were expressed by men and women, constructed in and affected by economic and political institutions, expressive of a range of relationships that included not only sex but also class and power. The results, it was argued, would throw new light not only on women's experience but on social and political practice as well.

For historians, studying gender has been largely a matter of method so far. It consists of comparing women's situation implicitly or explicitly to men's by focusing on law, prescriptive literature, iconographic representation, institutional structure, and political participation. Temma Kaplan's *Anarchists of Andalusia*, for example, examined the different appeals of that political movement to men and women and the different but complementary ways in which male and female peasants and workers were organized to revolutionary struggle. Her parallel treatment of men and women within anarchism shows how aspects of gender relationships in Andalusian society were used to articulate this particular political movement's attack on capitalism and the state. Tim Mason developed important insights about the "reconciliatory function of the family" in Nazi Germany as a result of an inquiry into the position of women and policies toward women. The factual material he gathered about women, who he says were largely "non-actors" in the politics of the period, "provided an exceptionally fruitful new vantage point from which the behaviour of the actors could be—indeed, had to be—reinterpreted." Taking Foucault's suggestion (in the *History of Sexuality*) that sexuality was not repressed, but at the center of modern discourses, Judith Walkowitz delved into Josephine Butler's campaign against the Contagious Diseases Acts in late Victorian England. She placed her account of this successful woman's movement, aimed at combating the double standard of sexual morality, in the context of economic, social, religious, and political divisions in English society. The study establishes the centrality for members of parliament as

well as for leading professional figures, male and female, of debates about sexual conduct. These debates were carried on "in public," and resulted in institutional and legal change. Sexual conduct was, therefore, an explicit political issue for at least several decades. The articulation of the meanings of sexual differences was also crucial at certain moments in the French Revolution, when citizenship and political participation were being defined. Darlene Levy and Harriet Applewhite have studied the proclamations that outlawed women's clubs in 1793 in the name of protecting femininity and domesticity. And Lynn Hunt has called attention to the way the Jacobins used masculinity to represent the sovereign people.

These studies share a common preoccupation with politics and more specifically with governments as the realm in which power relationships are formally negotiated. As such, they indicate the importance of connecting the study of gender with the study of politics. Since political structures and political ideas shape and set the boundaries of public discourse and of all aspects of life, even those excluded from participation in politics are defined by them. "Non-actors," to use Mason's term, are acting according to rules established in political realms; the private sphere is a public creation; those absent from official accounts partook nonetheless in the making of history; those who are silent speak eloquently about the meanings of power and the uses of political authority.

This emphasis brings women's history directly to political historians, those most committed to writing narratives with male subjects at their center. It also begins to develop a way of thinking historically about gender, for it draws attention to the ways in which changes happen in laws, policies, and symbolic representations. Furthermore, it implies a social rather than a biological or characterological explanation for the different behaviors and the unequal conditions of women and men. At the same time, however, it seems to undercut the feminist project by neglecting female agency and by implicitly diminishing the historical importance of personal and social life—family, sexuality, sociability—the very areas in which women have been visible participants.

The contradictions encountered by these various approaches to women's history have not prevented the production of new knowledge. That is evident in the multiplication of women's history jobs and courses and in the thriving journals and book market on which publishers have so readily capitalized. The contradictions have been productive in other ways as well. They have generated a search for resolution, an effort to formulate theories, and have set off reflection on the process of writing history itself. When put into dialogue with one another, these different approaches can move the entire discussion forward. But they can only do so, it seems to me, if the key terms of analysis are examined and redefined. These terms are three: woman as subject, gender, and politics.

Although there is a growing literature (informed especially by psychoanalysis) on the question of the "subject" that ought to be brought to bear on any discussion of women in history, I want to take up only a small point here. That has to do with the issue—made so apparent by the experience of "her-story"— of the particularity of women in relation to the universality of men. The abstract rights-bearing individual who came into being as the focus of liberal political debate in the seventeenth and eighteenth centuries somehow became embodied in male form and it is his-story that historians have largely told. Feminists' scholarship has repeatedly come up against the difficulty of including women in this universal representation since, as their work reveals, it is a contrast with feminine particularity that secures the universality of the masculine representation.

It seems clear that to conceive of women as historical actors, equal in status to men, requires a notion of the particularity and specificity of all human subjects. Historians cannot use a single, universal representative for the diverse populations of any society or culture without granting differential importance to one group over another. Particularity, however, raises questions about collective identities and about whether all groups can ever share the same experience. How do individuals become members of social groups? How are group identities defined and formed? What influences people to act as members of groups? Are processes of group identification common or variable? How do those marked by multiple differences (black women, or women workers, middle-class lesbians, or black lesbian workers) determine the salience of one or another of these identities? Can these differences, which together constitute the meanings of individual and collective identities, be conceived of historically? How could we realize in the writing of history Teresa de Lauretis's suggestion that differences among women are better understood as "differences within women?"

If the group or category "women" is to be investigated, then gender—the multiple and contradictory meanings attributed to sexual difference—is an important analytic tool. The term "gender" suggests that relations between the sexes are a primary aspect of social organization (rather than following from, say, economic or demographic pressures); that the terms of male and female identities are in large part culturally determined (not produced by individuals or collectivities entirely on their own); and that differences between the sexes constitute and are constituted by hierarchical social structures.

The turn to political history by those interested in writing about gender has introduced notions of contest, conflict, and power into the process of the cultural determination of the terms of sexual difference. But by studying power as it is exercised by and in relation to formal governmental authorities, historians unnecessarily eliminate whole realms of experience from consideration. This would not happen if a broader notion of "politics" were employed, one that took all unequal relationships as somehow "political" because involving unequal distributions of power, and asked how they were established, refused, or maintained. Here Foucault's discussion of power relations in Volume I of *The History of Sexuality* seems worth quoting at length:

> The question that we must address, then, is not: Given a specific state structure, how and why is it that power needs to establish a knowledge of sex? Neither is the question: What over-all domination was served by the

concern, evidenced since the eighteenth century, to produce true discourses on sex? Nor is it: What law presided over both the regularity of sexual behavior and the conformity of what was said about it? It is rather: In a specific type of discourse on sex, in a specific form of extortion of truth, appearing historically and in specific places (around the child's body, apropos of women's sex, in connection with practices restricting births and so on), what were the most immediate, the most local power relations at work? How did they make possible these kinds of discourses, and conversely, how were these discourses used to support power relations? . . . In general terms: rather than referring all the infinitesimal violences that are exerted on sex, all the anxious gazes that are directed at it, and all the hiding places whose discovery is made into an impossible task, to the unique form of a great Power, we must immerse the expanding production of discourses on sex in the field of multiple and mobile power relations.

This approach would end such seeming dichotomies as state and family, public and private, work and sexuality. And it would pose questions about the interconnections among realms of life and social organization now treated quite separately from one another. With this notion of politics, one could offer a critique of history that characterized it not simply as an incomplete record of the past but as a participant in the production of knowledge that legitimized the exclusion or subordination of women.

Gender and "politics" are thus antithetical neither to one another nor to recovery of the female subject. Broadly defined they dissolve distinctions between public and private and avoid arguments about the separate and distinctive qualities of women's character and experience. They challenge the accuracy of fixed binary distinctions between men and women in the past and present, and expose the very political nature of a history written in those terms. Simply to assert, however, that gender is a political issue is not enough. The realization of the radical potential of women's history comes in the writing of histories that focus on women's experiences *and* analyze the ways in which politics construct gender and gender constructs politics. Feminist history then becomes not the recounting of great deeds performed by women but the exposure of the often silent and hidden operations of gender that are nonetheless present and defining forces in the organization of most societies. With this approach women's history critically confronts the politics of existing histories and inevitably begins the rewriting of history.

14

Female Slave Resistance

The Economics of Sex

(1997)

Darlene Clark Hine

The question of the extent and nature of black resistance to slavery has been the subject of a number of recent historical studies. These works, concentrating as they do on the examination of black male resistance to the slave system, have demonstrated that such resistance was carried on both overtly in the form of slave rebellions and covertly in indirect attacks on the system, through resistance to the whip, feigning of illness, conscious laziness, and other means of avoiding work and impeding production. None of these studies, however, has considered in depth the forms of black female resistance to slavery, although they have suggested a methodology for attempting such an investigation. This paper is concerned with uncovering the means through which female slaves expressed their political and economic opposition to the slave system. What behavior patterns did enslaved black women adopt to protect themselves and their children and to undermine the system which oppressed and exploited them?

Unlike male slaves, female slaves suffered a dual form of oppression. In addition to the economic exploitation which they experienced along with black males, females under slavery were oppressed sexually as well. Sexual oppression and exploitation refer not only to the obvious and well-documented fact of forced sexual intercourse with white masters but also to those forms of exploitation resulting from the very fact of her female biological system. For example, the female slave in the role of the mammy was regularly required to nurse white babies in addition to and often instead of her own children. In his *Roll, Jordon, Roll: The World the Slaves Made,* Eugene Genovese acknowledges the uniquely difficult position in which this practice placed the mammy:

> More than any other slave, she had absorbed the paternalist ethos and accepted her place in a system of reciprocal obligations defined from above. In so doing, she developed pride, resourcefulness, and a high sense of responsibility to white and Black people alike. . . . She did not reject her people

Hine, Darlene Clark. "Female Slave Resistance." In *Hine Sight: Black Women and the Re-Construction of American History* Bloomington, IN: Indiana University Press, 1997. Reprinted by permission of the Indiana University Press.

in order to identify with stronger whites, but she did place herself in a relationship to her own people that reinforced the paternalist order.

While Genovese gives evidence of the mammy's manipulation of her favored position, the pivotal question of how it must have felt to be forced to nurse and raise her future oppressors remains unexamined.

Another major aspect of the sexual oppression of black women under slavery took the form of the white master's consciously constructed view of black female sexuality. This construct, which was designed to justify his own sexual passion toward her, also blamed the female slave for the sexual exploitation that she experienced at the hands of her master. Winthrop Jordan comments in his *White Over Black: American Attitudes toward the Negro, 1550–1812,* that white men,

> by calling the Negro woman passionate . . . were offering the best possible justifications for their own passions. Not only did the Negro woman's warmth constitute a logical explanation for the white man's infidelity, but, much more important, it helped shift responsibility from himself to her. If she was *that* lascivious—well, a man could scarcely be blamed for succumbing against overwhelming odds.

It is clear from several slave narratives that the female slave was well aware of the image of her sexuality that was fostered among the white male population. In her narrative, *Incidents in the Life of a Slave Girl,* Linda Brent offers a revealing observation on the effect of this image on the female slave: "If God has bestowed beauty upon her, it will prove her greatest curse. That which commands admiration in the white woman only hastens the degradation of the female slave." In his article "New Orleans: The Mistress of the Trade," Frederic Bancroft documents Brent's observation and shows how this image of black female sexuality gave rise to a section of the slave trade specifically designed to profit from the sale of attractive black women, or, as they were known at the time, "fancy girls." Bancroft points out that slave traders frequently prided themselves on the numbers of such women they had for sale and on the high prices commanded by their physical appearance. Often these women sold for prices that far exceeded those which planters were willing to pay for a field laborer. In 1857, for example, the *Memphis Eagle and Enquirer* ran an editorial in which it was observed that "a slave woman is advertised to be sold in St. Louis who is so surpassingly beautiful that $5,000 has already been offered for her, at private sale, and refused."

How, then, did a female slave resist both the economic and sexual oppressions which were a part of her daily life? Three intimately related forms of resistance peculiar to female slaves emerge from the narratives. The first method can be called sexual abstinence. This method ranged from refusing or attempting to avoid sexual intercourse with the white master to a strong wish to delay marriage to a male slave while hope remained that marriage and childbirth could occur in a free state. Elizabeth Keckley, who toward the end of her life became a seamstress for Mrs. Abraham Lincoln, discusses this form of resistance in her narrative, *Behind the Scenes: Thirty Years a Slave and Four Years in the White House.* Her story is typical in outlining the extent and duration of her attempt to avoid the designs of her licentious master. She recalls that she was "regarded as fair-looking for one of my race," and that as a result of her appearance her master pursued her for four years:

> I do not care to dwell upon this subject, for it is fraught with pain. Suffice it to say, that he persecuted me for four years, and I—I—became a mother. The child of which he was the father was the only child I ever brought into the world. If my poor boy ever suffered any humiliating pangs on account of birth, he could not blame his mother, for God knows that she did not wish to give him life; he must blame the edicts of that society which deemed it no crime to undermine the virtue of girls in my then position.

Presumably, Mrs. Keckley found this experience so upsetting that she could not bring herself to have another child—not even after she had gained her freedom.

Similarly, Linda Brent described her prolonged attempts to avoid sexual relations with her master, Dr. Flint. She recalls that she was able to use the presence of her grandmother on the plantation to avoid her master's advances because "though she had been a slave, Dr. Flint was afraid of her. He dreaded her scorching rebukes. Moreover, she was known and patronized by many people; and he did not wish to have his villainy made public."

Ellen Craft along with her future husband, William, escaped slavery in a most ingenious fashion. Mrs. Craft was so reluctant to have children while she remained in slavery that she and William agreed to delay their marriage until they reached the North. In their narrative, "Running a Thousand Miles for Freedom," William Craft perceptively explains his wife's motivations:

> My wife was torn from her mother's embrace in childhood, and taken to a distant part of the country. She had seen so many other children separated from their parents in this cruel manner, that the mere thought of her ever becoming a mother of a child, to linger out a miserable existence under the wretched system of American slavery, appeared to fill her very soul with horror; and as she had taken what I felt to be an important view of her condition, I did not, at first, press the marriage, but agreed to assist her in trying to devise some plan by which we might escape from our unhappy condition, and then be married.

A second method of female resistance to slavery in general and to sexual exploitation in particular took the form of abortion. Because abortion appears to have been less common than sexual abstinence, it seems fair to assume that destruction of the fetus extracted a higher psychological toll that did abstinence. In a recent study of the black family, Herbert Gutman observes that the conscious decision on the part of a slave woman to terminate her pregnancy was one act that was totally beyond the control of the master of the plantation. Gutman offers evidence of several southern physicians who commented upon abortion and the use of contraceptive methods among the slave population:

> The Hancock County, Georgia, physician E. M. Pendleton reported in 1849 that among his patients "abortion and miscarriage" occurred more frequently among slave than white free women. The cause was either "slave labor (exposure, violent exercise, etc.)" or "as the planters believe, that the Blacks are possessed of a secret by which they destroy the fetus at an early stage of gestation." All county practitioners, he added, "are aware of

the frequent complaints of planters about the unnatural tendency in the African female population to destroy her offspring. Whole families of women. . . . fail to have any children.

Gutman also recounts a situation in which a planter had kept between four and six slave women "of the proper age to breed" for twenty-five years and that "only two children had been born on the place at full term." It was later discovered that the slaves had concocted a medicine with which they were able to terminate their unwanted pregnancies. Gutman found evidence as well of a master who claimed that an older female slave had discovered a remedy for pregnancies and had been "instrumental in all. . . . the abortions on his place."

This last instance suggests that even those women who did not resist slavery through actually having an abortion themselves resisted even more covertly by aiding those who desired them. It is therefore possible that a sort of female conspiracy existed on the Southern plantation. This requires further study. In an interesting twist to the apparently chronic problem of unwanted and forced pregnancies, there is evidence that female slaves, recognizing the importance of their role in the maintenance of the slave systems, often feigned pregnancy as a method of receiving lighter work loads. The success, however limited, of this kind of ploy would also require the aid of other female slaves on the plantation—a midwife, for example, who might testify to the master that one of his female slaves was indeed pregnant.

In their illuminating article, "Day to Day Resistance to Slavery," Raymond and Alice Bauer note that "pretending to be pregnant was a type of escape in a class by itself, since the fraud must inevitably have been discovered." To illustrate, they include the following report in their article:

> I will tell you of a most comical account Mr.——has given of the prolonged and still protracted pseudo-pregnancy of a woman called Markie, who for many more months than are generally required for the process of continuing the human species, pretended to be what the Germans pathetically and poetically call "in good hope" and continued to reap increased rations as the reward of her expectation, till she finally had to disappoint the estate and receive a flogging.

Apparently, the increased allotment of food and the possibility of lighter work were enough inducement for this woman to risk the punishment which she must have known would follow. In this case the slave woman was perceptive enough of the importance of her procreative function for the maintenance of the slave system to manipulate to her own advantage the precise function for which she was most valued by the master.

Possibly the most psychologically devastating means which the slave parent had for undermining the slave system was infanticide. The frequency with which this occurred is by no means clear. Several historians have contended that infanticide was quite rare, and Genovese writes that "slave abortions, much less infanticide, did not become a major problem for the slave holders or an ordinary form of 'resistance' for the slaves. Infanticide occurred, but so far as the detected cases reveal anything, only in some special circumstances." The subject of infanticide under slavery is clearly in need of further study. For our purposes it is important to note that the relatively small number of documented cases is not as significant as the fact that it occurred at all. Raymond and Alice Bauer reveal how both infanticide and suicide were combined in the following account:

> Not only were slaves known to take the lives of their masters or overseers, but they were now and then charged with the murder of their own children, sometimes to prevent them growing up in bondage. In Covington, a father and mother, shut up in a slave baracoon and doomed to the southern market, "when there was no eye to pity them and no arm to save," did by mutual agreement "send the souls of their children to heaven rather than have them descend to the hell of slavery," then both parents committed suicide.

Genovese notes one instance in which "the white citizens of Virginia petitioned in 1822 to spare a slave condemned to death for killing her infant. The child's father was a respectable white man, and the woman insisted that she would not have killed a child of her own color." There are numerous instances in which a slave woman simply preferred to end her child's life rather than allow the child to grow up enslaved. Genovese writes that "for the most part, however, the slaves recognized infanticide as murder. They loved their children too much to do away with them; courageously, they resolved to raise them as best they could, and entrusted their fate to God." He does not appear to be acknowledging the motivations for infanticide offered repeatedly by the slave parents themselves. Far from viewing such actions as murder, and therefore indicating these as lack of love, slave parents who took their children's lives may have done so out of a higher form of love and a clearer understanding of the living death that awaited their children under slavery. Since this explanation is the one offered most frequently in the narratives, and since there does not seem to be any evidence at this time that contradicts the slaves' statements, they should be accepted as reflective of their true motivations.

It is also possible that there were other motivations behind infanticide. It may have occurred as a response to rape or forced pregnancy and it was an act which, along with sexual abstinence and abortion, had economic implications as well. The narratives reveal that slave children were sometimes used as pawns in a power struggle between plantation owners and their slaves. Owners used the sale or the threat of sale of slave children as a means of manipulating their recalcitrant or troublesome slaves, and the slaves in turn used their children to manipulate the behavior of their masters. There is one documented instance, for example, in which a particularly rebellious female slave, Fannie, is told that she must be sold following an incident in which she physically attacked her mistress. To increase the harshness of the punishment she is informed by her master that her infant will remain on the plantation. One of her older daughters recalls her mother's response:

> At this, ma took the baby by its feet, a foot in each hand, and with the baby's head swinging downward, she vowed to smash its brains out before she'd leave it. Tears were streaming down her face. It was seldom that ma cried and everyone knew that she meant every word. Ma took her baby with her.

In this instance the threat of infanticide on the part of the slave mother was transformed into an effective means for gaining power over the planter and control over at least part of her life. Thus, it seems that there were complex motivations involved in both infanticide and the threat of infanticide.

In attempting to evaluate the consequences for the slave system of these acts of resistance, Genovese's definition of paternalism is most helpful. He writes that, "Paternalism in any historical setting defines relations of superordination and subordination. Its strength as a prevailing ethos increases as the members of the community accept—or feel compelled to accept—these relations as legitimate. As was pointed out earlier, slave women were expected to serve a dual function in this system and therefore suffered a dual oppression. They constituted an important and necessary part of the work force and they were, through their child-bearing function, the one group most responsible for the size and indeed the maintenance of the slave labor pool. Therefore, when they resisted sexual exploitation through such means as sexual abstention, abortion, and infanticide, they were, at the same time, rejecting their vital economic function as breeders. This resistance, of course, became especially important after 1808, when it was no longer legal to import slaves into the United States from Africa.

The slave woman's resistance to sexual and therefore to economic exploitation posed a potentially severe threat to paternalism itself, for implicit in such action was the slave woman's refusal to accept her designated responsibilities within the slave system as legitimate. This acceptance of mutual responsibility on the part of both the slaves and the

masters was, as Genovese points out, at the heart of the maintenance of the paternalistic worldview. The female slave, through her sexual resistance, attacked the very assumptions upon which the slave order was constructed and maintained.

Resistance to sexual exploitation therefore had major political and economic implications. A woman who elected not to have children, or, to put it another way, engaged in sexual abstinence, abortion, or infanticide negated through individual or group action her role in the maintenance of the slave pool. To the extent that in so doing she redefined her role in the system, she introduced a unit of psychological heterogeneity into a worldview which depended, for its survival, on homogeneity, at least with respect to the assumptions of its ideology.

The examples quoted above strongly indicate that the slave woman's decision to participate in these particular forms of resistance was made consciously and with full awareness of the potential political and economic ramifications involved. In rejecting her role in the economic advancement of the slave system, she could reduce the numbers of slaves available for the slave trade and undermine her master's effort to profit from exploiting her sexually. The planters were the only beneficiaries of the increase in the numbers of slaves: $1,500 for a good, strong buck; $1,200 for a hardworking, childbearing wench, with no large scale investment necessary to insure future profit. The master could presumably simply sit back and wait for the children to be born. If there was no black male available, he could engage in the procreative process himself. The result was the same, made conveniently so, by laws that stipulated that the child inherited the condition of the mother.

In his *Once a Slave: The Slaves' View of Slavery*, Stanley Feldstein notes that Frederick Douglass makes explicit the importance of breeding slaves, even for the less wealthy planters:

> Frederick Douglass told of the case of a master who was financially able to purchase only one slave. Therefore, he bought her as a "breeder," and then hired a married man to live with her for one year. Every night he would place the man and woman together in a room; at the end of the year, the woman gave birth to twins. The children were regarded by the master as an important addition to his wealth, and his joy was such that the breeder was kept in the finest material comfort in the hope that she would continue providing good fortune to the master and his family.

Perhaps the most revealing example of the female slave's awareness of the sexual/economic nexus inherent in her dual role in the slave system is offered by Jane Blake in her narrative, *Memoirs of Margaret Jane Blake*. She commented that many slave women resisted pregnancy because they did not want their children to grow up in a state of bondage; she continued that if "all the bond women had been of the same mind, how soon the institution could have vanished from the face of the earth, and all the misery belonging to it,

been lifted from the hearts of the holders of slaves.'

One of the more striking aspects of the subject of female slave resistance is its complex nature. The decision to resist in the three ways that have been outlined involved sexual, emotional, economic, and political concerns. The examination of the strategies that were developed by the female slave to resist sexual and economic exploitation represents a legitimate and necessary area of inquiry if we are to understand slave resistance in general. In connection with this area, we need to know much more about the role that male slaves played in helping slave women resist both sexual and economic exploitation. The dynamics of female slave behavior cannot be fully understood if examined in a vacuum.

Instances of sexual abstinence, abortion, and of infanticide are important for the same reasons that historians study the three major slave rebellions of the nineteenth century. As with the rebellions, the important point with respect to these modes of female resistance is not the infrequency with which they occurred, if indeed they were infrequent, but the fact that these methods were used at all. Through a closer examination of the responses of black women to slavery, we can gain further insight into the interaction of males and females of both races on the southern plantation.

15

The Female World of Love and Ritual

Relations Between Women in Nineteenth-Century America

(1975)

Carroll Smith-Rosenberg

THE FEMALE FRIENDSHIP of the nineteenth century, the longlived, intimate, loving friendship between two women, is an excellent example of the type of historical phenomena which most historians know something about, which few have thought much about, and which virtually no one has written about. It is one aspect of the female experience which consciously or unconsciously we have chosen to ignore. Yet an abundance of manuscript evidence suggests that eighteenth- and nineteenth-century women routinely formed emotional ties with other women. Such deeply felt, same-sex friendships were casually accepted in American society. Indeed, from at least the late eighteenth through the mid-nineteenth century, a female world of varied and yet highly structured relationships appears to have been an essential aspect of American society. These relationships ranged from the supportive love of sisters, through the enthusiasms of adolescent girls, to sensual avowals of love by mature women. It was a world in which men made but a shadowy appearance.

Defining and analyzing same-sex relationships involves the historian in deeply problematical questions of method and interpretation. This is especially true since historians, influenced by Freud's libidinal theory, have discussed these relationships almost exclusively within the context of indi-

Smith-Rosenberg, "The Female World of Love & Ritual," SIGNS 1 (Autumn 1975): 1-29. Used with permission of the University of Chicago Press.

vidual psychosexual developments or, to be more explicit, psychopathology. Seeing same-sex relationships in terms of a dichotomy between normal and abnormal, they have sought the origins of such apparent deviance in childhood or adolescent trauma and detected the symptoms of "latent" homosexuality in the lives of both those who later became "overtly" homosexual and those who did not. Yet theories concerning the nature and origins of same-sex relationships are frequently contradictory or based on questionable or arbitrary data. In recent years such hypotheses have been subjected to criticism both from within and without the psychological professions. Historians who seek to work within a psychological framework, therefore, are faced with two hard questions: Do sound psychodynamic theories concerning the nature and origins of same-sex relationships exist? If so, does the historical datum exist which would permit the use of such dynamic models?

I would like to suggest an alternative approach to female friendships— one which would view them within a cultural and social setting rather than from an exclusively individual psychosexual perspective. Only by thus altering our approach will we be in the position to evaluate the appropriateness of particular dynamic interpretations. Intimate friendships between men and men and women and women existed in a larger world of social relations and social values. To interpret such friendships more fully they must be related to the structure of the American family and to the nature of sex-role divisions and of male-female relations both within the family and in society generally. The female friendship must not be seen in isolation; it must be analyzed as one

aspect of women's overall relations with one another. The ties between mothers and daughters, sisters, female cousins and friends, at all stages of the female life cycle constitute the most suggestive framework for the historian to begin an analysis of intimacy and affection between women. Such an analysis would not only emphasize general cultural patterns rather than the internal dynamics of a particular family or childhood; it would shift the focus of the study from a concern with deviance to that of defining configurations of legitimate behavioral norms and options.

This analysis will be based upon the correspondence and diaries of women and men in thirty-five families between the 1760s and the 1880s. These families, though limited in number, represented a broad range of the American middle class, from hard-pressed pioneer families and orphaned girls to daughters of the intellectual and social elite. It includes families from most geographic regions, rural and urban, and a spectrum of Protestant denominations ranging from Mormon to orthodox Quaker. Although scarcely a comprehensive sample of America's increasingly heterogeneous population, it does, I believe, reflect accurately the literate middle class to which the historian working with letters and diaries is necessarily bound. It has involved an analysis of many thousands of letters written to women friends, kin, husbands, brothers, and children at every period of life from adolescence to old age. Some collections encompass virtually entire life spans; one contains over 100,000 letters as well as diaries and account books. It is my contention that an analysis of women's private letters and diaries which were never intended to be published permits the historian to explore a very private world of emotional realities central both to women's lives and to the middle-class family in nineteenth-century America.

The question of female friendships is peculiarly elusive; we know so little or perhaps have forgotten so much. An intriguing and almost alien form of human relationship, they flourished in a different social structure and amidst different sexual norms. Before attempting to reconstruct their social setting, therefore, it might be best first to describe two not atypical friendships. These two friendships, intense, loving, and openly avowed, began during the women's adolescence and, despite subsequent marriages and geographic separation, continued throughout their lives. For nearly half a century these women played a central emotional role in each other's lives, writing time and again of their love and of the pain of separation. Paradoxically to twentieth-century minds, their love appears to have been both sensual and platonic.

Sarah Butler Wister first met Jeannie Field Musgrove while vacationing with her family at Stockbridge, Massachusetts, in the summer of 1849. Jeannie was then sixteen, Sarah fourteen. During two subsequent years spent together in boarding school, they formed a deep and intimate friendship. Sarah began to keep a bouquet of flowers before Jeannie's portrait and wrote complaining of the intensity and anguish of her affection. Both young women assumed nom de plumes, Jeannie a female name, Sarah a male one; they would use these secret names into old age. They frequently commented on the nature of their affection: "If the day should come," Sarah wrote Jeannie in the spring of 1861, "when you failed me either through your fault or my own, I would forswear all human friendship, thenceforth." A few months later Jeannie commented: "Gratitude is a word I should never use toward you. It is perhaps a misfortune of such intimacy and love that it makes one regard all kindness as a matter of course, as one has always found it, as natural as the embrace in meeting."

Sarah's marriage altered neither the frequency of their correspondence nor their desire to be together. In 1864, when twenty-nine, married, and a mother, Sarah wrote to Jeannie: "I shall be entirely alone [this coming week]. I can give you no idea how desperately I shall want you. . . . " After one such visit Jeannie, then a spinster in New York, echoed Sarah's longing: "Dear darling Sarah! How I love you & how happy I have been! You are the joy of my life. . . . I cannot tell you how much happiness you gave me, nor how constantly it is all in my thoughts. . . . My darling how I long for the time when I shall see you. . . . " After another visit Jeannie wrote: "I want you to tell me in your next letter, to assure me, that I am your dearest. . . . I do not doubt you, & I am not jealous but I long to hear you say it once more & it seems already a long time since your voice fell on my ear. So just fill a quarter page with caresses & expressions of endearment. Your silly Angelina." Jeannie ended one letter: "Goodbye dearest, dearest lover—ever your own Angelina." And another, "I will go to bed . . . [though] I could write all night—A thousand kisses—I love you with my whole soul—your Angelina."

When Jeannie finally married in 1870 at the age of thirty-seven, Sarah underwent a period of extreme anxiety. Two days before Jeannie's marriage, Sarah, then in London, wrote desperately: "Dearest darling—How incessantly have I thought of you these eight days—all today—the entire uncertainty, the distance, the long silence—are all new features in my separation from you, grevious to be borne. . . . Oh Jeannie. I have thought & thought & yearned over you these two days. Are you married I wonder? My dearest love to you wherever and *who*ever you are." Like many other women in this collection of thirty-five families, marriage brought Sarah and Jeannie physical separation; it did not cause emotional distance. Although at first they may have wondered how marriage would affect their relationship, their affection remained unabated throughout their lives, underscored by their loneliness and their desire to be together.

During the same years that Jeannie and Sarah wrote of their love and need for each other, two slightly younger women began a similar odyssey of love, dependence and—ultimately—physical, though not emotional, separation. Molly and Helena met in 1868 while both attended the Cooper Institute School of Design for Women in New York City. For several years these young women studied and explored the city together, visited each other's families, and formed part of a social network of other artistic young women. Gradually, over the years, their initial friendship deepened into a close intimate bond which continued throughout their lives. The tone in the letters which Molly wrote to Helena changed over these years from "My dear Helena," and signed "your attached friend," to "My dearest Helena," "My Dearest," "My Beloved," and signed "Thine always" or "thine Molly."

The letters they wrote to each other during these first five years permit us to reconstruct something of their relationship together. As Molly wrote in one early letter:

> I have not said to you in so many or so few words that I was happy with you during those few so incredibly short weeks but surely you do not need words to tell you what you must know. Those two or three days so dark without, so bright with firelight and contentment within I shall always remember as proof that, for a time, at least—I fancy for quite a long time—we might be sufficient for each other. We know that we can amuse each other for many idle hours together and now we know that we can also work together. And that means much, don't you think so?

She ended: "I shall return in a few days. Imagine yourself kissed many times by one who loved you so dearly."

The intensity and even physical nature of Molly's love was echoed in many of the letters she wrote during the next few years, as, for instance in this short thank-you note for a small present: "Imagine yourself kissed a dozen times my darling. Perhaps it is well for you that we are far apart. You might find my thanks so expressed rather overpowering. I have that delightful feeling that it doesn't matter much what I say or how I say it, since we shall meet so soon and forget in that moment that we were ever separated. . . . I shall see you soon and be content."

At the end of the fifth year, however, several crises occurred. The relationship, at least in its intense form, ended, though Molly and Helena continued an intimate and complex relationship for the next half-century. The exact nature of these crises is not completely clear, but it seems to have involved Molly's decision not to live with Helena, as they had originally planned, but to remain at home because of parental insistence. Molly was now in her late twenties. Helena responded with anger and Molly became frantic at the thought that Helena would break off their relationship. Though she wrote distraught letters and made despairing attempts to see Helena, the relationship never regained its former ardor—possibly because Molly had a male suitor. Within six months Helena had decided to marry a man who was, coincidentally, Molly's friend and publisher. Two years later Molly herself finally married. The letters toward the end of this period discuss the transition both women made to having male lovers—Molly spending much time reassuring Helena, who seemed depressed about the end of their relationship and with her forthcoming marriage.

It is clearly difficult from a distance of 100 years and from a post-Freudian cultural perspective to decipher the complexities of Molly and Helena's relationship. Certainly Molly and Helena were lovers—emotionally if not physically. The emotional intensity and pathos of their love becomes apparent in several letters Molly wrote Helena during their crisis: "I wanted so to put my arms round my girl of all the girls in the world and tell her. . . . I love her as wives do love their husbands, as *friends* who have taken each other for life—and believe in her as I believe in my God. . . . If I didn't love you do you suppose I'd care about anything or have ridiculous notions and panics and behave like an old fool who ought to know better. I'm going to hang on to your skirts. . . . You can't get away from [my] love." Or as she wrote after Helena's decision to marry: "You know dear Helena, I really was in love with you. It was a passion such as I had never known until I saw you. I don't think it was the noblest way to love you." The theme of intense female love was one Molly again expressed in a letter she wrote to the man Helena was to marry: "Do you know sir, that until you came along I believe that she loved me almost as girls love their lovers. *I know I loved her so*. Don't you wonder that I can stand the sight of you." This was in a letter congratulating them on their forthcoming marriage.

The essential question is not whether these women had genital contact and can therefore be defined as heterosexual or homosexual. The twentieth-century tendency to view human love and sexuality within a dichotomized universe of deviance and normality, genitality and platonic love, is alien to the emotions and attitudes of the nineteenth century and fundamentally distorts the nature of these women's emotional interaction. These letters are significant because they force us to place such female love in a particular historical context. There is every indication that these four women, their husbands and families—all eminently respectable and socially conservative— considered such love both socially acceptable and fully compatible with heterosexual marriage. Emotionally and cognitively, their heterosocial and their homosocial worlds were complementary.

One could argue, on the other hand, that these letters were but an example of the romantic rhetoric with which the nineteenth century surrounded the concept of friendship. Yet they possess an emotional intensity and a sensual and physical explicitness that is difficult to dismiss. Jeannie longed to hold Sarah in her arms; Molly mourned her physical isolation from Helena. Molly's love and devotion to Helena, the emotions that bound Jeannie and Sarah together, while perhaps a phenomenon of nineteenth-century society were not the less real for their Victorian origins. A survey of the correspondence and diaries of eighteenth- and nineteenth-century women indicates that Molly, Jeannie, and Sarah represented one very real behavioral and emotional option socially available to nineteenth-century women.

This is not to argue that individual needs, personalities, and family dynamics did not have a significant role in determining the nature of particular relationships. But the scholar must ask if it is historically possible and, if possible, important, to study the intensely individual aspects of psychosexual dynamics. Is it not the historian's first task to explore the social structure and the world view which made intense and sometimes sensual female love both a possible and an acceptable emotional option? From such a social perspective a new and quite different series of questions suggests itself. What emotional function did such female love serve? What was its place within the hetero- and homosocial worlds which women jointly inhabited? Did a spectrum of love-object choices exist in the nineteenth century across which some individuals, at least, were capable of moving? Without attempting to answer these questions it will be difficult to understand either nineteenth-century sexuality or the nineteenth-century family.

Several factors in American society between the mid-eighteenth and the mid-nineteenth centuries may well have permitted women to form a variety of close emotional relationships with other women. American society was characterized in large part by rigid genderrole differentiation within the family and within society as a whole, leading to the emotional segregation of women and men. The roles of daughter and mother shaded imperceptibly and ineluctably into each other, while the biological realities of frequent pregnancies, childbirth, nursing, and menopause bound women together in physical and emotional intimacy. It was within just such a social framework, I would argue, that a specifically female world did indeed develop, a world built around a generic and unself-conscious pattern of single-sex or homosocial networks. These supportive networks were institutionalized in social conventions or rituals which accompanied virtually every important event in a woman's life, from birth to death. Such female relationships were frequently supported and paralleled by severe social restrictions on intimacy between young men and women. Within such a world of emotional richness and complexity devotion to and love of other women became a plausible and socially accepted form of human interaction.

An abundance of printed and manuscript sources exists to support such a hypothesis. Etiquette books, advice books on child rearing, religious sermons, guides to young men and young women, medical texts, and school curricula all suggest that late eighteenth-and most nineteenth-century Americans assumed the existence of a world composed of distinctly male and female spheres, spheres determined by the immutable laws of God and nature. The unpublished letters and diaries of Americans during this same period concur, detailing the existence of sexually segregated worlds inhabited by human beings with different values, expectations, and personalities. Contacts between men and women frequently partook of a formality and stiffness quite alien to twentieth-century America and which today we tend to define as "Victorian." Women, however, did not form an isolated and oppressed subcategory in male society. Their letters and diaries indicate that women's sphere had an essential integrity and dignity that grew out of women's shared experiences and mutual affection and that, despite the profound changes which affected American social structure and institutions between the 1760s and the 1870s, retained a constancy and predictability. The ways in which women thought of and interacted with each other remained unchanged. Continuity, not discontinuity, characterized this female world. Molly Hallock's and Jeannie Fields's words, emotions, and experiences have direct parallels in the 1760s and the 1790s. There are indications in contemporary sociological and psychological literature that female closeness and support networks have continued into the twentieth century—not only among ethnic and working-class groups but even among the middle class.

Most eighteenth- and nineteenth-century women lived within a world bounded by home, church, and the institution of visiting—that endless trooping of women to each others' homes for social purposes. It was a world inhabited by children and by other women. Women helped each other with domestic chores and in times of sickness, sorrow, or trouble. Entire days, even weeks, might be spent almost exclusively with other women. Urban and town women could devote virtually every day to visits, teas, or shopping trips with other women. Rural women developed a pattern of more extended visits that lasted weeks and sometimes months, at times even dislodging husbands from their beds and bedrooms so that dear friends might spend every hour of every day together. When husbands traveled, wives routinely moved in with other women, invited women friends to teas and suppers, sat together sharing and comparing the letters they had received from other close women friends. Secrets were exchanged and cherished, and the husband's return at times viewed with some ambivalence.

Summer vacations were frequently organized to permit old friends to meet at water spas or share a country home. In 1848, for example, a young matron wrote cheerfully to her husband about the delightful time she was having with five close women friends whom she had invited to spend the summer with her; he remained at home alone to face the heat of Philadelphia and a cholera epidemic. Some ninety years earlier, two young Quaker girls commented upon the vacation their aunt had taken alone with another woman; their remarks were openly envious and tell us something of the emotional quality of these friendships: "I hear Aunt is gone with the Friend and wont be back for two weeks, fine times indeed I think the old friends had, taking their pleasure about the country . . . and have the advantage of that fine woman's conversation and instruction, while we poor young girls must spend all spring at home. . . . What a disappointment that we are not together. . . . "

Friends did not form isolated dyads but were normally part of highly integrated networks. Knowing each other, perhaps related to each other, they played a central role in holding communities and kin systems together. Especially when families became geographically mobile women's long visits to each other and their frequent letters filled with discussions of marriages and births, illness and deaths, descriptions of growing children, and reminiscences of times and people past provided an important sense of continuity in a rapidly changing society. Central to this female world was an inner core of kin. The ties between sisters, first cousins, aunts, and nieces provided the underlying structure upon which groups of friends and their network of female relatives clustered. Although most of the women within this sample would appear to be living within isolated nuclear families, the emotional ties between nonresidential kin were deep and binding and provided one of the fundamental existential realities of women's lives. Twenty years after Parke Lewis Butler moved with her husband to Louisiana, she sent her two daughters back to Virginia to attend school, live with their grandmother and aunt, and be integrated back into Vir-

ginia society. The constant letters between Maria Inskeep and Fanny Hampton, sisters separated in their early twenties when Maria moved with her husband from New Jersey to Louisiana, held their families together, making it possible for their daughters to feel a part of their cousins' network of friends and interests. The Ripley daughters, growing up in western Massachusetts in the early 1800s, spent months each year with their mother's sister and her family in distant Boston; these female cousins and their network of friends exchanged gossip-filled letters and gradually formed deeply loving and dependent ties.

Women frequently spent their days within the social confines of such extended families. Sisters-in-law visited each other and, in some families, seemed to spend more time with each other than with their husbands. First cousins cared for each others' babies—for weeks or even months in times of sickness or childbirth. Sisters helped each other with housework, shopped and sewed for each other. Geographic separation was borne with difficulty. A sister's absence for even a week or two could cause loneliness and depression and would be bridged by frequent letters. Sibling rivalry was hardly unknown, but with separation or illness the theme of deep affection and dependency reemerged.

Sisterly bonds continued across a lifetime. In her old age a rural Quaker matron, Martha Jefferis, wrote to her daughter Anne concerning her own half-sister, Phoebe: "In sister Phoebe I have a real friend—she studies my comfort and waits on me like a child. . . . She is exceedingly kind and this to all other homes (set aside yours) I would prefer—it is next to being with a daughter." Phoebe's own letters confirmed Martha's evaluation of her feelings. "Thou knowest my dear sister," Phoebe wrote, "there is no one . . . that exactly feels [for] thee as I do, for I think without boasting I can truly say that my desire is for thee."

Such women, whether friends or relatives, assumed an emotional centrality in each others' lives. In their diaries and letters they wrote of the joy and contentment they felt in each others' company, their sense of isolation and despair when apart. The regularity of their correspondence underlines the sincerity of their words. Women named their daughters after one another and sought to integrate dear friends into their lives after marriage. As one young bride wrote to an old friend shortly after her marriage: "I want to see you and talk with you and feel that we are united by the same bonds of sympathy and congeniality as ever." After years of friendship one aging woman wrote of another: "Time cannot destroy the fascination of her manner . . . her voice is music to the ear. . . ." Women made elaborate presents for each other, ranging from the Quakers' frugal pies and breads to painted velvet bags and phantom bouquets. When a friend died, their grief was deeply felt. Martha Jefferis was unable to write to her daughter for three weeks because of the sorrow she felt at the death of a dear friend. Such distress was not unusual. A generation earlier a young Massachusetts farm woman filled pages of her diary with her grief at the death of her "dearest friend" and transcribed the letters of condolence other women sent her. She marked the anniversary of Rachel's death each year in her diary, contrasting her faithfulness with that of Rachel's husband who had soon remarried.

These female friendships served a number of emotional functions. Within this secure and empathetic world women could share sorrows, anxieties, and joys, confident that other women had experienced similar emotions. One mid-nineteenth-century rural matron in a letter to her daughter discussed this particular aspect of women's friendships: "To have such a friend as thyself to look to and sympathize with her—and enter into all her little needs and in whose bosom she could with freedom pour forth her joys and sorrows—such a friend would very much relieve the tedium of many a wearisome hour. . . ." A generation later Molly more informally underscored the importance of this same function in a letter to Helena: "Suppose I come down . . . [and] spend Sunday with you quietly," she wrote Helena ". . . that means talking all the time until you are relieved of all your latest troubles, and I of mine. . . ." These were frequently troubles that apparently no man could understand. When Anne Jefferis Sheppard was first married, she and her older sister Edith (who then lived with Anne) wrote in detail to their mother of the severe depression and anxiety which they experienced. Moses Sheppard, Anne's husband, added cheerful postscripts to the sisters' letters—which he had clearly not read—remarking on Anne's and Edith's contentment. Theirs was an emotional world to which he had little access.

This was, as well, a female world in which hostility and criticism of other women were discouraged, and thus a milieu in which women could develop a sense of inner security and self-esteem. As one young woman wrote to her mother's longtime friend: "I cannot sufficiently thank you for the kind unvaried affection & indulgence you have ever shown and expressed both by words and actions for me. . . . Happy would it be did all the world view me as you do, through the medium of kindness and forbearance." They valued each other. Women, who had little status or power in the larger world of male concerns, possessed status and power in the lives and worlds of other women.

An intimate mother-daughter relationship lay at the heart of this female world. The diaries and letters of both mothers and daughters attest to their closeness and mutual emotional dependency. Daughters routinely discussed their mother's health and activities with their own friends, expressed anxiety in cases of their mother's ill health and concern for her cares. Expressions of hostility which we would today consider routine on the part of both mothers and daughters seem to have been uncommon indeed. On the contrary, this sample of families indicates that the normal relationship between mother and daughter was one of sympathy and understanding. Only sickness or great geographic distance was allowed to cause extended separation. When marriage did result in such separation, both viewed the distance between them with distress. Something of this sympathy and love between mothers and daughters is evident in a letter Sarah Alden Ripley, at age sixty-nine, wrote her youngest and recently married daughter: "You do not know how much I miss you, not only when I struggle in and out of my mortal envelop and pump

my nightly potation and no longer pour into your sympathizing ear my senile gossip, but all the day I muse away, since the sound of your voice no longer rouses me to sympathy with your joys or sorrows. . . . You cannot know how much I miss your affectionate demonstrations." A dozen aging mothers in this sample of over thirty families echoed her sentiments.

Central to these mother-daughter relations is what might be described as an apprenticeship system. In those families where the daughter followed the mother into a life of traditional domesticity, mothers and other older women carefully trained daughters in the arts of housewifery and motherhood. Such training undoubtedly occurred throughout a girl's childhood but became more systematized, almost ritualistic, in the years following the end of her formal education and before her marriage. At this time a girl either returned home from boarding school or no longer divided her time between home and school. Rather, she devoted her energies on two tasks: mastering new domestic skills and participating in the visiting and social activities necessary to finding a husband. Under the careful supervision of their mothers and of older female relatives, such late-adolescent girls temporarily took over the household management from their mothers, tended their young nieces and nephews, and helped in childbirth, nursing, and weaning. Such experiences tied the generations together in shared skills and emotional interaction.

Daughters were born into a female world. Their mother's life expectations and sympathetic network of friends and relations were among the first realities in the life of the developing child. As long as the mother's domestic role remained relatively stable and few viable alternatives competed with it, daughters tended to accept their mother's world and to turn automatically to other women for support and intimacy. It was within this closed and intimate female world that the young girl grew toward womanhood.

One could speculate at length concerning the absence of that mother-daughter hostility today considered almost inevitable to an adolescent's struggle for autonomy and self-identity. It is possible that taboos against female aggression and hostility were sufficiently strong to repress even that between mothers and their adolescent daughters. Yet these letters seem so alive and the interest of daughters in their mothers' affairs so vital and genuine that it is difficult to interpret their closeness exclusively in terms of repression and denial. The functional bonds that held mothers and daughters together in a world that permitted few alternatives to domesticity might well have created a source of mutuality and trust absent in societies where greater options were available for daughters than for mothers. Furthermore, the extended female network—a daughter's close ties with her own older sisters, cousins, and aunts—may well have permitted a diffusion and a relaxation of mother-daughter identification and so have aided a daughter in her struggle for identity and autonomy. None of these explanations are mutually exclusive; all may well have interacted to produce the degree of empathy evident in those letters and diaries.

At some point in adolescence, the young girl began to move outside the matrix of her mother's support group to develop a network of her own. Among the middle class, at least, this transition toward what was at the same time both a limited autonomy and a repetition of her mother's life seemed to have most frequently coincided with a girl's going to school. Indeed education appears to have played a crucial role in the lives of most of the families in this study. Attending school for a few months, for a year, or longer, was common even among daughters of relatively poor families, while middle-class girls routinely spent at least a year in boarding school. These school years ordinarily marked a girl's first separation from home. They served to wean the daughter from her home, to train her in the essential social graces, and, ultimately, to help introduce her into the marriage market. It was not infrequently a trying emotional experience for both mother and daughter.

In this process of leaving one home and adjusting to another, the mother's friends and relatives played a key transitional role. Such older women routinely accepted the role of foster mother; they supervised the young girl's deportment, monitored her health and introduced her to their own network of female friends and kin. Not infrequently women, friends from their own school years, arranged to send their daughters to the same school so that the girls might form bonds paralleling those their mothers had made. For years Molly and Helena wrote of their daughters' meeting and worried over each others' children. When Molly finally brought her daughter east to school, their first act on reaching New York was to meet Helena and her daughters. Elizabeth Bordley Gibson virtually adopted the daughters of her school chum, Eleanor Custis Lewis. The Lewis daughters soon began to write Elizabeth Gibson letters with the salutation "Dearest Mama." Eleuthera DuPont, attending boarding school in Philadelphia at roughly the same time as the Lewis girls, developed a parallel relationship with her mother's friend, Elizabeth McKie Smith. Eleuthera went to the same school and became a close friend of the Smith girls and eventually married their first cousin. During this period she routinely called Mrs. Smith "Mother." Indeed Eleuthera so internalized the sense of having two mothers that she casually wrote her sisters of her "Mamma's" visits at her "mother's" house—that is at Mrs. Smith's.

Even more important to this process of maturation than their mother's friends were the female friends young women made at school. Young girls helped each other overcome homesickness and endure the crises of adolescence. They gossiped about beaux, incorporated each other into their own kinship systems, and attended and gave teas and balls together. Older girls in boarding school "adopted" younger ones, who called them "Mother." Dear friends might indeed continue this pattern of adoption and mothering throughout their lives; one woman might routinely assume the nurturing role of pseudomother, the other the dependency role of daughter. The pseudomother performed for the other woman all the services which we normally associate with mothers; she went to absurd lengths to purchase items her "daughter" could have obtained from other sources, gave advice and func-

tioned as an idealized figure in her "daughter's" imagination. Helena played such a role for Molly, as did Sarah for Jeannie. Elizabeth Bordley Gibson bought almost all Eleanor Parke Custis Lewis's necessities—from shoes and corset covers to bedding and harp strings—and sent them from Philadelphia to Virginia, a procedure that sometimes took months. Eleanor frequently asked Elizabeth to take back her purchases, have them redone, and argue with shopkeepers about prices. These were favors automatically asked and complied with. Anne Jefferis Sheppard made the analogy very explicitly in a letter to her own mother written shortly after Anne's marriage, when she was feeling depressed about their separation: "Mary Paulen is truly kind, almost acts the part of a mother and trys to aid and *comfort me*, and also to *lighten my new cares.*"

A comparison of the references to men and women in these young women's letters is striking. Boys were obviously indispensable to the elaborate courtship ritual girls engaged in. In these teenage letters and diaries, however, boys appear distant and warded off—an effect produced both by the girls' sense of bonding and by a highly developed and deprecatory whimsy. Girls joked among themselves about the conceit, poor looks or affectations of suitors. Rarely, especially in the eighteenth and early nineteenth centuries, were favorable remarks exchanged. Indeed, while hostility and criticism of other women were so rare as to seem almost tabooed, young women permitted themselves to express a great deal of hostility toward peer-group men. When unacceptable suitors appeared, girls might even band together to harass them.

When one such unfortunate came to court Sophie DuPont she hid in her room, first sending her sister Eleuthera to entertain him and then dispatching a number of urgent notes to her neighboring sister-in-law, cousins, and a visiting friend who all came to Sophie's support. A wild female romp ensued, ending only when Sophie banged into a door, lacerated her nose, and retired, with her female cohorts, to bed. Her brother and the presumably disconcerted suitor were left alone. These were not the antics of teenagers but of women in their early and mid-twenties.

Even if young men were acceptable suitors, girls referred to them formally and obliquely: "The last week I received the unexpected intelligence of the arrival of a friend in Boston," Sarah Ripley wrote in her diary of the young man to whom she had been engaged for years and whom she would shortly marry. Harriet Manigault assiduously kept a lively and gossipy diary during the three years preceding her marriage, yet did not once comment upon her own engagement nor indeed make any personal references to her fiancé—who was never identified as such but always referred to as Mr. Wilcox. The point is not that these young women were hostile to young men. Far from it; they sought marriage and domesticity. Yet in these letters and diaries men appear as an other or out group, segregated into different schools, supported by their own male network of friends and kin, socialized to different behavior, and coached to a proper formality in courtship behavior. As a consequence, relations between young women and men frequently lacked the spontaneity and emotional intimacy that char-

acterized the young girls' ties to each other.

Indeed, in sharp contrast to their distant relations with boys, young women's relations with each other were close, often frolicsome, and surprisingly long lasting and devoted. They wrote secret missives to each other, spent long solitary days with each other, curled up together in bed at night to whisper fantasies and secrets. In 1862 one young woman in her early twenties described one such scene to an absent friend: "I have sat up to midnight listening to the confidences of Constance Kinney, whose heart was opened by that most charming of all situations, a seat on a bedside late at night, when all the household are asleep & only oneself & one's confidante survive in wakefulness. So she has told me all her loves and tried to get some confidences in return but being five or six years older than she, I know better. . . ." Elizabeth Bordley and Nelly Parke Custis, teenagers in Philadelphia in the 1790s, routinely secreted themselves until late each night in Nelly's attic, where they each wrote a novel about the other. Quite a few young women kept diaries, and it was a sign of special friendship to show their diaries to each other. The emotional quality of such exchanges emerges from the comments of one young girl who grew up along the Ohio frontier:

Sisters CW and RT keep diaries & allow me the inestimable pleasure of reading them and in turn they see mine—but O shame covers my face when I think of it; theirs is so much better than mine, that every time. Then I think well now I *will* burn mine but upon second thought it would deprive me the pleasure of reading theirs, for I esteem it a very great privilege indeed, as well as very improving, as we lay our hearts open to each other, it heightens our love & helps to cherish & keep alive that sweet soothing friendship and endears us to each other by that soft attraction.

Girls routinely slept together, kissed and hugged each other. Indeed, while waltzing with young men scandalized the otherwise flighty and highly fashionable Harriet Manigault, she considered waltzing with other young women not only acceptable but pleasant.

Marriage followed adolescence. With increasing frequency in the nineteenth century, marriage involved a girl's traumatic removal from her mother and her mother's network. It involved, as well, adjustment to a husband, who, because he was male came to marriage with both a different world view and vastly different experiences. Not surprisingly, marriage was an event surrounded with supportive, almost ritualistic, practices. (Weddings are one of the last female rituals remaining in twentieth-century America.) Young women routinely spent the months preceding their marriage almost exclusively with other women—at neighborhood sewing bees and quilting parties or in a round of visits to geographically distant friends and relatives. Ostensibly they went to receive assistance in the practical preparations for their new home—sewing and quilting a trousseau and linen—but of equal importance, they appear to have gained emotional support and reassurance. Sarah Ripley spent over a month with friends and relatives in Boston and Hingham before her wedding; Nelly Custis Lewis exchanged visits with her aunts and first cousins throughout Virginia.

Anne Jefferis, who married with some hesitation, spent virtually half a year in endless visiting with cousins, aunts, and friends. Despite their reassurance and support, however, she would not marry Moses Sheppard until her sister Edith and her cousin Rebecca moved into the groom's home, met his friends, and explored his personality. The wedding did not take place until Edith wrote to Anne: "I can say in truth I am entirely willing thou shouldst follow him even away in the Jersey sands believing if thou are not happy in thy future home it will not be any fault on his part. . . ."

Sisters, cousins, and friends frequently accompanied newlyweds on their wedding night and wedding trip, which often involved additional family visiting. Such extensive visits presumably served to wean the daughter from her family of origin. As such they often contained a note of ambivalence. Nelly Custis, for example, reported homesickness and loneliness on her wedding trip. "I left my Beloved and revered Grandmamma with sincere regret," she wrote Elizabeth Bordley. "It was sometime before I could feel reconciled to traveling without her." Perhaps they also functioned to reassure the young woman herself, and her friends and kin, that though marriage might alter it would not destroy old bonds of intimacy and familiarity.

Married life, too, was structured about a host of female rituals. Childbirth, especially the birth of the first child, became virtually a *rite de passage*, with a lengthy seclusion of the woman before and after delivery, severe restrictions on her activities, and finally a dramatic reemergence. This seclusion was supervised by mothers, sisters, and loving friends. Nursing and weaning involved the advice and assistance of female friends and relatives. So did miscarriage. Death, like birth, was structured around elaborate unisexed rituals. When Nelly Parke Custis Lewis rushed to nurse her daughter who was critically ill while away at school, Nelly received support, not from her husband, who remained on their plantation, but from her old school friend, Elizabeth Bordley. Elizabeth aided Nelly in caring for her dying daughter, cared for Nelly's other children, played a major role in the elaborate funeral arrangements (which the father did not attend), and frequently visited the girl's grave at the mother's request. For years Elizabeth continued to be the confidante of Nelly's anguished recollections of her lost daughter. These memories, Nelly's letters make clear, were for Elizabeth alone, "Mr. L knows nothing of this," was a frequent comment. Virtually every collection of letters and diaries in my sample contained evidence of women turning to each other for comfort when facing the frequent and unavoidable deaths of the eighteenth and nineteenth centuries. While mourning for her father's death, Sophie DuPont received elaborate letters and visits of condolence—all from women. No man wrote or visited Sophie to offer sympathy at her father's death. Among rural Pennsylvania Quakers, death and mourning rituals assumed an even more extreme same-sex form, with men or women largely barred from the deathbeds of the other sex. Women relatives and friends slept with the dying woman, nursed her, and prepared her body for burial.

Eighteenth- and nineteenth-century women thus lived in emotional proximity to each other. Friendships and intimacies followed the biological ebb and flow of women's lives. Marriage and pregnancy, childbirth and weaning, sickness and death involved physical and psychic trauma which comfort and sympathy made easier to bear. Intense bonds of love and intimacy bound together those women who, offering each other aid and sympathy, shared such stressful moments.

These bonds were often physical as well as emotional. An undeniably romantic and even sensual note frequently marked female relationships. This theme, significant throughout the stages of a woman's life, surfaced first during adolescence. As one teenager from a struggling pioneer family in the Ohio Valley wrote in her diary in 1808: "I laid with my dear R[ebecca] and a glorious good talk we had until about 4 [A.M.]—O how hard I do *love* her. . . ." Only a few years later Bostonian Eunice Callender carved her initials and Sarah Ripley's into a favorite tree, along with a pledge of eternal love, and then waited breathlessly for Sarah to discover and respond to her declaration of affection. The response appears to have been affirmative. A half-century later urbane and sophisticated Katherine Wharton commented upon meeting an old school chum: "She was a great pet of mine at school & I thought as I watched her light figure how often I had held her in my arms—how dear she had once been to me." Katie maintained a long intimate friendship with another girl. When a young man began to court this friend seriously, Katie commented in her diary that she had never realized "how deeply I loved Eng and how fully." She wrote over and over again in that entry: "Indeed I love her!" and only with great reluctance left the city that summer since it meant also leaving Eng with Eng's new suitor.

Peggy Emlen, a Quaker adolescent in Philadelphia in the 1760s, expressed similar feelings about her first cousin, Sally Logan. The girls sent love poems to each other (not unlike the ones Elizabeth Bordley wrote to Nellie Custis a generation later), took long solitary walks together, and even haunted the empty house of the other when one was out of town. Indeed Sally's absences from Philadelphia caused Peggy acute unhappiness. So strong were Peggy's feelings that her brothers began to tease her about her affection for Sally and threatened to steal Sally's letters, much to both girls' alarm. In one letter that Peggy wrote the absent Sally she elaborately described the depth and nature of her feelings: "I have not words to express my impatience to see My Dear Cousin, what would I not give just now for an hours sweet conversation with her, it seems as if I had a thousand things to say to thee, yet when I see thee, everything will be forgot thro' joy.... I have a very great friendship for several Girls yet it dont give me so much uneasiness at being absent from them as from thee.... [Let us] go and spend a day down at our place together and there unmolested enjoy each others company."

Sarah Alden Ripley, a young, highly educated woman, formed a similar intense relationship, in this instance with a woman somewhat older than herself. The immediate bond of friendship rested on their atypically intense scholarly interests, but it soon involved strong emotions, at least on Sarah's part. "Friendship," she wrote Mary Emerson, "is fast twining about her willing captive the silken hands of dependence, a dependence so sweet who would renounce it for the apathy of self-sufficiency?" Subsequent letters became far more emotional, almost conspiratorial. Mary visited Sarah secretly in her room, or the two women crept away from family and friends to meet in a nearby woods. Sarah became jealous of Mary's other young woman friends. Mary's trips away from Boston also thrust Sarah into periods of anguished depression. Interestingly, the letters detailing their love were not destroyed but were preserved and even reprinted in a eulogistic biography of Sarah Alden Ripley.

Tender letters between adolescent women, confessions of loneliness and emotional dependency, were not peculiar to Sarah Alden, Peggy Emlen, or Katie Wharton. They are found throughout the letters of the thirty-five families studied. They have, of course, their parallel today in the musings of many female adolescents. Yet these eighteenth- and nineteenth-century friendships lasted with undiminished, indeed often increased, intensity throughout the women's lives. Sarah Alden Ripley's first child was named after Mary Emerson. Nelly Custis Lewis's love for and dependence on Elizabeth Bordley Gibson only increased after her marriage. Eunice Callender remained enamored of her cousin Sarah Ripley for years and rejected as impossible the suggestion by another woman that their love might some day fade away. Sophie DuPont and her childhood friend, Clementina Smith, exchanged letters filled with love and dependency for forty years while another dear friend, Mary Black Couper, wrote of dreaming that she, Sophie, and her husband were all united in one marriage. Mary's letters to Sophie are filled with avowals of love and indications of ambivalence toward her own husband. Eliza Schlatter, another of Sophie's intimate friends, wrote to her at a time of crisis: "I wish I could be with you present in the body as well as the mind & heart—I would turn your *good husband out of bed*—and snuggle into you and we would have a long talk like old times in Pine St.— I want to tell you so many things that are not *writable*. . . . "

Such mutual dependency and deep affection is a central existential reality coloring the world of supportive networks and rituals. In the case of Katie, Sophie, or Eunice—as with Molly, Jeannie, and Sarah—their need for closeness and support merged with more intense demands for a love which was at the same time both emotional and sensual. Perhaps the most explicit statement concerning women's lifelong friendships appeared in the letter abolitionist and reformer Mary Grew wrote about the same time, referring to her own love for her dear friend and lifelong companion, Margaret Burleigh. Grew wrote, in response to a letter of condolence from another woman on Burleigh's death: "Your words respecting my beloved friend touch me deeply. Evidently . . . you comprehend and appreciate, as few persons do . . . the nature of the relation which existed, which exists, between her and myself. Her only surviving niece . . . also does. To me it seems to have been a closer union than that of most marriages. We know there have

been other such between two men and also between two women. And why should there not be. Love is spiritual, only passion is sexual."

How then can we ultimately interpret these long-lived intimate female relationships and integrate them into our understanding of Victorian sexuality? Their ambivalent and romantic rhetoric presents us with an ultimate puzzle: the relationship along the spectrum of human emotions between love, sensuality, and sexuality.

One is tempted, as I have remarked, to compare Molly, Peggy, or Sophie's relationships with the friendships adolescent girls in the twentieth century routinely form—close friendships of great emotional intensity. Helene Deutsch and Clara Thompson have both described these friendships as emotionally necessary to a girl's psychosexual development. But, they warn, such friendships might shade into adolescent and postadolescent homosexuality.

It is possible to speculate that in the twentieth century a number of cultural taboos evolved to cut short the homosocial ties of girlhood and to impel the emerging women of thirteen or fourteen toward heterosexual relationships. In contrast, nineteenth-century American society did not taboo close female relationships but rather recognized them as a socially viable form of human contact—and, as such, acceptable throughout a woman's life. Indeed it was not these homosocial ties that were inhibited but rather heterosexual learnings. While closeness, freedom of emotional expression, and uninhibited physical contact characterized women's relationships with each other, the opposite was frequently true of male-female relationships. One could thus argue that within such a world of female support, intimacy, and ritual it was only to be expected that adult women would turn trustingly and lovingly to each other. It was a behavior they had observed and learned since childhood. A different type of emotional landscape existed in the nineteenth century, one in which Molly and Helena's love became a natural development.

Of perhaps equal significance are the implications we can garner from this framework for the understanding of heterosexual marriages in the nineteenth century. If men and women grew up as they did in relatively homogeneous and segregated sexual groups, then marriage represented a major problem in adjustment. From this perspective we could interpret much of the emotional stiffness and distance that we associate with Victorian marriage as a structural consequence of contemporary sex-role differentiation and gender-role socialization. With marriage, both women and men had to adjust to life with a person who was, in essence, a member of an alien group.

I have thus far substituted a cultural or psychosocial for a psychosexual interpretation of women's emotional bonding. But there are psychosexual implications in this model which I think it only fair to make more explicit. Despite Sigmund Freud's insistence on the bisexuality of us all or the recent American Psychiatric Association decision on homosexuality, many psychiatrists today tend explicitly or implicitly to view homosexuality as a totally alien or pathological behavior—as totally unlike heterosexuality. I suspect that in essence they may have adopted an explanatory model similar to the one used in discussing schizophrenia. As a psychiatrist can speak of schizophrenia and of a borderline schizophrenic personality as both ultimately and fundamentally different from a normal or neurotic personality, so they also think of both homosexuality and latent homosexuality as states totally different from heterosexuality. With this rapidly dichotomous model of assumption, "latent homosexuality" becomes the indication of a disease in progress—seeds of a pathology which belie the reality of an individual's heterosexuality.

Yet at the same time we are well aware that cultural values can effect choices in the gender of a person's sexual partner. We, for instance, do not necessarily consider homosexual-object choice among men in prison, on shipboard or in boarding schools a necessary indication of pathology. I would urge that we expand this relativistic model and hypothesize that a number of cultures might well tolerate or even encourage diversity in sexual and nonsexual relations. Based on my research into this nineteenth-century world of female intimacy, I would further suggest that rather than seeing a gulf between the normal and the abnormal we view sexual and emotional impulses as part of a continuum or spectrum of affect gradations strongly effected by cultural norms and arrangements, a continuum influenced in part by observed and thus learned behavior. At one end of the continuum lies committed heterosexuality, at the other uncompromising homosexuality; between, a wide latitude of emotions and sexual feelings. Certain cultures and environments permit individuals a great deal of freedom in moving across this spectrum. I would like to suggest that the nineteenth century was such a cultural environment. That is, the supposedly repressive and destructive Victorian sexual ethos, may have been more flexible and responsive to the needs of particular individuals than those of midtwentieth century.

Science

Scientists employ a careful methodology to ensure objectivity and replication of results. Therefore, feminist criticism has often been dismissed as "unscientific" or seen as merely inapplicable. How can a perspective that sees power relations, exclusions, and distortions at work in intellectual endeavors have something relevant to say about the supposedly objective "hard sciences"? These three pieces show a range of feminist criticisms of the field, which together alter perceptions of neutral scientists working in laboratories to seek objective truths about how the world works. Natalie Angier is a feminist journalist whose book on women's bodies posed a serious challenge to accepted theories in many scientific fields. Marilyn Milloy's article on her book, its message, and its reception by the scientific community offers insights into the perceived opposition between feminism and science. Evelyn Fox Keller's article provides an overview of feminist critiques of science, from liberal to radical. She offers some compelling ideas about the association of masculinity with objectivity and how feminists might transform science without destroying its mission. In the final piece of this section, Phillida Bunkle asserts that medical knowledge is highly subjective and potentially dangerous, especially for women marginalized by poverty and race. Her piece uncovers unsettling connections between scientific research and multinational corporations, providing an alternative way to view the dissemination of knowledge about and for women.

Critical Thinking Questions

1. Why did Angier's book attract such scathing critiques from the scientific community? Does that mean her work is unscientific or too political?
2. What have you learned about your body and how it works from the field of science? How could science play a role in how individuals feel about themselves?
3. Compare the liberal and radical feminist critiques of science and fit yourself along the spectrum. Where would you place Angier and Bunkle on this spectrum?
4. Why does Keller reject the radical position of seeing science as "pure social product"? Do you agree with her?

5. How do insights from the field of psychology help Keller understand and explain the association of masculinity with objectivity?

6. Compare the results of the "scientific" studies of Depo-Provera with the feminist research done by Bunkle's group in New Zealand. Why and how are they different? Which research do you trust, if either?

7. Bunkle asserts that "contraception is an example of the technology created by the structures of capitalist patriarchy." Explain and assess this argument. If contraception is one example, can you think of others?

16

Turning the Tables on Science

(2000)

Marilyn Milloy

Okay, so it wasn't exactly what Natalie Angier would call the most affirming moment in her career.

There she was on a lovely spring day, quietly attending affairs of the home, when a letter arrived. It was from a biologist. An angry man in a huff not just over Angier's widely celebrated tome, *Woman: An Intimate Geography* (Houghton Mifflin, 1999) but over Angier, herself.

It was bad enough that she'd used her book to rally the "man-haters" of the world, the writer was saying, his furor stirring up a mighty dust. But Angier had had the audacity to turn for the facts to women scientists who were second-rate academics and suck-ups and, yes God, sexual predators, too.

"Whatever credibility you had, in my book, is now in the toilet," the man spewed. She'd had a chance to serve up a nuanced discussion, but, he wrote, "you've done little more than convince me that you're an embittered middle-aged fem crank with an attitude," unwilling to accept "that you're just not a player anymore."

Angier's jaw dropped. She certainly had expected criticism of this work of hers. It was, after all, a novel effort: science and medicine, psychology and culture, anatomy and history,

evolutionary theory and literature all woven into a provocative, rapturous—and brazenly feminist—ode to women. Angier had not only celebrated the female body and its parts with painstaking and lavish detail, pondered beauty, aggression, marriage, and strength with debunking zeal. She'd also eviscerated the notion of woman as "the second sex" and tossed mainstream wisdom about "the female nature" to the wind.

And so, yes, Angier knew some folks would accuse her of delivering a feminist manifesto and not a work grounded in science. She knew some would chastise her for letting her beliefs get in the way of "the facts." But she was totally unprepared for the magnificently personal floggings that came in the likes of the letter she got that spring day not long after *Woman* was published.

"At first I was getting very freaked out and depressed," she is confessing now in the living room of her Takoma Park, Maryland, home, plainly aware of how this must sound coming from a woman who calls herself a "female chauvinist sow."

Then *Woman* showed up on bestseller lists and best-books-of-the-year lists, wracked up a nomination for the National Book Award, garnered all manner of tributes declaring it a tour de force. And Angier, a Pulitzer Prize-winning science writer for the *New York Times*, knew for sure that hers were not the sensibilities of a lone failing fool.

Indeed, she came to see the skewering she got as the likely fate of anybody who would ask, "What makes a woman?" and answer not by simply waxing elegant about the breasts and the egg and the "almighty clitoris," but by flipping centuries-old thinking about the female body on its head. As Angier put it, woman's body "has been conceived of as the second sex, the first draft, the faulty sex, the default sex, the consolation prize, the succubus, the male interruptus. We are lewd, prim, bestial, ethereal. We have borne more illegitimate metaphors than we have unwanted embryos."

That Angier, a quietly incorrigible woman, would rake through the muck in an attempt to find Truth was ambitious enough. That she'd launch a scathing attack against an entire school of evolutionary science that says women are by nature a certain way—essentially monogamous and home-loving with a preference for "being" rather than "doing"—was asking for it.

So raw was the nerve she hit that, months after making its debut, *Woman* is still sending rumbles through the science community and beyond. Now, to Angier's delight, there is a public discourse about the misogynist thinking on evolution that's long permeated intellectual debate, and about the benign acceptance of it all by the culture at large.

What she put on the table was just a piece of that thinking, the part about how we mate and why. In a nutshell, this "wisdom" says that women are innately attracted to powerful, high-status men. That they're more interested in stable relationships and are less promiscuous than men. That they are more ho-hum about sex. That they can't help this any more than men can help that they are sex-huntin' rovers on a mission to deposit sperm throughout the land—preferably into cute young things, not middle-age fems or cranks or anybody not happily poised to make babies on their behalf.

Angier proposed, simply, that it couldn't be as black and white as all that and posited a host of "what ifs." What if it isn't biology that draws women to older men, but the fact that those men are actually less marketable and thus apt to treat women with more gratitude and respect? What if women want men who earn healthy wages because they know the income chasm between women and men leaves women wanting?

"I was so tired of women being told they are like 'this,' " Angier explains, the rarified tone of her voice more befitting the scholarly professor than an indignant rabble-rouser. "If you don't feel you fit the things they say about you, you're probably right. Unfortunately, if you have an alternative script. . . ." She pauses as if to ponder the insanity of it all. "Either you're made to feel weird, or you feel trapped."

The support for the accepted theories is so "anemic," Angier says, the methodology so riddled with holes, that the conclusions themselves are suspect. Why, for example, do the theorists point to differences in homosexual mating habits to buttress their claims, yet use homosexuals so unevenly, so whimsically: sometimes gay men are trotted out as supermasculine he-men and sometimes they're virtually women. And why, in one noted survey, did scientists distribute questionnaires to college students about the qualities they find attractive in the opposite sex, then seize on differences that scored low—she likes ambition, he likes beauty—even though both women and men said they prefer kind, funny, intelligent, considerate mates?

Suffice it to say that few of Angier's musings have sat well with her critics. It was heretic enough, some said, that she unabashedly set out to celebrate women, and that she did it using language that was at turns exuberant, hilarious, even poetic. On top of all that, they insisted, she ended up formulating gender stereotypes of her own.

"Over the years when she's written about animals and biology, it's been great," says Lionel Tiger, the preeminent Rutgers University anthropologist who added the phrase "male bonding" to the American lexicon. "But when she gets to humans, she goes Berkeley–Ms. magazine-feminism. I mean, it just doesn't make sense. It's sentimental Oprah stuff."

Now, Tiger ventures, "a whole generation of women are coming away thinking, 'Isn't it wonderful to be a woman, and aren't we so much better?' But that's not how it works. Males have to have a role—they can't go into relationships thinking they are defective from the outset."

Steven Pinker, the director of the McDonnell-Pew Center for Cognitive Neuroscience at the Massachusetts Institute of Technology, ratchets up the attack by claiming Angier is so "desperate" for science to fit her political agenda that it clouds her entire view of the field and ultimately undermines the cause of feminism. "She seems to think it would be more congenial to feminism if men's and women's minds were equal, but it's a terrible idea.

"Suppose there are biological differences. The idea that women should not be discriminated against, beaten up, and raped should be true regardless of why men do it." But the fact of the matter, he insists, is that there are differences. "It's not that men are highly sexed and women are sexless," he says. It's that their emotions and motivations around sex are different, and the amount of evidence that says so is "huge."

To all this, Angier expresses exasperation. No, she's not suggesting women and men are the same, or should be, or that women are superior to men. "If somebody says, 'You're this way,' and I say, 'No, I'm not,' I'm not in denial. I'm just saying you haven't explained it well enough. There are problems with the data."

Now, others are saying the same. Just in the last few months several significant works have surfaced that take a machete to the jungle of theories espoused by evolutionary psychologists. One paper, by researchers Wendy Wood and Alice Eagley, reanalyzes the data compiled by one of the leading scientists in the field, David Buss. It concludes that the gender differences that Buss identified are as easily attributable to social roles as to evolution. Another new work, by Jeffry Simpson and Steven Gangastead, contests the notion that all men have an impulse to be promiscuous. And so *Woman*, says Patricia Gowaty, an evolutionary biologist at the University of Georgia, has been good for science. "What Natalie was calling for was for us to get our house in order," says Gowaty. "She's done us a service."

Meredith Small, professor of anthropology at Cornell University, agrees. Angier's criticisms of evolutionary psychology, she says, "are things many of us have been saying among ourselves for 15 years. Natalie brought it out and she got it right. Unfortunately, she's the one who had to take the flak for it." Unfortunate, indeed.

Sitting in the cozy living room of her lilac-colored Victorian home while her three-year-old daughter, Katherine, darts in and out, she makes no bones about the fact that the flak is what she's relished least. For all the sass and opinionated fury that storms through her writing, she has little stomach for confrontation or public debate or anything, for that matter, that thrusts her in the spotlight and onto the chopping block.

This surprises, for in reading her work, you imagine a woman who, if not poised with sword in hand to take on her detractors, is certainly eager to humor them into oblivion. You imagine a you-go-girl kind of gal ready to rock, a dramatic personality around whom people flock.

But Angier is is not that. Despite her well-attended muscles and sturdy bearing, she has a reserved, almost fragile air about her. As though she might cower if you snap too hard. And though she has a big, easy laugh—a kind of wonderful hoot—the intensity of her voice rings more nerdy intellectual than kitchen-table pal.

Yet, as Angier tries to convey in her book, what you see or "know" about her or any human being is hardly all there is to the tale. Her fascination with how complex and layered we are, how different one from the other, is palpable. And so it's not surprising that she'd take on the "evo-psychos"

with the zeal she does, or that upon meeting her she'd openly ponder why, biologically and psychologically, she's wired in the confounding way she is.

It is a doozy of a contradiction. Here is a daughter, wife, and mother of gut-wrenching passion and emotion, a writer who oozes wit and ebullience, living in the same skin as the person who is—and always has been, she insists—"notoriously unhappy." A worry wart of the highest order. A brittle, weepy, sullen, defensive, insecure woman who, O.K., is a tad hostile, too. Her words.

By way of explanation, Angier ventures a connection to her father, who was not a happy man. But the answers still don't come easy, for he was a diagnosed schizophrenic, she says, and she is not. "But I'm borderline something," she says confidently, matter-of-factly. "There's definitely something."

It's all fodder for deep and everlasting thought, and if ever there were a person to turn it inside out until the heavens rage, it's Angier. Behavioral and biological science, after all, have been her life. Her off-beat curiosity over why animals and people move, sleep, harass, kiss, smell, and yes, fret the way they do is near legend among science lovers.

Those who know her tend toward terms like "amazing," "fascinating," and, as Dennis Overbye, a *New York Times* editor and longtime pal, says, "formidably bright." She's also fervidly feminist (since she was 12), with opinions about everything from men and babies to girls and lipstick (she wears it). It was perhaps only a matter of time, Angier acknowledges, before she poured some of her musings on gender into a book.

What excited her, she says, was the awesome stuff she'd been learning about women: how they're made; what their parts actually look like and do, and why they do them; the theories behind how they evolved and why they're different from, yet so similar to, females of other species. She has long believed that the body is a "map to meaning and freedom," but the female body has been so maligned and romanticized that many women don't quite know what to make of their own—how to read their bodies, so to speak.

Her first thought was to sort through all the madness by writing a book strictly about body parts, especially the uniquely female ones, like the egg, uterus, vagina, and breasts. "Then I started doing more and more research into hormones and their impact on behavior and thought there was a lot of interesting material there, too." At the same time, she was becoming intrigued about some of the thinking on evolution and was determined to say a thing or two about its bearing on female desires and actions. The glue that would hold it all together would be tone. "The basic message had to be taken from a position of strength and celebration and dynamism. Ultimately this would be its narrative thread."

Her critics may chide her for being too much the cheerleader, the queen of hear-me-roar, but she firmly believes girls and women can and must have a basis for loving themselves better. And Lord knows she had been in search of that herself. All her life, she figured it would be a far greater thing to be a man. But the process, she says, of "taking the trouble to say what womanhood is, rather than accept other's definition of it as something suboptimal" finally turned her around.

The task was to bring readers along for the ride. And so Angier became a ruthless miner of information. She plucked not merely from medicine and science, but from history, culture, myth, and literature, as well as from the everyday lives of women: women having hysterectomies, women donating eggs, women with both female and male genitalia. And at every turn, she says, she was wowed by what she found.

"I discovered that the female body is a very sturdily built piece of work, and this was very encouraging," she says, her eyes brightening in that I-love-this-stuff kind of way. She long knew that females survive at a higher rate than males; what she hadn't known was that it starts at conception. "The best thing that a premature baby can be is female because female preemies have a higher rate of survival and a lower incidence of birth defects. Now why is that?" she asks. "Well we don't know, but it suggests to me that the female is built to last."

This makes even more compelling, Angier says, a theory by the University of Utah anthropologist Kristen Hawkes: that in prehistoric times, grandmothers foraged for food far more successfully than the big-game hunting males, thereby seeing to the survival of the progeny, and saving the human race. Angier is downright gleeful here. "That really says a lot to me—that there may actually be a kind of evolutionary basis for our persistence and strength, that we are selected for longevity and endurance."

One of the intriguing implications of this theory is that it forces us to consider menopause in a different light: do our bodies become infertile because we once needed to be free from pregnancy and breastfeeding in order to roam for food? Knowing these things, she says, women might glean answers to practical questions such as whether to take estrogen and when. In much the same way, if they know that the scientific link between testosterone and aggression is tenuous, women can better appreciate their own rage without feeling aberrant. If they understand something so basic as why their bodies smell the way they do, they can be more confident about themselves. The bottom line, Angier says, is that there's power in knowledge.

She was astounded by how profoundly true this is for the clitoris. "There's so much to it that the evolutionary theorizing doesn't address—the fact that it is built solely for sexual pleasure and that it is so extraordinarily responsive. That's something we have to keep hearing since we obviously don't believe it." Angier is emphatic: when women are feeling most confident, this most exquisite of organs is at its best. "That's when you're most orgasmic. The more you take control of your sexuality, the better it's going to be."

The problem, she says, is that "men do not necessarily like a woman who is in charge of sexuality because we're both battling over the same turf, which is the female body, and they want to be in control of it."

The idea put forth by evolutionary psychologists that women are less promiscuous by nature than men is the dearest example, she believes, of the insidiousness of the problem. "In order to control female sexuality," she has said, "one good weapon is to tell women that A, if they're promiscuous they'll suffer and B, to try to mute the impulse in the first place." So a woman is condemned when she flaunts her sexuality; she's a tramp, a slut, "two notches below a goat in social status." In some cultures, her genitals are destroyed before they can give her pleasure. "Everything you look at culturally is aimed at curbing female sexuality. It makes sense to do that, and a very potent way is psychologically."

The notion that women fit some universal pattern grates on Angier deeply. Part of the reason stems from what she knows of herself, what she knows of other women and men, indeed, what she witnessed growing up as the third of four children in a wholly unconventional household in the Bronx.

"The relationship between my parents really defied so many of the rules," Angier says. Her father, Keith, was a would-be artist who worked as a machinist and her mother, Adele, daughter of immigrants, worked in a meatpacking plant before becoming a schoolteacher later in life. Both were Communist Youth party members when they met, and highly antiestablishment. Adele Angier was an ardent feminist who chose her husband, she says, not simply because he was "a bonafide intellectual" but because she figured if he was of a lower economic status, she would not have to be subordinate to him. But Keith Angier, for all his leftist politics, was, his daughter says, a "sexist pig" who demanded that women play out their "mother earth" nurturing roles often and in good spirit.

Needless to say, the parents clashed, many times violently, and the marriage ended when Natalie was 12. Still, their life was a testament to the notion that there is no distinctly male or female instinct. "My father had a certain feminine quality about him," says Angier. "He was definitely the more emotional one. He would cry. And my mother was much more a rationalist, and tough. So I think that I saw in both of them a certain degree of—androgyny is a such a boring word—but there was this kind of maleness and femaleness that would express itself in complex and always changing ways."

Even in the way they raised their four children, Angier says, there were clues that gender lines could easily be blurred. "There was no boys-did-the-sports-and-girls-did-the-dolls thing in my house." And in her rough-and-tumble Irish neighborhood, girls were as athletic and "boyish" as they come.

Angier was programmed to behold the world through a different lens, says her older brother, Joe, a television producer in Los Angeles. "Our parents taught us consciously or semiconsciously, don't take anything at face value. Don't believe what you're being told in school necessarily. Question even us."

And so Natalie did question and never took no for an answer. "She saw something she wanted and she went after it," Joe says. "We lived hand-to-mouth, but if Natalie came home with a notice to give a dollar to the PTA, she was on the floor if it wasn't done. It wasn't princessy behavior, it was just this sense that you don't settle for the answer you've been given."

Angier admits she was something apart. She drew and painted well, read incessantly, wrote short stories and poems, and delighted in the magic realism of writers E. Nesbit and Lewis Carroll. But she knew when she smelled a rat. "I remember in third grade going through my reader and noticing that all the stories were about boys, and I was really upset," she recalls.

By the time her parents split and her mother moved Natalie and her younger brother to rural New Buffalo, Michigan, Angier had become fed up with a lot of things. She was by then a brassy-tempered, 13-year-old militant feminist who was reading *The Dialectic of Sex* and *The Female Eunuch* and helping her mother start a consciousness-raising group. She also began trying to break through the thinking that said "girls were supposed to be good and boys could fuck around." So she asked boys out a lot, got rejected a lot, had a string of bummer relationships that involved sex "probably too early" and developed a reputation as a "weirdo." But quite a popular one.

And when kids came to the Angier house, they usually learned something. "There was always a debate going on. It was so different from what I was used to," says Marcia McKeague, Natalie's best friend since those days, now a vice president at Great Northern Paper Company. Birth control and expectations about sexuality, music, politics—it was all on the table, McKeague recalls.

That honesty of discussion, Angier thinks, was vital to her emergence as a thinker and self-starter and has already been instructive to her as a mother. "What worked for me was the expectation that I would be smart and responsible. That no matter what you do, you're intelligent. And that was an enormously powerful message."

Angier skipped two grades, cultivated a highly eclectic set of interests, including science, and excelled at them all. "I was really amazed at the power of science to tell us so much about the universe," Angier says, so by the time she went to the University of Michigan and then to

Barnard College, she was actively trying to figure out how to do what few had done: merge science and creative writing.

"I liked the fact that science could explain reality and that you could do an experiment and predict a particular result. But at the same time I felt that creativity was important, so the power of merging the two was enormous and the potential was unexplored." And, she concedes, "I guess I was looking for something to set me apart. Maybe it's part of my insecurity. If you write a novel, there are a zillion novelists; if you write about science in a way that's alluring, it seems a bit more unusual."

After leaving graduate school at City University of New York in 1979, she landed a job at *Discover* magazine as a reporter/researcher. But her energy and imagination quickly became evident, and she was promoted to writer. Angier launched full-bore into the world of molecular and evolutionary biology. Shannon Brownlee, a freelance writer who was also at *Discover* then, says part of what made Angier's work so muscular and fun was that she thought so deeply about things. "It was like, don't get into a discussion with her and come in with a bunch of opinions you haven't carefully thought about, because nine times out of ten, she's really thought about it, and your little opinion has no standing."

By 1984, when *Time* hired Angier as a science writer, her reputation as the consummate reporter was solid. So was her reputation as a whimsical, idiosyncratic writer. But within a few years, she was on the move again. After finishing her first book, *Natural Obsessions: The Search for the Oncogene* (Houghton Mifflin, 1988), a riv-

eting tale of the biology of cancer told through the soap-operalike lives of scientists in the field, she was lured to the prestigious science desk of the *New York Times*.

Within weeks, she was serving up groundbreaking pieces on animal infidelity (she discovered they cheat more than most people, even scientists, had suspected); on the intriguing lives of scorpions ("some of the biggest, meanest, longest-lived, most sensitive, most maternal, least fraternal, slowest, quickest, and certainly the most weirdly colored creatures among the arachnids and insects"); on the importance of sleep; on caloric restriction as a way to prolong life. And in less than a year, she'd won the Pulitzer, the most prestigious of a raft of awards that she'd already gotten and would get, including her personal favorite, the Science Journalism Award.

But on that day, Angier did as she had throughout her life: question whether she was good enough. "She called me and asked did I think it meant anything," says her brother Joe, still incredulous. It's what Angier has dubbed the Rocky Road Syndrome, that sad, worrisome plodding through life, never satisfied, never feeling fully worthy, always anxious. Her family and friends are convinced it is, in fact, what drives her success. But it is no less painful, says her husband, Rick Weiss.

"She suffers immensely over her writing," says Weiss, a science reporter at the *Washington Post*. "After anything is done, she'll roll around in bed all night and feel it's no good."

"She's one of those people for whom life isn't easy because she feels so intensely about even the little things," says Erica Goode, a *Times* colleague. Goode recalls the time Angier loaned her *Moby Dick* after she herself had put it down. "She stopped reading it when she got to where Ishmael concluded the whale was a fish. It was like, the whale's too noble a creature! That's very Natalie."

Angier's mother talks almost daily with her daughter and she marvels at Natalie's "confusion over how good she is. She has the perfect life," Adele Angier says, as only a mother could. "I wonder how she could have a moment's unhappiness."

Yet Angier says being able to revel in her life is not easy, and relief, medicinal and otherwise, has been elusive. "For me, to be happy is like trying to be taller. As much as I'm against genetic determinism, I think my temperament has been mine all my life." Yet there are things that give her fantastic jolts of joy. One is her daughter, Katherine Ida Angier (if she'd been a boy, Weiss would have been the last name), a kid who is as funny as all get-out and for whom life is still a romp. A kid who, Angier points out, likes bugs and trucks and hitting balls as much as she likes dressing up in high heels and lipstick.

The other source of her optimism is the promise of feminism. She believes women would do well to embrace more fervidly the idea that "there isn't a right or wrong way to do things, that there are variations in strategies, and different strategies work for different women at different times in their lives." And even though it's a jungle out there, for women and for men, "the war between the sexes is never really going to be over and so we are never really going to lose the war. There's always going to be feminism coming back, even if it may be submerged for a while." The trick, she says, is to "never get complacent and think, Oh we've done this, we're finished."

Somehow, Angier says, she suspects that won't happen.

"Even from someone as skeptical as me, I am hopeful that things are going to continue to evolve."

17

Feminism and Science

(1982)

Evelyn Fox Keller

In recent years, a new critique of science has begun to emerge from a number of feminist writings. The lens of feminist politics brings into focus certain masculinist distortions of the scientific enterprise, creating, for those of us who are scientists, a potential dilemma. Is there a conflict between our commitment to feminism and our commitment to science? As both a feminist and a scientist, I am more familiar than I might wish with the nervousness and defensiveness that such a potential conflict evokes. As scientists, we have very real difficulties in thinking about the kinds of issues that, as feminists, we have been raising. These difficulties may, however, ultimately be productive. My purpose in the present essay is to explore the implications of recent feminist criticism of science for the relationship between science and feminism. Do these criticisms imply conflict? If they do, how necessary is that conflict? I will argue that those elements of feminist criticism that seem to conflict most with at least conventional conceptions of science may, in fact, carry a liberating potential for science. It could therefore benefit scientists to attend closely to feminist criticism. I will suggest that we might even use feminist thought to illuminate and clarify part of the substructure of science (which may have been historically conditioned into distortion) in order to preserve the things that science has taught us, in order to be more objective. But first it is necessary to review the various criticisms that feminists have articulated.

The range of their critique is broad. Though they all claim that science embodies a strong androcentric bias, the meanings attached to this charge vary widely. It is convenient to represent the differences in meaning by a spectrum that parallels the political range characteristic of feminism as a whole. I label this spectrum from right to left, beginning somewhere left of center with what might be called the liberal position. From the liberal critique, charges of androcentricity emerge that are relatively easy to correct. The more radical critique calls for correspondingly more radical changes; it requires a reexamination of the underlying assumptions of scientific theory and method for the presence of male bias. The difference between these positions is, however, often obscured by a

Keller, "Feminism and Science," SIGNS 7:3 (1982): 589–602. Used with permission of the University of Chicago Press.

knee-jerk reaction that leads many scientists to regard all such criticism as a unit—as a challenge to the neutrality of science. One of the points I wish to emphasize here is that the range of meanings attributed to the claim of androcentric bias reflects very different levels of challenge, some of which even the most conservative scientists ought to be able to accept.

First, in what I have called the liberal critique, is the charge that is essentially one of unfair employment practices. It proceeds from the observation that almost all scientists are men. This criticism is liberal in the sense that it in no way conflicts either with traditional conceptions of science or with current liberal, egalitarian politics. It is, in fact, a purely political criticism, and one which can be supported by all of us who are in favor of equal opportunity. According to this point of view, science itself would in no way be affected by the presence or absence of women.

A slightly more radical criticism continues from this and argues that the predominance of men in the science has led to a bias in the choice and definition of problems with which scientists have concerned themselves. This argument is most frequently and most easily made in regard to the health sciences. It is claimed, for example, that contraception has not been given the scientific attention its human importance warrants and that, furthermore, the attention it has been given has been focused primarily on contraceptive techniques to be used by women. In a related complaint, feminists argue that menstrual cramps, a serious problem for many women, have never been taken seriously by the medical profession. Presumably, had the concerns of medical research been

articulated by women, these particular imbalances would not have arisen.[1] Similar biases in sciences remote from the subject of women's bodies are more difficult to locate—they may, however, exist. Even so, this kind of criticism does not touch our conception of what science is, nor our confidence in the neutrality of science. It may be true that in some areas we have ignored certain problems, but our definition of science does not include the choice of problem—that, we can readily agree, has always been influenced by social forces. We remain, therefore, in the liberal domain.

Continuing to the left, we next find claims of bias in the actual design and interpretation of experiments. For example, it is pointed out that virtually all of the animal-learning research on rats has been performed with male rats.[2] Though a simple explanation is offered—namely, that female rats have a four-day cycle that complicates experiments—the criticism is hardly vitiated by the explanation. The implicit assumption is, of course, that the male rat represents the species. There exist many other, often similar, examples in psychology. Examples from the biological sciences are somewhat more difficult to find, though one suspects that they exist. An area in which this suspicion is particularly strong is that of sex research. Here the influence of heavily invested preconceptions seems all

---

[1] Notice that the claim is not that the mere presence of women in medical research is sufficient to right such imbalances, for it is understood how readily women, or any "outsiders" for that matter, come to internalize the concerns and values of a world to which they aspire to belong.

[2] I would like to thank Lila Braine for calling this point to my attention.

but inevitable. In fact, although the existence of such preconceptions has been well documented historically,[3] a convincing case for the existence of a corresponding bias in either the design or interpretation of experiments has yet to be made. That this is so can, I think, be taken as testimony to the effectiveness of the standards of objectivity operating.

But evidence for bias in the interpretation of observations and experiments is very easy to find in the more socially oriented sciences. The area of primatology is a familiar target. Over the past fifteen years women working in the field have undertaken an extensive reexamination of theoretical concepts, often using essentially the same methodological tools. These efforts have resulted in some radically different formulations. The range of difference frequently reflects the powerful influence of ordinary language in biasing our theoretical formulations. A great deal of very interesting work analyzing such distortions has been done.[4] Though I cannot begin to do justice to that work here, let me offer, as a single example, the following description of a single-male troop of animals that Jane Lancaster provides as a substitute for the familiar concept of "harem": "For a female, males are a resource in her environment which she may use to further the survival of herself and her offspring. If environmental conditions are such that the male role can be minimal, a one-male group is likely. Only one male is necessary for a group of females if his only role is to impregnate them."[5]

These critiques, which maintain that a substantive effect on scientific theory results from the predominance of men in the field, are almost exclusively aimed at the "softer," even the "softest," sciences. Thus they can still be accommodated within the traditional framework by the simple argument that the critiques, if justified, merely reflect the fact that these subjects are not sufficiently scientific. Presumably, fair-minded (or scientifically minded) scientists can and should join forces with the feminists in attempting to identify the presence of bias—equally offensive, if for different reasons, to both scientists and feminists—in order to make these "soft" sciences more rigorous.

It is much more difficult to deal with the truly radical critique that attempts to locate androcentric bias even in the "hard" sciences, indeed in scientific ideology itself. This range of criticism takes us out of the liberal domain and requires us to question the very assumptions of objectivity and rationality that underlie the scientific enterprise. To challenge the truth and necessity of the conclusions of natural science on the grounds that they too reflect the judgment of men

[3] D. L. Hall and Diana Long. "The Social Implications of the Scientific Study of Sex," *Scholar and the Feminist* 4 (1977): 11–21.

[4] See, e.g., Donna Haraway, Animal Sociology and a Natural Economy of the Body Politic, Part I: A Political Physiology of Dominance"; and "Animal Sociology and a Natural Economy of the Body Politic, Part II: The Past Is the Contested Zone: Human Nature and Theories of Production and Reproduction in Primate Behavior Studies," *Signs: Journal of Women in Culture and Society* 4. no. 1 (Autumn 1978): 21–60.

[5] Jane Lancaster, *Primate Behavior and the Emergence of Human Culture* (New York: Holt, Rinehart & Winston, 1975), p. 34.

is to take the Galilean credo and turn it on its head. It is not true that "the conclusions of natural science are true and necessary, and the judgement of man has nothing to do with them";[6] it is the judgment of woman that they have nothing to do with.

The impetus behind this radical move is twofold. First, it is supported by the experience of feminist scholars in other fields of inquiry. Over and over, feminists have found it necessary, in seeking to reinstate women as agents and as subjects, to question the very canons of their fields. They have turned their attention, accordingly, to the operation of patriarchal bias on ever deeper levels of social structure, even of language and thought.

But the possibility of extending the feminist critique into the foundations of scientific thought is created by recent developments in the history and philosophy of science itself.[7] As long as the course of scientific thought was judged to be exclusively determined by its own logical and empirical necessities, there could be no place for any signature, male or otherwise, in that system of knowledge. Furthermore, any suggestion of gender differences in our thinking about the world could argue only too readily for the further exclusion of women from science. But as the philosophical and historical inadequacies of the classical conception of science have become more evident, and as historians and sociologists have begun to identify the ways in which the development of scientific knowledge has been shaped by its particular social and political context, our understanding of science as a social process has grown. This understanding is a necessary prerequisite, both politically and intellectually, for a feminist theoretic in science.

Joining feminist thought to other social studies of science brings the promise of radically new insights, but it also adds to the existing intellectual danger a political threat. The intellectual danger resides in viewing science as pure social product; science then dissolves into ideology and objectivity loses all intrinsic meaning. In the resulting cultural relativism, any emancipatory function of modern science is negated, and the arbitration of truth recedes into the political domain.[8] Against this background, the temptation arises for feminists to abandon their claim for representation in scientific culture and, in its place, to invite a return to a purely "female" subjectivity, leaving rationality and objectivity in the male domain, dismissed as products of a purely male consciousness.[9]

---

6 Galileo Galilei, *Dialogue on the Great World Systems*, trans, T. Salusbury, ed. G. de Santillana (Chicago: University of Chicago Press, 1953), p. 63.

7 The work of Russell Hanson and Thomas S. Kuhn was of pivotal importance in opening up our understanding of scientific thought to a consideration of social, psychological, and political influences.

8 See, e.g., Paul Feyerabend, *Against Method* (London: New Left Books, 1975); and *Science in a Free Society* (London: New Left Books, 1978).

9 This notion is expressed most strongly by some of the new French feminists (see Elaine Marks and Isabelle de Courtivron, eds., *New French Feminisms: An Anthology* [Amherst: University of Massachusetts Press, 1980]), and is currently surfacing in the writings of some American feminists. See, e.g., Susan Griffin, *Woman and Nature: The Roaring Inside Her* (New York: Harper & Row, 1978).

Many authors have addressed the problems raised by total relativism;[10] here I wish merely to mention some of the special problems added by its feminist variant. They are several. In important respects, feminist relativism is just the kind of radical move that transforms the political spectrum into a circle. By rejecting objectivity as a masculine ideal, it simultaneously lends its voice to an enemy chorus and dooms women to residing outside of the realpolitik modern culture; it exacerbates the very problem it wishes to solve. It also nullifies the radical potential of feminist criticism for our understanding of science. As I see it, the task of a feminist theoretic in science is twofold: to distinguish that which is parochial from that which is universal in the scientific impulse, reclaiming for women what has historically been denied to them; and to legitimate those elements of scientific culture that have been denied precisely because they are defined as female.

It is important to recognize that the framework inviting what might be called the nihilist retreat is in fact provided by the very ideology of objectivity we wish to escape. This is the ideology that asserts an opposition between (male) objectivity and (female) subjectivity and denies the possibility of mediation between the two. A first step, therefore, in extending the feminist critique to the foundations of scientific thought is to reconceptualize objectivity as a dialectical process so as to allow for the possibility of distinguishing the objective effort from the objectivist illusion. As Piaget reminds us:

> Objectivity consists in so fully realizing the countless intrusions of the self in everyday thought and the countless illusions which result—illusions of sense, language, point of view, value, etc.—that the preliminary step to every judgement is the effort to exclude the intrusive self. Realism, on the contrary, consists in ignoring the existence of self and thence regarding one's own perspective as immediately objective and absolute. Realism is thus anthropocentric illusion, finality—in short, all those illusions which teem in the history of science. So long as thought has not become conscious of self, it is a prey to perpetual confusions between objective and subjective, between the real and the ostensible.[11]

In short, rather than abandon the quintessentially human effort to understand the world in rational terms, we need to refine that effort. To do this, we need to add to the familiar methods of rational and empirical inquiry the additional process of critical self-reflection. Following Piaget's injunction, we need to "become conscious of self." In this way, we can become conscious of the features of the scientific project that belie its claim to universality.

The ideological ingredients of particular concern to feminists are

---

[10] See, e.g., Steven Rose and Hilary Rose, "Radical Science and Its Enemies." *Socialist Register 1979*, ed. Ralph Miliband and John Saville (Atlantic Highlands, N.J.: Humanities Press, 1979), pp. 317–35. A number of the points made here have also been made by Elizabeth Fee in "Is Feminism a Threat to Objectivity?" (paper presented at the American Association for the Advancement of Science meeting, Toronto, January 4, 1981).

[11] Jean Piaget, *The Child's Conception of the World* (Totowa, N.J.: Littlefield, Adams & Co., 1972).

found where objectivity is linked with autonomy and masculinity, and in turn, the goals of science with power and domination. The linking of objectivity with social and political autonomy has been examined by many authors and shown to serve a variety of important political functions.[12] The implications of joining objectivity with masculinity are less well understood. This conjunction also serves critical political functions. But an understanding of the sociopolitical meaning of the entire constellation requires an examination of the psychological processes through which these connections become internalized and perpetuated. Here psychoanalysis offers us an invaluable perspective, and it is to the exploitation of that perspective that much of my own work has been directed. In an earlier paper, I tried to show how psychoanalytic theories of development illuminate the structure and meaning of an interacting system of associations linking objectivity (a cognitive trait) with autonomy (an affective trait) and masculinity (a gender trait).[13] Here, after a brief summary of my earlier argument, I want to explore the relation of this system to power and domination.

Along with Nancy Chodorow and Dorothy Dinnerstein, I have found that branch of psychoanalytic theory known as object relations theory to be especially useful.[14] In seeking to account for personality development in terms of both innate drives and actual relations with other objects (i.e., subjects), it permits us to understand the ways in which our earliest experiences—experiences in large part determined by the socially structured relationships that form the context of our developmental processes—help to shape our conception of the world and our characteristic orientations to it. In particular, our first steps in the world are guided primarily by the parents of one sex—our mothers; this determines a maturational framework for our emotional, cognitive, and gender development, a framework later filled in by cultural expectations.

In brief, I argued the following: Our early maternal environment, coupled with the cultural definition of masculine (that which can never appear feminine) and of autonomy (that which can never be compromised by dependency) leads to the association of female with the pleasures and dangers of merging, and of male with the comfort and loneliness of separateness. The boy's internal anxiety about both self and gender is echoed by the more widespread cultural anxiety, thereby encouraging postures of autonomy and masculinity, which can, indeed may, be designed to defend against that anxiety and the longing that generates it. Finally, for all of us, our sense of reality

[12] Jerome R. Ravetz. *Scientific Knowledge and Its Social Problems* (London: Oxford University Press, 1971); and Hilary Rose and Steven Rose, *Science and Society* (London: Allen Lane, 1969).

[13] Evelyn Fox Keller, "Gender and Science," *Psychoanalysis and Contemporary Thought* 1 (1978): 409–33.

[14] Nancy Chodorow, *The Reproduction of Mothering: Psychoanalysis and the Sociology of Gender* (Berkeley: University of California Press, 1978); and Dorothy Dinnerstein. *The Mermaid and the Minotaur: Sexual Arrangements and Human Malaise* (New York: Harper & Row, 1976).

is carved out of the same develop-mental matrix. As Piaget and others have emphasized, the capacity for cognitive distinctions between self and other (objectivity) evolves con-currently and interdependently with the development of psychic auton-omy; our cognitive ideals thereby become subject to the same psycho-logical influences as our emotional and gender ideals. Along with auton-omy the very act of separating subject from object—objectivity itself—comes to be associated with masculinity. The combined psychological and cul-tural pressures lead all three ideals—affective, gender, and cognitive—to a mutually reinforcing process of exag-geration and rigidification.[15] The net result is the entrenchment of an ob-jectivist ideology and a correlative devaluation of (female) subjectivity.

This analysis leaves out many things. Above all it omits discussion of the psychological meanings of power and domination, and it is to those meanings I now wish to turn. Central to object relations theory is the recognition that the condition of psychic autonomy is double edged: it offers a profound source of pleasure, and simultaneously of potential dread. The values of autonomy are consonant with the values of compe-tence, of mastery. Indeed compe-tence is itself a prior condition for autonomy and serves immeasurably to confirm one's sense of self. But need the development of competence and the sense of mastery lead to a state of alienated selfhood, of denied connectedness, of defensive sepa-rateness? To forms of autonomy that can be understood as protections against dread? Object relations the-ory makes us sensitive to autonomy's range of meanings; it simultaneously suggests the need to consider the corresponding meanings of compe-tence. Under what circumstances does competence imply mastery of one's own fate and under what cir-cumstances does it imply mastery over another's? In short, are control and domination essential ingredi-ents of competence, and intrinsic to selfhood, or are they correlates of an alienated selfhood?

One way to answer these questions is to use the logic of the analysis sum-marized above to examine the shift from competence to power and con-trol in the psychic economy of the young child. From that analysis, the impulse toward domination can be understood as a natural concomitant of defensive separateness—as Jessica Benjamin has written, "A way of re-pudiating sameness, dependency and closeness with another person, while attempting to avoid the consequent feelings of aloneness."[16] Perhaps no one has written more sensitively than

---

[15] For a fuller development of this argument, see n. 12 above. By focusing on the contribu-tions of individual psychology, I in no way mean to imply a simple division of individual and social factors, or to set them up as alter-native influences. Individual psychological traits evolve in a social system and, in turn, so-cial systems reward and select for particular sets of individual traits. Thus if particular op-tions in science reflect certain kinds of psy-chological impulses or personality traits, it must be understood that it is in a distinct so-cial framework that those options, rather than others, are selected.

[16] Jessica Benjamin has discussed this same is-sue in an excellent analysis of the place of domination in sexuality. See "The Bonds of Love: Rational Violence and Erotic Domina-tion," *Feminist Studies* 6, no. 1 (Spring 1980): 144–74, esp. 150.

psychoanalyst D. W. Winnicott of the rough waters the child must travel in negotiating the transition from symbiotic union to the recognition of self and other as autonomous entities. He alerts us to a danger that others have missed—a danger arising from the unconscious fantasy that the subject has actually destroyed the object in the process of becoming separate.

Indeed, he writes, "It is the destruction of the object that places the object outside the area of control. . . . After 'subject relates to object' comes 'subject destroys object' (as it becomes external); then may come '*object survives* destruction by the subject.' But there may or may not be survival." When there is, "because of the survival of the object, the subject may now have started to live a life in the world of objects, and so the subject stands to gain immeasurably; but the price has to be paid in acceptance of the ongoing destruction in unconscious fantasy relative to object-relating."[17] Winnicott, of course, is not speaking of actual survival but of subjective confidence in the survival of the other. Survival in that sense requires that the child maintain relatedness; failure induces inevitable guilt and dread. The child is poised on a terrifying precipice. On one side lies the fear of having destroyed the object, on the other side, loss of self. The child may make an attempt to secure this precarious position by seeking to master the other. The cycles of destruction and survival are reenacted while the other is kept safely at bay, and as Benjamin writes, "the original self assertion is . . . converted from innocent mastery to mastery over and against the other."[18] In psychodynamic terms, this particular resolution of preoedipal conflicts is a product of oedipal consolidation. The (male) child achieves his final security by identification with the father—an identification involving simultaneously a denial of the mother and a transformation of guilt and fear into aggression.

Aggression, of course, has many meanings, many sources, and many forms of expression. Here I mean to refer only to the form underlying the impulse toward domination. I invoke psychoanalytic theory to help illuminate the forms of expression that impulse finds in science as a whole, and its relation to objectification in particular. The same questions I asked about the child I can also ask about science. Under what circumstances is scientific knowledge sought for the pleasures of knowing, for the increased competence it grants us, for the increased mastery (real or imagined) over our own fate, and under what circumstances is it fair to say that science seeks actually to dominate nature? Is there a meaningful distinction to be made here?

In his work *The Domination of Nature* William Leiss observes, "The necessary correlate of domination is the consciousness of subordination in those who must obey the will of another; thus properly speaking only other men can be the objects of domination."[19] (Or women, we might add.) Leiss infers from this observation that it is not the domination of physical nature we should worry

---

[17] D. W. Winnicott, *Playing and Reality* (New York: Basic Books, 1971), pp. 89–90.

[18] Benjamin, p. 165.

[19] William Leiss, *The Domination of Nature* (Boston: Beacon Press, 1974), p. 122.

about but the use of our knowledge of physical nature as an instrument for the domination of human nature. He therefore sees the need for correctives, not in science but in its uses. This is his point of departure from other authors of the Frankfurt school, who assume the very logic of science to be the logic of domination. I agree with Leiss's basic observation but draw a somewhat different inference. I suggest that the impulse toward domination does find expression in the goals (and even in the theories and practice) of modern science, and argue that where it finds such expression the impulse needs to be acknowledged as projection. In short, I argue that not only in the denial of interaction between subject and other but also in the access of domination to the goals of scientific knowledge, one finds the intrusion of a self we begin to recognize as partaking in the cultural construct of masculinity.

The value of consciousness is that it enables us to make choices—both as individuals and as scientists. Control and domination are in fact intrinsic neither to selfhood (i.e., autonomy) nor to scientific knowledge. I want to suggest, rather, that the particular emphasis Western science has placed on these functions of knowledge is twin to the objectivist ideal. Knowledge in general, and scientific knowledge in particular, serves two gods: power and transcendence. It aspires alternately to mastery over and union with nature.[20] Sexuality serves the same two gods, aspiring to domination and ecstatic communion—in short, aggression and eros. And it is hardly a new insight to say that power, control, and domination are fueled largely by aggression, while union satisfies a more purely erotic impulse.

To see the emphasis on power and control so prevalent in the rhetoric of Western science as projection of a specifically male consciousness requires no great leap of the imagination. Indeed, that perception has become a commonplace. Above all, it is invited by the rhetoric that conjoins the domination of nature with the insistent image of nature as female, nowhere more familiar than in the writings of Francis Bacon. For Bacon, knowledge and power are one, and the promise of science is expressed as "leading to you Nature with all her children to bind her to your service and make her your slave,"[21] by means that do not "merely exert a gentle guidance over nature's course; they have the power to conquer and subdue her, to shake her to her foundations."[22] In the context of the Baconian vision, Bruno Bettelheim's conclusion appears inescapable: "Only with phallic psychology did aggressive manipulation of nature become possible."[23]

The view of science as an oedipal project is also familiar from the writ-

---

[20] For a discussion of the different roles these two impulses play in Platonic and in Baconian images of knowledge, see Evelyn Fox Keller, "Nature as 'Her'" (paper delivered at the Second Sex Conference, New York Institute for the Humanities, September 1979).

[21] B. Farrington, "Temporis Partus Masculus: An Untranslated Writing of Francis Bacon," Centaurus 1 (1951): 193–205, esp. 197.

[22] Francis Bacon, "Description of the Intellectual Globe," in The Philosophical Works of Francis Bacon, ed. J. H. Robertson (London: Routledge & Sons, 1905), p. 506.

[23] Quoted in Norman O. Brown, Life against Death (New York: Random House, 1959), p. 280.

ings of Herbert Marcuse and Norman O. Brown.[24] But Brown's preoccupation, as well as Marcuse's, is with what Brown calls a "morbid" science. Accordingly, for both authors the quest for a nonmorbid science, an "erotic" science, remains a romantic one. This is so because their picture of science is incomplete: it omits from consideration the crucial, albeit less visible, erotic components already present in the scientific tradition. Our own quest, if it is to be realistic rather than romantic, must be based on a richer understanding of the scientific tradition, in all its dimensions, and on an understanding of the ways in which this complex, dialectical tradition becomes transformed into a monolithic rhetoric. Neither the oedipal child nor modern science has in fact managed to rid itself of its preoedipal and fundamentally bisexual yearnings. It is with this recognition that the quest for a different science, a science undistorted by masculinist bias, must begin.

The presence of contrasting themes, of a dialectic between aggressive and erotic impulses, can be seen both within the work of individual scientists and, even more dramatically, in the juxtaposed writings of different scientists. Francis Bacon provides us with one model;[25] there are many others. For an especially striking contrast, consider a contemporary scientist who insists on the importance of "letting the material speak to you," of allowing it to "tell you what to do next"—one who chastises other scientists for attempting to "impose an answer" on what they see. For this scientist, discovery is facilitated by becoming "part of the system," rather than remaining outside; one must have a "feeling for the organism."[26] It is true that the author of these remarks is not only from a different epoch and a different field (Bacon himself was not actually a scientist by most standards), she is also a woman. It is also true that there are many reasons, some of which I have already suggested, for thinking that gender (itself constructed in an ideological context) actually does make a difference in scientific inquiry. Nevertheless, my point here is that neither science nor individuals are totally bound by ideology. In fact, it is not difficult to find similar sentiments expressed by male scientists. Consider, for example, the following remarks: "I have often had cause to feel that my hands are cleverer than my head. That is a crude way of characterizing the dialectics of experimentation. When it is going well, it is like a quiet conversation with Nature."[27] The difference between conceptions of science as "dominating" and as "conversing with" nature may not be a difference primarily between epochs, nor between the sexes. Rather, it can be seen as representing a dual theme played out in the work of all scientists, in all ages. But the two poles of this dialectic do not

[24] Brown: and Herbert Marcuse, *One Dimensional Man* (Boston: Beacon Press, 1964).

[25] For a discussion of the presence of the same dialectic in the writings of Francis Bacon, see Evelyn Fox Keller, "Baconian Science: A Hermaphrodite Birth," *Philosophical Forum* 11, no. 3 (Spring 1980): 299–308.

[26] Barbara McClintock, private interviews. December 1, 1978, and January 13, 1979.

[27] G. Wald, "The Molecular Basis of Visual Excitation," *Les Prix Nobel en 1967* (Stockholm: Kungliga Boktryckerlet, 1968), p. 260.

appear with equal weight in the history of science. What we therefore need to attend to is the evolutionary process that selects one theme as dominant.

Elsewhere I have argued for the importance of a different selection process.[28] In part, scientists are themselves selected by the emotional appeal of particular (stereotypic) images of science. Here I am arguing for the importance of selection within scientific thought—first of preferred methodologies and aims, and finally of preferred theories. The two processes are not unrelated. While stereotypes are not binding (i.e., they do not describe all or perhaps any individuals), and this fact creates the possibility for an ongoing contest within science, the first selection process undoubtedly influences the outcome of the second. That is, individuals drawn by a particular ideology will tend to select themes consistent with that ideology.

One example in which this process is played out on a theoretical level is in the fate of interactionist theories in the history of biology. Consider the contest that has raged throughout this century between organismic and particulate views of cellular organization—between what might be described as hierarchical and nonhierarchical theories. Whether the debate is over the primacy of the nucleus or the cell as a whole, the genome or the cytoplasm, the proponents of hierarchy have won out. One geneticist has described the conflict in explicitly political terms:

Two concepts of genetic mechanisms have persisted side by side throughout

the growth of modern genetics, but the emphasis has been very strongly in favor of one of these. . . . The first of these we will designate as the "Master Molecule" concept. . . . This is in essence the Theory of the Gene, interpreted to suggest a totalitarian government. . . . The second concept we will designate as the "Steady State" concept. By this term . . . we envision a dynamic self-perpetuating organization of a variety of molecular species which owes its specific properties not to the characteristic of any one kind of molecule, but to the functional interrelationships of these molecular species.[29]

Soon after these remarks, the debate between "master molecules" and dynamic interactionism was foreclosed by the synthesis provided by DNA and the "central dogma." With the success of the new molecular biology such "steady state" (or egalitarian) theories lost interest for almost all geneticists. But today, the same conflict shows signs of reemerging—in genetics, in theories of the immune system, and in theories of development.

I suggest that method and theory may constitute a natural continuum, despite Popperian claims to the contrary, and that the same processes of selection may bear equally and simultaneously on both the means and aims of science and the actual theoretical descriptions that emerge. I suggest this in part because of the recurrent and striking consonance that can be seen in the way scientists work, the relation they take to their object of study, and the theoretical orientation they favor. To pursue the

---

[28] Keller, "Gender and Science."

[29] D. L. Nanney. "The Role of the Cyctoplasm in Heredity," in *The Chemical Basis of Heredity*, ed. William D. McElroy and Bentley Glass (Baltimore: Johns Hopkins University Press, 1957), p. 136.

example cited earlier, the same scientist who allowed herself to become "part of the system," whose investigations were guided by a "feeling for the organism," developed a paradigm that diverged as radically from the dominant paradigm of her field as did her methodological style.

In lieu of the linear hierarchy described by the central dogma of molecular biology, in which the DNA encodes and transmits all instructions for the unfolding of a living cell, her research yielded a view of the DNA in delicate interaction with the cellular environment—an organismic view. For more important than the genome as such (i.e., the DNA) is the "overall organism." As she sees it, the genome functions "only in respect to the environment in which it is found." In this work the program encoded by the DNA is itself subject to change. No longer is a master control to be found in a single component of the cell; rather, control resides in the complex interactions of the entire system. When first presented, the work underlying this vision was not understood, and it was poorly received. Today much of that work is undergoing a renaissance, al-though it is important to say that her full vision remains too radical for most biologists to accept.

This example suggests that we need not rely on our imagination for a vision of what a different science—a science less restrained by the impulse to dominate—might be like. Rather, we need only look to the thematic pluralism in the history of our own science as it has evolved. Many other examples can be found, but we lack an adequate understanding of the full range of influences that lead to the acceptance or rejection not only of particular theories but of different theoretical orientations. What I am suggesting is that if certain theoretical interpretations have been selected against, it is precisely in this process of selection that ideology in general, and a masculinist ideology in particular, can be found to effect its influence. The task this implies for a radical feminist critique of science is, then, first a historical one, but finally a transformative one. In the historical effort, feminists can bring a whole new range of sensitivities, leading to an equally new consciousness of the potentialities lying latent in the scientific project.

18

Calling the Shots?
The International Politics
of Depo-Provera

(1984)

Phillida Bunkle

Depo-Provera, the three-monthly contraceptive injection, is a case study in the dilemmas posed to women by the development of the new reproductive technology. On the one hand Depo's easy administration and contraceptive efficacy makes contraception potentially convenient for millions of underprivileged women; on the other hand these very features make it a powerful tool for the control of women.

Depo is exclusively manufactured by the multinational Upjohn Corporation. Upjohn not only manufactures the drug—it also manufactures most of the information about it. Responding 'rationally' to the economic system, naturally they promote knowledge favourable to their product.

Depo, or medroxyprogesterone acetate, is a progestogen, that is, an artificially created drug which has some properties similar to naturally occurring sex hormones called progesterones. Upjohn started testing Depo as a contraceptive in the early 1960s.

In 1967 Upjohn applied to the United States Food and Drug Administration (FDA) for a licence to sell Depo as a contraceptive (*The Depo-Provera Debate*, 1978). In the following year Upjohn began the seven-year dog and ten-year monkey studies required by FDA.

The dog trials showed dose-related increases in both benign breast nodules and breast cancer. As a result of initial findings in dogs, the oral form of the drug, called Provest, and four other progestogen contraceptive preparations were withdrawn in 1970. Controversy has surrounded the use of the injectable long-acting Depo form ever since.

In 1974 FDA responded to the licensing application by allowing marketing with very stringent restrictions (ibid.: 223–7). Even with these conditions final permission was stayed on request from a Congressional Committee. The debate continued with a series of Congressional Hearings. In

Bunkle, Phillida, "Calling the Shots? The International Politics of Depo-Provera," In Arditta et. al: *Test-Tube Women: What Future for Motherhood.* Harper Collins, 1989. Used by permission of the author.

1978 FDA finally rejected the application to market Depo as a contraceptive in the United States. In an extraordinary move Upjohn appealed against the decision. A Public Board of Enquiry heard this appeal in early 1983 (*Science*, 1982; *Time*, 1983). As of September 1983 the results of this and a similar appeal in the UK are not known.

The FDA ban meant effectively that Depo could not be manufactured in the USA. New Zealand, which had approved it for use in 1968, imports its supplies from an Upjohn subsidiary in Belgium. Not only was the company denied the lucrative US market, but, more importantly, because State Department policy prevented USAID (the main channel for American overseas aid) from supplying drugs banned in the US, Upjohn could not manufacture there for the huge Third World market (*Export of Hazardous Products*, 1980; Shaikh and Reich, 1981). Until President Reagan changed this policy in 1981 this was the primary cause of the company's concern. The ban not only inhibited willingness to buy by making the product look suspect, it cut off the large market that AID funds would make available.

Various population agencies were led, by their perception of the overriding need to make contraception available to all women, to evade this restriction (Ehrenreich, Dowie and Minkin, 1979; Sarra, 1982). It is alleged, for instance, that AID funds passed to International Planned Parenthood Federation (IPPF), whose headquarters are in London. IPPF purchased Depo for worldwide supply to national family planning associations. In this way family planning associations (FPA) became major

sources of Depo, although many of their well-intentioned medical workers are not aware of this background. When the propriety of laundering funds was questioned, IPPF defended their action by convening an international committee of medical experts especially to consider Depo. Some committee members had worked with FPA supplying Depo in their various countries. Their report was highly reassuring, as were the expert evaluations provided by other interested parties, the World Health Organisation and AID (*Bulletin of the World Health Organization*, 1982; *IPPF Medical Bulletin*, 1980; 1982; AID, *Report to USAID of the Ad Hoc Consultative Panel*, 1978). Sometimes FPA doctors who prescribe Depo in New Zealand appear to have only information from these reports and package inserts supplied by the company.

WHO USES DEPO-PROVERA?

The market potential of Depo was enormous. With half the world's population as potential users and manufacturing costs low, the market for contraceptive drugs is particularly large and profitable. In the West market saturation for contraceptive pharmaceuticals was reached with the pill by the late 1960s. Thereafter development of new products slowed. Market expansion depended on developing methods of administering contraceptives that would reach new populations. Here the interests of the drug companies and population controllers coincided. Unlike other expensive drugs, contraceptives are ones which Third World governments and international agencies are willing to spend money on. Although long-acting injectable drugs were ideal, the US ban meant that Up-john had to work hard to develop the market potential. Between 1971–4 Upjohn spent over $4 million in bribes to foreign governments and family planning officials to encourage the use of the drug (*Export of Hazardous Products*, 1980: 184–7). Upjohn's persistence in challenging FDA decisions kept the safety issue 'open' and kept the debate focussed on the distant issue of cancer rather than more immediate adverse effects, until Depo was firmly established as brand leader.

Sales increased throughout the 1970s, reaching 7 million doses per year in 1978 and 8 million by 1983 (*Population Reports*, 1983. K-21). Of the countries with the highest rates of use, Jamaica, Thailand, New Zealand, Mexico and Sri Lanka, only New Zealand is not a third world country (ibid.). In most rich countries, for example, in the USA, Australia and Great Britain, Depo is banned or heavily restricted (Rakusen, 1981). In these countries there is, however, significant use in sections of the population which most resemble Third World stereotypes. Depo is, for example, reportedly used extensively on West Indian and Asian women in Britain and Aboriginals in Australia (*Cultural Survival*, 1981; Floreman, 1981: 17; Lucas and Ware, 1981; Savage, 1983; Thomas, 1982; *The Times*, 1981).

In New Zealand it is used disproportionately on Polynesian women. One statistically reliable survey of family practice found that

> Maori and Non-Maori women had similar overall contraception consultation rates, but there was a striking difference between races in the type of contraception used. Maori women

were much more likely to get the Depo Provera injection. (Gimore, 1983: 8)

In this study Depo was prescribed to Maori women more often than any other form of contraception.

Company sales figures suggest that between 80,000 to 100,000 injections are sold in New Zealand each year. Dr Charlotte Paul of the University of Otago Medical School has estimated from surveys of contraceptive use that approximately 15 per cent of Pakeha (paleface) and 25 per cent of Maori women have used it at some time (Paul, 1981). A disturbing proportion of us, especially Maoris, will be at risk from any long-term effects Depo many turn out to have.

DEBATE OVER THE SAFETY OF DEPO-PROVERA

Upjohn's assertion that Depo 'is probably the safest hormonal contraceptive drug available' is based on their claim that after fifteen years' use and millions of prescriptions there is a 'low reported incidence of side effects' (Upjohn Corporation, 1980: 314). The company has a vested interest in not looking for such evidence. But the absence of information does not establish the safety of a drug.

Upjohn claims that Depo is one of the most studied drugs available. None of these studies, however, conclusively answers vital safety questions. This is apparent even from an exhaustive evaluation of the medical evidence that is very favourable to Depo by Ian Fraser, Australia's foremost advocate of Depo and consultant to WHO and FPA (Fraser and Weisberg, 1981).

The example of this review shows why the medical evidence does not answer women's questions. Fraser's review was published as part of the *Medical Journal of Australia*. Printing costs were, however, paid by Upjohn. Having paid for production, Upjohn distributes this 'reputable' medical opinion as part of their promotional literature. Corporate production of 'academic' knowledge is not usually so blatant. Political science journals do not carry party manifestos even as supplements. The medical literature is generally reassuring about Depo, not because the drug is safe, but because of the way medical knowledge is constructed and disseminated.

The claim made by medical literature that Depo is safe cannot in fact be scientifically evaluated because the evidence available is either (i) the result of experiments performed or funded by the Corporation and constructed to give them favourable results, (ii) is 'proprietary information', or (iii) has never been systematically examined at all. To illustrate this I shall examine each of the safety issues using these three categories.

(i) The corporate construction of knowledge

Cancer Three cancer sites are involved, the breast, cervix and uterus. There are questions about the carcinogenicity of oestrogen pills and IUDs, especially copper IUDs, but if Depo were licensed it would be the first contraceptive drug accepted by FDA which is known to have caused cancer in test animals.

Controversy has centred on the applicability of the findings of cancer in the dog and monkey studies to women. Upjohn argued, and the population control agencies echoed, that

the dog study is not significant because in Upjohn's view the beagles used in the dog studies were uniquely susceptible to breast cancers. Critics reply that while these results do not prove that Depo causes breast cancer in humans it must nevertheless be treated as presumptive evidence. Since animal tests have proved predictive for other known carcinogens, at the very least they shift the onus of proof of safety onto the manufacturer (Epstein, 1977).

When the results of the monkey study became available they added fuel to the controversy. At the end of the ten years, two of the high dose animals had endometrial cancers, and it was later revealed that three had had breast lumps. The debate on the validity of species-to-species extrapolation was promptly repeated for the monkeys. There has been little independent study of a possible cancer link in women. The evidence on breast cancer is described as 'sparse' (Fraser and Weisberg, 1981: 11). Upjohn rebuts the possibility that Depo causes uterine cancer by citing a 'study' done by Malcolm Potts in Thailand (McDaniel and Potts, 1979). In 1978 Potts, former medical director of IPPF, joined the International Fertility Research Program (IFRP), an organisation funded by USAID with lesser contributions from IPPF, Upjohn and others. IFRP has led the campaign for Depo. Potts went to Thailand for one month and with Edward McDaniel, the main distributor of Depo in Northern Thailand, he was able to trace nine of the sixty women who had been admitted to the region's hospital with uterine cancer (Minkin, 1981). He ascertained that none of the nine had had Depo. The inadequacies of the 'study' are obvious, indeed laughable, yet it has been cited repeatedly as 'evidence' that Depo does not cause cancer in women.

Very recently, Dr Potts, Dr Shelton from AID and others have published evidence from 5,000 black American Depo users showing no increase in breast, uterine or ovarian cancers (Liang, 1983). Unfortunately, short exposure, a limited follow-up period and wide 'confidence limits' prevent the study from being anything other than inconclusive.

In the meantime, however, concern had arisen over a possible relation in humans between Depo and cervical cancer, which is a much greater cause of concern than relatively rare uterine cancer. This is the shakiest, but in some ways most suggestive, human evidence on the carcinogenicity of Depo.

The human trials required from Upjohn were reported with no controls, little information of concurrent drug usage and zero follow-up. In 1974 an FDA analyst giving testimony to a Congressional Sub-Committee showed, however, that if the Third National Cancer Survey was used as a control to the Upjohn supplied data then it appeared that women on Depo had rates of cervical cancer in situ much greater than expected (Johnson, 1976).

FDA rejected the validity of using the National Cancer Survey as a control because the Upjohn group had been subject to more intense diagnostic scrutiny. Feminists were dissatisfied with FDA's dismissal of such suggestive evidence. They found two similarly screened groups to use as controls for the Upjohn data. Both suggested elevated rates of cervical cancer in Depo users (Corea, 1980).

Upjohn now needed evidence to refute the suspicion. The New Zealand Contraception and Health Study was the response. The 'primary objective' of the study 'is to examine the relative association between contraceptive practices and the development of dysplasia, carcinoma in situ, or invasive carcinoma of the cervix' (*Protocol*, 1982: 2). The study has a most prestigious executive committee, including the senior obstetrics/gynaecology professors from both New Zealand medical schools. The chairperson of the executive, Professor Liggins, from the National Women's Hospital, vehemently maintains that the study is independent and was initiated by him (*Close Up*, 1983). This is disputed by some scientists who were first consulted by Upjohn personnel. The fragmentary documentary history made public at a recent Statistical Association conference would seem to support the view that the early stages were initiated and designed by Upjohn (Renner, 1983a). The company seems less concerned than academics to maintain the appearance of independence from the study; their 'media package' says 'Upjohn is currently conducting long range studies in New Zealand' (Upjohn Interview, 1982). There appears to be no other study to which they might be referring.

New Zealand is convenient for an investigation of a possible link between Depo and cervical cancer. New Zealand has a higher rate of use than any other country with a social and ethnic composition similar to the United States and a comparable standard of health care. An internal Upjohn memo notes the public health care system as an advantage, presumably because it will relieve the company from having to pay for any medical treatment incurred by subjects (Weisblat, 1977). The minister of health, dedicated to the 'free market' of ideas, eschews any regulation of privately funded research, even on human subjects. More significantly, welfare state legislation precludes the possibility of suing a doctor or drug company for damages. Regulatory freedom and legal immunity must be extremely attractive to a company which is a party to multi-million dollar suits for damages from American women who feel they have been injured by DES or Depo.

The New Zealand Contraception and Health Study is a prospective observational study following three groups of 2,500 subjects using Depo, IUDs, or combined pills for five years. A PAP smear is taken at each annual examination and a questionnaire completed by the doctor. Completed questionnaires are forwarded to the study office located in a partitioned section of the Upjohn warehouse in Auckland, which is leased by the Executive Committee from Upjohn, with Upjohn funds. 'Sealed patient questionnaires are not opened in New Zealand' (*Protocol*, 1982: 13) but are sent direct to Upjohn headquarters in Kalamazoo, Michigan, where data are stored on the company computer (ibid.: 21). Data will be analysed by company scientists under the director of an Upjohn 'project manager' (ibid.). There is no undertaking to publish all or any results.

Professor Liggins maintains that this constitutes complete independence from the Upjohn Corporation (*Close Up*, 1983). There has been some discussion internal to the medical profession about why the pathology for the study is not being handled

in New Zealand, where the capacity to process PAP smears is well developed. Similarly the Protocol says that 'All data processing and analysis will be performed in Kalamazoo' (*Protocol*, 1982: 21). Some biostatisticians have asked why the statistical analysis has not been designed and carried out in New Zealand. The Report of the Survey Appraisals Committee of the New Zealand Statistical Association, which is critical of the study, draws attention to the fact that there will be no independent access to data to facilitate 'peer review' (Deely, 1983).

The design of the study will crucially affect its results. Papers by a statistical consultant at recent Statistical Association and Epidemiological conferences show that the duration and sample size are too small to allow the study the statistical power to discriminate even large increases in cervical dysplasia or cancer (Renner, 1983a; 1983b; 1983c). Study design will therefore ensure reassuring results, justified or not. Only one medical doctor in New Zealand has publicly voiced concern about the study (*Close Up*, 1983). Next day he was verbally assailed by the head of National Women's Hospital and told that his professional standing was in jeopardy. These remarks were later withdrawn but the collective silence of the medical profession is perhaps not surprising. It is unlikely that aspiring obstetricians and gynaecologists will risk their career prospects by publicly criticising senior professors of both medical schools, on an issue of little personal concern to themselves.

The most outspoken medical advocate of Depo in New Zealand is John Hutton, formerly junior colleague of

Professor Liggins, and recently promoted to the chair of obstetrics and gynaecology at Wellington Clinical School. At his aptly entitled inaugural lecture, 'Depo-Provera: Are the critics justified?' (Hutton, 1981; 1983), Professor Hutton defended Upjohn paying for a study in which they have a vested interest, on the grounds that 80 per cent of all medical research worldwide is funded by drug companies. Upjohn funding for this study was, he said, comparable to the annual budget of the Medical Research Council, the government source of medical research funds in New Zealand. Of course, such funds are important to those whose careers and prestige depend upon attracting them. By lending their names to research funded by drug companies, academics notch up the publication titles essential to career success. The more they do this, the more successful and powerful they will become, and the more able to attract funds (Mangold, 1983).

Upjohn money may also have influenced liberal doctors, many of whom work for FPA. Through affiliation with IPPF, FPA became the single largest supplier of Depo in New Zealand. FPA is chronically poorly funded. The company pay them $25 plus a consultation fee for each woman recruited into the study.

Upjohn have spent a great deal of money on the New Zealand Contraceptive and Health Study. It is unlikely that their funds will be wasted.

(ii) Corporate control of knowledge

Cancer is not, however, the only safety issue with Depo-Provera. In 1979 Stephen Minkin published a critical review of the evidence on Depo in which he claimed that company reports of the animal studies spoke of cancers but did not reveal other very important adverse effects, in particular that many dogs actually died of uterine disease (Minkin, 1979). Minkin's work has been widely discredited, especially for lax citation (Hutton, 1980). Some of these criticisms are justified, but nevertheless the central charge that important evidence of side effects was not released remains unrefuted (Corea, 1980). Since the company 'owns' the evidence it is not available for scrutiny and the charge cannot be evaluated. The safety debate has focussed on cancer with little investigation on other health risks to women.

Depo has been promoted worldwide as the ideal contraceptive for lactating mothers. This is a critical issue for Third World women. In New Zealand this is when it is likely to be prescribed for white, middle-class women. Apart from one study on rats, there is no evidence about the effect on neo-nates of Depo, absorbed from breast milk (Satayasthit et al., 1976). That Depo should have been promoted for this purpose before its effects on infants was established is another example of unwillingness to look for evidence that might injure prime markets.

Teratogenic effects The concern arises because of the known teratogenic effects of progestogens (Shapiro, 1978). Exposure during gestation is different and more significant but is nevertheless reasonable grounds for caution in exposing breast-fed neonates. As with cancer the evidence is a pattern of suggestive animal studies, backed by fragmentary human evidence.

In animal studies progestogens given in utero cause masculinisation of female foetuses. There is some slight but disturbing corroborative evidence from children who have been treated with Depo during gestation. Girl babies exposed to large doses of Depo in utero have been found to have 'clitoral hypertrophy'. 'Clitoral hypertrophy is an increase in the size of the clitoris in relationship to the size of the baby.' (*The Depo-Provera Debate*, 1978: 75–80). The doctors who gave this evidence to a Congressional Committee, however, testified that they found no evidence of birth defects. Clitoral enlargement 'becomes less obvious as the girl grows up' (ibid.) so that although it was a defect apparent at birth it was not a 'birth defect'.

Upjohn have used this remarkable logic to discredit critics concerned about a possible link between Depo and growth abnormalities (*Export of Hazardous Products*, 1980: 332). Now-you-see-it-now-you-don't definitions enable them to evade disturbing evidence and at the same time discredit opposition.

A recent evaluation in the prestigious *Journal of the American Medical Association* turns the lack of research on this issue into an argument for wider use to facilitate further experimentation (Rosenfield et al., 1983: 2925).

Upjohn recognises that more evidence is needed. In their submission to the FDA Board of Enquiry Upjohn say: 'follow-up of children exposed in utero is one aspect of the prospective observational study being conducted in New Zealand'. (Upjohn Corporation, 1982: 5)

The study *Protocol*, however, has no mention of such children. The *Protocol* simply provides no evidence for the existence of this aspect of the study (*Protocol*, 1982: 5, 10). This is similar to the 'six years of clinical trials' that the Upjohn consumer information pamphlet claims have taken place in New Zealand, but of which there is no trace (*Close Up*, 1983).

(iii) The invisibility of women's experience in medical research

If advocates of Depo discount animal evidence because it is animal, they also discount women's experience with the drug because it is 'subjective'.

When women report to their doctors effects of the drug unrelated to its contraceptive efficacy it does not appear to raise doubts about the drug, but, rather, reinforces the stereotype of women as 'complaining' or 'over-anxious'. Effects may be attributed to women's nature rather than recognised as drug-related. Many women have been told that the problems they report are 'most unusual'. The implication is that the problems are 'in' the women rather than 'in' the drug.

Women's experience has not been heard at all in the Depo debate. The definition of medical knowledge excludes the personal and invalidates our testimony. I have been part of a New Zealand feminist health group evaluating the medical evidence and asserting the primacy of women's experience in the debate. By gathering together many women's accounts of how they were prescribed Depo and their experience using it we have been able to reassure many women that they are not alone or unusual in experiencing adverse effects. For many women it has been a huge relief to feel it is not something 'wrong' with them.

In trying to gather information about the use of Depo in New Zealand, our group has been hampered not only by our lack of resources but also by the belief that we are paranoid or neurotic. Not being scientists or doctors, we are made to feel that we have no 'right' to such information. Our health and our bodies are none of our business. The chief O & G (obstetrician/gynecologist) of New Zealand described the letters that come to National Women's Hospital on 'forced sterilization and Depo-Provera' as 'not usually true, grossly distorted or psychotic' (Bonham, 1980). Feminist research is seen as the exaggeration of distorted minds having problems with 'authority'. This may seem like rather primitive abuse of psychiatric labels but it is effective in discrediting our individual and collective experience.

Some of the women who shared their experience with us found Depo helpful and experienced few side effects; others experienced side effects but considered them worthwhile for effective contraception; others experienced very severe effects. Because it is important that negative experiences be made visible I draw on them here.

Bleeding The medical literature recognises that bleeding 'disturbances' are the most common side effect of Depo. What is unacknowledged is how disabling these 'disturbances' can be.

Ruth: Within 24 hours of the injection I started bleeding. I flooded for 14 weeks. In that time I lost 3 stone (42 lbs). I couldn't go out. Sometimes I could only crawl around.

Upjohn does now admit that 1–2 per cent of women will have heavy bleeding on Depo. Bleeding is difficult to quantify. It has therefore been consistently minimised. Few studies investigate it. One study which does do so speaks of bleeding 'episodes' of eleven–thirty days a month (Nash, 1975; Toppozada, 1978). But how heavy, for how many months? Bleeding is perceived as a problem because it is the main reason of 'discontinuance'. The significance of side effects are measured by the effect on 'acceptance ratios'. This orientation is reflected in a World Health Organization study which set out to test how 'legitimate' women's reasons were for discontinuing Depo. They found that stopping Depo was positively correlated with bleeding 'episodes' of eighty days or more (WHO, 1978)!

There is no recognition in the medical literature of the meaning to otherwise healthy women of these 'disturbances', or of the utter debility they can cause. One 'expert' said 'one woman a week was admitted to National Women's Hospital with uncontrollable bleeding from Depo Provera' (Taylor, 1980). The issue is not just how many incapacitated women this adds up to, but that it trivialises women's, sometimes devastating, experience.

Christine: Christine is a maths teacher. She is married to a senior lecturer (assistant professor) of accountancy. She was given Depo in the maternity hospital after the birth of her second child. She believed it was administered routinely to all her doctor's patients and did not feel she had a choice. It seemed to make all her post-natal symptoms worse. She felt debilitated by the following eighteen months spotting and bleeding which was accompanied by sharp stabbing pains in the uterus. But it was feeling afraid to go out of the house because she had to be near a toilet that contributed most to her depression. She was prescribed psycho-active drugs but the gynaecologist offered no treatment for the bleeding.

When we talk openly of women's experiences and what they mean we are said to be 'sensationalising' the issue. The fact that they are often accompanied by acute distress and depression is used to discredit the testimony. We are accused of 'frightening' women but their months of fear are ignored.

There seems to be a discrepancy between what women experience and the evidence in the medical literature. The New Zealand Contraception and Health Study provides an example of how this discrepancy can come about. The study devises useful measures of bleeding 'disturbances'. The 'exclusion criteria', however, exclude subjects who stop their method of contraception within ninety days (*Protocol*, 1982: 7). Ninety days is only relevant to Depo. It means that women who only have one shot will be dropped from the study. Although heavy bleeding sometimes occurs when the drug is withdrawn, usually the worst bleeding occurs immediately after the first shot. The most severe bleeding will therefore be excluded by the study and will not be measured at all.

Such knowledge is constructed to discount women's actual experience. 'Objective facts' like these are used to show how feminists exaggerate.

Science is projected as 'pure', that is, independent of the interests that produce it. The authority of science obscures the political process in the construction of scientific knowledge. The 'facts', however, directly reflect the structures that create them.

The process by which facts are validated is very important in defining what is 'known'. Only events recorded in medical literature are recognised, yet such documentation is quite haphazard. The experience of our group suggests significant underreporting of serious effects. Fraser's review of the medical literature found 'one case of anaphylactic shock has been reported' and 'There does not appear to be a single well substantiated case' of permanent infertility 'in the literature' (Fraser and Weisberg, 1981: 8). Our group knows of four women who have had life-threatening anaphylactic reactions. Two followed the first and two followed the second injection. The ninety-day 'exclusion criterion' will predictably result in under-representation of anaphylaxis in the New Zealand Contraception and Health Study, which will contribute to 'knowledge' about the rarity of such events.

Infertility Similarly, we know of four women, two of 'proven fertility' who, having been regular before, have not had a period since taking Depo.

Gail had previously had a child. 'I took Depo 8 years ago and my cycle has never returned to normal. I have never had a period since then unless I took the pill.' Gail was later able to conceive with the help of fertility drugs.

Jane had previously had a child. 'I had two shots of Depo 7 years ago. I have not had a period since.' Jane has recently had some treatment with fertility drugs. She hopes they will make her fertile again as she felt that being made infertile was one reason why her relationship broke up.

The absence of 'objective' evidence of permanent infertility is used to show that continuing concern about Depo is irrational. Four women may not be many, but for them being unusual is no comfort.

The long delay in the return of fertility can cause havoc in women's lives. It is hard to plan your life when you are waiting in limbo to conceive, or worrying that you may be either pregnant or sterile.

The manufacturers do admit that there is a lengthy delay in the return of fertility. Two studies are quoted which show that, two years after stopping Depo injections, conception rates are comparable to the pill and higher than the IUD (Pardthaisong, 1980; Gardner and Mischell, 1970). The medical literature shows that, eighteen months after discontinuance, 85 per cent of women are menstruating again (*Population Reports*, 1983). The 15 per cent who are not disappear from the literature. Reversibility is of vital concern to women, yet it is given little attention in the research. Women's needs do not determine scientific priorities.

Depression and permanent weight gain No attempt at all is made to gather information on some 'side effects', no matter how important they are to women. Medical research tends to equate 'real' with 'quantifiable'. 'Real' means you can add it up. Everything else is psychosomatic or subjective. Evidence that does not fit into the objective quantifiable mode, such as depression, cannot be measured and is readily dismissed. There is an assumption that only clearly physical effects can be caused by a drug. It is a short step to seeing the person who reports such 'unreal' effects as unreal or unstable too.

Many women have told us how depressed they seemed to become while taking Depo. Most women recognised that it was difficult to tell whether Depo was a 'cause' of their depressed mood, although some said that they had never felt depressed before taking it. Quite a few women had treatment for depression while taking Depo. Depo is frequently given to women who are experiencing difficulties. It is routinely given to many mental hospital patients. No one knows how much it may contribute to keeping them in this state. Women who are given Depo post-natally may have weight gain, sexual turn-off and depression anyway, but Depo isn't going to help the situation. These women may have to struggle harder to climb out of their condition. The medical literature shows that the average weight gain is 5–10 lbs (*Population Reports*, 1983: K-27). Quite a lot of women are, however, really distressed by very large weight gains which they find hard to reverse. The literature shows gains of up to 45 lbs in a year. For some women this was associated with a sense of helplessness that contributed to depression.

Sexual turn-off The effect of Depo about which most women complained to us was that of being sexually turned off. Depo is used in two American clinics to chemically castrate male sex-offenders (Barry and Ciccone, 1975), but it is used on millions of women without any consideration of its effects on their sex lives. In the medical literature on Depo, the only discussion of this as a problem I have found was from a Chilean doctor who said that they gave up using six-monthly injections of a double dose because 'it caused a rather marked regression of the internal genitals that was accompanied frequently by poor libido and lack of orgasm, a matter that meant some conflict with the husband' (Zanartu, 1978). What it meant for the women themselves is not considered. It simply isn't important that women experience sexual pleasure. Is contraception for women, but sex for men? Only sexist science sees the chemical castration of women as a technical advance.

Two women who shared their experiences with us said they thought Depo was a good contraceptive but also said that they lost interest in sex. Some women are so concerned about pregnancy that they find being turned off an acceptable price to pay for secure contraception. That some of us do not feel free not to have sex we do not enjoy is probably a comment on how closely sex is associated with our dependence on men, rather than our pleasure. It is a telling measure of our powerlessness in a sexist society.

I have been told repeatedly that being turned off cannot be investigated at all because it would rely on what women say. It would mean believing that women actually know whether they are turned on or not. Such a belief cannot be incorporated into science. 'Hard' science has 'objective' evidence that women do not know the difference between an orgasm and a shiny floor.

Who calls the shots?

Depo is not unique. It is one example of the creation of authoritative knowl-edge in our society (Spender, 1981: 1–9). Technological knowledge is both a function and a source of power. Women must insist upon becoming informed participants in public debate over technology. But it is hard. We have been told we are incapable of this type of understanding. Not only do we have to convince ourselves that we can crack the medical code but be confident enough to offer a basic criticism of the distortions of male-defined science (Elston, 1981; Overfield, 1981).

Committed to an empirical, value-free mode, medics find it hard to perceive the basic contamination of the 'objectivity' of their data by the processes and structures within which it is defined and constructed (Fee, 1982; Whitbeck, 1982). From the industry's point of view the health care system exists only to market its products. The integration of the medical profession and corporate enterprise is obvious in marketing but is actually cemented in the production of medical data itself.

Contraception is an example of the technology created by the structures of capitalist patriarchy. The 'knowledge' on which it is based reflects these interests. It is not 'value-free' but generated to serve the interests that create it. Many doctors pass on the fruits of this knowledge in good faith because they do not see their own place in the structure that perpetuates such 'truths'. They then find themselves unable to treat the problems it creates.

The overwhelming reason most women who spoke to us use Depo is that they cannot solve the contraception problem. Many had run the gauntlet of contraceptive methods. All the other methods demand that we face the conflict over and over again, every day. Here at last is a method that promises we will not have to face the problem for a few weeks. No wonder it sounds attractive. For some it worked, but for some it was a false promise. For most of those of us who need birth control there is no answer to the problem.

The technology is the end product of the system that produced it. That system has nothing at all to do with women's needs. No wonder our needs are not met by it. Depo-Provera gives the illusion that women can control their reproductive destiny. Our need for that control is exploited. Our desire for that control is used against us. We are made to pay an enormous price for our reproductive 'power'.

Sociology

Sociologists study societies and social phenomena, making it one of the broadest fields in the academy. It was also one of the first that felt the impact of second wave feminism. In the first piece, Joan Acker casts doubt on the inroads feminists have made in the field and argues that power relations help to explain resistance to their participation. She contends that sociological theory both explains and tends to perpetuate power relations. Acker questions whether a paradigm shift in the field might require a shift in actual power relations. Next, Robin L. Jarrett explores the strategies employed by poor women to adapt to their economic circumstances. She uses interviews with unmarried African-American mothers as her data, through which she makes more general claims about discrimination, structural explanations for poverty, and individual resilience. Finally, Judith Lorber's piece offers an example of how gender itself has become a topic for sociological study. She asserts that gender is a social institution and one of the major ways that human beings organize their lives. Her feminist analysis encourages us to reevaluate many aspects of our lives and values that might have seemed natural or unproblematic.

Critical Thinking Questions

1. Should sociology (or any other discipline) be expected to produce "knowledge *for* rather than *of* women" as suggested by Acker?
2. Compare the obstacles to a feminist transformation of sociology to other disciplines we have encountered. Why does Acker assert that sociology might be particularly resistant?
3. What does Jarrett learn about poor women through qualitative ethnographic research that is not revealed through quantitative research? How does her research support the structural perspective on poverty and family life?
4. What coping strategies do single, poor women employ to deal with their circumstances? Did the interviews help you to better understand the choices made by women generally labeled as part of the "underclass"?
5. How has Lorber's piece made you aware of ways you "do gender" in your daily lives? Does her argument undermine your perception of your autonomy or individuality?
6. Lorber offers eight components of gender as a social institution. Rank these components in terms of their significance or influence in your own lives and in society at large.

19

Making Gender Visible

(1989)

Joan Acker

In "The Missing Feminist Revolution in Sociology," Judith Stacey and Barrie Thorne (1985) argue that feminist theory has made little impact on the core theoretical perspectives in sociology. On the contrary, they contend, feminist thought has been co-opted and ghettoized within sociology, and the paradigm shift that feminist scholars predicted in the early 1970s has not occurred. I believe that the general situation they describe continues— a vast accumulation of new empirical and theoretical work about women existing in relative isolation from a world of sociological theory that continues in a prefeminist mode.

This new research has revealed many anomalies, findings that cannot be accounted for in the old theoretical frameworks, that according to Kuhn (1964), are precursors to fundamental change. Perhaps a paradigm shift is in process but simply has not yet been fully achieved. In any case, producing sociological theory that incorporates the understanding that social life is deeply

gendered has been far more difficult than we thought a number of years ago, and the new understandings that we have developed neither have been integrated into, nor have they transformed, the old, "general" theories of society. Thus Stacey and Thorne's question about why this has occurred is still an important one.

In this chapter, I hope to contribute to the discussion initiated by Stacey and Thorne. First, I examine the concept of paradigm, asking what must change, and how, if we are to claim such a shift. Second, I develop the explanations offered by Stacey and Thorne, taking up some sociological dimensions of the question that they noted but did not elaborate. I suggest that an additional reason dominant sociological paradigms have not been transformed lies in their success, which is rooted in their relationship to the structuring of power. Further, I argue, again extending Stacey and Thorne's critique, that the feminist alternative has not yet been sufficiently well developed to

Acker, Joan, "Making Gender Visible." In *Feminism and Sociological Theory,* ed. Ruth Wallace. Sage Publications, 1989. Reprinted by permission of Sage Publications, Inc.

present a clear challenge to the dominant paradigms because of the way that gender is already incorporated within their fundamental terms. However, at the same time, the outlines of such an alternative are emerging within feminist sociology, particularly in the work of Dorothy Smith (1987a, 1987b), and, in certain areas of empirical and theoretical work outside the main domain of feminist sociology, one can also see the emerging impact of feminist thought. Finally, I question whether the acceptance of a new paradigm, the achievement of a paradigm shift, is possible within the present structure of social relations.

WHAT IS A PARADIGM AND WHAT SHALL WE CHANGE?

A paradigm consists of the "orienting assumptions and conceptual frameworks which are basic to a discipline" (Stacey and Thorne 1985, p. 302). Although Stacey and Thorne, noting that Kuhn uses the word *paradigm* in many different ways, only implicitly elaborate this definition, the word has additional meanings that can help us to identify more precisely in what ways a paradigm shift has not occurred. I want to emphasize two of these: First, a paradigm includes the central questions of a discipline and the concepts used to pose, think about, and answer those questions. Second, a paradigm can also be defined as the model for the critical investigation or experiment that illustrates to students and others how to do "science." This notion of paradigm implies assumptions about methodology and epistemology, even if these are not always clearly formulated and

articulated in the models. As Stacey and Thorne observe, although sociology today is a confusion of competing paradigms, a paradigm in this second meaning still has a predominant place in American sociology in the positivist model of the natural science investigation that produces quantifiable data organized as variables manipulated to test hypotheses. This dominant methodological paradigm cuts across different paradigms in the other sense, adapted to competing conceptual frameworks as different as Marxism and structural-functionalism. Alternative interpretive methodologies, developed by feminist theorists using—but going beyond—existing male-defined critical approaches (Stanley and Wise, 1984) have also been melded to a variety of conceptual frameworks. When feminist sociologists discuss a paradigm shift, I take it that they are talking about paradigms in, at least, these two meanings, both of which include competing and contradictory forms (see also Saarinen 1988).

A new paradigm would mean, then, a new methodological-epistemological approach and a new or altered conceptual framework depicting the empirical world. A new conceptual paradigm would encompass, probably redefine, at least some of the questions dealt with in the old paradigm; it would provide more adequate accounts of the phenomena covered by the old paradigm as well as including ways of understanding issues that were not dealt with in the old mode of thought. Thus, as Stacey and Thorne recognize (1985, p. 311), a gendered paradigm would provide a better understanding than we now have of, for example, class structure, the state, social revolution, and militarism, as well as a better understanding of the sex segregation of labor, male dominance in the family, and sexual violence. A new feminist paradigm would place women and their lives, and gender, in a central place in understanding social relations as a whole. Such paradigm would not only pose new questions about women and gender but also help to create a more complex and adequate account of industrial, capitalist society. A feminist paradigm would also contain a methodology that produces knowledge *for* rather than *of* women in their many varieties and situations (see, e.g., Harding 1987).

The task of creating both a new methodological paradigm and a new substantive conceptual framework and, at the same time, working out what one implies for the other, is huge in a field that aspires to include everything about human social life. Perhaps we should be amazed at the progress that feminist sociologists have made rather than distressed at how far we have to go. However, the size and complexity of the undertaking is not the only problem. There are more serious difficulties that at least partly account for the failure to achieve a paradigm shift.

WHY HAS THERE BEEN NO PARADIGM SHIFT?

Stacey and Thorne (1985, p. 306) discuss several reasons for the lack of a feminist transformation of sociology, including the "limiting assumptions of functionalist conceptualizations of gender, the inclusion of gender as a variable rather than as a central theoretical concept, and the ghettoization of feminist insights, especially within Marxist sociology." Additional

reasons, they also note, have to do with the dominance of positivism in sociology, the social organization of the discipline, and the underdevelopment of feminist theory. The strength of positivism in sociology has been, I agree, one of the factors inhibiting a feminist transformation. However, this strength needs explaining, as does the resistance to feminist insights that we find in substantive conceptual paradigms. I will look at these problems by further examining the social organization of the discipline, particularly its relation to the structuring of power in the society, and look again at the problem of developing an adequate alternative feminist theory.

Power and the Organization of the Discipline

Sociology, like political science and economics, has an underlying resistance, deeply embedded in the organization of the discipline, to acceptance of the feminist critique and possible new feminist frameworks. This resistance is also related to problems of constructing new feminist paradigms.

An academic discipline is an organized set of activities that define a discourse and who may participate in the discourse. We may look at sociology both as ongoing activities that maintain a variety of organizations and produce a discourse, and as the discourse itself. These two ways of viewing sociology reveal different facets of power.

Sociology as a discourse, produced within organizational processes that define and redefine its content and arguments (here I draw on the work of

Smith—1979, 1987a, 1987b), has, in common with other academic fields, a particular connection to power in society as a whole or to the relations of ruling; the almost exclusively male domain of academic thought is associated with abstract, intellectual, textually mediated processes through which organizing, managing, and governing are carried out (see also MacKinnon 1982). These processes constitute a particular location in our societies and it is from the perspective of that location that objective, rational, scientific sociology looks out upon society and defines its contours and what is significant about it. As Smith (1979, 1987a, 1987b) argues, the concepts and definitions of the problematic in sociology have their origins in the issues of interest to those involved in the business of organizing and ruling the dominant socioeconomic structures. Thus the standpoint of the knowledge creator is not outside the social relations she studies, not objective, but deeply embedded within them. The argument that the standpoint of the sociologist or any other knowledge worker is not objective in the sense of being value free is well known (for a discussion of several feminist versions of the argument, see Harding 1987), but we less often explicitly talk about another obvious fact: The perspectives that develop their concepts and problematics from within what is relevant to the relations of ruling are successful. Their success continues, even though disputed by those such as feminists who stand outside the limits of that domain and see very well that they are wrong, or at least incomplete, in their claims. This success of the dominant paradigms—and I include here the versions of Marxism that exclude the embodied and gendered human being and have adopted the natural science model of research—is one of the reasons that there has been no paradigm shift.

These paradigms are successful to the extent that they make sense of a world in which what is relevant has been decided from the perspective of the processes of ruling. Social science, in attempting to describe and explain the world as it is, often adopts the taken-for-granted categories of ruling and thus makes sense of the world as seen from the perspective of the location of the creation of those categories. For example, the idea of position or "empty slot" used in some theories of class is almost identical to—one might think adopted from—managerial categories that are used in organizing and controlling work organizations (Acker 1987; Smith 1987b). Even oppositional and critical theories, such as Marxism, often work within the boundaries of the problematic as defined in the institutions that structure the broad relations of power. For example, the Marxist definition of the sphere of the economic covers much the same territory as that covered by neoclassical economic theory (Thompson 1978).

The discourses, spoken and written, of the processes of ruling help to organize and shape the world they describe. That is what they are intended to do. Sociological frameworks not only use the concepts of that sphere but also often provide conceptualizations of the way the world works for managers and administrators, politicians, reformers, and political movements. This is another reason that the established paradigms have some success: They participate in the creation and recreation of the very structures they are meant to study. As Giddens (1987) argues, ideas about how societies work have a reflexive relationship with the social processes they seek to describe and explain. Sociological ideas are taken up by and inform the practice of those formulating social policy or those seeking to manage more effectively. I am not arguing that policies work, that management is effective, or that reform efforts are successful, but that, for example, policies get formulated, to some degree, in the terms invented by social science, which then is able to discover the same phenomena. Social science does not create fiction, it creates concepts anchored in the organization and problems of ruling.

For example, the recently popular concept of an underclass, which includes mothers on welfare, addicts, homeless mentally ill, and others with extreme problems of survival, groups together people defined as troublesome who might be dealt with through similar administrative means. The idea of an underclass makes some sense from the perspective of ruling, although it may make little sense from the perspective of, for example, welfare mothers. What is problematic to them is probably not what is problematic to the authorities. How women receiving public aid experience and think about their situations is probably quite distinct from the experiences of addicts, nor are all welfare mothers alike. Although this is not a a new argument, it points to the ways that old paradigms are successful: They do provide concepts to understand, locate, and organize aspects of ongoing societal processes that are problematic from a certain standpoint, that of the relations of ruling.

Sociological concepts may also give form to the experiences of ordinary people within bureaucratized, institutionally differentiated and complicated societies, organized and coordinated through abstract textually mediated means. I think that this helps to explain the continuing pervasive use of the concept of role. As Stacey and Thorne (1985, p. 307) point out, "Early on, contemporary feminists recognized the influence and limitations of functionalism as a framework for understanding gender." But, as they also say, "Much of feminist sociology is cast in the language of roles" with all its attendant functionalist assumptions. The language of roles is well adapted to the processes of ruling in which people, in multiple ways, are instructed, cajoled, and coerced into proper performance according to the demands of various organizations and institutions. Although an individual's experience is, feminists have argued, seamless, she is approached as a mother by the schools, as a debtor by the credit company, and as a female worker by the boss. The concept of role may help to make sense out of this reality, even while helping to perpetuate that reality by defining its personal consequences as a depoliticized role conflict or a psychological problem rather than, for example, the consequences of unequal power. In sum, I suggest that to understand better the persisting liveliness, even in the work of feminist researchers, of concepts that have been widely criticized as either androcentric or as inadequate for the development of feminist theory, we need to recognize their contradictory character. Many concepts both reflect recognizable reality and, at the same time, mystify the underlying relations, which include the complex connections between the discourse and the organization of power.

Existing paradigms are also supported by the system of universities, departments, associations, journals, and funding agencies—almost all still dominated by men at the top—that organize the power to allot money, job security, and status. To be a sociologist meant and still means to learn and to use the skills of survival within this complex (Smith 1979), which includes learning how to think within a discipline that had already excluded women and their concerns in the process of becoming a separate discipline.

Survival involves much more than learning the proper ways of thinking. This was illustrated to me in a recent conversation with another sociologist, a man, who told me about a colleague who had never learned "how to package a career." The colleague, who was quite competent, had failed to understand that "a career" demands publication in the right places and a deemphasis on teaching and community service. Because of the colleague's failure, others in the department had the unwelcome task of ending his appointment. A familiar story, it is also a cautionary tale understood in some form by all those who intend to survive. What we are about, at some level, is the packaging of careers, rather than the doing of intellectual work. A safe, easy, and quick way to package a career is by using old paradigms. Indeed, no other way may be visible, because to do sociology still means emersion in the established ways. The heavy prestige of the natural science model recommends it as the pattern to follow.

The fact that this model has been elaborated to specify how to proceed is important, for sociology is about concrete societies and people, and demands the collection and analysis of empirical data. One of the attractions of the natural science model is that one can get on with the work without having to think through its epistemological underpinnings—without, in other words, having to confront questions raised by the feminist critique of sociology. The result is perpetuation of an atheoretical sociology that Stacey and Thorne identify as one of the barriers to further feminist theoretical development. Much of the mass of new work on women and gender has been done within this implicit understanding of sociology. Thus women and gender have opened new topics around which to package careers and new avenues to survival, but with far less impressive theoretical results than we might wish.

The imperatives of survival in academia derive from the organization of power within the discipline that is integral to the maintenance of sociology as a "discipline" with boundaries that distinguish it from other disciplines. I think that we should not underestimate how much this organization of power acts as a barrier to the introduction of new ways of thinking. Sometimes men also feel such pressures, both subtle and direct, to get on with the career by doing "normal science." However, men are, I think, unlikely to propose changes as potentially radical as that of the feminist critique because they have not been excluded as part of the prior conditions upon which the discipline was erected. From their standpoint, the gendered nature of social relations is not so clearly problematic.

The success of the old paradigms—evident in both their congruence with the taken-for-granted ways that things are organized and their continuing power within the discipline as ongoing activity—is one of the reasons that feminist inroads have been so few. Why should sociologists abandon whatever version of sociology they are using if it seems to work, if it answers, or even only deals with, questions they and the discipline as an organization of resources and power define as the relevant ones?

The Underdevelopment of Feminist Theory

Although feminist social theory has developed rapidly, we have run into formidable problems that have prevented us, so far, from realizing the goal of theory that fully comprehends the gendered nature of social relations. We have not, as yet, been able to suggest new ways of looking at things that are obviously better than the old ways for comprehending a whole range of problems—from how organizations function to how capital accumulation processes alter class structure. We know a great deal more about how such things affect women, but are only beginning to know how gender is fundamentally involved in the processes.

We began, necessarily, looking for ways to conceptualize and explain female subordination. These efforts produced, in the main, new conceptual frameworks that were dual systems theories, innovative theorizing about women, male dominance, and patriarchy that still leave the old structural conceptualizations of the political-economic-social system essentially intact. Such theorizing goes part of the way, but is ultimately unsatisfactory because the very theories we have identified as part of the relations of male domination are unaltered, unaffected by the feminist insight that all social relations are gendered. This is, of course, a very summary assessment that skips over much complexity, but as a summary, I think it is still fair. In addition, we have had difficulties developing a methodology that deals satisfactorily with the criticisms we ourselves have made (Acker et al. 1983) and, with a few exceptions (Smith 1979, 1987; Esseveld 1988), proposals for a feminist methodology in sociology have not gone beyond proposals previously made by male critics of positivism.

The question is this: Why have we had this difficulty? The answer, I think, is at least partly that we have to use—start with—the successful. as I have argued, conceptual frameworks that exist. Even if we consciously attempt to start "in the work and practical reasoning of actual individuals," rather than in the received discourse, as Dorothy Smith (1987a, p. 165) suggests, we cannot avoid framing our interpretations in some conceptualization of the broader social context if we wish to go beyond description or beyond local experience to comprehend the constraints and possibilities that set the conditions for that experience.

The problem is, no doubt, different with different theoretical starting points; some of the existing perspectives are better, I believe, than others as a place to begin. Given a beginning in a Marxist framework concerned with understanding oppression, which seems to be most reasonable for a feminist theory, we have to talk about class, the state, capitalism, politics, even though we talk about them as gendered. There is no other way.

However, the ways of thinking at hand, which we want to transform but that still are where we start, appear to be gender neutral, but are deeply gendered. The discourse that excludes the female speaks from a male situation, but conceptualizes itself as gender neutral. Moreover, this is a discourse that shares a common conceptual ground with the rational, objective, organizing practices and principles of an increasingly abstract mode of managing and governing (Smith 1987a, 1987b). This gives the gender-neutral stance its authority, its appearance of accounting for and accurately reflecting reality.

Although we have realized, since the beginning of the contemporary feminist critique that the dominant theoretical voice is a masculine one, we are only now understanding how fundamental to central sociological conceptualizations is their gendered substructure, and how difficult this is to penetrate. It seems that, having assumed the masculine, but then framed conceptualizations of the human and of society in genderless terms, there is no easy way to bring the feminine or gender back into the framework in an explicit and conscious way. To talk about gender, too often meaning women, is to take the theorizing from the general to the specific, and this appears to undermine the theorizing about the abstract and the general. Consequently, talking about gender and women can be seen as trivializing serious theoretical questions, or it can be seen as beside the point. All of this rests upon obscuring of the gendered nature of fundamental concepts under the cloak of gender neutrality (Acker 1988).

Recent work of Carole Pateman (1983a, 1983b) on theories of democracy illustrates an attempt to deal with this problem. She analyzes the idea of the individual in liberal democratic theory and the importance of the disembodied abstract individual for the development of a general theory of liberal democracy. This individual must be disembodied, because if he were not it would be clear that he is a man and does not represent all humanity: thus there would be no general theory that applies to all people. Giving a body to the abstract individual also reveals that women cannot have the same standing in the theory of democracy as men because, as a human category, they do not have the same access to political participation and power as men. To argue that women should demand and seize the rights and responsibilities of the abstract individual is to argue that they should become like men, which ignores the fact that their lives are different from those of men and most women must be different until there is a fundamental change in the lives of men and the overall structure of our societies. This, of course, is the radical potential of liberal feminism (Eisenstein 1981). In the meantime, the abstract and disembodied individual is still present in a great deal of theorizing in the social sciences, not only in theories of liberal democracy.

Feminist efforts to develop a theory of gender and class provide another example of the difficulties in transforming concepts that contain a gendered substructure beneath an apparently gender-neutral surface. In spite of the long attention of numerous theorists, an adequate feminist theory of class has proved to be elusive (e.g., Acker 1980, 1988; Beechey 1987). Feminist thinkers now commonly recognize the importance of class and race as well as gender and argue that these are all interconnected (e.g., Lewis 1985). However, although many theorists now accept the need for one theory incorporating both gender and class, in practice we keep on talking about class and gender (and race) as separate (Cockburn 1986).

The unsolved problem for Marxist class theory is partly, as Stacey and Thorne (1985, p. 308) point out, that "the central Marxist categories which focus on production, labor, and class—as defined through men's relationship to production and labor—are . . . obviously androcentric." The development of a nonandrocentric concept of class may be so difficult because of the way that class has been conceptualized at a level of abstraction that erases the body and women and makes gender invisible. Contemporary U.S. academic neo-Marxists, for example, often use a structural notion of class that embeds it within an abstract mode of production, the domain of economic relations that constitutes the process of capital accumulation. The abstract worker in this domain is just as disembodied as the abstract individual of liberal theory, and just as fundamentally male. Theoretical treatment of capitalist processes remains indifferent to the gender-based organization of labor markets and to the unpaid work of women in spite of feminist efforts to insert this labor into the abstract theory. In this version of Marxist class theory, gender becomes visible only

with a move to a lower level of abstraction, from the mode of production to the social formation, where actual, concrete societies are the object of analysis. However, the labor of men is still privileged because only that labor, conceptualized as gender neutral, is theorized in the concepts that allow us to understand the system as a whole.

Feminists often implicitly ignore these theoretical twistings, perhaps wisely, and work with a general and somewhat vague notion of class, emphasizing processes and the linkages between employment and work in the home. However, this does not result in a new way of understanding the nature of class processes, which is what a feminist paradigm that could challenge the existing Marxist theories of class would do. The problem resides in the gendered substructure of the definition of the territory of the problematic, "the economy," seen from the perspective of the system of ruling (the male-defined and dominated ruling of capitalist societies). The solution must be to redefine the economic, to redefine the relations of class, not simply to add reproduction to production. However, this is difficult because the old frameworks, linked to the relations of ruling in various and complex ways, still "work," for feminists as well as others, even though, at the same time, they are inadequate. Thus the problems facing feminist sociological theorizing that starts from and uses a Marxist understanding lead back to the resistances of the old structural paradigm to feminist critique and to the contradictory nature of the old concepts—they *do* illuminate capitalist processes but cannot take into account their own gendered substructure. Their inadequacy becomes more and more evident as the contradictions of women's situations in contemporary societies become more evident and politically more problematic.

EMERGING ALTERNATIVES

The possibilities for a new feminist paradigm are better with some of the competing existing sociological frameworks than with others, as I have already argued. Structural functionalist assumptions, as Stacey and Thorne (1985, p. 307) also argue, "have posed significant obstacles to feminist rethinking of basic orienting assumptions within sociology." Feminist theory, which is about transformation and liberation, must start elsewhere, I believe, in ways of thinking that pose change and the elimination of oppression as central questions. Marxist theory, with all the problems and more noted above, is still an obvious place to start.

A number of developments in feminist-socialist-Marxist thinking provide some grounds for optimism. One promising direction is the discussion of a feminist standpoint, or taking the perspective of women, particularly the work of Dorothy Smith (1979, 1987a, 1987b). Smith proposes investigating the relations of ruling from the standpoint of women concretely located in a variety of places within societal structures. She avoids, I think, some of the problems of other "standpoint theories" (Harding 1986), which move either to a relativistic position or to an inter- and intrapsychic—often Freudian—analysis. Smith's approach remains anchored in the lives of actual—rather than textually created—people and focused on the processes and relations outside their immediate daily lives that help to create the conditions for those lives. She is also able to include the actions of women, and men, as they deal with and sometimes oppose the relations of ruling. Thus she is proposing a method to understand the relations of ruling from the perspective of women who themselves define the problematic, rather than from the perspective of the problematics of those who manage and organize those relations.

The assumption that all social relations are gendered is another relatively new development that promises to contribute significantly to a new paradigm. This assumption, only recently made explicit in much work (see, for example, Smith 1987; Flax 1987), changes the nature of the debate from an exclusive focus on women to a focus on how gender shapes and is implicated in all kinds of social phenomena (see also Scott 1986). I think that we are only at the beginning of working out what we mean, in concrete terms, when we say that social relations and processes are gendered. The reshaping of the meaning of gender is under way in all disciplines, but it could have a particularly profound effect in sociology in helping us move toward a more penetrating critique of our concepts and frameworks than we have yet had.

The development of the concept of reproduction as the hidden substructure upon which production relations depend—not in the rather narrow terms of a political economy of domestic labor or a theory of the reproduction of labor power, or even of nurturing and caring activities, but as the organization of activities and relations that make possible human survival—is also a promising direction.

Studies of Third World societies and developing areas make visible how daily life and reproduction are shattered and sometimes reconstituted by capitalist transformation, moving reproduction to the center of the analysis (for example, Redclift and Mingione 1985). At the other end of affluence, feminist analyses of the welfare state focus on reproduction, increasingly seeing contradictions around reproduction as indications of a deep crisis in capitalism (see, for example, Sassoon 1987). Even a non-feminist male Marxist such as Therborn (1986) recognizes that the welfare state has to do with reproduction, although he fails to make the obvious links to gender and the subordination of women.

CONCLUSION: IS A PARADIGM SHIFT POSSIBLE?

A paradigm shift means not only the transformation of existing conceptual frameworks, but also the acceptance of the new framework in the field (Stacey and Thorne 1985, p. 302). Historically, as Kuhn (1964) observed, a shift does not come about simply because the new perspective is more persuasive and provides "better" knowledge than the old one, but also as a result of a struggle for organizational power and intellectual dominance. Moreover, previous paradigm shifts have always occurred within societal structures dominated by men. This suggests a problem for feminists and their theories. If a paradigm shift can only occur with a shift in power, and if that means taking power in institutions that are already structured within the historical context of gendered relations of domination, what are the chances for the survival of critical feminist theories? Can a shift occur at all, at the fundamental level about which we have been talking, within some reasonable short run? Or is a paradigm shift part of the process of transforming those relations of domination, probably a very long-run project? What will new theory look like? Will it be a *new grand theory* with the totalizing aims that term implies? How do we put together the myriad standpoints of women? Must that lead us to the end of theory and out of the mode of thinking that posits competing paradigms, as some feminists suggest? That is, do we expect too much, or the wrong thing, when we search for a paradigm shift as an accomplished transformation?

20

Living Poor

Family Life among Single Parent, African-American Women

(1994)

Robin L. Jarrett

INTRODUCTION: "BUT WHERE ARE THE PEOPLE?"

In the years since the media's rediscovery of race and poverty in America's inner cities, much has been written about . . . low-income housing projects. . . . [They] have become must-stops for anyone writing about the nation's so-called "underclass." Yet for all the ink and air time devoted to them, it is amazing how little we still know about the people who live there . . . . [R]arely do we get to know the people of the projects as anything other than sociological types . . . one-dimensional portraits of third- or fourth-generation welfare mothers, violence-prone, drug-dealing gang members or street smart man-children living by their wits. Seldom do writers dare to look beyond the sociology and statistics . . . to see people as individuals rather than as examples of predrawn stereotypes (Monroe 1991:1).

Recent increases in the number of households headed by poor African-American women, the result of non-marital, adolescent childbearing, have encouraged researchers to once again debate the relationship between family structure, race, and poverty. Like past discussions, both structural and cultural arguments have been advanced to explain changing household and family formation patterns. Recent quantitative studies (see Baca Zinn 1990b; Marks 1991; Patterson 1981 for an overview), as well as past ethnographic research (see Jarrett in press for an overview), offer support for the structural argument, challenging the cultural position. These data indicate that economic forces are closely correlated with female headship and non-marital child-bearing among poor African-American women. The structural perspective correctly documents the link between economic forces and family patterns. But it obscures many of the processes associated with living in poverty.

This paper expands on the structural explanation by describing the ways that African-American women live in poverty, dynamically adapting to larger economic forces. I use qualitative interview data to explore the following question: How do poor African-American women, in their daily lives, respond to conditions of economic marginality?

This paper is divided into four sections. Section One provides an overview of the current issues regarding family life and poverty among African Americans. Substantive themes and explanatory frameworks derived from the "underclass debate" are critically discussed and compared to earlier discussions of poverty in the United States. Section Two describes the qualitative group interviews that were conducted with a sample of never-married, African-American mothers. These data are used to examine issues raised in Section One, concentrating on unmarried women because they figure so prominently in the underclass debate. Section Three presents empirical findings from the focus group interviews. Verbatim excerpts from these discussions are used to examine key components of the structural argument. Observations from the focus group study are also compared with earlier ethnographic and qualitative research to explore continuity in family patterns. Finally, Section Four explores the broader theoretical implications of the research. The discussion addresses how the focus group data elaborate on the structural explanation and offer direction for future research.

FAMILY STRUCTURE, RACE, AND POVERTY: "FEMALE HOUSEHOLDER, NO HUSBAND PRESENT"

At the heart of the deterioration of the fabric of Negro society is the deterioration of the Negro family. It is the fundamental source of the weakness of the Negro community . . . . In essence, the Negro community has been forced into a matriarchal structure which, because it is so out of line with the rest of the American society, seriously retards the progress of the group as a whole (Moynihan 1965:5, 29).

How could it be that, despite the combination of economic growth and huge increases in expenditures on the poor, the number of poor stopped shrinking in the early 1970s? . . . We have encountered a variety of explanations . . . . Now we have an additional explanation: the increasing prevalence of a certain type of family—a young mother with children and no husband present (Murray 1984:133).

Under the new rubric of the "underclass debate," researchers have returned to old questions of the relationship between family structure, race, and poverty (Katz 1989; Piven et al. 1987; Wilson and Aponte 1985). Little consensus exists in its key dimensions—such as size, origins, defining characteristics—or if, in fact, such a group exists. Most researchers, however, use the term "underclass" to convey a group of minority poor who represent a persistent and more dangerous form of poverty (see Auletta 1982; Glasgow 1980; Lemann 1986; Mead 1986; Murray 1984; Ricketts and Sawhill 1988).

Several distinct groups are hypothesized to comprise the underclass, such as criminals, hustlers in the underground economy, the chronically unemployed, and the long-term working poor, but households headed by women are cited as key contributors to its growth (Auletta 1982; Glasgow 1980; McLanahan, Garfinkel, and Watson 1988; Ricketts and Sawhill 1988; Wilson 1987). For example, demographic data indicate that the proportion of poor African-American families headed by women increased from 30 percent in 1959 to 72 percent in 1977—more than doubling in one generation. Since then it has remained slightly above 70 percent. Female heads of household comprised, respectively, one-third of the poor in 1982 and 71 percent of all poor African-American families (Wilson, 1987).

Two conceptual frameworks, the cultural and the structural, provide competing arguments to explain changes in family patterns. The cultural explanation maintains that changing household and family formation patterns among low-income African Americans are the result of deviant values. Researchers cite various factors generating distinctive values, but cultural formulations that stress the role of liberal welfare reforms in exacerbating deviant values have been particularly influential (Mead 1986; Murray 1984). The basic argument is that ghetto-specific norms differ from their mainstream counterparts, positively endorsing single motherhood, out-of-wedlock childbearing, welfare dependency, male irresponsibility, criminal behavior, low mobility aspirations, and, more generally, family instability (Auletta 1982; Lemann 1986; Mead 1986; Murray 1984; see also Cook and Curtin 1987 for an overview).

The structural explanation argues that demographic shifts in household and family formation patterns reflect larger economic trends. Researchers cite macro-structural changes in the economy—including the decline in entry-level jobs, the relocation of jobs away from the inner-city, and the mismatch between job requirements and employee skills—and parallel declines in rates of male employment, marriage, and child-bearing within marriage as evidence of external or situational pressures on family life. The fundamental thesis is that economic factors impede the construction and maintenance of mainstream family patterns: they encourage poor African-American women to forego marriage, bear children out-of-wedlock, head their own households, and rely on welfare income (Darity and Meyers 1984; Joe 1984; Staples 1985; Testa et al. 1989; Wilson 1987).

Current discussions about poverty and the underclass are similar in two ways to the poverty discussions that took place from the early 1960s to the mid-1970s when such issues were last seriously discussed. Then, as now, both structural and cultural arguments were the dominant explanatory frameworks as researchers debated the competing role of economic and cultural factors. Furthermore, recent and past studies concentrate on family structure or, more precisely, household structure. During both periods, structural and cultural perspectives focused on the idea that particular family arrangements—either as a consequence or as a cause—were associated with poverty status (Lemann 1986; Lewis 1965, 1966; Mead 1986; Moynihan 1965; Murray 1984; Garfinkel and McLanahan 1986; Wilson 1987).

Current discussions about poverty differ, however, from earlier discussions, in three key ways: in the analytic focus of research studies; in the disciplines of theorists who propose explanatory frameworks; and in the types of evidence used to support conceptual claims. First, current poverty studies are primarily concerned with female headship and a variety of demographic correlates, particularly welfare (Bane and Ellwood 1984a, 1984b; Ellwood and Bane 1984; Garfinkel and McLanahan 1986; Murray 1984; Nichols-Casebolt 1988; see also Baca Zinn 1989, 1990b; Piven et al. 1987; and Wilson and Aponte 1985 for an overview). By contrast, research from the 1960s and 1970s was principally interested in how poor families coped and adapted to poverty (Aschenbrenner 1975; Hannerz 1969; Jeffers 1967; Lewis 1965, 1966; Rainwater 1970; Schulz 1969; Stack 1974).

Second, current conceptualizations of the cultural perspective derive largely from journalists (Auletta 1982; Lemann 1986; see also Marks 1991; Williams 1992a). By contrast, in previous decades, cultural formulations emanated from anthropologists and sociologists (Gans 1969; Hannerz 1969; Leacock 1971; Lewis 1965, 1966; Rainwater 1970; Stack 1974; Valentine 1968; see also Rainwater 1987 for an overview). During both periods, discussions of the structural position have come primarily from social scientists. Third, current poverty studies use demographic analyses to substantiate or challenge particular theoretical claims (Baca Zinn 1989; Williams 1992a). By contrast, during the 1960s and 1970s both ethnographic research (see Hannerz 1975; Jarrett in press; and Rainwater 1987 for an overview) and demographic analyses were used to assess the cultural and structural arguments (Wilson and Aponte 1985; Katz 1989).

Yet, both recent and past poverty research are similar in that they both rely on cultural and structural frameworks as the dominant explanations. They also demonstrate a continued concern with family structure as a key causal or explanatory variable. As a consequence of their differences, poverty researchers today know more about the demographic profiles of poor African-American families than about their internal dynamics; they more frequently respond to journalistic conceptualizations of cultural processes than those of anthropologists and sociologists; and they possess a wealth of quantitative data and a dearth of qualitative and ethnographic research to explore the issue of family life and poverty.

The evidence marshalled by myriad studies favors the structural argument and challenges the cultural argument. Reviews of longitudinal panel data that focus on the link between welfare and marital status, reproductive behavior, and living arrangements indicate that welfare has little or no effect on these behaviors (see Baca Zinn 1989; Ellwood and Bane 1984; Garfinkel and McLanahan 1986; Marks 1991; Patterson 1981). Nor do these data provide evidence for the intergenerational transfer of poverty and welfare dependence as a result of normative orientations (Baca Zinn 1989; Corcoran et al. 1985; McLanahan, Garfinkel, and Watson 1988; Wilson and Aponte 1985). Other quantitative studies demonstrate a strong relationship between male unemployment, female headship, and out-of-wedlock childbearing (Darity and Meyers 1984; Joe 1984; Staples 1985; Testa et al. 1989; Wilson 1987).

Ethnographic research, though largely untapped in the current debate, can contribute to the current discussion of poverty in several ways. First, it can add further support to the structural argument, as it can serve to describe in detail how economic factors impinge on family life and the ways that the poor respond to these conditions. These data also reveal that the poor share conventional aspirations concerning family life, rather than exhibit a deviant set of values (Anderson 1976; Jeffers 1967; Ladner 1971; Liebow 1967; Stack 1974; Valentine 1978; see also Jarrett in press). Furthermore, qualitative data are the most appropriate type to assess cultural arguments (Rainwater 1987) and to critique improper conceptualizations of cultural processes as formulated in the culture of poverty framework (Gans 1969; Leacock 1971; Lewis 1965, 1966; Rainwater 1970, 1987; Valentine 1968; see also Swidler 1986).

The structural perspective challenges the culture of poverty argument and documents the association between economic factors and family patterns. Nevertheless, it is flawed in two critical ways. First, it assumes the superiority of the two-parent household (Cerullo and Erlien 1986). The structural perspective uses an idealized, if not mythic, model of the nuclear family to assess poor African-American families (Reed 1988). Consequently, it fails to acknowledge the diversity of family forms as well as their viability among the poor and non-poor alike (Baca Zinn and Eitzen 1992; Thorne and Yalom 1982; Williams 1992b; see also Baca Zinn 1990a). Second, the structural perspective takes an economic deterministic position and ignores the role of human agency. It posits a direct and unmediated relationship between economic factors and family patterns. Moen's and Wethington's (1992:243) general critique of structural models is applicable: the inordinate concentration on external factors encourages the overgeneralized view that families are "at the mercy of forces beyond their control, their responses constrained to the point of total conformity to structural forces." Consequently, we know little about how poor women actually respond to conditions of economic marginality.

Despite its conceptual limitations, the structural perspective has received consistent empirical support. This suggests that the continued rejuvenation of the cultural perspective reflects larger racial divisions within U.S. society, rather than actual findings from academic research (Gresham 1989; Wilkerson and Gresham 1989). Historically, poverty research has been permeated by political controversies based on speculation and stereotyping, rather than sound theories and methods (Davis and Davis 1989; Rainwater and Yancey 1967; Suttles 1976). These observations highlight the need to move beyond stagnant debates that center on improperly conceptualized cultural models (Gans 1969; Leacock 1971; Rainwater 1987; Swidler 1986) as well as on deterministic and overgeneralized structural models.

SAMPLE AND METHODOLOGY: "RESEARCH TOUCHED BY HUMAN HANDS"

Qualitative methods ... as they get close to the subjects of their research ... necessarily reflect social reality from the bottom upwards (Finch 1986:113).

The data reported in this paper derive from a series of focus group interviews (see Jarrett 1993 for a detailed methodological discussion). The interviews were broadly conceived as an exploratory examination of how women in poor families adapt to conditions of poverty. I concentrated on various aspects of family life, including family formation patterns, household living arrangements, childcare and socialization patterns, intergenerational relations, male-female relations, and welfare, work, and social opportunities.

Ten focus groups, comprised of a total of 82 low-income African-American women, were conducted between January and July 1988. Each focus group session lasted approximately two hours and was held with groups of no more than 8–10 women. The tape recorded discussions were relatively unstructured but topically oriented, allowing for comparisons across groups. The ten focus group interviews conducted represent a larger than average number for such research projects and fell within the upper range for serious research (see Calder 1977; Hedges 1985).

The criteria for selection of the women was based on the profiles of women discussed in the current underclass debate. They included: (1) never-married mothers, (2) who received AFDC, and (3) lived in high poverty or economically transitional neighborhoods in the city of Chicago. Most of the women were in their early to middle twenties and began their childbearing careers as adolescents. A purposive sample was drawn from Chicago-area Head Start programs since such programs are located in low-income communities and serve women fitting the above profile.

A team of research assistants transcribed and coded the interviews thematically by topical area. The initial codes were based on the broad topical areas guiding the research but were expanded to include unanticipated information that emerged in the discussion. Once this task was completed, key issues and themes were identified for each area.

THE EMPIRICAL DATA: "IN THEIR OWN WORDS"

[T]he actor's 'own story,' is a live and vibrant message from 'down there,' telling us what it means to be a kind of person we have never met face to face (Becker 1970:70).

In this section, I present empirical data that offer insights on the lives of real women and that address the limitations of the structural framework. As a point of departure, I examine the normative and behavioral dimensions of familial roles among the sample of never-married, African-American mothers. The concentration on the conflict between norms and behaviors provides a dynamic example of how women who hold conventional aspirations concerning family patterns respond in their daily lives. Around this broad topic, I explore four issues: (1) Marriage, the ideal; (2) Marriage, the reality; (3) Economic impediments to conventional marriage; and (4) Alternatives to conventional marriage.

Marriage, the Ideal: "Everybody Wants to Be Married"

Women consistently professed adherence to mainstream patterns. For virtually all of the women interviewed, legal marriage was the cornerstone of conventional family life. Marriage represented a complex of behaviors, including independent household formation, economic independence, compatibility, and fidelity and commitment that were generally associated with the nuclear family. Representative excerpts from group members illustrate:

Independent Household Formation We were talking about marriage and all of that . . . . We was staying with his mother . . . . I told him we'll get married and we'll get our own place.

> He lives with his grandmother. I don't want to move into his grandmother's home. I live at my mother's. I don't want him to move in there. When we get married, I want us to live in our own house, something we can call ours.

Economic Independence He asked me [to get married] . . . . We never did. It's more like we waiting to get more financial.

> Charles, [my boyfriend] be half-stepping [financially]. That's why I'm not really ready for marriage.
>
> I plan on getting married. But I would rather wait. He said he wanted to wait until he made 22. He works two jobs, but he said he want to wait until he gets a better job, where he can support both of us.
>
> He's always nagging me to get married. I ask him: 'Are you going to be able to take me off aid and take care of all four of my children?' So when I say that he just laugh.

Compatibility I think a person should never get married unless it's for love. . . . [If] you want to spend the rest of your life with that person, you all [should] have a good understanding. If you marry somebody just because you pregnant, just because you have four or five kids by them, or because society or whoever pressured you into it, you goin' to become mean and resentful. And if that person turns out to not be what you thought or that marriage turns out to be something less than you hoped it would be, it's not goin' to be worth it.

> I'm not married to him so I can do what I want to do. But when I get married, I can't do it at all. But it's not supposed to be like that. He says: 'I pay all the bills.' But you don't get to boss me.
>
> I don't want to marry him 'cause me and him would never get along; but I like him.
>
> You know, I like him a whole lot. But then [my mother] say: 'Well then why you don't a marry him?' [It's] because . . . somehow our waves just won't click.
>
> A lotta' time you can't get along with the children's father. . . . Me and Carmen's father could not get along, point blank. [I]t wasn't the money. It's not 'cause I didn't have a father; he had a father. We came from good homes. We just could not get along. We don't even know how we made the baby. [laughter]

Fidelity and Commitment If I get married, I believe in being all the way faithful.

> I want you to take care of me. I'm not looking to jump into bed and call this a marriage. I want you to love me, care for me, be there when I need you because I'm going to be there for you when you need me.
>
> As soon as [men] get married and things change and he's looking for somebody else. Man! Why didn't they find that person before they marry you

and you start going through all those changes.

Nita, a mother of two children provided one of the most eloquent statements on the meaning of marriage. She said:

> I would love to be married. . . . I believe I would make a lovely wife. . . . I would just love to have the experience of being there married with a man. I imagine me and my children, my son basketball player . . . playing for the [Chicago] Bulls. My daughter . . . playing the piano, have a secretary job or going to college. . . . Me, I'm at home playing the wifely duties. This man, not a boy, coming home with his manly odors. . . . My husband comes home, takes off his work boots and have dinner. . . . I would like to have this before I leave this earth, a husband, my home, my car.

Likewise, Charmaine, who despite her own unmarried status, firmly asserted:

> I think everybody wants to get married. Everybody wants to have somebody to work with them . . . and go through life with. . . . I would like to be married. . . . I want to be married. I'm not gonna lie. I really do.

Women, despite their insistent statements concerning the importance of marriage as the cornerstone of mainstream family life, were well aware of the unconventionality of their actual behaviors. Women openly acknowledged that their single status, non-marital childbearing, and in some cases, female-headship, diverged from mainstream household and family formation patterns. Tisha said with a mixture of humor and puzzlement:

> Is this what it's supposed to be like? So, I'm going backwards. Most people say:

'Well, you go to school, you get married, and you have kids.' Well, I had my kids. I'm trying to go to school and maybe, somewhere along the line, I'm going to catch up with everybody else.

Natty, the mother of an active preschooler who periodically appeared at the door of the meeting room, further observed:

> I really would like to have two children but I'm not married . . . and I would like to be married before I do have another child. . . . So maybe one day we might jump the broom or tie the knot or whatever.

Sherry's comments were similar:

> I wanted to marry him because we had talked about it so long. . . . We always talked about it . . . gettin' married, then have our kids and stuff and everything.

Tisha's, Natty's, and Sherry's observations indicate that the desired sequence of events entails economic independence, then marriage, and, finally, childbearing.

Women's observations in this study are consistent with past ethnographic research (Aschenbrenner 1975; Clark 1983; Holloman and Lewis 1978; Ladner 1971; Stack 1974; see also Anderson 1976). Even in Lee Rainwater's (1970) study of the purportedly notorious Pruitt-Igoe housing project in St. Louis, impoverished residents routinely professed adherence to mainstream values concerning marriage and family. He observed:

> The conventionality and ordinariness of Pruitt-Igoeans' conception of good family life is striking. Neither in our questionnaires nor in open-ended interviews or observational contexts did we find any consistent elaboration of an unconventional ideal. In the working class, a good family life is seen to have at its core a stable marriage be-

tween two people who love and respect each other and who rear their children in an adequate home, preferably one that has its own yard. If only things went right, according to most Pruitt-Igoeans, their family life would not differ from that of most Americans (Rainwater 1970:48).

Marriage, the Reality: "That's a Little White Girl's Dream"

Women were pessimistic about actually contracting family roles as defined in the mainstream manner. Their aspirations for conventional family roles were tempered by doubt and, in some cases, outright pessimism.

Karen's comment reflected her sense of uncertainty:

I would like to get married one day . . . to somebody that's as ready as I am . . . But it's so scary out here. You scared to have a commitment with somebody, knowing he's not on the level. . . . They ready to get their life together; they looking for a future.

Denise and Chandra were most pessimistic about their chances for a conventional and stable family life:

I used to have this in my head, all my kids got the same daddy, get married have a house. That's a little white girl's dream. That stuff don't happen in real life. You don't get married and live happily ever after.

It doesn't work in that way. Just because you have a baby don't mean they gone stay with you. . . . Even if you married, that don't mean he gone stay with you; he could up and leave.

Even Dee Dee's initially firm assertions were laced with doubt:

I'm goin' to get married one day. I'm goin' to say I know I'm getting' married

one day, if it is just for a month. I'm gettin' married, I know that. [laughter] I know I am . . . well maybe.

Earlier in their lives most of these women assumed that their household and formation patterns would follow conventional paths. Remaining single, bearing children outside of marriage, and heading a household were not foregone conclusions. Rather, pessimism about the viability of mainstream patterns grew out of their first-hand experiences. Women related conflictual and depriving situations that caused them to reassess their expectations.

Andrea described her attempt to forge a long-term relationship and its disappointing outcome:

I would rather live by myself, me and my two kids, because I used to stay with somebody. . . . Me and him did not work out. We used to have to go scrape up some food to eat. I would rather stay by myself.

Both Pat and Lisa, recount similar tribulations:

It makes me angry to think about it. . . . I go through changes [with him] and . . . sometimes I just throw up my hands in the air—excuse the expression—I just say 'Fuck it! Had it! I'm tired! Sometime I say: 'Man disappear!'

[Men cause] a lot of headache and heartache. . . . All the time you taking to set that man straight, you could be spending with your child. . . . Instead of having time with your kids, you got to get him together.

Kara, like Pat and Lisa, expressed feelings of frustration:

You want to see [men] do something one way and they don't see it that way. They want to do it the way they want to do it. . . . You get mad. You frustrated. It's just emotionally draining.

Women's experiences were augmented by the experiences of others. Through the processes of observation of and comparison to older women in the community, younger women gauged their chances of contracting ideal family forms. Comments from Regina and Tennye, respectively, illustrated this:

> A good husband has a good job where I can stay home with the family, raise the kids like on TV. But then it's hard. You don't find too many, not like when our mothers was coming up.
>
> I don't think I'll ever find a husband because of the way I feel. I want it like my mother had it. [My father] took care of us. She been married to him since she was sixteen. He took care of her, took her out of her mother's house. She had four kids, he took care of all the kids.

These comments suggest that even as younger women compare themselves with older women, conventional patterns remain their reference point. Women's views also signal their awareness of declining opportunities for attaining mainstream family patterns within impoverished African-American communities.

Women's first-hand experiences indicate a more general point. Economic forces are not experienced in impersonal ways; nor are they experienced by solitary individuals, as implied by the structural perspective. Economic constraints are, instead, mediated through social relationships and interaction processes. Individuals ponder their situations with others in similar circumstances. As a result of his own ethnographic work, Hannerz (1969) critiqued the mechanistic components of the structural argument:

> [I]t is made to look as if every couple were left on its own to work out anew a solution to problems which have confronted many of both their predecessors and their contemporaries in the black community (Hannerz 1969:76).

His comment also suggests that the generational persistence and reaffirmation of particular strategies occur because the socioeconomic conditions that support them are still operant (cf. Franklin 1988). This point is aptly illuminated by Myesha and Pam, whose circumstances mirrored their mothers':

> My father wasn't around. But you know he tried. . . . He calls [me] now. Well, with my boyfriend, he [may] stay by my side. If he leaves, he just leave. . . . So, if my mama could do it, I know I can raise Daniel [my son].
>
> My mother had eight of us. I sympathize with what she go through because she doesn't get any help. But she raised us all by herself and we doing okay. It's a lot of women that don't need no man to help raise her kids because I know I can take care of mine by myself.

Economic Impediments to Marriage: "I Could Do Bad by Myself"

The women's own interpretations concerning changes in household and family formation patterns are consistent with the structural explanation of poverty. Economic factors, according to women, played a prominent role in their decisions to forego marriage, bear children outside of marriage, and, in some cases, head households.

Iesha described how economic factors influenced her decisions. She said:

> I had a chance to get married when I first had my two [children]. We had planned the date and everything, go

down to city hall. . . . When the day came along, I changed my mind. Right today I'm glad I did not marry him because he still ain't got no job. He still staying with his sister and look where I am. Ever since I done had a baby I been on my own. I haven't lived with no one but myself. I been paying bills now.

Renee, who was considering marriage to her current companion, also recounted how economic considerations influenced her decisions:

I could do bad by myself. . . . If we get married and he's working, then he lose his job. I'm going to stand by him and everything. I don't want to marry nobody that don't have nothing going for themselves. . . . I don't see no future. . . . I could do bad by myself.

Cheryl echoed her views:

As far as I'm concerned about marriage and kids, I want to be married; but I also want to be married to somebody who is responsible, who can give me somethin' out of life. . . . I would like that security.

Pat was even more direct in her preference for an economically stable mate:

If he's out of a job, he can't sit here too long. I can't do it alone. . . . I got to see a place where he's helping me. But if you don't help, I got no time.

Tina, who was currently uninvolved ("on my own"), further described the link between male economic marginality and marriage:

I wanted to get married when I first found out I was pregnant, but he didn't want to get married. And I'm glad that he didn't. . . . It would have been terrible; he wasn't working. Maybe that was one of the reasons why he did not want to get married.

Other qualitative and ethnographic studies also describe the depressing effect that economic pressures have on marriage among poor women and men (Aschenbrenner 1975; Liebow 1967; Hannerz 1969; Rainwater 1970; Stack 1974; Sullivan 1985). The absence of legal marriage or economically stable partnerships, however, did not preclude the formation of strong and stable male-female relationships. Many of the women were involved in a variety of unions. As previously described, some of these relationships were indeed conflictual. Others were remarkably stable, considering the economic constraints that both women and men faced. Several women described long-term relationships, some of which had endured for over a decade.

One said:

I'm not married. I got three kids. But their father is there with the kids. He been there since I was 16. . . . I been with the same guy since I was 16 years old and I'm still with him now. I only had really one man in my life.

Another one echoed:

We been together for so many years; I really think we could work it out. . . . I go over his house, me and the kids, and stay for weeks. Then we come back home.

Still another one underlined:

I been with my baby's father for 12 years. We still not married. So maybe one day we might jump the broom or tie the knot or whatever.

These comments are important because they identify the existence of strong alternative relationships that are not detected in demographic profiles that recognize only legal marriages. They also confirm the result of earlier ethnographic studies that identify a variety of male-female arrangements that exist outside of marriage (Aschenbrenner 1975; Jarrett 1992; Liebow 1967; Rainwater 1970; Schulz 1969; Stack 1974; Sullivan 1985). Such arrangements varied from casual friendships to fully committed partnerships. The information gathered from the focus groups and the detailed accounts resulting from ethnographic case studies suggest the need to explore the spousal and parental roles that men assume outside of marriage. These arrangements have significant implications for the support and well-being of women and children.

Women's decisions regarding household and family formation patterns were not surprising in light of the economic profiles of potential marital partners. Even when men worked, their employment options were limited. The prospective mates of the women interviewed were generally unemployed, underemployed, or relegated the most insecure jobs in the secondary labor market. Within the context of the larger discussion on perceptions of social and economic opportunities, women described the types of jobs their male companions and friends assumed. They included: car wash attendants; drug dealers; fast food clerks; grocery store stock and bag clerks; informal car repairmen; lawn workers; street peddlers; and street salvage workers.

The focus group data thus confirm the structural explanation of poverty and its emphasis on economic factors, such as joblessness. But they also go beyond the primary concentration on the economic instability of men and its consequences for family maintenance. The focus group interviews indicate that women also considered their own resources in addition to those of the men. They assessed their own educational backgrounds, job experiences, welfare resources, and childcare arrangements. For example, women reviewed their educational qualifications and assessed their potential for economic independence.

Educational Attainment As far as working, I have to be serious. I don't have any skills and I prefer to go to school. . . . do something progressive, you know, to try to get off of [welfare].

> Now I'm trying to go back to school 'cause when I dropped out. . . . I was in the 11th grade and was pregnant. . . . I was pregnant with her then, so I had to leave school. . . . Now I'm trying to go back to school for nursing assistant, so I can get off all public aid: find somethin' else to do 'stead of being on welfare all my life.
>
> I try to do what I can. And it's hard out there when you dropped out of high school or you may have a G.E.D. And you have a child . . . and then go and try to find a job.

Work Experiences

Contrary to common stereotypes, many of the women had worked. Women's past work experiences served to clarify the limitations of using the types of jobs available to them as a strategy of mobility. The women's comments focused on low wages, job access, and job inflexibility.

Low Wages It don't make sense to go to McDonald's to make 3.35 an hour when you know you got to pay 4 dollars an hour to baby-sit and you got to have bus fare.

> If you got to get something, you need something that's going to pay some-

thing, that's going to make a difference and not take away from it. And you know when they had that discussion like that on Oprah [Winfrey talk show], they don't really see that. They tell you get out there. One girl get on there talking about she'll scrub the floor for 3.50 [an hour], but what it's going to do for you? You still losing out. You not bringing in as much as you get if you were at home.

Job Access It was too far. . . . I would have to get up at 4 o'clock in the morning in order to be at work at seven. [I] leave work at 3:30 and still wouldn't make it home until 8 o'clock. And it was too far when I wasn't making anything. . . . I didn't have no time for my kids, no time for myself.

Job Inflexibility [I] miss[ed] a day on the weekend and they fire[d] me. I didn't understand. They call me, but I wouldn't go back, because ain't no telling when I get sick like I was sick then. I told them no I didn't want it. And I been looking, putting in applications hoping that somebody call.

Welfare Experiences Welfare, like low-wage jobs, also represented an institutionalized impediment to mobility. The women's comments highlighted the need for benefits, the stigma of public aid, welfare regulations, and their need for childcare.

Need for Benefits If [public aid is] going to do something, I prefer if they would take me off but leave my kids on. Because they would need it more and I figure I can take care of myself a little bit more than they can. You need that medical for them.

> One reason, seriously . . . that I do not want [public aid] to take my check [is] because I need my medical card. They

can take the money, but I need that medical card and I need those food stamps.

Stigma of Public Aid You got to go out there on your own using [your] public aid background . . . because a lot of companies not going to hire you because you coming from public aid.

Welfare Regulations They give you the runaround for nothing. . . . This money not coming out . . . their pockets. . . . [I]t's not like it's coming out they paycheck every week. . . . It's coming from your parents paying they state taxes. . . . You trying to take care of your children the best way you can and this is one of the ways that you can take care of your children.

> How you goin' to get ahead? Somebody needs to explain it to me. . . . I know a lot of people that graduated from college and stuff, they ain't got jobs. If you do get a job you got to know somebody. . . . Soon as you get the job guess who be on your back? Mr. A.D.C.
>
> They make you go through so many changes . . . so many changes for nothing. . . . When I was goin' to school, they call [me for an appointment. I said:] 'Can I come after I get out of school?' [They said:]
> 'No, come now.' [I said:] 'I have finals.' [They said:] 'So, come or you will be cut off.'

Childcare Needs Women, unlike men, had to factor childcare into their work schedules:

> Well, I want to wait until my kids get about 5 [to work], so if something's going on [at the babysitter's] they can tell me. I don't want to be worried. I don't have nobody. I keep my own kids.
>
> If I want to go out and get a job, I ain't going to pick any daycare in the city, because they ain't so safe either.

I just feel it was harder for a woman . . . with children . . . to find a job. When I was working it was always Keisha [my daughter], this, Keisha, that, Keisha this, that. She did this today; she scribbled on my wall. . . . So, my mother died. I quit working. . . . I didn't have nobody to keep her. And so that was that.

As a result of their limited educational attainment, low-paying jobs, welfare disincentives, and childcare needs, most women came to perceive their economic options as severely limited. Consequently, when women sought other opportunities, they took both men's economic limitations and their own into account.

Alternatives to Conventional Marriage: "You Can Depend on Your Mama"

The focus group interviews expand on the structural explanation of poverty in yet another way. They serve to identify the strategic processes and sequences of events that follow women's decisions to forego marriage, bear children as single mothers, and in some cases, head households. Women responded to their poverty in three ways: they extended domestic and childcare responsibilities to multiple individuals; they relaxed paternal role expectations; and they assumed a flexible maternal role.

Domestic Kin Networks The extension of domestic and childcare responsibilities beyond the nuclear family represented a primary response to economic marginality. Extended kin networks that centered around women provided assistance

to single mothers and their children. For example, LaDawn, whose unintended pregnancy interrupted her plans to leave home, attend college, and get "real wild," described how living with her mother provides valuable support for her:

When you money is gone and you at home with your mama, you don't have to worry about where you getting your next meal from because mama is always going to figure out a way how you can get your next meal. . . . And your mama would be there to depend on; you can depend on your mama.

Likewise, Rita, who currently lives alone with her son, also receives assistance from her mother and other female kin. She described the complex, but cooperative pattern, that characterizes the care of her child:

Well, on the days Damen has school, my mother picks him up at night and keeps him at her house. And then when she goes to work in the morning, she takes him to my grandmother's house. And when my little sister gets out of school, she picks him up and takes him back to my mother's house. And then I go and pick him up.

Sheila, the mother of a preschooler and a newborn and who lives alone, described her situation:

I had a hard struggle. I had to ask my mama for a lot of help. . . . I needed help for food . . . to go to school . . . help to watch my kids.

Ebony, who now lives alone, described the childcare benefits of living with her mother:

I'm on my own. . . . I wish my mother would come stay with me . . . to help me out. Because when I was at home . . . it was things that she knew I didn't know nothing about. Why the baby crying so much. Well, you had it outside [the blanket] with no covers on. Letting me know so when the next [child] came I knew not to do this.

Diana also described the childcare benefits of living with her mother. She further hinted how her mother's assistance facilitates Diana's role as the primary caregiver:

> My mother gives me good advice . . . if something's wrong. [My twins] had the chicken pox. What am I gonna do? . . . They itching. What should I put on them? She helps me out that way. And I stays with my mother. Me and my mother sit down and talk. We don't have no kind of problems as far as her trying to raise [my kids].

The women's accounts in these focus group interviews are paralleled in similar ethnographic studies. Aschenbrenner (1975), Jarrett (1992), and Sullivan (1985), in their works, highlight the importance of grandmothers, as well as other women kin, in the lives of poor women and children. Grandmothers provide money on loan, childcare on a daily basis, and help with cooking and cleaning. These services allow some young mothers to finish school and get a job, staying off public assistance. Other qualitative studies provide comparable descriptions of supportive kin who provide care for poor children (Anderson 1990; Burton 1991; Holloman and Lewis 1978; Liebow 1967; Stack 1974; Williams and Kornblum 1985; Zollar 1985). These examples are important in another way. They indicate that house-holds labeled as female-headed are often embedded in larger kinship networks. Interhousehold family arrangements and the domestic activities shared be-tween them are usually overlooked in quantitative studies. Consequently, female-headship as a living arrangement and family as a set of social relationships that may transcend household boundaries are often confounded (Jarrett 1992; Stack 1974; Yanagisako 1979).

Expansion of the Paternal Role
Living in poverty issued yet other strategies. A second type of strategy concentrated on paternal role performance. Women lowered their expectations of men and extended the paternal role to non-biological fathers as ways of facilitating the involvement of men in childcare. Evaluations of paternal role performance that hinged on providing for the family economically were replaced by assessments that centered on men's efforts to find work and assist with day-to-day child welfare (see also Rainwater 1970). For example, Jaleesa, an ebullient mother of one child, said of her daughter's father:

> Even though he don't have a job, sometimes what counts is he spends time with his child. That child will think about that: 'Well, my father's here when my mother's not here.' [That child will] have someone else to turn to. And the father say: 'Well I ain't got no job. I ain't going to be around a child.' That's not all to it.

Anna, who openly proclaimed her strength in the face of many obstacles, echoed Jaleesa's sentiments:

> I got three kids all by him and he try to help out when he can. He's not working now but [he] did try to help. And . . . he be going out looking for a job. I don't try to pressure. [Men] care about their kids. They wanna try to help.

Anita, who with her mother, forms a strong coalition around the care of her children, elaborated on Jaleesa's and Anna's comments:

> If he ain't out there trying to find a job doing something . . . he can be there with that baby, holding that baby, changing that baby's Pampers and let that mommy get rest or let her go out there and do what she have to do to support that baby.

According to Yvette, simply showing interest in one's child was positively evaluated:

> It's not what you do, it's how you do it. I don't expect him to buy my baby snowsuits and boots . . . [I]t's just the thought. When Keith's [my son's] birthday come around, [his father] ain't got to give him a quarter, he ain't got to send him a card. You could pick up the phone and wish him a happy birthday.

The way that poor unmarried fathers assist in their care of their children, both directly and indirectly, is also exemplified in Sullivan's (1985) ethnographic study. Men in his study provided food, clothing, and supervision for their children. Women's willingness to lower their expectations of their children's fathers reflected a fundamental reality. Most men lacked the resources to fully support their children. Yvette summarized this point aptly: "If they don't have it, they just don't have it. You can't get blood from a turnip."

Additionally, women extended the paternal role to men other than the biological fathers of their children. This strategy ensured that there was a male who provided nurturance and discipline, as well as economic support. For example, Alisha, asserted:

> It's not a father, but a male image. . . . My daughter will mind my brother better than she do me. I will tell her to sit down, whereas I would probably have to tell her four or five times; whereas my brother will come in with that manly image and will say sit down one time and she be sitting down.

Debra, whose male companion is not the father of her child, provided another example:

> It don't have to be blood to be like a father to somebody. . . . You can meet a man that will be a better father to your child than the natural father and it's nothing wrong with that.

LaDawn offered a similar view:

> The guy I'm with is not my daughter's father; but he accepts my daughter. With him accepting and helping me out with her, that's all right. Most men they not going to do too much except maybe like buy her a little something, play with her and call it a day. But he accepts my daughter. And seeing that it is not his, I think that's a big responsibility. Because if I ask him for something for my daughter, he'll give it to me. So I figure that right there is a man.

Several ethnographic studies also provide examples of how non-biological fathers supply support for poor African-American children (Aschenbrenner 1975; Burton 1991; Holloman and Lewis 1978; Liebow 1967; Schulz 1969; Stack 1974; Sullivan 1985). These studies identify an array of male figures, such as uncles, grandfathers, neighbors, fictive kin, and male companions who played significant roles in the lives of many children.

Expansion of the Maternal Role A third strategy used by women to facilitate the care of children entailed the expansion of the maternal role. Women, when necessary, broadened their role repertoire to include both expressive and instrumental role responsibilities. Irrespective of the presence or absence of men in the home, women expressed similar views about role flexibility. Under conditions of economic marginality women understood that at some point in their lives they would assume extensive household and family obligations.

Ethnographic research has consistently found that strong and competent mothers are greatly admired in low-income African-American communities (Aschenbrenner 1975; Ladner 1971; Rainwater 1970; Stack 1974). The focus group interviews provided corroboration. Women's comments illustrated their strength and competence as mothers. For example, Jeannie and Connie, who were currently living with the fathers of their children, respectively claimed:

> It does not take a man to make those kids strong. When I tell my kids to do something, they going to look at me first.
>
> I can be their mother and father and teach them values, teach them the right things. . . . I don't think they have to have a father in the home to teach them the right things.

Crystal, Sharon, and Shelly, who, currently were not living with male companions, individually asserted:

> I can discipline [my children] myself. I have that bass in my voice. . . . I raise my voice and they'll . . . sit down. They'll mind me; they'll mind my mother.
>
> I think a father should be around. But it can't always be. I'm raising my children by myself.
>
> [My daughter] is well taken care of and I feel good about myself that I can give her everything she needs without his help.

In addition to describing how poor African-American women respond to conditions of poverty, the interviews highlighted the meanings that women attributed to the alternative family roles that they assumed. Motherhood, irrespective of women's single marital status, conferred them with a valued role. Moreover, women's ability to garner scarce resources, provide care for children, and in some cases, maintain households under stark conditions of poverty led to enhanced self-esteem. For example, Diane, mother of twin daughters, expressed her views on motherhood:

> It's some fun parts in it and then you got some down parts when you got to do this and got to do that. But I enjoy my daughters. . . . They make me happy. . . . They're what get me up in the morning.

Lois, who cared for her children as well as her sister's, gave a similar view:

> People compliment [me]: 'You really take time [with your kids].' Just because . . . I got three kids and not married, that don't mean I'm running the streets all the time. I'm at home helping my children.

Roberta, a mother of four children, who freely admitted that "sometimes my children drive me up the wall," also said:

> I feel proud that I'm a mother. I'm going to see them grow up and get big. . . . The best thing about being a mother is having my kids close to me, knowing that I love them, and just to know that I'm going to be there for my kids if they ever need me.

Contrary to common assumptions, women's accounts described some of the positive consequences of heading one's own household. Tammy, who shares a small apartment with her mother, two sisters, and her children mused:

> I never had a place of my own ... [but] I'm ready for responsibility. I'm ready to raise my family by myself without my mother or sisters telling me: 'Well, you shouldn't do this, and you should do that'. ... I'm ready to do it by myself, now.

Iesha, who lives alone with her children, elaborated:

> The person that's out there on their own is more responsible. You have to think about they are actually taking care of their home now. If they're paying rent, light bill, gas bill, they got to be responsible.

Lareesa, who described how she has been labeled "slow" in school, offered one of the most articulate statements on the relationship between household independence and personal development:

> I [and my son] live with my grandmother. ... She says I have to listen to what she says because as long as I'm living under her roof, I got to obey her rules. ... I'm not saying I'm grown [emphasis], grown [sic], but I want responsibility. That's just like taking an exam. If somebody gives you the answers, that's cheating me out of my life, if I can't do what I want, learn from myself.

DISCUSSION: "BRINGING PEOPLE BACK IN"

> As I got to know and to absorb a great deal about the daily routines and the physical and social contexts of the lives of many parents and children, the logic of many of the choices and much of the behavior of these low-income families became clearer (Jeffers 1967:117).

The primary goal of this paper is to expand on the structural explanation of poverty. The structural perspective correctly documents changes in household and family formation patterns and the relationship of these changes to economic factors. Nevertheless, it ignores alternative family arrangements and omits the role of personal agency in understanding poverty among the poor. The focus group data address these two limitations by concentrating on African-American women's first-hand accounts of their lives. Women's narratives describe family arrangements that were, indeed, different from mainstream patterns but that were viable, nonetheless. Significantly, these differences in household and family formation patterns do not represent abandonment of conventional aspirations (see also Rainwater 1987; Staples 1985; Williams 1992b). Further, women's accounts highlight the active roles that they played in caring for children and maintaining households. Women do not mechanistically respond to economic forces. Rather, they assess their options and make choices that allow them to forge meaningful lives despite the harsh economic conditions in which they and their children find themselves.

The findings from the focus group interviews corroborate those from existing ethnographic studies. This underscores the importance of qualitative and ethnographic data, rather than quantitative census and survey data, for understanding family processes and dynamics. New qualitative data, such as that derived from the focus group interviews, serve several functions: they expand quantitative conceptualizations and interpretations; update our current understanding of family processes among poor African-American families; enhance our confidence in past studies; and counter the tendency to use past qualitative studies as timeless explanations (Williams 1992a).

The data derived from this study suggest several directions for future research. First, researchers should look seriously at alternative family arrangements and cease to assume the superiority of mainstream family patterns. Certainly it is conceivable that a two-parent household with adequate economic resources provides more opportunities for its children than an impoverished family with inadequate resources. However, researchers should not automatically assume that *all* middle-class families are stable and that *all* low-income families are unstable (see, for example, Coontz 1992).

Second, researchers should explore issues of coping and adaptation among poor families, rather than just document female headship and its demographic correlates. We need to identify more precisely the family dynamics that allow poor African-American families to cope (or fail to cope) with economic marginality. We know from past ethnographic research that a variety of family and household strategies can exist under the same social and economic condi-

tions (see, for example, Clark 1983; Jarrett in press; di Leonardo 1984). Thus, the most theoretically compelling studies will be those that identify variations in coping strategies and seek explanations for these differences.

Finally, researchers should focus on gender as a major orienting framework. Mainstream poverty research, in general, and structural arguments, in particular, concentrate on poor African-American women but give little sustained analysis to the implications of gender (Baca Zinn 1989; Mullings 1989). Research that uses gender as an analytic framework can potentially answer such questions as how the conditions of poverty impact gendered ideologies and gendered strategies among poor African-American women and men.

The focus group data serve to not only expand the structural explanation of poverty, but also to highlight the humanity of the people who are too starkly described by statistical profiles and policy regulations. Leslie's comments underscore this point:

> Just because you poor, you want someone to love too. Just because you poor, you might have to live off welfare, that doesn't mean that you're not eligible to have children. Like once you reach a certain income that you not eligible to have children because you too poor.

21

"Night to His Day"
The Social Construction of Gender
(1995)

Judith Lorber

first question we ask about a newborn baby?

—*Ursula Le Guin (1969, 94)*

Talking about gender for most people is the equivalent of fish talking about water. Gender is so much the routine ground of everyday activities that questioning its taken-for-granted assumptions and presuppositions is like thinking about whether the sun will come up. Gender is so pervasive that in our society we assume it is bred into our genes. Most people find it hard to believe that gender is constantly created and re-created out of human interaction, out of social life, and is the texture and order of that social life. Yet gender, like culture, is a human production that depends on everyone constantly "doing gender" (West and Zimmerman 1987).

And everyone "does gender" without thinking about it. Today, on the subway, I saw a well-dressed man with a year-old child in a stroller. Yesterday, on a bus, I saw a man with a tiny baby in a carrier on his chest. Seeing men taking care of small children in public is increasingly common—at least in New York City. But both men were quite obviously stared at—and smiled at, approvingly. Everyone was doing gender—the men who were changing the role of fathers and the other passengers, who were applauding them silently. But there was more gendering going on that probably fewer people noticed. The baby was wearing a white crocheted cap and white clothes. You couldn't tell if it was a boy or a girl. The child in the stroller was wearing a dark blue T-shirt and dark print pants. As they started to leave the train, the father put a Yankee baseball cap on the child's head. Ah, a boy, I thought. Then I noticed the gleam of tiny earrings in the child's ears, and as they got off, I saw the little flowered sneakers and lace-trimmed socks. Not a boy after all. Gender done.

Lorber, Judith, "Night to His Day: The Social Constructive Gender." In *Paradoxes of Gender* (1993). New Haven, CT: Yale University Press. Reprinted by permission of the Yale University Press.

Gender is such a familiar part of daily life that it usually takes a deliberate disruption of our expectations of how women and men are supposed to act to pay attention to how it is produced. Gender signs and signals are so ubiquitous that we usually fail to note them—unless they are missing or ambiguous. Then we are uncomfortable until we have successfully placed the other person in a gender status; otherwise, we feel socially dislocated. In our society, in addition to man and woman, the status can be *transvestite* (a person who dresses in opposite-gender clothes) and *transsexual* (a person who has had sex-change surgery). Transvestites and transsexuals carefully construct their gender status by dressing, speaking, walking, gesturing in the ways prescribed for women or men—whichever they want to be taken for—and so does any "normal" person.

For the individual, gender construction starts with assignment to a sex category on the basis of what the genitalia look like at birth. Then babies are dressed or adorned in a way that displays the category because parents don't want to be constantly asked whether their baby is a girl or a boy. A sex category becomes a gender status through naming, dress, and the use of other gender markers. Once a child's gender is evident, others treat those in one gender differently from those in the other, and the children respond to the different treatment by feeling different and behaving differently. As soon as they can talk, they start to refer to themselves as members of their gender. Sex doesn't come into play again until puberty, but by that time, sexual feelings and desires and practices have been shaped by gendered norms and expectations.

Adolescent boys and girls approach and avoid each other in an elaborately scripted and gendered mating dance. Parenting is gendered, with different expectations for mothers and for fathers, and people of different genders work at different kinds of jobs. The work adults do as mothers and fathers and as low-level workers and high-level bosses, shapes women's and men's life experiences, and these experiences produce different feelings, consciousness relationships, skills—ways of being that we call feminine or masculine. All of these processes constitute the social construction of gender.

Gendered roles change—today fathers are taking care of little children, girls and boys are wearing unisex clothing and getting the same education, women and men are working at the same jobs. Although many traditional social groups are quite strict about maintaining gender differences, in other social groups they seem to be blurring. Then why the one-year-old's earrings? Why is it still so important to mark a child as a girl or a boy, to make sure she is not taken for a boy or he for a girl? What would happen if they were? They would, quite literally, have changed places in their social world.

To explain why gendering is done from birth, constantly and by everyone, we have to look not only at the way individuals experience gender but at gender as a social institution. As a social institution, gender is one of the major ways that human beings organize their lives. Human society depends on a predictable division of labor, a designated allocation of scarce goods, assigned responsibility for children and others who cannot care for themselves, common values and their systematic transmission to new members, legitimate leadership, music, art, stories, games, and other symbolic productions. One way of choosing people for the different tasks of society is on the basis of their talents, motivations, and competence—their demonstrated achievements. The other way is on the basis of gender, race, ethnicity—ascribed membership in a category of people. Although societies vary in the extent to which they use one or the other of these ways of allocating people to work and to carry out other responsibilities, every society uses gender and age grades. Every society classifies people as "girl and boy children," "girls and boys ready to be married," and "fully adult women and men," constructs similarities among them and differences between them, and assigns them to different roles and responsibilities. Personality characteristics, feelings, motivations, and ambitions flow from these different life experiences so that the members of these different groups become different kinds of people. The process of gendering and its outcome are legitimated by religion, law, science, and the society's entire set of values.

In order to understand gender as a social institution, it is important to distinguish human action from animal behavior. Animals feed themselves and their young until their young can feed themselves. Humans have to produce not only food but shelter and clothing. They also, if the group is going to continue as a social group, have to teach the children how their particular group does these tasks. In the process, humans reproduce gender, family, kinship, and a division of labor—social institutions that do not exist among animals. Primate social groups have been re-ferred to as families, and their mating patterns as monogamy, adultery, and harems. Primate behavior has been used to prove the universality of sex differences—as built into our evolutionary inheritance (Haraway 1978a). But animals' sex differences are not at all the same as humans' gender differences; animals' bonding is not kinship; animals' mating is not ordered by marriage; and animals' dominance hierarchies are not the equivalent of human stratification systems. Animals group on sex and age, relational categories that are physiologically, not socially, different. Humans create gender and age-group categories that are socially, and not necessarily physiologically, different.

For animals, physiological maturity means being able to impregnate or conceive; its markers are coming into heat (estrus) and sexual attraction. For humans, puberty means being available for marriage; it is marked by rites that demonstrate this marital eligibility. Although the onset of physiological puberty is signaled by secondary sex characteristics (menstruation, breast development, sperm ejaculation, pubic and underarm hair), the onset of social adulthood is ritualized by the coming-out party or desert walkabout or bar mitzvah or graduation from college or first successful hunt or dreaming or inheritance of property. Humans have rituals that mark the passage from childhood into puberty and puberty into full adult status, as well as for marriage, childbirth, and death; animals do not (van Gennep 1960). To the extent that infants and the dead are differentiated by whether they are male or female, there are different birth rituals for girls and boys, and different funeral rituals for men and women (Biersack 1984, 132–33). Rituals of puberty, marriage, and becoming a parent are gendered, creating a "woman," a "man," a "bride," a "groom," a "mother," a "father." Animals have no equivalents for these statuses.

Among animals, siblings mate and so do parents and children; humans have incest taboos and rules that encourage or forbid mating between members of different kin groups (Lévi-Strauss 1956, [1949] 1969). Any animal of the same species may feed another's young (or may not, depending on the species). Humans designate responsibility for particular children by kinship; humans frequently limit responsibility for children to the members of their kinship group or make them into members of their kinship group with adoption rituals.

Animals have dominance hierarchies based on size or on successful threat gestures and signals. These hierarchies are usually sexed, and in some species, moving to the top of the hierarchy physically changes the sex (Austad 1986). Humans have stratification patterns based on control of surplus food, ownership of property, legitimate demands on others' work and sexual services, enforced determinations of who marries whom, and approved use of violence. If a woman replaces a man at the top of a stratification hierarchy, her social status may be that of a man, but her sex does not change.

Mating, feeding, and nurturant behavior in animals is determined by instinct and imitative learning and ordered by physiological sex and age (Lancaster 1974). In humans, these behaviors are taught and symbolically reinforced and ordered by so-cially constructed gender and age grades. Social gender and age statuses sometimes ignore or override physiological sex and age completely. Male and female animals (unless they physiologically change) are not interchangeable; infant animals cannot take the place of adult animals. Human females can become husbands and fathers, and human males can become wives and mothers, without sex-change surgery (Blackwood 1984). Human infants can reign as kings or queens.

Western society's values legitimate gendering by claiming that it all comes from physiology—female and male procreative differences. But gender and sex are not equivalent, and gender as a social construction does not flow automatically from genitalia and reproductive organs, the main physiological differences of females and males. In the construction of ascribed social statuses, physiological differences such as sex, stage of development, color of skin, and size are crude markers. They are not the source of the social statuses of gender, age grade, and race. Social statuses are carefully constructed through prescribed processes of teaching, learning, emulation, and enforcement. Whatever genes, hormones, and biological evolution contribute to human social institutions is materially as well as qualitatively transformed by social practices. Every social institution has a material base, but culture and social practices transform that base into something with qualitatively different patterns and constraints. The economy is much more than producing food and goods and distributing them to eaters and users; family and kinship are not the equivalent of having sex and procreating; morals and religions cannot be equated with the fears and ecstasies of the brain; language goes far beyond the sounds produced by tongue and larynx. No one eats "money" or "credit"; the concepts of "god" and "angels" are the subjects of theological disquisitions; not only words but objects, such as their flag, "speak" to the citizens of a country.

Similarly, gender cannot be equated with biological and physiological differences between human females and males. The building blocks of gender are *socially constructed statuses*. Western societies have only two genders, "man" and "woman." Some societies have three genders—men, women, and *berdaches* or *hijras* or *xaniths*. Berdaches, hijras, and xaniths are biological males who behave, dress, work, and are treated in most respects as social women; they are therefore not men, nor are they female women; they are, in our language, "male women." There are African and American Indian societies that have a gender status called *manly hearted women*—biological females who work, marry, and parent as men; their social status is "female men" (Amadiume 1987; Blackwood 1984). They do not have to behave or dress as men to have the social responsibilities and prerogatives of husbands and fathers; what makes them men is enough wealth to buy a wife.

Modern Western societies' *transsexuals* and *transvestites* are the nearest equivalent of these crossover genders, but they are not institutionalized as third genders (Bolin 1987). Transsexuals are biological males and females who have sex-change operations to alter their genitalia. They do so in order to bring their physical anatomy in congruence with the way they want to live and with their own sense of gender identity. They do not become a third gender; they change genders. Transvestites are males who live as women and females who live as men but do not intend to have sex-change surgery. Their dress, appearance, and mannerisms fall within the range of what is expected from members of the opposite gender, so that they "pass." They also change genders, sometimes temporarily, some for most of their lives. Transvestite women have fought in wars as men soldiers as recently as the nineteenth century; some married women, and others went back to being women and married men once the war was over. Some were discovered when their wounds were treated; others not until they died. In order to work as a jazz musician, a man's occupation, Billy Tipton, a woman, lived most of her life as a man. She died recently at seventy-four, leaving a wife and three adopted sons for whom she was husband and father, and musicians with whom she had played and traveled, for whom she was "one of the boys" (*New York Times* 1989). There have been many other such occurrences of women passing as men to do more prestigious or lucrative men's work (Matthaei 1982, 192–93).

Genders, therefore, are not attached to a biological substratum. Gender boundaries are breachable, and individual and socially organized shifts from one gender to another call attention to "cultural, social, or aesthetic dissonances" (Garber 1992, 16). These odd or deviant or third genders show us what we ordinarily take for granted—that people have to learn to be women and men. Men who cross-dress for performances or for pleasure often learn from women's magazines how to "do femininity" convincingly (Garber 1992, 41–51). Because transvestism is direct evidence of how gender is constructed, Marjorie Garber claims it has "extraordinary power . . . to disrupt, expose, and challenge, putting in question the very notion of the 'original' and of stable identity" (1992, 16).

GENDER BENDING

It is difficult to see how gender is constructed because we take it for granted that it's all biology, or hormones, or human nature. The differences between women and men seem to be self-evident, and we think they would occur no matter what society did. But in actuality, human females and males are physiologically more similar in appearance than are the two sexes of many species of animals and are more alike than different in traits and behavior (C. F. Epstein 1988). Without the deliberate use of gendered clothing, hairstyles, jewelry, and cosmetics, women and men would look far more alike. Even societies that do not cover women's breasts have gender-identifying clothing, scarification, jewelry, and hairstyles.

The case with which many transvestite women pass as men and transvestite men as women is corroborated by the common gender misidentification in Westernized societies of people in jeans, T-shirts, and sneakers. Men with long hair may be addressed as "miss," and women with short hair are often taken for men unless they offset the potential ambiguity with deliberate gender markers (Devor 1987, 1989). Jan Morris, in *Conundrum*, an autobiographical account of events just before and just after a sex-change operation, described how easy it was to shift back and forth from being a man to being a woman when testing how it would feel to change gender status. During this time, Morris still had a penis and wore more or less unisex clothing; the context alone made the man and the woman:

> Sometimes the arena of my ambivalence was uncomfortably small. At the Travellers' Club, for example, I was obviously known as a man of sorts—women were only allowed on the premises at all during a few hours of the day, and even then were hidden away as far as possible in lesser rooms or alcoves. But I had another club, only a few hundred yards away, where I was known only as a woman, and often I went directly from one to the other, imperceptibly changing roles on the way— "Cheerio, sir," the porter would say at one club, and "Hello, madam," the porter would greet me at the other. (1975, 132)

Gender shifts are actually a common phenomenon in public roles as well. Queen Elizabeth II of England bore children, but when she went to Saudi Arabia on a state visit, she was considered an honorary man so that she could confer and dine with the men who were heads of a state that forbids unrelated men and women to have face-to-unveiled-face contact. In contemporary Egypt, lower-class women who run restaurants or shops dress in men's clothing and engage in unfeminine aggressive behavior, and middle-class educated women of professional or managerial status can take positions of authority (Rugh 1986, 131). In these situations, there is an important status change: These women are treated by the others in the situation as if they are men. From their own point of view, they are still women. From the social perspective, however, they are men.

In many cultures, gender bending is prevalent in theater or dance—the Japanese kabuki are men actors who play both women and men; in Shakespeare's theater company, there were no actresses—Juliet and Lady Macbeth were played by boys. Shakespeare's comedies are full of witty comments on gender shifts. Women characters frequently masquerade as young men, and other women characters fall in love with them; the boys playing these masquerading women, meanwhile, are acting out pining for the love of men characters. In *As You Like It*, when Rosalind justifies her protective crossdressing, Shakespeare also comments on manliness:

> Were it not better,
> Because that I am more than common tall,
> That I did suit me all points like a man:
> A gallant curtle-axe upon my thigh,
> A boar-spear in my hand, and in my heart
> Lie there what hidden women's fear there will,
> We'll have a swashing and martial outside,
> As many other mannish cowards have
> That do outface it with their semblances. (I, i, 115–22)

Shakespeare's audience could appreciate the double subtext: Rosalind, a woman character, was a boy dressed in girl's clothing who then dressed as a boy; like bravery, masculinity and femininity can be put on and taken off with changes of costume and role (Howard 1988, 435).

M Butterfly is a modern play of gender ambiguities, which David Hwang (1989) based on a real person. Shi Peipu, a male Chinese opera singer who sang women's roles, was a spy as a man and the lover as a woman of a Frenchman, Gallimard, a diplomat (Bernstein 1986). The relationship lasted twenty years, and Shi Peipu even pretended to be the mother of a child by Gallimard. "She" also pretended to be too shy to undress completely. As "Butterfly," Shi Peipu portrayed a fantasy Oriental woman who made the lover a "real man" (Kondo 1990b). In Gallimard's words, the fantasy was "of slender women in chong sams and kimonos who die for the love of unworthy foreign devils. Who are born and raised to be perfect women. Who take whatever punishment we give them, and bounce back, strengthened by love, unconditionally" (D. H. Hwang 1989, 91). When the fantasy woman betrayed him by turning out to be the more powerful "real man," Gallimard assumed the role of Butterfly and, dressed in a geisha's robes, killed himself: "because 'man' and 'woman' are oppositionally defined terms, reversals . . . are possible" (Kondo 1990b, 18).

But despite the ease with which gender boundaries can be traversed in work, in social relationships, and in cultural productions, gender statuses remain. Transvestites and transsexuals do not challenge the social construction of gender. Their goal is to be feminine women and masculine men (Kando 1973). Those who do not want to change their anatomy but do want to change their gender behavior fare less well in establishing their social identity. The women Holly Devor called "gender blenders" wore their hair short, dressed in unisex pants, shirts, and comfortable shoes, and did not wear jewelry or makeup. They described their everyday dress as women's clothing: One said, "I wore jeans all the time, but I didn't wear men's clothes" (Devor 1989, 100). Their gender identity was women, but because they refused to "do femininity," they were constantly taken for men (1987, 1989, 107–42). Devor said of them: "The most common area of complaint was with public washrooms. They repeatedly spoke of the humiliation of being challenged or ejected from women's washrooms. Similarly, they found public change rooms to be dangerous territory and the buying of undergarments to be a difficult feat to accomplish" (1987, 29). In an ultimate ironic twist, some of these women said "they would feel like transvestites if they were to wear dresses, and two women said that they had been called transvestites when they had done so" (1987, 31). They resolved the ambiguity of their gender status by identifying as women in private and passing as men in public to avoid harassment on the street, to get men's jobs, and, if they were lesbians, to make it easier to display affection publicly with their lovers (Devor 1989, 107–42). Sometimes they even used men's bathrooms. When they had gender-neutral names, like Leslie, they could avoid the bureaucratic hassles that arose when they had to present their passports or other proof of identity, but because most had names associated with women, their appearance and their cards of identity were not conventionally congruent, and their gender status was in constant jeopardy. When they could, they found it easier to pass as men than to try to change the stereotyped notions of what women should look like.

Paradoxically, then, bending gender rules and passing between genders does not erode but rather preserves gender boundaries. In societies with only two genders, the gender dichotomy is not disturbed by transvestites, because others feel that a transvestite is only transitorily ambiguous—is "really a man or woman underneath." After sex-change surgery, transsexuals end up in a conventional gender status—a "man" or a "woman" with the appropriate genitals (Eichler 1989). When women dress as men for business reasons, they are indicating that in that situation, they want to be treated the way men are treated; when they dress as women, they want to be treated as women:

> By their male dress, female entrepreneurs signal their desire to suspend the expectations of accepted feminine conduct without losing respect and reputation. By wearing what is "unattractive" they signify that they are not intending to display their physical charms while engaging in public activity. Their loud, aggressive banter contrasts with the modest demeanor that attracts men. . . . Overt signalling of a suspension of the rules preserves normal conduct from eroding expectations. (Rugh 1986, 131)

FOR INDIVIDUALS, GENDER MEANS SAMENESS

Although the possible combinations of genitalia, body shapes, clothing, mannerisms, sexuality, and roles could produce infinite varieties in human beings, the social institution of gender depends on the production and maintenance of a limited number of gender statuses and of making the members of these statuses similar to each other. Individuals are born sexed but not gendered, and they have to be taught to be masculine or feminine. As Simone de Beauvoir said:

"One is not born, but rather becomes, a woman ... ; it is civilization as a whole that produces this creature ... which is described as feminine." (1952, 267).

Children learn to walk, talk, and gesture the way their social group says girls and boys should. Ray Birdwhistell, in his analysis of body motion as human communication, calls these learned gender displays *tertiary* sex characteristics and argues that they are needed to distinguish genders because humans are a weakly dimorphic species—their only sex markers are genitalia (1970, 39–46). Clothing, paradoxically, often hides the sex but displays the gender.

In early childhood, humans develop gendered personality structures and sexual orientations through their interactions with parents of the same and opposite gender. As adolescents, they conduct their sexual behavior according to gendered scripts. Schools, parents, peers, and the mass media guide young people into gendered work and family roles. As adults, they take on a gendered social status in their society's stratification system. Gender is thus both ascribed and achieved (West and Zimmerman 1987).

The achievement of gender was most dramatically revealed in a case of an accidental transsexual—a baby boy whose penis was destroyed in the course of a botched circumcision when he was seven months old (Money and Ehrhardt 1972, 118–23). The child's sex category was changed to "female," and a vagina was surgically constructed when the child was seventeen months old. The parents were advised that they could successfully raise the child, one of identical twins, as a girl. Physicians assured

them that the child was too young to have formed a gender identity. Children's sense of which gender they belong to usually develops around the age of three, at the time that they start to group objects and recognize that the people around them also fit into categories—big, little; pink-skinned, brown-skinned; boys, girls. Three has also been the age when children's appearance is ritually gendered, usually by cutting a boy's hair or dressing him in distinctively masculine clothing. In Victorian times, English boys wore dresses up to the age of three, when they were put into short pants (Garber 1992, 1–2).

The parents of the accidental transsexual bent over backward to feminize the child—and succeeded. Frilly dresses, hair ribbons, and jewelry created a pride in looks, neatness, and "daintiness." More significant, the child's dominance was also feminized:

> The girl had many tomboyish traits, such as abundant physical energy, a high level of activity, stubbornness, and being often the dominant one in a girls' group. Her mother tried to modify her tomboyishness: "... I teach her to be more polite and quiet. I always wanted those virtues. I never did manage, but I'm going to try to manage them to—my daughter—to be more quiet and lady-like." From the beginning the girl had been the dominant twin. By the age of three, her dominance over her brother was, as her mother described it, that of a mother hen. The boy in turn took up for his sister, if anyone threatened her. (Money and Ehrhardt 1972, 122)

This child was not a tomboy because of male genes or hormones; according to her mother, she herself had also been a tomboy. What the mother had learned poorly while growing up as a "natural" female she insisted that her physically reconstructed son-daughter learn well. For both mother and child, the social construction of gender overrode any possibly inborn traits.

People go along with the imposition of gender norms because the weight of morality as well as immediate social pressure enforces them. Consider how many instructions for properly gendered behavior are packed into this mother's admonition to her daughter: "This is how to hem a dress when you see the hem coming down and so to prevent yourself from looking like the slut I know you are so bent on becoming" (Kincaid 1978).

Gender norms are inscribed in the way people move, gesture, and even eat. In one African society, men were supposed to eat with their "whole mouth, wholeheartedly, and not, like women, just with the lips, that is half-heartedly, with reservation and restraint" (Bourdieu [1980] 1990, 70). Men and women in this society learned to walk in ways that proclaimed their different positions in the society:

> The manly man . . . stands up straight into the face of the person he approaches, or wishes to welcome. Ever on the alert, because ever threatened, he misses nothing of what happens around him. . . . Conversely, a well brought-up woman . . . is expected to walk with a slight stoop, avoiding every misplaced movement of her body, her head or her arms, looking down, keeping her eyes on the spot where she will next put her foot, especially if she happens to have to walk past the men's assembly. (70)

Many cultures go beyond clothing, gestures, and demeanor in gendering children. They inscribe gender directly into bodies. In traditional Chinese society, mothers bound their daughters' feet into three-inch stumps to enhance their sexual attractiveness. Jewish fathers circumcise their infant sons to show their covenant with God. Women in African societies remove the clitoris of prepubescent girls, scrape their labia, and make the lips grow together to preserve their chastity and ensure their marriageability. In Western societies, women augment their breast size with silicone and reconstruct their faces with cosmetic surgery to conform to cultural ideals of feminine beauty. Hanna Papanek (1990) notes that these practices reinforce the sense of superiority or inferiority in the adults who carry them out as well as in the children on whom they are done: The genitals of Jewish fathers and sons are physical and psychological evidence of their common dominant religious and familial status; the genitals of African mothers and daughters are physical and psychological evidence of their joint subordination.

Sandra Bem (1981, 1983) argues that because gender is a powerful "schema" that orders the cognitive world, one must wage a constant, active battle for a child not to fall into typical gendered attitudes and behavior. In 1972, *Ms. Magazine* published Lois Gould's fantasy of how to raise a child free of gender-typing. The experiment calls for hiding the child's anatomy from all eyes except the parents' and treating the child as neither a girl nor a boy. The child, called X, gets to do all the things boys *and* girls do. The experiment is so successful that all the children in X's class at school want to look and behave like X. At the end of the story, the creators of the experiment are asked what will happen when X grows up. The scientists' answer is that by then it will be quite clear what X is, implying that its hormones will kick in and it will be revealed as a female or male. That ambiguous, and somewhat contradictory, ending lets Gould off the hook; neither she nor we have any idea what someone brought up totally androgynously would be like sexually or socially as an adult. The hormonal input will not create gender or sexuality but will only establish secondary sex characteristics; breasts, beards, and menstruation alone do not produce social manhood or womanhood. Indeed, it is at puberty, when sex characteristics become evident, that most societies put pubescent children through their most important rites of passage, the rituals that officially mark them as fully gendered—that is, ready to marry and become adults.

Most parents create a gendered world for their newborn by naming, birth announcements, and dress. Children's relationships with same-gendered and different-gendered caretakers structure their self-identifications and personalities. Through cognitive development, children extract and apply to their own actions the appropriate behavior for those who belong in their own gender, as well as race, religion, ethnic group, and social class, rejecting what is not appropriate. If their social categories are highly valued, they value themselves highly; if their social categories are low status, they lose self-esteem (Chodorow 1974). Many feminist parents who want to raise androgynous children soon lose their children to the pull of gendered norms (T. Gordon 1990, 87–90). My son attended a carefully nonsexist elementary school, which didn't even have girls' and boys' bathrooms. When he was seven or eight years old,

I attended a class play about "squares" and "circles" and their need for each other and noticed that all the girl squares and circles wore makeup, but none of the boy squares and circles did. I asked the teacher about it after the play, and she said, "Bobby said he was not going to wear makeup, and he is a powerful child, so none of the boys would either." In a long discussion about conformity, my son confronted me with the question of who the conformists were, the boys who followed their leader or the girls who listened to the woman teacher. In actuality, they both were, because they both followed same-gender leaders and acted in gender-appropriate ways. (Actors may wear makeup, but real boys don't.)

For human beings there is no essential femaleness or maleness, femininity or masculinity, womanhood or manhood, but once gender is ascribed, the social order constructs and holds individuals to strongly gendered norms and expectations. Individuals may vary on many of the components of gender and may shift genders temporarily or permanently, but they must fit into the limited number of gender statuses their society recognizes: In the process, they re-create their society's version of women and men: "If we do gender appropriately, we simultaneously sustain, reproduce, and render legitimate the institutional arrangements. . . . If we fail to do gender appropriately, we as individuals—not the institutional arrangements—may be called to account (for our character, motives, and predispositions)" (West and Zimmerman 1987, 146).

The gendered practices of everyday life reproduce a society's view of how women and men should act (Bourdieu [1980] 1990). Gendered social arrangements are justified by religion and cultural productions and backed by law, but the most powerful means of sustaining the moral hegemony of the dominant gender ideology is that the process is made invisible; any possible alternatives are virtually unthinkable (Foucault 1972; Gramsci 1971).

FOR SOCIETY, GENDER MEANS DIFFERENCE

The pervasiveness of gender as a way of structuring social life demands that gender statuses be clearly differentiated. Varied talents, sexual preferences, identities, personalities, interests, and ways of interacting fragment the individual's bodily and social experiences. Nonetheless, these are organized in Western cultures into two and only two socially and legally recognized gender statuses, "man" and "woman." In the social construction of gender, it does not matter what men and women actually do; it does not even matter if they do exactly the same thing. The social institution of gender insists only that what they do is *perceived* as different.

If men and women are doing the same tasks, they are usually spatially segregated to maintain gender separation, and often the tasks are given different job titles as well, such as executive secretary and administrative assistant (Reskin 1988). If the differences between women and men begin to blur, society's "sameness taboo" goes into action (G. Rubin 1975, 178). At a rock and roll dance at West Point in 1976, the year women were admitted to the prestigious military academy for the first time, the school's administrators "were report-

edly perturbed by the sight of mirror-image couples dancing in short hair and dress gray trousers," and a rule was established that women cadets could dance at these events only if they wore skirts (Barkalow and Raab 1990, 53). Women recruits in the U.S. Marine Corps are required to wear makeup—at a minimum, lipstick and eye shadow—and they have to take classes in makeup, hair care, poise, and etiquette. This feminization is part of a deliberate policy of making them clearly distinguishable from men Marines. Christine Williams quotes a twenty-five-year-old woman drill instructor as saying: "A lot of the recruits who come here don't wear makeup; they're tomboyish or athletic. A lot of them have the preconceived idea that going into the military means they can still be a tomboy. They don't realize that you are a *Woman* Marine" (1989, 76–77).

If gender differences were genetic, physiological, or hormonal, gender bending and gender ambiguity would occur only in hermaphrodites, who are born with chromosomes and genitalia that are not clearly female or male. Since gender differences are socially constructed, all men and all women can enact the behavior of the other, because they know the other's social script: " 'Man' and 'woman' are at once empty and overflowing categories. Empty because they have no ultimate, transcendental meaning. Overflowing because even when they appear to be fixed, they still contain within them alternative, denied, or suppressed definitions." (J. W. Scott 1988a, 49). Nonetheless, though individuals may be able to shift gender statuses, the gender boundaries have to hold, or the whole gendered social order will come crashing down.

Paradoxically, it is the social importance of gender statuses and their external markers—clothing, mannerisms, and spatial segregation—that makes gender bending or gender crossing possible—or even necessary. The social viability of differentiated gender statuses produces the need or desire to shift statuses. Without gender differentiation, transvestism and transsexuality would be meaningless. You couldn't dress in the opposite gender's clothing if all clothing were unisex. There would be no need to reconstruct genitalia to match identity if interests and lifestyles were not gendered. There would be no need for women to pass as men to do certain kinds of work if jobs were not typed as "women's work" and "men's work." Women would not have to dress as men in public life in order to give orders or aggressively bargain with customers.

Gender boundaries are preserved when transsexuals create congruous autobiographies of always having felt like what they are now. The transvestite's story also "recuperates social and sexual norms" (Garber 1992, 69). In the transvestite's normalized narrative, he or she "is 'compelled' by social and economic forces to disguise himself or herself in order to get a job, escape repression, or gain artistic or political 'freedom'" (Garber 1992, 70). The "true identity," when revealed, causes amazement over how easily and successfully the person passed as a member of the opposite gender, not a suspicion that gender itself is something of a put-on.

GENDER RANKING

Most societies rank genders according to prestige and power and construct them to be unequal, so that moving from one to another also means moving up or down the social scale. Among some North American Indian cultures, the hierarchy was male men, male women, female men, female women. Women produced significant durable goods (basketry, textiles, pottery, decorated leather goods), which could be traded. Women also controlled what they produced and any profit or wealth they earned. Since women's occupational realm could lead to prosperity and prestige, it was fair game for young men—but only if they became women in gender status. Similarly, women in other societies who amassed a great deal of wealth were allowed to become men—"manly hearts." According to Harriet Whitehead (1981):

> Both reactions reveal an unwillingness or inability to distinguish the sources of prestige—wealth, skill, personal efficacy (among other things)— from masculinity. Rather there is the innuendo that if a person performing female tasks can attain excellence, prosperity, or social power, it must be because that person is, at some level, a man. . . . A woman who could succeed at doing the things men did was honored as a man would be. . . . What seems to have been more disturbing to the culture—which means, for all intents and purposes, to the men—was the possibility that women, within their own department, might be onto a good thing. It was into this unsettling breach that the berdache institution was hurled. In their social aspect, women were complimented by the berdache's imitation. In their anatomic aspect, they were subtly insulted by his vaunted superiority. (108)

In American society, men-to-women transsexuals tend to earn less after surgery if they change occupations; women-to-men transsexuals tend to increase their income (Bolin 1988, 153–60; Brody 1979). Men who go into women's fields, like nursing, have less prestige than women who go into men's fields, like physics. Janice Raymond, a radical feminist, feels that transsexual men-to-women have advantages over female women because they were not socialized to be subordinate or oppressed throughout life. She says:

> We know that we are women who are born with female chromosomes and anatomy, and that whether or not we were socialized to be so-called normal women, patriarchy has treated and will treat us like women. Transsexuals have not had this same history. No man can have the history of being born and located in this culture as a woman. He can have the history of *wishing* to be a woman and of *acting* like a woman, but this gender experience is that of a transsexual, not of a woman. Surgery may confer the artifacts of outward and inward female organs but it cannot confer the history of being born a woman in this society. (1979, 114)

Because women who become men rise in the world and men who become women fall, Elaine Showalter (1987) was very critical of the movie. *Tootsie*, in which Dustin Hoffman plays an actor who passes as a woman in order to be able to get work. "Dorothy" becomes a feminist "woman of the year" for standing up for women's rights not to be demeaned or sexually harassed. Showalter feels that the message of the movie is double-edged: "Dorothy's 'feminist' speeches . . . are less a response to the oppression of women than an instinctive situational male reaction to being treated like a woman. The implication is that women must be taught by men how to

win their rights. . . . It says that feminist ideas are much less threatening when they come from a man" (123). Like Raymond, Showalter feels that being or having been a man gives a transsexual man-to-woman or a man cross-dressed as a woman a social advantage over those whose gender status was always "woman." The implication here is that there is an experiential superiority that doesn't disappear with the gender shift.

For one transsexual man-to-woman, however, the experience of living as a woman changed his/her whole personality. As James, Morris had been a soldier, foreign correspondent, and mountain climber; as Jan, Morris is a successful travel writer. But socially, James was far superior to Jan, and so Jan developed the "learned helplessness" that is supposed to characterize women in Western society:

> We are told that the social gap between the sexes is narrowing, but I can only report that having, in the second half of the twentieth century, experienced life in both roles, there seems to me no aspect of existence, no moment of the day, no contact, no arrangement, no response, which is not different for men and for women. The very tone of voice in which I was now addressed, the very posture of the person next in the queue, the very feel in the air when I entered a room or sat at a restaurant table, constantly emphasized my change of status.
>
> And if other's responses shifted, so did my own. The more I was treated as woman, the more woman I became. I adapted willy-nilly. If I was assumed to be incompetent at reversing cars, or opening bottles, oddly incompetent I found myself becoming. If a case was thought too heavy for me, inexplicably I found it so myself. . . . Women treated

me with a frankness which, while it was one of the happiest discoveries of my metamorphosis, did imply membership of a camp, a faction, or at least a school of thought; so I found myself gravitating always towards the female, whether in sharing a railway compartment or supporting a political cause. Men treated me more and more as junior, . . . and so, addressed every day of my life as an inferior, involuntarily, month by month I accepted the condition. I discovered that even now men prefer women to be less informed, less able, less talkative, and certainly less self-centered than they are themselves; so I generally obliged them. (1975, 165–66)

COMPONENTS OF GENDER

By now, it should be clear that gender is not a unitary essence but has many components as a social institution and as an individual status.

As a social institution, gender is composed of:

Gender statuses, the socially recognized genders in a society and the norms and expectations for their enactment behaviorally, gesturally, linguistically, emotionally, and physically. How gender statuses are evaluated depends on historical development in any particular society.

Gendered division of labor, the assignment of productive and domestic work to members of different gender statuses. The work assigned to those of different gender statuses strengthens the society's evaluation of those statuses—the higher the status, the more prestigious and valued the work and the greater its rewards.

Gendered kinship, the family rights and responsibilities for each gender status. Kinship statuses reflect and reinforce the prestige and power differences of the different genders.

Gendered sexual scripts, the normative patterns of sexual desire and sexual behavior, as prescribed for the different gender statuses. Members of the dominant gender have more sexual prerogatives; members of a subordinate gender may be sexually exploited.

Gendered personalities, the combinations of traits patterned by gender norms of how members of different gender statuses are supposed to feel and behave. Social expectations of others in face-to-face interaction constantly bolster these norms.

Gendered social control, the formal and informal approval and reward of conforming behavior and the stigmatization, social isolation, punishment, and medical treatment of nonconforming behavior.

Gender ideology, the justification of gender statuses, particularly, their differential evaluation. The dominant ideology tends to suppress criticism by making these evaluations seem natural.

Gender imagery, the cultural representations of gender and embodiment of gender in symbolic language and artistic productions that reproduce and legitimate gender statuses. Culture is one of the main supports of the dominant gender ideology.

For an individual, gender is composed of:

Sex category to which the infant is assigned at birth based on appearance of genitalia. With prenatal testing and sex-typing, categorization is prenatal. Sex category may be changed later through surgery or reinspection of ambiguous genitalia.

Gender identity, the individual's sense of gendered self as a worker and family member.

Gendered marital and procreative status, fulfillment or nonfulfillment of allowed or disallowed mating, impregnation, childbearing, kinship roles.

Gendered sexual orientation, socially and individually patterned sexual desires, feelings, practices, and identification.

Gendered personality, internalized patterns of socially normative emotions as organized by family structure and parenting.

Gendered processes, the social practices of learning, being taught, picking up cues, enacting behavior already learned to be gender-appropriate (or inappropriate, if rebelling, testing), developing a gender identity, "doing gender" as a member of a gender status in relationships with gendered others, acting deferent or dominant.

Gender beliefs, incorporation of or resistance to gender ideology.

Gender display, presentation of self as a certain kind of gendered person through dress, cosmetics, adornments, and permanent and reversible body markers.

For an individual, all the social components are supposed to be consistent and congruent with perceived physiology. The actual combination of genes and genitalia, prenatal, adolescent, and adult hormonal input, and procreative capacity may or may not be congruous with each other and with sex-category assignment, gender identity, gendered sexual orientation and procreative status, gender display, personality, and work and family roles. At any one time, an individual's identity is a combination of the major ascribed statuses of gender, race, ethnicity, religion, and social class, and the individual's achieved statuses, such as education level, occupation or profession, marital status, parenthood, prestige, authority, and wealth. The ascribed statuses substantially limit or create opportunities for individual achievements and also diminish or enhance the luster of those achievements.

GENDER AS PROCESS, STRATIFICATION, AND STRUCTURE

As a social institution, gender is a process of creating distinguishable social statuses for the assignment of rights and responsibilities. As part of a stratification system that ranks these statuses unequally, gender is a major building block in the social structures built on these unequal statuses.

As a *process*, gender creates the social differences that define "woman" and "man." In social interaction throughout their lives, individuals learn what is expected, see what is expected, act and react in expected ways, and thus simultaneously construct and maintain the gender order: "The very injunction to be a given gender takes place through discursive routes: to be a good mother, to be a heterosexually desirable object, to be a fit worker, in sum, to signify a multiplicity of guarantees in response to a variety of different demands all at once" (J. Butler 1990, 145). Members of a social group neither make up gender as they go along nor exactly replicate in rote fashion what was done before. In almost every encounter, human beings produce gender, behaving in the ways they learned were appropriate for their gender status, or resisting or rebelling against these norms. Resistance and rebellion have altered gender norms, but so far they have rarely eroded the statuses.

Gendered patterns of interaction acquire additional layers of gendered sexuality, parenting, and work behaviors in childhood, adolescence, and adulthood. Gendered norms and expectations are enforced through informal sanctions of gender-inappropriate behavior by peers and by formal punishment or threat of punishment by those in authority should behavior deviate too far from socially imposed standards for women and men.

Everyday gendered interactions build gender into the family, the work process, and other organizations and institutions, which in turn reinforce gender expectations for individuals. Because gender is a process, there is room not only for modification and variation by individuals and small groups but also for institutionalized change (J. W. Scott 1988a, 7).

As part of a *stratification* system, gender ranks men above women of the same race and class. Women and men could be different but equal. In practice, the process of creating difference depends to a great extent on differential evaluation. As Nancy Jay (1981) says: "That which is defined, separated out, isolated from all else is A and pure. Not-A is necessarily impure, a random catchall, to which nothing is external except A and the principle of order that separates it from Not-A" (45). From the individual's point of view, whichever gender is A, the other is Not-A; gender boundaries tell the individual who is like him or her, and all the rest are unlike. From society's point of view, however, one gender is usually the touchstone, the normal, the dominant, and the other is different, deviant, and subordinate. In Western society, "man" is A, "wo-man" is Not-A. (Consider what a society would be like where woman was A and man Not-A.)

The further dichotomization by race and class constructs the gradations of a heterogeneous society's stratification scheme. Thus, in the United States, white is A, African American is Not-A; middle class is A, working class is Not-A, and "African-American women occupy a position whereby the inferior half of a series of these dichotomies converge" (P. H. Collins 1990, 70). The dominant categories are the hegemonic ideals, taken so for granted as the way things should be that white is not ordinarily thought of as a race, middle class as a class, or men as a gender. The characteristics of these categories define the Other as that which lacks the valuable qualities the dominants exhibit.

In a gender-stratified society, what men do is usually valued more highly than what women do because men do it, even when their activities are very similar or the same. In different regions of southern India, for example, harvesting rice is men's work, shared work, or women's work: "Wherever a task is done by women it is considered casy, and where it is done by [men] it is considered difficult" (Mencher 1988, 104). A gathering and hunting society's survival usually depends on the nuts, grubs, and small animals brought in by the women's foraging trips, but when the men's hunt is successful, it is the occasion for a celebration. Conversely, because they are the superior group, white men do not have to do the "dirty work," such as housework; the most inferior group does it, usually poor women of color (Palmer 1989).

230 *Part 2 / Women's Studies in Action*

Freudian psychoanalytic theory claims that boys must reject their mothers and deny the feminine in themselves in order to become men: "For boys the major goal is the achievement of personal masculine identification with their father and sense of secure masculine self, achieved through superego formation and disparagement of women" (Chodorow 1978, 165). Masculinity may be the outcome of boys' intrapsychic struggles to separate their identity from that of their mothers, but the proofs of masculinity are culturally shaped and usually ritualistic and symbolic (Gilmore 1990).

The Marxist feminist explanation for gender inequality is that by demeaning women's abilities and keeping them from learning valuable technological skills, bosses preserve them as a cheap and exploitable reserve army of labor. Unionized men who could be easily replaced by women collude in this process because it allows them to monopolize the better paid, more interesting, and more autonomous jobs: "Two factors emerge as helping men maintain their separation from women and their control of technological occupations. One is the active gendering of jobs and people. The second is the continual creation of sub-divisions in the work processes, and levels in work hierarchies, into which men can move in order to keep their distance from women" (Cockburn 1985, 13).

Societies vary in the extent of the inequality in social status of their women and men members, but where there is inequality, the status "woman" (and its attendant behavior and role allocations) is usually held in lesser esteem than the status "man." Since gender is also intertwined with a society's other constructed statuses of differential evaluation—race, religion, occupation, class, country of origin, and so on—men and women members of the favored groups command more power, more prestige, and more property than the members of the disfavored groups. Within many social groups, however, men are advantaged over women. The more economic resources, such as education and job opportunities, are available to a group, the more they tend to be monopolized by men. In poorer groups that have few resources (such as working-class African Americans in the United States), women and men are more nearly equal, and the women may even outstrip the men in education and occupational status (Almquist 1987).

As a *structure*, gender divides work in the home and in economic production, legitimates those in authority, and organizes sexuality and emotional life (Connell 1987, 91–142). As primary parents, women significantly influence children's psychological development and emotional attachments, in the process reproducing gender. Emergent sexuality is shaped by heterosexual, homosexual, bisexual, and sadomasochistic patterns that are gendered—different for girls and boys, and for women and men—so that sexual statuses reflect gender statuses.

When gender is a major component of structured inequality, the devalued genders have less power, prestige, and economic rewards than the valued genders. In countries that discourage gender discrimination, many major roles are still gendered; women still do most of the domestic labor and child rearing, even while doing full-time paid work; women and men are segregated on the job and each does work considered "appropriate"; women's work is usually paid less than men's work. Men dominate the positions of authority and leadership in government, the military, and the law; cultural productions, religions, and sports reflect men's interests.

In societies that create the greatest gender difference, such as Saudi Arabia, women are kept out of sight behind walls or veils, have no civil rights, and often create a cultural and emotional world of their own (Bernard 1981). But even in societies with less rigid gender boundaries, women and men spend much of their time with people of their own gender because of the way work and family are organized. This spatial separation of women and men reinforces gendered differentness, identity, and ways of thinking and behaving (Coser 1986).

Gender inequality—the devaluation of "women" and the social domination of "men"— has social functions and a social history. It is not the result of sex, procreation, physiology, anatomy, hormones, or genetic predispositions. It is produced and maintained by identifiable social processes and built into the general social structure and individual identities deliberately and purposefully. The social order as we know it in Western societies is organized around racial ethnic, class, and gender inequality. I contend, therefore, that the continuing purpose of gender as a modern social institution is to construct women as a group to be the subordinates of men as a group. The life of everyone placed in the status "woman" is "night to his day—that has forever been the fantasy. Black to his white. Shut out of his system's space, she is the repressed that ensures the system's

functioning" (Cixous and Clément [1975] 1986, 67).

THE PARADOX OF HUMAN NATURE

To say that sex, sexuality, and gender are all socially constructed is not to minimize their social power. These categorical imperatives govern our lives in the most profound and pervasive ways, through the social experiences and social practices of what Dorothy Smith calls the "everyday / everynight world" (1990, 31–57). The paradox of human nature is that it is *always* a manifestation of cultural meanings, social relationships, and power politics; "not biology, but culture, becomes destiny" (J. Butler 1990, 8). Gendered people emerge not from physiology or sexual orientation but from the exigencies of the social order, mostly, from the need for a reliable division of the work of food production and the social (not physical) reproduction of new members. The moral imperatives of religion and cultural representations guard the boundary lines among genders and ensure that what is demanded, what is permitted, and what is tabooed for the people in each gender is well known and followed by most (C. Davies 1982). Political power, control of scarce resources, and, if necessary, violence uphold the gendered social order in the face of resistance and rebellion. Most people, however, voluntarily go along with their society's prescriptions for those of their gender status, because the norms and expectations get built into their sense of worth and identity as a think, the way we see and hear and speak, the way we fantasy, and the way we feel.

There is no core or bedrock human nature below these endlessly looping processes of the social production of sex and gender, self and other, identity and psyche, each of which is a "complex cultural construction" (J. Butler 1990, 36). *For humans, the social is the natural.* Therefore, "in its feminist senses, gender cannot mean simply the cultural appropriation of biological sexual difference. Sexual difference is itself a fundamental—and scientifically contested—construction. Both 'sex' and 'gender' are woven of multiple, asymmetrical strands of difference, charged with multifaceted dramatic narratives of domination and struggle" (Haraway 1990, 140).

Communication

In its purest form, the field of communication is concerned with sending and receiving information. Scholars in this discipline are charged with the task of analyzing both the forces that complicate or modify the intended message and the events that occur as result of the communication process. With roots in the rhetoric of the Ancient Greeks, the modern discipline has now grown to include advertising, journalism, public relations, broadcasting, film and television theory and criticism, publishing, and new media studies. Feminist inquiry in this field is imperative as the ideology that is disseminated by the media is culturally pervasive yet often operates invisibly. As such, feminists seek to uncover the ways that women's voices are silenced or distorted by the hegemonic messages that surround us. The articles in this text provide an introduction to the work of feminist scholars in three different concentrations. Cynthia Carter, Gill Branston, and Stuart Allan explore the sexual politics of news broadcasting. They show how the field of journalism is still highly gendered in their discussion of organizational practices, "professionalized norms," and content decisions. Karlyn Kohrs Campbell offers an innovative study of the rhetoric of the early Women's Liberation Movement. She argues that its rhetoric is unique; both style and substance are aimed at sparking reform by attacking our reality structure. Finally, E. Ann Kaplan provides an overview of the work of feminist film critics. In this piece, she discusses pleasure in narrative cinema, exploring the relationship between patriarchy, visual images, and the subconscious mind.

Critical Thinking Questions

1. "Critical Theory" posits that those with economic influence act as gate-keepers and dictate the dissemination of information, especially news. Explain how Critical Theory can be applied to each Critical Mode of Enquiry as set forth by Carter, Branston, and Allan.
2. Feminists and nonfeminists alike have argued for the existence of a "woman's perspective." Does this exist? Should we seek to include all women in roles of power (in the media and elsewhere), or is there a specific kind of woman we want in these roles?

3. How do current news practices perpetuate the active male/passive female stereotypes as explained by Carter, Branston, and Allen? What other dichotomies are at work within the gender biased news industry?

4. Based on Kohrs Campbell's explanation of early women's liberation rhetoric, should contemporary feminists employ these same tactics to achieve equality? Would they work today?

5. Kohrs Campbell describes the major resistance to feminist rhetoric as existing within individuals as they attempt to "fight an enemy who has outposts in your head." Have your own preconceived notions of feminism stood in opposition to what you have encountered this semester? How have you resolved this?

6. Explain how the genre of melodrama can be simultaneously attractive to, and oppressive for, women. What assumptions about femininity underlie this specific type of film?

7. Identify the three Male Gazes as discussed by Kaplan. Explain how they work together to manipulate the viewer. Can you recall an experience with this type of manipulation?

8. Does feminist criticism take the pleasure out of watching a film? How might a feminist film be different from a traditional Hollywood movie?

9. Kaplan insists that psychoanalytic theory is a powerful tool for film criticism. To what extent can attention to the unconscious enrich our understanding of pleasure, power, and art?

22

Setting New(s) Agendas

An Introduction

(1998)

Cynthia Carter, Gill Branston, and Stuart Allan

'The story of modern journalism', declared British journalist Emilie Hawkes Peacocke in her book *Writing for Women* published in 1936, 'is that of the rise of the Woman's Story' (Peacocke 1936: 129). By a 'woman's story', she was referring both to the late nineteenth-century development of the newspaper 'Woman's Department', responsible for covering such topics as 'beauty', 'fashion', 'shopping', 'social affairs', 'gossip', 'home decoration' and 'child care', as well as to a corresponding rise in the number of women working in journalism as a vocation.[1] These sweeping changes were largely derivative of the 'New Journalism' which was also developing at that time. In general terms, this emergent form of presenting the news sought to emphasise 'human interest' stories, particularly those which were likely to appeal to the 'uneducated mass of all classes'. In the words of Matthew Arnold, who was arguably the first to coin the phrase, writing in the May 1887 issue of *The Nineteenth Century* magazine:

It has much to recommend it . . . it is full of ability, novelty, variety, sensation, sympathy, generous instincts, its one great fault is that it is featherbrained. It throws out assertions at a venture because it wishes them true; does not correct either them or itself, if they are false; and to get at the seat of things as they truly are seems to feel no concern whatever.

(Arnold 1887: 638–9;
see also Griffiths 1992)

The emergent news values which informed the New Journalism were explicitly gendered at a number of different levels, in part so as to direct journalistic attention beyond the preoccupations of propertied, educated and leisured male readers. A range of factors were responsible for this shift, not least of which was the fact that newspaper proprietors and advertisers (especially in the domestic goods markets) alike were becoming increasingly inclined to regard women consumers as an important audience on their own

Carter, Branston, and Allan, "Setting New(s) Agendas: An Introduction." In *News, Gender, and Power*. London: Taylor & Francis, 1998.

terms. This movement also created spaces for the re-articulation of bourgeois definitions of 'femininity' at a time when longstanding power-differentials based on sexual difference were undergoing extensive transformations across British society. 'The new press,' as Margaret Beetham writes, 'came to be associated with a range of characteristics which were traditionally "feminine", especially its tendency towards sensation and the personalising of information' (Beetham 1996: 118; see also Bateson 1895; Carter and Thompson 1997; Fry 1929; Grieve 1964; Head 1939; Hunter 1992; Knight 1937; Leslie 1943; Mills 1990; Sebba 1994).

Tellingly, though the contemporary 'story of modern journalism' now includes both press and broadcast histories, it continues to refer to similar types of developments, albeit often employing (in our view inappropriately) a language of 'post-feminism'. In Britain at the beginning of the 1990s, for example, many media commentators were insisting that this would be 'The Decade of Women'. Demographic statistics appeared to indicate that there would not be enough graduates to fill job demand, thus 'the female factor' suddenly became an important issue for employers, including those in the media industries (see Dougary 1994: xi). The Conservative government launched its 'Opportunity 2000' programme in 1990 to facilitate the movement of women into 'top jobs' so as to shatter the 'glass ceiling'. That same year would see three women appointed to editorial positions on national newspapers. As the recession started to take grip, however, the optimism of the beginning of the decade began to fade. Those

women who had been successful in negotiating senior media posts were increasingly being portrayed in news accounts in either ambivalent or hostile terms.[2] More to the point, they were often the first to be 'let go' as 'efficiency gains' began to dictate moves toward 'downsizing' news organisations (at the time of writing, there is only one female national-newspaper editor, at the *Daily Express* and *Express on Sunday*).

Today, as we approach the start of a new century, the day-to-day culture of most newsrooms is still being defined in predominantly male terms. Whilst there has been a dramatic increase in the number of women securing jobs in journalism, white middle-class men continue to occupy the vast majority of positions of power throughout the sector. Women are still not being promoted to senior decision-making posts in proportion to the overall rôle they play in the profession. At a time when both broadcast and print news organisations are facing ever more intensive (and increasingly globalised) forms of competition, and when female readers, listeners and viewers remain as elusive as ever, the costs of this failure to treat women fairly in the journalistic workplace continue to mount. A study of British journalism by Anne Sebba documents the varied types of discrimination female newsworkers often encounter with their male counterparts, 'some of whom may feel themselves threatened by the star status accorded to several women reporters, others of whom resent what they see as special privileges granted them; a few merely patronise their female colleagues' (Sebba 1994: 9; see also Christmas 1997; Tunstall 1996). Still, this is not to deny that women have made crucial gains in the field of news reporting which have fundamentally altered the types of sexist dynamics which once characterised the profession, as described by Peacocke (1936) above. Nevertheless, Sebba (1994: 10) is not alone when she looks forward to the day when 'women reporters are working in sufficient numbers that they are no longer judged by their looks, their personalities or their private lives and when we, the audience, are able to absorb merely the news they are reporting'.

CRITICAL MODES OF ENQUIRY

To point out that journalism is central to the study of the modern mass media across a range of academic disciplines is to state the obvious. Even a cursory glance at the research literature, however, confirms that insufficient consideration is being given to an array of pressing questions regarding how gender relations shape its forms, practices, institutions and audiences. It was a commitment to addressing this exigency which led, in turn, to the project that would eventually culminate in this volume.

The contributors to *News, Gender and Power* were invited to demonstrate from their respective analytical perspectives precisely why the media politics of gender deserve much more critical attention than they have typically received to date. Shared by each of the following chapters is a specific politics of intervention, that is, a desire to disrupt the familiar assumptions characteristic of conventional thinking about these issues. In highly varied ways, each of them draws upon the rich resources of feminist and gender-sensitive critique with the aim of providing fresh insights into a vigorous set of debates. A common thread running throughout the collection is a recognition of the need to rethink the organising tenets of earlier research with an eye to facilitating new work in this rapidly developing area of enquiry.

In this introductory essay, we would like to briefly highlight a series of important research problematics which underpin many of the themes later taken-up in a substantive way across a range of the chapters. Although we can offer only a sketch of several of the attendant conceptual and methodological issues here, it is hoped that the general contours of distinct modes of enquiry will begin to emerge as they inform the multiple interconnections between 'news', 'gender' and 'power'. Accordingly, we can identify, in schematic terms, eight interrelated problematics as follows.

1 Ownership and control

Feminist and gender-sensitive studies of journalism are becoming increasingly concerned with the changing patterns of news media ownership, especially with regard to the growing levels of concentration, conglomeration and integration, within local, national and global contexts. The dynamics of ownership are directly linked to a range of issues associated with control over journalistic content: media power is being restricted to an ever smaller number of (white male) hands; the corporate priority of profit maximisation is leading to a commercialisation of news formats whereby content becomes ever more uniform and the spaces available to articulate dissent are being reduced; and, fears over 'the bottom line' are reshaping news values in ways which frequently define feminist concerns as 'controversial', and thus potentially threatening to 'market sensitive' news organisations and their advertisers. The implications of reducing news to a commodity form like any other are profound, particularly when women's voices are struggling just to be heard within the confines of ideological parameters conditioned by these competing logics of capital. Proposed strategies for change call for a fundamental re-organisation of the current dynamics of media ownership and control, a process to be achieved through the radical re-structuring of state regulatory frameworks (see Domhoff 1978; Gallagher 1981; Jallov 1996; Mattelart 1986; Riaño 1994; Simonton 1995; Soothill and Walby 1991; Valdivia 1992; Wasko 1996).

2 Employment

At this level, and in light of the developments described above, new investigations are focusing on the changing nature of women's occupational status within news organisations. In general, the growing commodification of news has led these organisations to 'trim back' the number of journalists they employ, just as women are beginning to make serious inroads into the profession (a language of 'efficiency' is similarly used to justify a shift away from investigative reporting so as to focus on 'pre-packaged' news events which are easier, and cheaper, to cover). An organising assumption of much of this research is that the increased presence of women in the newsroom will necessarily encourage substantive changes in news-

work practices: women, it is often argued, are more inclined than men to endorse informal, non-hierarchical management structures and to support collectively-based decision-making processes. In terms of news content, more female reporters means that the lines between 'hard' and 'soft' news will continue to blur, leading to a news agenda defined more closely with 'human interest' news (see Beasley 1993; Buresh 1984; Christmas 1997; Cramer 1993; Deakin 1984; Dougary 1994; Fritz 1979; Gallagher 1995; Grist 1984; Higgins 1997; Lafky 1993; Mills 1990, 1997; Norris 1997; Schulman 1995). At the same time, however, other researchers have questioned the extent to which arguments such as these can be supported as a general rule (see B. Smith 1989; van den Wijngaard 1992; van Zoonen 1991, 1994). Many are sceptical of the claim that there is a 'woman's perspective' which female journalists inevitably bring to their reporting. In any case, as Jane Arthurs contends in her discussion of the televisual industry in Britain: 'More women in the industry is not enough: there need to be more women with a politicised understanding of the ways in which women's subordination is currently reproduced, and with the will to change it' (Arthurs 1994: 100).

3 Professional identity

Feminist studies of the processes of socialisation, which reporters undergo when learning the skills necessary for their job, continue to raise awareness of how gender relations underwrite journalism as a profession (see Baehr 1996; Epstein 1978; Foote 1995; Gill 1993; Lafky 1995; Makins

1975; Mata 1994; Molotch 1978; Rhodes 1992, 1995; Schultz-Brooks 1984; Smith 1980; Stott 1973; van Zoonen 1994; Weaver 1997). In the 1930s, Emilie Peacocke (1936) told aspiring female journalists that reporters learnt their craft through a system of reward and punishment. Rewards included being given the 'good assignments' ('serious' news stories), peer acknowledgement, praise, promotion and acclaim; punishments included increased demands for story re-writes as well as the outright rejection of their work, being given less prestigious assignments ('Society news', the women's department, obituaries), and being relegated to 'trite' beats such as 'Lifestyles'. Today, feminist researchers have sought to elucidate how certain 'common sensical' attitudes, values and beliefs about gender inform the criteria underpinning what counts as 'professionalism' and how they, in turn, shape the forms of sexism regularly encountered by female journalists both in the newsroom and in the field (see Bradley 1995; Christmas 1997; Coles 1997; Dougary 1994; Elwood-Akers 1988; Graham 1997; Higgins 1997; Hoffman 1970–1; Kaufman 1995; Mills 1990; Sanders and Rock 1988; Sebba 1994; Skard 1989; Skidmore 1995; Smith *et al.* 1993; Steiner 1997b; Walkowitz 1993). As much of this work suggests, it is the very taken-for-grantedness of the professionalised norms that govern journalistic routines and conventions which makes them difficult to identify, let alone challenge.

4 News sources

News sources, routinely organised by the journalist into a 'hierarchy of cred-ibility' (Hall *et al.* 1978), are encouraged to speak the social world in certain preferred ways. Studies of media-source relations show that journalists tend to rely primarily upon white, middle-class, middle-aged, professional males as sources, particularly when 'expert' opinions are being accessed (see Beasley 1993; Bridge 1995; Croteau and Hoynes 1992; Holland 1987; Rakow and Kranich 1991). 'News is not simply mostly . . . about and by men', John Hartley writes, 'it is overwhelmingly seen through men' (1982: 146). When women are included as news sources, as several feminist researchers have argued, they tend to be defined in terms of their status *vis-à-vis* the principal (typically male) news actor in a particular story. As Patricia Holland points out, women are routinely presented:

> either as an anonymous example of uninformed public opinion, as housewife, consumer, neighbour, or as mother, sister, wife of the man in the news, or as victim—of crime, disaster, political policy. Thus not only do they speak less frequently, but they tend to speak as passive reactors and witnesses to public events rather than as participants in those events.

(Holland 1987: 138–9)

This gendered division is linked, in turn, to an alignment of 'serious' news values with public-sphere events deemed to be of interest to men, whilst so-called 'women's issues' are more likely to be framed in relation to the 'private' or domestic sphere (see C. F. Epstein 1978; Finn 1989–90; Hanmer and Saunders 1993; Lees 1995; McCormick 1995; Meyers 1994; Nava 1988; Norris 1997; Pingree and Hawkins 1978; Robinson 1978; Rupp 1980; Simpson 1979; Skidmore 1995;

Tuchman 1978a, 1978c; van Zoonen 1991, 1992; Voumvakis and Ericson 1984).

5 Representation

Feminist research has long been concerned with how women are portrayed in news media texts, and much of this work has employed the notion of 'stereotypes' to advantage (see Allen *et al.* 1996; Baehr 1980; Baehr and Spindler-Brown 1987; Barr 1977; Benedict 1992; Caputi 1987; Davies *et al.* 1987; C. F. Epstein 1978; Gist 1993; King and Stott 1977; Koerber 1977; Lang 1978; Luebke 1989; McNeill 1996; Robinson 1978; Root 1986; Soothill 1995; Steenland 1995; Stratford 1987; Tuchman 1978b; Tunks and Hutchinson 1991). It is often argued that the journalist's deployment of these stereotypes, far from being harmless, is instead likely to result in 'negative and undesirable social consequences' for women (Lazier and Kendrick 1993). Stereotypes are usually defined as standardised mental pictures which provide sexist judgements about women such that their subordinate status within patriarchal society is symbolically reinforced. Demands to reform these types of stereotypical practices in journalism have tended to centre on the need to make news texts more 'accurate' or 'true to real life' in their depiction of women's experiences. At the same time, however, some feminists query the value of this notion of 'stereotyping', arguing that it succeeds in obscuring the fluidly contradictory, and often contested, dynamics that it should otherwise be at pains to render visible (see Beetham 1996; Brake 1994; Cirkensa and Cuklanz

1992; Creedon 1993; Douglas 1994; Ganguly 1992; Holland 1983, 1987; Houston 1992; Macdonald 1995; Rakow 1992; Shevelow 1989; Steeves 1987; van Zoonen 1994; Wykes 1995; see also Adam and Allan 1995; Weedon 1997; Women's Studies Group 1978). Much of this work has initiated a conceptual shift to rethink the attendant issues of representation in terms of the ideological gendering of news as an androcentric form of discourse.

6 Narrative forms and practices

Another line of feminist research, as suggested by the problematic above, has sought to argue that news discourse constitutes a 'masculine narrative form'. Lana F. Rakow and Kimberlie Kranich maintain, for example, that in these masculinised narratives, women function not as speaking subjects but as 'signs'. In examining these narrative structures, they argue that 'since women are found so infrequently in news stories, and since they always sign as "woman" (unlike men, who do not ordinarily carry meaning as "man" because the culture assumes maleness as given), their function as sign is unique' (Rakow and Kranich 1991: 13). Moreover, they point out that the meaning of the sign 'woman' is similarly bound up with the assumption of whiteness: 'Both race and gender depend on linguistically categorising people, ostensibly to reflect biological (e.g., skin colour) differences but actually to create a political and hierarchical system of difference' (1991: 19–20). Also relevant here is John Fiske's critique of televisual news as 'masculine soap opera', where he observes that news and soap opera share several characteristics, including 'lack of final closure, multiplicity of plots and characters, repetition and familiarity' (Fiske 1987: 308). It follows from these modes of analysis that the narrative forms and practices routinely held to constitute 'news' will have to undergo critical reconsideration if the imperatives of male hegemony are to be challenged (see Carter and Thompson 1997; Clark 1992; Cuklanz 1996; Holland 1987; Kitzinger and Skidmore 1995; Meyers 1997; Rakow and Kranich 1991; Sanders 1993; Steiner 1992; Valdivia 1992; van Zoonen 1988; 1991; see also Tolson 1977). The same is true for the research process itself, as certain alternative forms of news discourse which often claim to speak more directly to women's experiences, such as talk shows, documentaries, magazines, and breakfast television, have tended to be overlooked–frequently being dismissed by male researchers as being 'infotainment' rather than 'proper news', and hence unworthy of scholarly attention.

7 Feminisation and sexualisation

'There is a move right across the media towards making the news more fun, more sexy, more entertaining', writes British journalist Suzanne Moore, 'as though there is an implicit understanding that news on its own is just too straight, too dull and too boring to attract those peculiar minorities, women and young people' (1997: 21). It would appear that for many different news organisations the division between 'hard' ('serious'; 'fact-based') news and 'soft' ('light' or 'human interest'; 'interpretation-based') news is slowly being dissolved or 'feminised',

in part as a response to demands from advertisers that female readers be more actively pursued as a distinct audience-demographic group (see Branston 1993; Christmas 1997; Dougary 1994; Grindstaff 1997; Hartley 1996; Mills 1990; Rapping 1995; Shuttac 1997; Squires 1997; van Zoonen 1991). Several researchers maintain that this process of feminisation is dramatically recasting 'mainstream' (or 'malestream') news narratives. One recent example of such a shift has been the coverage of the death and global mourning of Princess Diana. Specifically, some argue that it illustrates the ways in which the representation of certain highly privileged news celebrities allows a range of feminist debates to be articulated, and in a way which retains an emphasis on expressive feelings and emotions that would otherwise be disallowed under the constraints of 'objective' reporting or 'dispassionate' and 'detached' commentary. Feminised forms of reporting this tragic event elicited worldwide tributes from women for whom certain personal concerns (bulimia, the experience of divorce, very gender-specific feelings of worthlessness) had been given a greater public voice.

8 News audiences

Researchers interested in investigating the actual ways in which people relate to news discourse have drawn upon a range of methodological strategies, including interviews, participant observation and ethnography (see Bird 1997; Brunsdon and Morley 1978; Gillespie 1995; Grindstaff 1997; Hobson 1980, 1990; Morley 1980, 1986; Philo 1990; Reid 1989; Schlesinger *et al.* 1992; see also Allan 1998, 1997b). Evidence drawn from these ethnographic accounts often indicates that how people watch televisual news, for example, is much less determined by the actual programming than it is conditioned by the social relations of its consumption. In tracing the contours of the social contexts of viewing within everyday domestic life in the household, a range of studies have highlighted the need to explicate the gendered nature of both televisual technology and the practices by which it is negotiated. In an early study, entitled 'Housewives and the mass media', Dorothy Hobson (1980) examines how a range of factors inform a sexual division of household labour which, in turn, conditions a gender-specificity with regard to programming preferences. Her female interviewees (young working-class mothers of small children) revealed a tendency to demarcate televisual news into a 'masculine' domain. In Hobson's words:

> There is an *active* choice of programmes which are understood to constitute the 'woman's world', coupled with a complete *rejection* of programmes which are presenting the 'man's world' [predominantly news, current affairs, 'scientific' and documentary programmes]. However, there is also an acceptance that the 'real' or 'man's world' is important, and the 'right' of their husbands to watch these programmes is respected: but it is not a world with which the women in this study wanted to concern themselves. In fact, the 'world', in terms of what is constructed as of 'news' value, is seen as both alien and hostile to the values of women.

(Hobson 1980: 109)

The social world, as represented in news discourse, is generally seen by the women in this study to be 'depressing' and 'boring'. Still, Hobson points out that 'the importance of accepted 'news values' is recognised, and although their own world is seen as more interesting and relevant to them, it is also seen as secondary in rank to the 'real' or 'masculine' world' (1980: 111). As more recent research studies have similarly argued, the varied social uses to which televisual news is put need to be examined in association with the (usually unspoken) rules by which the very 'normality' of everyday life, especially its patriarchal structures, is defined and reproduced (see also Brunsdon and Morley 1978; Dines and Humez 1995; Gillespie 1995; Gray 1992, 1996; Grindstaff 1997; Hobson 1978, 1980; Lull 1990; Mattelart 1986; Morley 1980, 1986; Nightingale 1990; Press 1991; Silverstone 1996).

Overall, then, this brief sketch of several particularly salient problematics (located, as they are, amongst a host of others) illuminates some of the rudimentary features of the ongoing debates we regard as being central to this volume's analytical and strategic agendas. In electing to outline them in this fashion, it has been our intention to help establish a conceptual point of departure for the critical discussions to follow in the various contributions. As will quickly become apparent, each of the respective chapters provides a unique vantage point from which its author(s) engages with the challenge of extending these types of problematics into new areas of concern.

NOTES

1. Similarly, Kay Mills (1990: 24), in her account of US journalism at about this time, argues that female reporters

tended to be restricted to these same types of stories to cover. There were exceptions to this general rule, however, and she describes how a limited number of female reporters became their newspaper's 'stunt girl'. Such women wrote about controversial subjects, such as divorce and prostitution, and often placed themselves in physically dangerous situations to get 'sensational' stories on topics like the failure of social welfare programmes for women and children. Still others assumed the rôle of 'sob sister', whose function it was to report on court trials where they would "watch for the tear-filled eye, the widow's veil, the quivering lip, the lump in the throat, the trembling hand" (Ross cited in Mills 1990: 26;

see also Banks 1902; Beasley and Gibbons 1993; Carpenter 1946; Furman 1949; Henry 1993; Marzolf 1977, Ross 1936; Schlipp and Murphy 1983; Steiner 1992, 1997a; Steiner and Gray 1985).

2. At that time, a BBC report on the first three women newspaper editors was broadcast under the title: 'Killer Bimbos on Fleet Street'. Ginny Dougary (1994: xiii) claims that 'the shorthand has stuck, and set the trivialising tone for subsequent articles on Eve Pollard. When she moved from the *Sunday Mirror* to become the first female editor of a mid-market newspaper, the *Sunday Express*, the *Observer's* interviewer described her as "A 'Killer Bimbo' who knows how to use her bosom as cosh" '.

23

The Rhetoric of Women's Liberation

An Oxymoron

(1973)

Karlyn Kohrs Campbell

Whatever the phrase "women's liberation" means, it cannot, as yet, be used to refer to a cohesive historical-political movement. No clearly defined program or set of policies unifies the small, frequently transitory groups that compose it, nor is there much evidence of organizational unity and cooperation. At this point in time, it has produced only minor changes in American society, although it has made the issues with which it is associated major topics of concern and controversy. As some liberation advocates admit, it is a "state of mind" rather than a movement. Its major manifestation has been rhetorical, and as such, it merits rhetorical analysis.

Because any attempt to define a rhetorical movement or genre is beset by difficulties, and because of the unusual status of women's liberation I have briefly described, I wish to state explicitly two presuppositions informing what follows. First, I reject historical and socio-psychological definitions of movements as the basis for rhetorical criticism on the grounds that they do not, in fact, isolate a genre of *rhetoric* or a distinctive body of *rhetorical* acts. The criteria defining a rhetorical movement must be rhetorical; in Aristotelian terminology, such criteria might arise from the relatively distinctive use or interpretation of the canons and modes of proof. However, rather than employing any codified critical scheme, I propose to treat two general categories—substance and style. In my judgment, the rhetoric of women's liberation (or any other body of discourses) merits *separate* critical treatment if, and only if, the symbolic acts of which it is composed can be shown to be distinctive on both substantive and stylistic grounds. Second, I presume that the style and substance of a genre of rhetoric are interdependent. Stylistic choices are deeply influenced by subject-matter and context, and issues are formulated and shaped by stylistic strategies. The central argument of this essay is that the rhetoric of women's liberation is a distinctive genre because it evinces unique *rhetorical*

Campbell, Karlyn Kohrs, "The Rhetoric of Women's Liberation: An Oxymoron," 59 QJS (February 1973), no. 1: pp. 74–86.

qualities that are a fusion of substantive and stylistic features.

DISTINCTIVE SUBSTANTIVE FEATURES

At first glance, demands for legal, economic, and social equality for women would seem to be a reiteration, in a slightly modified form, of arguments already familiar from the protest rhetoric of students and blacks. However, on closer examination, the fact that equality is being demanded *for women* alters the rhetorical picture drastically. Feminist advocacy unearths tensions woven deep into the fabric of our society and provokes an unusually intense and profound "rhetoric of moral conflict." The sex role requirements for women contradict the dominant values of American culture— self-reliance, achievement, and independence. Unlike most other groups, the social status of women is defined primarily by birth, and their social position is at odds with fundamental democratic values. In fact, insofar as the role of rhetor entails qualities of self-reliance, self-confidence, and independence, *its very assumption is a violation of the female role*. Consequently, feminist rhetoric is substantively unique by definition, because no matter how traditional its argumentation, how justificatory its form, how discursive its method, or how scholarly its style, it attacks the entire psychosocial reality, the most fundamental values, of the cultural context in which it occurs. As illustration, consider the apparently moderate, reformist demands by feminists for legal, economic, and social equality—demands ostensibly based on the shared value of equality. (As presented here, each of these demands is a condensed version of arguments from highly traditional discourses by contemporary liberationists.)

The demand for legal equality arises out of a conflict in values. Women are not equal to men in the sight of the law. In 1874, the Supreme Court ruled that "some citizens could be denied rights which others had," specifically, that "the 'equal protection' clause of the Fourteenth Amendment did not give women equal rights with men," and reaffirmed this decision in 1961, stating that "the Fourteenth Amendment prohibits any arbitrary class legislation, except that based on sex." The legal inferiority of women is most apparent in marriage laws. The core of these laws is that spouses have reciprocal—not equal—rights and duties. The husband must maintain the wife and children, but the amount of support beyond subsistence is at his discretion. In return, the wife is legally required to do the domestic chores, provide marital companionship, and sexual consortium but has no claim for direct compensation for any of the services rendered. Fundamentally, marriage is a property relationship. In the nine community property states, the husband is considered the head of the "community," and so long as he is capable of managing it, the wife, acting alone, cannot contract debts chargeable to it. In Texas and Nevada, the husband can even dispose of the property without his wife's consent, property that includes the income of a working wife. The forty-one common law states do not recognize the economic contribution of a wife who works only in the home. She has no right to an allowance, wages, or income of any sort, nor can she claim joint ownership upon divorce. In addition, every married woman's surname is legally that of her husband, and no court will uphold her right to go by another name.

It seems to me that any audience of such argumentation confronts a moral dilemma. The listener must either admit that this is not a society based on the value of equality or make the overt assertion that women are special or inferior beings who merit discriminatory treatment.

The argument for economic equality follows a similar pattern. Based on median income, it is a greater economic disadvantage to be female than to be black or poorly educated (of course, any combination of these spells economic disaster). Although half of the states have equal pay laws, dual pay scales are the rule. These cannot be justified economically because, married or single, the majority of women who work do so out of economic necessity, and some forty percent of families with incomes below the poverty level are headed by women. Occupationally, women are proportionately more disadvantaged today than they were in 1940, and the gap between male and female income steadily increases. It might seem that these data merely indicate a discrepancy between law and practice—at least the value is embodied in some laws—although separating values and behavior is somewhat problematic. However, both law and practice have made women economically unequal. For example, so long as the law, as well as common practice, gives the husband a right to the domestic services of his wife, a woman must perform the equivalent of two jobs in order to hold one outside the home. Once again, the audience of such argumentation confronts a moral dilemma.

The most overt challenge to cultural values appears in the demand for so-cial or sexual equality, that we dispense forever with the notion that "men are male *humans* whereas women are human *females*," a notion enshrined in the familiar phrase, "I now pronounce you *man* and wife." An obvious reason for abolishing such distinctions is that they lead to cultural values for men as men and women as wives. Success for men is defined as instrumental, productive labor in the outside world whereas "wives" are confined to "woman's place"—child care and domestic labor in the home. As long as these concepts determine "masculinity" and "femininity," the woman who strives for the kind of success defined as the exclusive domain of the male is inhibited by norms prescribing her "role" and must pay a heavy price for her deviance. Those who have done research on achievement motivation in women conclude that: "Even when legal and educational barriers to achievement are removed, the motive to avoid success will continue to inhibit women from doing 'too well'— thereby risking the possibility of being socially rejected as 'unfeminine' or 'castrating,'" and "The girl who maintains qualities of independence and active striving (achievement-orientation) necessary for intellectual mastery defies the conventions of sex appropriate behavior and must pay a price, *a price in anxiety*." As long as education and socialization cause women to be "unsexed" by success whereas men are "unsexed" by failure, women cannot compete on equal terms or develop their individual potentials. No values, however, are more deeply engrained than those defining "masculinity" and "femininity." The fundamental conflict in values is evident.

Once their consequences and implications are understood, these apparently moderate, reformist demands are rightly seen as revolutionary and radical in the extreme. They threaten the institutions of marriage and the family and norms governing child-rearing and male-female roles. To meet them would require major, even revolutionary, social change. It should be emphasized, however, that these arguments are drawn from discourses that could not be termed confrontative, alienating, or radical in any ordinary sense. In form, style, structure, and supporting materials, they would meet the demands of the strictest Aristotelian critic. Yet they are substantively unique, inevitably radical, because they attack the fundamental values underlying this culture. The option to be moderate and reformist is simply not available to women's liberation advocates.

DISTINCTIVE STYLISTIC FEATURES

As a rhetoric of intense moral conflict, it would be surprising indeed if distinctive stylistic features did not appear as strategic adaptations to a difficult rhetorical situation. I propose to treat "stylistic features" rather broadly, electing to view women's liberation as a persuasive campaign. In addition to the linguistic features usually considered, the stylistic features of a persuasive campaign include, in my view, characteristic modes of rhetorical interaction, typical ways of structuring the relationships among participants in a rhetorical transaction, and emphasis on particular forms of argument, proof, and evidence. The rhetoric of women's liberation is distinctive stylistically in rejecting certain tradi-

tional concepts of the rhetorical process—as persuasion of the many by an expert or leader, as adjustment or adaptation to audience norms, and as directed toward inducing acceptance of a specific program or a commitment to group action. This rather "anti-rhetorical" style is chosen on substantive grounds because rhetorical transactions with these features encourage submissiveness and passivity in the audience—qualities at odds with a fundamental goal of feminist advocacy—self-determination. The paradigm that highlights the distinctive stylistic features of women's liberation is "consciousness raising," a mode of interaction or a type of rhetorical transaction uniquely adapted to the rhetorical problem of feminist advocacy.

The rhetorical problem may be summarized as follows: women are divided from one another by almost all the usual sources of identification—age, education, income, ethnic origin, even geography. In addition, counterpersuasive forces are pervasive and potent—nearly all spend their lives in close proximity to and under the control of males—fathers, husbands, employers, etc. Women also have very negative self-concepts, so negative, in fact, that it is difficult to view them as an audience, i.e., persons who see themselves as potential agents of change. When asked to select adjectives to describe themselves, they select such terms as "uncertain, anxious, nervous, hasty, careless, fearful, dull, childish, helpless, sorry, timid, clumsy, stupid, silly, and domestic . . . understanding, tender, sympathetic, pure, generous, affectionate, loving, moral, kind, grateful, and patient." If a persuasive campaign directed to this audience is to be effective, it must transcend alienation to create "sister-hood," modify self-concepts to create a sense of autonomy, and speak to women in terms of private, concrete, individual experience, because women have little, if any, publicly shared experience. The substantive problem of the absence of shared values remains: when women become part of an audience for liberation rhetoric, they violate the norms governing sex appropriate behavior.

In its paradigmatic form, "consciousness raising" involves meetings of small, leaderless groups in which each person is encouraged to express her personal feelings and experiences. There is no leader, rhetor, or expert. All participate and lead: all are considered expert. The goal is to make the personal political: to create awareness (through shared experiences) that what were thought to be personal deficiencies and individual problems are common and shared, a result of their position as women. The participants seek to understand and interpret their lives as women, but there is no "message," no "party line." Individuals are encouraged to dissent, to find their own truths. If action is suggested, no group commitment is made; each must decide whether, and if so which, action is suitable for her. The stylistic features heightened in this kind of transaction are characteristic of the rhetoric as a whole: affirmation of the affective, of the validity of personal experience, of the necessity for self-exposure and self-criticism, of the value of dialogue, and of the goal of autonomous, individual decision making. These stylistic features are very similar to those Maurice Natanson has described as characteristic of genuine argumentation":

What is at issue, really, in the risking of the self in genuine argument is the immediacy of the self's world of feeling, attitude, and the total subtle range of its affective and conative sensibility. . . . I open myself to the viable possibility that the consequence of an argument may be to make me *see* something of the structure of my immediate world . . . the personal and immediate domain of individual experience. . . .

. . . feeling is a way of meaning as much as thinking is a way of formulating. Privacy is a means of establishing a world, and what genuine argument to persuade does is to publicize that privacy. The metaphor leads us to suggest that risking the self in argument is inviting a stranger to the interior familiarity of our home. . . .

Even a cursory reading of the numerous anthologies of women's liberation rhetoric will serve to confirm that the stylistic features I have indicated are characteristic. Particularly salient examples include Elizabeth Janeway's *Man's World; Woman's Place.* "The Demise of the Dancing Dog," "The Politics of Housework." *A Room of One's Own,* and "Cutting Loose." The conclusion of the last essay cited will serve as a model:

The true dramatic conclusion of this narrative should be the dissolution of my marriage; there is a part of me which believes that you cannot fight a sexist system while acknowledging your need for the love of a man. . . . But in the end my husband and I did not divorce. . . . Instead I raged against him for many months and joined the Woman's Liberation Movement, and thought a great deal about myself, and about whether my problems were truly all women's problems, and decided that some of them were and that some of them were not. My sexual rage was the most powerful single emotion of my life, and the feminist analysis has become for me, as

I think it will for most women of my generation, as significant an intellectual tool as Marxism was for generations of radicals. But it does not answer every question. . . . I would be lying if I said that my anger had taught me how to live. But my life has changed because of it. I think I am becoming in many small ways a woman who takes no shit. I am no longer submissive, no longer seductive. . . .

My husband and I have to some degree worked out our differences. . . . But my hatred lies within me and between us, not wholly a personal hatred, but not entirely political either. And I wonder always whether it is possible to define myself as a feminist revolutionary and still remain in any sense a wife. There are moments when I still worry that he will leave me, that he will come to need a woman less preoccupied with her own rights, and when I worry about that I also fear that no man will ever love me again, that no man could ever love a woman who is angry. And that fear is a great source of trouble to me, for it means that in certain fundamental ways I have not changed at all.

I would like to be cold and clear and selfish, to demand satisfaction for my needs, to compel respect rather than affection. And yet there are moments, and perhaps there always will be, when I fall back upon the old cop-outs. . . . Why should I work when my husband can support me, why should I be a human being when I can get away with being a child?

Women's liberation is finally only personal. It is hard to fight an enemy who has outposts in your head.

This essay, the other works I have cited here, and the bulk of women's liberation rhetoric stand at the farthest remove from traditional models of rhetorical discourse, judged by the stylistic features I have discussed. This author, Sally Kempton, invites us into the interiority of her self, disclosing the inner dynamics of her feelings and the specific form that the problem of liberation takes in her life. In a rhetorically atypical fashion, she honors her feelings of fear, anger, hatred, and need for love and admits both her own ambivalence and the limits of her own experience as a norm for others. She is self-conscious and self-critical, cognizant of the inconsistencies in her life and of the temptation to "cop out," aware of both the psychic security and the psychic destruction inherent in the female role. She is tentatively describing and affirming the beginnings of a new identity and, in so doing, sets up a dialogue with other women in a similar position that permits the essay to perform the ego-functions that Richard Gregg has described. The essay asks for the participation of the reader, not only in sharing the author's life as an example of the problems of growing up female in this society, but in a general process of self-scrutiny in which each person looks at the dynamics of the problems of liberation in her own life. The goal of the work is a process, not a particular belief or policy; she explicitly states that her problems are not those of all women and that a feminist analysis is not a blue-print for living. Most importantly, however, the essay exemplifies "risking the self" in its most poignant sense. The Sally Kempton we meet in the essay has been masochistic, manipulative, an exploiter of the female role and of men, weak, murderous, vengeful and castrating, lazy and selfish. The risk involved in such brutal honesty is that she will be rejected as neurotic, bitchy, crazy, in short, as not being a "good" woman, and more importantly, as *not like us*. The risk may lead to alienation or to sisterhood. By example, she asks other women to confront themselves, recognize their own ambivalence, and face their own participation and collaboration in the roles and processes that have such devastating effects on both men and women. Although an essay, this work has all the distinctive stylistic features of the "consciousness raising" paradigm.

Although the distinctive stylistic features of women's liberation are most apparent in the small group processes of consciousness raising, they are not confined to small group interactions. The features I have listed are equally present in essays, speeches, and other discourses completely divorced from the small group setting. In addition, I would argue that although these stylistic features show certain affinities for qualities associated with psychotherapeutic interaction, they are rhetorical rather than expressive and public and political rather than private and personal. The presumption of most psychotherapy is that the origins of and solutions to one's problems are personal; the feminist analysis presumes that it is the social structure and the definition of the female role that generate the problems that individual women experience in their personal lives. As a consequence, solutions must be structural, not merely personal, and analysis must move from personal experience and feeling to illuminate a common condition that all women experience and share.

Finally, women's liberation rhetoric is characterized by the use of confrontative, non-adjustive strategies designed to "violate the reality structure." These strategies not only attack the psycho-social reality of the culture, but violate the norms of decorum, morality, and "femininity" of the women addressed. Essays on frigidity and orgasm, essays by prostitutes and lesbians, personal accounts of promiscuity and masochism, and essays attacking romantic love and urging man-hating as a necessary stage in liberation "violate the reality structure" by close analysis of tabooed subjects, by treating "social outcasts" as "sisters" and credible sources, and by attacking areas of belief with great mythic power. Two specific linguistic techniques, "attack metaphors" and symbolic reversals, also seem to be characteristic. "Attack metaphors" mix matrices in order to reveal the "nonconscious ideology" of sexism in language and belief, or they attempt to shock through a kind of "perspective by incongruity." Some examples are: "Was Lurleen Wallace *Governess* of Alabama?" A drawing of Rodin's "Thinker" as a female. "Trust in God; She will provide." "Prostitutes are the only honest women because they charge for their services, rather than submitting to a marriage contract which forces them to work for life without pay." "If you think you are emancipated, you might consider the idea of tasting your menstrual blood— if it makes you sick, you've got a long way to go, baby." Or this analogy:

Suppose that a white male college student decided to room or set up a bachelor apartment with a black male friend. Surely the typical white student would not blithely assume that his black roommate was to handle all the domestic chores. Nor would his conscience allow him to do so even in the unlikely event that his roommate would say: "No, that's okay. I like doing housework. I'd be happy to do it. . . ." But change this hypothetical black roommate to a female marriage partner, and somehow the student's conscience goes to sleep.

Symbolic reversals transform devil terms society has applied to women into god terms and always exploit the power and fear lurking in these terms as potential sources of strength. "The Bitch Manifesto" argues that liberated women are bitches—aggressive, confident, strong. W.I.T.C.H., the Women's International Terrorist Conspiracy from Hell, says, in effect, "You think we're dangerous, creatures of the devil, witches? You're right! And we're going to hex you!" Some feminists have argued that the lesbian is the paradigm of the liberated female; others have described an androgynous role. This type of reversal has, of course, appeared in other protest rhetorics, particularly in the affirmation that "black is beautiful!" But systematic reversals of traditional female roles, given the mystique associated with concepts of wife, mother, and loving sex partner, make these reversals especially disturbing and poignant. Quite evidently, they are attempts at the radical affirmation of new identities for women.

The distinctive stylistic features of women's liberation rhetoric are a result of strategic adaptation to an acute rhetorical problem. Women's liberation is characterized by rhetorical interactions that emphasize affective proofs and personal testimony, participation and dialogue, self-revelation and self-criticism, the goal of autonomous decision making through self-persuasion, and the strategic use of techniques for "violating the reality structure." I conclude that, on stylistic grounds, women's liberation is a separate genre of rhetoric.

THE INTERDEPENDENCE OF SUBSTANTIVE AND STYLISTIC FEATURES

The rhetorical acts I have treated in the preceding section, particularly as illustrated by the excerpt from an essay by Sally Kempton, may seem to be a far cry from the works cited earlier demanding legal, economic, and social equality. However, I believe that all of these rhetorical acts are integral parts of a single genre, a conclusion I shall defend by examining the interdependent character of the substantive and stylistic features of the various discourses already discussed.

Essays such as that of Sally Kempton are the necessary counterparts of works articulating demands for equality. In fact, such discourses spell out the meaning and consequences of present conditions of inequity and the implications of equality in concrete, personal, affective terms. They complete the genre and are essential to its success as a persuasive campaign. In the first section, I argued that demands for equality for women "attack the entire psycho-social reality."

> threatening; the bitch is the reversal of the private role of wife—instead of being comforting, loving, and serious, she is selfish, teasing, emasculating. The point she is making is that these are not new, creative roles, merely reversals of existing, socially defined roles. (Pp. 119-123, 126-127, 199-201.)

That phrase may conceal the fact that such an attack is an attack on the *self* and on the roles and relationships in which women, and men too, have found their identities traditionally. The effect of such an argument is described by Natanson, "When an argument hurts me, cuts me, or cleanses and liberates me it is not because a particular stratum or segment of my world view is shaken up or jarred free but because *I* am wounded or enlivened—*I* in my particularity, and that means in my existential immediacy: feelings, pride, love, and sullenness, the world of my actuality as I live it." The only effective response to the sensation of being threatened existentially is a rhetorical act that treats the personal, emotional, and concrete directly and explicitly, that is dialogic and participatory, that speaks from personal experience to personal experience. Consequently, the rhetoric of women's liberation includes numerous essays discussing the personal experiences of women in many differing circumstances— black women, welfare mothers, older women, factory workers, high school girls, journalists, unwed mothers, lawyers, secretaries, and so forth. Each attempts to describe concretely the personal experience of inequality in a particular situation and/or what liberation might mean in a particular case. Rhetorically, these essays function to translate public demands into personal experience and to treat threats and fears in concrete, affective terms.

Conversely, more traditional discourses arguing for equality are an essential counterpart to these more personal statements. As a process, consciousness raising requires that the personal be transcended by moving toward the structural, that the individual be transcended by moving toward the political. The works treating legal, economic, and social inequality provide the structural analyses and empirical data that permit women to generalize from their individual experiences to the conditions of women in this society. Unless such transcendence occurs, there is no persuasive campaign, no rhetoric in any public sense, only the very limited realm of therapeutic, small group interaction.

The interrelationship between the personal and the political is central to a conception of women's liberation as a genre of rhetoric. All of the issues of women's liberation are simultaneously personal and political. Ultimately, this interrelationship rests on the caste status of women, the basis of the moral conflict this rhetoric generates and intensifies. Feminists believe that sharing personal experience is liberating, i.e., raises consciousness, because all women, whatever their differences in age, education, income, etc., share a common condition, a radical form of "consubstantiality" that is the genesis of the peculiar kind of identification they call "sisterhood." Some unusual rhetorical transactions seem to confirm this analysis. "Speakouts" on rape, abortion, and orgasm are mass meetings in which women share extremely personal and very negatively valued experiences. These events are difficult to explain without postulating a radical form of identification that permits such painful self-revelation. Similarly, "self-help clinics" in which women learn how to examine their cervixes and look at the cervixes of other women for purposes of comparison seem to require extreme identification and trust. Feminists would argue that "sisterhood is powerful" because it grows out of the recognition of pervasive, common experience of special caste status, the most radical and profound basis for cooperation and identification.

This feminist analysis also serves to explain the persuasive intent in "violating the reality structure."

From this point of view, women in American society are always in a vortex of contradiction and paradox. On the one hand, they have been, for the most part, effectively socialized into traditional roles and values, as research into their achievement motivation and self-images confirms. On the other hand, "femininity" is in direct conflict with the most fundamental values of this society—a fact which makes women extremely vulnerable to attacks on the "reality structure." Hence, they argue, violations of norms may shock initially, but ultimately they will be recognized as articulating the contradictions inherent in "the female role." The violation of these norms is obvious in discourses such as that of Sally Kempton; it is merely less obvious in seemingly traditional and moderate works.

CONCLUSION

I conclude, then, that women's liberation is a unified, separate genre of rhetoric with distinctive substantive-stylistic features. Perhaps it is the only genuinely *radical* rhetoric on the contemporary American scene. Only the oxymoron, the figure of paradox and contradiction, can be its metaphor. Never is the paradoxical character of women's liberation more apparent than when it is compared to conventional or familiar definitions of rhetoric, analyses of rhetorical situations, and descriptions of rhetorical movements.

Traditional or familiar definitions of persuasion do not satisfactorily account for the rhetoric of women's liberation. In relation to such definitions, feminist advocacy wavers between the rhetorical and the non-rhetorical, the persuasive and the non-persuasive. Rhetoric is usually defined as dealing with public issues, structural analyses, and social action, yet women's liberation emphasizes acts concerned with personal exigences and private, concrete experience, and its goal is frequently limited to particular, autonomous action by individuals. The view that persuasion is an enthymematic adaptation to audience norms and values is confounded by rhetoric which seeks to persuade by "violating the reality structure" of those toward whom it is directed.

Nor are available analyses of rhetorical situations satisfactory when applied to the rhetoric of women's liberation. Parke Burgess' valuable and provocative discussion of certain rhetorical situations as consisting of two or more sets of conflicting moral demands and Thomas Olbricht's insightful distinction between rhetorical acts occurring in the context of a shared value and those occurring in its absence do not adequately explicate the situation in which feminists find themselves. And the reason is simply that the rhetoric of women's liberation appeals to *what are said to be* shared moral values, but forces recognition that those values are *not* shared, thereby creating the most intense of moral conflicts. Lloyd Bitzer's more specific analysis of the rhetorical situation as consisting of "one controlling exigence which functions as the organizing principle" (an exigence being "an imperfection marked by urgency" that "is capable of positive modification"), an audience made up "only of those persons who are capable of being influenced by discourse and of being mediators of change," and of constraints that can limit "decision and action needed to modify the exigence"—this more specific analysis is also unsatisfactory. In women's liberation there are dual and conflicting exigences not solely of the public sort, and thus women's liberation rhetoric is a dialectic between discourses that deal with public, structural problems and the particularly significant statements of personal experience and feeling which extend beyond the traditional boundaries of rhetorical acts. A public exigence is, of course, present, but what is unavoidable and characteristic of this rhetoric is the accompanying and conflicting personal exigence. The concept of the audience does not account for a situation in which the audience must be *created under the special conditions* surrounding women's liberation. Lastly, the notion of constraints seems inadequate to a genre in which to act as a mediator of change, either as rhetor or audience member, is itself the most significant constraint inhibiting decision or action—a constraint that requires the violation of cultural norms and risks alienation no matter how traditional or reformist the rhetorical appeal may be.

And, similarly, nearly all descriptions of rhetorical movements prove unsatisfactory. Leland Griffin's early essay on the rhetoric of historical movements creates three important problems: he defines movements as occurring "at some time in the past"; he says members of movements "make efforts to alter their environment"; and he advises the student of rhetoric to focus on "the pattern of public discussion." The first problem is that the critic is prevented from examining a contemporary movement

and is forced to make sharp chronological distinctions between earlier efforts for liberation and contemporary feminist advocacy; the second problem is that once again the critic's attention is diverted from efforts to change the self, highly significant in the liberation movement, and shifted toward efforts to change the environment; and the third is a related deflection of critical concern from personal, consciousness-raising processes to public discussion. Herbert Simons' view of "a leader-centered conception of persuasion in social movements" defines a movement "as an uninstitutionalized collectivity that mobilizes for action to implement a program for the reconstitution of social norms or values." As I have pointed out, leader-centered theories cannot be applied profitably to the feminist movement. Further, women's liberation is not characterized by a *program* that mobilzes feminist advocates to reconstitute social norms and values. Dan Hahn and Ruth Gonchar's idea of a movement as "socially shared activities and beliefs directed toward the demand for change in some aspect of the social order" is unsuitable because it overlooks the extremely important elements of the personal exigence that require change in the self. There are, however, two recent statements describing rhetorical movements that are appropriate for women's liberation. Griffin's later essay describing a dramatistic framework for the development of movements has been applied insightfully to the inception period of contemporary women's liberation. What makes this description applicable is that it recognizes a variety of symbolic acts, the role of drama and conflict, and the essentially moral or value-related character of rhetorical movements. Also, Robert Cathcart's formulation, again a dramatistic one, is appropriate because it emphasizes *"dialectical enjoinment in the moral arena"* and the *"dialectical tension growing out of moral conflict."*

And so I choose the oxymoron as a label, a metaphor, for the rhetoric of women's liberation. It is a genre without a rhetor, a rhetoric in search of an audience, that transforms traditional argumentation into confrontation, that "persuades" by "violating the reality structure" but that presumes a consubstantiality so radical that it permits the most intimate of identifications. It is a "movement" that eschews leadership, organizational cohesion, and the transactions typical of mass persuasion. Finally, of course, women's liberation is baffling because it has no program, because there is no clear answer to the recurring question, "What do women want?" On one level, the answer is simple; they want what every person wants—dignity, respect, the right to self-determination, to develop their potentials as individuals. But on another level, there is no answer—not even in feminist rhetoric. While there are legal and legislative changes on which most feminists agree (although the hierarchy of priorities differs), whatever liberation is, it will be something different for each woman as liberty is something different for each person. What each woman shares, however, is the paradox of having "to fight an enemy who has outposts in your head."

24

Is the Gaze Male?

(1983)

E. Ann Kaplan

Since the beginning of the recent women's movement, American feminists have been exploring the representation of female sexuality in the arts—in literature, painting, film, and television. As we struggle towards meaningful theory, it is important to note that feminist criticism, as a new way of reading texts, emerged from the daily, ongoing concerns of women re-evaluating the culture in which they had been socialized and educated. In this sense, feminist criticism differs in basic ways from earlier critical movements which evolved out of reaction to dominant theoretical positions (i.e. out of a reaction which took place on an intellectual level). Feminism is unusual in its combination of the theoretical and (loosely speaking) the ideological (Marxist literary theory alone shares a similar dual focus, but from very different premises).

The first wave of feminist critics adopted a broadly sociological approach, looking at sex roles women occupied in various imaginative works, from high art to mass entertainment.

They assessed roles as "positive" or "negative" according to some externally constructed criteria describing the fully autonomous, independent woman. While this work was important in initiating feminist criticism (Kate Millett's *Sexual Politics* was a ground-breaking text), feminist film critics, influenced by developments taking place in film theory at the start of the 1970s, were the first to point out its limitations. First, influenced by semiology, feminist theorists stressed the crucial role played by the artistic form as the medium for expression; second, influenced by psychoanalysis, they argued that Oedipal processes were central to the production of art works. That is, they gave increasing attention to *how meaning is produced* in films, rather than to the "content," which had preoccupied sociological critics; and they stressed the links between the processes of psychoanalysis and cinema.

Before summarizing in more detail the French theorists whose influence

Kaplan, "Is the Gaze Male?" In *Women and Film: Both Sides of the Camera*. London: Taylor & Francis, 1990.

shaped currents in feminist film theory, let me deal briefly with the reasons for using psychoanalytic methodology in chapters 2 to 5 of this book, those devoted to the Hollywood film. Why, given many feminists' hostile rejection of Freudian and Lacanian theory, do I see psychoanalysis as a useful tool?

First, let me make clear that I do not see psychoanalysis as necessarily uncovering essential "truths" about the human psyche which exist across historical periods and different cultures. Making trans-historical generalizations about human psychic processes is difficult since the means for verifying those generalizations barely exist. Nevertheless, the history of literature in western civilization does show a surprising recurrence of Oedipal themes. We could say that Oedipal themes occur at those historical moments when the human family is structured in specific ways that elicit Oedipal traumas: for my purposes here, since I am concerned with a recent art form, film, and the recent theory of Oedipal problems (dating back to Freud), I am prepared to make claims for the relevance of psychoanalysis only to the state of industrial social organization characteristic of the twentieth century.

One could argue that the psychic patterns created by capitalist social and interpersonal structures (especially the late-nineteenth-century forms that carried over into our century) required at once a machine (the cinema) for their unconscious release and an analytic tool (psychoanalysis) for understanding, and adjusting, disturbances caused by the structures that confine people. To this extent, both mechanisms (film and psychoanalysis) support the status quo: but,

rather than being necessarily eternal and unchanging in the forms in which we have them, they are inserted in history, linked, that is, to the particular moment of bourgeois capitalism that gave both their birth.

If this is so, it is extremely important for women to use psychoanalysis as a tool, since it will unlock the secrets of our socialization within (capitalist) patriarchy. If we agree that the commercial film (and particularly the genre of melodrama that this book focuses on) took the form it did in some way to satisfy desires and needs created by nineteenth-century familial organization (an organization that produces Oedipal traumas), then psychoanalysis becomes a crucial tool for explaining the needs, desires, and male-female positionings that are reflected in film. The signs in the Hollywood film convey the patriarchal ideology that underlies our social structures and that constructs women in very specific ways—ways that reflect patriarchal needs, the patriarchal unconscious.

Psychoanalytic discourse may indeed have oppressed women, in the sense of bringing us to accept a positioning that is inherently antithetical to being a subject and to autonomy: but if that is the case, we need to know exactly *how* psychoanalysis has functioned to repress what we could potentially become; for this, we must master the terms of its discourse and ask a number of questions. First, is the gaze *necessarily* male (i.e. for reasons inherent in the structure of language, the unconscious, symbolic systems and thus all social structures)? Could we structure things so that women own the gaze? If this were possible, would women want to own the gaze? Finally, in either case, what does it mean to be a female spectator? Only through asking such questions within the psychoanalytic framework can we begin to find the gaps and fissures through which we can insert woman in a historical discourse that has hitherto been male-dominated and has excluded women. In this way, we may begin to change ourselves as a first step toward changing society.

Using psychoanalysis to deconstruct Hollywood films enables us to see clearly the patriarchal myths through which we have been positioned as Other (enigma, mystery), and as eternal and unchanging. We can also see how the family melodrama, as a genre geared specifically to women, functions both to expose the constraints and limitations that the capitalist nuclear family imposes on women and, at the same time, to "educate" women to accept those constraints as "natural," inevitable—as "given." For part of what defines melodrama as a form is its concern explicitly with Oedipal issues—illicit love relationships (overtly or incipiently incestuous), mother–child relationships, husband–wife relationships, father–son relationships: these are the staple fare of melodrama as surely as they are largely excluded from the dominant Hollywood genres, the western and the gangster film, that melodrama compensates for.

Using the framework developed by Peter Brooks, we might say that the western and gangster genres aim to duplicate the functions that tragedy once fulfilled, in the sense of placing man within the larger cosmic scene. But Brooks points out that we are now in a period when "mythmaking [can] only be personal and individual" since we lack "a clear transcendent value to be reconciled to;" so

that even these genres, broadly speaking, fall into melodrama. All Hollywood films, taking this large view, require what Brooks considers essential to melodrama, namely "a social order to be purged, a set of ethical imperatives to be made clear."

It is important that women are excluded from the central role in the main, highly respected Hollywood genres: women, and female issues, are only central in the family melodrama (which we can see as an offshoot of other melodramatic forms). Here Brooks's definition of the way characters in melodrama "assume primary psychic roles, Father, Mother, Child, and express basic psychic conditions" seems particularly relevant, as is also his explicit linking of psychoanalysis and melodrama at the end of the book. Psychoanalytic processes themselves, he notes, reveal the "melodrama aesthetic" (we will see in chapter 11 that the directors of a recent feminist film, *Sigmund Freud's Dora*, also view psychoanalysis as melodrama); but important for our purposes here is his comment that the melodramatic form deals with "the processes of repression and the status of repressed content." Brooks concludes that "the structure of ego, superego and id suggests the subjacent manichaeism of melodramatic persons."

Laura Mulvey (the British filmmaker and critic whose theories are central to new developments) also views melodrama as concerned with Oedipal issues, but she sees it primarily as a female form, acting as a corrective to the main genres that celebrate male action. The family melodrama is important, she says, in "probing pent-up emotion, bitterness and disillusion well known to women."

For Mulvey, melodrama serves a useful function for women who lack any coherent culture of oppression. "The simple fact of recognition has aesthetic importance," she notes; "there is a dizzy satisfaction in witnessing the way that sexual difference under patriarchy is fraught, explosive and erupts dramatically into violence within its own private stomping ground, the family." But Mulvey concludes that if melodrama is important in bringing ideological contradictions to the surface, and in being made for a female audience, events are never reconciled at the end in ways beneficial to women.

So why is it that women are drawn to melodrama? Why do we find our objectification and surrender pleasurable? This is precisely an issue that psychoanalysis can help to explain: for such pleasure is not surprising if we consider the shape of the girl's Oedipal crisis. Following Lacan for a moment, we see that the girl is forced to turn away from the illusory unity with the Mother in the prelinguistic realm and has to enter the symbolic world which involves subject and object. Assigned the place of object (lack), she is the recipient of male desire, passively appearing rather than acting. Her sexual pleasure in this position can thus be constructed only around her own objectification. Furthermore, given the male structuring around sadism, the girl may adopt a corresponding masochism.

In practice, this masochism is rarely reflected in more than a tendency for women to be passive in sexual relations; but in the realm of myth, masochism is often prominent. We could say that in locating herself in fantasy in the erotic, the woman places herself as either pas-sive recipient of male desire or, at one remove, as *watching* a woman who is passive recipient of male desires and sexual actions. Although the evidence we have to go on is slim, it does seem that women's sexual fantasies would confirm the predominance of these positionings. (We will look shortly at some corresponding male fantasies.)

Nancy Friday's volumes provide discourses on the level of dream and, however questionable as "scientific" evidence, show narratives in which the woman speaker largely arranges events for her sexual pleasure so that things are done to her, or in which she is the object of men's lascivious gaze. Often, there is pleasure in anonymity, or in a strange man approaching her when she is with her husband. Rarely does the dreamer initiate the sexual activity, and the man's large erect penis usually is central in the fantasy. Nearly all the fantasies have the dominance-submission pattern, with the woman in the latter place.

It is significant that in the lesbian fantasies that Friday has collected, women occupy *both* positions, the dreamer excited either by dominating another woman, forcing her to have sex, or enjoying being so dominated. These fantasies suggest either that the female positioning is not as monolithic as critics often imply or that women occupy the "male" position when they become dominant. Whichever the case may be (and I will say more about this in a moment), the prevalence of the dominance–submission pattern as a sexual turn-on is clear. At a discussion about pornography organized by Julia LeSage at the Conference on Feminist Film Criticism (Northwestern University, 1980), both gay and straight women admitted their pleasure (in both fantasy and actuality) in being "forced" or "forcing" someone else. Some women claimed that this was a result of growing up in Victorian-style households where all sexuality was repressed, but others denied that it had anything to do with patriarchy. Women wanted, rightly, to accept themselves sexually, whatever the turn-on mechanism. But simply to celebrate whatever gives us sexual pleasure seems to me both too easy and too problematic: we need to analyze *how it is* that certain things turn us on, how sexuality has been constructed in patriarchy to produce pleasure in the dominance–submission forms, before we *advocate* these modes.

It was predictable that many of the male fantasies in Friday's book *Men in Love* show the speaker constructing events so that he is in control: again, the "I" of identity remains central, as it is not in the female narrations. Many male fantasies focus on the man's excitement in arranging for his woman to expose herself (or even give herself) to other men, while he watches.

The difference between this male voyeurism and the female form is striking. For the woman does not own the desire, even when she watches; her watching is to place responsibility for sexuality at yet one more remove, *to distance herself from sex*. The man, on the other hand, *owns the desire and the woman*, and gets pleasure from exchanging the woman, as in Lévi-Strauss's kinship system.

Yet, some of the fantasies in Friday's book show men's wish to be taken over by an aggressive woman, who would force them to become helpless, like the little boy in his mother's hands. A tour of Times Square in 1980 (the organization Women Against Pornography runs them regularly) corroborated this. After a slide show that focused totally on male sadism and violent sexual exploitation of women, we were taken to sex shops that by no means stressed male domination. We saw literature and films expressing as many fantasies of male as of female submission. The situations were the predictable ones: young boys (but sometimes men) seduced by women in a form of authority—governesses, nursemaids, nurses, schoolteachers, stepmothers, etc. (Of course, it is significant that the corresponding dominance-submission fantasies of women have men in authority positions that carry much more status — professors, doctors, policemen, executives: these men seduce the innocent girls or young wives who cross their paths.)

Two interesting things emerge here. One is that dominance–submission patterns are apparently a crucial part of both male and female sexuality as constructed in western civilization. The other is that men have a far wider range of positions available: more readily both dominant and submissive, they vacillate between supreme control and supreme abandonment. Women, meanwhile, are more consistently submissive, but not excessively abandoned. In their own fantasies, women do not position themselves as exchanging men, although a *man* might find being exchanged an exciting fantasy.

The passivity revealed in women's sexual fantasies is reinforced by the way women are positioned in film. In an interesting paper on "The 'woman's film': possession and address," Mary Ann Doane has shown that in the one film genre (i.e. melodrama) that, as we have seen, constructs a female spectator, the spectator is made to participate in what is essentially a masochistic fantasy. Doane notes that [in the major classical genres, the female body is sexuality.] [providing the erotic object for the male spectator.] In the woman's film, the gaze must be de-eroticized (since the spectator is now assumed to be female), but in doing this the films effectively disembody their spectator. The repeated, masochistic scenarios effectively immobilize the female viewer. [She is refused pleasure in that imaginary identification which, as Mulvey has shown, repeats for men the experience of the mirror phase. The idealized male screen heroes give back to the male spectator his more perfect mirror self, together with a sense of mastery and control. In contrast, the female is given only powerless, victimized figures who, far from perfect, reinforce the basic sense of worthlessness that already exists.]

Later on in her paper, Doane shows that Freud's "A child is being beaten" is important in distinguishing the way a common masochistic fantasy works out for boys and for girls. In the male fantasy, "sexuality remains on the surface" and the man "retains his own role and his own gratification in the context of the scenario. The 'I' of identity remains." But the female fantasy is first desexualized and second, "necessitates the woman's assumption of the position of spectator, outside of the event." In this way, the girl manages, as Freud says, "to escape from the demands of the erotic side of her life altogether."

But the important question remains: when women are in the domi-nant position, are they in the *masculine* position? Can we envisage a female dominant position that would differ qualitatively from the male form of dominance? Or is there merely the possibility of both sex genders occupying the positions we now know as "masculine" and "feminine?"

The experience of films of the 1970s and 1980s would support the latter possibility, and explain why many feminists have not been excited by the so-called "liberated" woman on the screen, or by the fact that some male stars have recently been made the object of the "female" gaze. Traditionally male stars did not necessarily (or even primarily) derive their "glamor" from their looks or their sexuality but from the power they were able to wield within the filmic world in which they functioned (e.g. John Wayne); these men, as Laura Mulvey has shown, became ego-ideals for the men in the audience, corresponding to the image in the mirror, who was more in control of motor coordination than the young child looking in. "The male figure," Mulvey notes, "is free to command the stage . . . of spatial illusion in which he articulates the look and creates the action."

Recent films have begun to change this pattern: stars like John Travolta (*Saturday Night Fever, Urban Cowboy, Moment by Moment*) have been rendered object of woman's gaze and in some of the films (e.g. *Moment by Moment*) placed explicitly as a sexual object to a woman who controlled the film's action. Robert Redford likewise has begun to be used as object of "female" desire (e.g. in *Electric Horseman*). But it is significant that in all these films, when the man steps out of his traditional role as the one who controls the whole action, and when he is set up as sex object, the woman then takes on the "masculine" role as bearer of the gaze and initiator of the action. She nearly always loses her traditionally feminine characteristics in so doing—not those of attractiveness, but rather of kindness, humaneness, motherliness. She is now often cold, driving, ambitious, manipulating, just like the men whose position she has usurped.

Even in a supposedly "feminist" film like *My Brilliant Career*, the same processes are at work. The film is interesting because it foregrounds the independently minded heroine's dilemma in a clearly patriarchal culture: in love with a wealthy neighbor, the heroine makes him the object of her gaze, but the problem is that, as female, her desire has no power. Men's desire naturally carries power with it, so that when the hero finally concedes his love for her, he comes to get her. However, being able to conceive of "love" only as "submission," an end to autonomy and to her life as a creative writer, the heroine now refuses him. The film thus plays with established positions, but is unable to work through them to something else.

What we can conclude from the discussion so far is that our culture is deeply committed to myths of demarcated sex differences, called "masculine" and "feminine," which in turn revolve first on a complex gaze apparatus and second on dominance-submission patterns. This positioning of the two sex genders in representation clearly privileges the male (through the mechanisms of voyeurism and fetishism, which are male operations, and because his desire carries power/action where woman's usually does not). However,

as a result of the recent women's movement, women have been permitted in representation to assume (step into) the position defined as "masculine," as long as the man then steps into *her* position, thus keeping the whole structure intact.

It is significant, of course, that while this substitution is made to happen relatively easily in the cinema, in real life any such "swapping" is fraught with immense psychological difficulties that only psychoanalysis can unravel. In any case, such "exchanges" do not do much for either sex, since nothing has essentially changed: the roles remain locked into their static boundaries. Showing images of mere reversal may in fact provide a safety valve for the social tensions that the women's movement has created by demanding a more dominant role for women.

We have thus arrived at a point where we must question the necessity for the dominance-submission structure. The gaze is not necessarily male (literally), but to own and activate the gaze, given our language and the structure of the unconscious, is to be in the "masculine" position. It is this persistent presentation of the masculine position that feminist film critics have demonstrated in their analysis of Hollywood films. Dominant, Hollywood cinema, they show, is constructed according to the unconscious of patriarchy; film narratives are organized by means of a male-based language and discourse which parallels the language of the unconscious. [Women in film thus do not function as signifiers for a signified (a real woman), as sociological critics have assumed, but signifier and signified have been elided into a sign that represents something in the male unconscious.]

Two basic Freudian concepts—voyeurism and fetishism—have been used to explain what exactly woman represents and the mechanisms that come into play for the male spectator watching a female screen image. (Or, to put it rather differently, voyeurism and fetishism are mechanisms the dominant cinema uses to *construct* the male spectator in accordance with the needs of his unconscious.) The first, voyeurism, is linked to the scopophilic instinct (i.e. the male pleasure in his own sexual organ transferred to pleasure in watching other people having sex). Critics argue that the cinema relies on this instinct, making the spectator essentially a voyeur. The drive that causes little boys to peek through keyholes of parental bedrooms to learn about their sexual activities (or to get sexual gratification by thinking about these activities) comes into play when the male adult watches films, sitting in a dark room. The original eye of the camera, controlling and limiting what can be seen, is reproduced by the projector aperture which lights up one frame at a time; and both processes (camera and projector) duplicate the eye at the keyhole, whose gaze is confined by the keyhole "frame." The spectator is obviously in the voyeur position when there are sex scenes on the screen, but screen images of women are sexualized no matter what the women are doing literally or what kind of plot may be involved.

According to Laura Mulvey, this eroticization of women on the screen comes about through the way the cinema is structured around three explicitly male looks or gazes: there is the look of the camera in the situation being filmed (called the pro-

filmic event); while technically neutral, this look, as we've seen, is inherently voyeuristic and usually "male" in the sense that a man is generally doing the filming; there is the look of the men within the narrative, which is structured so as to make women objects of their gaze; and finally there is the look of the male spectator (discussed above) which imitates (or is necessarily in the same position as) the first two looks.

But if women were simply eroticized and objectified, matters might not be too bad, since objectification, as I have already shown, may be an inherent component of both male and female eroticism as constructed in western culture. But two further elements suggest themselves. To begin with, men do not simply look; their gaze carries with it the power of action and of possession which is lacking in the female gaze. [Women receive and return a gaze, but cannot act upon it. Second, the sexualization and objectification of women is not simply for the purposes of eroticism; from a psychoanalytic point of view, it is designed to annihilate the threat that woman (as castrated and possessing a sinister genital organ) poses.] In her article "The dread of women" (1932) Karen Horney goes to literature to show that "Men have never tired of fashioning expressions for the violent force by which man feels himself drawn to the woman, and side by side with his longing, the dread that through her he might die and be undone." Horney goes on to conjecture that even man's glorification of women "has its source not only in his cravings for love, but also in his desire to conceal his dread. A similar relief, however, is also sought and found in the disparagement of women that men often display ostentatiously in their attitudes." Horney then explores the basis of the dread of women not only in castration (more related to the father) but in fear of the vagina.

But psychoanalysts agree that, for whatever reason—fear of castration (Freud) or in an attempt to deny the existence of the sinister female genital (Horney), men endeavor to find the penis in women. Feminist film critics have seen this phenomenon (clinically known as fetishism) operating in the cinema; the camera (unconsciously) fetishizes the female form, rendering it phallus-like so as to mitigate woman's threat. Men, that is, turn "the represented figure itself into a fetish so that it becomes reassuring rather than dangerous (hence overvaluation, the cult of the female star)."

The apparently contradictory attitudes of glorification and disparagement pointed out by Horney thus turn out to be a reflection of the same ultimate need to annihilate the dread that woman inspires. In the cinema, the twin mechanisms of fetishism and of voyeurism represent two different ways of handling this dread. As Mulvey points out, fetishism "builds up the physical beauty of the object, turning it into something satisfying in itself," while voyeurism, linked to disparagement, has a sadistic side, and is involved with pleasure through control or domination and with punishing the woman (guilty for being castrated). For Claire Johnston, both mechanisms result in woman not being presented qua *woman* at all. Extending the *Cahiers du Cinéma* analysis of *Morocco*. Johnston argues that Von Sternberg represses "the idea of woman as a social and sexual being," thus replacing the opposition man—woman with male—non-male.

With this look at feminist film theories and at the issues around the problem of the gaze and of the female spectator that psychoanalysis illuminates, we can begin to see the larger theoretical issues the psychoanalytic methodology involves, particularly in relation to possibilities for change. It is this aspect of the new theoretical approaches that has begun to polarize the feminist film community. For example, in a round-table discussion in 1978, some women voiced their displeasure with theories that were themselves originally devised by men, and with women's preoccupation with how we have been seen/placed/positioned by the dominant male order. Julia LeSage, for instance, argued that the use of Lacanian criticism has been destructive in reifying women "in a childlike position that patriarchy has wanted to see them in"; for LeSage, the Lacanian framework establishes "a discourse which is totally male." And Ruby Rich objected to theories that rest with the apparent elimination of women from both screen and audience. She asked how we can move beyond our placing, rather than just analyzing it.

As if in response to Rich's request, some feminist film critics have begun to take up the challenge to move beyond the preoccupation with how women have been constructed in patriarchal cinema. Judith Mayne, for example, in a useful summary of issues in recent feminist film criticism, argues that the context for discussion of women's cinema needs to be "opened up" to include the film spectator: "The task of criticism," she says, "is to examine the processes that determine how films evoke responses and how spectators produce them." A little later on, Mayne suggests that the proper place for the feminist critic may well be close to the machine that is the agency for the propulsion of images onto the screen, i.e. the projector. By forcing our gaze to dwell on the images by slowing down or stopping the projection that creates patriarchal voyeurism, we may be able to provide a "reading against the grain" that will give us information about our positioning as spectators.

If Mayne's, LeSage's, and Rich's objections lead in a fruitful direction, those of Lucy Arbuthnot and Gall Seneca are problematic, but useful here for the purposes of illustration. In a paper on *Gentlemen Prefer Blondes* Arbuthnot and Seneca attempt to appropriate for themselves some of the images hitherto defined as repressive. They begin by expressing their dissatisfactions not only with current feminist film theory as outlined above, but also with the new theoretical feminist films, which, they say, "focus more on denying men their cathexis with women as crotic objects than in connecting women with each other." In addition, these films by "destroying the narrative and the possibility for viewer identification with the characters, destroy both the male viewer's pleasure and our pleasure." Asserting their need for identification with strong, female screen images, they argue that Hollywood films offer many examples of pleasurable identification; in a clever analysis, the relationship between Marilyn Monroe and Jane Russell in *Gentlemen Prefer Blondes* is offered as an example of strong women, who care for one another, providing a model we need.

However, looking at the construction of the film as a whole, rather than simply isolating certain shots, it is clear that Monroe and Russell are positioned, and position themselves, as objects for a specifically male gaze. The men's weakness does not mitigate their narrative power, and the women are left merely with the limited control they can wield through their sexuality. The film constructs them as "to-be-looked-at," and their manipulations end up as merely comic, since "capturing" the men involves their "being captured." The images of Monroe show her fetishized placement, aimed at reducing her sexual threat, while Russell's stance becomes a parody of the male position. The result is that the two women repeat, in exaggerated form, dominant gender stereotypes.

The weakness of Arbuthnot and Seneca's analysis is that it ignores the way that all dominant images are basically male constructs. Recognizing this has led Julia Kristeva and others to say that it is impossible to know what the "feminine" might be, outside of male constructs. Kristeva says that while we must reserve the category "women" for social demands and publicity, by the word "woman" she means "that which is not represented, that which is unspoken, that which is left out of meanings and ideologies." For similar reasons, Sandy Flitterman and Judith Barry have argued that feminist artists must avoid claiming a specific female power residing in the body of women and representing "an inherent feminine artistic essence which could find expression if allowed to be explored freely." The impulse toward this kind of art is understandable in a culture that denies satisfaction in being a woman, but it results in Motherhood being redefined as the seat of female creativity, while women "are proposed as the bearers of culture, albeit an alternative one."

Flitterman and Barry argue that this form of feminist art, along with some others that they outline, is dangerous in not taking into account "the social contradictions involved in 'femininity'." They suggest that "A radical feminist art would include an understanding of how women are constituted through social practices in culture" and argue for "an aesthetics designed to subvert the production of 'woman' as commodity," much as Claire Johnston and Laura Mulvey had earlier stated that to be feminist a cinema had to be a counter-cinema.

But the problem with this notion of a counter-cinema hinges on the issue of pleasure. Aware that a feminist counter-cinema would almost by definition deny pleasure. Mulvey argued that this denial was a necessary prerequisite for freedom but did not go into the problems involved. In introducing the notion of pleasure. Arbuthnot and Seneca have located a central and little-discussed issue, namely our need for feminist films that at once construct woman as spectator without offering the repressive identifications of Hollywood films and that satisfy our craving for *pleasure*. They have pinpointed a paradox in which feminist film critics have been caught without realizing it, namely our fascination with Hollywood films, rather than with, say, avant-garde films, because they bring us pleasure; but we have (rightly) been wary of admitting the degree to which the pleasure comes from identification with objectification. Our positioning as "to-be-looked-at," as object of the (male) gaze, has come to be sexually pleasurable.

However, it will not do simply to enjoy our oppression unproblematically; to appropriate Hollywood images to ourselves, taking them out of the context of the total structure in which they appear, will not get us very far. As I suggested above, in order fully to understand *how it is* that women take pleasure in objectification one has to have recourse to psychoanalysis.

Christian Metz, Stephen Heath, and others have shown that the processes of cinema mimic in many ways those of the unconscious. The mechanisms Freud distinguishes in relation to dream and the unconscious have been likened to the mechanism of film. In this analysis, film narratives, like dreams, symbolize a latent, repressed content, except that now the "content" refers not to an individual unconscious but to that of patriarchy in general. If psychoanalysis is a tool that will unlock the meaning of dreams, it should also unlock that of films.

The psychoanalytic methodology is thus justified as an essential first step in the feminist project of understanding our socialization in patriarchy. My analyses of Hollywood films amply demonstrate the ways in which patriarchal myths function to position women as silent, absent, and marginal. But, once we have fully understood our placing and the way that both language and psychoanalytic processes, inherent in our particular form of nuclear family, have constructed it, we have to think about strategies for changing discourse, since these changes would, in turn, affect the structuring of our lives in society. (I am not here excluding the possibility of working from the other end, i.e. finding gaps in patriarchal discourse through which to establish alternate practices, such as collective child-rearing, which might, in turn, begin to affect patriarchal discourse;

but this approach requires constant vigilance about the effect on our thoughts and actions of dominant signifying practices.)

As we'll see in the second part of the book, some feminist filmmakers have begun the task of analyzing patriarchal discourses, including cinematic representation, with a view to finding ways to break through them. The analysis of *Sigmund Freud's Dora*, undertaken in chapter 11, shows the filmmakers' belief that the raising of *questions* is the first step to establishing a female discourse, or perhaps that asking questions is the only discourse available to women as a resistance to patriarchal domination. Since questions lead to more questions, a kind of movement is in fact taking place, although it is in a non-traditional mode. Sally Potter structured her film *Thriller* (also analyzed in chapter 11) around this very notion and allowed her heroine's investigation of herself as heroine to lead to some (tentative) conclusions. And Laura Mulvey has suggested that, even if one accepts the psychoanalytic positioning of women, all is not lost, since the Oedipus complex is not completed in women; she notes that "there's some way in which women aren't colonized," having been "so specifically excluded from culture and language."

From this position, psychoanalytic theory allows us to see that there is a possibility for women to change themselves (and perhaps to bring about social change) just because they have not been processed, as have men as little boys, through a clearly defined, and ultimately simple, set of psychic stages. It is this possibility that we will discuss in the book's conclusion, after looking at responses by women directors to repressive Hollywood representations.

English/Literary Studies

The discipline of "English" is most often associated with the study and evaluation of literary texts. Many feminists in this field have argued that patriarchal standards have shaped discussions and assessment of literary work, thereby ignoring or distorting women's literary contributions. Feminist scholars have sought to recover and reassess the work of forgotten women writers, identify the biases and cultural forces that have stifled women's creativity, and examine the relationship between writing and gender. Sandra Gilbert and Susan Gubar were two of the earliest feminist literary critics to identify distinct areas of inquiry for studying women writers and establish the notion of a female literary tradition. Their essay illustrates the power of feminist insights to pose new questions of old texts and uncover connections among texts that had been overlooked or unexplored. Nellie McKay's essay examines a black female literary tradition. She claims that black women writers depict an authentic and complex portrait of black women's experience in defiance of stereotypes that abound in culture and the literary works of others. McKay recovers and explores a long ignored tradition and then argues for its significance in the larger American literary landscape. Finally, Tey Diana Rebolledo comments on the state of Chicano/a criticism, exploring its purpose and tensions. Her essay shows how those who have been traditionally marginalized in the academy may bring special insights into "the politics" of their scholarly work. Note the use of the first person in Rebolledo's discussion of Chicana criticism, and compare its effectiveness to the more traditional presentations of the other literary scholars.

Critical Thinking Questions

1. Do you agree that women authors constitute a separate literary subculture that is marked by distinct "anxieties" and therefore require attention an analysis separate from male writers?
2. To what extent does our culture shape or limit individual creativity? Are you aware of any restraints placed on your own creativity?

3. Upon what criteria should texts be chose for inclusion in the literary canon? To what degree is it important to create or sustain a canon that "makes more complete the reality of the multi-faceted American experience?

4. What is the connection between literature and politics? Should exposure to literature by diverse authors be a personal or curricular goal?

5. To what extent has the African-American women's literary tradition, as outlined by McKay, reflected progress and change since the eighteenth century?

6. How does Rebolledo's critique of the ascendancy of theory relate to the concerns of other feminist scholars.

7. What are the politics of poetics for Chicanos? How are they more complicated for them than for either Chicanos or white women?

25

Infection in the Sentence

The Woman Writer and the Anxiety of Authorship

(1979)

Sandra Gilbert and Susan Gubar

The man who does not know sick women does not know women.

—*S. Weir Mitchell*

I try to describe this long limitation, hoping that with such power as is now mine, and such use of language as is within that power, this will convince any one who cares about it that this "living" of mine had been done under a heavy handicap. . . .

—*Charlotte Perkins Gilman*

A Word dropped careless on a Page
May stimulate an eye
When folded in perpetual seam
The Wrinkled Maker lie

Infection in the sentence breeds
We may inhale Despair
At distances of Centuries
From the Malaria—
      —*Emily Dickinson*

I stand in the ring
in the dead city
and tie on the red shoes
. . . .
They are not mine,
they are my mother's,
her mother's before,
handed down like an heirloom
but hidden like shameful letters.
    —*Anne Sexton*

Gilbert and Gubar, "Infection in the Sentences: The Woman Writer and the Anxiety of Authorship." In *Madwoman in the Attic* (1984). New Haven, CT: Yale University Press. Reprinted by permission of the Yale University Press.

What does it mean to be a woman writer in a culture whose fundamental definitions of literary authority are, as we have seen, both overtly and covertly patriarchal? If the vexed and vexing polarities of angel and monster, sweet dumb Snow White and fierce mad Queen, are major images literary tradition offers women, how does such imagery influence the ways in which women attempt the pen? If the Queen's looking glass speaks with the King's voice, how do its perpetual kingly admonitions affect the Queen's own voice? Since his is the chief voice she hears, does the Queen try to sound like the King, imitating his tone, his inflections, his phrasing, his point of view? Or does she "talk back" to him in her own vocabulary, her own timbre, insisting on her own viewpoint? We believe these are basic questions feminist literary criticism—both theoretical and practical—must answer, and consequently they are questions to which we shall turn again and again, not only in this chapter but in all our readings of nineteenth-century literature by women.

That writers assimilate and then consciously or unconsciously affirm or deny the achievements of their predecessors is, of course, a central fact of literary history, a fact whose aesthetic and metaphysical implications have been discussed in detail by theorists as diverse as T. S. Eliot, M. H. Abrams, Erich Auerbach, and Frank Kermode. More recently, some literary theorists have begun to explore what we might call the psychology of literary history—the tensions and anxieties, hostilities and inadequacies writers feel when they confront not only the achievements of their predecessors but the traditions of genre, style, and metaphor that they inherit from such "forefathers." Increasingly, these critics study the ways in which, as J. Hillis Miller has put it, a literary text "is inhabited . . . by a long chain of parasitical presences, echoes, allusions, guests, ghosts of previous texts."

As Miller himself also notes, the first and foremost student of such literary psychohistory has been Harold Bloom. Applying Freudian structures to literary genealogies, Bloom has postulated that the dynamics of literary history arise from the artist's "anxiety of influence," his fear that he is not his own creator and that the works of his predecessors, existing before and beyond him, assume essential priority over his own writings. In fact, as we pointed out in our discussion of the metaphor of literary paternity, Bloom's paradigm of the sequential historical relationship between literary artists is the relationship of father and son, specifically that relationship as it was defined by Freud. Thus Bloom explains that a "strong poet" must engage in heroic warfare with his "precursor," for, involved as he is in a literary Oedipal struggle, a man can only become a poet by somehow invalidating his poetic father.

Bloom's model of literary history is intensely (even exclusively) male, and necessarily patriarchal. For this reason it has seemed, and no doubt will continue to seem, offensively sexist to some feminist critics. Not only, after all, does Bloom describe literary history as the crucial warfare of fathers and sons, he sees Milton's fiercely masculine fallen

Satan as *the* type of the poet in our culture, and he metaphorically defines the poetic process as a sexual encounter between a male poet and his female muse. Where, then, does the female poet fit in? Does she want to annihilate a "forefather" or a "foremother"? What if she can find no models, no precursors? Does she have a muse, and what is its sex? Such questions are inevitable in any female consideration of Bloomian poetics. And yet, from a feminist perspective, their inevitability may be just the point; it may, that is, call our attention not to what is wrong about Bloom's conceptualization of the dynamics of Western literary history, but to what is right (or at least suggestive) about his theory.

For Western literary history *is* overwhelmingly male—or, more accurately, patriarchal—and Bloom analyzes and explains this fact, while other theorists have ignored it, precisely, one supposes, because they assumed literature had to be male. Like Freud, whose psychoanalytic postulates permeate Bloom's literary psychoanalyses of the "anxiety of influence," Bloom has defined processes of interaction that his predecessors did not bother to consider because, among other reasons, they were themselves so caught up in such processes. Like Freud, too, Bloom has insisted on bringing to consciousness assumptions readers and writers do not ordinarily examine. In doing so, he has clarified the implications of the psychosexual and sociosexual contexts by which every literary text is surrounded, and thus the meanings of the "guests" and "ghosts" which inhabit texts themselves. Speaking of Freud, the feminist theorist Juliet Mitchell has remarked that "psychoanalysis is not a recommendation *for* a patriarchal society, but an analysis of one." The same sort of statement could be made about Bloom's model of literary history, which is not a recommendation for but an analysis of the patriarchal poetics (and attendant anxieties) which underlie our culture's chief literary movements.

For our purposes here, however, Bloom's historical construct is useful not only because it helps identify and define the patriarchal psychosexual context in which so much Western literature was authored, but also because it can help us distinguish the anxieties and achievements of female writers from those of male writers. If we return to the question we asked earlier—where does a woman writer "fit in" to the overwhelmingly and essentially male literary history Bloom describes?— we find we have to answer that a woman writer does *not* "fit in." At first glance, indeed, she seems to be anomalous, indefinable, alienated, a freakish outsider. Just as in Freud's theories of male and female psychosexual development there is no symmetry between a boy's growth and a girl's (with, say, the male "Oedipus complex" balanced by a female "Electra complex") so Bloom's male-oriented theory of the "anxiety of influence" cannot be simply reversed or inverted in order to account for the situation of the woman writer.

Certainly if we acquiesce in the patriarchal Bloomian model, we can be sure that the female poet does not experience the "anxiety of influence" in the same way that her male counterpart would, for the simple reason that she must confront precursors who are almost exclusively male, and therefore significantly different from her. Not only do these precursors incarnate patriarchal authority (as our discussion of the metaphor of literary paternity argued), they attempt to enclose her in definitions of her person and her potential which, by reducing her to extreme stereotypes (angel, monster) drastically conflict with her own sense of her self—that is, of her subjectivity, her autonomy, her creativity. On the one hand, therefore, the woman writer's male precursors symbolize authority; on the other hand, despite their authority, they fail to define the ways in which she experiences her own identity as a writer. More, the masculine authority with which they construct their literary personae, as well as the fierce power struggles in which they engage in their efforts of self-creation, seem to the woman writer directly to contradict the terms of her own gender definition. Thus the "anxiety of influence" that a male poet experiences is felt by a female poet as an even more primary "anxiety of authorship"—a radical fear that she cannot create, that because she can never become a "precursor" the act of writing will isolate or destroy her.

This anxiety is, of course, exacerbated by her fear that not only can she not fight a male precursor on "his" terms and win, she cannot "beget" art upon the (female) body of the muse. As Juliet Mitchell notes, in a concise summary of the implications Freud's theory of psychosexual development has for women, both a boy and a girl, "as they learn to speak and live within society, want to take the father's [in Bloom's terminology the precursor's] place,

and *only the boy will one day be allowed to do so*. Furthermore both sexes are born into the desire of the mother, and as, through cultural heritage, what the mother desires is the phallus-turned-baby, *both* children desire to be the phallus for the mother. Again, *only the boy can fully recognize himself in his mother's desire*. Thus *both* sexes repudiate the implications of femininity," but the girl learns (in relation to her father) "that her subjugation to the law of the father entails her becoming the representative of 'nature' and 'sexuality,' a chaos of spontaneous, intuitive creativity."

Unlike her male counterpart, then, the female artist must first struggle against the effects of a socialization which makes conflict with the will of her (male) precursors seem inexpressibly absurd, futile, or even—as in the case of the Queen in "Little Snow White"—self-annihilating. And just as the male artist's struggle against his precursor takes the form of what Bloom calls revisionary swerves, flights, misreadings, so the female writer's battle for self-creation involves her in a revisionary process. Her battle, however, is not against her (male) precursor's reading of the world but against his reading of *her*. In order to define herself as an author she must redefine the terms of her socialization. Her revisionary struggle, therefore, often becomes a struggle for what Adrienne Rich has called "Revision—the act of looking back, of seeing with fresh eyes, of entering an old text from a new critical direction . . . an act of survival." Frequently, moreover, she can begin such a struggle only by actively seeking a *female* precursor who, far from representing a threatening force to be denied or killed, proves by example that a revolt against patriarchal literary authority is possible.

For this reason, as well as for the sound psychoanalytic reasons Mitchell and others give, it would be foolish to lock the woman artist into an Electra pattern matching the Oedipal structure Bloom proposes for male writers. The woman writer—and we shall see women doing this over and over again—searches for a female model not because she wants dutifully to comply with male definitions of her "femininity" but because she must legitimize her own rebellious endeavors. At the same time, like most women in patriarchal society, the woman writer does experience her gender as a painful obstacle, or even a debilitating inadequacy; like most patriarchally conditioned women, in other words, she is victimized by what Mitchell calls "the inferiorized and 'alternative' (second sex) psychology of women under patriarchy." Thus the loneliness of the female artist, her feelings of alienation from male predecessors coupled with her need for sisterly precursors and successors, her urgent sense of her need for a female audience together with her fear of the antagonism of male readers, her culturally conditioned timidity about self-dramatization, her dread of the patriarchal authority of art, her anxiety about the impropriety of female invention—all these phenomena of "inferiorization" mark the woman writer's struggle for artistic self-definition and differentiate her efforts at self-creation from those of her male counterpart.

As we shall see, such sociosexual differentiation means that, as Elaine Showalter has suggested, women writers participate in a quite different literary subculture from that inhabited by male writers, a subculture which has its own distinctive literary traditions, even—though it defines itself *in relation to* the "main," male-dominated, literary culture—a distinctive history. At best, the separateness of this female subculture has been exhilarating for women. In recent years, for instance, while male writers seem increasingly to have felt exhausted by the need for revisionism which Bloom's theory of the "anxiety of influence" accurately describes, women writers have seen themselves as pioneers in a creativity so intense that their male counterparts have probably not experienced its analog since the Renaissance, or at least since the Romantic era. The son of many fathers, today's male writer feels hopelessly belated; the daughter of too few mothers, today's female writer feels that she is helping to create a viable tradition which is at last definitively emerging.

There is a darker side of this female literary subculture, however, especially when women's struggles for literary self-creation are seen in the psychosexual context described by Bloom's Freudian theories of patrilineal literary inheritance. As we noted above, for an "anxiety of influence" the woman writer substitutes what we have called an "anxiety of authorship," an anxiety built from complex and often only barely conscious fears of that authority which seems to the female artist to be by definition inappropriate to her sex. Because it is based on the woman's socially determined sense of her own biology, this anxiety of authorship is quite distinct from the anxiety about creativity that could be traced in such male writers as Hawthorne or Dostoevsky. Indeed, to the extent that it forms one of the unique bonds that link women in what we might call the secret sisterhood of their literary subculture, such anxiety in itself constitutes a crucial mark of that subculture.

In comparison to the "male" tradition of strong, father-son combat, however, this female anxiety of authorship is profoundly debilitating. Handed down not from one woman to another but from the stern literary "fathers" of patriarchy to all their "inferiorized" female descendants, it is in many ways the germ of a dis-ease or, at any rate, a disaffection, a disturbance, a distrust, that spreads like a stain throughout the style and structure of much literature by women, especially—as we shall see in this study—throughout literature by women before the twentieth century. For if contemporary women do now attempt the pen with energy and authority, they are able to do so only because their eighteenth- and nineteenth-century foremothers struggled in isolation that felt like illness, alienation that felt like madness, obscurity that felt like paralysis to overcome the anxiety of authorship that was endemic to their literary subculture. Thus, while the recent feminist emphasis on positive role models has undoubtedly helped many women, it should not keep us from realizing the terrible odds against which a creative female subculture was established. Far from reinforcing socially oppressive sexual stereotyping, only a full consideration of such problems can reveal the extraordinary strength of women's literary accomplishments in the eighteenth and nineteenth centuries.

Emily Dickinson's acute observations about "infection in the sentence," quoted in our epigraphs, resonate in a number of different ways, then, for women writers, given the literary woman's special concept of her place in literary psychohistory. To begin with, the words seem to indicate Dickinson's keen consciousness that, in the purest Bloomian or Millerian sense, pernicious "guests" and "ghosts" inhabit all literary texts. For any reader, but especially for a reader who is also a writer, every text can become a "sentence" or weapon in a kind of metaphorical germ warfare. Beyond this, however, the fact that "infection in the sentence *breeds*" suggests Dickinson's recognition that literary texts are coercive, imprisoning, fever-inducing; that, since literature usurps a reader's interiority, it is an invasion of privacy. Moreover, given Dickinson's own gender definition, the sexual ambiguity of her poem's "Wrinkled Maker" is significant. For while, on the one hand, "we" (meaning especially women writers) "may inhale Despair" from all those patriarchal texts which seek to deny female autonomy and authority, on the other hand "we" (meaning especially women writers) "may inhale Despair" from all those "foremothers" who have both overtly and covertly conveyed their traditional authorship anxiety to their bewildered female descendants. Finally, such traditional, metaphorically matrilineal anxiety ensures that even the maker of a text, when she is a woman, may feel imprisoned within texts—folded and "wrinkled" by their pages and thus trapped in their "perpetual seam[s]" which perpetually tell her how she *seems*.

Although contemporary women writers are relatively free of the infection of this "Despair" Dickinson defines (at least in comparison to their nineteenth-century precursors), an anecdote recently related by the American poet and essayist Annie Gottlieb summarizes our point about the ways in which, for all women, "Infection in the sentence breeds":

> When I began to enjoy my powers as a writer, I dreamt that my mother had me sterilized! (Even in dreams we still blame our mothers for the punitive choices our culture forces on us.) I went after the mother-figure in my dream, brandishing a large knife; on its blade was writing. I cried, "Do you know what you are doing? You are destroying my femaleness, my *female power*, which is important to me *because of you!*"

Seeking motherly precursors, says Gottlieb, as if echoing Dickinson, the woman writer may find only infection, debilitation. Yet still she must seek, not seek to subvert, her *"female power*, which is important"* to her because of her lost literary matrilineage. In this connection, Dickinson's own words about mothers are revealing, for she alternately claimed that "I never had a mother," that "I always ran Home to Awe as a child. . . . He was an awful Mother but I liked him better than none," and that "a mother [was] a miracle." Yet, as we shall see, her own anxiety of authorship was a "Despair" inhaled not only from the infections suffered by her own ailing physical mother, and her many tormented literary mothers, but from the literary fathers who spoke to her—even "lied" to her—sometimes near at hand, sometimes "at distances of Centuries," from the censorious looking glasses of literary texts.

It is debilitating to be *any* woman in a society where women are warned that if they do not behave like angels they must be monsters. Recently, in fact, social scientists and social historians like Jessie Bernard, Phyllis Chesler, Naomi Weisstein, and Pauline Bart have begun to study the ways in which patriarchal socialization literally makes women sick, both physically and mentally. Hysteria, the disease with which Freud so famously began his investigations into the dynamic connections between *psyche* and *soma*, is by definition a "female disease," not so much because it takes its name from the Greek word for womb, *hyster* (the organ which was in the nineteenth century supposed to "cause" this emotional disturbance), but because hysteria did occur mainly among women in turn-of-the-century Vienna, and because throughout the nineteenth century this mental illness, like many other nervous disorders, was thought to be caused by the female reproductive system, as if to elaborate upon Aristotle's notion that femaleness was in and of itself a deformity. And, indeed, such diseases of maladjustment to the physical and social environment as anorexia and agoraphobia did and do strike a disproportionate number of women. Sufferers from anorexia—loss of appetite, self-starvation—are primarily adolescent girls. Sufferers from agoraphobia—fear of open or "public" places—are usually female, most frequently middle-aged housewives, as are sufferers from crippling rheumatoid arthritis.

Such diseases are caused by patriarchal socialization in several ways. Most obviously, of course, any young girl, but especially a lively or imaginative one, is likely to experience her education in docility, submissiveness, self-lessness as in some sense sickening. To be trained in renunciation is almost necessarily to be trained to ill health, since the human animal's first and strongest urge is to his/her *own* survival, pleasure, assertion. In addition, each of the "subjects" in which a young girl is educated may be sickening in a specific way. Learning to become a beautiful object, the girl learns anxiety about—perhaps even loathing of—her own flesh. Peering obsessively into the real as well as metaphoric looking glasses that surround her, she desires literally to "reduce" her own body. In the nineteenth century, as we noted earlier, this desire to be beautiful and "frail" led to tight-lacing and vinegar-drinking. In our own era it has spawned innumerable diets and "controlled" fasts, as well as the extraordinary phenomenon of teenage anorexia. Similarly, it seems inevitable that women reared for, and conditioned to, lives of privacy, reticence, domesticity, might develop pathological fears of public places and unconfined spaces. Like the comb, stay-laces, and apple which the Queen in "Little Snow White" uses as weapons against her hated step-daughter, such afflictions as anorexia and agoraphobia simply carry patriarchal definitions of "femininity" to absurd extremes, and thus function as essential or at least inescapable parodies of social prescriptions.

In the nineteenth century, however, the complex of social prescriptions these diseases parody did not merely urge women to act in ways which would cause them to become ill; nineteenth-century culture seems to have actually admonished women to *be* ill. In other words, the "female diseases" from which Victorian women suffered were not always byproducts of their training in femininity; they were the goals of such training. As Barbara Ehrenreich and Deirdre English have shown, throughout much of the nineteenth century "Upper- and upper-middle-class women were [defined as] 'sick' [frail, ill]; working-class women were [defined as] 'sickening' [infectious, diseased]." Speaking of the "lady," they go on to point out that "Society agreed that she was frail and sickly," and consequently a "cult of female invalidism" developed in England and America. For the products of such a cult, it was, as Dr. Mary Putnam Jacobi wrote in 1895, "considered natural and almost laudable to break down under all conceivable varieties of strain—a winter dissipation, a houseful of servants, a quarrel with a female friend, not to speak of more legitimate reasons. . . . Constantly considering their nerves, urged to consider them by well-intentioned but short-sighted advisors, [women] pretty soon become nothing but a bundle of nerves."

Given this socially conditioned epidemic of female illness, it is not surprising to find that the angel in the house of literature frequently suffered not just from fear and trembling but from literal and figurative sicknesses unto death. Although her hyperactive stepmother dances herself into the grave, after all, beautiful Snow White has just barely recovered from a catatonic trance in her glass coffin. And if we return to Goethe's Makarie, the "good" woman of *Wilhelm Meister's Travels* whom Hans Eichner has described as incarnating her author's ideal of "contemplative purity," we find that this "model of selflessness and of purity of heart . . . this embodiment of *das Ewig-Weibliche*, suffers from migraine headaches." Implying ruthless self-suppression, does the "eternal feminine" necessarily imply illness? If so, we may have found yet another meaning for Dickinson's assertion that "Infection in the sentence breeds." The despair we "inhale" even "at distances of centuries" may be the despair of a life like Makarie's, a life that *"has no story."*

At the same time, however, the despair of the monster-woman is also real, undeniable, and infectious. The Queen's mad tarantella is plainly unhealthy and metaphorically the result of too much storytelling. As the Romantic poets feared, too much imagination may be dangerous to anyone, male or female, but for women in particular patriarchal culture has always assumed mental exercises would have dire consequences. In 1645 John Winthrop, the governor of the Massachusetts Bay Colony, noted in his journal that Anne Hopkins "has fallen into a sad infirmity, the loss of her understanding and reason, which had been growing upon her divers years, by occasion of her giving herself wholly to reading and writing, and had written many books," adding that "if she had attended her household affairs, and such things as belong to women . . . she had kept her wits." And as Wendy Martin has noted

> in the nineteenth century this fear of the intellectual woman became so intense that the phenomenon . . . was recorded in medical annals. A thinking woman was considered such a breach of nature that a Harvard doctor reported during his autopsy on a Radcliffe graduate he discovered that her uterus had shrivelled to the size of a pea.

If, then, as Anne Sexton suggests (in a poem parts of which we have also used here as an epigraph), the red shoes passed furtively down from woman to woman are the shoes of art, the Queen's dancing shoes, it is as sickening to be a Queen who wears them as it is to be an angelic Makarie who repudiates them. Several passages in Sexton's verse express what we have defined as "anxiety of authorship" in the form of a feverish dread of the suicidal tarantella of female creativity:

> All those girls
> who wore red shoes,
> each boarded a train that would not
> stop.
> . . . .
> They tore off their ears like safety pins.
> Their arms fell off them and became
> hats.
> Their heads rolled off and sang down
> the street.
> And their feet—oh God, their feet in
> the market place—
> . . . the feet went on.
> The feet could not stop.
> . . . .
> They could not listen.
> They could not stop.
> What they did was the death dance.
>
> What they did would do them in.

Certainly infection breeds in these sentences, and despair: female art, Sexton suggests, has a "hidden" but crucial tradition of uncontrollable madness. Perhaps it was her semiconscious perception of this tradition that gave Sexton herself "a secret fear" of being "a reincarnation" of Edna Millay, whose reputation seemed based on romance. In a letter to DeWitt Snodgrass she confessed that she had "a fear of writing as a woman writes," adding, "I wish I were a man—I would rather write the way a man writes." After all, dancing the death dance, "all those girls/who wore the red shoes" dismantle their own bodies, like anorexics renouncing the guilty weight of their female flesh. But if their arms, ears, and heads fall off, perhaps their wombs, too, will "shrivel" to "the size of a pea"?

In this connection, a passage from Margaret Atwood's *Lady Oracle* acts almost as a gloss on the conflict between creativity and "femininity" which Sexton's violent imagery embodies (or dis-embodies). Significantly, the protagonist of Atwood's novel is a writer of the sort of fiction that has recently been called "female gothic," and even more significantly she too projects her anxieties of authorship into the fairy-tale metaphor of the red shoes. Stepping in glass, she sees blood on her feet, and suddenly feels that she has discovered

> The real red shoes, the feet punished for dancing. You could dance, or you could have the love of a good man. But you were afraid to dance, because you had this unnatural fear that if you danced they'd cut your feet off so you wouldn't be able to dance.... Finally you overcame your fear and danced, and they cut your feet off. The good man went away too, because you wanted to dance.

Whether she is a passive angel or an active monster, in other words, the woman writer feels herself to be literally or figuratively crippled by the debilitating alternatives her culture offers her, and the crippling effects of her conditioning sometimes seem to "breed" like sentences of death in the bloody shoes she inherits from her literary foremothers.

Surrounded as she is by images of disease, traditions of disease, and invitations both to disease and to disease, it is no wonder that the woman writer has held many mirrors up to the discomforts of her own nature. As we shall see, the notion that "Infection in the sentence breeds" has been so central a truth for literary women that the great artistic achievements of nineteenth-century novelists and poets from Austen and Shelley to Dickinson and Barrett Browning are often both literally and figuratively concerned with disease, as if to emphasize the effort with which health and wholeness were won from the infectious "vapors" of despair and fragmentation. Rejecting the poisoned apples her culture offers her, the woman writer often becomes in some sense anorexic, resolutely closing her mouth on silence (since—in the words of Jane Austen's Henry Tilney—"a woman's only power is the power of refusal"), even while she complains of starvation. Thus both Charlotte and Emily Brontë depict the travails of starved or starving anorexic heroines, while Emily Dickinson declares in one breath that she "had been hungry, all the Years," and in another opts for "Sumptuous Destitution." Similarly, Christina Rossetti represents her own anxiety of authorship in the split between one heroine who longs to "suck and suck" on goblin fruit and another who locks her lips fiercely together in a gesture of silent and passionate renunciation. In addition, many of these literary women become in one way or another agoraphobic. Trained to reticence, they fear the vertiginous openness of the literary marketplace and rationalize with Emily Dickinson that "Publication—is the Auction / Of the Mind of Man" or, worse, punningly confess that "Creation seemed a mighty Crack—/To make me visible."

As we shall al so see, other diseases and dis-eases accompany the two classic symptoms of anorexia and agoraphobia. Claustrophobia, for instance, agoraphobia's parallel and complementary opposite, is a disturbance we shall encounter again and again in women's writing throughout the nineteenth century. Eye "troubles," moreover, seem to abound in the lives and works of literary women, with Dickinson matter-of-factly noting that her eye got "put out," George Eliot describing patriarchal Rome as "a disease of the retina," Jane Eyre and Aurora Leigh marrying blind men, Charlotte Brontë deliberately writing with her eyes closed, and Mary Elizabeth Coleridge writing about "Blindness" that came because "Absolute and bright, / The Sun's rays smote me till they masked the Sun." Finally, aphasia and amnesia—two illnesses which symbolically represent (and parody) the sort of intellectual incapacity patriarchal culture has traditionally required of women—appear and reappear in women's writings in frankly stated or disguised forms. "Foolish" women characters in Jane Austen's novels (Miss Bates in *Emma*, for instance) express Malapropish confusion about language, while Mary Shelley's monster has to learn language from scratch and Emily Dickinson herself childishly questions the meanings of the most basic English words: "Will there really be a 'Morning'? / Is there such a thing as 'Day'?" At the same time, many women writers manage to imply that the reason for such ignorance of language—as well as the reason for their deep sense of alienation and inescapable feeling of anomie—is that they have *forgotten* something. Deprived of the power that even their pens don't seem to confer, these women resemble Doris Lessing's heroines, who have to fight their in-ternalization of patriarchal strictures for even a faint trace memory of what they might have become.

"Where are the songs I used to know, / Where are the notes I used to sing?" writes Christina Rossetti in "The Key-Note," a poem whose title indicates its significance for her. "I have forgotten everything / I used to know so long ago." As if to make the same point, Charlotte Brontë's Lucy Snowe conveniently "forgets" her own history and even, so it seems, the Christian name of one of the central characters in her story, while Brontë's orphaned Jane Eyre seems to have lost (or symbolically "forgotten") her family heritage. Similarly, too, Emily Brontë's Heathcliff "forgets" or is made to forget who and what he was; Mary Shelley's monster is "born" without either a memory or a family history; and Elizabeth Barrett Browning's Aurora Leigh is early separated from—and thus induced to "forget"—her "mother land" of Italy. As this last example suggests, however, what all these characters and their authors really fear they have forgotten is precisely that aspect of their lives which has been kept from them by patriarchal poetics: their matrilineal heritage of literary strength, their "female power" which, as Annie Gottlieb wrote, is important to them *because of* (not in spite of) their mothers. In order, then, not only to understand the ways in which "Infection in the sentence breeds" for women but also to learn how women have won through disease to artistic health we must begin by redefining Bloom's seminal definitions of the revisionary "anxiety of influence." In doing so, we will have to trace the difficult paths by which nineteenth-century women overcame their "anxiety of authorship," repudiated debilitating patriarchal prescriptions, and recovered or remembered the lost foremothers who could help them find their distinctive female power.

To begin with, those women who were among the first of their sex to attempt the pen were evidently infected or sickened by just the feelings of self-doubt, inadequacy, and inferiority that their education in "femininity" almost seems to have been designed to induce. The necessary converse of the metaphor of literary paternity, as we noted in our discussion of that phenomenon, was a belief in female literary sterility, a belief that caused literary women like Anne Finch to consider with deep anxiety the possibility that they might be "Cyphers," powerless intellectual eunuchs. In addition, such women were profoundly affected by the sort of assumptions that underly an assertion like Rufus Griswold's statement that in reading women's writing "We are in danger . . . of mistaking for the efflorescent energy of creative intelligence, that which is only the exuberance of personal 'feelings unemployed.' " Even if it was not absurd for a woman to try to write, this remark implies, perhaps it was somehow sick or what we would today call "neurotic." "We live at home, quiet, confined, and our feelings prey upon us," says Austen's Anne Elliot to Captain Harville, not long before they embark upon the debate about the male pen and its depiction of female "inconstancy" which we discussed earlier. She speaks in what Austen describes as "a low, feeling voice," and her remarks as well as her manner suggest both her own and her author's acquiescence in the notion that

women may be more vulnerable than men to the dangers and diseases of "feelings unemployed."

It is not surprising, then, that one of Finch's best and most passionate poems is an ambitious Pindaric ode entitled "The Spleen." Here, in what might almost be a response to Pope's characterization of the Queen of Spleen in *The Rape of the Lock*, Finch confesses and explores her own anxiety about the "vaporous" illness whose force, she feared, ruled her life and art. Her self-examination is particularly interesting not only because of its rigorous honesty, but because that honesty compels her to reveal just how severely she herself has been influenced by the kinds of misogynistic strictures about women's "feelings unemployed" that Pope had embedded in *his* poem. Thus Pope insists that the "wayward Queen" of Spleen rules "the sex to fifty from fifteen"—rules women, that is, throughout their "prime" of female sexuality—and is therefore the "parent" of both hysteria and (female) poetry, and Finch seems at least in part to agree, for she notes that "In the Imperious *Wife* thou Vapours art." That is, insubordinate women are merely, as Pope himself would have thought, neurotic women. "Lordly *Man* [is] born to Imperial Sway," says Finch, but he is defeated by splenetic woman; he "Compounds for Peace . . . And *Woman* arm'd with Spleen, do's servilely Obey." At the same time, however, Finch admits that she feels the most pernicious effects of Spleen within herself, and specifically within herself *as an artist*, and she complains of these effects quite movingly, without the self-censure that would seem to have followed from her earlier vision of female insubordination. Addressing Spleen, she writes that

> O'er me alas! thou dost too much prevail:
> I feel thy Force, whilst I against thee rail;
> I feel my Verse decay, and my crampt Numbers fail.
> Thro' thy black Jaundice I all Objects see,
> As Dark, and Terrible as Thee,
> My Lines decry'd, and my Employme. thought
> An useless Folly, or presumptuous Fault.

Is it crazy, neurotic, splenetic, to want to be a writer? In "The Spleen" Finch admits that she fears it is, suggesting, therefore, that Pope's portrayal of her as the foolish and neurotic Phoebe Clinket had—not surprisingly—driven her into a Cave of Spleen in her own mind.

When seventeenth- and eighteenth-century women writers—and even some nineteenth-century literary women—did not confess that they thought it might actually be mad of them to want to attempt the pen, they did usually indicate that they felt in some sense apologetic about such a "presumptuous" pastime. As we saw earlier, Finch herself admonished her muse to be cautious "and still retir'd," adding that the most she could hope to do as a writer was "still with contracted wing, / To some few friends, and to thy sorrows sing." Though her self-effacing admonition is riddled with irony, it is also serious and practical. As Elaine Showalter has shown, until the end of the nineteenth century the woman writer really was supposed to take second place to her literary brothers and fathers. If she refused to be modest, self-deprecating, sub-servient, refused to present her artistic productions as mere trifles designed to divert and distract readers in moments of idleness, she could expect to be ignored or (sometimes scurrilously) attacked. Anne Killigrew, who ambitiously implored the "Queen of Verse" to warm her soul with "poetic fire," was rewarded for her overreaching with charges of plagiarism. "I writ, and the judicious praised my pen: / Could any doubt ensuing glory then?" she notes, recounting as part of the story of her humiliation expectations that would be reasonable enough in a male artist. But instead "What ought t'have brought me honour, brought me shame." Her American contemporary, Anne Bradstreet, echoes the frustration and annoyance expressed here in a discussion of the reception she could expect *her* published poems to receive:

> I am obnoxious to each carping tongue
> Who says my hand a needle better fits,
> A poet's pen all scorn I should thus wrong,
> For such despite they cast on female wits:
> If what I do prove well, it won't advance,
> They'll say it's stol'n, or else it was by chance.

There is such a weary and worldly accuracy in this analysis that plainly, especially in the context of Killigrew's experience, no sensible woman writer could overlook the warning implied: be modest or else! Be dark enough thy shades, and be thou there content!

Accordingly, Bradstreet herself, eschewing Apollo's manly "bays," asks only for a "thyme or parsley wreath," suavely assuring her male readers that "This mean and unrefined ore of mine / Will make your glist'ring gold but more to shine." And though once again, as with Finch's self-admonitions, bitter irony permeates this modesty, the very pose of modesty necessarily has its ill effects, both on the poet's self-definition and on her art. Just as Finch feels her "Crampt Numbers" crippled by the gloomy disease of female Spleen, Bradstreet confesses that she has a "foolish, broken, blemished Muse" whose defects cannot be mended, since "nature made it so irreparable." After all, she adds—as if to cement the connection between femaleness and madness, or at least mental deformity—"a weak or wounded brain admits no cure." Similarly, Margaret Cavendish, the Duchess of Newcastle, whose literary activities actually inspired her contemporaries to call her "Mad Madge," seems to have tried to transcend her own "madness" by deploying the kind of modest, "sensible," and self-deprecatory misogyny that characterizes Bradstreet's *apologia pro vita sua*. "It cannot be expected," Cavendish avers, that "I should write so wisely or wittily as men, being of the effeminate sex, whose brains nature has mixed with the coldest and softest elements." Men and women, she goes on to declare, "may be compared to the blackbirds, where the hen can never sing with so strong and loud a voice, nor so clear and perfect notes as the cock; her breast is not made with that strength to strain so high." But finally the contradictions between her attitude toward her gender and her sense of her own vocation seem really to have made her in some sense "mad." It may have been in a fleeting moment of despair and self-confrontation that

she wrote, "Women live like Bats or Owls, labour like Beasts, and die like Worms." But eventually, as Virginia Woolf puts it, "the people crowded round her coach when she issued out," for "the crazy Duchess became a bogey to frighten clever girls with."

As Woolf's comments imply, women who did *not* apologize for their literary efforts were defined as mad and monstrous: freakish because "unsexed" or freakish because sexually "fallen." If Cavendish's extraordinary intellectual ambitions made her seem like an aberration of nature, and Finch's writing caused her to be defined as a fool, an absolutely immodest, unapologetic rebel like Aphra Behn—the first really "professional" literary woman in England—was and is always considered a somewhat "shady lady," no doubt promiscuous, probably self-indulgent, and certainly "indecent." "What has poor woman done, that she must be / Debarred from sense and sacred poetry?" Behn frankly asked, and she seems just as frankly to have lived the life of a Restoration rake. In consequence, like some real-life Duessa, she was gradually but inexorably excluded (even exorcized) not only from the canon of serious literature but from the parlors and libraries of respectability.

By the beginning of the bourgeois nineteenth century, however, both money and "morality" had become so important that no serious writer could afford either psychologically or economically to risk Behn's kind of "shadiness." Thus we find Jane Austen decorously protesting in 1816 that she is constitutionally unable to join "manly, spirited Sketches" to the "little bit (two Inches wide) of Ivory," on which, figuratively speaking, she claimed to inscribe her novels, and

Charlotte Brontë assuring Robert Southey in 1837 that "I have endeavored ... to observe all the duties a woman ought to fulfil." Confessing with shame that "I don't always succeed, for sometimes when I'm teaching or sewing, I would rather be reading or writing," she dutifully adds that "I try to deny myself; and my father's approbation amply reward[s] me for the privation." Similarly, in 1862 we discover Emily Dickinson telling Thomas Wentworth Higginson that publication is as "foreign to my thought, as Firmament to Fin," implying that she is *generically* unsuited to such self-advertisement, while in 1869 we see Louisa May Alcott's Jo March learning to write moral homilies for children instead of ambitious gothic thrillers. Clearly there is conscious or semiconscious irony in all these choices of the apparently miniature over the assuredly major, of the domestic over the dramatic, of the private over the public, of obscurity over glory. But just as clearly the very need to make such choices emphasizes the sickening anxiety of authorship inherent in the situation of almost every woman writer in England and America until quite recently.

What the lives and lines and choices of all these women tell us, in short, is that the literary woman has always faced equally degrading options when she had to define her public presence in the world. If she did not suppress her work entirely or publish it pseudonymously or anonymously, she could modestly confess her female "limitations" and concentrate on the "lesser" subjects reserved for ladies as becoming to their inferior powers. If the latter alternative seemed an admission of failure, she could rebel, accepting the ostracism that must have seemed inevitable. Thus, as Virginia Woolf observed, the woman writer seemed locked into a disconcerting double bind: she had to choose between admitting she was "only a woman" or protesting that she was "as good as a man." Inevitably, as we shall see, the literature produced by women confronted with such anxiety-inducing choices has been strongly marked not only by an obsessive interest in these limited options but also by obsessive imagery of confinement that reveals the ways in which female artists feel trapped and sickened both by suffocating alternatives and by the culture that created them. Goethe's fictional Makarie was not, after all, the only angelic woman to suffer from terrible headaches. George Eliot (like Virginia Woolf) had them too, and perhaps we can begin to understand why.

26

Reflections on Black Women Writers
Revising the Literary Canon
(1987)

Nellie McKay

There is no doubt that black women as writers have made drastic inroads into the American literary consciousness since the beginning of the 1970s, and the film success of Alice Walker's *The Color Purple* has indeed placed the entire group within a new dimension in the national consciousness. Aside from its merits (or demerits) as book and/or movie, *The Color Purple* is important for what its popularity means in terms of the recognition it compels for the works of black women. Thousands, perhaps millions, of people who had not, until now, ever heard the name of Alice Walker, and countless others who had, but who were able to ignore her (although she has been publishing fiction and poetry since the late 1960s), have seen and will see the film—learn her name, and respond to her work, whether they acknowledge its richness, or see it as a misrepresentation of the black experience. Above the din of the controversy that *The Color Purple* has

sparked inside and outside of the black community, many will discover something new about the experiences of black women in America. For what black women as writers have consistently provided for themselves and others has been a rendering of the black woman's place in the world in which she lives, as she shapes and defines that from her own impulses and actions.

Before *The Color Purple* the only comparable achievement for a black woman writer was made by Lorraine Hansberry's *A Raisin in the Sun*, which was first staged in 1959. This play, for which Hansberry won the New York Drama Critics Circle Award of "Best Play of the Year," over Tennessee Williams's *Sweet Bird of Youth*, Archibald MacLeish's *JB*, and Eugene O'Neill's *A Touch of the Poet*, made her not only the youngest American, the first woman, and the first black person to achieve that honor, but also the first black woman to have her work produced on Broadway. *A Raisin in*

McKay, Nellie, "Reflections on Black Women Writers: Revising the Literary Canon" In *The Impact of Feminist Research in the Academy* ed. Christie Farnham. Indianapolis: Indiana University Press, 1987. Reprinted by permission of the author.

the Sun, seen by millions of Americans on stage, screen, and television, has been translated into more than thirty languages and produced on all continents of the globe. It foreshadowed the emergence of a new movement in black theater, a new place in letters for black women writers, and opened one artistic door onto the large stage of the Civil Rights Movement of the 1960s and 1970s.

A Raisin in the Sun is not autobiographical. Lorraine Hansberry came from a black middle-class family which had long overcome the problems faced by the characters in her play. But if Hansberry was economically removed from the dilemma of the Youngers, the family she writes about, she was nevertheless emotionally attached to the issues she explored through them, issues that remained at the core of the lives of the majority of black people in America in the 1950s. The experiences of her dramaturgical family were part of the collective three-hundred-year-old consciousness of what it meant to be born black in America. In giving several of the key roles in her play to women, she had also followed in the footsteps of her less well-known earlier sisters who had sought to write out of their black female awareness and point of view on that reality.

At the center of *Raisin* is that most memorable Mama: Lena Younger, whose grandeur takes vengeance for all the black mammies previously presented in American literature. For black women in American literature, from the beginning, having been depicted as either sexually loose and therefore tempters of men, or obedient and subservient mammies, loving and tender to the white children they raised and forever faithful to the owners they served. Lena Younger defies more than two hundred years of such stereotyping of black women, and turns black female strength, too often maligned by everyone else, into the means by which her son Walter shapes his emerging manhood. Lorraine Hansberry was not the first black woman who gave us such a positive image of black women, but she was the first in her own time whose voice reached as wide an audience as hers did. Her achievement opened a wider way for the black women writers who came after her.

What is significant in the Lena Younger image in *Raisin* for the purposes of this paper is that she is the central force that holds her family together, that she has no ambivalences regarding the inherent human worth and dignity of herself and those whom she loves, and that speaking from inside of her own experiences, she demonstrates that the black struggle to transcend dwarfs the victimization that would otherwise have destroyed black people a long time ago. And while Mama Younger stands as the force at the center of her family, there are also the other women in that drama whose roles are fully as important as her own: daughter Beneatha, who wants to be a doctor so that she will be able to heal sick and broken black bodies, but whose sophisticated cynicism meets with the stern rebuke of her mother; and Ruth, Walter's wife, whose concerns for the welfare and well-being of her children precipitates a family controversy over abortion that belies the notion that poor and/or black people produce babies without consideration for what happens after they arrive. Years later, when Ruth will tell Travis and his siblings stories about their grandmother, or when Beneatha recalls her young adulthood and the conflicts she had with her mother, the scripts to those narratives will bear no resemblances to the majority of those concerning black mothers and/or women that appear in the literature written by black men or white men or women.

Since the success of *A Raisin in the Sun* the names of an impressive number of black women writers have become fairly well known to large numbers of Americans, and at the same time new and different images of black women have emerged from their pens. But while it is accurate to give credit to Hansberry's success as foreshadowing the contemporary wider recognition of black women writers and critics, the momentum it signalled had its beginnings more than two hundred years earlier. The history of the creative efforts of black women in America began with the beginnings of literacy, in 1746 with Lucy Terry's "Bars Fight," a poem about an Indian raid on the white settlement of Deerfield, Massachusetts, and continued with Phillis Wheatley's *Poems on Various Subjects, Religious and Moral* in 1773. Terry's and Wheatley's extant works confirm that black women in the eighteenth century had literary voices which they made bold to use, while black women of the nineteenth century, building on what preceded them, authenticated their voices by speaking to local and national issues that had direct impact on the lives of black people. From Sojourner Truth, abolitionist and feminist, who could neither read nor write but whose words were recorded by others, to Jarena Lee, evangelist, who documented the hundreds of miles she logged across the

country preaching and teaching and saving souls, to Maria Stewart, the first woman in the country to make a profession of the public lecture circuit, and Anna Julia Cooper and Frances Watkins Harper, whose feminist, antiracist writings are as contemporary as today, we know that these women spoke loud and clear in celebration of the positive characteristics of human life, and in strong criticism of racial and gender oppression. This history assures us that black women have not ever been artistically or critically silent, even though for most of the past their voices went largely ignored by those who did not wish to hear them. In their own voices, black women have always confirmed and authenticated the complexity of the black American female experience, and in so doing have debunked the negative stereotypes that others created of them while denying them audience for their words. Now, finally admitted to a larger hearing than they ever previously enjoyed, both past and present black female literary voices combine to alter the historical nature of the discourse and to play a prominent role in revising the canon from which they were long excluded.

There is no need here to again recite the history of the stereotyping of black women in American literature by others than themselves. That has been adequately done by several critics. It is important, however, to note that the efforts to reverse the negative images of black women in literature began as early as these women began to find an opportunity to write: with the slave narratives, fiction, poetry, and nonfiction prose of the nineteenth century. The spoken words of women like Sojourner

Truth, and the writings of other women like Stewart, Cooper, and Watkins-Harper, among others, were primary in the struggle against slavery and the abuses of women, especially of black women. Their boldness and assertiveness define these women as a highly intelligent, morally outraged group in a struggle against white injustice to blacks and male dominance of women.

In the earliest known novel by a black woman, *Our Nig or Sketches from the Life of a Free Black* (1859), by Harriet Wilson, the abused heroine, Frado, is a hardworking, honest child of mixed racial parentage who is caught in a web of white hatred and cruelty. Frado is neither an immoral woman nor a mammy, the most frequent of the stereotypes of black women in that time, and Wilson uses her characterization of the helpless child to emphasize the unfairness of a social structure that permitted individuals to treat black people in a less-than-human fashion. In writing this novel, Wilson, of whom not a great deal is known, was the flesh-and-blood example of the rebel against the treatment she outlined in her book. As such, she provided another concrete example of black women's estimation of their self-worth. For one thing, she explicitly wrote her narrative as a means of earning money to take care of herself and her ailing son. Wilson, who lived in Boston and other areas of New England, and who sets her work in that geographical location, took advantage of the tradition of the sentimental female novel, which at that time enjoyed enormous popularity. The form of her book—the epigraphs, style, and structure of the narrative—shows that she was well aware of many of the conventions of novel writing at the time, and that she considered them valuable to plead the case, not of the poor white heroine who eventually achieves a good marriage and a happy home, as they did in the white female novels, but of an abused black child and woman who was unable to realize the goals of white protagonists. Wilson, deserted by her husband, was sufficiently self-assured to imagine that writing held the possibilities of a vocation for her.

But the slave narrative, not fiction, was the mode that dominated the earliest Afro-American attempts at literature, which through its existence revised the nature of the American "Self." Until recently, most of the attention to this body of work has focused on the writings of men, with *The Narrative of Frederick Douglass, An American Slave, Written by Himself* receiving the majority of the plaudits. It is now recognized that the female slave narrative deserves attention for its own sake—for its unique contributions to the genre. The narrative of Harriet Jacobs, in particular, *Incidents in the Life of a Slave Girl*, published in 1861 under the name of Linda Brent, is a stunning literary success, equal in every way to the preeminent male slave narrative. Jacobs, a South Carolina slave who became a fugitive at age twenty-seven, told a story that brilliantly deconstructs the meaning of the female slave experience in relationship to that of her male counterpart and the white world around her. The literary prowess she displayed in her careful delineation of the sexual harassment she suffered from her owner, her masterly circumvention of his intentions toward her, her patience and determination to free herself and her children, and her understanding of the differences between psychological and physical freedom make her tale a female classic. As an early narrative by a black woman, one of the most significant contributions that *Incidents* makes to the history is its identification of the existence of and effectiveness of a woman's community in which black and white, slave and free women sometimes joined forces to thwart the brutal plans of masters against helpless slave women. In Harriet Wilson's *Our Nig*, the cruel stepmother of the fairy-tale convention is replaced by the cruel mistress and her equally cruel daughter, while the men in the story, sympathetic to Frado, are ineffective against the wickedness of the female members of their family. On the contrary, Jacobs, who hides in the crawl-space of her grandmother's house for seven years, in real life, is assisted in this effort by a number of women until she can safely escape. Similarly, other black women's slave narratives pay tribute to the roles that women play as models and inspiration in their struggle to rise above oppression. The "sisterhood" of black women and the peculiarity of relations between black and white women that appears in later black women's literature were already well documented in the black female slave narrative tradition.

If the slave narrative as a genre revised the concept of the American self, then, as a separate body of work, the narratives written by slave women are especially important for their revisionist elements in relationship to the narratives of ex-slave men and the American female experience in the autobiographical accounts of white women. We are indebted to Frances Foster's study,

" 'In Respect to Females . . . ': Differences in the Portrayals of Women by Male and Female Narrators," for alerting us to the implications of gender in slave narratives a few years ago. Of necessity, the experiences of white women in the age of the "cult of true womanhood" were very separate from those of black slave women, but slave men and women also had different perceptions of their common condition. In the narratives of ex-slave men, for instance, slave women appear completely helpless and fully exploited. Much of this is identified as the result of their sexual vulnerability, and the women are pictured as victims without recourse to means of protecting or of defending themselves. Images of these women on auction blocks, stripped to their waists, their children having been sold away from them—all because of the licentiousness of their masters—are among those that abound in the literature. In Douglass's narrative for instance, he is painstaking in his descriptions of the beatings slave women were often given. His accounts of the sounds of the whips against their flesh and the flow of the blood from their backs are graphic. On the other hand, in telling their own stories, ex-slave women did not concentrate on the sexual exploitation they suffered. They did not deny it, but they made it clear that there were other elements in their lives which were important to them as well. In short, they saw themselves as more than victims of rape and seduction. As Foster points out, when they wrote, they not only wanted to witness to the atrocities of slavery, but also to celebrate their hard-won escapes. Their stories show them to be strong, courageous, dignified, and spirited in spite of the world in which they were forced to live. They depicted themselves as complex human beings with a desire to engage in discourse that took the breadth of their experiences into consideration. In writing, they were no longer secondary characters in someone else's script, but heroines in their own creations. As noted earlier, these black women writers focused less on individual performance and more on the positive roles that engaged women. They allotted time to the value of family relationships, not only to beatings and mutilations by slave masters. As they related their stories, ex-slave women took control of their narratives in much the same way as they took control of the circumstances that enabled them to survive and escape captivity.

Jacobs's narrative provides a good example of this mode. While she tells us of her dilemma with her master, the focus of *Incidents* is largely on her attempts to become free and to free her children. She demonstrates that she had power over her master while she was concealed in her grandmother's house, and she used this power to lead him to believe that she had left the state. She further tells us of her success in finding employment after her escape, and of the happy union she had with her children in the North. Her self-confidence was never destroyed by the abuses of slavery, and her self-esteem remained strong through the difficulties of her escape. Taking up where Foster left off, other critics have noted, from textual evidence in *Incidents*, how well Jacobs understood the meaning of freedom in her dealings with northern whites, especially in her

contacts with women. Associated with both the feminist and abolitionist movements, she analyzed her situation and wrote perceptively of the racism of white feminists. Like Wilson, she made use of the sentimental tradition in women's fiction, but skillfully subverted that tradition for her own purposes. It is interesting that both Wilson and Jacobs rejected the convention of marriage and the happy ending of popular white female fiction. There are several less fully developed ex-slave women narratives, but all are equally confirming in their assertion of the positive identity of their authors. Among them we have Elizabeth Keckley, a seamstress who later made a successful living by tending the wardrobes of presidential first ladies in Washington; Susie King Taylor, a woman of many talents, from laundress to schoolteacher; and Amanda Berry Smith, a preacher. All wrote, not only to expose the evils that had been done to them, but also to demonstrate their abilities to gain physical and psychological liberty by transcending those evils.

The poetry, fiction, and nonfiction prose of black women to come out of the latter part of the nineteenth century wage open warfare against racism and gender oppression, on one hand, and on the other, encourage and castigate blacks in an effort to promote the "uplift" of the race. As other critics have often noted, the novels by black men and women with the mulatto heroine were often an appeal to whites for the elimination of atrocities, based on racial prejudices, against blacks, especially in the face of the evidences of the extent of blood co-mingling between the races. Barbara Christian has done an excellent exploration of the range of the intentions of Frances

Watkins Harper, for instance, who was responsible for the publication of some eleven volumes of poetry, religious in tone and mainly directed toward the less fortunate, in her effort to "make songs for the people," who spoke out and wrote overtly scathing essays against white racism and sexism. She wrote a novel as well, *Iola LeRoy, Shadows Uplifted* (1892), with a mulatta heroine who revises this type of protagonist as s/he appears in novels such as William Wells Brown's *Clotel; or The President's Daughter* (1853). Unlike the tragic character whom Brown and others portray, Harper's heroine, given a chance to escape from her race, chooses to marry an Afro-American and dedicate her life to helping unfortunate black people. Anna Julia Cooper, who wrote no fiction, used didactic prose in *A Voice from the South: By a Black Women of the South*, not only to admonish white Americans for their injustices against other Americans, but to celebrate the achievements of black women and to sternly reproach the shortcomings of black men, particularly when those failings diminished the value of what black women strove to achieve.

A much neglected black female voice that spans the period between the end of the nineteenth century and the activities of the Harlem Renaissance of the 1920s is that of Alice Dunbar Nelson, who for a short time was married to the famous Paul Laurence Dunbar. Her importance to the history of Afro-American letters continues to be eclipsed by his. But the recent publication of Dunbar Nelson's diary, *Give Us Each Day, The Diary of Alice Dunbar-Nelson*, edited by Gloria Hull, has added an important work to the corpus of black women's writings. While twentieth-century black women's autobiographies have often proved to be frustrating documents because of their lack of openness, and the tendency of the authors to avoid private disclosures, this diary reveals the side of Dunbar Nelson that would otherwise remain unknown to the world. Dunbar Nelson, who was born in 1875 and died in 1935, like many of the writers of that era, was middle-class, educated, and highly sophisticated, a journalist as well as short-story writer, dramatist, and poet. In the ease with which she handled more than one literary form, she belongs to a group that includes women like Georgia Johnson and Angelina Grimké, both poets and dramatists, whose pens made known that black women were not only involved with the practical problems of education and economics for black people, but also with the creation of art and literature. Most of these women earned a living by teaching, the only respectable profession that was open to them, but one that was also in line with their ideas of service to others. Especially as dramatists, Dunbar Nelson, Johnson, and Grimké addressed many of the social problems facing the black community, and agitated for changes to alter them. Racism of all kinds, including lynching, were topics of their plays, and these women went as far as to take up the issue of poor women and the need for birth control education in the struggle against poverty and ignorance.

On the opposite side of the coin of achievement, from Dunbar Nelson's diary we learn some details of how women of her standing coped with many of the problems that confronted them in their private lives, away from the long days and busy schedules which make their histories as impressive as they are. Space does not permit an accounting of the financial difficulties which she faced for almost all of her life, or the strength and creativity she put into protecting her public image from the chaos of her private world. Suffice it to say that she worried a great deal over an accumulation of debts; that a fear of bouncing checks is one of the themes in the book; and that she was a woman who could pawn her jewelry to pay her water bill, and go immediately from that second task to address a meeting of wives of professional white men, dressed like a "certified check." From the diary too, there is further confirmation of the strength of the women's community which female slave narrators introduced into the literature. Not only did Dunbar Nelson live in a family in which women were pre-eminent, regardless of the men who entered their lives at different times, but her world outside of her family was peopled by women like Mary McLeod Bethune and Nannie Burroughs, famous educators, in addition to the Club Women and the writers and artists of her time.

Dunbar Nelson and the women who appear in her diary are complex figures who do not fit the stereotypes of black women of their day in the literature of others. They were exciting and strong, but they were also very human in the ways in which they responded to experience. They worked, laughed, loved, cried, and survived because they were tough-minded and respected themselves and others. They transgressed the boundaries of the expectations of women in that day, and created themselves in their own images. In respect to what she discloses of their private lives, Dunbar Nelson's diary is extremely important in the process of the revision of the literary images of ambitious upwardly mobile black women of the early part of the century.

The 1920s were the years in which black culture flourished as it has not done before in America, and the center of the activity was in Harlem, New York City. Following on the heels of the large black migration from a rural to an urban environment that began early in the century, and an increase in the West Indian and African populations in the country, the artistic and scholarly communities, as a group, set themselves to the task of defining the black experience in as positive a way as they could. It is now common knowledge that Jessie Fauset, black woman poet and novelist, in her role as W. E. B. DuBois's assistant at the *Crisis* (one of the most important journals of the time), was instrumental in bringing all of the important writers of the period into public view. In addition, Fauset was the only member of the group to publish three novels between the early 1920s and early 1930s. She, along with Nella Larsen, author of two novels in the late 1920s, have received less attention as writers than their male counterparts because of a perception that their works belong to the genteel tradition of the novel of manners. That condition is moving toward rapid change, however, as contemporary black women critics re-evaluate the writings of women before the 1960s; as cooperative publishers make out-of-print texts available for classroom use; and teachers and professors in Women's Studies and Afro-American and other literature courses make use of them.

Not all the women who came of age in the 1920s or who were associated with the Harlem Renaissance emerged then or did their best work in that period. Dorothy West, novelist, short fiction writer, and journalist, and Pauli Murray, family chronicler, poet, and civil rights activist were young women attracted to the verve of the cultural movement, but whose work appeared later in the 1930s and 1940s. The most illustrious of the women in the later-blooming group to have had an association with the Renaissance was Zora Neale Hurston. In the early 1970s, her work was rediscovered and it did more than any single writer's work to mobilize the energy of contemporary black women critics. Hurston arrived in New York from Florida by way of Baltimore and Washington, D.C., in 1925, after having won a prize for short fiction published in *Opportunity* magazine. Before her mature work in the 1930s and 1940s she continued to write short stories, earned herself a degree in anthropology from Columbia University, did fieldwork in the South and the West Indies, and was a colorful figure among the Harlem literati. In her time she received only minor praise for her work, and long before her death in 1960 she was forgotten by most of the literary world and derided by those who remembered her. In the early 1970s, her now-acclaimed novel, *Their Eyes Were Watching God* (1937), retrieved her name from oblivion and set the wheels rolling for the new black feminist criticism of the 1970s and 1980s. In relationship to black literature until then, this novel turned aside from the literature of protest against racism and racial discrimination to explore the inner dynamics of black culture, and to introduce, as heroine, the ordinary, uneducated black woman in search of a self-defined identity. Taking place al-most entirely within the black community, *Their Eyes* explores primal relations between black men and women as they had never been done before. Here are rural people without concern for "social uplift," but whose lives are rich with a heritage that has fostered black survival for generations. Janie, her central character, is the first black feminist heroine in the fictional canon. At the same time, the folklore in all of her books makes Hurston's work an important source of information far beyond the boundaries of literature. Unfortunately, her other works have often been adjudged "lesser" than *Their Eyes*, even by her most ardent supporters. This too is a judgment that may well be revised in the near future, as at least one other novel of hers, *Moses, Man of the Mountain* (1939), a black folk rendition of the biblical myth, has finally begun to attract critical attention. Her autobiography, *Dust Tracks on a Road*, is a problematical text from the point of view of its concealments and evasions. But again, new studies in black women's autobiographies suggest that such concealments are a prominent convention in the tradition. As black women's autobiography stands, Hurston may not be the exception most people now think she is. However, had she written nothing of importance other than *Their Eyes Were Watching God*, her place in history would still be fully assured. She did indeed change the nature of the black female heroine in American literature.

From the end of the nineteenth century through the conclusion of the 1940s, the women mentioned above were among those who produced works that were representative of the kinds of writings that black women were engaged in for the first part of the century. Although, except for rare exceptions, they never received the public recognition they deserved, they wrote. They were ambitious, versatile in what they could do, and very productive. As nineteenth-century black women writers had done before them, they continued to explore racism and gender oppression in their writings, especially in fiction and autobiography. Because they were working within the black tradition of protest against white racism, they handled this issue more overtly than they tended to do with gender oppression, especially as that existed within the black community. Since most of these writers were members of the intellectual middle class as well, they also gave a good deal of attention to the "progress" of black people as a whole, an idea that tended to place white middle-class values in a position of superiority in relationship to values inherent in Afro-American culture. In the autobiographical literature of the period the emphasis was on the level of achievement women had made in education and economic independence, although many narratives focused on the ways in which these women worked to "elevate" young women and children, mainly by rescuing them from lives of poverty and immorality and leading them to paths of industry and morality. Hurston, as noted above, unlike many of the writers in her time, deviated from popular black trends and looked backwards to the black folk culture for the materials of her art. As a result, she often incurred the anger of her peers, who felt that her stance in applauding the inner

vitality of that culture and her lack of attention to the deprivations of racism worked at cross purposes to their goals. They felt that her position undermined their efforts to force social change since it diluted their efforts to present a united front in confronting the white world.

Between 1940 and the beginning of the 1960s there was a good deal of creative activity on the part of black women writers. In 1949 Gwendolyn Brooks received the Pulitzer Prize for poetry, and became the first black American to be so honored. Brooks, whose work began appearing in 1945, continues to be a poet with enormous energy. Her excursions away from poetry produced a novel, *Maud Martha*, in 1953, and an autobiographical narrative that resembles a prose poem, *Report From Part One*, in 1972. Brooks's work, until 1970, though highly stylized, turned to face the plight of urban blacks in her home city of Chicago. Life on the segregated South Side, with its many disadvantages, was the subject of her prize-winning poetry. Her poetry did for blacks in this urban ghetto what Langston Hughes had earlier done for their counterparts in Harlem. In her novel she examined the inner thoughts of a young woman who is not pretty by conventional standards, or dynamic, or specially gifted, but who has the confidence in herself to seek her happiness. Since 1970, Brooks's work has taken on a decided black militant posture.

A number of other writers made important contributions to the literature of black women during these decades. Particularly deserving of special mention are Margaret Alexander Walker, another prize-winning novelist and poet; Adrienne Kennedy, playwright; Alice Childress, play-wright and fiction writer; and Ann Petry, journalist, short-story writer, and author of three novels. After some years of neglect, Petry is experiencing a return to acclaim with the 1985 re-publication of her most well-known work, *The Street*, originally issued in 1943. In this novel, written in the naturalistic mode, the heroine, Lutie Johnson, bright, beautiful, ambitious, hard-working, and a single mother, is defeated by the hostile environment of the ghetto, represented by a Harlem street. In choosing to use the conventions that she did, Petry creates a character who, unlike most black women's heroines, is alienated from all the support systems available to poor black people: the church, extended family, and a network of friends. Other works of the period emphasize the distressing results of racism on black life, but most demonstrate that survival is possible when their protagonists make use of black support institutions. Especially missing in this novel is the community of women that had for so long been a mainstay in the conventions of black women's fiction.

The 1950s ended on a note of great promise for black American women writers, and in spite of the politics of white racism and of gender, and the sexism of many black men, the rising tide of the Civil Rights Movement was helpful to many of these writers. While Lorraine Hansberry's play received the most outstanding acclaim of all in 1959, there were other women who came to public view with less fanfare, but who were of no less importance to the tradition. One such was Paule Marshall, whose novel, *Brown Girl, Brownstones*, was

the first black narrative to probe the sensibilities of an American-born adolescent girl of West Indian parents. Marshall, since then, has built her literary career around the interconnections blacks of West Indian heritage feel with white western civilization in the United States. For although most of the Islands were colonized by different European countries, African residuals remained stronger in them than among American blacks, largely because the populations in the islands contained a majority of African descendants. In her second novel, *The Chosen Place, The Timeless People*, published a decade after *Brown Girl*, Marshall's heroine is a West Indian woman who, after several years of living in England, returns to her island home to battle the ills of imperialism there. In *Praise Song For the Widow*, her 1983 work, she examines the recovery of "roots" by a middle-aged West Indian American woman on a journey back to her West Indian past. This is a theme that Marshall, a first-generation American with a West Indian background, seems to find fruitful to pursue. Between her novels she has produced a number of short stories as well, most of them with some "island" flavor.

Writers like Gwendolyn Brooks, Margaret Walker, Alice Childress, Paule Marshall, and Ann Petry continue to be productive in the 1980s. Within the last three decades, however, a remarkable number of new writers have joined their company, many of whom have produced an astonishing volume of writings. Those of us who have been privileged to follow the careers of writers Toni Morrison, whose first novel was *The Bluest Eye* (1970), Alice Walker, since her novel *The Third Life of Grange Copeland* (1970), and Maya Angelou, whose first volume of autobiography was called *I Know Why the Caged Bird Sings* (1970), are aware of how large the output has been in a short time. All of these women have produced multiple volumes of fiction, poetry, autobiography, and essays. Even the newest writers to emerge, like Ntozake Shange and Gloria Naylor, who did not publish until the beginning of the 1980s, have been prolific.

The literature of black women of the 1960s, 1970s, and 1980s follows in the tradition of the earlier times, but is also very different from what went before. Previously, in the slave narrative tradition and the fiction, autobiography, and drama, black women worked hard to debunk the negative stereotypes that other writers had imposed on them. In some instances what they produced were counterstereotypes that depicted black women as strong, and always overcoming hardships. The writers of the present generation see no need to perpetuate only those images, and are now exploring all aspects of black women's experiences— their weaknesses and failings, as well as their strengths and ability to transcend race and gender oppression. Writing from inside of their own experiences, and the knowledge of the experiences of black women for more than three hundred years in America, they examine the innate humanity of the characters they portray— characters who embody qualities that make them neither flawless heroines, immoral individuals, or helpless victims. A good example of this reconciliation of human traits shows up in Toni Morrison's first novel, in which a young black girl, driven insane in her quest for the white western ideal of female beauty—blue eyes—is balanced by the second black girl who understood and rejected the self-destructiveness inherent in a black woman's identifying with such an ideal. In like manner, the conflicts between black men and women that Alice Walker exposes in *Grange Copeland* and other novels are more than an accounting of how brutal some black men can be to their women, but rather a search for the roots of that brutality as a means toward reconciliation between the embattled sexes. Morrison, Walker, and dozens of other new black women writers are "prophets for a new day," in which black American women writers are demanding honor in their own country.

The hallmark of contemporary black women's writings is the impulse toward an honest, complicated, and varied expression of the meaning of the black woman's experiences in America. There is little effort to conceal the pain, and just as little to create the ideal, but a great deal to reveal how black women incorporate the negative and positive aspects of self and external reality into an identity that enables them to meet the challenges of the world in which they must live. Not all black women are strong and enduring, yet a core of resistance to emotional and physical oppression, and a will to discover the path to survival and beyond resides even in those works in which these women do not transcend. As I noted earlier, a long history of black women and the art-of-words exists, and the literature of black America, in its oral and written contexts, has been within the province of its women from the beginning of the American experience. The work of the writers has been ongoing, and has included every branch of the literary family. From the perceived utility of the slave narrative of antebellum days to the more highly crafted and sophisticated forms of the present time, black women have told their own stories both as a way of self-confirmation and a means of correcting the erroneous white and male record of their inner reality. Black women writers project a dynamic "I" into the canon, one that makes more complete the reality of the multifaceted American experience.

27

The Politics of Poetics

Or, What Am I, a Critic, Doing in This Text Anyhow?

(1987)

Tey Diana Rebolledo

In an essay "Retrieving our Past, Determining our Future" poet Pat Mora chose to begin with a pre-Colombian poem:

> Also they grow cotton
> of many colors:
> red, yellow, pink,
> purple, green, bluish-green,
> blue, light green,
> orange, brown, and dark gold.
> These were the colors of the cotton itself.
> It grew that way from the earth,
> no one colored it.
> And also they raised these
> fowl of rare plumage:
> small birds the color of turquoise,
> some with green feathers,
> with yellow, with flame-colored breasts.
> Every kind of fowl
> that sang beautifully,
> like those that warble in the mountains.

Mora chose this poem because she liked the images of music, color and nature. But then she is a poet. I would like to underscore Mora's choice and begin with some definitions. "*Politics*:

intrigue or maneuvering within a group; one's position or attitude on political subjects. *Poetics*: literary criticism dealing with the nature, form and laws of poetry; a study of or treatise on poetry or aesthetics. *Criticism*: the art, skill or profession of making discriminating judgements, especially of literary or artistic works, detailed investigation of the origin and history of literary documents. *Discourse*: to run about, to speak at length, the process or power of reasoning."

My understanding several months ago was that this symposium "Chicana Creativity and Criticism: Charting New Frontiers in American Literature," would undertake a dialogue between Chicana creative writers and Chicana literary critics with regard to several topics: are Chicana critics friends or foes to the writers? What function do or can we Chicana critics play in relationship to our literature? And, what the heck are we doing in and to these texts anyway? As Chicanas we are all in this *revoltura*

Rebolledo, Tey Diana, "The Politics of Poetics." In *Chicana Creativity and Criticism*, eds. Herrera-Sobek & Viramontes (1988). Reprinted by permission of the University of New Mexico Press.

and explosion of literature and poetics together. It is time, perhaps, to take a step back and analyze where we are and where we might be going.

I do not mean the remarks I am about to make to be anti-intellectual, anti-theoretical or anti-aesthetic. Nor do I mean to assume the position of any critic other than myself. Nor am I criticizing the work of any particular literary critic. Nevertheless, I am commenting on what I see as a general phenomenon: one that we need to take stock of and one which affects Chicano male critics as well as the females, Juan Bruce-Novoa, in his recent article "Canonical and Non-canonical Texts," thinks there is now a "body of work" which constitutes Chicano literature and which is recognized as such. He recognizes that previously "any mention of canon was clearly understood as a reference to mainstream literature" and, he adds, "to state we were excluded from the canon was to state the obvious. Moreover, there was an ironic sense of worth associated with being outside the canon, almost a sense of purity, because, beyond the exclusionary ethnocentrism implied by the canon, Chicanos infused the term with a criticism of the very existence of a privileged body of texts."

It seems to me that in spite of the explosion of creative and critical activity on the part of both critics and writers, Chicana writers and critics are still within a framework of marginality among Chicano writing as well as in mainstream writing. Some of this may be attributed to time; that is, time for the maturing of our literature as well as of our criticism. In addition to the creation of new insights and perspectives, we are also at a moment of rupture in which we are just beginning to look back to uncover our traditions, whether they be written or oral, and to talk back—to unsay what had been said and frozen in time and place. We are at the moment of questioning everything, even ourselves. Only when it is accomplished can we, with clear conscience, proceed towards some understanding of critical difference.

At the recent Chicano Studies Conference in Salt Lake City (1987), it became clear that for the past several years social scientists and literary critics alike have been engaged in a desperate search for a theoretical/critical discourse in which to situate what is happening to us. There have been discourses and counter-discourses. We talk about historical/materialist perspectives, transformative perspectives, pluralism (which some called a pre-prostituted dominant discourse) and the word hegemony was used in one session alone thirty-two times. Some of the talks began with a few of the questions to be asked, then discussed the methods used to answer those questions, mostly the methods used. I would say a typical talk could be summarized in the following way: the speaker begins, "This paper will focus on the ideology of cultural practice and its modes of signifying." S/he then spends twenty minutes discussing how the works of whatever theoretical greats s/he selects will define, inform and privilege the work s/he is doing. Such names as Jameson, Said, Williams, Hall, Burke and other contemporary *meros*, *meros* (mostly male) will be invoked over and over. The speaker is then sent a note by the chair of the panel that there is no time left. And whatever the Chicano/a writing or phenomenon that was to be discussed is quickly summarized in two minutes.

The talk is over. We have talked so much about theory we never get to our conclusion nor focus on the texts. By appropriating mainstream theoreticians and critics we have become so involved in intellectualizing that we lose our sense of our literature and therefore our vitality. This priority of placing our literature in a theoretical framework to "legitimize" it, if the theory overshadows it, in effect undermines our literature or even places it, once again, in a state of oblivion. Privileging the theoretical discourse de-privileges ourselves.

In puzzling over this scenario, which in fact occurred many times in Salt Lake, one could be left with various insights about what is happening to us:

1. We have internalized the dominant ideology so that only by talking theory (construed as a superior form of logic) can our literature and our cultural practices be intellectually viable, that is, accepted within the traditional academic canon as "legitimate."
2. We are trying to impress ourselves and others with our ability to manipulate theoretical discourse, to use buzz words such as hegemony, signifying and even the word discourse. Someone once said to me "you are so articulate. You are able to talk in *their* language." I am not sure what this means. On the one hand they may be telling me I am totally assimilated or they may, in reality, be saying that no Chicana can truly be articulate. (I myself often feel that it is only our baroque *conceptismo* that has been transferred into English.)
3. We have entered into the "Age of Criticism" which could be defined as a preoccupation with theoretical structures often not internalized: we feel that theory is power.
4. We have a genuine desire to look beyond the elements (the texts) to the conditions that structured them. We are truly in search of a theoretical framework which yet eludes us or at least some of us (and I count myself among those eludees).

I would like to outline some of the problems that I think we Chicana critics face or that at least I, as a critic in training, think about from time to time. They often as not deal with the question, what am I doing in this text anyhow?

1. First of all I am a reader. But I am not just a reader. My job, as a university professor, is to bring the attention of my students to the text itself. How can I do this if the text is not included in the general course curriculum, in the anthologies or in any way accessible to the student or to the population at large? Perhaps my primary responsibility, therefore, is the promulgation of the works of these writers, to make the writers known. We all know that the material production of Chicana writers is often limited to chapbooks, journals and the few texts that are accepted by Arte Publico Press and Bilingual Press. It is limited even to the Chicano audience and from one region to the next, from one big city to the next, we may not know what is happening. The work being done by Juan Rodríguez, *Third Woman* and the Centro de Escritores de Aztlán, for example, helps but as these texts go out of print, this production becomes more difficult to find. At Salt Lake City a copy of the first printing of Quinto Sol's *El Grito* was proudly held up as the rarity it has become. Of the chapbooks that were and are produced in the 1960s, 1970s and 1980s, many will end up in a rare book room in a library if we are fortunate. Fortunate because they will be preserved as artifacts—the same phenomenon which will make the book even more inaccessible.

If this product is inaccessible to those who are its target, in terms of interest, it is virtually unavailable to a larger audience. The role of the Chicana critic then becomes one of facilitator: reproducing and making known the texts of our authors. In itself this may not be an insignificant task since, for example, in a recent struggle with some of my coauthors (not the editors) of a book to be published by Yale University Press, I was told that my method of writing, that is, including entire poems written by Chicanas instead of dissecting them by including between slashes "pertinent" quotes from the text, made my article "hard to read" and "jumpy." While this may be true of my own writing, it certainly was not true of those texts of the authors I had included. I was very troubled by the inadequacies of a vision which presumed to have me speak for all Chicanas when they were perfectly able to speak for themselves. My arguments for entire text inclusion were the following: a) These texts were unknown and therefore needed to be reproduced in their entirety; b) These writers were more passionate, forceful and graphic than I; c) I did not want to do to these writers what others have been doing to all of us for centuries, that is, to appropriate their discourse through my discourse. I commented that I had no problem with my strategy and if they were not happy with publishing my chapter as it was, I did not wish it to be included in the volume. Fortunately the article will be published in its jumpy entirety in The Desert Is No Lady, title poem by Pat Mora.

2. The second function of a critic may be to analyze the content of the literary production—stepping back from the product in order to see what may be the dominant concerns and themes. I myself have indulged in this type of descriptive thematic analysis (adding, I hope, some analysis in depth as to cultural context and history). One example is a paper I wrote on *abuelitas*, noting the scope and complexity of this recurring figure and offering an explanation as to why this figure was approaching what I considered to be mythic proportions. This article has brought mixed reviews. My secretary,

who was typing it, asked to take it home to read to her children, and many others have used it in their classrooms for teaching. Recently, a contemporary writer remarked to me about critics writing descriptively about things that "everyone already knew about," such as *abuelitas*. Yet descriptive thematic analysis serves its purpose too, particularly as it grows in sophistication, and as historical and cultural analysis are linked to it. I hope that since my *abuelitas* article was published and as I have grown as a scholar that my analysis has too.

3. Another important current function for us as critics is to remember our literary history. While contemporary writers may feel that they are seeing the world anew, those of us who are searching out our literary roots are finding women writers who were raising many of the same concerns women voice today—written in a different tone and style and conforming to a different mode; nevertheless, contemporary writers have not arisen from a complete void. If the written word did not survive in enough texts to be known today, nonetheless the oral forms of women's concerns, of women's images have lived in the tradition from one generation, from one century to another. Thus the critic as literary historian is able to fill in the lacunae and to connect the past and the present.

4. Chicana literary discourse, like most feminist discouse, is a troubled one. It is always searching, questioning and fraught with tensions and contradictions, just as is the creative writing arising from the same creative context. A truly Chicana literary theory would result from the attempt to resolve these things, to mend the rift between doers and thinkers. I think we would all agree that Chicana criticism and theory are still in a state of flux looking for a theoretical, critical framework that is our own, whatever the perspective. I personally find it difficult to have theory (male-oriented, French feminist, post-structural or whatever is the current fad) be what dictates what we find in our literature. I prefer to have the

literature speak for itself and as a critic try to organize and understand it. Perhaps from a more open perspective our own theoretical critical analysis will arise, rather than finding the theory first and imposing it upon the literature.

Recently several Chicana critics have taken up the issue of a theoretical approach to our literature. Norma Cantú in "The Chicana Poet and Her Audience: Notes Towards a Chicana Feminist Aesthetic" acknowledges the lack of a methodological approach in our work but feels that it is a sense of place and world as embedded in particular language use that the Chicana poet communicates to her Chicana audience. For Cantú it is the special relationship between writer and listener, the shared cultural referents that make the poems work. Norma Alarcón, in her perceptive study on the image of La Malinche, reevaluates and reconstructs the symbolic and figurative meaning this figure holds for us as Chicana writers and critics, dealing with the significance of language use and silence within our literature. She also sees significant evolution of the Chicana as "speaking subject," one who brings within herself her race, class and gender, expressing this from a self-conscious point of view. Both of these critics, it seems to me, in addition to being theoretically well-grounded, look at literature from within, in an integrative sense.

5. It is very difficult to work on living authors: authors who read what you write and agree or don't agree. But it is just as difficult to work on authors no longer living. In the practice of literary criticism one (or perhaps I speak for myself only) must practice sound and honorable as well as rigorous criticism. That is, facts must be checked, scholarship must be sound. There is always the danger that the critic, immersed in pursuing some essential point, will become over enthusiastic and confuse the authorial voice with that of the narrative or poetic voice. If structuralism has taught us anything at all, it is that the lyric/narrative speaker is just that. As critics we must be careful not to confuse author with speaker.

When dealing with a vigorously living author we must also not be too timid to analyze symbolically what we, as critics, may see in the text—that which the author may not consciously have intended. We know that there are many levels of symbolic discourse that we may not be aware of at any given moment. When the text is published, when the author gives it up to the public domain, it is released and opened up to interpretation by the reader. It exists on its own, separate from the author. The textual interpretation, therefore, is one of integration between the authorial intent, and the text itself, *and* the third (and separate) interpretation or grasping of those two aspects by the reader.

6. We must, as critics, also be careful in our criticism to be honest. I think Chicana critics are often too benign. Our close network between writers and critics makes it difficult to have caustic criticism (which might ruin friendships) but at the same time we may hesitate to be as critical as we should be. One way I know I cope with this, and I imagine others have the same problem is simply to ignore those texts I don't like of writers that I do like or to ignore those writers who say nothing to me. This seems to me to be a function of human nature. What is important, however, is that the critic be conscious of her biases. And while we women may be benign to each other, there are still many Chicano critics who refuse to recognize their own biases and misogyny. Raymond Paredes, in a recent review article, is only able to see Chicana literature through a particularly phallocentric focus. If we were to accept his views we would see "if there is one quality that runs consistently through *their* (italics mine) stories, plays and novels, it is the conviction that men know and care very little about women and that everyone is the worse for it." His review continues with the assumption that men are the focus of Chicana literature, as he assails Beverly Silva, Cherrie Moraga and Ana Castillo as faulted writers, their work, he says, is more interesting "ideologically"

than aesthetically. Back to the old notion of "Are They Any Good?" Those writers whose perspectives Paredes does not agree with he considers superficial, and Denise Chávez, with whom he is more in agreement, is merely "flawed."

7. Perhaps more dangerous than ignoring texts we dislike is excluding the works of authors whose perspective we do not share or whose perspective we might feel uncomfortable with. Here I mean specifically the perspective of sexual preference. There are some fine Lesbian writers such as Cherríe Moraga, Gloria Anzaldúa, and Veronica Cunningham whose works are often excluded (although less so recently) from our critical thinking. Certainly if critics are serious about historical, cultural and gender context, then all writers need to be included within the general cultural framework. Then too some critics feel more comfortable with socially conscious literature and exclude that coming from the middle class. As the complexities and shades of our literature grows, we must be careful not to canonize a certain few to the exclusion of other equally fine writers.

8. While some scholars see the need for some resolution of dichotomies, for example of Chicana and feminist, Chicana and poet—as if they were mutually exclusive—others examine the relationship between dominant and ethnic communities. The dominant discourse, if we internalize it, would have us believe that we function under such labels, and to some extent we do. I believe, however, as Bernice Zamora so succinctly expressed it, that our complexities are infinite: that we have grown up and survived along the edges, along the borders of so many languages, worlds, cultures and social systems that we constantly fix and focus on the spaces in between, Nepantla as Sor Juana would have seen it. Categories that try to define and limit this incredibly complex process at once become diminished for their inability to capture and contain. Those of us who try to categorize these complexities inevitably fail.

Margarita Cota-Cárdenas in her novel *Puppet* examines the way in which this ideology is imposed. She sees this in part as arising from a single vision of what being Chicana should be.

> Are you Malinche a malinche? Who are you (who am I Mal inche)? Seller or buyer? Sold or bought and at what price? What is it to be what so many should say sold-out malinchi who is who are/are we what? At what price without having been there naming putting label tags what who have bought sold malinchismo what other-ismos invented shouted with hate reacting, striking like vipers like snakes THEIR EYES like snakes what who what

Her Malinche breaks the silence of centuries and she does not do so quietly:

> yes yes I went yelling loud too why why and they said tie her up she's too forward too flighty she thinks she's a princess thinks she's her father's daughter thinks she's hot stuff that's it doesn't know her place a real threat to the tribe take her away haul her off she's a menace to our cause that's it only learned to say crazy things accuse with HER EYES and they didn't want then troublemakers in their country.

These labels, specific here to La Malinche but clearly extended to all Chicanas, are of course the very labels culture uses to restrict and limit women's activity, socially as well as intellectually. Women are so silenced that they are only left to speak with "their eyes." In a country defined as "their" country, one that does not belong to her, Cota-Cárdenas makes the connection between Mexico and the United States:

> This country, well I suppose Mexico, Aztlán . . . ? Well, it could have been a little more to the north or a little more to the south, it makes no difference

now, what I was telling you was my version, that's it, my version . . . as a woman, that's right, and they can establish the famous dialectic with the other versions that you already know very well.

Cota-Cárdenas thus introduces the complexities, the ambiguities in our lives and, while she does not deny the legitimacy of the other versions (acknowledging them for what they are), overlays another perspective that is hers alone.

These remarks I have made may seem to be arising from some simplistic assumptions. I myself was trained as a structuralist, semiotic critic. But increasingly I have become suspicious and yes, even bored, by a criticism which seems alien to the text about which it purports to talk: by a theoretical basis of patriarchal norms or a theory which does not take the particular concerns of minority writers and culture into account. I am suspicious of criticism which ignores the texts of our writers and which turns the vitality and the passion of those texts of our writers into an empty and meaningless set of letters. This sort of criticism, it seems to me, might as well be analyzing a menu or a telephone directory, and would perhaps be better directed in doing so. As Sor Juana criticized Aristotle—he would have been a better philosopher had he studied cooking—I believe that our critical discourse should come from within, within our cultural and historical perspective. This is not to say that I am advocating limited, regional, small-minded descriptive literary analysis. But I think we should internalize and revolutionize theoretical discourse that comes from outside ourselves, accepting that which is useful and discarding that which is merely meant to impress. In the search for our own aesthetic, for our own analytical direction, we need to look to each other, to recognize that our literature and our cultural production does not need legitimization from the academy, that it already is legitimate in itself. Above all, we must not forget that the most important aspect of our analysis are the texts themselves. As we ask ouselves where are we, what are we doing, we must never appropriate into our own discourse the discourse of the writer herself. If we are to diffuse, support, promote, analyze and understand the work of our writers, we must let them speak for themselves. As a critic I desire the same as poet Pat Mora, I want to see the cotton of many colors, the small birds the color of turquoise and hear the birds that warble in the mountains.

Economics

The increasing power of global capitalism along with the glaring reality of women's poverty around the world makes the field of economics particularly in need of feminist perspectives. These essays illustrate both the obstacles to the inclusion of feminist perspectives in the field of economics and the important work being done by feminist economists. Marianne A. Ferber and Julie A. Nelson offer a comprehensive overview of feminist critiques of and contributions to the field. Their piece provides a helpful introduction to masculinist biases, past and present, and feminist strategies to remedy those biases. Deborah Barndt's essay shows how including the experiences of women and the insights of feminist theory may challenge conventional notions of "globalization" and the "free market." A professor of environmental studies whose research focuses on community development, women, globalization, and food, Barndt's work provides a fascinating example of how interdisciplinary feminist scholarship may reveal new insights into productivity, flexibility, and labor policy. Randy Albelda's piece turns our attention toward domestic economic policy in its examination of poor mothers, welfare, and work. Albelda shows that omitting certain realities from policy discussions has serious consequences for women and families in the United States.

Critical Thinking Questions

1. How do issues of power, dependency, and tradition influence people's economic "choices"? Do you perceive yourself to be free to make these choices, or do you recognize limitations as explained by feminist economists?
2. Which factors—institutional and disciplinary—seem to play the largest role in keeping feminist concerns outside mainstream economics? Can these factors be characterized as omissions or exclusions as discussed by Minnich?
3. To what extent does a feminist perspective force a reconsideration of globalization and the free market?
4. Can you imagine an economic policy that concerns itself with profit, freedom, and justice? Or, do these three goals seem incompatible?

5. What are the connections between Mexican agricultural workers and Canadian supermarket cashiers? Can you see how you might be part of the food chain as described in Barndt's essay?

6. What preconceptions did you have about welfare and welfare reform? How has Albelda's essay influenced your ideas?

7. Would it be fair or productive for employers or the state to attempt to make jobs "mother-ready"? What might this shift entail?

28

The Social Construction of Economics and the Social Construction of Gender

(1993)

Marianne A. Ferber and Julie A. Nelson

Is the development of the discipline of economics a story of continuous refinement and unidirectional progress, guided only by the internal requirement of logical coherence and the self-evident "nature" of external economic phenomena? If this is so, then social distinctions such as gender and social movements such as feminism are largely irrelevant for the development of economic analysis. If this is so, then, as one of the most influential books on the history of economic thought suggests, the story of economics can be written as "yesterday's blunders now corrected . . . , undiluted by entertaining historical digressions or biographical coloring" (Blaug 1962, ix).

Many feminists find such an ahistorical, disembodied account of the discipline bizarre. In the extreme it suggests that the ideals and definition of economics have been given to humankind through divine intervention, or perhaps dropped from a Friedmanesque helicopter. If we instead recognize that the discipline we call economics has been developed by particular human actors, it is hard to see how it could fail to be critically influenced by the limitations implicit in human cognition and by the social, cultural, economic, and political milieu in which it has been created. Acknowledging the importance of human factors and social influences by no means implies a wholesale rejection of current practices or an abandonment of the pursuit of objectivity. As the chapters show, it can improve the objectivity of practice.

This introduction begins by reviewing how the role of people within economics, and the attention given to their experiences, has differed according to their sex. We then turn to feminist theory, which explores the links between the social construction of scientific disciplines and the social construction of gender, to suggest reasons why such differences in experience

Ferber and Nelson, "Introduction: The Social Construction of Economics and the Social Construction of Gender." From *Beyond Economic Man*, pp. 1–22. Used with permission of the University of Chicago Press.

should not be dismissed as just "historical digressions or biographical coloring."

MEN, WOMEN, AND ECONOMICS

The most obvious point to be made about gender and the social construction of economics is that historically, and continuing to the present day, men have dominated the community of scholars who have created the discipline. Equally important, gender also affects the construction of the discipline in terms of the standpoint from which the world is perceived, and the way the importance and relevance of questions are evaluated. Certain activities and experiences that are historically of greater concern to women than to men have all too frequently been neglected. Further, even when economists have attempted to understand phenomena from such traditionally feminine realms as the home and family, the results are often judged as unsatisfactory by feminists who believe that the analysis of women's experiences is inadequate or even biased.

Economists Are (Mostly) Male

The small number of women listed in Mark Blaug's *Who's Who in Economics* is one indication of the extent to which women have been absent from the ranks of prestigious economists who have played a significant part in shaping the discipline. A mere thirty-one out of one thousand entries are women. Only five of these women were born before the turn of the century; seventeen have been born since 1930.[1] Other evidence points in the same direction. No woman has yet received the Nobel Prize in economics. All seven recipients of the Francis A. Walker medal, bestowed by the American Economic Association every five years between 1947 and 1972, have been men, as have the twenty-one recipients of the John Bates Clark medal awarded between 1947 and 1989, and the thirty-seven honorary members from other countries in 1989. Of the forty distinguished fellowships awarded between 1965 and 1989, only one was bestowed on a woman.[2] There has been one woman president of the American Economic Associatin since it was founded in 1886.[3]

The proportion of economists who are women has increased in recent years, but women continue to be underrepresented among recipients of advanced degrees and among faculties of colleges and universities, particularly in senior ranks and at the most prestigious institutions. Between 1949–50 and 1985–86, the share of B.A. degrees in economics awarded to women rose from 8 percent

---

1. Blaug's selections were based on the number of citations each author had during the years 1972–83. The five female economists born before 1900 are Rosa Luxemburg, Jane Marcet, Mary P. Marshall, Harriet Martineau, and Beatrice P. Webb; those born between 1900 and 1930 are Carolyn S. Bell, Barbara R. Bergmann, Mary J. Bowman, Phyllis M. Deane, Selma Mushkin, Barbara R. B. Reagan, Joan Robinson, Anna Schwartz, and Barbara M. Ward. Dorothy Lampen Thomson's *Adam Smith's Daughters* (1973) claims to "fill a void that exists in most treatises on the history of economics" by discussing the contribution of six women: five from Blaug's list, plus Millicent G. Fawcett.
2. Margaret G. Reid.
3. Alice M Rivlin, who was president in 1986.

to 34 percent, the share of M.A. degrees rose from 12 percent to 26 percent, and the share of Ph.D. degrees rose from 5 percent to 20 percent (National Center for Education Statistics 1977–78, 1988). The Committee on the Status of Women in the Economics Profession (1990) reports that while women made up 16 percent of the faculty of undergraduate institutions in 1988–89, only 9 percent of the faculty and only 3 percent of the full professors at universities with graduate programs were women.

One frequently suggested explanation for the low number of women majoring in economics is that women are inadequately prepared in mathematics. However, in 1985–86 fully 47 percent of bachelor's degrees and 35 percent of master's degrees in mathematics were awarded to women. (NCES 1977–78, 1988).[4] Assuming that the equivalent of an M.A. in mathematics is currently adequate for an economist, there appears to be little support for this explanation. There is somewhat more reason to believe that a differential by sex in the understanding of undergraduate economics could be part of an explanation: an extensive review of the literature on economic education yielded some evidence that female undergraduate students tend to do less well in economics courses than male students, even though females' overall grade point averages tend to be higher (Siegfried 1979). The reasons for females' poorer performance have been little researched.

Two studies found that when essay questions were used instead of the standard multiple-choice questions, men's and women's scores were no longer significantly different (Ferber, Birnbaum, and Green 1983; Morawetz 1976). In addition, the "classroom climate" may be relatively unfriendly toward women students because of lack of support by predominantly male faculty[5] and because stereotypical or disparaging references to women continue to be found in undergraduate textbooks.[6] Or the construction of economics itself may continue to signal to students its status as a distinctively masculine preserve.

Women who do go on to get doctoral degrees and take jobs in academia advance to associate and full professor levels in lower numbers than would be expected, given the number of female assistant professors (CSWEP 1990). While direct discrimination is one possible explanation, research has focused on the extent to which lower measured productivity may play a role. Far less attention has focused on the question of whether women have equal opportunity to become productive.

Mary Fish and Jean Gibbons (1989) found that in a sample of persons who received Ph.Ds between 1969 and 1984, matched by subfield and year of degree (but not by the quality of the institution at which they were employed), men published

---

4. Even the percentage of women among Ph.D.s has been about as high in mathematics as in economics.

5. Teachers have been found to be more supportive of students of the same sex (Tidball 1976).

6. Feiner and Morgan (1987) cite a number of such stories about women, for example, the story of a female graduate student who has to learn about supply from an old roadside vegetable vendor (Leftwich 1984). Ferber (1990) also discusses the "classroom climate" in undergraduate economics courses.

more than women. Two studies have compared women's and men's acceptance rates by economics journals with and without double-blind refereeing.[7] The first (Ferber and Teiman 1980) found that women did relatively better under double-blind refereeing, while the second, more recent study found no significant difference (Blank 1991). In addition to quantity of publications, number of citations increasingly has been used as a measure of economists' quality in promotion decisions. Two studies—one that focused specifically on labor economics (Ferber 1986), another that considered five different fields (Ferber 1988)— determined that scholars are more inclined to cite work by authors of the same sex, a clear disadvantage to women as long as the field remains predominantly male.

One very recent study (Dillingham, Ferber, and Hamermesh 1991) has looked at another factor that may be taken into account in promotion decisions: election to offices in professional societies. This examination of a regional economics association found not only that female voters favored women candidates significantly but that male voters also favored them, albeit very slightly. Thus some recent evidence suggests that the situation for women may be improving. But long-term effects of past discrimination, a continuing lack of women mentors, and employment structures that put the highest emphasis on professional achievement during the potential childbearing years may continue to take their toll.[8]

The World of "Economic Man"

Women have been largely absent not only as economic researchers but also as the subjects of economic study. Margaret Reid intensively studied the traditional "women's realm" of household production in the 1930s (e.g., Reid 1934), but such analysis was not given a permanent place in mainstream economics until much later. The first edition of Paul Samuelson's *Economics* (1948) had only two references to "females" and none to "women," both included in a segment on "minorities." Even today, women and families remain strangely absent from many "general" discussions of economic matters.

A few examples will serve to illustrate this point. Consider this recent textbook discussion: "The unit of analysis in economics is the individual

_____

7. In single-blind refereeing, the referee knows the author's name, and thus, in most cases, is also likely to know the author's sex. Experimental studies often have shown that if evaluators are told the sex of the author of an article or application, evaluations are lower for women than for men even on identical written work. A review in Wallston and O'Leary (1981) concluded that such "competence biases favoring men are more pronounced when women engage in tasks or seek jobs typically reserved for men" (20).

_____

8. On the importance of mentors, see Berg and Ferber (1983). On the potential problems created by the "clockwork of academic careers" see Hochschild (1975). The effects of family responsibilities, however, should not be overemphasized: not all women economists choose family involvement, and, in spite of continuing inequities in the division of household tasks (and in contradiction of the theory of Becker 1985), there is little evidence that women put forth less effort on the job (Bielby and Bielby 1988). Further, there is no evidence that the productivity of mothers is lower than that of other women (Hamovitch and Morgenstern 1977).

... [although] individuals group together to form collective organizations such as corporations, labor unions, and governments" (Gwartney, Stroup, and Clark 1985). Somehow the family escaped attention. Or consider this recent argument that consumption is individual while production is social: "If you ask a modern individual who they are, they will usually not tell you about their religion, their hobbies, or the clubs to which they belong. They will first tell you where they work and their occupation. Work is the domain from which one gets esteem in the modern world. . . . We are individual consumers in nuclear families but we are social producers" (Thurow 1988). One must ask whether the "individual" and "we" do not display a distinctively masculine tendency toward identification from work rather than relationships, and whether the notion of "individual consumers in nuclear families" is not fundamentally confused. Such a blind spot when it comes to women's traditional identification through family relations, and disregard of the possibility that the same may be true of men, implies "invisibility" of women and families in the analysis of "human" behavior.

Similarly, little attention is given to the economic value of household work, traditionally done mostly by women. Again taking an example from a textbook, the complete discussion of this issue consists of three sentences: "Many people, particularly leaders of the women's movement, argue that household work should be given a value and included in GNP. This is worth thinking about. Would it be a reasonable thing to do? If so, how would one go about valuing household production?" (Reynolds 1988).

Marilyn Waring (1988) and Nancy Folbre (1991) have discussed additional incidents of such neglect and the consequences they have for social statistics and policy. Standard discussions of human capital formation (e.g., Ehrenberg and Smith 1991) start with a discussion of secondary schooling; they ignore the socialization and education processes undertaken at home as well as the care from birth (or even from before birth, as in maternal health and nutrition) devoted to creating and developing a child's capacities.

Even when a topic that is particularly relevant to women is discussed, the gender aspect of the question may be ignored. Lloyd Reynolds (1988), for example, devotes four pages to problems of poverty without ever mentioning the disproportionate representation of women (and particularly women of color) among the ranks of the poor. To the extent that such a tendency to neglect women's issues discourages women students from pursuing study in economics, or to the extent that it goes hand in hand with evaluation of research done on these issues as less important, the patterns of underrepresentation of women discussed in the last section may be reinforced.

Are Women's Experiences Distorted?

Women's rising participation in the paid labor force, and the "women's realm" of the home and family, received noticeably more attention from mainstream economists starting in the mid-1960s. Gary Becker's "A Theory of the Allocation of Time" (1965) and Reuben Gronau's "Leisure, Home

Production and Work" (1977) formally introduced work at home as another third alternative in models of individual choice in addition to paid labor and leisure.[9] In "A Theory of Marriage" (1973, 1974), Becker developed a neoclassical model of household behavior that posited a "caring" or "altruistic" household head. A 1974 volume, *Economics of the Family*, edited by Theodore Schultz, included several more papers pursuing these themes. Together, these works laid the foundation for what came to be called the "new home economics."

Directing attention to women and families was certainly a move in the right direction. However, simply adding women as the subjects without changing the tools of analysis has been described as "add women and stir" in the feminist literature. It is interesting to note that the birth of the "new home economics" was accompanied by a contemporaneous, if less well-known, critique by feminist economists. Carolyn Shaw Bell (1974), Marianne Ferber and Bonnie Birnbaum (1977), and Isabel Sawhill (1977) all expressed early reservations about this line of research, in part because such research often served to reinforce outdated assumptions about "natural" male and female behavior. For example, they raised the question "whether economists have done anything more than describe the status quo in a society where sex roles are 'givens' " (Sawhill, 120). They also pointed out the circular reasoning in early arguments, which claimed that, on the one hand, women earn less in the market-place

because of "their" household responsibilities while, on the other hand, women specialize in home production because they earn less in the labor market. Becker's assumption of an "altruistic" household head raised feminist ire, both for its patriarchal bias and because the "heads' " unique capability was ascribed to his altruism rather than his power over household resources.

More fundamentally, these and later authors have suggested that, in general, models of free individual choice are not adequate to analyze behavior fraught with issues of dependence, interdependence, tradition, and power. Tradition, in particular, may be a far more powerful force in determining the allocation of household tasks than rational optimization. Sawhill (1977) suggested that "received microeconomic doctrine" may sometimes be a "Procrustean bed," "obliterating" areas of interest such as intrahousehold conflict. Myra Strober (1987) has challenged a number of widely accepted fundamental assumptions of neoclassical economics: "that human beings are rational and maximizing; that efficiency is 'good' because it produces greater welfare; that consumers and workers are hedonistic; that welfare is equivalent to, or at least approximated by, income; and that consumers and workers are atomistic and exhibit constant tastes" (136).

This is not the place for a complete analysis of the "new home economics" in its many varieties, or of the appropriateness of neoclassical tools. More recent criticisms of masculine biases in work on women and families can be found in several works, including those by Nancy Folbre and Heidi Hartmann (1988)

---

9. This was, of course, in some sense a rediscovery and extension of Reid (1934).

and Barbara Bergmann (1986, 1987).[10] Amartya Sen has investigated the applicability of the usual conception of "utility" when women may be socialized to expect little (1990) and has pointed out limitations on the usefulness of bargaining models to examine intrahousehold conflict (1985).

WHAT IS A FEMINIST TO DO?

As we have seen, feminists have noted and commented on the frequent exclusion of women and their experiences, and what they perceive as distortions of women's experiences by mainstream economists.[11] At a minimum, gender ideology can make a difference in what problems are selected for research, how research is operationalized, and how findings are interpreted (Blau 1981). Normative judgments enter even when only measurement of existing relationships appears to be involved. For instance, when investigating whether equally qualified men and women on university faculties receive equal rewards, rank may be used as an independent variable influencing salary or may itself be regarded as one of the rewards to be

investigated. Similarly, value judgments enter when interpreting outcomes, since, contrary to general belief, facts do not speak for themselves. For example, the fact that women and men are often found in different occupations may be assumed to be the result of differences in tastes, or the possibility of discrimination may be considered.

In many other disciplines as well as in the cross-disciplinary field of women's studies, a more extensive process of identifying such biases and seeking solutions has been going on for a much longer time.[12] Only a thumbnail sketch of some major currents is offered here. Responses to perceived inadequacies in the academic disciplines can be loosely grouped into five, not necessarily mutually exclusive, categories: what we shall call "affirmative action," "feminist empiricism," "feminist 'difference,'" "feminist postmodernism," and "feminist constructionism." The last alternative, being the one most authors in this volume find most congenial, will be described in greater detail.

Four Suggested Alternatives

In the "affirmative action" view, the central problem with the discipline is the underrepresentation of women. The Committee on the Status of

---

10. Bergmann writes that Gary Becker "explains, justifies, and even glorifies role differentiation by sex. . . . To say that the 'new home economists' are not feminist in their orientation would be as much of an understatement as to say that Bengal tigers are not vegetarians" (1987, 132–33).

11. Other published or soon-to-be-published works on feminist perspectives on mainstream economics not cited elsewhere include Barrett (1981), Cohen (1982, 1985), Feiner and Roberts (1990), Ferber and Teiman (1980, 1981), Nelson (1987), and Seiz (1989).

12. See, for example, Aiken et al. (1988), Bleier (1986), Eisenstein and Jardine (1980), Farnham (1987), J. Harding (1986), S. Harding (1987), Harding and O'Barr (1987), Jaggar and Bordo (1989), Keller (1985), Lowe and Hubbard (1983), Spender (1981), and Tuana (1989).

Women in the Economics Profession (CSWEP) of the American Economic Association emphasizes this approach. It has taken on the job of monitoring and encouraging women's advancement, publishing regular reports and newsletters and sponsoring sessions at the national and regional meetings. While complementary to several of the other approaches, the affirmative action view need not imply dissatisfaction with the way a discipline is practiced, only with the underrepresentation of women among its practitioners.

Sandra Harding coined the term "feminist empiricism" to refer to the position that "social biases [are] correctable by stricter adherence to the existing methodological norms of scientific inquiry" (1986, 24). Thus, it is not the tools of the discipline that need improvement, only the way they are applied. As the Swedish economist Siv Gustaffson says, for example, "It is not the [neoclassical economic] theory that is patriarchic, but the questions male economists have asked and the conclusions they have drawn and particularly the policy implications based on the research" (1990, 6). Casual conversation suggests that most feminist economists currently adhere to this view.[13]

The next two positions appear to have considerably lower representa-

tion among economists. Proponents of "feminist 'difference' " emphasize distinctions between men and women. They often make claims for women's superiority in creating knowledge based on women's experiences, including experiences of oppression or what they call women's "ways of knowing." Some suggest that since the failures and biases of men's past inquiry are the result of their "masculinist" methods, women should use "gynocentric" or women-centered methods in their research. At the extreme, values of objectivity, reason, and analytical inquiry might simply be overthrown in favor of their feminine-identified opposites: subjectivity, emotion, and a holistic approach. There is obviously little common ground for dialogue between those who hold this extreme view and practicing economists and scientists. Indeed there is little likelihood (given self-selection, cognitive dissonance, and professional pressure) that an active economist would subscribe to these views. However, works such as Belenky et al. (1986), Stanley and Wise (1983), Gilligan (1982), and Ruddick (1989), which are sometimes caricatured as taking a radical "difference" stance, contain a more subtle and complex analysis. The extreme "feminist 'difference' " position often serves as a handy *mis*conception in the discussion about science, particularly for those unfamiliar with more sophisticated views. Thus, for instance, Evelyn Fox Keller, a noted writer on the subject of gender and science, recounts with apparent frustration how she has been interpreted as advocating a "female science" (1986, 170).

The intellectual movement of "postmodernism" in general has had little

---

13. Given the preponderance of antifeminist and afeminist ("I haven't thought about it") views among economists, including some women economists, espousal of feminist opinions, even of the affirmative action or feminist empiricist sort, may still constitute some risk to professional advancement and hence require courage on the part of the individual.

impact on economics; for practical purposes, feminist discussions and uses of postmodernism or deconstructionism are unknown in economics. Associated with the work of Jacques Derrida (1976), Jean-François Lyotard (1984), Michel Foucault (1976), and others in philosophy and literary criticism, this intellectual movement seeks to "deconstruct" traditional understandings. Discussions of feminist postmodernism include Alcoff (1988), Scott (1988), Poovey (1988), and Nicholson (1990). A crucial issue in their discussions is the extent to which gender is a meaningful categorization or whether it also requires deconstruction. As is true of " 'difference' feminism," the majority of economists (who tend to view delving into literary criticism an endeavor of small marginal value) are likely to find little intellectual common ground with feminist postmodernism in its more highbrow forms.

Feminist Constructionism

Studies of the intertwining of the social construction of gender and the social construction of science, sometimes considered "postmodern" in the broader sense of being "after modernism," hold the most appeal for the majority of social scientists writing in this volume. At present, this approach probably provides the best basis for a dialogue between feminist theory and economics. Even here, however, a careful introduction of the central ideas and vocabulary of a feminist and social constructivist view is necessary to provide a foundation for understanding. Let us now briefly explain some of the key concepts of what we call "feminist constructionism."[14]

1. "Gender," as the word is used by many feminists, means something quite different from biological sex. Gender is the *social meaning* given to biological differences between the sexes; it refers to cultural constructs rather than to biological givens.

2. It is a basic tenet of feminism that many of the characteristics traditionally attributed to either women or men on the basis of biology are more general human characteristics whose identification as "feminine" or "masculine" is a matter of social belief. Patterns of gender attribution are, in fact, subject to considerable historical and cross-cultural variation. Therefore, facile conflation of biological men with constructions of masculinity, or of women with femininity, is condemned as *essentialism*—the mistaken belief that a certain trait is "of the essence" of man or woman instead of socially constructed.

3. Another problem with the word "gender" is that it is often read as "pertaining to women." This confusion arises because it is often assumed that attributes traditionally associated with men are "human," neutral, and universal while only those traits associated with women contain the "contamination" of gender. Such a view is labeled *masculinist* or *androcentric* (i.e., centered about a masculine ideal, with feminine aspects considered marginal and inferior). Feminist discussions of the ideals of science focus, in fact, not so much on the problems created by the absence of women as on the problems created by the power of myths of masculinity.

---

14. The explanations are derived from a wide range of feminist discussion, although particular aspects of their meaning may remain in dispute. Blame for oversimplification remains with the authors of this chapter.

4. The predominance or *privileging* of masculine ideals is seen as based on an unjust and damaging disparagement of qualities perceived as feminine. In order to remedy the situation, women's experiences and ideals (and at least certain aspects of traditional femininity) must be elevated or *valorized;* in some cases where gender systems used to be different, they must be *revalorized.*

5. Modern Western culture associates masculinity with ideals of *separation* or *separativeness*, femininity with ideals of *connection* or *relation*. In the masculine model, people are perceived primarily as individuals who are separated both from nature and from other humans. In the feminine model, people are regarded as more integrally connected to human and ecological communities. For example, European and American men traditionally have been identified through their individual exploits or their jobs while women have been identified by their relationships as wives and mothers. Many institutions developed under male domination, including science, are likely to display an unjustified affinity with masculine attitudes of detachment and autonomy.

Feminist theory, as applied to science in general and economics in particular, accordingly claims that peculiarly masculine ideals have influenced the formation of science, probably to our benefit but also to our harm. As Sandra Harding writes in *The Science Question in Feminism:*

> Mind vs. nature and the body, reason vs. emotion and social commitment, subject vs. object and objectivity vs. subjectivity, the abstract and the general vs. the concrete and particular—in each case we are told that the former must dominate the latter lest human life be overwhelmed by irrational and alien forces, forces symbolized in science as the feminine. All these dichotomies play important roles in the intellectual structures of science, and all appear to be associated both historically and in contemporary psyches with distinctively masculine sexual and gender identity projects. (1986, 25)

The issue, then, is whether valorization of some or all of the "feminine" aspects previously excluded would improve the practice of science, and of economics.

An immediate question may be raised about whether the introduction of "feminine" qualities, such as emotion and social commitment, might destroy the objectivity of the scientific enterprise. But this question misses the point. The valorization of feminine-identified qualities discussed here does not imply either the introduction of gender or the creation of a "female science." Gender is already deeply embedded in scientific practice—it just happens to be gender of the masculine kind and hence less noticeable to those who have come to accept masculine values as the only admissible ones. We do not seek to excise all of the values traditionally associated with science but to investigate and remedy the biases that may arise from an unexamined emphasis on masculinity. Objectivity, the search for knowledge that does not reflect particularistic biases, is still a goal. However, it is no longer assumed that objectivity can be reached by the individual researcher, even when he or she follows certain correct methods of investigation. Scholarly work on the social construction of science (e.g., Kuhn 1962, 1970; Feyerabend 1976; works reviewed in Gergen 1985) suggests that objectivity is more of a social than an individual phenomenon. Helen Longino's description of objectivity makes a useful sixth entry to our glossary:

6. The *objectivity* of individuals . . . consists in their participation in the collective give-and-take of critical discussion and not in some special relation (of detachment, hardheadedness) they may bear to their observations. Thus understood, objectivity is dependent upon the depth and scope of the transformative interrogation

that occurs in any given scientific community. This community-wide process ensures (or can ensure) that the hypotheses ultimately accepted as supported by some set of data do not reflect a single individual's idiosyncratic assumptions about the natural world. To say that a theory or hypothesis was accepted on the basis of objective methods does not entitle us to say it is true but rather that it reflects the critically achieved consensus of the scientific community. In the absence of some form of privileged access to transempirical (unobservable) phenomena it's not clear we should hope for anything better. (1990, 79; emphasis added)

This does not imply that it is acceptable for any group of people to choose to believe any theory they wish; there is a real world, and a scientific approach requires that we seek evidence from that world to support or disprove our hypotheses. However, decisions about whether hypotheses deserve investigation as well as about what constitutes acceptable and convincing evidence are made by scientific communities. From this perspective, the idea that objectivity is individually attainable through rigorous methods, emotional detachment, and "separation" from both the object of study and other researchers itself appears to be an emotionally loaded, culturally created construct. The general devaluation of women and of all things culturally associated with femininity may be partly responsible for resistance to the idea of science as connected to and practiced for the benefit of the community.

WHY A FEMINIST ANALYSIS?

Many of the criticisms of current economic practice that will be voiced in this volume have been voiced elsewhere without feminist identification.

Among numerous attempts to move beyond the usual practice are critical discussions of efficiency by Harvey Leibenstein (1969, 1976); of the neglect of social considerations by Robert Frank (1985); of the emphasis on formalism by Nicholas Georgescu-Roegen (1966) and Donald McCloskey (1991); of rationality in a collection edited by Karen Schweers Cook and Margaret Levi (1990); of self-interest in a collection edited by Jane Mansbridge (1990); of the importance of language by Donald McCloskey (1985, 1990); of the neglect of policy by Alan Blinder (1988); of the importance of power by Kenneth Boulding (1989); and of neoclassical labor market theory by Robert Solow (1990). At the same time, no coherent body of new theory has emerged from these piecemeal critiques, no matter how valuable they have been individually.

Further, to a surprising degree these authors have failed to apply their innovative ideas to subjects that have been of special concern to women. Three examples will suffice to make this point. Harvey Leibenstein's "X-efficiency" theory posits that the behavior of interacting individuals is determined by differences in personality and varying conditions rather than by the usual model of autonomous, rationally optimizing agents. While such a theory would seem to have particularly important implications for analysis of households, emphasis has been placed largely on application to firms, and Leibenstein's (1976) own discussion of intrahousehold consumption is curiously genderfree. Robert Solow (1990) has raised the question of how systems of wages may be the result of commonly accepted rules of equity and institutional controls, both of which could constitute substantial hurdles to the operation of equilibrating forces. He even suggests that wages have to be regarded as an independent variable, likely to be important in determining the productivity of labor. Yet he fails to note the relevance of this view to "comparable worth," an issue that has been high on the agenda of many feminists. Donald McCloskey (1985) put great faith in the "body of enlightened scholars" rather than positivist methodological rules to guide economic research. Yet only two of the ninety-two economists and economic historians in the group of scholars he mentions in his acknowledgments are women.

Ironically, the fact that these criticisms have remained piecemeal and have failed to become the new mainstream views may—in spite of their neglect of women's viewpoints—have something to do with sexism. Eliminating androcentrism would involve not merely localized modifications but altering a self-image and a worldview with deep emotional as well as intellectual roots. Is it easier to ignore or to misunderstand these critiques, or merely to label them "interesting" and then forget them, in part because they seem "soft" and "touchy-feely," or "feminine"?

This is not to say, of course, that the feminist analysis presented here pretends to remedy all difficulties in the profession. For one, women have not been the only group historically excluded from the construction of economics. The authors of this volume, while challenging male hegemony in the profession, are all professionals, United States citizens, and, with only one exception, of European descent. Our views are therefore unavoidably partial, and further work from the per-spective of women and men of other ethnicities, races, classes, nationalities, and cultures is needed to ensure the sort of objectivity described earlier. An interesting dialogue has, in fact, arisen between the African-American male economist Vernon Dixon (1970, 1976) and the feminist theorist Sandra Harding (1987) regarding similarities and differences between feminist and African-American worldviews. Such discussions are likely to enrich the analysis by revealing previously invisible biases and limitations.

In this book we focus on how economics could be improved by being freed from the straitjacket of masculine mythology. As noted earlier, such a view does not require that all of the methods of scientific investigation developed to date be rejected. Rather, it requires a new conception of where such methods fit in the overall picture of human knowledge and a willingness to consider methods previously rejected, not because they were bad or ineffective but simply because they were perceived as "feminine." One should not infer that this position attributes "feminine" cognitive traits only to women. The point is that while men can think in stereotypically feminine ways and women can think in stereotypically masculine ways, both men and women have become accustomed to regarding the feminine as being of lesser value. For this reason, the simple entry of women into economics is not likely to be sufficient to change economic practice. However, the denial of entry to women is one indicator of the strength and persistence of strong cultural sexism; it indicates the distance that remains to be traveled before economic practice can be freed from its masculine biases.

ELEMENTS OF A FEMINIST ANALYSIS OF ECONOMICS

This volume explores the implications of feminist theories of the construction of science with specific application to economics. Four essays, by Julie A. Nelson, Paula England, Diana Strassmann, and Donald N. McCloskey, focus on mainstream or "neoclassical" economics; Nancy Folbre looks at socialist economic thought; and Ann L. Jennings writes about the institutionalist school of economics. Rebecca M. Blank and Robert M. Solow provide commentary on these main chapters from the point of view of mainstream economics, Rhonda M. Williams offers reflections informed by considerations of postmodernism and race and Helen E. Longino offers a review from the perspective of a feminist philosopher of science. Within these broad subject categories, many of the themes outlined above emerge and reemerge.

Julie A. Nelson concentrates on controversy about the definition of economics. She argues that economists' overwhelming reliance on mathematical models of individual choice, to the exclusion of other approaches, reflects masculinist biases rooted in Cartesian divisions between rationality and embodiment. She also suggests that the discipline should not be concerned merely with goods and services traded in the market but with all necessities and conveniences that sustain and improve life. She concludes that the discipline would be far richer if it became a fully "human" science that made full use of the tools of "imaginative rationality."

Paula England takes as her subject the androcentric biases in the basic assumptions of neoclassical economics. She points out that three crucial postulates—the impossibility of interpersonal utility comparisons, exogenous and unchanging tastes, and selfish behavior in market transactions—flow from the premise that each economic agent is a "separative self," emotionally disconnected from others. She contrasts these postulates with the opposite assumption that individuals are entirely altruistic in families. She discusses the origin of the separative self assumption and its consequences for economic practice, and argues that these two polarized assumptions together serve to hide women's disadvantage in markets and in their families.

Have the assumptions of self-interested individualism and contractual exchange become dominant in economics because they have won out in a competitive "marketplace of ideas"? Diana Strassmann's chapter challenges such a view, maintaining instead that these core concepts serve as exclusionary devices, insulating the discipline from alternative, and more adequate, perspectives. She discusses four "stories" that serve to exclude issues of values and power—stories of the benevolent patriarch, the woman of leisure, free choice, and the "marketplace of ideas" itself. Because models are by nature incomplete, she argues, a greater openness to alternative perspectives would allow the discipline to capture the complexity of economic activities more successfully.

Unlike the earlier chapters, which tend to focus on gender as a social construct, Donald N. McCloskey takes as his starting point the premise that men and women tend to differ in their approach to economics because they live different lives. In this view, some of the limitations of economics can be traced to the virtual exclusion of the feminine perspective. Nonetheless, he hopes, much as Nelson does, that a "conjective" economics would enlarge and humanize the field, giving its practitioners, male and female alike, a "tolerant confidence" they now often lack.

Nancy Folbre is concerned with the interaction between socialism and feminism in economics. She points out that Marx and Engels downplayed feminist concerns, partly to establish political economy as a science. This distinction between scientific socialism and the utopian socialism of reformers who were more concerned with values and morality for the most part has been uncritically accepted by historians of economic thought. Hence the views of this latter group were largely ignored, and the strongest advocates of women's rights were placed essentially outside the purview of economics. Folbre includes both schools within the broader context of feminist socialism.

Ann L. Jennings examines economics from a perspective that combines feminist and institutionalist approaches. She argues that the way the American-European tradition of institutionalism conceives of "culture" leads to a criticism of dualistic thinking, a criticism that has significant parallels in feminist thought. Yet Thorstein Veblen's recognition of feminist issues at the turn of the century has not been reflected in most later institutionalist work. Jennings uses feminist and institutionalist arguments to challenge dualistic compartmentalization both in knowledge and in social life.

In her commentary, Rebecca M. Blank reflects on the main chapters in the volume from the perspective of a neoclassical economist. Although she defends the use of the neoclassical model, she agrees with several of the other authors that economics would be enriched by a greater diversity of theoretical and methodological approaches. She urges the authors to give more specific examples of how a feminist economics would lead to new insights and questions why the approach they describe should be labeled "feminist."

Rhonda M. Williams's commentary evaluates the main chapters from a postmodernist perspective. She compares feminist and Afrocentrist theories both to each other and to a postmodernist alternative, which deconstructs both gender and race. She suggests that insufficient attention to the complexities of race and class leaves the economic theories outlined in the main chapters regrettably incomplete.

Robert M. Solow, like McCloskey, takes the issue of gender to be largely an issue of differences between men and women. He focuses on the question of whether men and women have different cognitive styles. He suggests that male dominance, in addition to influencing which subjects are considered interesting, may have something to do with the "atmosphere" in which work is done. He is skeptical, however, of the notion that a move away from male dominance would change what he considers to be the substance of the discipline.

In the final commentary, Helen E. Longino reviews what she sees as the main points of the chapters regarding women, households, and economic agents. She finds the arguments regarding the masculine construction of the discipline compelling, but challenges feminist economists to explore the normative influences and purposes of conventional research programs further and to develop new research programs that better represent a diversity of interests.

The authors of the main chapters were not given the opportunity to reply (or to revise) in response to the commentaries. We leave many issues unresolved, with the intention of stimulating further discussion not only among the contributors to this volume but also among a larger community of scholars.

29

Whose "Choice"?

"Flexible" Women Workers in the Tomato Food Chain

(1999)

Deborah Barndt

My whole family [works] at McDonald's: my mother, my sisters, my boyfriend, often at different times. And my dad, a police officer, works from eleven in the night 'til six in the morning. So there's no time we can eat together. We just grab something and put it in the microwave.

THIS NARRATIVE, BY TANIA, a York University student working at McDonald's, may resonate with many young women in the North. At the Southern end of the NAFTA food chain, Tomasa, a Mexican fieldworker for Santa Anita Packers, one of the biggest domestic producers of tomatoes, describes her daily food preparations during the harvest season: "I get up at three a.m. to make tortillas for our lunch, then the truck comes at six to take us to the fields to start working by seven a.m." An hour away at a Santa Anita greenhouse, Sara, a young tomato packer, tells us that the foreign management of Eco-Cultivos has just eliminated the two-hour lunch break, so workers no longer go

home for the traditional noontime meal.

These changes in the eating practices of women workers in the continental food system reflect several dimensions of the global economic restructuring that has reshaped the nature of their labour. Shifts in family eating practices have not been the "choice" of the women whose stories are told here, nor have they "chosen" the work shifts that involve them around the clock in growing and preparing food for other people.

"McDonaldization," initiated in the North and spreading to the South, and "maquilization," initiated in the South and now appearing in the North, are interrelated processes in the new global economy. McDonaldization, as George Ritzer describes it, is the model that the fast-food restaurant has offered as a way to reorganize work in all other sectors. This model is based on efficiency, predictability, calculability or quantifiability, substitution of non-human technology,

Barndt, Deborah, ""Whose Choice"? "Flexible" Women Workers in the Tomato Food Chain." From *Women Working the NAFTA Food Chain: Women, Food and Globalization* ed. Deborah Barndt. Toronto: Sumach Press, 1999.

control and the irrationality of rationality. Central to this model is "flexible" part-time labour.

"Maquilization," originating in the maquila free trade zones of northern Mexico, now refers to a more generalized work process characterized by 1) the feminization of the labour force, 2) extreme segmentation of skill categories, 3) the lowering of real wages and 4) a non-union orientation. In the traditional maquila sectors, such as the garment and electronic industries, there is full-time (though not necessarily stable) employment. However, the trade liberalization epitomized by NAFTA has opened the door for the development of maquilas throughout Mexico. "Agromaquilas," in particular, depend on more temporary, part-time and primarily female labour.

Central to both the McDonaldization of the retail and service sectors and the maquilization of the agro-industrial and manufacturing sectors in the continental food chain are the interrelated processes of the "feminization of poverty" and the "flexibilization of labour." Since the 1960s when export processing zones such as the Mexican maquilas began to employ primarily young women in low-skilled and low-wage jobs, women have been key players in this new global formula. In the reorganization of work by global capital, women workers have also become key players in new flexible labour strategies, building on an already established sexual division of labour and institutionalized sexism and racism in the societies where transnational corporations set up shop. In these sectors of the global food system, women bring their own meaning to flexible labour as they juggle their lives as both producers and consumers of food, as both part-time salaried workers and full-time domestic workers in managing households.

TOMASITA COMES NORTH WHILE BIG MAC GOES SOUTH

In the Tomasita Project, the journey of the tomato from the Mexican field through the United States to the Canadian fast-food restaurant reveals the dynamics of globalization. While food production and consumption takes place in all three countries, deep inequities, upon which NAFTA was based, remain among them.

The basic North–South contradiction of this continental (and increasingly hemispheric) system is that Mexico produces fresh fruit and vegetables (in this case, the tomato) for North American consumers, while Northern retail supermarkets and fast-food restaurants, such as McDonald's, are moving South at record speed to market new foods, work and food practices, particularly as a result of NAFTA's trade liberalization. This contradiction is revealed in retail advertising. In its promotion of President's Choice products, Loblaws proclaims "Food Means the World to Us." We are seduced by such images into consuming an increasing "diversity" and seemingly endless array of fresh, "exotic" and non-traditional foods. Meanwhile, there are hidden costs under which these foods were produced—the appropriation of Indigenous lands; the degradation of the environment and the health and dignity of workers; increasing poverty; deepening sexist and racist employment practices—which are kept (carefully and consciously) from our view.

The Tomasita Project aims to uncover these costs, particularly by exposing the living and working conditions of the women workers whose labour (not by choice) brings the "world of food" to us. A deconstruction of the Loblaws' ad would reveal these women workers as the producers behind the food product, and show that they, too, are part of a global system that links agro-export economies (such as Mexico) with the increasing consumer demand in the North for fresh produce all year round.

Tomasita is a both a material and symbolic "ecofeminist" tomato within globalized food production—from biogenetic engineering to intensive use of agrochemicals, from long journeys in refrigerated trucks to shorter journeys across supermarket counters where their internationally standardized "product look up" numbers are punched in. Its fate is paralleled by the intertwining fates of women workers in the different stages of its production, preparation and consumption. If the tomato is shaped by "just-in-time" production practices, women workers make this supply-on-demand possible through their flexible labour.

The tracing of the tomato chain builds on the tradition of "commodity chain analysis," which examines three interlocking processes: 1) raw material production, 2) combined processing, packaging and exporting activities, and 3) marketing and consumptive activities. The women workers who make the tomato chain come alive represent four different sectors of the food system—two in Mexico and two in Canada. In Mexico, they are the pickers and packers in Santa Anita Packers, a large export-oriented agribusiness, and the assembly line workers producing ketchup in Del Monte, a well-established multinational food processor. In Canada, the workers are cashiers in Loblaws supermarkets and service workers in McDonald's restaurants. How do these women workers (both as producers and consumers) reflect, respond to and resist the "flexible labour strategy" so central to corporate restructuring? There are, of course, obvious differences between the Mexican Indigenous workers moving from harvest to harvest to pick tomatoes and the Canadian women slicing these tomatoes and stacking them into a hamburger. Yet, since NAFTA, there are increasing similarities in the feminization and flexibilization of the labour force in all four sectors and in all three countries. One of the similarities is the increasing participation of young female workers, who, from the perspective of the companies, are seen as both cheaper and more productive than comparable male labour. Gender ideologies, culturally entrenched and reinforced by managerial practices, strongly shape this socially constructed reality.

FLEXIBILIZATION: FROM ABOVE AND FROM BELOW

Key to global economic restructuring is the notion of flexibility. The term, however, changes meaning depending on whose perspective it represents. The perspective from above, from the vantage point of corporate managers, is different than the perspective from below, from the new global workforce. To some, flexibility implies "choice," but "*whose choice*" rules in a food system built on structural inequalities, which are based on differences of national identity, race, class, gender and age? For large transnational corporations, flexibility has meant greater freedom (provided by NAFTA and increasing support from the Mexican government) to set up businesses in Mexico, where businesses are offered lower trade barriers, property laws that allow greater foreign investment, decreasing subsidies, decentralization of production through subcontracting and so forth. For large Mexican domestic producers such as Santa Anita Packers, trade liberalization has meant entering a globally competitive market with comparative advantages of land, climate and cheap labour. Once producing primarily for national consumption, Santa Anita has become ever more export-driven—it now produces 85 percent of crops for export and, in the case of greenhouse production, 100 percent for export. The fruit and vegetable sector is one of the few winners of NAFTA in Mexico.

The meaning of flexibility changes when set in the context of the new global marketplace, where borders and nation–states are less and less relevant, and where production is increasingly decentralized while decision-making is increasingly centralized. In this context, flexibility also refers to the shift from Fordist to post-Fordist production practices. Fordism was based on scientific management principles and organization of tasks in assembly lines for mass production, with the production of large volumes being the objective. Post-Fordist or "just-in-time" production responds to more diversified and specific demands in terms of quality and quan-

tity. It is ultimately very rationalized, of course, as demonstrated by the processes of workplace McDonaldization in which new technologies allow greater control of inventory and labour, while decentralization of production allows companies to shift many of the risks to subcontractors. In talking about the globalized corporate world, or "globalization from above," then, flexibility is ultimately about maximizing profits and minimizing obstacles (such as trade tariffs, government regulations, underused labour, trade union organization).

WOMEN WORKERS' EXPERIENCES OF FLEXIBILITY

What does flexibility mean, though, for the women moving the tomato through this continental food system, from Mexican field to Canadian table? If we first look at the consumption-end of the food chain, the fast-food and supermarket workers in Canada, and then move to the source, where women plant, pick, pack and process tomatoes in Mexico, we can learn how flexibilization has affected these women's daily lives.

McDonald's

"Flexible labour strategies" have been key to the model of production of McDonald's and its competitors. McJobs, whether filled by students, seniors or underemployed women, have always been primarily part-time (up to twenty-four hours a week). Part-time jobs do not require certain benefits and, because they are limited to short three- to four-hour shifts, do not require many breaks. Women student workers might be sent home after an hour or two if sales for the day are not reaching their predetermined quota. Karen, a university student, explains:

> They're supposed to make a certain amount of money an hour, say $1,300 between twelve noon and one p.m., and if they make less than that, for every $50 (under the quota), they cut half an hour of labour. Especially if you're newer, there's pressure to go home. It takes me an hour to get to work by bus, and I could be asked to go home after an hour of work.

Flexibility of this temporary labour force is reinforced by the lack of trade union organization. Strong company-induced loyalty is fed by perks such as team outings, weekly treats and training that inculcate a family orientation. It is meant to dissuade employees from seeking unionization or from complaining about their hours. Nonetheless, there are increasing efforts to organize McDonald's workers and there have been recent union successes in BC and Quebec.

Loblaws

The experience of flexibility for women workers in the larger chains of the retail food sector, such as Loblaws in Canada, are just as precarious. Even though they are unionized, the working conditions of part-time workers have been eroded through recent labour negotiations. In the case of Loblaws, for example, the most recent contract negotiated by the United Food and Commercial Workers Union eliminated almost all of the full-time cashier positions. Part-time cashiers are dependent on

seniority for being able to choose their working hours. This particularly affects new cashiers, such as Wanda: "When you are low on the seniority list, you are lucky to get any hours. They might call you in once every two weeks for a four-hour shift." This restriction on available hours also affects the cashiers' earning power. A cashier must complete five hundred hours before being eligible for a raise. At this pace, she could work at the starting wage for over two years. From the company's perspective, this shift to primarily part-time flexible labour is a conscious strategy; it is part of "lean production."

Del Monte

What does flexibility look like in the Del Monte food processing plant in Irapuato, Mexico? The production of ketchup in Del Monte takes place during a four-month period, from February through May. In part, this coincides with the peak period for harvesting tomatoes; thus flexibility in the agromaquilas depends, in part, on the seasonal nature of agricultural production (becoming less pronounced with the increasing phenomenon of year-round greenhouse production).

Another reason that production is limited to one period is to maximize the use of the food processing machinery and the skilled labour force. Del Monte's ketchup production employs a combination of Fordist and post-Fordist processes: it is an assembly line production from the dumping and cooking of tomatoes in big vats to the bottling, capping and labelling on a mechanized line. Because other food processing (such as marmalade) uses the same machinery, the same full-time workers can easily shift from one product to another. Many are, in fact, multiskilled and are moved from one process to another, reflecting post-Fordist practices. Such multitasking is another form of flexibility in the experience of the new global workforce. Part-time women workers are brought on for the peak season only and for less skilled tasks. These women sometimes sit in the waiting room of the plant, hoping for a few hours of work, which are determined day by day. Flexibility reigns in a context where there is an oversupply of cheap labour, so companies can make such decisions on the spot, hiring and dismissing workers on a daily basis. This is another example of lean production, dependent on a disposable supply of female labour.

Santa Anita Packers

Finally we reach the source, Santa Anita Packers—the agribusiness that organizes production of tomatoes, from the importing of seeds to the exporting of waxed and packaged tomatoes in refrigerated trucks. Santa Anita, headquartered in Jalisco, in central Mexico, uses a mixture of production practices and diverse applications of the notion of flexibility. It is important to understand the historical development of the agro-export industry in Mexico in the context of North–South political economic relations, which are based on ever-deepening inequalities, both between and within nations. Since the early part of the century, Mexican agriculture has been led by Northern demand for fresh fruit and vegetables,

and by the use of cheap Mexican labour by US agribusinesses on both sides of the border. While the Depression in the 1930s led to American workers taking over farm labour jobs from Mexican workers in the US and also to a spurt of farm labour organizing, the availability of cheap Mexican Indigenous migrant labour fed the post-war development of large agribusinesses in both countries from the 1950s onward. This transnationalization of the economy was built upon institutionalized racism and sexism within Mexico and the US, employing Indigenous workers often as family units who were brought by the companies from the poorer states.

The sexual division of labour is seen most strongly in the packing plants, where a gendered ideology is used to justify the employment of women, as echoed by one of the company owners:

> Women "see" better than men, they can better distinguish the colours and they treat the product more gently. In selection, care and handling, women are more delicate. They can put up with more than men in all aspects: the routine, the monotony. Men are more restless, and won't put up with it.

The feminization of the global labour force, and thus the feminization of global poverty, has been based on the marginal social role that women play and on a social consensus that their domestic duties are primary. As Lourdes Beneria argues, "the private sphere of the household is at the root of continuing asymmetries between men and women."

In the case of Mexican agro-industry, women are among the most marginalized workers, along with children, students, the elderly and

Indigenous peoples. Sara Lara notes that agribusinesses exploit their common situation of "mixedness," referring to the fact that these workers already play socially marginal roles based on their gender, race or age: "women as housewives, Indigenous peoples as 'poor peasants', children as sons and daughters, young people as students, all as the ad hoc subjects of flexible processes." It is important to integrate national identity, gender, race, class, age and marital status into any analysis of the new global labour force.

DEEPENING INEQUALITIES: FLEXIBILITY FOR WHOM?

In their restructuring, corporations have adopted a dual employment strategy that deepens the inequalities within the workforce and divides it into two groups: a "nucleus" of skilled workers who are trained in new technologies and post-Fordist production processes (quality circles, multiskilling and multitasking) and who have stable employment, and a "periphery" of unskilled workers whose jobs are very precarious. McDonald's and Loblaws both have a small full-time workforce, mainly male, while women make up the majority of the more predominant part-time workforce. Tomato production in Mexico also mirrors this dualism. Small numbers of permanent workers prepare the seedlings and the land for production, and later pack and process the tomatoes; a large number of temporary part-time workers pick tomatoes during the harvest seasons. Santa Anita, for example, employs Mestizos from the local area for the jobs of cultivating the tomato plants, while hundreds of poor Indigenous workers, brought in by trucks and housed in conditions of squalor in makeshift camps, do much of the picking during the three-to-five month harvest season. In this dual employment strategy, Indigenous workers are again required to be the most flexible, which is yet another form of discrimination and exploitation.

Such flexibility has been integral to labour-intensive and seasonal agricultural production for decades, though the composition of the migrant labour force has shifted over time. It is not uncommon for entire families to work together in the field, when the demand for labour is up. Children of local Mestizo peasant workers join their families on weekends during peak season, while children of Indigenous migrant workers, with neither school nor extended family to care for them, often work alongside their parents. With increasing unemployment in Mexico, however, men are taking on agricultural jobs done previously by women, such as picking, and because the current economic crisis has increased the surplus of labour, companies choose the youngest and heartiest workers above the older ones (the ideal age seems to be fifteen to twenty-four, so workers in their thirties can already be considered less desirable). The flexible labour strategies of Mexican agribusinesses are predicated on race, gender and age. And once again, flexibility is determined by the companies and not the workers.

Technological changes within the production process are integral to the application of flexibilization. Differences among workers (of gender, race and skill) are accentuated with the increasingly sophisticated modes of greenhouse production and packing.

Tomatoes in those plants, for example, are now weighed and sorted by colour in a computerized process, which at the same time records the inventory and monitors the productivity of the workers. Through these changes, foreign managers and technicians are reorganizing production relations and the workday in ways that are also shifting social relations, both in the workplace and at home.

In a Santa Anita greenhouse, unproductive workers are dismissed daily, as there is always a plentiful pool of surplus labour to choose from. There are echoes here of the McDonald's worker being sent home when quotas are down and the Loblaws cashier not being called for weeks when she's not needed, as well as Mexican women waiting for a few hours of work on Del Monte's ketchup production line. Flexibility serves the companies' need to maximize production and profits; it does not always serve the needs of Mexican or Canadian women in this food chain to survive, to complement their family income or to organize their lives and their double-day responsibilities. And as Sara Lara concludes, "Flexibility is not a choice for women," and "labour force management by companies is at the same time family management, that is, it reinforces particular family power relations."

With NAFTA, the Mexican fruit and vegetable industry has been one of the only sectors to benefit from trade liberalization and has maintained an international competitiveness. Mexico has the advantage over its Northern partners in terms of land, climate and cheap labour. The expansion of the agro-export industry, however, reflects a basic North–South contradiction between a "negotiated flexibility" and a "primitive flexibility." Large domestic companies in Mexico, such as Santa Anita, are becoming increasingly multinational, yet are still in the periphery of production decisions (controlled outside Mexico) and often lag behind in technological development. In the agro-export economy of Mexico, there is a growth of unstable and temporary employment in the still labour-intensive processes of production, sorting, packing and processing. In these jobs, women, children and Indigenous peoples (the most flexible workers in a rural labour market) are managed by "primitive flexibility." Transnational companies, however, are located primarily in the more industrialized North and control production through ownership, subcontracting and advanced technology (biogenetic engineering, sophisticated food processing, production of most of the inputs and machinery of production, and architects of the commercialization and distribution systems). These transnationals employ the "nucleus" of skilled workers, with relatively stable employment, and manage this workforce through "negotiated flexibility."

COMPARISONS ACROSS BORDERS: WOMEN WORKERS AS PRODUCERS AND CONSUMERS

Yet there are also increasing similarities between women workers in Mexican agribusinesses and food processing plants and women working as supermarket cashiers and fast-food service workers in Canada. They play key roles in the implementation of corporate flexible labour strategies. As a result, they experience similar contradictions in their efforts to fulfill their dual roles as salaried workers in the food system and as consumers or providers of food for their families. Wanda, a Canadian cashier, feels some common bonds with Tomasa, a Mexican tomato fieldworker:

> Tomasa used to make her own tortillas but now she has to go and work, so she buys ready-made tortillas. And she's feeling that pull just like the North American women are: Should I stay at home with the kids? Should I go to work? She's feeling the economic thing, because everybody has to survive, everybody has to eat. She's taking care of the family, that's a priority in her life; I'd like to think that in my life that's a priority.

Wanda has reached a point in her career, after twenty-three years as a part-time cashier, where she now has seniority and so may choose her hours. She "chooses" to work three eight-hour days instead of six four-hour shifts, for example, because she moved out of town a few years ago and must now commute one hour to work, adding two hours to her workday. That "choice" is framed by the fact that if she transferred to a Loblaws that was closer to her home, she would lose her seniority. She also "chooses" to work on weekends, because, as a single mother, it is the only time her former husband can take care of her children, saving her childcare expenses. Her "choice" of hours allows her to be at home during most weekdays:

> As a single parent, I'm taking my kids to school, doing the piano lessons, the Brownies, that kind of thing. So I know which days I don't want to come down to Toronto to work, because it's quite a ways for me. Or if they have a PD day [professional development day for teachers], I don't go into work that day.

Here is where the flexibility of women's labour comes head to head with other social contradictions of an institutionalized sexist culture. Corporate managers, in fact, often point out that their flexible labour strategy suits women who "choose" to have more time with their families, and therefore don't want to work full-time. And there is certainly some truth to this. Even some feminists argue that flexibilization can be reappropriated by women and men, if it challenges the sexual division of labour in the home and promotes more shared responsibility, while also shortening the workweek. But it usually has little to do with "choice" and is often based on the assumption that women, not men or public childcare, will take care of children and feed their families.

In the Mexican context, there is even less of an illusion of "choice" for Indigenous women who are at the bottom of the hierarchy of workers, both locally and globally. While Santa Anita Packers brings Indigenous families to work during the harvest season, they provide neither adequate housing nor childcare, and it has been a struggle to get the children into the local school. It has been reported that company foremen became angry with Indigenous women workers who brought their children tied to their backs to the fields and who stopped work, periodically, to breastfeed them. Here, in the most basic sense, the primary role that women fulfill in feeding their children is regulated by the company's rules. And though they have little choice but to bring their children to the fields, they also take tremendous risks in doing so. When we visited their camp, one baby was reportedly dying because, as the Indigenous workers explained, pesticide residue on the mother's hand had entered the child's mouth during breastfeeding.

Since NAFTA, and with the deepening impoverishment of the rural population in Mexico, these Indigenous families are forced to migrate from one harvest to another for even longer periods of the year. Whereas previously they may have been able to remain home for a few months and raise some of their own food, they are now permanently moving, by necessity, ready to go to wherever there is work.

The Mestizo workers who live near the Santa Anita plant and only work seasonally experience the insecurity in another way. Due to erratic weather conditions, their work periods have been cut short, and the jobs available for them peter out. Describing the situation, Tomasa said:

> In the end, we were working one or two days a week, and then not at all. They don't even say thanks 'til the day that they return. Only when they begin to plant again in the next season, they come with their truck to take us back to the fields, no?

This sense of never knowing when you are going to work, and often in the case of Indigenous migrant workers even where, is a permanent condition of agricultural fieldworkers. Canadian cashiers and fast-food workers may know a week or two in advance what their shifts are to be, but the constantly changing hours often affect family routines, interactions and, especially, eating practices. It is not uncommon for a family to have no time when they can all sit down to a meal together.

Whose interests are served by this flexible labour strategy? Flexibilization as it plays out in the continental food system, and particularly in the lives of women workers in this food chain from Mexico to Canada, must be seen as "an ideology propagated by firm owners as a desirable future end state, and supported by conservative pro-business forces and governments in order to assist the private sector in achieving this goal." It is part and parcel of lean production, maximizing efficiency and profits and leaving the most vulnerable and marginalized workers bound to the shifting winds of just-in-time production. In the end, they become just-in-time workers with no time of their own.

And what are the real choices for women in this system? Wanda, the Loblaws cashier, has taken a keen interest in this study and has read the stories of the Mexican workers. She concludes:

> I feel an overwhelming sadness and connection to all the women in the "tomato food chain." We all play a seemingly small part, but the ramifications of our work are enormous . . . We are all entrapped in the corporate workings of flexibilization. However, the dilemma still exists for all of us in the food chain: we're trying to survive.

NOTES

I gratefully acknowledge the tremendous efforts of the graduate research assistants who worked from 1995 to 1999 on the Tomasita Project, helping to shape it and carrying out the interviews referred to in this chapter. Special thanks to Emily Levitt, Deborah Moffer, Lauren Baker (Mexican interviews), Ann Eyerman (McDonald's interviews), Stephanie Conway (Loblaw's interviews), Egla Martinez-Salazar (review of Mexican interviews), Karen Serwonka (McDonald's interviews), Anuja Mendiratta, and Melissa Tkachyk (glossary).

This chapter also refers to ideas more fully discussed elsewhere in this volume. See Kirsten Appendini, "From Where Have All the Flowers Come?"; Antonieta Barrón, "Mexican Women on the Move"; Ann Eyerman, "Serving Up Service"; Harriet Friedmann, "Remaking 'Traditions'"; Egla Martinez-Salazar, "The 'Poisoning' of Indigenous Migrant Women Workers and Children"; and Ester Reiter, "Serving the McCustomer."

1. Tania (pseudonym), interview with author, Toronto, Ontario, February 1998.
2. Tomasa (pseudonym), interview with author, Gomez Farias, Mexico, April 1997.
3. Sara (pseudonym), interview with author, San Isidro Mazatepec, Mexico, April 1997.
4. See George Ritzer, *The McDonaldization of Society* (Thousand Oaks, CA: Pine Forge Press, 1993). Ritzer notes that the new model of rationalization in our culture is no longer the bureaucracy, as Max Weber suggested, but the fast-food restaurant. He outlines the characteristics of this work organization based on 1) efficiency (from the factory-farm production of the ingredients to the computer scanners at the counter), 2) predictability (from the ambience and the personnel to the limited menu), 3) calculability or quantity, 4) substitution of non-human technology (the techniques, procedures, routines and machines make it almost impossible for workers to act autonomously), 5) control (the rationalization of food preparation and serving gives control over the employees), and 6) the irrationality of rationality (for example, we see McDonald's as rational despite the reality that the chemicals in the food are harmful and that we can gain weight from the high calories and cholesterol levels).
5. The four dimensions of maquilization, developed by J. Carillo as he observed restructuring in the auto industry, are elaborated by Kathryn Kopinak in *Desert Capitalism: What Are the Maquiladoras?* (Montreal: Black Rose Books, 1997), 13.
6. Gita Sen and Caren Grown, *Development, Crises, and Alternative Visions: Third World Women's Perspectives* (New York: Monthly Review Press, 1987), 25.
7. Kirsten Appendini, "Revisiting Women Wage-Workers in Mexico's Agro-Industry: Changes in Rural Labour Markets," Working Paper 95, no. 2, Centre for Development Research (Copenhagen, 1995), 11–12.
8. The categorizing of so-called "low-skilled" work needs to be problematized, particularly when describing the kinds of tasks allotted to women in food production.

30

Fallacies of Welfare-to-Work Policies

(2002)

Randy Albelda

With the draconian changes to welfare at the state and federal levels, a great many scholars are cashing in on the waves of foundation and government money attached to studying the impacts of welfare reform. A hefty share of these researchers are examining how adults leaving welfare are faring, with an emphasis on their earnings and employment situations. What is astonishing about the results from these "leaver" studies is how similar they are, despite the supposed diversity of programs adopted by the states. Between two-thirds and three-quarters of adults are employed most often for about 35 hours a week, earning an average hourly wage of about $7.50 in jobs that as often as not do not have health care benefits, rarely provide any sick days, and offer little or no vacation time.[1] Evidence is mounting that many leavers do not stay employed for very long, reproducing a pattern well established before welfare reform of cycling in and out of the labor market. Soon, however, some will not cycle back onto welfare because time limits preclude that.

Average income levels of the families leaving welfare are still at or near poverty levels. Families in the bottom 20 percent of the income distribution—most of whom are poor—have more earnings-related income (wages and the earned income tax credit [EITC]) but a lot less government income associated with being poor (welfare and food stamps). Overall, the loss of public assistance swamps increases in earnings and tax credits, leaving families with about the same or even less income, despite the high levels of employment generated since welfare reform.

These not-so-spectacular results occurred during the best economic expansion in 40 years and before most states hit time limits on welfare receipt. In short, these are the best results we can expect from welfare reform. Still, politicians are thrilled with the results. Almost universally they tout declines in caseloads as evi-

Albelda, Randy, "Fallacies of Welfare to Work Policies" In *Lost Ground*. Cambridge, MA: South End Press, 2002.

dence of the resounding success of welfare reform (see the article by Sanford F. Schram and Joe Soss in this volume). Researchers argue that most of those who were once on welfare are now employed and see this as a positive result.[2]

The effort to place former welfare mothers in jobs is not costless or effortless. States, nonprofit organizations, and advocates are spending enormous amounts of resources trying to make welfare-to-work policy work. Researchers are busily documenting the types of support women need to make a successful transition into the low-wage labor market. Despite claims of success, lurking under the surface are problems and structural impediments. Problems such as whether there are enough jobs and if the jobs former welfare recipients get pay living wages are being raised and sometimes get play in the press (and other outlets). Some of these problems are being addressed head-on, like the issue of whether mothers are job-ready. However, there are other problems, ones that are much more structural and symbolic, that are not being raised. These problems revolve around the nature of the low-wage labor market and the overriding reality that poor mothers are primary caretakers. It is not only that the jobs pay far too little—even with financial incentives—but that they are not mother-ready.

Most accept the general strategy of replacing public assistance with earnings but do not dare address the dramatic changes needed in low-wage labor markets or the implementation of adequate caregiving policies that must accompany this strategy. As currently implemented, the welfare-to-work solution is a match made in hell. It joins together poor mothers with few resources whose family responsibilities require employment flexibility with jobs in the low-wage labor market that often are the most inflexible, have the least family-necessary benefits (vacation time, health care, sick days), and provide levels of pay that often are insufficient to support a single person, let alone a family. This mismatch will not be resolved by providing the types of support that are currently being discussed and provided: short-term job training, work vans, poor-quality child care, or refundable earned income tax credits.

The welfare-to-work mismatch is more than an individual problem to be resolved by sympathetic counseling and financial incentives. It is a political, social, and economic problem that must be addressed in our policies as well as in our national psyche. It starts with valuing the work that families do. Raising children—with or without two adults in a family—is deserving work and absolutely vital to our individual and collective well-being.

Overlooking or not counting unpaid work conceptually and empirically overestimates the "success" of welfare reform and undermines women's progress for economic equality. Promoting more family-based benefits for low-income workers will help immensely. But we will not be able to totally eliminate public income support for low-income parents who are taking care of families. The ideological base for providing employment-based benefits is well established in the United States, but the base for appreciating the value of care is not. We will need to make more progress by engaging in a new kind of family values debate, one that argues that the work families do is valuable and worth supporting, even—or especially—if the family is poor.

WELFARE TO WHAT?

Before addressing the welfare-to-work strategy, we must think about the other ways in which poor women leave welfare. This is important because time limits and full-family sanctions virtually assure that the majority of families who receive welfare will be cut off, at least from federal funding. Not having access to welfare poses some historically familiar alternatives for women. First, instead of being dependent on the state, women can be dependent on family members—a much more acceptable form of dependency. Single mothers can get their income or in-kind support from parents, sisters, boyfriends, or former husbands. Efforts to crack down on deadbeat dads and fatherhood initiatives are a modern corollary to family dependency (see the article by Gwendolyn Mink in this volume). Getting recipients married and keeping them married was of course the fond hope and major inspiration for conservatives who sponsored the 1996 federal welfare reform legislation.[3]

A second way families without public assistance or income from other family members support themselves is to give up their children—by choice or by force. Newt Gingrich was lambasted for floating the idea of orphanages in the mid-1990s, but it seems totally plausible that the states will be seriously discussing this option soon. Newspaper accounts across the country often report on overloaded child protection agencies increasingly removing children from families for poverty-related reasons. Preliminary data are consistent with this scenario: the percentage of child-only cases on the welfare rolls has increased steeply in a short period of time, from 17 percent in 1994 to 29 percent in 1999 (U.S. Department of Health and Human Services 1999, exhibit 1).

Promoting marriages and discussing ways to snatch children, while important ways to end welfare, are not usually the main focus of welfare reform. Instead, most states, as well as the ancillary not-for-profit agencies and for-profit companies that get lucrative welfare-to-work-related contracts, are putting their energies into getting adult welfare recipients to work. In this case, work is always intended to mean paid employment or unpaid community or public service placements (that is, workfare).

Welfare-to-work policies embody a wide range of methods for promoting paid work instead of welfare. These include the punitive work-first strategies pursued by more than half the states as well as the more liberal strategies that include a generous package of training and education options, financial incentives, day care, transportation, and health care. And despite its current popularity, the notion of putting welfare mothers to work is hardly new. Gwendolyn Mink (1998) traces the history of work requirements in the Aid to Families with Dependent Children (AFDC) program since the legislation's inception and argues that by the late 1960s work requirements were seen as an important way to get women, particularly black women, off the welfare rolls. It was only in the early 1990s, however, that paid work was viewed as the main alternative in light of time-limit benefits.

Most researchers, politicians, agency heads, and advocates assume that work is good and that people on public assistance, if physically possible, should be working. It is easy to see why they, as well as liberals and progressives, find work appealing. Employment breaks welfare recipients' presumed (although not empirically validated) cycle of dependency. Further, when adult recipients work, even if they receive hefty supplements, they are not perceived as receiving handouts and hence are deserving. It would seem, then, putting welfare mothers to work solves the welfare problem of growing welfare rolls and plays into American values that will help restore safety nets for the poor. There are other reasons to want to see women employed as well, such as the benefits of being economically independent. This allows for a much larger range of choices and less control by men or by the state.

THE WORK DEBATE

These are clearly important and laudable reasons to want to see low-income mothers employed, but there should be considerable unease with current efforts to put welfare mothers to work.

One issue is whether there are jobs at all and what happens to the low-wage labor market when millions of welfare mothers look for paid employment. Outside of exceptional expansions, the macroeconomic structure makes jobs for workers with low educational attainment and few marketable skills difficult if not impossible to get and keep (see, for example, Hoynes 2000; Smith and Woodbury 2000). Further, wage pressures caused by the increased ranks of the low-wage labor market caused by welfare-to-work policies could serve to reduce wages for all workers at the bottom (Burtless 2000; Bartik 2000). With black adults facing unemployment rates twice that of whites, the availability of jobs and the persistence of labor market discrimination cannot be dismissed.

The economic expansion of the 1990s has both accompanied and accommodated welfare-to-work policies. The economy has almost seamlessly absorbed close to a million new workers from welfare, but come the downturn, many who did get jobs will lose them and case-loads will creep back up. Smith and Woodbury (2000) estimate that in the last recession over a million low-wage jobs were lost. The long expansion has allowed states to be slack, if not entirely unimaginative, in their training and education efforts, relying on the economic expansion to reduce rolls.

Another problem with welfare-to-work policy is the low pay women get. Without having to do much academic heavy lifting, Nobel prize winner Robert Solow (1998a, 1998b) combines basic macroeconomic theory on labor markets, data on the previous welfare program (AFDC), some common sense, and compassion to make a forceful case that welfare reform is both wishful thinking and pure folly. Current policy will turn those who are already poor and receiving cash assistance into the working poor, at the same time making some of the non-welfare-receiving poor worse off. For Solow, the economics of the problem are quite simple. Society cannot expect single mothers to enter low-wage labor markets and exit poverty. Recent examinations of the low-wage labor force come to similar conclusions (Bernstein and Hartmann 2000). The obvious solutions are to improve low-wage jobs and to improve the supplements to workers with low-wage jobs.

There have been important efforts toward supplementing earnings. The federal government has expanded the EITC, which serves to both boost low wages and provide financial incentives to employment. Several states have established or expanded their own EITC programs as well. Generous financial incentives—like high earnings disregards and the EITC—seem to work not only in encouraging employment but in reducing poverty (Miller et al. 2000; Blank, Card, and Robins 2000). However, most states are not implementing generous financial incentives, and at least one state that did—Minnesota—saw welfare use increase because truly supporting families when a caregiver is employed requires a sustained commitment to providing cash benefits. Instead, most states use time-limited financial incentives that have low-income thresholds of eligibility (including the EITC). This is precisely why women who leave welfare for earnings or who combine welfare and earnings are still poor (see, for example, Danziger 2000). As a result, current wage supplements are not proving a recipe for welfare reduction. Despite the fact that more families rely on earnings rather than on public aid, the income of the bottom quintile of single mothers has declined (Porter and Primus 1999;

Primus et al. 1999). There is little doubt that carrots—financial incentives like EITC and higher earnings disregards—are better than sticks like sanctions and time limits, both in terms of outcomes and welfare policy gestalt. However, they have yet to be very successful in taking most poor families off the poverty track for long.

A third problem with welfare-to-work policies is the issue of the job readiness of welfare mothers. Research confirms that many welfare mothers have low educational attainment and lack recent job experience (although the vast majority have been employed at some point). Both of these characteristics impede entry into the labor market and all but assure low wages for those who do find work. Recent research is uncovering another set of barriers to work that have little to do with individual motivation, human capital investments, or self-help. These barriers include women's learning disabilities, severe bouts of depression, and experiences with domestic violence.

There is growing evidence that states, especially those that promote work-first strategies, are finding that the easy-to-place recipients have left the welfare system, but those who require much more training to get paid employment remain (see, for example, Danziger 2000). Ironically, or perhaps cynically, welfare is becoming more and more as it was portrayed for years—a system that serves very low-functioning women with many children who need assistance for many years. Women with barriers to employment will need time and long-term training to move up and out, something welfare reform is discouraging or prohibiting.

Finding a job, earning enough to support a family, removing barriers to employment, and developing marketable skills are challenges faced by any poor adult in the United States. However, what distinguishes welfare recipients from other poor people is that the vast majority are children being raised, most often, by a mother on her own. Not surprisingly, a fourth concern with or critique of welfare-to-work policy revolves around the set of ancillary supports that mothers need to get to work. While there are several needs, such as transportation and health care coverage, by far the biggest and most expensive is child care.

Although states are using TANF money to purchase child care, there still is not enough. There already is a child care crisis without welfare mothers boosting demand. The cost of quality care is typically far beyond the reach of many low-income parents. Very little attention has been paid to the quality of child care that women leaving welfare are finding. Who knows what is happening to children, including school-age children, when mothers are employed? These are problems that have not been solved and will have enormous implications for both the sustainability of welfare-to-work policies and the well-being of families now and in the future.

THE PROBLEMS NOT DISCUSSED

As pressing as these concerns are, they are by now relatively well established. Resolving them will be a necessary, but not sufficient, part of constructing any decent system of welfare.

What is almost always ignored or conveniently forgotten in critiques of welfare-to-work policies is that the U.S. labor market has always failed women who have little formal education and sporadic job experience. Women have a very hard time supporting themselves, let alone supporting families. Low-income women are still segregated into low-paying occupations, despite the vast improvements for college-educated women. In 1998, 54 percent of all women worked in sales, service, or administrative support occupations (U.S. Bureau of Labor Statistics 2000, 176). Over one third (35.3 percent) of all women in 1997 earned too little to pull themselves up to the poverty level for a family of four, even if they worked 40 hours a week, 52 weeks a year (Bernstein and Hartmann 2000, 20).

For former welfare recipients, the likelihood of being in low-paying work is remarkably high. One study found that between 1984 and 1990 two out of every three women moving off welfare worked in sales, service, or clerical jobs (Spalter-Roth et al. 1995). Recent leaver studies indicate little change in these results. Even though the new solution to welfare is immediate employment, there are still the same old problems that single mothers have always faced: a low-wage labor market, family demands, barriers to employment, and a shortage of ancillary supports.

Jobs that pay family-sustaining wages are not mother ready, nor are the jobs that low-income mothers are finding, even when they get training, find work, have child care arrangements, and receive wage supplements. The needs jobs cannot meet include remarkably mundane events such as sick children, school and medical appointments, school vacations, and early-release school days. Employers, especially those who employ low-wage workers, will not tolerate workers who come in late because a school bus did not show up, miss days because there was no child care or a kid was sick, or worry about their children at 3 p.m. instead of doing their work.

The work of taking care of families is often inconsistent with the demands of being a family breadwinner. Yet, this work-family dilemma is overlooked in welfare reform research and policy. For example, the work of taking care of children is not seen as work or as an important family and economic input in the welfare-to-work strategy; rather, it is seen as a cost of going to work and only once women get jobs are their family responsibilities recognized as important to replace.

What much of the welfare-to-work debate fails to confront is the complex nature of paid and unpaid work for all families, particularly those with children and those that are poor. Adults responsible for children many times cannot (and probably should not) put their jobs—especially low-wage ones—before the needs (mundane or profound) of their children. Instead of trying to reform poor mothers to become working-poor mothers, we need to take a closer look at job structures and what it will take to make work possible for mothers who support families.

THE VALUE DEBATES

The obsession with employment for poor mothers is the culmination of a major value shift in thinking about women and public assistance. The Social Security Act of 1935 entitled poor single mothers to receive AFDC, although the levels received were far lower than in the other two major programs included in that historic legislation, Social Security and Unemployment Insurance. Further, the value set governing aid for single mothers was in direct contrast to that guiding both the benefit levels and the allocation of Social Security and Unemployment Insurance. These programs offer employment-based cash assistance doled out to those who can document long-term, continuous employment participation. In the 1930s, paid work became the entry door to entitlements, and the benefits were not based on need—although they were initially based on type of employment, which effectively excluded black and female workers. In 1935, single mothers in the industrial North were not expected to do paid labor—indeed, white women were discouraged from it in the 1930s. However, for those who were eligible the benefits were kept intentionally low so as not to discourage marriage (Gordon 1994). Widows were seen as deserving, whereas divorced, separated, and never-married mothers were not. Benefit levels continue to reinforce these values. Widows and their children receive much more generous funds from Social Security then did non-widowed single mothers receiving AFDC (and now TANF).

Today, what makes a single mother entitled and deserving has changed. It is no longer sufficient to be a parent raising children on one's own. Indeed, the most salient factor in determining the level and length of support one might receive is if one is engaged in paid labor. This emphasis on paid work is only possible now that most women are in the paid labor market and the moral sanctions against women without men has dissipated. Making the demand that single mothers work because other mothers do is politically, although not necessarily economically, feasible. Few seem to notice that the majority of married mothers do not work in year-round, full-time jobs, yet for single mothers to move from welfare to self-sufficiency, they would need to be employed more than 40 hours a week, every week of the year. In order to deserve the generosity of American taxpayers, single mothers need to give back something in return. Importantly, this goes beyond doing the work of raising children. In the words of Mary Jo Bane (1997), "The public, rightly, wanted welfare reform that expected work and parental responsibility" (47).

The positive value of employment has been accompanied by the negative value placed on receiving welfare. Led by Ronald Reagan and Charles Murray in the 1980s, critics derided women on welfare with the title of welfare queen. Women on welfare were presumed to have loads of children and then pass down the legacy of welfare receipt to their children. Receiving welfare, in these accounts, constituted dysfunctional behavior. So-called liberal poverty researchers carried this banner as well. Notably, William Julius Wilson (1987) and Christopher Jencks (1991), as well as their left detractors, such as William Darity and Samuel Myers (1994), discuss welfare receipt as a pathology—one of the many "bad" behaviors that help reproduce poverty.

Jencks (1991, 83) even refers to women receiving welfare as the "reproductive underclass." In this debate, paid work is good, and welfare receipt is bad. Therefore, to make progress, poor mothers need to be in the labor force and off welfare.

I am not arguing that paid work is bad. Indeed, earnings can and do buy economic security and some independence from men, especially from abusive relationships. In a society that values paid work, employment can build one's self-esteem as well. There is no doubt that women's ability to earn wages has the potential to set them free. However, welfare-to-work policy is a setup. The types of jobs many poor mothers get and keep do not provide much dignity or sufficient wages. Working enough hours at low wages to support a family is often untenable. Women fail too often. This is not only demoralizing; it is economically debilitating. For many, welfare-to-work policies are a cruel hoax that makes legislators feel better about themselves but leaves poor families in the lurch.

Ironically, for different reasons, many conservatives and some progressives are not so comfortable with the new welfare values of putting mothers to work—at least as they apply to middle- and upper-income mothers. Many would prefer to see all mothers in heterosexual marriages rather than on welfare or working. But conservatives are having a very hard time mandating marriage for anyone. Instead, they will settle for bullying welfare mothers, making sure gays and lesbians cannot get married, and providing hefty tax breaks for married stay-at-home moms.

The antifeminist version of this argument is that feminists have played a cruel hoax on the American people by insisting that women can do it all—have fulfilling careers and be terrific mothers. For example, Danielle Crittenden (1999) argues that feminism is unnatural because women need to raise their own children and not be working in the labor force full-time and hiring nannies. Women should stay home and let their husbands support them.

While the antifeminists' analysis and solution are faulty, the problem of having it all is real. Even assuming, as these authors typically do, that everyone is white and college educated, the fault is not in women's wanting to be employed but, rather, in what it means for both men and women to be in full-time jobs that pay living wages. Our current job structure is built on the assumption that unpaid labor is free and plentiful, while family-supporting jobs (with high pay and benefits) preclude the actual work of taking care of families. For families without the benefit of college education or that face other barriers to high-paying employment, men's falling wages and families' need for women's income mean that all parents must be employed in order to have enough income to make ends meet.

For progressives, the sole focus on making employment a deserving behavior without also reevaluating the nature of care work is both practically and politically problematic. Rather than be preoccupied with the value of paid work in building a safety net, more progress for all might be made by focusing on the value of the economic work performed in the home and what constitutes a family.

WHAT WE NEED

A national discussion about the value of women's work in the home and the nature of low-wage work for women with children might redirect our nation's priorities. Rather than tax breaks, we might consider an infusion of public funds to help raise and take care of family members. Such a discussion might promote employers and the government to construct policies that revamp paid work to accommodate unpaid work, rather than the other way around.

At a minimum, we need universal early-education programs, extended school day programs, and child allowances. We should consider a shorter workweek or at least income supplements to low-income workers who take part-time jobs so that families can still pay for basic needs like housing, health insurance, child care, food, and clothing. Paid family and medical leave and expanding unemployment insurance to cover less continuous and low-paying part-time work must also be in place. Pay equity would help, since women's wages are lower than men's in jobs that require comparable skills and effort. Enforcement of antidiscrimination laws and affirmative action would help low-income women of color.

If we as a nation recognized the value of women's work, we would not have welfare reform that substitutes public assistance with the earnings of mothers in low-wage jobs and a shallow set of supports that vanish quickly. Seeing the work of raising children as a benefit to families and society, not merely as a barrier to going to work, would mean developing a welfare-to-work regime that truly supports part-time waged work. Further, it might make us more cognizant that for some families having the sole adult in the labor force is not always possible or desirable. Public income supports for poor single mothers will always need to exist precisely because we value the work of mothers taking care of their children. Arbitrary time limits, meager benefits, and a fractured system of welfare defined by individual states (and sometimes counties) all work against a real safety net.

If there is an opportunity in welfare-to-work welfare reform, it is in recognizing that jobs, especially at the low end of the pay scale, do not pay enough to support families and do not provide the flexibility that parents need. It is an opportunity, however, only if we can get past the welfare-to-work mentality.

NOTES

1. There are many leaver studiest—too many to mention. A catalog of them can be found at www.researchforum.org. For an excellent list of studies, go to www.welfareinfo.org/trackingstudies. htm. In addition, Appendix L to the 2000 congressional *Green Book* includes findings from leaver studies (U.S. House of Representatives 2000).

2. For example, the introduction of a recent edited volume on employment and welfare reform by highly respected and relatively liberal labor economists concludes, "So far, the evidence suggests that welfare reform is proceeding as well as or better than most analysts had expected. In terms of declining caseloads and increasing work effort among single mothers, welfare reform has been an astonishing success. . . . The research in this book suggests we are on the right track with many policy efforts" (Blank and Card 2000, 17–18).

3. This is made very clear in the findings section (101) of the 1996 Personal Responsibility and Work Opportunity Reconc iliation Act (H.R. 3734),

Philosophy

Philosophy has been described as "thinking about thinking." Philosophers apply reason, systematic thinking, and argument in their quest to understand concepts such as truth, knowledge, and existence. Feminists have challenged the both the content and the structure of the discipline. In particular, feminist philosophers have critiqued Western philosophy's tendency toward dualistic thinking whereby reason and objectivity are linked to masculinity, and emotion and subjectivity are linked to femininity. Susan Sherwin questions the compatibility of feminism and philosophy and explores the nature of the tension between the two enterprises. She offers overviews of philosophical and feminist agendas that help to illuminate their divergent and overlapping paths towards truth (and justice). Karen J. Warren discusses the connections between feminism and the environment that are being made by feminist philosophers. Her piece illustrates how feminists have altered the scope of the field and posed challenges to its most basic conceptions. Feminist environmentalism also exemplifies the politicization of scholarship that is associated with the women's movement. The final piece in this section presents a decidedly unorthodox scholarly dialogue between graduate students in philosophy who identify themselves as third wave feminists. This e-mail discussion between Rita Alfonso and Jo Trigilio covers the topics of feminism's contributions to and interactions with philosophy, postmodernism, the relationship between theory and practice, and the place of philosophy in the academy.

Critical Thinking Questions

1. What arguments does Sherwin offer that support the incompatibility of feminism and philosophy? How do her observations relate to feminist critiques in other disciplines?
2. What do philosophy and feminism have to offer each other? Should feminist philosophy remain a subset or tangent of the larger field, adhering to its own agreed-upon standards and criteria, or should feminists keep trying to enter and alter the mainstream?
3. What are some connections proposed by feminist philosophers between the domination/abuse of women and the domination/abuse of nature? Do

you find these connections valid, and if so, do you believe the women's movement should concern itself or even merge with the environmental movement?

4. Whose input would you find most valuable in a discussion of ethics in general and environmental ethics in particular—a mainstream philosopher or a feminist philosopher? In what ways might their perspectives and methods differ?

5. In what ways do Alfonso and Trigilio imagine third wave feminism as transforming the field of philosophy? To what extent do they seek to build on the accomplishments of the second wave and to what extent to remedy its flaws?

6. Do Alfonso and Trigilio present a hopeful picture of the future of feminist philosophy? To what extent do the issues they raise about the compatibility of the two enterprises mirror or differ from Sherwin?

31

Philosophical Methodology and Feminist Methodology
Are They Compatible?
(1988)

Susan Sherwin

Both "philosophy" and "feminism" are broad terms covering a variety of activities and subject matter. Each identifies an area of central concern to me: I frequently tend, in fact, to define myself in terms of them (I do philosophy; I am a feminist—though, curiously, I seldom say I am a philosopher; never I do feminism). But, more and more, I find myself wondering just how compatible these two interests are. They often seem to present different, and conflicting, demands.

The tension I experience revolves around the question of method. This is a particularly serious issue, since some philosophers recommend that we make method the defining characteristic of philosophy. Jay Rosenberg, for instance, says in *The Practice of Philosophy*, "Philosophy as a discipline is perhaps thought of most fruitfully as being distinguished by its method rather than by a subject matter." The question then naturally arises of what that methodology is,

and, whether it is compatible with the methodology of feminism.

In "Feminism, Marxism, Method, and the State," Catharine A. MacKinnon defines feminist methodology as consciousness-raising: "consciousness-raising is the major technique of analysis, structure of organization, method of practice, and theory of social change of the women's movement." We must ask, then, whether this methodology of consciousness-raising falls within the scope of acceptable philosophical methodology.

Immediately, we are confronted by the problem of which methodology to use to examine the question of the compatability of philosophical and feminist method without distortion. Reflecting my deep ambivalence on this matter, I have chosen to consider the various aspects of the question alternately from each perspective to see what insight I can derive as to whether I may keep both hats, only one, or, perish the thought, none. (Hence, as some critics have noticed,

Sherwin, Susan, "Philosophical Methodology and Feminist Methodology: Are They Compatible?" In *Feminist Perspectives: Philosophical Essays on Method and Morals*, ed., Lorraine Code, Sheila Mullett, & Christine Overall. Toronto: University of Toronto Press, 1988.

this paper rather schizophrenically reflects virtues and vices of each approach at various points. I see no way to avoid that dilemma in this particular case.)

This is not a disinterested or purely academic question. This paper is motivated by a particular personal experience. Hence, following feminist methodology, I shall begin by describing and interpreting that experience. Here we come quickly to the first point of departure from philosophy, for there is no comparable beginning from a philosophical orientation. Philosophy does not encourage focusing on particular personal experiences such as this.

> THE EXPERIENCE: A paper I submitted to the Canadian Philosophical Association (CPA) in 1984, entitled "Ethics: A Feminist Approach," was rejected by the CPA; it was, however, accepted by the Canadian Society for Women in Philosophy (C-SWIP) and enthusiastically received at the C-SWIP session of those same meetings. An earlier draft was also read at the annual meeting of the Canadian Research Institute for the Advancement of Women (CRIAW) meeting, where it received a great deal of encouragement (and two requests for publication).

Among the referees' comments from the CPA were the following remarks:

> REFEREE 1: "The discussion at the bottom on p. 4 implies that there is 'a common experience of being female' that women generally share, that is distinctive of the sex and that is morally significant so that a correct moral theory must take it into account. What is this 'common experience' and what is the evidence for its prevelance? Also, why is it morally relevant?" [These questions are precisely the ones addressed by the paper.]

> REFEREE 2: "This essay is . . . not up to the standards we should expect for CPA philosophy papers. . . . The author's thesis is likely false. Much of contemporary feminism is individualistic in ways criticized by the author. . . ."

> REFEREE 3: "Exactly what thesis does the paper profess? Is it a philosophical thesis? (To put the question differently, does the paper seek to prescribe a morality different from those it identifies as dominant or traditional? Or does it seek to produce a moral theory which describes morality more accurately than the disfavoured theories?) If (as it seems to this reader) the paper seeks to do the first, what is its relevance to a philosophical congress?" [In fact, it was a first step toward developing a feminist approach to a normative theory; I continue to consider such a project relevant to a philosophical congress.]

The experience of receiving such scathing reviews is painful. Like many women, I am inclined to accept deprecating judgements of my limited philosophical ability. I've certainly made similar judgements myself often enough. But, under my feminist hat, I know that I am obliged to look more deeply. The personal may just be political even here.

I consider it significant that I continue to run into nonfeminist philosophers who insist that what I do is "not philosophy." The viciousness with which feminist work is dismissed by such philosophers is a frequent source of concern. It is helpful, though, to note that this hostility is not directed exclusively at me; other feminist philosophers have experienced similar sorts of attack from the pens and word-processors of mainstream (malestream) philosophers. The target of this rage is often difficult to determine, for the objectors usually insist that they have no problem with the feminist content of the work per se; they are always very eager to make clear their tolerance for radical thought. Rather, they say, the problem is with the sloppiness, the ignorance, the incompetence of the author qua philosopher. If they were to write feminist philosophy, they suggest, they would do a far more "professional" job of it. I believe they might, but would it be equally good by feminist standards?

I imagine they would produce work something like the books on feminist themes that have been published over the last few years by writers who are clear about their philosophical identity, and who are prepared to use unquestioningly their certified philosophic expertise to provide helpful guides for feminists, generously showing them how philosophy can clarify their thinking; I have in mind such works as *Women's Choices* by Mary Midgley and Judith Hughes, and *Women, Reason, and Nature* by Carol McMillan. Implicit in their promise to bring the clear light of philosophy to feminist thought is a patronizing attitude—recognizable by the third person references to feminism by which they dissociate themselves from most feminist thought; the distancing, patronizing tone limits the value of their work to feminist thinking. Janet Radcliffe Richards provides a borderline case in *The Sceptical Feminist*, for she oscillates between including herself in and distancing herself from feminist thinkers. There is a striking contrast in tone and content between these books and others by explicitly self-identified feminist philosophers, such as Marilyn Frye, Alison Jaggar, or the collection edited by Sandra Harding and Merrill Hintikka. The latter books, produced by self-proclaimed feminist philosophers, expand and deepen feminist thought, rather than constrain and reduce it. There are important differences in approach that reflect the divergent paradigms of the two models.

Feminist methodology directs us to look for the political significance of personal experience. What is the political message underlying the scorn with which our individual work is frequently received within the profession? Clearly, the work of feminist philosophers generally is not of lower quality than the norm for mainstream philosophical meetings, so it is puzzling that a paper welcomed at feminist forums is not even worthy of a hearing at "regular" philosophical association meetings. Hence, we are left to wonder whether the feminist content is so threatening that the males who dominate the standards of scholarship in philosophy cannot bear to allow it a hearing, or whether there are different methodological criteria operating in the different forums.

The question is partly empirical, and in that sense, it is already suspect by purely philosophical standards. Philosophy assumes that there exist objective criteria by virtue of which any paper, whatever its political orientation, could be evaluated. A suspicion of political resistance on the part of referees is a claim most philosophers would find profoundly offensive.

It may just be, though, that there is no way to do genuinely feminist research and have it thoroughly respected by one's nonfeminist colleagues. Feminism, after all, is ultimately extremely radical, challenging the status quo in thought as well as in practice. Feminist philosophy does not just offer new truths, or new perspectives on truth, nor is it simply another point of view in these relativist philosophic times. I believe that feminism demands a distinct way of doing philosophy and challenges the very practice most philosophers pride themselves on having mastered. Hence, I shall proceed to explore this intuition—which, qua philosopher, I find disturbing—to see whether or not it is possible to discuss feminism in a way that is "philosophically respectable."

What, then, are the methods that characterize philosophy, and are they compatible with feminist methodology? As with most things, philosophers tend to disagree about the method. Throughout this paper, I will be referring to the style of philosophy that is characteristic of the Anglo-American approach, a method that has its roots in analytic philosophy and prizes a "scientific" approach to thought. This is the tradition dominant in philosophy departments throughout the English-speaking world and is the approach to philosophy in which I was trained and continue to function. I readily acknowledge that other approaches to philosophy differ in many significant respects, and some of my specific comments may not be applicable to other styles of philosophy. Although I suspect there are other specific barriers between modern feminist methodology and the various other styles of philosophy, I shall not attempt to review them here.

Even within the Anglo-American style of philosophy, there are differences about what constitutes appropriate methodology. Rosenberg (in *The Practice of Philosophy*) characterizes the method of philosophy as "the application of reason to its own operations, the rational study of rational practices" (p. 6). He considers philosophy to be primarily a "second-order" activity occupied with abstract "radical generalizations." He recommends that we appeal to the history of philosophy as a major methodological tool, seeing it as our common *"medium"* of inquiry. "It provides philosophers with a common expository idiom, a shared vocabulary of *concepts*, and a set of paradigms of philosophical reasoning, which can serve as shared starting points for contemporary reexplorations of central philosophical concerns" (p. 11). In other words, we do philosophy by learning the traditions the masters have handed down to us and carrying on in a similar vein; philosophy is defined by what philosophers have done.

If we take Rosenberg's advice seriously and look to the history of philosophy for the common assumptions of method and concepts, feminists are bound to have some concerns. The first thing feminists are sure to notice is that there are seldom any women listed among the philosophic greats, and, as Genevieve Lloyd puts it, the female philosophers we find in the history of philosophy "have been philosophers despite, rather than because of, their femaleness; there has been no input of femaleness into the formation of ideals of Reason." The tradition, it would seem, has long been biased against the perspective of women.

The next thing feminists observe is that the work of the leading historical figures is embarrassingly filled with powerful misogynist statements. Apart from Plato, Augustine, and Mill, it is difficult to find a major historical figure who had a good word to say about women; and the claims of equality from these three are so qualified as to be almost as offensive as their less generous colleagues to some feminists. Most contemporary philosophers are more careful in their discussions of gender than the historical figures were; they tend to be "liberal" on such matters, and generally excuse their predecessors as naively misguided by the culture of their times when it came to the question of women. It is commonly accepted that we can simply excise the offensive empirical claims from their philosophy and maintain the pure intellectual core. Feminist historians are far less certain about the externality and peripheral character of an author's views on women. Many recent papers have argued that the misogyny runs right through to the core of most major philosophers. Again quoting Lloyd, "It is clear that what we have in the history of philosophical thought is no mere succession of surface misogynist attitudes, which can now be shed, while leaving intact the deeper structures of our ideals of Reason. . . . women cannot easily be accommodated into a cultural ideal which has defined itself in opposition to the feminine" (pp. 103–104).

If we look to the method recommended by history we find that although philosophers disagree about the best method of doing philosophy, the debates tend to include agreement about certain principles that psychologists have identified as male-oriented. Descartes, for instance, urged a method that he expressly claimed would be suitable "even for women." It was the method of pure thought, moving privately from general universals to particulars by the pure activity of the mind uncontaminated by the influence of the body. Being more generous than many other philosophers, he assumed that women had minds as well as bodies; hence, apparently, he genuinely believed that women, too, were capable of truth. Unfortunately, he did not take into account his further claims that such activity required a concentration that necessitates freedom from concern with practical demands. It is still common to think that philosophic activity demands total concentration; for example, "The real philosopher, it might be said, exhibits a full, intense commitment to his work, as Socrates did. . . . The 'real' philosopher, it might be argued, spends most of his time doing philosophy." Yet, as Virginia Woolf observed in *A Room of One's Own*, such a luxury was/is available only to men, for the culture provides that women will see to the demands of practical living, leaving men free for the "important work." Given our socialization and the real demands on our time for nontheoretical tasks, it is hardly surprising that few women are perceived as engaged in "real philosophy." In contrast, we should note, within feminist circles, practical work is an important component of one's contribution to theory.

Moreover, in our society at least, men are inclined towards abstract general thought, and tend to find universals clearer and more comfortable than particulars, just as Descartes imagined. Women, however, seem to think most readily in terms of particulars. Universal, abstract ideas are things they can think towards, but seldom are they the place where thought begins for women. In this sense, perhaps the Socratic model of reasoning from the particular to the general is more suitable for women. If so, it is unfortunate that it passed out of philosophic style for so many centuries.

Turning now to feminism, several important differences in norms are apparent. The methodology of consciousness-raising is very much a "first-order" methodology, where we begin by focusing on the concrete and the specific, and delay abstraction and generalization to a later stage. Consciousness-raising involves "collective critical reconstitution of the meaning of women's social experience, as women live through it." Thus, where philosophers are encouraged to seek abstract generalization, feminists try to learn to uncover the personal. So while philosophers seek objective truth, defined as truth valid from any possible viewpoint, feminists consider it important to look to the actual point of view of the individual speaking. Philosophers tend to believe that emotion and personal feeling are impediments to truth, since they can seldom be generalized objectively, but feminists, who consider direct, personal experience an important component of truth, pay particular attention to the emotional content of claims. The quest for abstract universality is reflected in the fascination philosophers have with hypothetical counter-examples. Feminists, however, tend to concentrate on the texture of a complex range of different but related real experiences.

Psychologists have observed that women tend to prefer social, interactive processes, unlike men who long for the isolation of completely private thought. In this sense, then, the methodology of feminism is the methodology of women's thought: consciousness-raising begins with personal experience, focusing on the details of experience, and then collectively moves to a broader analysis. Generalizations come after a number of particulars are presented. This is an interactive activity, and not the sort of private process Descartes envisioned.

Feminists do not assume that the truth is readily accessible if only we concentrate hard enough. Recognizing that what has been claimed to be objective and universal is in reality the male point of view, feminists seek to concentrate on women's own experience and explicitly avoid any claims of being "objective, abstract or universal." Feminists acknowledge that their perspective is not universal or unpremised, recognizing that women's perspective may in fact be different in a different world. After all, women's experience is experience within patriarchy, and "the male perspective is systematic and hegemonic." Philosophers, in contrast, continue to hope to find the pure, general, universal point of view. Thus, feminists readily admit to "bias" in our perspective, embracing it as a virtue, while other philosophers continue to assume bias should, and can be, avoided. This is, then, a point of serious conflict between the two approaches.

Another area of difference is that feminist scholarship is explicitly interdisciplinary. Feminist scholars have argued that they are constrained in their work by limits connected with the established frameworks of existing disciplines. Such constraint has been cited as constituting one of the most insidious barriers to development of feminist thought, and it is of as much concern to those with a background in philosophy as it is to those from other disciplines. Hence, by definition, feminists will rely on an eclectic methodology, having its roots in various disciplines, and will not restrict themselves entirely to any single disciplinary approach, neither that of philosophy, nor any other. Although there is a sense in which philosophy is also interdisciplinary, it views its relation to other disciplines in metatheoretic terms, and so it is not interdisciplinary in the methodological sense of involving genuine collective cross-disciplinary thought. It maintains its own sense of method and sees its task as criticially examining the presuppositions of other disciplines, but not specifically adopting the methods of the disciplines it examines (though, in fact, scientific methodology has been highly attractive to modern philosophers).

Another area of apparent difference is found in the definition of the criteria of acceptability and criticism within each field. In philosophy, the emphasis on universality makes positive claims virtually impossible to prove and renders counterexamples potentially devastating, hence commenting on a philosopher's thought is often taken to require a furious search for the decisive counterexample, however hypothetical it may be. Negative theses, disproving the analysis someone else has offered, is the most natural route for a critical philosopher to take. The logic of the argument is the most important feature of a philosophic position, far more important than the plausibility of the claims or the usefulness of the insight to other questions. In commenting on a philosophic thesis, one may identify a logical flaw, challenge the underlying assumptions, or note the inadequacy of its explanatory power. It is taken for granted that the task of colleagues discussing this work is to test the thesis along these logical dimensions, seeking to demolish it to make room for their own clever innovations.

In feminist scholarship, logic is also important—as Richards et al. take delight in pointing out—and theories that are logically flawed, or clearly false, or lacking in explanatory power are subject to criticism among feminists as well. But feminists have political as well as intellectual aims, which they are quite willing to admit to. (Feminists have provided powerful arguments to show that historically, philosophers commonly have political agendas, as well, and suspect their contemporary philosophic colleagues of also having political aims, but, apart from Marxists and feminists, few philosophers will admit to politics shaping their work.) What this means in practice is that a theoretical claim in feminism must be consistent with overall feminist values, and, in fact, it should further the pursuit of those values. The effect, as well as the logic, of a theory is significant. A theory that did not contribute to political change is of only limited interest. In other words, feminists view political effects as one measure of acceptability, though certainly not the only measure. Philosophers tend to be appalled by such frank admissions of bias.

Moreover, it is commonly accepted among feminists that theory alone is not sufficient—that the theorist should also be directly involved in social activism. In this way, we guard against the danger of ungrounded theory. So, where philosophers are deeply suspicious of explicit political concerns shaping one's intellectual exploration, feminists are suspicious of theoretic arguments that deny any political implications. Philosophers, for the most part, now recognize that value-free reasoning is an impossible goal in science, yet they continue to aspire to it within their own discipline.

Feminists are also unlikely to tolerate a theory that rejects or denies personal experience. Many philosophers, for their part, seem to take a perverse delight in shocking others by providing an analysis that appears to fly in the face of experience. And where feminists consider it important to fit their ideas into the broader picture of developing feminist thought, philosophers are often most pleased if they can turn existing philosophic thought on its head and present some radically original position that brings much prior work into question.

This difference in standards of acceptability and grounds of criticism leads to differences in style of interaction within the area of study. Janice Moulton has provided a clear feminist critique of the standard model of interaction among modern philosophers. As she argued in "A Paradigm of Philosophy: The Adversary Method" (Chapter One of this volume), the model of philosophic debate is that of a contest of adversaries, where aggression is at least as important as truth is to the outcome. Aggression, however, is not an attractive or desirable model for anyone to pursue in professional debates, and it is particularly alien and dangerous for women, let alone feminists. There are clear defects in such an approach as a means of arriving at the goal of philosophic activity, truth. By making debating skill a chief criterion of success, the profession of philosophy rewards traits such as aggression and competitiveness; but feminists reject

the view that these traits are desirable, for they see them to be central to patriarchy. By making truth an all or nothing affair, and encouraging us to seek any hole in a colleague's argument by which her/his position might be demolished, we foster a rather frightening model of the pursuit of truth. More than one clever philosopher has abandoned the profession because she lacks the taste for the combative search for truth. Moreover, it is a difficult tool to use in the pursuit of truth. Recognizing that the truth is complex and elusive, philosophers nonetheless expect one another to pursue it at all stages with air-tight arguments and supreme confidence. It often is the case, though, that one's first attempts in a new direction are tentative and exploratory, and not best pursued by subjecting them, alone and unassisted, to the strongest opponent.

Feminist scholarship, in contrast, holds onto an ideal of cooperative, collective work. Scholarship in pursuit of a shared goal is to be undertaken as a collective enterprise where different people do piece work on different aspects of the problem. Ideas are shared as part of this collective enterprise, and, as long as they contribute to the overall goals of feminist activity and are not thoroughly false, the goal of criticism is to help develop those ideas further in the direction begun. Assumptions are shared and, hence, one can get immediately to the business at hand of furthering the argument, rather than reviewing it yet again. Each contribution is related to the larger system of ideas, the larger project, and not offered as a private theory to then bear one's name. (It is a feminist view of justice we seek, not a Kantian, Marxist,

Rawlsian, or Nozikian one—or even a Fryian, Jaggarian, or Hardingist theory.)

This, of course, is an idealized description of feminist work. There are different approaches to feminism, and the disputes among various interpretations can be significant. Certainly many feminist scholars have felt shocked and betrayed to find their work (and often themselves) under attack by other feminists. The reason for the shock, however, is that it really is a violation of feminist values and norms to attack destructively (rather than criticize in some constructive way) another's work. It happens, but, unlike the widely held philosophic norm, it is not an explicit ideal of the discipline to view debate as a pitched battle. Feminists consciously aim at cooperative solutions and seek to avoid personally devastating attacks.

My philosophy colleagues sometimes express puzzlement on how to criticize feminist work if the adversary system is not acceptable. One approach is to try to understand how the paper at issue fits into the larger picture of feminist goals, and the broad view of social and political or ethical (or epistemological, metaphysical, etc.) thought. Feminists begin with a spirit of charity in trying to decipher the thrust of a colleague's work. For feminists, the nit-picking inherent in the current Anglo-American approaches to philosophy comes after a general consideration of the plausibility of the problem. In fairness, I must add that it does seem true, lately, that many nonfeminist philosophers are recognizing the limits of the adversary method; more and more sessions at conferences seem to eschew that approach and see the task at hand as a collective search for the truth. (I think, in fact, feminist philosophers can take some of the credit for this shift in style. We really do offer a more attractive paradigm.)

Consider now another aspect of academic activity, namely teaching, from both perspectives. Here, too, there is a different ideal envisioned in philosophy classes from that in feminist studies. In academic contexts, feminist teaching does not proceed by the Socratic method where the wise but humble teacher skillfully directs the unreflective student to the truth he/she has overlooked; rather it involves a cooperative exploration of perceptions and experience toward a new understanding for all members of the class. Feminist teaching incorporates feminist values. Hence, feminist classrooms are noted for "an acceptance of, and even emphasis on, the personal/affective element in learning; and a warm human relationship among persons in the class, students and teachers." As Marilyn Webb notes, feminist teachers are conscious of the politics of the classroom:

> When we teach about sexual politics, it's a class hierarchy we are attacking. If we recreate this class division within our teaching, our analysis is "devoid of form." That's why as feminist teachers, it's just as important for us to look at how we teach as to look at what we teach.

More precisely, Webb goes on to sketch the methods of achieving these ideals, including: the attempt to teach without imposing authoritarian structures; the attempt to build a "consciousness of an alternative, e.g., collective learning and action" rather than individual isolation and competition; an attempt to incorporate "actual experience of what we are talking about in our teaching"; and a general commitment to an emphasis on the experiential (p. 417). These aspects of feminist teaching are not explicitly rejected in general philosophic pedagogy, but they are certainly not accepted as central to the enterprise either. In fact, in philosophy, as in other disciplines, feminist pedagogy tends to contradict mainstream methods, creating hostility and rejection of our approach within the model of other academic classes.

It seems, then, that there are many important differences in the approach I see taken by philosophers and feminists. Nonetheless, there are many of us who believe ourselves to be both feminists and philosophers, and much high quality work has been produced that seems to satisfy the norms of both disciplines. There must, then, be room for overlap. Hence, what I am really seeking here is a way of characterizing that area of overlap, of identifying some method of feminist philosophy which is acceptable from both perspectives.

One aspect I can perceive of shared approach is the important fact that both are committed to a strong and general skepticism about authoritative pronouncements of the truth. Both disciplines train initiates not to accept statements of fact without question. It is not really such a surprise that some philosophers are pursuing radical feminist alternatives to the standard problems of philosophy. Philosophy has always tolerated, and perhaps from time to time has even encouraged, radical rethinking of its underlying assumptions. It is not unreasonable for feminists to align themselves with this time-honored philosophic tradition.

Moreover, philosophers have never actually agreed on any single method. While individual philosophers and schools have identified particular methods as paradigm, other philosophers have always challenged such restrictions and introduced different approaches as legitimate. (And some, like Rorty, seem to deny that there is any proper philosophic method—as it is now conceived by Anglo-American philosophers—at all.) There is no single authorized method, wholly original and unique to the discipline, which does not have counterparts and inspiration in other disciplines. So, too, for feminism, where there is a great diversity of opinion on the best approach. In fact, both philosophy and feminism have always involved rather an eclectic variety of methods. Thus, there is no single, accepted method by which philosophers can reject feminist methodology out of hand.

Perhaps more importantly, it would be a violation of feminist principles to reject philosophic methods. Feminism relies on whatever morally and epistemologically acceptable methods are available and can contribute toward its overall ends, and surely philosophy can help in that enterprise. Those feminists who have expressed skepticism over the rational methods of philosophy are recording a well-deserved distrust of methods and ideas which have been used to limit women's freedom and imagination. But, as philosophers never tire of pointing out, feminists can only express their case by use of such rational methods themselves, and in most cases the difficulty they have with rationality can be attributed in part to their unexamined— and mistaken—assumptions about what rationality involves. What is seen by some feminists as a methodological barrier is actually the result of abuses of a rational approach by misogynist philosophers.

One of the dangers that feminists have pointed to within traditional methodologies is the hazard of accepting dichotomies. Dichotomous thinking forces ideas, persons, roles, and disciplines into rigid polarities. It reduces richness and complexity in the interest of logical neatness, and, in doing so, it distorts truth. Moreover, the creation and use of dichotomies seem to be important elements in the very structure of patriarchy; the institution of patriarchy involves power relations that rest on the assumption of fundamental and unbridgeable differences between the sexes reflected in multiple forms of polarity. Hence, I believe that it is important for feminists to resist the temptation to pursue dichotomies from our own perspective; i.e., we should take care not to define philosophic methodology as inherently opposed to feminist thought or imagine the differences in approach to involve a schism that cannot be forded.

I cannot, therefore, conclude that feminist and philosophic methodologies are incompatible. They are, however, made compatible only with significant effort from each end. Many standard approaches and assumptions in philosophy are not acceptable from a feminist point of view, so it is not all of philosophy that can be seen as compatible with feminism. Philosophers, from their perspective, must make some noticeable effort to understand the feminist enterprise before dismissing it as not meeting the usual professional norms. They must recognize that feminists have much ground to cover in rethinking the philosophic activity of the past 2500 years, and they should be prepared to tolerate a bit of sketchiness and hand-waving as feminists explore the ways in which ethics, epistemology, and metaphysics may have to be revised when we change their underlying political assumptions. Perhaps the greatest challenge comes from the need to pay attention to the genuine criticisms of their discipline which feminists have to offer. Philosophers should consider whether the particular approaches feminists take to philosophic questions can in fact serve philosophic ends. I seem still to believe that feminism can enrich philosophy and that it behooves philosophers to learn to be open to feminist style and commitments.

For our part as feminists, in order to help philosophers make such modifications in their usual methods of evaluation, we should continue to try to put our thoughts into a language they can understand and relate our analysis to familiar issues when possible. In doing so, though, I believe we must remain conscious of the risks involved. It is important to be able to rely on one another for the support necessary when philosophers fail to notice the significant differences involved in adopting a feminist perspective. We should never forget that philosophic gatherings and journals are still predominantly hostile environments for feminists, and we ought not to venture far into such terrain without adequate support from one another.

Postscript. I noticed as I concluded this paper that I experienced a familiar sense of unease that the ideas seem tentative and lacking in drama and surprise. Writing this paper was a valuable cathartic exercise for me, for I now realize that this deja vu feeling of dissatisfaction is in fact yet another symptom of my ambivalence about appropriate standards. Under my philosopher's hat, the ideal is to come up with the decisive conclusion, settling the question once and for all; I feel as if I ought now to be prepared to defend my view against all comers. On that criterion, this paper, like the earlier one so disliked by the referees, is flawed.

But as a feminist paper, the agenda is different. Under my feminist hat, I see my task to be an exploration of my views and feelings on this broadly abstract and deeply personal question. Having done that, I am quite comfortable to pass the issue on to others who will share the responsibility of following these ideas through, taking them in directions I cannot clearly foresee. From that perspective, it is acceptable to be reflective about a matter that troubles me without presuming to have entirely settled it. Clearly, this dilemma is a piece of a greater puzzle, and it is open to modification in light of the experience and insight of others who approach it constructively. Or, in other words, this is a paper that is best read at a conference for feminist philosophers.

32

Feminism and the Environment

An Overview of the Issues

(1991)

Karen J. Warren, Macalester College

INTRODUCTION

The past few decades have witnessed an enormous interest in the women's movement and the ecology (or, environmental) movement. Many feminists have argued that the goals of these two movements are mutually reinforcing and ultimately involve the development of worldviews and practices which are not based on models of domination. One of the first feminists to do so was Rosemary Radford Ruether who, in 1974, wrote in *New Women/New Earth*,

> Women must see that there can be no liberation for them and no solution to the ecological crisis within a society whose fundamental model of relationships continues to be one of domination. They must unite the demands of the women's movement with those of the ecological movement to envision a radical reshaping of the basic socioeconomic relations and the underlying values of this [modern industrial] society (204).

Subsequent feminist writings by animal rights activists, ecological and other environmental feminists have reinforced Ruether's basic point: there are important connections between feminism and environmentalism, an appreciation of which is essential for the success of the women's and ecological movements.

Just what are some of the connections between "feminism and the environment"? How has recognition of these connections affected and informed the theoretical perspectives of feminism and environmental ethics? What is the philosophical significance of the topic "feminism and the environment"?

In this essay I attempt to answer these questions by doing three things: First, I identify some of the connections between the domination of women and the domination of nature which have been suggested in the scholarly literature on "feminism and the environment." Second, I identify a range of philosophical positions which have emerged, particu-

Warren, Karen, "Feminism and the Environment: An Overview of the Issues." *The American Philosophical Association Newsletter* 90, no. 3: 108–116.

larly in the field of environmental ethics, in an attempt to provide a theoretical framework for understanding the connections between feminism and the environment. Third, I suggest what the philosophical significance of this emerging literature is, not only for feminism and environmental ethics but for mainstream philosophy as well. While no attempt is made to provide an exhaustive account, hopefully this overview highlights some of the relevant issues and acquaints the newcomer with the nature and range of philosophical positions on "feminism and the environment."

SOME ALLEGED CONNECTIONS BETWEEN FEMINISM AND THE ENVIRONMENT

In what follows I identify eight sorts of connections which feminists, particularly "ecological feminists" (ecofeminists), have identified as important to understanding the connections between feminism and the environment. No attempt is made here to critically assess the claims made about these connections. Furthermore, these eight categories are not to be viewed as competing or mutually exclusive. Indeed, many of the important claims made about one kind of connection (e.g., conceptual and theoretical) often depend on insights gleaned from others (e.g., historical and empirical). The aim in this section is simply to present for consideration the various elements of the overall "feminism and the environment" picture.

1. **Historical and causal.** One sort of alleged connection between feminism and the environment discussed is historical. When historical data is used to generate theories concerning the sources of the twin dominations of women and nature, it is also causal. In fact, some feminists characterize ecofeminism in terms of just such historical and causal claims: "Eco-feminism is a recent development in feminist thought which argues that the current global environmental crisis is a predictable outcome of patriarchal culture (Salleh 1988, 138, n.1). What are some of these historical and causal claims?

Some feminists (e.g., Spretnak 1990; Reiser 1989, 1990) trace the historical and causal connections to prototypical patterns of domination begun with the invasion of Indo-european societies by nomadic tribes from Eurasia about 4500 B.C. (Lahar 1991). Riane Eisler describes the time before these invasions as a "matrilocal, matrilineal, peaceful agrarian era." Others (e.g., Griffin 1978; Plumwood 1991; Reuther 1974) focus on the historical role played by rationalism and important conceptual dualisms (discussed at 2, below) in classical Greek philosophy. Still other feminists (e.g., Merchant 1980, 1989; Shiva 1988) focus on cultural and scientific changes that occurred during the scientific revolution and sanctioned the exploitation of nature, unchecked commercial and industrial expansion, and the subordination of women.

What prompts and explains these alleged historical and causal connections between the domination of women and the domination of nature? What *else* was in place to permit and sanction these twin dominations? To answer these questions, many have turned to the conceptual props which keep the historical dominations of women and nature in place.

2. **Conceptual.** Many feminists (e.g., Cheney 1987; Gray 1981; Griffin 1978; Y. King 1981, 1983, 1989a; Merchant 1980, 1990; Plumwood 1986, 1991; Reuther 1974; Salleh, 1984; Warren 1987, 1988, 1990) have argued that, ultimately, historical and causal links between the dominations of women and of nature are located in conceptual structures of domination and in the way women and nature have been conceptualized, particularly in the

western intellectual tradition. Four such conceptual links have been suggested.

One account locates the conceptual basis of the twin dominations of women and nature in *value dualisms,* i.e., disjunctive pairs in which the disjuncts are seen as oppositional (rather than as complementary) and exclusive (rather than as inclusive), and *value hierarchies,* i.e., perceptions of diversity organized by a spatial Up-Down metaphor which attribute higher value (status, prestige) to that which is higher ("Up") (see Gray 1981; Griffin 1978, 1989a; Y. King 1981, 1983, 1990; Ruether 1974; Zimmerman 1987). Frequently cited examples of these hierarchically organized value dualisms include reason/emotion, mind/body, culture/nature, human/nature, and man/woman dichotomies. These theorists argue that whatever is (historically) associated with emotion, body, nature, and women is regarded as inferior to that which is (historically) associated with reason, mind, culture, human (i.e., male) and men. One role of feminism and environmental ethics, then, is to expose and dismantle these dualisms, and to rethink and reconceive those mainstay philosophical notions (e.g., reason, rationality, knowledge, objectivity, the self as knower and moral agent) which rely on them.

A second, related account houses the value dualistic, value hierarchical thinking (described above) in larger, oppressive patriarchal conceptual frameworks—ones undergirding *all* social "isms of domination," e.g., racism, classicism, heterosexism, as well as sexism as well as "naturism" or, the unjustified domination and subordination. An oppressive conceptual framework is patriarchal when it explains, justifies and maintains the subordination of women by men. Oppressive and patriarchal conceptual frameworks are characterized not only by value dualisms and value hierarchies, but also by "power-over" conceptions of power and relationships of domination (Warren 1991) and by a "logic of domination," i.e., a structure of argumentation which justifies subordi-

nation on the grounds that *superiority justifies subordination* (Warren 1987, 1990). On this view, it is oppressive and patriarchal conceptual frameworks (and the behaviors which they give rise to) which sanction, maintain, and perpetuate the twin dominations of women and nature. Revealing and overcoming oppressive and patriarchal conceptual frameworks as they are manifest in theories and practices regarding women and nature are important tasks of feminism, environmentalism, and environmental ethics.

A third account locates the conceptual basis in sex-gender differences, particularly in differentiated personality formation or consciousness (see Cheney 1987; Gray 1981; Leland 1983; O'Brien 1981; Salleh 1984). The claim is that female bodily experiences (e.g., of reproduction and childbearing), not female biology *per se,* situate women differently with respect to nature than men. This difference is revealed in a different consciousness in women than men; it is rooted conceptually in "paradigms that are uncritically oriented to the dominant western masculine forms of experiencing the world: the analytic, non-related, delightfully called 'objective' or 'scientific' approaches" (Salleh 1988, 130)— just the sort of value dualisms which are claimed (above) to separate and inferiorize what is historically female-gender identified. These sociopsychological factors provide a conceptual link insofar as they are embedded in different conceptualization structures and strategies (different "ways of knowing"), coping strategies and ways of relating to nature for women and men. A goal of feminism and environmental ethics, then, is to develop gender-sensitive language, theory, and practices which do not further the exploitative experiences and habits of dissociated, male-gender identified culture toward women and nature.

A fourth account draws on some of the historical connections mentioned earlier (at 1). It locates the conceptual link between feminism and the environment in the metaphors and models of mechanistic science which began during both the Enlightenment and pre-Enlightenment period (see Merchant 1980; Easlea 1981). The claim is that prior to the seventeenth century, nature was conceived on an organic model as a benevolent female, a nurturing mother; after the scientific revolution, nature was conceived on a mechanistic model as a (mere) machine, inert, dead. On both models, nature was female. The claim is that the move from the organic to the mechanistic model conceptually permitted and ethically justified the exploitation of the (female) earth, by removing the sorts of barriers to such treatment that the metaphor of nature as a living organism previously prevented. The challenge to feminists, environmentalists, and the environmental ethicists, then, is to overcome metaphors and models which feminize nature *and* naturalize women to the mutual detriment of both nature and women.

3. **Empirical and experiential.** Many feminists have documented empirical evidence linking feminism and the environment. Some point to various health and risk factors caused by the presence of low-level radiation, pesticides, toxics, and other pollutants and borne disproportionately by women and children (see Caldecott and Leland 1983; Diamond 1990; Kheel 1989; Philipose 1989; Westra, this issue). Others provide data to show that First World development policies foster practices regarding food, forests, and water which directly contribute to the inability of women to provide adequately for themselves and their families (e.g., Mies 1986; Salleh 1990; Shiva 1988; Warren 1988, 1989). Feminist animal rights scholars argue that factory farming, animal experimentation, hunting, and meat-eating are tied to patriarchal concepts and practices (Adams 1988, 1991; Collard with Contrucci 1988; Kheel 1985, 1987–88). Appeal to such empirical data are intended to document the very real, felt, lived connections between the dominations of women and nature and to motivate the need for feminist critical analysis of environmental concerns.

Some feminists cite experiential connections which honor and celebrate important cultural and spiritual ties of women and indigenous peoples to the earth (see Allen 1986, 1990; Bagby 1990; Doubiago 1989; LaChapelle 1978; *Woman of Power* 1988). Indeed documenting such connections and making them integral to the project of "feminism and the environment" is often heralded as one of the most important contributions to the creation of liberating, life-affirming, and post-patriarchal worldviews and earth-based spirituality or theology (see Christ, 1990; McDaniels 1989, 1990; Ruether 1989; Spretnak 1989a, 1990; Starhawk 1989, 1990). Appreciating these connections and understanding the "politics of women's spirituality" is viewed as an important aspect of feminism, environmentalism, and environmental ethics.

4. **Epistemological.** The various historical, conceptual, and empirical/experiential connections which have been claimed to link feminism and the environment (discussed at 1–3, above) have also motivated the need for different feminist environmental epistemologies. Typically these emerging epistemologies build on scholarship currently underway in feminist philosophy which challenges mainstream views of reason, rationality, knowledge, and the nature of the knower (see APA *Newsletter on Feminism and Philosophy* 1989; Cheney 1989a; Code 1987; Garry and Pearsall 1989; Harding and Hintikka 1983; Jaggar and Bordo 1989). Douglas Buege, for instance, argues for a feminist environmental epistemology that builds on Lorraine Code's responsibilist epistemology (Buege, 1991). As Val Plumwood suggests, if one mistakenly construes environmental philosophy as only or mainly concerned with ethics, one will neglect "a key aspect of the overall problem which is concerned with the definition of the human self as separate from nature, the connection between this and the instrumental view of nature, and broader *political* aspects of the critique of instrumentalism" (Plumwood 1991). A

feminist environmental epistemology would address these political aspects of the human/nature dichotomy.

Other feminists appeal to the Critical Theory of Horkheimer (1974), Balbus (1982) and the Frankfurt circle, claiming that "their epistemology and substantive analysis both point to a convergence of feminist and ecological concerns, anticipating the more recent arrival of ecofeminism" (Salleh 1988, 131). For those feminists, Critical Theory provides a critique of the "nature versus culture" and an epistemological structure for critiquing the relationship between the domination of women and the domination of nature (see Salleh 1988; Mills 1987, 1991).

5. **Symbolic.** Many theorists (see, e.g., *Heresies #13*; Bell 1988; Murphy 1990; Salleh 1988) explore the symbolic association and devaluation of women and nature that appears in art, literature, religion, and theology. Drawing on feminist literature (e.g., the literature of Atwood 1985; Bagby 1990; Corrigan and Hoppe 1989, 1990; Doubiago 1990; Gearhart 1979; Kolodny 1975; LeGuin 1985, 1987, 1988; Oliver 1983; Piercy 1976; Rich 1986; Silko 1987; Zahava 1988), some argue that patriarchal conceptions of nature and women have justified "a two-pronged rape and domination of the earth and the women who live on it" (Murphy 1988, 87), often using this as background for developing an ecofeminist literary theory (Murphy 1991). Others explore the potential of (eco)feminism for creating alternative languages (e.g., Daly 1978, Griffin 1978), religious/spiritual symbols (e.g., "Goddess" symbols), hypotheses (e.g., feminist-inspired interpretations of the "Gaia hypothesis"), theologies (e.g., Christ 1990; Daly 1978; Gray 1988; Ruether 1989; Spretnak 1982, 1989a; Starhawk 1989, 1990) and societies (e.g. the feminist utopias suggested by Gearhart 1979 and Piercy 1976).

Other theorists explore the symbolic connections between sexist and naturalist language, i.e., language which inferiorizes women and nonhuman nature. This may involve raising questions about whether the sex-gendered language used to describe "Mother nature" is, in Ynestra King's words, "potentially liberating or simply a rationale for the continued subordination of women (King 1981, 12; see also Griscom 1981; Ortner 1974; Roach 1991). It may involve establishing connections between the languages used to describe women, nature, and nuclear weaponry (see Adams 1988; Cohn 1989; Strange 1989). For instance, women are often described in animal terms (e.g., as cows, foxes, chicks, serpents, bitches, beavers, old bats, pussycats, cats, bird-brains, hare-brains). Nature is often described in female and sexual terms: Nature is raped, mastered, conquered, controlled, mined. Her secrets are penetrated and her womb is put into the services of the "man of science." Virgin timber is felled, cut down. Fertile soil is tilled and land that lies fallow is "barren," useless. The claim is that language which so feminizes nature and naturalizes women describes, reflects, and perpetuates the domination and inferiorization of both by failing to see the extent to which the twin dominations of women and nature (including animals) are, in fact, culturally (and not merely figuratively) analogous (Adams 1988, 61). The development of feminist theory and praxis which does not perpetuate this language and the power-over systems of domination they reinforce is, therefore, a goal of feminist environmentalism.

6. **Ethical.** Much of the philosophical literature on feminism and the environment has linked the two ethically. The claim is that the interconnections among the conceptualizations and treatment of women, animals, and (the rest of) nonhuman nature require a feminist ethical analysis and response. Minimally, the goal of feminist environmental ethics is to develop theories and practices concerning humans and the natural environment which are not male-biased and which provide a guide to action in the pre-feminist present (see Warren 1990; Warren and Cheney 1991b). Since a discussion of ethical concerns is intimately

tied with alleged theoretical connections between feminism and the environment, consider now the range of theoretical positions which have emerged.

7. **Theoretical.** The varieties of alleged connections between feminism and the environment (identified at 1-6, above) have generated different, sometimes competing, theoretical positions in all areas of feminist and environmental scholarship. Nowhere is this more evident than in the field of environmental ethics. For reasons of space and audience, the discussion of "theoretical connections" is limited here to the field of environmental ethics.

In many respects, contemporary environmental ethics reflects the range of positions in contemporary normative philosophical ethics. The latter includes traditional consequentialist (e.g., ethical egoist, utilitarian) and non-consequentialist or deontological (e.g. Kantian, rights-based, virtue-based) positions, as well as challenges to them by non-traditional (e.g., some feminist, existentialist, Marxist, Afrocentric) positions. Similarly with environmental ethics. There are consequentialist (e.g., eco-utilitarian, utilitarian-based animal liberation, land stewardship) positions that extend traditional ethical considerations to animals and the nonhuman environment. There also are non-traditional approaches (e.g., holistic Leopoldian land ethics, social ecology, deep ecology, ecological feminism). Feminists who address environmental issues can be found defending each of these sorts of positions.

However, one position stands out as being expressly committed to making visible the nature of the connections between feminism and the environment: ecological feminism. Is there, then, one ecofeminism and one ecofeminist ethic?

In each case the answer is "No." Just as there is not one feminism, there is not one ecofeminism. 'Ecological feminism' is the name of a variety of different feminist perspectives on the nature of the connections between the domination of women (and other oppressed humans) and the domination of nature. These different perspectives reflect not only different feminist perspectives (e.g., liberal, traditional Marxist, radical, socialist); they also reflect different understandings of the nature, and solution to, pressing environmental problems (see Warren 1987). By extension, there is not one ecofeminist ethic. Given the newness of ecofeminism as a theoretical position, the nature of ecofeminist ethics is still emerging. Among the most visible feminist-inspired positions are feminist animal rights positions (e.g., Adams 1988, 1991; Kheel 1985; Slicer, 1991) and feminist environmental ethics based on an ethic of care (e.g., Curtain 1991; see also R. King 1991, this issue), themes in social ecology (e.g., Y. King 1981, 1983, 1989, 1990) and themes in bioregionalism (e.g., Cheney 1989b; Plant 1990). They all recognize important connections between the indefensible treatment of women and of nature, and involve a commitment to developing ethics which are not male-biased. It remains an open question how may, which, and on what ground *any* of the various positions in environmental ethics which acknowledge such feminist concerns are ecofeminist positions.[1]

8. **Political (Praxis).** Francoise d'Eaubonne introduced the term 'ecofeminisme' in 1974 to bring attention to women's potential for bringing about an ecological revolution (1974, 213–52). Ecofeminist and other feminist concerns for women and the environment have always grown out of pressing political and practical concerns. These range from issues of health concerning women and the natural environment, to development and technology, the treatment of animals, and peace, anti-nuclear, anti-militarism activism (see Griffin 1989b; Harris and King 1989; Lahar 1991; Spretnak 1989b). The varieties of feminist theoretical perspectives on the environment are properly seen as an attempt to take seriously such grassroots activism and political concerns by developing analyses of domination which explain, clarify, and guide that

praxis (see *The Ecofeminist Newsletter*; Harris and King 1989; Y. King 1981, 1983, 1989, 1990; Spretnak 1989b; Warren 1991).

PHILOSOPHICAL IMPORTANCE OF THE LITERATURE CONNECTING FEMINISM AND THE ENVIRONMENT

In the preceding I have identified eight sorts of connections between feminism and the environment in the literature. I have indicated why and how, if indeed there are these connections, feminism, environmentalism, and environmental ethics will need to take them seriously. What are some of the implications of these connections for mainstream philosophy? I suggest a few here.

The conceptual links (given above at 2) suggest that philosophical conceptions of the self, knowledge and the "knower," reason and rationality, objectivity, and "nature versus culture"— mainstay philosophical notions in ethics, epistemology, metaphysics, philosophy of science, history of philosophy, political philosophy—will need to be reconceived. The value dualisms which seem to pervade the western philosophical tradition since the early Greeks (e.g., reason/emotion, mind/body, culture/nature, human/nature) and the historical sex-gendered association of women with emotion, body, and nature, will need to be examined for male-gender bias.

The historical and empirical links (given at 1 and 3, above) suggest that social scientific data on women and the environment is relevant to theoretical undertakings in many areas of philosophy. For example, in ethics, this data on raises issues of anthro-

pocentric and androcentric bias. Can mainstream normative ethical theories generate an environmental ethic which is not male biased? In epistemology, data on the "indigenous technical knowledge" (see Warren 1988) of women who globally constitute the main agricultural production force (e.g., at least 80% of the farmers in Africa are women) raises issues about women's "epistemic privilege" about farming and forestry (see Warren 1988). If there is such privilege, does it generate the need for "feminist standpoint epistemologies" (see Garry and Pearsall 1989; Harding 1986; Harding and Hintikka 1983; Jaggar and Bordo 1989)? In metaphysics, data of the cross-cultural variability of women-nature connections raises issues about the concept of nature and the nature/cultural dichotomy. Is "nature" a given, a cross-cultural constant that stands in contrast to socially evolving and created "culture"? Or is nature, like culture, a social construct? That is, even if there really are material trees, rivers, and ecosystems, does the way nature is conceived and theorized about reflect historical, socioeconomic factors in much the same way that, according to many feminists, conceptions and theories about "humans and "human nature" do? In political philosophy, data about the inferior standards of living of women globally raises issues about political theories and theorizing. What roles do unequal distributions of power and privilege play in the maintenance of systems of domination over both women and nature? How do they affect the content and methodology of political theories and theorizing? In the history of philosophy, data on the historical inferiorization and associations of women and nature raises issues about and the philosophical theories advanced in any given time period. Do these theories contain biases against women and nature which bear on the substantive content of the theories themselves? In philosophy of science, particularly philosophy of biology, such data raises issues about the relationships between feminism and science, particularly the science of ecology. As Carolyn Merchant asks, "Is there a set of assumptions basic to the science of ecology that also holds implications for the status of women? Is there an ecological ethic that is also a feminist ethic?" (Merchant 1985, 229). Are there important parallels between contemporary feminist environmental ethics and ecosystems ecology which suggest ways in which they are engaged in mutually supportive projects (see Y. King 1989; Warren and Cheney 1991)? These are the sort of questions raised by a philosophical look at the significance of issues concerning "feminism and the environment."

CONCLUSION

In this essay I have identified some of the alleged connections between "feminism and the environment" and discussed some of the issues these connections raise for feminism, environmentalism, environmental ethics, and mainstream philosophy. Presumably, taking these issues seriously involves revising the courses we teach (see Adams, this issue) and rethinking much of our scholarship. As with any attempt to incorporate the scholarship on women and feminism into our curricula and scholarship, such revising projects may be quite challeng-

ing. With regard to feminism and the environment, they also may be vital—not only for women, animals, and planet Earth, but for the development of worldviews and practices which are ecologically responsible and socially just for us all.

NOTES

1. Indeed, just what the similarities and differences are between ecological feminism and "deep ecology," "social ecology," and "animal rights" positions in environmental ethics is an issue which receives considerable scholarly attention, particularly in the leading journal in the field, *Environmental Ethics*. The so-called debate between ecofeminism and deep ecology (the position advocated by Bill Devall and George Sessions 1985, Arne Naess 1973, 1985, 1986 and Warwick Fox 1985, 1989, to name a few) has probably received the most attention. The "debate" between them will undoubtedly continue. In his preface to the Spring 1989 issue of *Environmental Ethics* marking the beginning of the journal's second decade, editor Eugene C. Hargrove committed the journal to providing a forum for that debate:

   In the coming decade the journal can be expected to chart some new territory. Much attention is currently being given to deep ecology and ecofeminism and the various conflicts between the two, both as movements and as philosophies. Because deep ecologists and ecofeminists are as yet not even completely in agreement about what they are disagreeing about, this debate can be expected to be rather lengthy (1989, 3).

33

Surfing the Third Wave

A Dialogue Between Two Third Wave Feminists

(1997)

Rita Alfonso and Jo Trigilio

As third wave feminist philosophers attending graduate schools in different parts of the country, we decided to use our e-mail discussion as the format for presenting our thinking on the subject of third wave feminism. Our dialogue takes us through the subjects of postmodernism, the relationship between theory and practice, the generation gap, and the power relations associated with feminist philosophy as an established part of the academy.

From: Jo Trigilio
(trigilio@oregon.uoregon.edu)
To: Rita Alfonso
(dralfonso@cc.memphis.edu)
Subject: Catching the third wave

I am excited by our decision to write a dialogue through e-mail for the special issue of *Hypatia* on third wave feminism. I know that we did not decide whether we should eventually take it out of dialogue form and transform it into a collaborative essay, but I think we should keep its original form as an e-mail dialogue. I think that as third wavers, it is important for us to recognize and give value to forms of feminist philosophy that fall outside the boundaries of traditional academic philosophy. I also think that the very possibility of having a philosophical conversation through electronic mail—instant communication through computers and phone lines—will play a role in the development of feminist thinking in our generation. The Internet opens new lines of communication and provides a new kind of support for young academic feminists. Many graduate students cannot afford to go to feminist conferences and SWIP (Society for Women in Philosophy) meetings. Being able to communicate with feminist philosopher friends in different parts of the country helps alleviate potential feelings of isolation.

From: Rita Alfonso
(dralfonso@cc.memphis.edu)
To: Jo Trigilio
(trigilio@oregon.uoregon.edu)
Subject: Re: Catching the third wave

There are certain advantages to the new communication media, that is for sure. For example, I usually have a wide variety of conversations simultaneously over the Internet, which is difficult to manage in a

Alfonso and Trigilio,"Surfing the Third Wave: A Dialogue Between Two Third Wave Feminists." *Hypatia* 12, no. 3: 7–17.

physical setting like a classroom. In this way, I am exposed to many, and more diverse, points of view. I like to think that I bring some of these perspectives into the classroom with me, and that this alters the discussions in that physical space. E-mail has been not only personally but also professionally enriching. It has been instrumental to my gaining access to everything from information on graduate philosophy programs that are inclusive of feminist perspectives to feminist bibliographies, to conference announcements. The Internet can be a powerful tool for the dissemination of information because of its inexpensiveness and speed; and it is likely to play a central role in the organization and deployment of future feminist campaigns. There are also difficulties related to a virtual reality forum; sustaining a substantial discussion in a virtual space is a tricky business, I think because a lack of physical proximity and temporal linearity tends to fragment the continuity of a virtual conversation. By using the e-mail format for a philosophical dialogue, we are certainly pushing against the limits of the whats and the hows not only of philosophy, but also of the dialogue form.

From: Jo Trigilio
(trigilio@oregon.uoregon.edu)
To: Rita Alfonso
(dralfonso@cc.memphis.edu)
Subject: What third wave?

Maybe we should begin our dialogue by situating ourselves as third wave feminists. I'm curious about what it means for you to be a third wave feminist because, to be honest, I have trouble understanding the construction of a third wave. First wave and second wave feminisms are marked by large, distinct activist movements. A great deal of first wave feminism was concerned with women's suffrage, and second wave feminism with the radical reconstruction or elimination of sex roles and the struggle for equal rights. No large, distinctive activist feminist movement seems to be occurring, out

of which a third wave of feminism is rising. Third wave feminism seems to be more of an academic construction, used to mark the development of postmodernist critiques of second wave feminism. I cannot help feeling that one must be a postmodernist to be a third waver.

I came to feminism in the mid-1980s as a radical interested in activism. As someone who is critical of certain aspects of second wave feminism, but even more critical of postmodernism, I feel as if I am standing on the beach with my surfboard, too late to catch the peak of the second wave and unwilling to conform to the rules of pack riding the third.

From: Rita Alfonso
(dralfonso@cc.memphis.edu)
To: Jo Trigilio
(trigilio@oregon.uoregon.edu)
Subject: Re: What third wave?

I certainly do not hold either that you have to be a postmodernist—whatever the meaning du jour for this term may be—in order to identify as a third wave feminist, or that not being hip to a postmodernist scene places you squarely outside the third wave camp. Consider the critiques of women of color, which do not fall neatly into the second or the third wave. Although they share feminist commitments to combat the oppression of women, they have taken issue with the construction of "woman" as white-centered. A better example may be found with the grassroots AIDS activist working under the rubric of "Queer Nation" (Stein 1993). These are two examples of feminist positions that are not necessarily postmodernist nor second wave; notice also that the latter example is more clearly identifiable as a third wave position. This leads me to suspect that we are construing both waves of feminism too narrowly; but in any case, the two positions—postmodernism and third wave feminism—are not equatable.

I do think there are various posts from which to measure the distances between second and first wave feminisms. The most obvious post is a generational one, where the differences between these are, correspondingly, the differences between the baby boomer generation and the so-called generation X—which roughly works out to be those who were born after the 1960s and those who came of age during the Reagan administration (Coupland 1991; Howe and Strauss 1993). I strongly hold that the experiences that led me to identify as a feminist were significantly different from those that inspired the previous generation (Findlen 1995, xi). I also wish to acknowledge, however, that there are women of my age group who identify with the struggles of the second wave of feminists in a straightforward manner, and there are women of the baby boomer generation who are acutely aware of the experiences and issues informing a third wave of feminism.

Modifying the perhaps simplistic account of a generation gap in feminism is notion of a "political generation," understood as "a group of people (not necessarily of the same age) that experiences shared formative social conditions at approximately the same point in their lives, and that holds a common interpretive framework shaped by historical circumstances" (Whittier 1995, 180). I believe that this theory of "political generations" can account for subject positions across historical waves of feminism, as well as for the existence of two relatively distinct waves of feminism; for these reasons, it can help us measure the differences between a third and a second wave of feminism.

From: Jo Trigilio
(trigilio@oregon.uoregon.edu)
To: Rita Alfonso
(dralfonso@cc.memphis.edu)
Subject: Can I surf without a surfboard?

This idea of a "political generation" is a useful alternative to simplistic accounts of a generation gap; but in using it, we should ask which groups of people are empowered to give voice to their concerns. I have to wonder what this emerging discourse about third wave feminism means for feminist philosophy. I am concerned that third wave feminism may be nothing more than academic discourse about discourse, instead of thinking that arises out of and is closely associated with the social and political problems ordinary women face. The reason I bring this up is that I fear that third wave feminism, because it is not arising from a mass-based social movement, may be even less class-conscious than much second wave feminism has been. More and more, the problems feminist thinkers take up are problems that arise out of academic discourses. They are not the socio-political problems ordinary women of different races, classes, sexualities, ethnicities face in their everyday lives. As I see it, feminist philosophy has to play its part in promoting feminist change, and this change cannot be limited to the world of academic philosophy. Feminist philosophers are responsible to all aspects of feminism. In selecting the kind of work they do, feminist philosophers should not ask, "What seems most interesting to me?" but instead, "What needs to be done?" U.S. feminists need theories about race, class, poverty, eating disorders, families, homophobia, work—theories they can "hold in their hands" and use and share easily. If I had to prescribe something for feminist philosophy, it would be pragmatism. I was very excited about the special issue of *Hypatia* devoted to feminism and pragmatism. That a number of feminist philosophers are interested in pragmatism gives me a sense of hope.

I also have serious concerns about the difficult, specialized, jargonistic language in which much recent feminist philosophy is being presented. These theories are accessible only to the most highly educated. I would like to think it ironic that theories about oppression are being presented in a manner that the majority of those who are oppressed cannot understand. But finding it ironic would not adequately convey the gravity of the problem this poses. This type of language perpetuates elitist power relations associated with who gets to speak about oppression. Every time I bring this up, people treat me as if I am so pedestrian that I cannot understand the significance of the insights of these theories, as if form and content were separable. I do not think feminist philosophers have seriously addressed the problem of power relations and of who is empowered to speak, write, and publish about oppression in our country. I find it beyond ironic that this type of specialized theorizing about oppression is emerging at the very same time that the gap between the rich and the poor has widened in the United States, that higher education is seriously suffering financially, and that it has become significantly more difficult for people from low-income families to go to college. Feminist theory is becoming the product of the privileged few who hold academic positions, a product to which non-academics do not have access.

From: Rita Alfonso
(dralfonso@cc.memphis.edu)
To: Jo Trigilio
(trigilio@oregon.uoregon.edu)
Subject: Surfing the third wave

Since I came to identify as a feminist while in the academy, one of the experiences that has strongly marked my own feminism is that of formally being taught about feminism by second wave feminists in an academic environment. I belong to the first generation to have the good fortune to learn, in an academic setting, from the lived experiences of women, and to have female role models in nearly all the traditionally male-dominated fields; but because the medium shapes the message to some extent, I am convinced that acquiring a feminist consciousness has

been different for those of us who encountered feminism in academe. The feminist theories and texts with which we are presented in the academy necessarily fall short of the experiences that originally animated them—the consciousness-raising experiences that led radical and liberal women of the late 1960s and early 1970s to identify as feminist, at a time when political activism provided the impetus and the focus for feminist theorizing. Although this has been my experience, and it is not an uncommon one, I recognize that it is not at all a universal one.

While it may seem that what characterizes my "political generation" is a general lack of cohesiveness or continuity, as well as a lack of political conviction in the face of a more politically conservative environment, we should remember that this is with respect to the liberalism of the 1960s. As a consequence of changed political conditions, the goals and strategies that some third wave feminists elect do not always coincide with the goals and strategies associated with the second wave of feminism; sometimes they even go against some perceived second wave feminist positions. Again, even if third wave feminists perform their feminism in ways that may, in many cases, be continuous with second wave feminism, these performances might not even register as feminist performances on a traditional, liberal feminist scale.

From: Jo Trigilio
(trigilio@oregon.uoregon.edu)
To: Rita Alfonso
(dralfonso@cc.memphis.edu)
Subject: Sexy sexuality

I went to a dyke punk show the other night. Tribe 8 was one of the bands. It made me seriously consider the differences between second and third wave feminists. Their antics most likely would have seemed offensive and male-identified to feminists twenty years ago. Two members of the band are hard core butches, one is a sexy femme complete with a low-cut shirt, and the lead singer performed bare-breasted and with a big black dildo hanging out of her pants zipper. She cut it off with a giant knife and flung it into the audience during the second to last song.

All of this led me to think about feminist theorizing about sexuality. Second wave feminism has been marked by strands that appear prudish. For example, some early radical feminist groups such as the Feminists and Cell 16, believed that all sexual relations were oppressive (Echols 1989, 173–74). By the 1980s, huge debates about pornograpy, butch-femme and s/m had arisen (Vance 1989). These tensions persist to this day. Tribe 8 served to remind me that many younger lesbians who are feminists are faced with the task of reconciling feminism with sexuality centered around neo-butch-femme or s/m (Nestle 1992; Morgan 1993). Second wave feminism seems to say no to these forms of sexuality. It seems that second wave feminism has put up more restrictions than green lights when it comes to sexuality. This is not to say that it has not seriously challenged the institution of compulsory heterosexuality and sex defined as male-centered intercourse. These challenges have been liberatory, but more needs to be done. Second wave feminism has not been successful at producing new, interesting forms of sexuality. It has, in part, relied on popular essentialist notions of sexuality as an empowering force within, as per Helene Cixous and Audre Lorde.

On the other hand, postmodernism seems to say yes indiscriminately to all forms of "disruptive" sexuality. By doing so, it sanctions the production of new sexualities without providing coherent political strategies through which to evaluate them. Madonna is a good example of this. She is constantly changing identities, resisting definition, transgressing boundaries; but it is not clear that her disruptions constitute positive feminist change. My point is that I do not think that second wave feminism has done a very good job of offering viable redefinitions of sexuality. This leaves young feminists either alienated, confused, or in the sex shop, spending lots of money on overpriced sex toys.

From: Rita Alfonso
(dralfonso@cc.memphis.edu)
To: Jo Trigilio
(trigilio@oregon.uoregon.edu)
Subject: Riot grrrls

The antics of Tribe 8 remind me of the riot grrrl movement, which has intrigued me since the early 1990s. From what I have gathered, riot grrrls was originally the name of an all-girl punk rock band based in Olympia, Washington. They quickly disbanded, but they lent their name to a surge, around 1991, of all-girl bands in Olympia and Seattle. What was special about the riot grrrls was their antics and strategies, which reminded me of those I have read were used by the early radical feminists, the Redstockings (Redstockings 1975). For example, riot grrrls started up what they called "rags," which were magazines written and published on personal computers, and distributed both electronically and through a more conventional grassroots operation. These "rags" were devoted to the expression (from poems and short stories, to letters and sketches) of dissatisfaction with the status quo, heterosexual arrangement between the sexes. The riot grrrls conducted their own versions of consciousness-raising sessions, according to Amy Raphael, who has researched and formally written about them (Raphael 1994, xxvii). Similarly, Kathie Sarachild writes that the first thing which the Redstockings did as a group was to put out a journal devoted to their common experiences as women (Sarachild 1975, 147).

Among the riot grrrls antics was dressing up in baby doll dresses, usually worn with combat boots, colorful but torn stockings, and any number of tiny plastic hair barrettes, but writing "slut" on their bodies to preempt society's judgment of them. I interpret these antics as an intentional "putting on" of the girlishness and innocence preserved with the societal ideal of femininity, (remembering that these were post-pubescent women) while simultaneously writing over and naming the performance of femininity as such, revealing femininity to be exactly its opposite—sluttishness. What this performance speaks to is the essential sameness of these two opposite poles of femininity; and it is a play on the ancient virgin/whore dichotomy. Unlike the Redstockings, who protested by throwing items used in the oppression of women into the "freedom trashcan" at the 1968 Miss America Beauty Pageant, the riot grrrls donned and reclaimed, in a perverse manner, the accoutrements of femininity. They made a display of the power that these accoutrements brought to them, and simultaneously mocked this power through parody. More than about performing music, the riot grrrls were about performing their gender.

What is unfortunate about the riot grrrls, though is that they never really managed to gain momentum because they were quickly co-opted and merchandised. The surge of all-girl bands—including Bikini Kill, 7 Year Bitch, and best known of all, Hole—had been incorporated into the Seattle grunge scene by 1993. But I think that their example still speaks to the great difficulties of sustaining a feminist movement today. "All" the Redstockings did to catch the attention of the national and international media, according to Sarachild herself, was to throw some items representing "femininity" into a trashcan, while this same act today, I should think might only serve as a ten-second sound bite (Sarachild 1975, 147). The example of the riot grrrls also invokes a way of performing feminism that pushes against the conceptual boundaries of the Anglo-American, liberal feminist tradition. This issue of femininity

provides one of the notable differences between second and third wave feminists. Whether it makes sense or not, young women today seem to be experiencing femininity and reacting to its exhortations in another way—they seem to be reclaiming it, taking it on—in contrast with the predominant androgyny of the earlier wave. Beyond the rise of political conservatism, this might be a plausible explanation for the increasing popularity not only of the work of the feminist Carol Gilligan and her care-based ethics, but also of the theorists of sexual difference—Irigaray, Cixous, and Kristeva—in the United States.

From: Jo Trigilio
(trigilio@oregon.uoregon.edu)
To: Rita Alfonso
(dralfonso@cc.memphis.edu)
Subject: Surfing freestyle

How to understand and situate femininity has been a subject that has haunted second wave feminism. Second wave feminists faced the difficult task of saying that women are not naturally feminine but socialized to be feminine, while at the same time trying to give value to feminine traits. They have broken ground for third wave feminists to redefine femininity, to perform it differently. But this will be no easy task for third wave feminists, because we have to contend with new forms of oppressive and objectifying femininity. The normalization of cosmetic surgery—of breast implants, facial reconstruction, and liposuction in particular—is creating new racist, classist, thin-centered, sexually objectifying forms of femininity. Femininity is no longer just about make-up and high heels. It is now being constructed surgically. Perhaps the normalization of cosmetic surgery should be taken as an indication that second wave feminism has in some way failed to provide viable practices and redefinitions of appearance. Second wave feminism has been astoundingly successful in changing socio-political structures and attitudes associated with sexual assault, sexual harassment, and domestic violence. Public consciousness has been transformed with regard to these issues. This is not the case with appearance.

As I see it, feminist philosophy has only begun its work. Being an academic feminist philosopher comes with a price. Surviving in academic philosophy involves proving to the boys that you can "do" philosophy. As a result, I fear that different kinds of philosophizing are not being facilitated. Academic philosophy in general suffers from having replaced the love of wisdom with the love of linearity and the love of citing other academic philosophers. Feminist philosophy has not done enough to challenge the dominant form of philosophy as linear and rationalistic. While feminist philosophy, in just a short time, has been amazingly successful at challenging the content of Western philosophy, it has not done much by way of challenging its form. Nonlinear writing, imbued with passion and emotion, has not found its way into the mainstream of feminist philosophy. When power relations have changed to the extent that feminists no longer have to prove they can "do" philosophy in the dominant, traditional form, radical fundamental change can take place. As it is, established feminist philosophers are still training feminist students to prove that they can "do" philosophy the traditional academic way. There are other ways of "doing" philosophy: storytelling, narratives, dialogues, aphorisms, to name a few. These forms of philosophizing are better suited for conveying emotion, passion, and wonder. They also make philosophy potentially more accessible to non-philosophers and non-academics.

I think feminist philosophers have not yet learned the art of freestyle thinking. I want to tell a story to illustrate this point. I studied calligraphy intensively for months with a very good but very strict teacher. I spent hours on hours drawing carefully measured guidelines for the letters and then making perfectly uniform, beautiful letters. The calligraphy society was impressed by my work, and accepted it into a show. To my surprise, my calligraphy teacher told me after the show that I was too constrained, that I needed to be freer, to let go. This made me feel both anxious and confused. It made me feel anxious because the thought of drawing outside the lines was scary. Staying within the lines was safe—not necessarily easy, but familiar. It confused me because the very teacher who seemed to have demanded that I stay within the lines, was telling me something "else." To draw outside the lines? To not have lines? To use different kinds of guidelines? I have come to realize that what she was saying was that the real art lies not in mastering how to make beautiful letters within the lines but in using what you learn from drawing within the lines to do something "else."

This is the lesson feminist philosophers have not yet learned. We are all very busy drawing within the lines of different traditions and schools of thought. The "liberties" we take are within the realm of safety, like taking the serifs of a different character set and putting them on the character set with which we are familiar.

Anthropology

Anthropology is the scientific study of human beings in their physical and social aspects. Physical anthropologists study human origins and evolution through an examination of fossil remains, while cultural anthropologists study the development of human society and culture. Scholars in this field pose essential questions about what makes us human: what aspects of our behavior are culturally constructed and what aspects biologically based, and why institutions, customs, and beliefs reflect so much diversity across time and cultures. These questions have proven extremely tantalizing to feminist scholars who also seek answers about the power of culture to shape individuals. In the first selection, Sally Slocum offers a compelling critique of male bias in the field. Her work illustrates the power of a feminist perspective to uncover methodological and interpretive problems that can distort and corrupt theory building. Arguing for the centrality of the mother-infant relationship, Slocum reinterprets archeological evidence and suggests a version of evolution in which hunting does not play a pivotal role. Next, Deborah A. Gordon explores the development of and implications for feminist ethnography. Ethnographers are anthropologists who study a particular group of living people, exploring how they interact, what they believe, and what they do. Gordon provides an example of an innovative critical literacy project that had a profound impact on both the anthropologists and the "subjects" they were studying. Finally, Mary Daly provides a radical feminist critique of anthropology as a discipline. She contends that the scholarly objectivity claimed by this "science" merely masks an agenda of misogyny. Daly offers a serious challenge to traditional scholarly methods, standards, and goals, which reflects one facet of the many voices within Women's Studies.

Critical Thinking Questions

1. Which version of human evolution sounds more plausible or logical to you—the traditional one or Slocum's feminist reconstruction?
2. Gordon states that in the El Barrio literacy project, anthropologists considered themselves as participant witnesses rather than observers or guides. What does she mean by this, and would Daly approve of such an arrangement?

3. Do the terms "applied anthropology" or "advocacy anthropology" seem fundamentally contradictory?
4. Why is it important to distinguish functional literacy from critical literacy? In what ways does literacy work to shape women's identities?
5. In what ways were the goals of the El Barrio project similar to the goals of the Mississippi Freedom Schools?
6. To what extent can Daly's position be interpreted as ethnocentric as well as feminist?
7. Are you comfortable with Daly's unabashed political advocacy of victims and her rejection of objectivity?

34

Woman the Gatherer
Male Bias in Anthropology
(1975)

Sally Slocum

The perspective of women is, in many ways, equally foreign to an anthropology that has been developed and pursued primarily by males. There is a strong male bias in the questions asked, and the interpretations given. This bias has hindered the full development of our discipline as "the study of the human animal" (I don't want to call it "the study of man" for reasons that will become evident). I am going to demonstrate the Western male bias by reexamining the matter of evolution of Homo sapiens from our nonhuman primate ancestors. In particular, the concept of "Man the Hunter" as developed by Sherwood Washburn and C. Lancaster (1968) and others is my focus. This critique is offered in hopes of transcending the male bias that limits our knowledge by limiting the questions we ask.

Though male bias could be shown in other areas, hominid evolution is particularly convenient for my purpose because it involves speculations and inferences from a rather small

amount of data. In such a case, hidden assumptions and premises that lie behind the speculations and inferences are more easily demonstrated. Male bias exists not only in the ways in which the scanty data are interpreted, but in the very language used. All too often the word "man" is used in such an ambiguous fashion that it is impossible to decide whether it refers to males or to the human species in general, including both males and females. In fact, one frequently is led to suspect that in the minds of many anthropologists, "man," supposedly meaning the human species, is actually synonymous with "males."

This ambiguous use of language is particularly evident in the writing that surrounds the concept of Man the Hunter. Washburn and Lancaster make it clear that it is specifically males who hunt, that hunting is much more than simply an economic activity, and that most of the characteristics which we think of as specifically

Slocum, Sally, "Woman the Gatherer: Male Bias in Anthropology." In *Toward an Anthropology of Women*, edited by Rayna Reiter. New York: Monthly Review Press. Reprinted by permission of Monthly Review Foundation.

human can be causally related to hunting. They tell us that hunting is a whole pattern of activity and way of life: "The biology, psychology, and customs that separate us from the apes—all these we owe to the hunters of time past" (1968:303). If this line of reasoning is followed to its logical conclusion, one must agree with Jane Kephart when she says:

> Since only males hunt, and the psychology of the species was set by hunting, we are forced to conclude that females are scarcely human, that is, do not have built-in the basic psychology of the species: to kill and hunt and ultimately to kill others of the same species. The argument implies built-in aggression in human males, as well as the assumed passivity of human females and their exclusion from the mainstream of human development. (1970:5)

To support their argument that hunting is important to human males, Washburn and Lancaster point to the fact that many modern males still hunt, though it is no longer economically necessary. I could point out that many modern males play golf, play the violin, or tend gardens: these, as well as hunting, are things their culture teaches them. Using a "survival" as evidence to demonstrate an important fact of cultural evolution can be accorded no more validity when proposed by a modern anthropologist than when proposed by Tylor.

Regardless of its status as a survival, hunting, by implication as well as direct statement, is pictured as a male activity to the exclusion of females. This activity, on which we are told depends the psychology, biology, and customs of our species, is strictly male. A theory that leaves out half the human species is unbalanced. The theory of Man the Hunter is not only unbalanced; it leads to the conclusion that the basic human adaptation was the desire of males to hunt and kill. This not only gives too much importance to aggression, which is after all only one factor of human life, but it derives culture from killing. I am going to suggest a less biased reading of the evidence, which gives a more valid and logical picture of human evolution, and at the same time a more hopeful one. First I will note the evidence, discuss the more traditional reading of it, and then offer an alternative reconstruction.

The data we have to work from are a combination of fossil and archeological materials, knowledge of living nonhuman primates, and knowledge of living humans. Since we assume that the protohominid ancestors of Homo sapiens developed in a continuous fashion from a base of characteristics similar to those of living nonhuman primates, the most important facts seem to be the ways in which humans differ from nonhuman primates, and the ways in which we are similar. The differences are as follows: longer gestation period; more difficult birth; neoteny, in that human infants are less well developed at birth; long period of infant dependency; absence of body hair; year-round sexual receptivity of females, resulting in the possibility of bearing a second infant while the first is still at the breast or still dependent; erect bipedalism; possession of a large and complex brain that makes possible the creation of elaborate symbolic systems, languages, and cultures, and also results in most behavior being under cortical control; food sharing; and finally, living in families. (For the purposes of this paper I define families as follows: a situation where each individual has defined responsibilities and obligations to a specific set of others of both sexes and various ages. I use this definition because, among humans, the family is a *social* unit, regardless of any biological or genetic relationship which may or may not exist among its members.)

In addition to the many well-known close physiological resemblances, we share with nonhuman primates the following characteristics: living in social groups; close mother-infant bonds; affectional relationships; a large capacity for learning and a related paucity of innate behaviors; ability to take part in dominance hierarchies; a rather complex nonsymbolic communication system which can handle with considerable subtlety such information as the mood and emotional state of the individual, and the attitude and status of each individual toward the other members of the social group.

The fossil and archeological evidence consists of various bones labeled Ramapithecus, Australopithecus, Homo habilis, Homo erectus, etc.; and artifacts such as stone tools representing various cultural traditions, evidence of use of fire, etc. From this evidence we can make reasonable inferences about diet, posture and locomotion, and changes in the brain as shown by increased cranial capacity, ability to make tools, and other evidences of cultural creation. Since we assume that complexity of material culture requires language, we infer the beginnings of language somewhere between Australopithecus and Homo erectus.

Given this data, the speculative reconstruction begins. As I was taught

anthropology, the story goes something like this. Obscure selection pressures pushed the protohominid in the direction of erect bipedalism— perhaps the advantages of freeing the hands for food carrying or for tool use. Freeing the hands allowed more manipulation of the environment in the direction of tools for gathering and hunting food. Through a hand-eye-brain feedback process, coordination, efficiency, and skill were increased. The new behavior was adaptive, and selection pressure pushed the protohominid further along the same lines of development. Diet changed as the increase in skill allowed the addition of more animal protein. Larger brains were selected for, making possible transmission of information concerning tool making, and organizing cooperative hunting. It is assumed that as increased brain size was selected for, so also was neoteny—immaturity of infants at birth with a corresponding increase in their period of dependency, allowing more time for learning at the same time as this learning became necessary through the further reduction of instinctual behaviors and their replacement by symbolically invented ones.

Here is where one may discover a large logical gap. From the difficult-to-explain beginning trends toward neoteny and increased brain size, the story jumps to Man the Hunter. The statement is made that the females were more burdened with dependent infants and could not follow the rigorous hunt. Therefore they stayed at a "home base," gathering what food they could, while the males developed cooperative hunting techniques, increased their communicative and organizational skills through hunting, and brought the meat back to the dependent females and young. Incest prohibitions, marriage, and the family (so the story goes) grew out of the need to eliminate competition between males for females. A pattern developed of a male hunter becoming the main support of "his" dependent females and young (in other words, the development of the nuclear family for no apparent reason). Thus the peculiarly human social and emotional bonds can be traced to the hunter bringing back the food to share. Hunting, according to Washburn and Lancaster, involved "cooperation among males, planning, knowledge of many species and large areas, and technical skill" (1968:296). They even profess to discover the beginnings of art in the weapons of the hunter. They point out that the symmetrical Acheulian biface tools are the earliest beautiful man-made objects. Though we don't know what these tools were used for, they argue somewhat tautologically that the symmetry indicates they may have been swung, because symmetry only makes a difference when irregularities might lead to deviations in the line of flight. "It may well be that it was the attempt to produce beautiful, symmetrical objects" (1968:298).

So, while the males were out hunting, developing all their skills, learning to cooperate, inventing language, inventing art, creating tools and weapons, the poor dependent females were sitting back at the home base having one child after another (many of them dying in the process), and waiting for the males to bring home the bacon. While this reconstruction is certainly ingenious, it gives one the decided impression that only half the species—the male half— did any evolving. In addition to containing a number of logical gaps, the

argument becomes somewhat doubtful in the light of modern knowledge of genetics and primate behavior.

The skills usually spoken of as being necessary to, or developed through, hunting are things like coordination, endurance, good vision, and the ability to plan, communicate, and cooperate. I have heard of no evidence to indicate that these skills are either carried on the Y chromosome, or are triggered into existence by the influence of the Y chromosome. In fact, on just about any test we can design (psychological, aptitude, intelligence, etc.) males and females score just about the same. The variation is on an individual, not a sex, basis.

Every human individual gets half its genes from a male and half from a female; genes sort randomly. It is possible for a female to end up with all her genes from male ancestors, and for a male to end up with all his genes from female ancestors. The logic of the hunting argument would have us believe that all the selection pressure was on the males, leaving the females simply as drags on the species. The rapid increase in brain size and complexity was thus due entirely to half the species; the main function of the female half was to suffer and die in the attempt to give birth to their large-brained male infants. An unbiased reading of the evidence indicates there was selection pressure on both sexes, and that hunting was not in fact the basic adaptation of the species from which flowed all the traits we think of as specifically human. Hunting does not deserve the primary place it has been given in the reconstruction of human evolution, as I will demonstrate by offering the following alternate version.

Picture the primate band: each individual gathers its own food, and the major enduring relationship is the mother-infant bond. It is in similar circumstances that we imagine the evolving protohominids. We don't know what started them in the direction of neoteny and increased brain size, but once begun the trends would prove adaptive. To explain the shift from the primate individual gathering to human food sharing, we cannot simply jump to hunting. Hunting cannot explain its own origin. It is much more logical to assume that as the period of infant dependency began to lengthen, *the mothers would begin to increase the scope of their gathering to provide food for their still-dependent infants*. The already strong primate mother-infant bond would begin to extend over a longer time period, increasing the depth and scope of social relationships, and giving rise to the first sharing of food.

It is an example of male bias to picture these females with young as totally or even mainly dependent on males for food. Among modern hunter-gatherers, even in the marginal environments where most live, the females can usually gather enough to support themselves and their families. In these groups gathering provides the major portion of the diet, and there is no reason to assume that this was not also the case in the Pliocene or early Pleistocene. In the modern groups women and children both gather and hunt small animals, though they usually do not go on the longer hunts. So, we can assume a group of evolving protohominids, gathering and perhaps beginning to hunt small animals, with the mothers gathering quite efficiently both for themselves and for their offspring.

It is equally biased, and quite unreasonable, to assume an early or rapid development of a pattern in which one male was responsible for "his" female(s) and young. In most primate groups when a female comes into estrus she initiates coitus or signals her readiness by presenting. The idea that a male would have much voice in "choosing" a female, or maintain any sort of individual, long-term control over her or her offspring, is surely a modern invention which could have had no place in early hominid life. (Sexual control over females through rape or the threat of rape seems to be a modern human invention. Primate females are not raped because they are willing throughout estrus, and primate males appear not to attempt coitus at other times, regardless of physiological ability.) In fact, there seems to me no reason for suggesting the development of male-female adult pair-bonding until much later. Long-term monogamy, is a fairly rare pattern even among modern humans—I think it is a peculiarly Western male bias to suppose its existence in protohuman society. An argument has been made (by Morris, 1967, and others) that traces the development of male-female pair-bonding to the shift of sexual characteristics to the front of the body, the importance of the face in communication, and the development of face-to-face coitus. This argument is insufficient in the first place because of the assumption that face-to-face coitus is the "normal," "natural," or even the most common position among humans (historical evidence casts grave doubt on this assumption). It is much more probable that the coitus position was invented *after* pair-bonding had developed for other reasons.

Rather than adult male-female sexual pairs, a temporary consort-type relationship is much more logical in hominid evolution. It is even a more accurate description of the modern human pattern: the most dominant males (chief, headman, brave warrior, good hunter, etc.), mate with the most dominant females (in estrus, young and beautiful, fertile, rich, etc.), for varying periods of time. Changing sexual partners is frequent and common. We have no way of knowing when females began to be fertile year-round, but this change is not a necessary condition for the development of families. We need not bring in any notion of paternity, or the development of male-female pairs, or any sort of marriage in order to account for either families or food sharing.

The lengthening period of infant dependency would have strengthened and deepened the mother-infant bond; the earliest families would have consisted of *females and their children*. In such groups, over time, the sibling bond would have increased in importance also. The most universal, and presumably oldest, form of incest prohibition is between mother and son. There are indications of such avoidance even among modern monkeys. It could develop logically from the mother-children family: as the period of infant dependency lengthened, and the age of sexual maturity advanced, a mother might no longer be capable of childbearing when her son reached maturity. Another factor which may have operated is the situation found in many primates today where only the most dominant males have access to fertile females. Thus a young son, even after reaching sexual maturity, would still have to spend time working his way up the male hierarchy before gaining access to females. The length of time it would take him increases the possibility that his mother would no longer be fertile.

Food sharing and the family developed from the mother-infant bond. The techniques of hunting large animals were probably much later developments, after the mother-children family pattern was established. When hunting did begin, and the adult males brought back food to share, the most likely recipients would be first their mothers, and second their siblings. In other words, a hunter would share food *not* with a wife or sexual partner, but with those who had shared food with him: his mother and siblings.

It is frequently suggested or implied that the first tools were, in fact, the weapons of the hunters. Modern humans have become so accustomed to the thought of tools and weapons that it is easy for us to imagine the first manlike creature who picked up a stone or club. However, since we don't really know what the early stone tools such as hand-axes were used for, it is equally probable that they were not weapons at all, but rather *aids in gathering*. We know that gathering was important long before much animal protein was added to the diet, and continued to be important. Bones, sticks, and hand-axes could be used for digging up tubers or roots, or to pulverize tough vegetable matter for easier eating. If, however, instead of thinking in terms of tools and weapons, we think in terms of *cultural inventions*, a new aspect is presented. I suggest that two of the *earliest and most important* cultural inventions were containers to hold the products of gathering, and some sort of sling or net to carry babies. The latter in particular must have been extremely important with the loss of body hair and the increasing immaturity of neonates, who could not cling and had less and less to cling to. Plenty of material was available—vines, hides, human hair. If the infant could be securely fastened to the mother's body, she could go about her tasks much more efficiently. Once a technique for carrying babies was developed, it could be extended to the idea of carrying food, and eventually to other sorts of cultural inventions—choppers and grinders for food preparation, and even weapons. Among modern hunter-gatherers, regardless of the poverty of their material culture, food carriers and baby carriers are always important items in their equipment.

A major point in the Man the Hunter argument is that cooperative hunting among males demanded more skill in social organization and communication, and thus provided selection pressure for increased brain size. I suggest that longer periods of infant dependency, more difficult births, and longer gestation periods also demanded more skills in social organization and communication—creating selective pressure for increased brain size without looking to hunting as an explanation. The need to organize for feeding after weaning, learning to handle the more complex social-emotional bonds that were developing, the new skills and cultural inventions surrounding more extensive gathering—all would demand larger brains. Too much attention has been given to the skills required by hunting, and too little to the skills required for gathering and the raising of dependent young. The techniques required for efficient gathering include location and iden-

tification of plant varieties, seasonal and geographical knowledge, containers for carrying the food, and tools for its preparation. Among modern hunting-gathering groups this knowledge is an extremely complex, well-developed, and important part of their cultural equipment. Caring for a curious, energetic, but still dependent human infant is difficult and demanding. Not only must the infant be watched, it must be taught the customs, dangers, and knowledge of its group. For the early hominids, as their cultural equipment and symbolic communication increased, the job of training the young would demand more skill. Selection pressure for better brains came from many directions.

Much has been made of the argument that cooperation among males demanded by hunting acted as a force to reduce competition for females. I suggest that competition for females has been greatly exaggerated. It could easily have been handled in the usual way for primates—according to male status relationships already worked out—and need not be pictured as particularly violent or extreme. The seeds of male cooperation already exist in primates when they act to protect the band from predators. Such dangers may well have increased with a shift to savannah living, and the longer dependency of infants. If biological roots are sought to explain the greater aggressiveness of males, it would be more fruitful to look toward their function as protectors, rather than any supposedly basic hunting adaptation. The only division of labor that regularly exists in primate groups is the females caring for infants and the males protecting the group from predators. The possibilities for both cooperation and aggression in males lies in this protective function.

The emphasis on hunting as a prime moving factor in hominid evolution distorts the data. It is simply too big a jump to go from the primate individual gathering pattern to a hominid cooperative hunting-sharing pattern without some intervening changes. Cooperative hunting of big game animals could only have developed *after* the trends toward neoteny and increased brain size had begun. Big-game hunting becomes a more logical development when it is viewed as growing out of a complex of changes which included sharing the products of gathering among mothers and children, deepening social bonds over time, increase in brain size, and the beginnings of cultural invention for purposes such as baby carrying, food carrying, and food preparation. Such hunting not only needed the prior development of some skills in social organization and communication; it probably also had to await the development of the "home base." It is difficult to imagine that most or all of the adult primate males in a group would go off on a hunting expedition, leaving the females and young exposed to the danger of predators, without some way of communicating to arrange for their defense, or at least a way of saying, "Don't worry, we'll be back in two days." Until that degree of communicative skill developed, we must assume either that the whole band traveled *and hunted* together, or that the males simply did not go off on large cooperative hunts.

The development of cooperative hunting requires, as a prior condition, an increase in brain size. Once such a trend is established, hunting

skills would take part in a feedback process of selection for better brains just as would other cultural inventions and developments such as gathering skills. By itself, hunting fails to explain any part of human evolution and fails to explain itself.

Anthropology has always rested on the assumption that the mark of our species is our ability to *symbol*, to bring into existence forms of behavior and interaction, and material tools with which to adjust and control the environment. To explain human nature as evolving from the desire of males to hunt and kill is to negate most of anthropology. Our species survived and adapted through the invention of *culture*, of which hunting is simply a part. It is often stated that hunting *must* be viewed as the "natural" species' adaptation because it lasted as long as it did, nine-tenths of all human history. However:

Man the Hunter lasted as long as "he" did from no natural propensity toward hunting any more than toward computer programming or violin playing or nuclear warfare, but because that was what the historical circumstances allowed. We ignore the first premise of our science if we fail to admit that "man" is no more natural a hunter than "he" is naturally a golfer, for after symboling became possible our species left forever the ecological niche of the necessity of any one adaptation, and made all adaptations possible for ourselves. (Kephart, 1970:23)

That the concept of Man the Hunter influenced anthropology for as long as it did is a reflection of male bias in the discipline. This bias can be seen in the tendency to equate "man," "human," and "male"; to look at culture almost entirely from a male point of view; to search for examples of the behavior of males and assume that this is sufficient for explanation, ignoring almost totally the female half of the species; and to filter this male bias through the "ideal" modern Western pattern of one male supporting a dependent wife and minor children.

The basis of any discipline is not the answers it gets, but the questions it asks. As an exercise in the anthropology of knowledge, this paper stems from asking a simple question: what were the females doing while the males were out hunting? It was only possible for me to ask this question after I had become politically conscious of myself as a woman. Such is the prestige of males in our society that a woman, in anthropology or any other profession, can only gain respect or be attended to if she deals with questions deemed important by men. Though there have been women anthropologists for years, it is rare to be able to discern any difference between their work and that of male anthropologists. Learning to be an anthropologist has involved learning to think from a male perspective, so it should not be surprising that women have asked the same kinds of questions as men. But political consciousness, whether among women, blacks, American Indians, or any other group, leads to reexamination and reevaluation of taken-for-granted assumptions. It is a difficult process, challenging the conventional wisdom, and this paper is simply a beginning. The male bias in anthropology that I have illustrated here is just as real as the white bias, the middle-class bias, and the academic bias that exist in the discipline. It is our task, as anthropologists, to create a "study of the human species" in spite of, or perhaps because of, or maybe even by means of, our individual biases and unique perspectives.

35

Border Work

Feminist Ethnography and the Dissemination of Literacy

(1996)

Deborah A. Gordon

IN 1991, on completing my Ph.D. thesis, I came across a letter from Peggy Sanday, Sanday, who published her earliest work on the status of women in *Woman, Culture and Society,* had answered a letter I had written to feminist anthropologists in the initial stages of my research. I wanted to understand the traffic in academia and politics from 1967 to 1975 and the intermeshing of social activism and technical debates among a cohort of feminist anthropologists in the late 1960s. I asked a number of feminist anthropologists to reflect on how feminism had affected their professional practice and on how anthropology had shaped their feminism. Although Sanday wrote the longest response to my request, I put her letter away, being vaguely put off by the fact that it did not "fit" the type of textual experimentation I was looking for. Rereading her letter, I was dismayed that I had dismissed her words so lightly:

I am now working on a book that begins with an ethnography of an incident that occurred at Penn in Feb. 1982. One of my students alleged that she was raped by 6–8 fraternity brothers after a party. I am writing on that incident as a lens for looking at male dominance on college campuses, particularly date and the group rape by fraternity brothers. The person who influenced me was my student.

When she told me about the incident, I felt that it was essential to go to bat for her. I was also influenced by my own work on rape that taught me that rape is publicly condemned only where it is publicly aired. I convinced the student that rather than hide the incident it was important to fight it openly on campus. I am writing the book with a male journalist who wrote a very important story about the incident in the *Philadelphia Inquirer* Sunday magazine. Because he wrote the story with feminist eyes he did a lot to swing the climate that makes incidents like the one at Penn quite common. It will be an ethnography of sexuality. In this book, anthropology will definitely contribute to a political effort on my part to change American understanding of sexual abuse and use of young women.

Gordon, Deborah, "Border Work: Feminist Ethnography and the Dissemination of Literacy." In *Women Writing Culture,* edited by Behar and Gordon. Berkeley, California: University of California Press, 1995.

384

I consider this book to be extremely important from an action standpoint.

I dismissed the letter not only because I could not locate Sanday's project within a framework of experimentation but also because of the subject matter. By 1991, action-oriented research seemed academically dated. Sanday published the results of her research in *Fraternity Gang Rape*, a study of fraternities, rape, and masculinity among white college men. Using interviews with college students and university administrators as well as written accounts by students, Sanday and a team of student researchers accessed the "sexual subculture that encourages and supports rape." *Fraternity Gang Rape* mixes different types of analysis—sociological, social psychological, legal, and culturally symbolic. Sanday's book has not made it into the canon of experimental ethnography, nor does it fit with the turn toward fiction, genre-mixing, and autobiography that anthropologists have exploited in the search for a feminist ethnography. It is also not likely to reach a broad feminist audience, for it is difficult to read. Detailed descriptions of fraternity initiation rituals, of turning young men into "brothers," disturb the academic penchant for interesting writing that is not too emotionally disturbing. Judge Lois Forer, who overrode the University of Pennsylvania's refusal to prosecute the rape of Sanday's student, wrote the book's foreword. While feminists clearly support the full use of the law to stop sexual violence against women, there is a more general mistrust of feminist alignments with the regulative power of the state. In addition, despite tenacious efforts to make college campuses habitable and equally supportive for women students, the fear that ethnography might expose university negligence threatens distorted notions of academic freedom that many men and women still hold. Indeed, Judge Forer's foreword to *Fraternity Gang Rape* functions as a shield for the institutional radicalness of this account by demanding that university officials enforce rape laws. Sanday's odd proximity to genre shifts in feminist anthropology serves less as a model and more as a point of departure for exploring ethnographic form and social change.

FEMINIST ETHNOGRAPHY AND SOCIAL ACTION

Sanday's phrase "from an action standpoint" provides a critical perspective on the emergence of recent attempts by feminist social scientists to carve "feminist ethnography out of the literary turn in anthropology." *Fraternity Gang Rape* locates ethnography where ethnographers live, that is, in the halls of academe. A recent wave of feminist anthropology "at home" responds to new-right political and intellectual agendas of the 1980s that carried particular consequences for women. Yet Sanday's study of gang rape in fraternities is more than an ethnography at home. It registers the unstable character of ethnographic form. This timely ethnography serves as a counterpoint to a potential hardening of "experimental" ethnography. I consider the problematic nature of ethnographic form not simply within its present literary moment but also within a growing cultural hostility toward higher education and especially academic research on the part of citizens outside universities, regents of public systems, and the media. When academic research and publication are under intense public scrutiny, we need to articulate why and how feminist research matters. Poor journalism and sensationalized editorials exploit middle-class frustration and encourage a public content with mass illiteracy. It seems necessary for feminists, who are only too aware of the gender and race barriers to publication, to counter myths that publishing necessitates abandoning students for the archives and the library. Defining and supporting women's research and publication in the face of budget crises must be a priority for feminist faculty members, particularly those with tenure.

Of all feminist academics, feminist ethnographers may be uniquely suited to articulate the "public" as an essentially contested category. As the meanings surrounding culture shift from bounded, timeless objects to heterogeneous codes, ethnography may be a growing political resource in battles over the public interest, if only to underline that there is no such thing as "the public" in the singular. Consider, for example, how both conservative and liberal politicians distinguish the public from the immigrants and the homeless. California's Proposition 187 is only the most dramatic sign of widespread anti-immigrant sentiment in which liberal Democrats and Republicans are allied. The urge to exploit demographic shifts and xenophobia motivated people in Florida and Washington to pursue similar legislation, to support border enforcement. In a new twist on a long discursive history of Malthusian practice in the West, newspapers fuel middle-class blaming of these "populations" for its decline. Feminist ethnography might counter the racism and class hostility that seeks to punish immigrants and those left homeless by discovering field sites in immigration and welfare offices, government agencies, and on literal borders.

As part of the anthropological turn toward "home" in the 1980s, feminist anthropologists moved away from more traditional area studies to study the symbolism and practices surrounding reproductive technologies, abortion politics, medical and legal discourse, and gay and lesbian communities. While the ethnography produced by this wave of scholarship has been particularly rich, we need feminist fieldwork in the United States that participates in political activist and advocacy-oriented research. Interdisciplinary dialogue with oral historians who work within a disciplinary tradition of public advocacy might pull feminist anthropology at home toward grittier intellectual alliances such as with community educators and activists.

Locating feminist ethnography at the crossroads of anthropology at home and advocacy-oriented oral history speaks to what may turn out to be the critical political terrain for feminism in the 1990s—women's literacy. Access to formal education and literacy among white women and people of color in the United States has always been unevenly distributed. During a period of deep economic change fueled by deindustrialization and global corporate capitalism, access to formal education increasingly determines material reality for women. Recent research on the economic status of women in the United States suggests an intensified earnings gap between white women and women of color. Given present conditions, which include dynamics of multinational capitalism, limited access for some women to low-paid service-sector jobs, poor labor conditions at home and abroad in industry, and federal, state, and city budget crises, contests over and for literacy become directly political.

Testifying before the Senate Committee on Labor and Human Resources, economists Heidi Hartmann and Roberta Spalter-Roth have argued that a dominant trend in the workplace has been the deterioration of relationships between workers and employers. But deteriorating labor conditions, particularly the growth of involuntary part-time and low-wage work, have affected women more than men. The preliminary results of Hartmann and Spalter-Roth's 1991 study suggest that the factors contributing most to increasing earnings of both African American and white mothers were, above all, higher education, followed by full-time employment, work experience, and union membership. Without making the mistake of expecting education to solve the problem of global economic restructuring, Hartmann and Spalter-Roth's policy prescriptions make women's access to higher education a priority.

If we consider policy research alongside the growing awareness that differences among women are substantive not superficial, feminist ethnography as literacy work becomes a compelling model of politically grounded research that does not reduce intellectual acts to political acts or vice versa. Critical literacy creates new notions of women writing culture to fit patterns of global migration under multinational capitalism. Resisting assimilationist logic, Latino scholars have retheorized knowledge, identity, and citizenship by affirming the process whereby disenfranchised groups assert their own sense of human, legal, and social rights. During a period of increased immigrant-bashing, especially in the wake of the North American Free Trade Agreement, feminist ethnographers may be uniquely suited to address the racist fantasy that holds immigrants responsible for adverse economic conditions such as downsizing. Feminist ethnography as a practice of critical literacy situates ethnographic writing within these daily life struggles of women who are pulled away from their homes and toward the United States.

In the wake of collections such as *Writing Culture*, anthropologists have exploited the conceptual slipperiness of the term *ethnographic writing*. The pull toward writing as individual authorship has encouraged critics to take individual ethnographies to be the main unit of analysis in the critique of ethnographic representation. In turn, the political aim of decolonized knowledge has rested on individual writing experiments. The hope of challenging that larger, weightier sense of social inscription gets funneled through publishing practices, which are based in the ideologies of authorship as unique, individual expression.

How will feminist ethnographers negotiate the conceptual ambiguity surrounding ethnographic writing? In considering the political connection of ethnography to knowledge, one must have a sense of the political terrain on which objects such as ethnographic canons and cultural authority are built. In a compelling analysis of the antidisciplinary character of anthropology's present moment, George Marcus argues that the rhetoric of canon formation obscures the fact that cultural authority rests more on oral modes of communication, such as corridor talk, than on print media. Marcus's ordering of the oral as the authoritative form of communication and print as secondary downplays their mutual dependency. His argument for more ethnographically based studies of the production of knowledge, however, nicely dovetails with a feminist ethnography that charts global capitalism's impact on women's literacy. Without ethnography among women, it is difficult to know what literacy means to women who negotiate different cultural practices and political dynamics. Where literacy work politically focuses Marcus's call for accounts of cultural migrations is in its pursuit of women's own effort to define citizenship in cultural rather than legal terms. Feminist literacy work recognizes that reading and writing may have radically different meanings for those groups that have historically struggled for literacy rather than taken it for granted.

LITERACY WORK AND FEMINIST ETHNOGRAPHY

Research based on literacy work already functions to make feminist research travel between academic offices and community-based classrooms. The El Barrio project exemplifies this mobile research. In the heart of New York City, this community-based program of action research initiated by the Center for Puerto Rican Studies (El Centro de Estudios Puertorriqueños) at Hunter College ran from 1985 until 1989. In 1985 the center initiated a Spanish-language adult literacy program in the Puerto Rican community of East Harlem. Researchers at Hunter created the project to study educational patterns in a community with a high rate of high-school dropouts. Directed by Rosa Torruellas in collaboration with Pedro Pedraza, an instructional and counseling staff, students, and a board of directors, the project eventually included the oral historians Ana Juarbe and Rina Benmayor. Torruellas, Benmayor, and Juarbe participated in classes on a regular basis, collecting life-histories that contributed to curriculum development. Most of the women who participated in the El Barrio project were female heads of households with sole responsibility for childrearing. Most had extensive experience dealing with the loss of jobs brought by deindustrialization combined with the indignities of the welfare system and grossly inadequate social services. The neighborhood women had no access to formal education, and the project's primary goal was to "promote empowerment through native-language literacy training and education of Spanish-speaking adults."

The greatest achievement of the El Barrio project was its making of feminist ethnography a partner in women's evolving sense of entitlement. Literacy work took place beyond the classroom as the women formed a culture of support in their daily lives. The participants in the program referred to it as their "second family," attesting to both their significant emotional investment in the term *family* and their ability to subvert its patriarchal meaning. As the women learned to read and write, they challenged power dynamics that structured family relations and were able to continue their education without risking the isolation that so often accompanies women's withdrawal from taking care of men and children. During a period of great gender and class instabilities, women whose identities have rested on their roles as mothers, wives, and family members need a sustained social community in order to exercise choice in a range of political circumstances. The research of the El Barrio project participated in the political empowerment of women through the institutionalization of social alternatives to families that emerged out of the classroom. In the El Barrio project, literacy work became a lifestyle of resistance forged by the women participants, with researchers and tutors acting as guides and interpreters.

The centerpiece of the El Barrio project, one critical in any discussion of feminist ethnography, is research that attempts to redistribute educational privilege. That redistribution is centered in teaching critical rather than functional literacy. Critical literacy assumes that disempowered communities need forms of knowledge to negotiate and change the inequities that keep them disadvantaged. The pedagogical commitments in critical literacy work urge the subversion of power between literate and "illiterate" women. An important contributing factor to redistributing power through critical literacy in the project was the willingness to continually redefine oral history and ethnography based on their pedagogical values. Initially, they were part of a long-term and extensive oral history project on Puerto Rican immigrants in New York. When they joined the literacy

project oral history became part of the teaching of literacy skills. In addition, the researchers also moved from doing oral history to utilizing "classroom ethnography." Their detailed notes and their observations on what occurred in the classroom aided the teaching process. Class assignments intersected oral histories through tutors' request that women participants write autobiographies. Life histories were collected by teaching women participants to write in a way that changed their sense of self and led to collective empowerment. For example, as women reinterpreted their lives through the life-history process, they became more willing to resist welfare workers. Rather than seeing themselves negatively in the ugly mirror the state holds up to them, these women came to realize that, as citizens, they had a right to welfare. Their perception of welfare as a political right grew from their articulation of fulfilling gendered and cultural responsibilities in their labor as mothers and wage laborers. More recently, the oral historians assessed how classroom processes interact with students' domestic lives. Their fieldwork shifted to visiting students' homes and accompanying them on their rounds. Like many anthropologists, they worked in distinct spaces in which informants acted out different identities. By pushing beyond oral-history collecting to an interdisciplinary practice of classroom ethnography, combined with interviewing in spaces outside the classroom, the Hunter College researchers tracked the shifts in identity that are critical to the women's expressed sense that they can act on their own behalf despite the humiliations of the welfare system.

From the perspective of traditional patterns of career and research development in the discipline, the practice of classroom ethnography and the use of oral history as the material of critical literacy violate anthropology's traditional romanticism and exoticism. The "work" of classroom ethnography is not prestigious, because it does not involve travel to geographic regions that compose departmental hirings, curricula, and reputations. Because prestigious university departments with long-standing traditions of sending graduate students abroad are well funded, they are able to attract faculty and students who are insisting on new, unorthodox definitions of the "field." A crucial example of this process of reconstituting the field is the attempt to theorize and describe processes such as cultural diasporas. As "home" becomes a problematic site of identity construction in the wake of mass migrations, anthropologists increasingly study the neighborhoods in which they grew up or the immigrant communities that border many urban universities. Calling classroom ethnography "fieldwork" assumes that the process of literacy is immanently a site of cultural politics, a "site" for participating in what Arjun Appadurai designated as ethnoscapes: "As groups migrate, regroup in new locations, reconstruct their histories, and reconfigure their ethnic 'projects,' the *ethno* in ethnography takes on a slippery, non-localized quality, to which the descriptive practices of anthropology respond."

As ethnic and cultural groups lose their spatial rootings as a result of tourism, migration, and warfare, human mobility and patterns of forced travel become obvious anthropological objects. Critical literacy projects that are enmeshed in the traffic of immigration are important places where the reconfiguration of ethnicity occurs. How women reconstruct gender identity through immigration, through guest work in foreign countries, and through becoming refugees must be a crucial area of feminist ethnography. The "feminism" of feminist ethnography will carry greater political weight if it is grounded in social change as a collective project. Critical literacy projects are ideal sites for further ethnographic experiments with advocacy work. Critical literacy involves commitment to classroom dynamics, tutoring, and staffing the program so that the self-redefinition that frequently accompanies education is shared. The sharing goes in two directions as researchers gain theoretical insights into social life. In the case of the El Barrio project, researchers noted how the gendered nature of class relations became increasingly clearer as they listened to participants' reconstruction of their identities in their life stories. A heightened sense that class must be understood as carved with the knife of gender became one of the lessons the women students provided. Carefully monitored engagement with the women participants over time suggested that intersecting relations of race, gender, class, and culture shift with the gains of writing and reading. Researchers and women students are not equal partners in this collective learning process, but in the face of that inequality they do reshape each other's intellectual skill.

The El Barrio project promotes reciprocity and mutual gains among community members and researchers, but its idealism does not work through a language of coauthorship. The idiom of empowerment present in the publications of the El Barrio research team does not offer images of dispersing ethnographic authority through shared authorship but evokes collective action. Ironically, the actual writing practice of the project includes joint authorship, use of quotations by the women participants, and extensive space for the women's autobiographies. The latter calls up the discourse of leftist women working in urban projects to ameliorate poverty in the 1960s, the same women who would come to participate in women's liberation activism. The relatively greater emphasis on community rather than on authority emerges from ethnic identity among an immigrant group that values cultural practices in deep tension with the dominant, nativist, Anglo-American, Puritan myths of individualism. The language of community, however, does not draw static and impenetrable lines between insiders and outsiders but rather signifies political struggle for material resources. In Rina Benmayor's words, the project converges on the "common bonds of interests and solidarity" shared by the neighborhood women in the project and the oral historians serving their desire to read and write. The "identity politics" of the project thus move toward a goal—acquisition by the women of the ability to act on their own behalf. It is clear from the project's publications that researchers do not believe that community interests don't have to be created, yet they also recognize the motivating character of the belief in the promise of common interests in making claims on the state and in enabling new subjectivity. The project's reports suggest that these women use the term *community* to signify an ongoing process of cultural reinvention that is deeply political. Cultural affirmation works through and with the construction of community interests. For these women the shared desire to be able to read and, especially, to write has motivated them to claim citizenship on the basis of positive cultural expression rather than assimilation.

Theoretical insights also include the realization that race and gender are not the sole categories through which communities are articulated in the United States. Here the El Centro researchers' care in attending to participants' language reveals the importance of the category "uneducated" to the women in the literacy program. According to Benmayor, an important bond among participants is their stigmatized identity as uneducated. She argues that it is this stigma that motivates women to take part in a process of countering the dominant definitions of women on welfare as either lazy or products of a culture of poverty. At a time in which the once-discredited notion that poverty is a result of behavioral deviance has reemerged in government policy and popular imagination, these women's collective identification with the category "uneducated" does not so much signal their enactment of the regulative power of state disciplining of "populations" as it moves them to write so that they may attain dignity, formal education, and jobs.

Given what appears to be the upward mobility of at least some of the women who went through the program, can literacy work such as in the El Barrio project merely be celebrated and used as a model for feminist ethnography in other sites of transnational cultures? What political dilemmas are eclipsed by an optimistic claim that literacy can be the site of collective empowerment? One trenchant response to characteristically North American naüiveté based on voluntarism suggests that attempts to empower others hide patronizing inequities. A critical moment in the debate over anthropology's debt to colonial "benevolence" appeared in the infamous *Signs* exchange between Frances Mascia-Lees et al. and Vicki Kirby. In a dramatic critique of the literary turn in anthropology, Mascia-Lees et al. argued that applied anthropology might be more appropriate for feminists in the discipline than engagement with textual theory and criticism. In a reply, Kirby warned of the dangers of misunderstanding "alterity, assuming that this space of negation is something we should work to overcome, an unfairness to be redressed rather than an enduring structural asymmetry with constitutive force." Applying Kirby's insistence on the force of asymmetry to the action-oriented life-history and classroom ethnography of the El Barrio project highlights the limits of pragmatic politics, even among women who have a shared purpose in tying ethnicity to citizenship. In fully entering the dilemmas of action-oriented research, however, we confront the need for less permanent and fixed concepts of asymmetry. We need to understand social processes in a manner that does not flatten all research between relatively privileged women and disenfranchised women into images of well-intentioned but naive ethnographers who cannot think about the structures within which they work.

To not caricature feminist ethnographers, a nonreductive theory of agency must be central to any assessment of specific research projects. In a post-Foucauldian and post-Lacanian theoretical moment, agency emerges as the negotiation of the regulative fictions in which subjectivity is an effect, not a cause, of social order. Feminist social theory has greatly benefited from Foucault's productive and dispersed view of power. Yet even Foucault's impact on new feminist theories of identity and agency seems overly bound up with legal rhetoric. The language of order, restraint, regulation, and management dominates in an attempt to hold on to power. As Judith Butler so nicely puts it, "Neither power nor discourse are rendered anew at every moment; they are not as weightless as the utopics of radical resignification might imply." At the same time, the contingencies of participants in specific fieldwork sites make clear the need for low-level generalizations about agency within asymmetrical relations among women. Although Kirby corrects the relative ease with which Mascia-Lees et al. claim that feminists are one with their politics, fully certain and in control of their enactment and meaning, theorizing action-oriented or advocacy research must grasp the texture of struggle for shared understanding that accompanies self-conscious efforts for collective empowerment of those marginalized in capitalist economies. Context-specific judgments as to which kinds of social, economic, and political privilege can be changed by literacy projects and which need more massive challenges to the welfare system, corporate practices, and global political alliances must be foregrounded in feminist theory.

Gayatri Spivak has offered one ethical model for assessing how women respond to and enact a politics of translation, which is highly suggestive for feminist literacy work. In her view, translation offers an opportunity to discover the trace of the other in the self. How one responds to that trace determines one's accountability to another's language. Because feminist ethnography is always bound up with situations of translation, the politics of its form lie in the conditions of both its production—including its modes of travel, and technologies of listening, recording, and writing— and its dissemination. There are important parallels between literary translation and the translation of ethnography, but also specific circumstances that give life to ethical dilemmas and their potential resolution. For example, Spivak's meditation on translation concerns her position as a postcolonial Indian woman, working in the American academy and translating contemporary literary work in Bengali, her native language. As she reminds us, Bengali divides into class dialects that suggest social layers which cry out for attention in translation.

The El Barrio researchers present a quite different situation of translation. Like Spivak, the researchers are fluent in the language of the women they work with in constructing histories. Class distinctions in language use are less centrally noted than in Spivak's discussion. The fieldwork situation allows for dialogue between the Hunter researchers and women students, which centers more on the women's expressed struggle and pleasure in learning to write. The differences between Spivak's and the El Barrio researchers' attention to language speaks to disciplinary, methodological, geographical, historical, and ethnic locations. In addition, the El Barrio researchers' ability to speak intimately with these women may be the result of the relatively long history of neighborhood relations between the Center for Puerto Rican Studies at Hunter and East Harlem. They may also emerge from who pays for and/or publishes the translation. In the case of the El Barrio researchers, it is the Center for Puerto Rican Studies that funds publication of their reports.

Given the ways in which languages carry social divisions and given the political complexities of research, how might one know whether one has actually learned another's tongue? Spivak suggests two tests of solidarity with women whose native tongue differs from one's own. The first is whether one can converse about intimate matters in the other's language. The second is whether one is capable "of distinguishing between good and bad writing by women, resistant and conformist writing by women. In Spivak's ethics, one has to be able and willing to judge the quality of writing within its local scene. Does it make sense to draw parallels between the translator and the translated and between the researcher/ teacher and studied/student in literacy projects? Are Spivak's ethical guidelines appropriate to the literacy work of the El Barrio project? The researcher and teacher of literacy is obliged to learn her students' language not simply to communicate but to enter the delicate process of leading and being led, which involves change. In the pedagogy of critical literacy is an especially intimate experience, because its pleasures and frustrations go to the core of women's shifting conception of self and community. The researchers include quotations from women attesting to their growing sense of deserving education, a good life, and support from family members to pursue their education. Spivak's second ethical test of translation concerns translators' ability to distinguish good writing from bad writing. While Spivak's focus is the politics of literacy translation, attention to student writing demands the same kind of nonpatronizing and nonracist stance of teachers.

The ethnographic form of the El Barrio project's writings registers that process of being led into and deeply learning another's language that subverts individual authorship. The students' building of support networks nicely parallels the team authorship of the project's publications. Paperbound reports to its funding sources circulate out of El Centro for little money. One such report is "Responses to Poverty among Puerto Rican Women: Identity, Community, and Cultural Citizenship." Rich description of the interplay between structural, cultural, and symbolic processes juxtaposed with women's life stories reveals the collective character of authorship when literacy is defined as a mode of constructing new subjectivities for disenfranchised communities.

In discussing how the women students led them to understand the role literacy played in their gender identities as well as their sense of citizenship, the authors call up their status as witnesses rather than as sympathetic observers, writers, or guides. This report suggests another figure in the history of anthropology, the participant witness rather than observer. Carrying a host of conflicting associations, including informant, litigant, function of the Holy Ghost, and spectator, a witness is less an observer than a teller—that is, one who translates what s/he sees and hears for an audience. The notion of the litigant calls up the courtroom as scene of performing the law with all of its theatricality, finesse, and savvy. As an informant, the witness purposely informs or tells, with all of the potential for betrayal implied. Yet witnessing in the context of the Americas also brings to mind the long-standing indigenous tradition of personal testimony, with the witness calling up a broken humanity to redeem it. Characteristically American traditions of African American preachers, Latin American human-rights activists, and advocates for the poor continually reinvent stories of redemption through suffering to challenge social injustice. The El Barrio project's classroom pedagogy relied heavily on personal testimony, in which women literally altered their life possibilities through witnessing their lives and those of other women. In participant witnessing, the lines between ethnographer and informant blur as each hears the other in a way that encourages self-representation. By portraying themselves as more closely akin to participants witnessing change than to classroom observers, the oral historians mark the instabilities of power dynamics in the project.

The El Barrio project researchers thus must be viewed as students and actors in literacy politics and not simply as instruments of state power. The careful qualifying of their research by continual insistence that they are not "insiders" in the Puerto Rican women's community despite the fact that they include second-generation Puerto Rican women who grew up in the neighborhood attests to the limits of social policy work. Spivak nicely designates the state's hold on political meaning as "global social work." In the face of a difficult political situation, cultural differences became the imaginative basis for U.S. citizenship rather than legal categories that enforce homogenization. Researchers' "complicity" with the actual economic realities of global, postindustrial conditions is inevitable—but no more so than library research, close readings, or any other disciplinary method. One of Spivak's and Kirby's points in their cautionary tales about women's cross-cultural research is that of the depth and endurance of Western feminism's complicity with the history of colonialism. My impression of anthropology is that as it has come to terms with its colonial legacy, it has designated applied anthropology, advocacy, and action-oriented research as entirely politically dirty compared with the more theoretically informed self-reflexive field account. Low rungs on the ladder of the disciplinary reward systems, advocacy-oriented fieldwork and applied anthropology are too obviously caught up in government and global aid bureaucracies that are laden with anthropology's complicity with colonial ventures. Yet these kinds of anthropology and their specific ethnographic forms need to be rethought for feminist purposes.

Precisely because so much Western feminism has enacted the colonial logic of either saving non-Western women from themselves or their men or turning them into curious, quaint relics through government or missionary work, applied or advocacy anthropology needs not to be abandoned but to be reconstructed.

The El Barrio project provides a beginning sense of what that reconstruction might look like. One central fact of this project is the researchers' upfront acknowledgment of the inequalities of their undertaking. Instead of essentializing ethnicity and claiming the space of the Puerto Rican community of East Harlem, they opt instead for what I would call the equalizing of power relations. Equalizing is a process, uncertain and ongoing. Equalizing inequality through research in this popular education project could not take place without the historical involvement of El Centro de Estudios Puertorriqueños in the immigration of Puerto Ricans to New York City after World War II. More importantly, the commitment of El Centro to the immigrant neighborhood built research that has not so much completely subordinated individual, academic achievement to community goals but has struggled for reciprocity between professional and neighborhood agendas. The neighborhood women participate in the project to learn to read and write Spanish. In 1989 the project's center, Casita Maria, made a transition from being managed by Hunter College to self-management by the neighborhood. This goal of community management was central to the education project from its beginning. Because researchers had responsibilities for directing or coordinating the literacy project, they agreed to perform multiple roles and fulfill multiple demands. Structuring literacy projects so that researchers are an integral part of the daily work of the center avoids a division of labor that would separate them from the hands-on running of the program, including classroom activities. Especially given that the El Barrio project implemented community leadership and self-management of the project, this kind of feminist ethnography highlights the achievements of accountability to those studied, to the neighborhood, and to a vision of public life that is peopled by more than taxpayers. Equalizing strategies in feminist ethnography appear to come both from an experimental flexibility in method that continually shifts over time and from researchers' willingness to help run the project.

There is a distinction between claiming equality and working to equalize that is not merely semantic. In the former, the image of giving voice to the disempowered suggests a troubling "matronization" of women who have not benefited from affirmative action policies and professional employment. Building equalizing strategies connotes participation in an uneven process that considers how power and resources are redistributed. The intellectual pleasures of research and writing get disseminated beyond the academy by widening education's scope. Feminist academics need to institutionally defend and promote ethnographic projects that involve research teams and jointly authored publications. Academic feminists, especially those with tenure and in positions of relative institutional strength, must not simply legitimate

this type of research even in universities that are not located in urban centers such as New York City, but treat it as serious theoretical, epistemological, and ethical material for considering what "counts" as feminist ethnography. Overprivileging one kind of cultural anthropology as the sole arena for an ethnographic politics that interrogates neocolonialism, inequality, and knowledge runs the risk of containing critical insight within very limited circles.

Deconstructing the border between oral history and ethnography introduces new feminist networks that reach out in two directions: toward other scholars and toward creating new kinds of intellectual communities. I am not arguing that feminists should rally around some naive politics that is stripped of ethnographic form, writing, or rhetoric. This is not a call for the "real" struggle over and against the mere "literary." On the contrary, the feminist ethnographic work I have examined rejects false distinctions between practice and writing, but it does so less through a focus on representing the experiencing individual than through grappling with the politics of academic research and writing. Although there are significant differences between ethnography and oral history, recent reflection on power in feminist fieldwork suggests a need for further dialogue among historians, anthropologists, and sociologists who work with interview and participant-observation methods. If ethnography is the process and product of cultural translation, feminist ethnography brings the dilemmas and limits of that exercise into an interdisciplinary feminist dialogue. In the 1980s the rhetoric of coalition politics within academic feminism often belied half-hearted attempts at crossing lines of race, class, culture, and sexuality. Literacy work provides one limited avenue for forming coalitions among women that situate the utopian impulse of dispersing ethnographic authority within a class-conscious politics. Donna Haraway has argued that information is our ontology, as being collapses into textualization in a world no longer captured by the traditionally Marxian sense of labor but by an "informatics of domination." Clearly, much of a woman's life experience in a world structured by information will turn on the types of literacy and access to formal education she has. Feminist ethnography as critical literacy gives a "politics" of ethnographic writing some weight. It deeply socializes the meaning of ethnographic form. Questions of ethnographic form, then, move beyond the staging of voices and textual authority to modes of description that change who reads and who writes, for what purposes and with what effects.

CONCLUSION

We have seen how Sanday's words, "from an action point of view," fit into the border between oral history and ethnography, community organizing and academic research, ethnicity and gender. Feminist anthropology is undergoing a transformation as ethnography becomes an object of reflection not only for poststructuralist critics and historians but also for women ethnographers who are struggling to account for their relations with women in postcolonial conditions.

The critique of ethnographic authority has compelled feminist anthropologists to account differently for how they come to know or not know women living outside Western feminist demands. Fieldwork and research in "homes" that are woven with cultural and political conflict expand feminism to encompass more than the usual media lineup of reproductive rights, affirmative action, the glass ceiling, the mommy track, and sexual harassment. Action-oriented research is not a panacea. Research similar to that generated by the Center for Puerto Rican Studies at Hunter may only be realistically possible among people who are culturally familiar enough with each other's backgrounds to warrant the type of trust that supports literacy projects. Finally, advocacy-oriented research is more physically dangerous and politically impossible for anthropologists in some geographical regions and under certain political circumstances (such as military dictatorship and occupation) than in others.

It seems fitting to end not on a celebratory note but with caution. The advantages of locating feminist ethnography in politicized textual experimentation are obvious. Feminist ethnographic efforts to alter textual voice, representation, and style in their widest and most radical senses move the profession in a way that makes daily work of anthropology accountable to feminism. Shifts in genre conventions to action, however complicated and nonessential its meaning has become after the decentering of the subject, will increasingly need to be theorized if feminist ethnography wants to accept challenges to its own authority. I purposely keep open what the politics of representation means. I continue to ask what kind of change makes what kind of difference to whom. And I ask these questions very much from within, not from outside, anthropology's "textual turn." We have no choice but to think in these "old-fashioned" terms if women's lives are to be of value. The question for feminist ethnography must be how to situate writing culture within those sometimes imaginary, sometimes real, communities we call women's movements while not reifying politics.

36

Indian *Suttee*

The Ultimate Consummation of Marriage

(1978)

Mary Daly

Slow advancing, halting, creeping,
Comes the Woman to the hour!
She walketh veiled and sleeping,
For she knoweth not her power.

*Charlotte Perkins Gilman, from "She Walketh
Veiled and Sleeping,"* In This Our World

"I have not deserved it. . . . Why must I die like this,
alone with my mortal enemy?"

Willa Cather, My Mortal Enemy

"Widow" is a harsh and hurtful word. It comes from the
Sanskrit and it means "empty." . . . I resent what the term has
come to mean. I am alive. I am part of the world.

Lynn Caine, Widow

They speak together of the threat they have constituted
towards authority, they tell how they were burned on pyres to
prevent them from assembling in future.

Monique Wittig, Les Guérillères

The Indian rite of *suttee*, or widow-burning, might at first appear totally alien to contemporary Western society, where widows are not ceremoniously burned alive on the funeral pyres of their husbands.* Closer examination unveils its connectedness with "our" rituals. Moreover, the very attempt to examine the ritual and its social context through the re-sources of Western scholarship demonstrates this connectedness. For the scholars who produced these re-sources exhibit by their very language their complicity in the same social order which was/is the radical source of such rites of female sacrifice.

The hindu rite of *suttee* spared widows from the temptations of impurity by forcing them to "immolate themselves," that is, to be burned alive, on the funeral pyres of their husbands. This ritual sacrifice must be understood within its social context. Since their religion forbade remarriage and at the same time taught that the hus-

---

*Although *suttee* was legally banned in 1829, and despite the existence of other legal reforms, it should not be imagined that the lot of most Indian women has changed dramatically since then, or since the publication of Katherine Mayo's *Mother India* in 1927. The situation of most widows is pitiable. An article in an Indian paper, the *Sunday Standard*, May 11, 1975, described the wretched existence of the 7,000 widows of the town of Brindaban, "the living spectres whose life has been eroded by another's death." These poverty-stricken women with shaved heads and with a single white cloth draped over their bare bodies are forced every morning to chant praise ("*Hare Rama, Hare Rama, Rama Rama, Hare Hare, Hare Krishna*" . . . ad nauseam) for four hours in order to get a small bowl of rice. In mid-afternoon they must chant for four more hours in order to receive the price of a glass of tea. A not unusual case is that of a sixty-nine-year-old widow who was married at the age of nine and widowed at eleven, and has been waiting ever since for the "day of deliverance." Surveys carried out by an Indian Committee on the Status of Women revealed that a large percentage of the Indian population still approves of such oppression of widows.

An Indian woman need not be widowed to be victimized. Many are literally starved to death. An article in an Indian magazine, *Youth Times*, March 7, 1975, states: "Our marriage ceremony puts her two steps behind the sacrificial fire—like a puppy that must follow its master. It is a place that spells disaster for millions. For it is a medical fact that the malnutrition and anaemia that plague such a vast number of our women have a basis in the habit of the women eating after they have served their husbands, a practice which in poor homes means virtual starvation" (p. 23). A look at tables of age-specific death rates is revealing. In 1969, in rural India, it was estimated that 70.2 females per thousand under the age of four died, while the death rate for males was 58.3. Since infant mortality generally is higher among males, it is reasonable to believe that these girl children got less to eat or were purposefully starved. The death rate for females is significantly higher in each age group up to the age of thirty-four (Devaki Jain, ed., *Indian Women* [Publications Division, Ministry of Information and Broadcasting, Government of India, 1975], p. 148). A number of sources, including Jain, refer obliquely to the high rate of "suicide" among women. Jain suggests that suicide "must seem an attractive way out of an intolerable situation" (p. 77). Jain is here referring to victims of the dowry system. The bride is often tormented and pressured to extract more money from her parents. In some cases she is murdered by her in-laws when her parents fail to come through. On January 13, 1977, the *New York Times* reported the details of one such murder of a twenty-year-old wife, who was strangled and burned in kerosene by her husband and in-laws. The article suggested that there are many such "dowry murders" in India each year, most of them disguised as kitchen accidents. These are occasionally reported in the Indian press in brief notices (as are cases of women murdered for not bearing sons). Although there was a Dowry Prohibition Act in 1961, according to the *Sunday Standard* (New Delhi, November 10, 1974), it is doubtful whether there has been even one instance of its enforcement. In addition to these horrors there is high maternal mortality resulting from extremely early marriage, too many pregnancies, maternal malnutrition, and unspeakably filthy and destructive methods of "delivery."

band's death was the fault of the widow (because of her sins in a previous incarnation if not in this one), everyone was free to despise and mistreat her for the rest of her life. Since it was a common practice for men of fifty, sixty, or seventy years of age to marry child-brides, the quantitative surplus of such unmarriageable widows boggles the imagination. Lest we allow our minds to be carried away with astronomic numerical calculations, we should realize that this ritual was largely confined to the upper caste, although there was a tendency to spread downward. We should also realize that in some cases—particularly if the widow was an extremely young child before her husband's unfortunate (for her) death—there was the option of turning to a life of prostitution, which would entail premature death from venereal disease. This, however, would be her only possible escape from persecution by in-laws, sons, and other relatives. As a prostitute, of course, she would be held responsible for the spread of more moral and physical impurity.

If the general situation of widowhood in India was not a sufficient inducement for the woman of higher caste to throw herself gratefully and ceremoniously into the fire, she was often pushed and poked in with long stakes after having been bathed, ritually attired, and drugged out of her mind. In case these facts should interfere with our clear misunderstanding of the situation, Webster's invites us to re-*cover* women's history with the following definition of *suttee:* "the act or custom of a Hindu woman *willingly* cremating herself or being cremated on the funeral pyre of her husband as an indication of her *devotion* to him [emphases mine]." It is thought-provoking to consider the reality behind the term *devotion*, for indeed a wife must have shown signs of extraordinarily slavish devotion during her husband's lifetime, since her very life depended upon her husband's state of health. A thirteen-year-old wife might well be concerned over the health of her sixty-year-old husband.

Joseph Campbell discusses *suttee* as the Hindu form of the widely practiced "custom" of sending the family or part of it "into the other world along with the chief member." The time-honored practice of "human sacrifice," sometimes taking the form of live burial, was common also in other cultures, for example in ancient Egypt. Campbell notes that Professor George Reisner excavated an immense necropolis in Nubia, an Egyptian province, and found, without exception, "a pattern of burial with human sacrifice—specifically, female sacrifice: of the wife and, in the more opulent tombs, the entire harem, together with the attendants." After citing Reisner's descriptions of female skeletons, which indicated that the victims had died hideous deaths from suffocation, Campbell writes:

In spite of these signs of suffering and even panic in the actual moment of the pain of suffocation, we should certainly not think of the mental state and experience of these individuals after any model of our own more or less imaginable reactions to such a fate. For these sacrifices were not properly, in fact, individuals at all; that is to say, they were not particular beings, distinguished from a class or group by virtue of any sense or realization of a personal, individual destiny or responsibility.

I have not italicized any of the words in this citation because it seemed necessary to stress *every* word. It is impossible to make any adequate comment.

At first, *suttee* was restricted to the wives of princes and warriors, but as one scholar (Benjamin Walker) deceptively puts it, "in course of time *the widows* of weavers, masons, barbers and others of lower caste *adopted the practice* [emphases mine]." The use of the active voice here suggests that the widows actively sought out, enforced, and accepted this "practice." Apparently without any sense of inconsistency the same author supplies evidence that relatives forced widows to the pyre. He describes a case reported in 1796, in which a widow escaped from the pyre during the night in the rain. A search was made and she was dragged from her hiding place. Walker concludes the story of this woman who "adopted the practice" as follows:

> She pleaded to be spared but her own son insisted that she throw herself on the pile as he would lose caste and suffer everlasting humiliation. When she still refused, the son with the help of some others present bound her hands and feet and hurled her into the blaze.

The same author gives information about the numerical escalation of *suttee*:

> Among the Rājputs and other warrior nations of northern India, the observance of suttee took on staggering proportions, since wives and concubines *immolated themselves* by the hundred. It became customary not only for wives but for mistresses, sisters, mothers, sisters-in-law and other near female relatives and retainers *to burn themselves* along with their deceased master. With Rājputs it evolved into

the terrible rite of *jauhar* which took place in times of war or great peril *in order to save the honour of the womenfolk of the clan* [emphases mine].

Again the victims, through grammatical sleight of hand, are made to appear as the agents of their own destruction. The rite of *jauhar* consisted in heaping all the females of the clan into the fire when there was danger of defeat by the enemy. Thousands of hindu women were murdered this way during the muslim invasion of India. Their masters could not bear that they should be raped, tortured, and killed by foreign males adhering to "different" religious beliefs, rather than by themselves.

The term *custom*—a casual and neutral term—is often used by scholars to describe these barbarous rituals of female slaughter. Clearly, however, they were religious rites. Some scholars assert that an unscrupulous priesthood provided the religious legitimation for the practice by rigging the text of the Rig Veda. Priests justified the ritual atrocity by their interpretations of the law of Karma. Furthermore, the typical mind-diverting orderliness of murderous religious ritual was manifested not only in the ceremonial bathing and dressing of the widows, but included other details of timing and placement. If the widow was menstruating, she was considered impure, and thus a week had to pass after the cessation of her period before she could commit *suttee*. Since impurity also resulted from pregnancy, *suttee* had to be delayed two months after the birth of the child. For the event itself, the widow was often required to sit with the corpse's head in her lap or on her breast. The orderliness is that of ritual: repetitive, compulsive, delusional.

This horror show was made possible by the legitimating role of religious rite, which allows the individual to distinguish between the real self, who may be fearful or scrupulous, and the self as role-performer. This schizoid perception on the part of those participating in the ritual carries over to the scholars who, though temporally or spatially distanced from the rite, identify with *it* rather than with the victims. Joseph Campbell placidly writes of the tortured and sacrificed woman:

> *Sati*, the feminine participle of *sat*, then, is the female who really *is* something in as much as she is truly and properly a player of the female part: she is not only good and true in the ethical sense but true and real ontologically. In her faithful death, she is at one with her own true being.

Thus the ontological and moral problems surrounding female massacre are blandly dismissed. Campbell is simply discussing a social context in which, for a woman, to be killed is "good and true," and to cease to exist is to be. His androcratically attached de-tachment from women's agony is manifested in paragraph after paragraph. After describing the live burial of a young widow which took place in 1813, this devotee of the rites of detached scholarship describes the event as "an *illuminating*, though *somewhat* appalling, glimpse into the deep, silent pool of the Oriental, archaic soul ... [emphases mine]." What eludes this scholar is the fact that the "archaic soul" was a woman destroyed by Patriarchal Religion (in which he is a true believer), which demands female sacrifice.

The bland rituals of patriarchal scholarship perpetuate the legitimation of female sacrifice. The social re-ality, unacknowledged by such myth-masters, is that of minds and bodies mutilated by degradation. The real social context included the common practice of marrying off small girls to old men, since brahmans have what has been called a "strange preference for children of very tender years." Katherine Mayo, in an excellent work entitled with appropriate irony, *Mother India*, shows an understanding of the situation which more famous scholars entirely lack. Her work is, in the precise sense of the word, exceptional. She writes:

> That so hideous a fate as widowhood should befall a woman can be but for one cause—the enormity of her sins in a former incarnation. From the moment of her husband's decease till the last hour of her own life, she must expiate those sins in shame and suffering and self-immolation, chained in every thought to the service of his soul. Be she a child of three, who knows nothing of the marriage that bound her, or be she a wife in fact, having lived with her husband, her case is the same. By his death she is revealed as a creature of innate guilt and evil portent, herself convinced when she is old enough to think at all, of the justice of her fate.

BLAMING THE VICTIM

Western scholars have acknowledged this problem, but in such a way that they have succeeded perfectly in blaming the child victim. For example, a nineteenth-century catholic priest-scholar, the Abbé Dubois, wrote:

> Experience has taught that young Hindu women do not possess sufficient firmness, and sufficient regard for their own honor, to resist the ardent solicitations of a seducer.

The evidence offered by the Abbé for his view of the situation was the fact that mothers admitted they were afraid to leave their eleven- and twelve-year-old daughters at home and accessible to male relatives. The christian priest thus perceives the situation through the lenses of his own tradition, which does not differ profoundly from the one he is observing.* The logic of the evidence which he offers for the "insufficient firmness" of hindu girls may seem strangely familiar to feminists of christian "background," who will recall being told repeatedly by their "confessors" and ministers that the onus of sexual responsibility was on the girl since males had "stronger sex drives."

It would be a mistake, however, to imagine that such ridiculous reasoning is restricted to the christian priesthood, for the priesthood of scholars devoted to the Rites of Re-Search has a more diverse membership. Thus David and Vera Mace, commenting upon the Abbáe's interpretation, appear to find nothing wrong with it, stating themselves that "from an early age, girls in the East were accustomed to the idea that they could not be trusted to guard their own virtue." It requires cultivated obtuseness to fail to grasp the fact that an eleven- or twelve-year-old

girl—particularly one who has had no training in self-defense and who has been trained to view males as gods—would hardly be able to fight off one or several full-grown rapist relatives.

Such horrors have not ceased.* Meanwhile, of the few women in "advanced" countries who have some idea of the facts of sexism and some knowledge of "women's history," far fewer glimpse the continued massacre that is masked by the rituals of re-search which repeatedly re-cover the interconnected crimes of planetary patriarchy. By the dogma of female worthlessness and the device of "blaming the victim" the priests of "objective scholarship" continue to justify a context in which *suttee* can be seen as reasonable and virtuous. From early childhood to old age, women are somehow made to appear at fault. Thus P. Thomas, describing the miserable life of an Indian widow in the house of her deceased husband, writes that "the mother-in-law, never too soft towards her daughters-in-law, could only look upon the widow as the virtual destroyer of her son who would not have died, according to *the then prevalent interpretations* of the law of Karma, if his wife was virtuous [emphasis mine]." Subtly his style lays the blame on that traditional scapegoat, the mother-in-law. His use of the nominalized passive, "the then prevalent interpretations," hides the true agents of the atrocity by suppressing the question: Just *who* created and enforced these interpretations

---

*In the mid-sixties in Rome, during a conversation with roman catholic archbishop Roberts (one of the "radicals" at the Second Vatican Council) who had lived for years in India, he "informed" me that *suttee* is the "logical conclusion" of female nature. Although that prelate was not actively promoting the practice, he was clearly expressing a basic agreement with its underlying asssumptions— assumptions shared by his own particular sect of patriarchal religion.

---

*Nor are they restricted to India. In April 1977 *Time* carried a story exposing a billion-dollar pornography industry in the United States specializing in children as subjects.

which could infect the minds of women who were cast into the role of "mother-in-law"?

Scholarly mystification continues to dull all sense of the unrightness of such rites as *suttee*, regarding them with detached interest and making them appear isolated and unrelated to "our" culture. It thus keeps minds/imaginations in a state of readiness to accept similar or comparable practices which carry out the same program—the killing of female divinity—ultimately requiring the extinction of female life and will to live.

Writing in 1960, David and Vera Mace masterfully muddied the issues illustrated in the rite of *suttee* for anyone searching in their book for insight. They wrote:

> Although *custom* and *duty* left many widows in the East no alternative but to suffer and even to die, it would be a grave *injustice* to explain all their sacrifices in these terms. In many, many cases the widow walked into the fire *proudly* and by *deliberate choice*. This was her way of showing the depth of her *affection*, her *devotion*, her *fidelity*. It was a strange way, and to us a gravely *mistaken* one. But leaving aside the *inappropriateness* of the action and looking at the motive, dare we say that these women of the East knew less of *true love* than their Western sisters [emphases mine]?

The authors erase such obvious questions as: Why did not widowers walk "proudly" into the fire? And, what does "proudly" mean? At times, hundreds, even thousands, of women died in *suttee* for *one* royal male. Who could speak of "pride" in dying for such godmen? How could anyone continue to use such language in the face of such frank admissions as the following statement of a hindu, cited by Mayo:

> We husbands so often make our wives unhappy that we might well fear they would poison us. Therefore did our wise ancestors make the penalty of widowhood so frightful—in order that the woman may not be tempted.

The fear expressed here is clearly a terror of deserved retaliation, for among other things, a wife risked receiving lethal doses of venereal disease by penile injection. The Maces' use of the term *injustice* to describe an attitude of horror and outrage at the widows' fate is worse than absurd. It throws the reader off the track of asking *who* was/is responsible for the real injustice which she finds so horrifying. She is tempted to feel guilty for not understanding women in "another culture." *Mistaken* and *inappropriateness* are bizarre terms in this context. They suggest that there was a real choice involved, and they belittle/distort the horrible reality. As for *true love, devotion*, et cetera, one can speculate that true masochism may be an ideal cherished more by these Western authors than by the widows whose options were so desperately narrowed.

One can find endless examples of such patriarchal scholarship. My purpose here is to detect in these perpetuations of murder patterns whose effect is mental murder. This pattern-detecting—the development of a kind of positive paranoia—is essential for every feminist Searcher, so that she can resist the sort of mind-poisoning to which she must expose herself in the very process of seeking out necessary information. I have already suggested that the feminist Searcher must be particularly aware of subtle mystification through language in books which take a liberal feminist approach and which have become institutionally acceptable materials for Women's Studies. Another example from Vern Bullough illustrates this kind of trap. He writes:

> Nowhere was the concept of inferiority of women more exemplified than in the *custom* of suttee, the Hindu rite of *suicide* of widows by *self-immolation* [emphases mine].

One might well ask whether any scholar would dare to describe the massacre of the Jews in Germany as a Nazi "custom." It is important also to note that even such a liberal scholar uses the terms *suicide* and *self-immolation*. It is abundantly obvious that if there was voluntariness, it consisted in "choosing" to jump from the frying pan into the pyre.

IDENTIFICATION WITH THE OPPRESSOR

If one seeks a probable explanation for such muddying language, I suggest that it may be found in the fact that the authors identify on some level with the agents of the atrocities, while being incapable of identifying with the victims—a subjective condition which is masked by the pose of "objective scholarship." Feminists have learned to expect such blunting of sensibilities in male scholars. Unfortunately, however, many female scholars also use similar language, for the temptation to identify with the male viewpoint—which is legitimated by every field—is strong, and the penalties for not doing so often intimidate women into self-deception. One also finds in teaching Women's Studies that some female students will at first resist seeing obvious implications of the material. A professor of Feminist Ethics described her experience in presenting gynocidal atrocities to her class of undergraduate women. Although most were able to respond intellectually and emotionally to the reality, a minority insisted that the women who died in *suttee* had "free choice." No amount of evidence or reasoning from the rest of the class could move them. However, it is important to recognize that the reasons for women's resistance to consciousness are different from those of men who actually or potentially hold power. For a woman, to begin to allow herself to see is to begin the Feminist Journey, whose hazards she can intuit even before experiencing them.

Yet another dimension of the significance of androcracy's woman-killing rituals is illustrated by *suttee*. That is, the after-effects—including both continued practice and scholarly legitimation of this—extend beyond official termination of the rite. Thus it is not surprising that "practical *suttee*"* has continued to occur among widows in India, even though the public ceremony was legally banned in 1829. Deceptively, this is called "suicide." The remarkable obtuseness of scholars regarding practical *suttee* is illustrated in the writing of Benjamin Walker, who apparently finds *suttee* distasteful only if the victim is "unwilling." He writes:

> Reports of eyewitnesses do record the *heroism* of some women who sought this form of death *of their own free will.*

---

*Katherine Mayo uses this expression to name instances where "the newly widowed wife deliberately pours oil over her garments, sets them afire and burns to death, in a connived-at secrecy" (*Mother India*, p. 83).

Quoting a number of instances from accounts of foreign travellers, Dr. A. S. Altekar speaks of his own sister who as late as 1946 *with indescribable fortitude* carried out her resolve, committing herself to the flames within twenty-four hours of her husband's death in spite of the pressing entreaties of her relations [emphases mine].

Given the immense "knowledge" of this scholar concerning the attitudes toward widows in India, his ignorance is demonic, though typical.

It is enlightening to compare Walker's account of "heroic" *suttee* with Katherine Mayo's realistic assessment of the situation. She writes:

She has seen the fate of other widows. She is about to become a drudge, a slave, starved, tyrannized over, abused—and this is the sacred way out—"following the divine law." Committing a pious and meritorious act, in spite of all foreign-made interdicts, she escapes a present hell and may hope for a happier birth in the next incarnation.

RESISTANCE TO FEMINIST SEARCHERS

Since Katherine Mayo stands as a startling exception among scholars who have written about women in India, it is interesting to look at what happened to her work from the perspective of fifty years later. *Mother India* was published in 1927. It aroused a storm of protest in the East and in the West. There was a flurry of books and articles, replies and counter-replies. Titles of volumes that appeared in the controversy include: *My Mother India; Sister India; Father India; Living India; Understanding India; A Son of Mother India Answers; Neighbour India; Unhappy India; In-*

dia, Step-Mother; India: Its Character, A Reply to Mother India; Shiva or The Future of India. Obviously Mayo had struck a nerve. As a result of her exploration and boldness, the literature multiplied. She herself wrote later books defending her position: *Slaves of the Gods* (1929) and *The Face of Mother India* (1935).

The sort of defensiveness which Mayo's exposé evoked is exemplified in *My Mother India* by Dalip Singh Saund. Defending the hindu married woman's condition, he pictures her as "dropping longingly into his [her husband's] embrace with almost divine confidence . . ." He speaks for his sister (who of course is not allowed to speak for herself):

And when the ideal of her childhood was realized, no wonder she found in his company that height of emotional exaltation which springs from the proper union of the sexes and is the noblest gift of God to man. The American girl thinks my sister married a stranger; but she had married an ideal, a creation of *her* imagination, and a part of her own being [emphasis mine].

In fact, his sister had been trained to worship her appointed husband as a god. She had no choice. The contrast between such defensive rhetoric and Mayo's eyewitness account and analysis speaks for itself.

The evaluation of Mayo's work and its impact has been left to such scholars as the authors of *Marriage: East and West*, who write:

The dust finally settled. It *was conceded* that Katherine Mayo's *facts, as facts,* were substantially accurate. It *was recognized* that she had taken up a serious issue and drawn attention to it, which had helped in some measure to *hasten much-needed reforms.* But at the same time her book had done a *grave injustice to India,* in presenting a one-sided and distorted picture of *an aspect of Indian life* that could only be properly understood *within the context of the entire culture* [emphases mine].

Thus Mayo is put in her place. We find here the familiar use of the passive voice, which leaves unstated just *who* conceded, *who* recognized. We find also the familiar balancing act of scholars, which gives a show of "justice" to their treatment of the attacked author. The qualifying expression, "as facts," added to "facts," has the effect of managing to minimize the factual. Women who counter the patriarchal reality are often accused of "merely imagining," or being on the level of *"mere polemic."* Here we have "mere" facts. Then the authors graciously concede that Mayo hastened "much-needed reforms," which gives the impression that everything has now been taken care of, that the messy details have been tidied up. Then comes the peculiarly deceptive and unjust expression "grave injustice to India." Mayo was concerned about grave injustice to living beings, women. Injustice is done to individual living beings. One must ask how it is possible to do injustice to a social construct, for example, India, by exposing its atrocities. We might ask such re-searchers whether they would be inclined to accuse critics of the Nazi death camps of "injustice" to Germany, or whether they would describe writers exposing the history of slavery and racism in America as guilty of "injustice" to the United States. The Maces go on to accuse Mayo of distorting "an aspect of Indian life." But what *is* "Indian life"? Mayo is concerned not with defending this vague abstraction (presumably meaning customs, beliefs, social

arrangements, et cetera), but with the *lives* of millions of women who happened to live in that part of patriarchy called "India."

The final absurdity in this scholarly obituary is the expression "properly understood within the context of the entire culture." It is Katherine Mayo who demonstrates an understanding of the cultural context, that is, the *entire culture*, refusing to reduce women to "an aspect." Her critics, twenty years after her death, attempted to absorb the realities she exposed into a "broad vision," which turns out to be a meaningless abstraction.

Feminist Searchers should be aware of this device, commonly repeated in the re-searchers' rituals. It involves intimidation by accusations of "one-sidedness," so that others will not listen to the discredited Searcher-Scholar who refused to follow the "right" rites. The device relies upon fears of criticizing "another culture," so that the feminist is open to accusations of imperialism, nationalism, racism, capitalism, or any other "-ism" that can pose as broader and more important than gynocidal patriarchy. Thus the just accuser becomes unjustly sentenced to erasure. Her life's meaning, as expressed in her life's work, is belittled, reversed, wiped out.

Feminist Seekers/Spinsters should search out and claim such sisters as Katherine Mayo. Her books are already rare and difficult to find. It is important that they do not become extinct. Spinsters must unsnarl phallocratic "scholarship" and also find our sister weavers/dis-coverers whose work is being maligned, belittled, erased, deliberately forgotten. We must learn to name our true sisters, and to save their work so that it may be continued rather than re-covered, re-searched, and re-done on the endless wheel of re-acting to the Atrocious Lie which is phallocracy. In this dis-covering and spinning we expand the dimensions of feminist time/space.

In the process of seeking out these sister Seekers/Spinsters, it is essential to look at *their own* writings. Secondary sources, even those which one would hope to be just, are often misleading. The entry on Katherine Mayo by Mary F. Handlin in *Notable American Women*, for example, would throw the reader completely off the track. Handlin gives a disproportionately small amount of space to Mayo's major work, *Mother India*, subtly discredits Mayo's motives, and gives no indication of the content or importance of the book. She distracts the reader by her use of pop psychology, stating that Mayo could confront her own sexual anxiety openly "only in writing about distant places and alien cultures." This is an unsubstantiated and irrelevant personality attack, a device which could be used on any scholar who studies a foreign culture. In order to recognize its inappropriateness, one could look at biographical entries concerning male historians and anthropologists and note the absence of such speculations, as well as the focus upon content and importance of their works. This ultimate burial of the Spinster (and Mayo was "unmarried," a point stressed snidely by Handlin) takes place quietly. Only ashes can be found in such "biographical entries," which softly intone the "last rites" in the series of cross-cultural rituals designed to make us *forget* the murder and dismemberment of the Goddess, that is, the killing of be-ing, of the creative divine life and integrity in concrete, existing women.

Psychology

The field of psychology has received much criticism since the second wave of feminism, when women argued that its theories historically limited women's potential and marked them as mentally ill if they sought to break out of the traditional feminine role. Simultaneously, feminists have also been attracted to a field that promises to unlock the secrets of the mind, help people find happiness, and explain why people think and behave the way they do. In these essays, spanning over thirty years, we have examples of feminist critiques and feminist contributions to the field. Naomi Weisstein's essay offers an early critique of the sexist assumptions that permeated the field and kept psychologists from understanding women. A second wave radical, Weisstein paints a devastating picture of a field that is unable to help women due to its ignorance and distortion of the circumstances that prescribe women's lives. By the 1980s feminists had entered the field and offered new theories that were not only compatible with but consciously sought to facilitate women's liberation and gender equality. Hester Eisenstein provides an overview of some of the important ideas and debates that animated feminist psychologists. Finally, Stephanie Riger's article offers a current assessment of the state of research on gender differences. How much has changed in the field since 1968? Does Riger offer hope that feminism and psychology can be compatible?

Critical Thinking Questions

1. How are Weisstein's criticisms similar in tone and content to other early second wave feminists?
2. Is there an irony in her accusation that the field has been too subjective and unempirical?
3. Does the concept of androgyny sound appealing to you as a means toward gender equality? Why did some feminists find it problematic? Do you agree with their critiques?
4. In what ways is Miller's "new psychology of women" more radical than the androgyny ideal, in what ways more conservative?
5. Weisstein argues that behavior can be predicted from the social situation rather than an individual psychological profile. Thirty years later, Riger

states that what appear to be stable sex differences in behavior might be the product of situational factors. Why have feminist insights been so consistent over time?

6. Do you believe psychological differences exist between males and females? If so, what are these differences and what accounts for them? Must equality be based on sameness?

7. Do Riger's calls for more qualitative and interdisciplinary work mark her argument as "unscientific" or "political"? What reception might these suggestions receive in the academy?

37

"Kinde, Kuche, Kirche" As Scientific Law

Psychology Constructs the Female

(1968)

Dr. Naomi Weisstein

It is an implicit assumption that the area of psychology which concerns itself with personality has the onerous but necessary task of describing the limits of human possiblity. Thus when we are about to consider the liberation of women, we naturally look to psychology to tell us what "true" liberation would mean: what would give women the freedom to fulfill their own intrinsic natures.

Psychologists have set about describing the true natures of women with an enthusiasm and absolute certainty which is rather disquieting. Bruno Bettelheim of the University of Chicago, tells us that:

> We must start with the realization that, as much as women want to be good scientists or engineers, they want

first and foremost to be womanly companions of men and to be mothers.[1]

Erik Erikson of Harvard University, upon noting that young women often ask whether they can "have an identity before they know whom they will marry, and for whom they will make a home," explains somewhat elegiacally that "Much of a young woman's identity is already defined in her kind of attractiveness and in the selectivity of her search for the man (or men) by whom she wishes to be

---

[1] Bruno Bettelheim, "The Commitment Required of a Woman Entering a Scientific Profession in Present Day American Society," *Woman and the Scientific Professions*, MIT symposium on American Women in Science and Engineering, 1965.

Weisstein, Naomi, Kinde, Kuche, Kirche' as Scientific Law: Psychology Constructs the Female. In *Sisterhood Is Powerful: An Anthology of Writings from the Women's Liberation Movement*, ed. Robin Morgan. Random House, 1970. Printed by permission of the author.

sought . . . "[2] Mature womanly fulfillment, for Erikson, rests on the fact that a woman's ". . . somatic design harbors an 'inner space' destined to bear the offspring of chosen men, and with it, a biological, psychological, and ethical commitment to take care of human infancy."[3] Some psychiatrists even see the acceptance of woman's role by women as a solution to societal problems. "Woman is nurturance . . . ," writes Joseph Rheingold, a psychiatrist at Harvard Medical School, ". . . Anatomy decrees the life of a woman . . . When women grow up without dread of their biological functions and without subversion by feminist doctrine, and therefore enter upon motherhood with a sense of fulfillment and altruistic sentiment, we shall attain the goal of a good life and a secure world in which to live it."[4]

These views from men of high prestige reflect a fairly general consensus within psychology: liberation for women will consist first in their attractiveness, so that second, they may obtain the kinds of homes, and the kinds of men, which will allow joyful altruism and nurturance.

Business does not disagree. If views such as Bettelheim's and Erikson's do indeed have something to do with real liberation for women, then seldom in human history has so much money and effort been spent on helping a group of people realize their "true potential" . . . :

Mother, for a while this morning, I thought I wasn't cut out for married life. Hank was late for work and forgot his apricot juice and walked out without kissing me, and when I was all alone I started crying. But then the postman came with the sheets and towels you sent, that look like big bandanna handkerchiefs, and you know what I thought? That those big red and blue handkerchiefs are for girls like me to dry their tears on so they can get busy and do what a housewife has to do. Throw open the windows and start getting the house ready, and the dinner, maybe clean the silver and put new geraniums in the box. *Everything to be ready for him when he walks through that door.*[5]

It is an interesting but limited exercise to show that psychologist's ideas of women's nature fit so remarkably the common prejudice and serve industry and commerce so well. Just because it's good for business doesn't mean it's wrong. What we will show is that it *is wrong;* that there isn't the tiniest shred of evidence that these fantasies of servitude and childish dependence have anything to do with women's true potential; that the idea of the nature of human possibility which rests on the accidents of individual development or genitalia, on what is possible today because of what happened yesterday, on the fundamentalist myth of sex-organ causality, has strangled and deflected psychology so that it is relatively useless in describing, explaining, or predicting humans and their behavior.

It then goes without saying that present psychology is less than worthless in

---

[2] Erik Erikson, "Inner and Outer Space: Reflections on Womanhood," *Daedalus* (93), 1964.

[3] *Ibid.*

[4] Joseph Rheingold, *The Fear of Being a Woman* (New York: Grune & Stratton, 1964), p. 714.

[5] Fieldcrest advertisement in the *New Yorker* (1965). Italics mine.

contributing to a vision which could truly liberate—men as well as women.

My central argument, then, is this. Psychology has nothing to say about what women are really like, what they need and what they want, essentially, because psychology does not know. I want to stress that this failure is not limited to women; rather, the kind of psychology which has addressed itself to how people act and who they are has failed to understand, in the first place, why people act the way they do, and certainly failed to understand what might make them act differently.

The kind of psychology which has addressed itself to these questions has been in large part clinical psychology and psychiatry. Here, the causes of failure are obvious and appalling: Freudians and neo-Freudians, Adlerians and neo-Adlerians, classicists and swingers, clinicians and psychiatrists in general have simply refused to look at the evidence against their theory and their practice, and have used as evidence for their theory and their practice stuff so flimsy and transparently biased as to have absolutely no standing as empirical evidence. But even psychology which conforms to rigorous methodology (academic personality research) has gone about looking at people in such a way as to have limited usefulness. This is because it has been a central assumption for most psychologists of human personality that human behavior rests primarily on an individual and inner dynamic, perhaps fixed in infancy, perhaps fixed by genitalia, perhaps simply arranged in a rather immovable cognitive network. But this assumption is rapidly losing ground as personality psychologists fail again

and again to find consistency in the assumed personalities of their subjects[6] and as the evidence demonstrates that what a person does and who he believes himself to be, will in general be a function of what people around him expect him to be, and what the over-all situation in which he is acting implies that he is. Compared to the influence of the social context within which a person lives, his or her history and "traits," as well as biological makeup may simply be random variations, "noise" superimposed on the true signal which can predict behavior. To summarize: the first reason for psychology's failure to understand what people are and how they act, is that clinicians and psychiatrists, who are generally the theoreticians on these matters, have essentially made up myths without any evidence to support these myths; the second reason for psychology's failure is that personality theory has looked for inner traits when it should have been looking at social context.

Let us turn to the first cause of failure: the acceptance by psychiatrists and clinical psychologists of theory without evidence. If we inspect the literature of personality, it is immediately obvious that the bulk of it is written by clinicians and psychiatrists, and that the major support for their theories is "years of intensive clinical experience." This is a tradition started by Freud and taken up by even his most vehement adversaries. Freud's "insights" occurred during the course of his work with his patients. Now there is nothing wrong

---

[6] J. Block, "Some Reasons for the Apparent Inconsistency of Personality," *Psychological Bulletin* (70) 1968.

with such an approach to theory *formulation;* a person is free to make up theories with any inspiration which works: divine revelation, intensive clinical practice, a random numbers table. However, he is not free to claim any validity for his theory until it has been tested and confirmed, and theories are treated in no such tentative way in ordinary clinical practice. Consider Freud. What he thought constituted evidence violated the most minimal conditions of scientific rigor. In *The Sexual Enlightenment of Children,* the classic document which is supposed to demonstrate empirically the existence of a castration complex and its connection to a phobia, Freud based his analysis on the reports of the father of the little boy, himself in therapy, and a devotee of Freudian theory. I really don't have to comment further on the contamination in this kind of evidence. It is remarkable that only recently has Freud's classic theory on the sexuality of women—the notion of the double orgasm—been actually tested physiologically and found just plain wrong. Now those who claim that fifty years of psychoanalytic experience constitute evidence enough of the essential truths of Freud's theory should ponder the robust health of the double orgasm. Did women, until Masters and Johnson, believe they were having two different kinds of orgasm? Did their psychiatrists cow them into reporting something that was not true? If so, were there other things they reported that were also not true? Did psychiatrists ever learn anything different than their theories had led them to believe? If clinical experience means anything at all, surely we should have been done with the double orgasm myth long before the Masters and Johnson studies.

But certainly, you may object, "years of intensive clinical experience" is the only reliable measure in a discipline which rests its findings on insight, sensitivity, and intuition. The problem with insight, sensitivity, and intuition, is that it can confirm for all time the biases that one started out with. People used to be absolutely convinced of their ability to tell which of their number were engaging in witchcraft. All it required was some sensitivity to the workings of the devil.

Years of intensive clinical experience is not the same thing as empirical evidence. The first thing an experimenter learns in any kind of experiment which involves humans is the concept of the "double blind." The term is taken from medical experiments, where one group is given a drug which is presumably supposed to change behavior in a certain way, and a control group is given a placebo. If the observers or the subjects know which group took which drug, the result invariably comes out on the positive side for the new drug. Only when it is not known which subject took which pill, is validity remotely approximated. In addition, with judgments of human behavior, it is so difficult to precisely tie down just what behavior is going on, let alone what behavior should be expected, that one must test again and again the reliability of judgments. How many judges, blind, will agree in their observations? Can they replicate their own judgments at some later time? When, in actual practice, these judgment criteria are tested for clinical validity, then we find that the judges cannot judge reliably nor can they judge consistently: they do no better than chance in identifying which of a certain set of stories were written by men and which by women; which of a whole battery of clinical test results are the products of homosexuals and which are the products of heterosexuals[7] and which, of a battery of clinical test results *and* interviews (where questions are asked such as "do you have delusions" and "what are your symptoms?"[8]) are products of psychotics, neurotics, psychosomatics, or normals. Lest this summary escape your notice, let me stress the implications of these findings. The ability of judges, chosen for their clinical expertise, to distinguish male heterosexuals from male homosexuals on the basis of three widely used clinical projective tests—the Rorschach, the TAT, and the MAP, was *no better than chance*. The reason this is such devastating news, of course, is that clinicians and psychiatrists assume sexuality to be of fundamental importance in the deep dynamic of personality; if what is considered gross sexual deviance cannot be caught, then what are psychologists talking about when they, for instance, claim that the basis of paranoid psychosis is "latent homosexual panic?" They can't even identify what homosexual anything is, let alone "latent homosexual panic." More alarming, expert clinicians cannot be consistent on what diagnostic category to assign to a person, again on the basis of both tests and interviews; a number of normals in the Little and Schneidman study were described as

psychotic, in such categories as "schizophrenic with homosexual tendencies" or "schizoid character with depressive trends." But most disheartening, when the judges were asked to rejudge the test protocols some weeks later, their diagnoses of the same subjects on the basis of the same protocol, differed markedly from their initial judgments. It is obvious that even simple descriptive conventions in clinical psychology cannot be consistently applied; that these descriptive conventions have any explanatory significance is therefore, of course, out of the question.

As a student in a graduate class at Harvard, some years ago, I was a member of a seminar which was asked to identify which of two piles of a clinical test, the TAT, had been written by males, and which of the two piles had been written by females. Only four students out of twenty identified the piles correctly, and this was after one and a half months of intensively studying the differences between men and women. Since this result is below chance, that is, this result would occur by chance about four out of a thousand times, we may conclude that there *is* finally a consistency here; students are judging knowledgeably within the context of psychological teaching about the differences between men and women; the teachings themselves are simply erroneous.

A frequent argument is that the theory may be scientifically "unsound" but at least it cures people. There is no evidence that it does. In 1952, Eysenck reported the results of what is called an "outcome of therapy" study of neurotics which show that, of the patients who received psychoanalysis, the improvement rate was

[7] E. Hooker, "Male Homosexuality in the Rorschach," *Journal of Projective Techniques* (21), 1957.

[8] K.B. Little and E.S. Schneidman, "Congruences among Interpretations of Psychological Test and Anamnestic Data," *Psychological Monographs* (73) 1959.

44 percent; of the patients who received psychotherapy, the improvement rate was 64 percent; and the patients who received no treatment at all, the improvement rate was 72 percent. These findings have never been refuted; subsequent studies have confirmed the negative results of the Eysenck study.[9] How can clinicians and psychiatrists then, in all good conscience, continue to practice? Largely by ignoring these results and being careful not to do outcome-of-therapy studies. The attitude is nicely summarized by Rotter: "research studies in psychotherapy tend to be concerned more with some aspects of the psychotherapeutic procedure and less with outcome . . . to some extent, it reflects an interest in the psychotherapy situation as a kind of personality laboratory."[10] Some laboratory.

Thus, we can conclude that since clinical experience and tools can be shown to be worse than useless when tested for consistency, efficacy, agreement, and reliability, we can safely conclude that theories of a clinical nature advanced about women are also worse than useless.

I want to turn now to my second major point, which is that, even when psychological theory is constructed so that it may be tested, and rigorous standards of evidence are used, it has become increasingly clear that in order to understand why people do what they do, and certainly in order to change what people do, psychologists must turn away from the theory of the causal nature of the inner dynamic and look to the social context within which individuals live.

Before examining the relevance of this approach for the question of women, let me first sketch the groundwork for this assertion.

In the first place, it is clear that personality tests never yield consistent predictions; a rigid authoritarian on one measure will be an unauthoritarian on the next.[11] But the reason for this inconsistency is only now becoming clear, and it seems overwhelmingly to have much more to do with the social situation in which the subject finds himself than with the subject himself.

In a series of brilliant experiments, Rosenthal and his co-workers have shown that if one group of experimenters has one hypothesis about what they expect to find, and another group of experimenters has the opposite hypothesis, both groups will in fact obtain results in accord with their hypotheses.[12] The results obtained are not due to mishandling of data by biased experimenters; rather, somehow, the bias of the experimenter creates a changed environment in which subjects actually act

---

[9] F. Barron and T. Leary, "Changes in Psychoneurotic Patients with and without Psychotherapy," *Journal of Counseling Psychology* (19) 1955; A.E. Bergin, "The Effects of Psychotherapy: Negative Results Revisited," *Journal of Counseling Psychology* (10) 1963; R.D. Cartwright and J.L. Vogel, "A Comparison of Changes in Psychoneurotic Patients During Matched Periods of Therapy and No-therapy," *Journal of Counseling Psychology* (24) 1960; C.B. Traux, "Effective Ingredients in Psychotherapy: An Approach to Unreveling the Patient-Therapist Interaction," *Journal of Counseling Psychology* (10) 1963; E. Powers and H. Witmer, *An Experiment in the Prevention of Delinquency* (New York: Columbia University Press. 1951).

[10] J.B. Rotter, "Psychotherapy," *Annual Review of Psychology* (11) 1960.

[11] J. Block, *op. cit.*

differently. For instance, in one experiment, subjects were to assign numbers to pictures of men's faces, with high numbers representing the subject's judgment that the man in the picture was a successful person, and low numbers representing the subject's judgment that the man in the picture was an unsuccessful person. One group of experimenters was told that the subjects tended to rate faces high; another group of experimenters was told that subjects tended to rate the faces low. Each group of experimenters was instructed to follow precisely the same procedure: they were required to read a set of instructions to subjects and to say nothing else. For the 375 subjects run, the results showed clearly that those subjects who performed the task with experimenters who expected high ratings gave high ratings; those subjects who performed the task with experimenters who expected low ratings gave low ratings. (The results would have happened by chance about one in one thousand times.) How did this happen? The experimenters all used the same words; it was something in their conduct which made one group of subjects do one thing, and another group of subjects do another thing.

The concreteness of the changed conditions produced by expectation is a fact, a reality: even with animal subjects, where there can be no verbal communication, in two separate studies[13] those experimenters who were told that rats learning mazes had been especially bred for brightness obtained better learning from their rats than did experimenters believing their rats to have been bred for dullness. In a recent study, Rosenthal and Jacobson extended their analysis to the natural classroom situation. Here, they tested a group of students and reported to the teachers that some among the students tested "showed great promise." Actually, the students so named had been selected on a random basis. Some time later, the experimenters retested the group of students; those students whose teachers had been told that they were promising showed real and dramatic increments in their I.Q.'s as compared to the rest of the students. Something in the conduct of the teachers towards the "bright" students made them brighter.

Thus, even in carefully controlled experiments, and with no outward or conscious difference in behavior, the hypotheses we start with will influence enormously the behavior of another organism. These studies are extremely important when assessing the validity of psychological studies of women. Since it is fairly safe to say that most of us start with hypotheses as to the nature of men and women, the validity of a number of observations on sex differences is questionable, even when these observations have been taken under carefully controlled conditions. Second, and more importantly, the Rosenthal experi-

[12] R. Rosenthal and L. Jacobson, *Pygmalion in the Classroom: Teacher Expectation and Pupil's Intellectual Development* (New York: Holt, Rinehart & Winston, 1968); R. Rosenthal, *Experimenter Effects in Behavioral Research* (New York: Appleton-Century Crofts, 1966).

[13] R. Rosenthal and K. L. Fode, "The Effect of Experimenter Bias on the Performance of the Albino Rat" (Harvard University, 1961); R. Rosenthal and R. Lawson, "A Longitudinal Study of the Effects of Experimenter Bias on the Operant Learning of Laboratory Rats" (Harvard University, 1961).

ments point quite clearly to the influence of social expectation. In some extremely important ways, people are what you expect them to be, or at least they behave as you expect them to behave. Thus, if women, according to Bruno Bettelheim, want first and foremost to be good wives and mothers, it is extremely likely that that is what Bruno Bettelheim (and the rest of society) want them to be.

There is another series of social psychological experiments which points to the inescapable, overwhelming weight of social context in an extremely vivid way. These are the obedience experiments of Stanley Milgram,[14] concerned with the extent to which subjects in psychological experiments will obey the orders of unknown experimenters, even when these orders carry with them the distinct possibility that the subject is killing somebody.

In Milgram's experiments a subject is told that he is administering a learning experiment, and that he is to deal out shocks each time the other "subject" (in reality, a confederate of the experimenter) answers incorrectly. The equipment appears to provide graduated shocks ranging upwards from 15 to 450 volts; for each four consecutive voltages there are verbal descriptions such as "mild shock," "danger, severe shock," and finally, for the 435 and 450 volt switches, simply a red XXX marked over the switches. Each time the stooge answers incorrectly the subject is supposed to increase the voltage. As the voltage increases the stooge begins to cry in pain; he demands that the ex-

periment stop; finally, he refuses to answer at all. When he stops responding, the experimenter instructs the subject to continue increasing the voltage; for each shock administered, the stooge shrieks in agony. Under these conditions, about 62.5 percent of the subjects administered shock that they believed to be possibly lethal.

No tested individual differences between subjects predicted which of the subjects would continue to obey, and which would break off the experiment. When forty psychiatrists predicted how many of a group of one hundred subjects would go on to give the maximum shock, their predictions were far below the actual percentages; most expected only one-tenth of one percent of the subjects to obey to the end. But even though psychiatrists have no idea of how people are going to behave in this situation (despite the fact that one of the central phenomena of the twentieth century is that people have been made to kill enormous numbers of other people), and even though individual differences do not predict which subjects will obey and which will not, it is easy to predict when subjects will be obedient and when they will be defiant. All the experimenter has to do is change the social situation. In a variant of Milgram's experiment, two stooges were present in addition to the "victim"; these worked along with the subject in administering electric shocks. When these two stooges refused to go on with the experiment, only ten percent continued to the maximum voltage. This is critical for personality theory. It says that the lawful behavior is the behavior that can be predicted from the social situation, not from the individual history.

---

[14] Stanley Milgram, "Liberating Effects of Group Pressure," *Journal of Personality and Social Psychology* (1) 1965.

Finally, an ingenious experiment by Schachter and Singer[15] showed that subjects injected with adrenalin (which produces a state of physiological arousal in all but minor respects identical to that which occurs when subjects are extremely afraid) became euphoric when they were in a room with a stooge who was acting euphoric, and became extremely angry when they were placed in a room with a stooge who was acting extremely angry.

To summarize: if subjects under quite innocuous and noncoercive social conditions can be made to kill other subjects and under other types of social conditions will positively refuse to do so; if subjects can react to a state of physiological fear by becoming euphoric because there is somebody else around who is euphoric, or angry because there is somebody else angry; if students become intelligent because teachers expect them to be intelligent, and rats run mazes better because experimenters are told that the rats are bright, then it is obvious that a study of human behavior requires first and foremost, a study of the social contexts within which people move, the expectations as to how they will behave, and the authority which tells them who they are and what they are supposed to do.

Two theories of the nature of women, which come not from psychiatric and clinical tradition, but from biology, can be disposed of now with little difficulty. The first argument notices social interaction in primate groups, and observes that females are submissive and passive. Putting aside for a moment the serious problem of experimenter bias,[16] the problem with the argument from primate groups is that the crucial experiment has not been performed. The crucial experiment would manipulate or change the social organization of these groups, and watch the subsequent behavior. Until then, we must conclude that, since primates are at present too stupid to change their social conditions by themselves, the "innateness" and fixedness of their behavior is simply not known. As applied to humans, the argument becomes patently irrelevant, since the most salient feature of human social organization is its variety; and there are a number of cultures where there is at least a rough equality between men and women.[17] Thus, primate arguments tell us very little.

The second theory of sex differences argues that since females and males differ in their sex hormones, and sex hormones enter the brain, there must be innate differences in "nature."[18] But the only thing this argument tells us is that there are differences in physiological state. The

---

[15] S. Schachter and J.E. Singer, "Cognitive, Social, and Physiological Determinants of Emotional State," *Psychological Review* (69) 1962.

---

[16] For example, H. F. Harlow, "The Heterosexual Affectional System in Monkeys," *The American Psychologist* (17) 1962. After observing differences between male and female rhesus monkeys, Harlow quotes Lawrence Sterne to the effect that women are silly and trivial, and concludes that "men and women have differed in the past and they will differ in the future."

[17] Margaret Mead, *Male and Female: A Study of the Sexes in a Changing World* (New York: Mentor, 1955).

problem is whether these differences are at all relevant to behavior. Recall that Schachter and Singer[19] have shown that a particular physiological state can itself lead to a multiplicity of felt emotional states, and outward behavior, depending on the social situation.

In brief, the uselessness of present psychology with regard to women, is simply a special case of the general conclusion: one must understand social expectations about women if one is going to characterize the behavior of women.

How are women characterized in our culture, and in psychology? They are inconsistent, emotionally unstable, lacking in a strong conscience or superego, weaker, "nurturant" rather than productive, "intuitive" rather than intelligent, and, if they are at all "normal," suited to the home and the family. In short, the list adds up to a typical minority group stereotype of inferiority: if they know their place, which is in the home, they are really quite lovable, happy, childlike, loving creatures.[20] In a review of the intellectual differences between little boys and little girls, Eleanor Maccoby[21] has shown that there are no intellectual differences until about high school, or, if there are, girls are slightly ahead of boys. At high school, girls begin to do worse on a few intellectual tasks, such as arithmetic reasoning, and beyond high school, the achievement of women now measured in terms of productivity and accomplishment drops off even more rapidly. There are a number of other, nonintellectual tests which show sex differences; I choose the intellectual differences since it is seen clearly that women start becoming inferior. It is no use to talk about women being different but equal; all of the tests I can think of have a "good" outcome and a "bad" outcome. Women usually end up at the "bad" outcome. In light of social expectations about women, what is surprising is not that women end up where society expects they will; what is surprising is that little girls don't get the message that they are supposed to be stupid until high school; and what is even more remarkable is that some women resist this message even after high school, college, and graduate school.

I began with remarks on the task of discovering the limits of human potential. Until psychologists realize that it is they who are limiting discovery of human potential, by their refusal to accept evidence, if they are clinical psychologists, or, if they are rigorous, by their assumption that people move in a context-free ether, with only their innate dispositions and their individual traits determining what they will do, then psychology will have nothing of substance to offer in this task. I don't know what immutable differences exist between men and women apart from differences in their genitalia; perhaps there are some other unchangeable differences; probably there are a number

---

[18] D.A. Hamburg and D.T. Lunde, "Sex Hormones in the Development of Sex Differences in Human Behavior," in Maccoby, ed., *The Development of Sex Differences* (Stanford: Stanford University Press, 1966), pp. 1–24.

[19] S. Schachter and J.E. Singer, *op cit.*

[20] H.M. Hacker, "Women as a Minority Group," *Social Forces* (30) 1951.

[21] Eleanor E. Maccoby, "Sex Differences in Intellectual Functioning," in Maccoby, *op. cit.*

of irrelevant differences. But it is clear that until social expectations for men and women are equal, until we provide equal respect for both men and women, our answers to this question will simply reflect our prejudices.

38

Androgyny and the Psychology of Women

(1983)

Hester Eisenstein

If lesbian feminism was one source of the woman-centered perspective, another was the debate over the psychology of women. An early focus of contemporary feminist thought was the psychological damage done to women by the system of sex-role stereotyping. Their traditional role prescribed a character structure and a set of values for women that evoked contempt from men toward women, and from women toward themselves. The condition of being subordinated by and to men had turned women into an inferior "species." Women had fulfilled their role expectations all too successfully. As a result, they were genuinely ill-fitted for equality with men. By a kind of self-fulfilling prophecy, women had become the poor creatures that men thought they were.

An influential exponent of this point of view was the psychologist Phyllis Chesler. In *Women and Madness,* she documented the results, among women, of the social process of conditioning for appropriate sex-role behavior. Chesler took the argument from sex roles to its logical conclusion. Millett, Janeway, Naomi Weisstein, and others had pointed out that, in the division of characteristics that governed sex-role stereotyping, women had received the worst of the deal. In establishing such a rigid difference between "male" and "female," society appeared to have allocated to "female" all of the qualities that males thought were undesirable. If the evidence from the practice of psychoanalysts was to be credited, it appeared that expectations for normal behavior in males—for so-called "masculinity"— were the same as expectations for normal behavior in human beings generally. But expectations for normal behavior in females—for so-called "femininity"—if abstracted from their connection to women, were in fact expectations for abnormal or nonfunctioning human beings. In other words, if a man acted like a woman (or, more precisely, in the manner expected of a woman), he would be adjudged to be sick or disturbed, and would be treated accordingly. But if a woman acted like a woman, this identical behavior in her case would be adjudged to be "normal" and as expected.

What, then, was society saying about women? It was saying, said Chesler, that women were supposed to be sick. For women, sickness—and specifically, mental illness—was an expected condition, part of the definition of what and how women were. To conform to the stereotype of "womanly" or "feminine" meant to display those characteristics that distinguished women from men. It meant, therefore, behavior that was passive or weak, compliant, and indecisive. It meant being easily moved to tears ("hysterical"), susceptible to suggestion from others, easily led or persuaded. It meant being nonaggressive and noncompetitive, and dependent, in need of direction, as well as companionship and affection. In short, women were meant to be inadequate, self-doubting, and essentially incapable of a strong, independent, and autonomous existence. The sex-role stereotype for women, Chesler maintained, was a prescription for failure, for victimization, and in extreme cases, for severe mental illness.

What about the woman who refused to conform to the social and familial expectations that she encountered, who declined to become "feminine"? Chesler argued that the rebellious woman—whether lesbian or straight—was likely to be caught in the worst kind of no-win situation, a kind of "Catch-22." Society, and society's representatives and guardians, the members of the psychological profession, would punish such a woman severely for her failure to conform. They would label her "deviant," abnormal or mentally ill, and would attempt to bring her back to the kind of behavior and attitudes deemed suitable for women. Thus a lesbian woman would find her psychologist attempting to "cure" her of her sexual preference for women and persuade her to learn how to "need" men. Similarly, a straight woman with ambitions for a career in a male-dominated profession would find her therapist arguing that she should learn to give up her abnormally high rate of aspirations and learn to become a good wife. Thus, to be a "normal" woman was to be sick or mad, and to be an "abnormal" woman was to be called, and treated as, sick or mad. Often, Chesler argued, these kinds of reactions could in fact drive rebellious women mad, that is, back to normality for women, which, she said, was inevitably madness.

What, then, was the way out for women? How could they emerge from the cultural and psychological trap set for them by the prescribed feminine role? What less damaging alternatives for women could be imagined? Consciousness-raising, to be sure, was a first step: becoming aware of the limits and dangers of femininity, both as an individual psychological state, and as a wider social phenomenon, was a prerequisite for change. But where did women go from there?

One suggestion, much debated among feminists, feminist-influenced academics, and popularizers of feminism in the early 1970s was a return to the ancient concept of androgyny. Carolyn Heilbrun argued that, in Western literature and mythology, there was a long-standing tradition defining the human as combining the best qualities of men and women. The exaggerated and polarized traits of conventional masculinity and femininity that characterized modern culture could be replaced with a balanced vision drawing on the best of each. Androgyny, an

> ancient Greek word—from *andro* (male) and *gyn* (female)—. . . seeks to liberate the individual from the confines of the appropriate. . . . [It] suggests . . . a full range of experience open to individuals who may, as women, be aggressive, as men, tender; it suggests a spectrum upon which human beings choose their places without regard to propriety or custom.

While Heilbrun traced the path of the "hidden river" of androgyny through the Western tradition from Plato to Virginia Woolf, others turned their attention to institutionalizing the concept in the practice of contemporary psychology. As Phyllis Chesler and others had noted, psychology made radical distinctions between expectations for males and females. These expectations were enshrined in personality tests, used widely to judge the "normality" or "abnormality" of a given subject. Standardized separate sets of criteria were used to check for normality in males and females, respectively. Sandra Bem designed what she termed an "androgynous" test, one that would blend the traits usually allocated to "masculine" and "feminine" subjects into a series of traits that were both crucial to the mental health of any individual, male or female. On her new androgynous personality scale, the Bem Sex-Role Inventory (BSRI), the most healthy and well-adjusted subjects, male or female, registered the most extensive and complete range of traits traditionally considered "normal" for male and female. That is, the well-adjusted, androgynous person

registered on the scale as possessing the full range of so-called female qualities—nurturance, compassion, tenderness, sensitivity, affiliativeness, cooperativeness—along with the full range of so-called masculine qualities—aggressiveness, leadership, initiative, competitiveness—all at the same time. Bem reported that it was the brightest and most accomplished people (using other criteria such as intelligence testing and educational achievement) who measured as most androgynous, that is, as least reflective of traditional male or female sex-role stereotypes.

In the thinking of Bem and like-minded psychologists, the problems created by sex-role stereotyping—what Heilbrun called "the macho-sex-kitten dichotomy, the inevitable quarterback-cheerleader assignment of life's roles"—could be eliminated by means of the concept of androgyny. In a new "psychology of androgyny," sex-role stereotypes would be set aside. Alternative criteria of mental health would separate sex from gender once and for all. In this new world maleness and femaleness would be experienced as elements of one's physical awareness—one would be conscious of inhabiting a body supplied with the biological capacities and characteristics of male or female—but in no other way. In Bem's view,

> a healthy sense of maleness or femaleness involves little more than being able to look into the mirror and to be perfectly comfortable with the body that one sees there. . . . But beyond being comfortable with one's body, one's gender need have no other influence on one's behavior or life style.

In Bem's analysis, the problem that had so troubled Shulamith Firestone—that of the biological capacity of women to bear children—became a nonproblem. Once "all people" had become "psychologically androgynous," the relationship of women to childbearing would be a simple matter of free choice: "although I would suggest that a woman ought to feel comfortable about the fact that she can bear children if she wants to, this does not imply that she ought to want to bear children, nor that she ought to stay home with any children that she does bear." Presumably, under the regime of androgyny, any problems of childcare could be solved by tapping men's newly developed nurturant instincts.

Popularized versions of the androgyny model received widespread attention and a good deal of apparent acceptance. Media interpretations such as Marlo Thomas's *Free to Be . . . You and Me*, in book, record, and film form, with Roosevelt Grier giving the example of a symbolic black football hero not embarrassed about crying, and the children's book about a gender-free child named "X." about whom no one could form rigid gender-expectations, helped to publicize the concept. Adrienne Rich remarked that "[a]ndrogyny has recently become a "good" word (like "motherhood" itself!) implying many things to many people, from bisexuality to a vague freedom from imposed sexual roles."

On one level, androgyny was a solution to the problem of sex-role stereotyping. Logically speaking, there was a certain inevitability in the progression from the analysis of sex-role stereotypes to the endorsement of psychological androgyny. If the problems encountered by women stemmed primarily from their allocation to a limiting feminine sex role, then the abolition of sex-role stereotyping was a plausible solution. If the

major element in the oppression of women was the enforcement of their differences from men, that is, the exaggeration of femininity as different from or other than masculinity, then it made sense to argue for the psychological homogenization of the two sexes.

Critics of androgyny among feminists, however, queried just how radical a model it was, in the form presented by Heilbrun, Bem, and others. Some noted that, while masquerading as a progressive concept, it still contained a reactionary core, in that it enshrined, and perpetuated, the association of certain traits with women and others with men. The androgynous ideal hoped to put back together that which had been split asunder by culture, like the beings in the Platonic myth, who, cut in half and severed from their mates, wandered the world seeking to be reunited and become once again a complete human being. But in this idealized reunification of what should never have been artificially separated, the androgynous ideal remained a static concept, in which traditional notions of the masculine and the feminine were simply stitched back together, in a "split-level hybrid or integration model. . . ." Catharine Stimpson pointed out that "the androgyne still fundamentally thinks in terms of 'feminine' and 'masculine.' It fails to conceptualize the world and to organize phenomena in a new way that leaves 'feminine' and 'masculine' behind."

In fact, the concept of psychological androgyny had a certain congruency, on the psychic level, with the demands of bourgeois feminism on the economic level. Feminist activists were fighting for the abolition of sex-linked job qualifications, and for the right of women to have access to all areas of the paid workforce. As Janeway, Millett, and others had pointed out, distinctions about women's capacities in the workforce were often linked to the allegedly intrinsic differences between women and men, which had been used to keep women out of male-dominated jobs. If women wished to have the full range of work opened to them, one way to accomplish this was to show that women had or could develop all of the important "male" characteristics demanded by employers.

Psychological androgyny meant that women, like men, could exercise hitherto masculine qualities: they could be "aggressive, ambitious, analytical, assertive, athletic, competitive, . . . dominant, forceful, . . . self-reliant, . . . willing to take risks. . . ." Of course, proponents of androgyny pointed out the value of males acquiring the "feminine" values, as well, such as being "affectionate, cheerful, childlike, compassionate, . . . flatterable, gentle, gullible, . . . sensitive to the needs of others, . . . understanding, warm, yielding." But these qualities tended to have less of a market value. The impact of the androgynous ideal in the capitalist marketplace appeared to be the demonstration that, in the competition for access to all areas of work, in particular, in the competition for access to positions of power, leadership, and authority, women were as good as men. That men could be as good as women did not, in this context, appear to be an important consideration.

In fact, the argument that, by means of psychological androgyny, women could be or become as good as men assumed that, in itself, the so-cialization of men left nothing to be desired. To be sure, according to the androgynous ideal, men were to learn to develop those parts of themselves left under-developed in their socialization as men. They were to learn, like Rosie Grier, to cry, to express their pent up feelings, and they were to legitimize their nurturing instincts. But the suggestion was that these traits would be added on, as a welcome addition to or enrichment of the male character. The BSRI revealed no critique of male characteristics. Indeed, the androgynous concept embodied an uncritical vision of maleness and of masculinity: the qualities of aggression, competitiveness, leadership, and so on were taken to be good in themselves, and therefore important for all people to acquire.

Above all, the androgynous ideal appeared to ignore or to gloss over issues of power. It held out a promise of social change via individual psychological transformation. There was no room in the androgyny concept for market forces or other material factors. And there certainly was little or no acknowledgment of the political dimension of relations between women and men. As Janice Raymond wrote, "the language and imagery of androgyny is the language of dominance and servitude combined. One would not put master and slave language or imagery together to define a free person." As with much of the academic literature on sex roles, the fundamental feminist critique of male dominance over women tended to disappear from the debate. Jean Baker Miller remarked that combining aspects of maleness and femaleness might appear to be an appealing conceit. But "[t]he idea remains a fanciful notion unless we ask seriously who really runs the world. . . . "

Instead of androgyny, Miller, a psychoanalyst, proposed an alternative: a new psychology of women. Miller began with the feminist premise that women had been what she called "subordinates," and men "dominants," and that this arrangement had only come into question in recent times. But, she asked, what if one chose to regard women's historic oppression as a potential source of strength and power for women? Miller proposed to think about the victimization of women dialectically (although she did not use this term). She sought to examine not only what had been done to women by virtue of their subordination to men, but also, what women had become, and made of themselves, in response to this condition. Was it possible that the attribution to women by men of certain psychological characteristics had not been an entirely negative phenomenon, needing to be remedied by the "adding-on" of "masculine" characteristics, but rather that this process had had positive, life-enhancing effects as well? Were there aspects of woman's condition that had some intrinsic psychological and social value?

In Miller's analysis, the historic subordination of women was a fundamental underpinning of Western civilization. Freud had maintained that civilization was built upon the repression of sexuality. In Miller's elaboration of Freud, the male "dominants" had repressed not only sexuality, but that group with whom they associated, and onto whom they projected the idea of sexuality, namely, women. In all societies, she argued, those who held the dominant position determined what aspects of life and culture had the most importance and the greatest value, and then took charge of those aspects for themselves. The other aspects, those deemed to be of lower value or of lesser importance, or those that the dominants wished to be relieved of, to keep buried and out of sight, would be assigned to the subordinates. In Western culture, the ruling groups valued and kept for themselves intellectual and managerial functions, and above all, abilities "related to 'managing' and overcoming the perceived hazards of the physical environment." The aspects that the dominants would assign to subordinates would be those that were "perceived as uncontrollable or as evidence of weakness and helplessness." These would include sexuality; "the realm of 'object relations,' " that is, intense interpersonal relationships; and things associated with the physical and bodily functions, generally. All of these aspects of human experience, Miller held, had been relegated to subordinates, and specifically, to women. Thus "women . . . [became] the 'carriers' for society of certain aspects of the total human experience. . . . "

Psychoanalysis itself, Miller suggested, had only become necessary because of this act of dissociation and repression by the dominant male culture. That is, the division of labor which resulted in the assignment of these realms to women, themselves subordinated in the culture as a whole, made it necessary to create a special science to dredge up that which had been so repressed and buried among the male dominants.

It seems possible that Freud had to discover the very specialized technique of psychoanalysis because there were crucial parts of the human experience that were not well provided for in fully acceptable and socially open ways within the culture of the dominant group. That is, they were not well provided for by the dominants *for the* dominants *themselves.*

Thus, in Miller's view, the things "assigned" to women were human skills crucial to the functioning of a healthy human society. These had been in some sense cast off by men, and relegated to women. At the same time, these necessary qualities were devalued, as "women's" and therefore inferior. This process distorted the human realities, according to a system of values that governed a very distorted culture.

Miller's analysis led to a reinterpretation, for example, of the conventional division between "rational" and "emotional" faculties. Men cultivated rationality, and attempted to diminish their vulnerability to emotions. Women, on the other hand, were encouraged to be attuned to emotions, especially those of others. As she put it, "[m]en are encouraged from early life to be active and rational; women are trained to be involved with emotions and with the feelings occurring in the course of all activity." Women learned their emotional skills at least to some degree as a result of their subordination.

> Most women do have a much greater sense of the emotional components of all human activity than most men. This is, in part, a result of their training as subordinates; for anyone in a subordinate position must learn to be attuned to the vicissitudes of mood, pleasure, and displeasure of the dominant group. Black writers have made this point very clearly.

But in Miller's view the devaluing of emotions was a serious cultural error. The skills often dismissed as "womanly intuition" or "womanly wiles," she argued, were in fact evidence of women's possessing "a basic ability that is very valuable. It can hardly be denied that emotions are essential aspects of human life."

In Miller's concept, the contemporary psychological condition of women pointed in two directions. She grouped some of the capacities and characteristics currently *"more highly developed in women as a group"* in a chapter labeled "Strengths," even though she pointed out that those characteristics had traditionally been called "weaknesses." Specifically, women's ability to express vulnerability, weakness, and helplessness; their capacity to experience, express, and interpret emotions; their capacity to cultivate cooperativeness, and to encourage coordination and working together, especially in the family—all of these, said Miller, were "two-sided" qualities.

> In a situation of inequality and powerlessness, these characteristics can lead to subservience and to complex psychological problems. . . . On the other hand, the dialogue is always with the future. These same characteristics represent potentials that can provide a new framework, one which would have to be inevitably different from that of the dominant male society.

In a society that was differently organized, Miller was suggesting, the very facts about women's psychology that had been treated as aspects of their inferiority could become the building blocks of a new and more humane culture.

Miller's view of the way out for women was, then, rather different from that proposed by the androgynous ideal. She was not proposing some kind of amalgam of "masculine" and "feminine" to create a new, "whole" personality that could be comfortably inhabited by men and women alike. Rather, she was suggesting that in the creation of the new woman—the woman produced by feminism—the crucial ingredients would come from the traditional strengths of women developed during the long period of their subordination. She believed that what women had learned in subordination would be the "psychic starting point" for "an entirely different (and more advanced) approach to living and functioning—very different, that is, from the approach fostered by the dominant culture." Thus, for Miller, women were *not* in need of being "cured" of their disabilities as developed under the debilitating impact of a male-dominated culture. Rather, the culture itself was desperately in need of those qualities that it had foolishly relegated only to women.

On one level, Miller's view of the damage done to women was not that different from that of Phyllis Chesler. She acknowledged the pain and the difficulty that women encountered in attempting to fill their traditional roles of wife and mother, as well as the fears and terrors experienced by the women who were attempting to step out of these roles into a new sense of self-definition and self-concept. Where she differed from Chesler was in the weight and importance that she attributed to the strengths of women, in the struggle for self-determination that they were undertaking under the influence of feminist ideas. In these traditional qualities of women, Miller saw the

seeds of a new set of social values. The goal for women, she argued, should by no means be to learn to act like, think like, and adopt the values of, men and the male-dominant culture. Rather, concepts such as autonomy, power, authenticity, self-determination—all of these should be reexamined and redefined by women, in order to incorporate within them some of the features of their "old" strengths while acquiring new ones. In the new psychology of women envisioned by Miller, some of the dichotomies decreed by male culture, and the traditional psychology it had produced—aggressiveness versus passivity; leadership, independence, and autonomy versus affiliativeness; power versus powerlessness—could be dissolved or transcended. Thus, for example, the concept of autonomy as it had been developed to apply to men was, she argued, inappropriate for women.

[A] word like *autonomy*, which many of us have used and liked, may need revamping for women. It carries the implication—and for women therefore the threat—that one should be able to pay the price of giving up affiliations in order to become a separate and self-directed individual.

Being autonomous, for men, usually meant the enhancement, rather than the sacrifice, of relationships, while for women it could in fact mean the opposite, given the usual reluctance of most men to tolerate a self-directed woman in intimate relationship. But, in addition, Miller argued that women needed a broadened concept of autonomy, or even, a more "complete" notion than autonomy. "Women are quite validly seeking something more complete than autonomy as it is defined for

men, a fuller not a lesser ability to encompass relationships to others, *sim-
ultaneous with the fullest development
of oneself*" (my italics). For women,
then, a new concept of autonomy
would mean a sense of self-direction
and self-determination that grew in
relation to, and with the help of, a
sense of affiliation and connection
with others, rather than in competition against them. Thus autonomy, in
the new psychology of women, would
be unhooked from its links to aggression and violence toward others.

The "new psychology of women,"
then, meant in general a development
that took as its base the psychological
characteristics that had been fostered
in women while they were "subordinates." It built on this base a set of
strengths growing out of women's

new aspiration to be equals. Miller
saw that the major resources for
women's growth in the era of feminism would come from women's own
experience in an era of subordination. She did not prescribe to women
that they should abandon what they
knew, as defective and faulty, now
that they sought equality. Rather, she
called upon them to remember it, because it was their experience, rather
than that of men, that in her view
held the seeds for a possible human
future. Miller's interpretation of the
psychology of women, then, was an
important expression of a woman-
centered analysis. Not only did she
focus on women rather than men as
her object of study: she took the condition of women as potentially normative for all human beings.

39

From Snapshots to Videotape

New Directions in Research on Gender Differences

(1997)

Stephanie Riger

As director of a women's studies program, people often besiege me with questions about sex differences. Their questions typically are prompted by stories that appear in the media reporting the latest supposedly "scientific" findings of gender differences. Is it true, they ask me, that men can park their cars better than women? That women cannot read maps? What do the experts say? Sit down, I tell them, this is going to take a while.

There are at least five different responses to the question of whether there are sex differences. These five answers derive from different traditions within psychology. The earliest tradition, an individual differences model, produced what I call "snapshot" research, that is, one-time, quick, narrowly focused studies in which people's performance is assumed to be the product of internal factors, be they biology or socialization. This model has been expanded at least to some extent by a social psychological model that incorporates situational factors as causal possibilities. I believe that both of these models are limited, and here I advocate further expansion into what I will describe as "video-tape" rather than "snapshot" research, which would enable us both to capture the dynamic qualities of gendered behavior and to widen our lens to include larger cultural, historic, and economic forces as causal agents.

THE MAIN ARGUMENTS

First, let me describe the five answers to the question of whether there are sex differences:

The "Sociobiology" Argument

Some researchers state clearly and unequivocally that there are significant sex differences, that those differences are, at least in part, biologically based, and that they affect our social lives in important ways. Perhaps the form of this argument most widely broadcast these days is the evolutionary psychology of David Buss and his colleagues (vigorously popularized

Riger, Stephanie, "From snapshots to videotape." *Journal of Social Issues*, V53 (1997): 395–408.

by Robert Wright in *Time* and *The New Republic*, among other venues). Buss argues that sex differences have a biological basis in reproductive roles: women face the need for life-sustaining resources while they are pregnant and lactating, and men face the need to reduce uncertainty about the paternity of the offspring they support. These different adaptive challenges have produced different psychological mechanisms in men and women which, in turn, are moderated by social factors.

However, as Fausto-Sterling points out, evolutionary theories in psychology are not grounded in actual data about human evolution. A key challenge to those who hold such positions is to identify specific links between biological mechanisms and social behavior over generations; until they do so, their theories remain on the level of speculation.

The "Differently Situated" Argument

Advocates of this position agree that there are important sex differences but consider them socially, not biologically, based. Various forms of this argument have been made, for example Eagly's claim that the division of labor between the sexes produces gender-role expectations and sex-typed skills and beliefs that in turn lead to sex differences in social behavior. Miller also believes that sex differences exist, but she places causal primacy on women's subordinate and men's dominant status.

These approaches identify particular antecedents of differences and put them in a theoretical context that highlights the fact that women are differently situated in society than men are, but they tend to overlook the fact that not all women are similarly situated. One challenge to these researchers is to identify particular social or structural factors that produce specific differences, whether those factors be roles, expectancies, or power positions. Lott provides numerous examples of how a belief in gender differences influences behavior and social policies.

The "Contingent" Argument

Advocates of this position claim that what appear to be sex differences tend to disappear or are mitigated when other factors are taken into account; hence the existence of sex differences is contingent on situational or social factors. Feingold, for example, points out that findings of differences in spatial visualization have declined by 59 percent over the years. It is possible that changes in testing methods have led to more precise measurement or that societal factors that either produced or minimized differences have changed. In this case, sex differences seem to be made up in part by cohort effects.

Brody reviews research on gender and emotion that demonstrates that expression of emotion by males and females is contingent on other factors, such as culture; Americans may differ by gender more than other cultural groups. As Epstein asserts, "what is regarded as uniquely female in one culture, group or subgroup may be regarded as male in another." A great deal of research on sex differences is done on members of one culture and assumes that those findings generalize across cultures. Markus and Oyserman point out that the relational sense of self as interdependent, embedded, and continuous with others, which is thought to characterize Western women, is in many ways little different from the collectivist sense of self that characterizes both men and women in some Eastern and African cultures. Furthermore, Wink and his colleagues argue that conceptualizing individualism and collectivism as dichotomous and oppositional may itself be a mistake, since individuals could be high (or low) on both these dimensions.

Others make a similar point when they underscore the need to look at race, social class, and other within-sex groupings, not just differences between males and females. One key question here is the relative importance of sex compared with other variables that demarcate subgroups of populations. Unger advocates an increase in the number and kind of group differences studied: "The more differences we explore, the less important any single difference can be."

In comparing group differences, however, the usual practice has been to adopt the dominant group as a standard and see how closely the subordinate group matches it. According to Hurtado, this deficit model leaves the dominant group unexamined and assumes that influence is unidirectional. Instead, she advocates a model that permits examination of the fluid nature of individuals' multiple group identities.

The "No Differences" Argument

Some psychologists emphatically respond "no" when asked if there are important sex differences. For exam-

ple, Tavris asserts that: "Meta-analysis of social behaviors, such as helpfulness, find that differences are due more to role than to gender, and meta-analyses of intellectual skills, such as math, verbal, and spatial abilities, find that differences have virtually vanished or are too trivial to matter." To Hyde, most differences are small and unimportant, but a few differences—such as those in sexual attitudes and behaviors—are large and should be studied. In her view, a key challenge is to identify which few differences are large enough to merit close inspection. Others would argue that the central task should be to identify similarities rather than give primacy to differences.

Some differences identified in past research may have been an artifact of research paradigms. Barnett points out that earlier research on the relationship between work, family, and mental health assumed that social roles had a differential impact on women and men, with women more influenced by family and men by work. These assumptions influenced both the research questions that were asked and the way in which findings were interpreted. In contrast, current paradigms assume that both work and family roles influence both women and men. Barnett concludes that, as women and men occupy similar work and family roles, the relationship between those roles and mental health does not differ by gender.

The "Disadvantage, Not Difference" Argument

Those who fall into this category believe that there may be sex differences; if they exist, in most cases they are small, but they are often: (a) magnified, and (b) made into justifications for inequality. To advocates of this position, a central task is to identify the social processes involved that amplify differences and interpret them as inadequacies, that is, how traits and behaviors attributed to women acquire the social meaning of deficits. The emphasis here is on the consequences of difference and how social institutions interpret the ways in which females differ from males as female disadvantage. As James puts it, "The extent to which the sexes differ is far less important than the consequences of emphasizing such differences in particular contexts."

Hare-Mustin and Maracek go further, suggesting that the important question is that of the political utility of either affirming or minimizing gender differences. From their constructivist perspective, there is no correct answer to the question of sex differences: "theories of gender, like other scientific theories, are representations of reality organized by particular assumptive frameworks and reflecting certain interests." In their opinion, research on sex differences is part of the social processes that construct gender and support the status quo. Instead of this research, they advocate the study of "privilege, power, subordination and rebellion" among individuals and social groups.

By now, the people who have queried me for simple answers to the question of sex differences are bewildered: Why the multiplicity of answers? In part, this stems from the varying "thresholds of convincibility" among researchers, making us more easily persuaded by research that confirms our beliefs. But the multiplicity of answers derives also from the different research traditions, with contradictory assumptions about human behavior, that underlie various arguments about the question of sex differences.

TWO MODELS OF RESEARCH ON SEX DIFFERENCE

Research on sex differences began with the "individual differences model" that goes back to the earliest days of scientific psychology. Subsequent research on sex differences has been based on other models, primarily the "social psychological" model. Each of these traditions has limits for the study of women and gender.

The Individual Differences Model

When nonprofessionals ask whether there are "truly" sex differences, they are usually referring to abilities and personality traits as studied from an "individual differences" model. This tradition goes back more than 100 years to the work of Francis Galton, a cousin of Charles Darwin. Galton set up a laboratory at the 1884 International Health Exhibition in London in which, for a threepence charge, he would measure the mental abilities of members of the public. He tested about 9,000 people by the time the exhibition closed, giving them information about their relative performance. Underlying Galton's work are assumptions that permeate interpretations of research on sex differences.

First, Galton saw the individual as a bundle of traits and abilities; tests of simple motor abilities and perception provided a measure of people's mental capacities. Galton believed that a quick "snapshot" at one point in time of someone's performance, taken under contrived conditions, could provide a full measure of that person on a particular dimension. Underlying Galton's work is a belief in radical individualism: that mental abilities are composed of stable and unalterable individual characteristics that owed nothing to social conditions; rather, the self is contained in the individual body. The origins of our actions (and responsibility for those actions) lies within the individual, rather than in some social group larger than the individual, such as the family or one's racial or ethnic group, or other extra-individual factors.

Today many studies of sex differences bring Galton's emphasis on mental abilities into contemporary terms by looking at particular cognitive skills, such as visual-spatial abilities and verbal and math ability, and ask whether there are sex differences in these abilities and whether these differences are large enough to be socially meaningful. But problems with this model limit its usefulness for understanding women's and men's behavior.

A key question is whether these studies are measuring abilities (i.e., what women and men are capable of doing) or simply performance (i.e., what people actually do). If what we are measuring is actually performance, then we cannot discount the effects of training and culture when considering findings. Even in the area of spatial abilities, where some of the most robust findings of difference have been identified, there is evidence that training and sociocultural experiences play a role.

A further problem with the individual differences model is the assumption that groups of males and females tested are homogeneous, not heterogeneous. Indeed, this assumption is built into the very statistics we use. Typical research strategies in psychology emphasize differences in central tendencies among groups and arrange these differences in hierarchical order. Often we begin with the belief that the population falls into a bell-shaped curve, and that what is defined as "normal" falls under 95 percent of that curve. But the groups that we test may be bimodal or multimodal, not bell-shaped. Within groups of males and females, subgroups may exist that do not fall neatly into the bell-shaped curve. In that situation, the "average" score will tell us little about the actual shape of the curve, and a higher percentage than 5 percent may fall under the "not normal" part of the curve. When we assume homogeneity, we cannot detect the presence of diverse subgroups. There are statistical solutions to these problems. For example, we could look at the overall shape of the distribution or the tails of curves as closely as we look at the means. Such solutions will become routine only when homogeneity is no longer the guiding assumption of our research.

Moreover, we do not know with certainty what it is we have learned when we discover the presence or absence of sex differences. Galton assumed that biology caused differences among individuals. More recently, researchers have added socialization and culture to the causal mix. In the absence of tests of specific causes of difference, we are left with long lists of studies, some of which show differences and some of which do not, but we have little means of understanding why these divergent findings occur.

Nonetheless, the most serious problem with the individual differences model may be the limits it places on the kinds of things that can be studied. Some of the most interesting phenomena, such as aggression or leadership, are most clearly manifested in social situations, and behavior may vary depending on whether a person is tested individually, in a dyad, or in a group. Maccoby found that pairs of young children engaged in much higher levels of social behavior when playing with a same-sex partner than when playing with a child of the other sex. Girls seldom acted passively when paired with other girls, but when paired with boys, their behavior patterns changed. "Girls frequently stood on the sidelines and let the boys monopolize the toys." Distinctive styles of interaction occurred in all-boy and all-girl groups, with boys focusing more on dominance and girls on social enabling behaviors. Mixed sex groups, consequently, combine styles that may be incompatible or at least divergent. These differences in style may not be present when children are tested individually.

This research demonstrates that presenting a female with a male is not equivalent to presenting a male with another male, or vice versa. Experimental psychologists refer to this as a problem in "stimulus equivalency"; I would reframe it as a problem in the assumption of individualism. One solution to this problem is to consider that research findings may well be the product of the interaction of the pair rather than the abilities or performance of the individual, highlighting the limits of the individual differences model.

The Social Psychological Model

The individual differences model has been superseded to some degree by a view of human behavior that considers extra-individual factors as potential causal agents. In the tradition of social psychology initiated by Kurt Lewin and his colleagues (many of them female), the focus is on the person embedded in a social situation. Lewin held that behavior is not solely a function of one's inner traits or abilities or preferences, but rather is partly the product of the social context that surrounds the person. In contrast to Galton's focus on the individual, Lewin took the effect of situational variation on behavior as his object of study.

A great deal of research in this tradition demonstrates that what appear to be stable sex differences in behavior may actually be the product of situational factors. Because this research has been catalogued so ably in books by Epstein and others, I will give only a few examples. In studies of power relations, when status is not assigned, men tend to exhibit patterns of dominance and women patterns of subordinate behaviors. When, however, status is manipulated experimentally, both women and men act in accord with their status, not with gender expectations. The most intriguing studies are those that demonstrate that the same participants exhibit both dominant and subordinate behaviors depending on their assigned status.

A social psychological approach sees behavior as the product of social interaction, as adaptive rather than fixed. The underlying theme is one of influence and counterinfluence, of being molded by the social environment and simultaneously shaping that environment rather than being free from contextual influences. But one limitation of the social psychological tradition is that, in its focus on the immediate situation, it may overlook the individual's place in the larger social system, ignoring economic or political or historical forces that shape women's and men's behavior. The ahistorical nature of social psychology conflates behaviors that are the product of contemporaneous conditions with universal, timeless principles of human behavior.

At the other end of the causal spectrum, the social psychological model also ignores the potential relationship of biological factors and behavior. If, for example, social conditions have an impact on human behavior, they may also affect one's biology. Considering only social factors, while ignoring biological ones, reifies the nature/nurture distinction that wrongly treats biology and culture as separable and competing sources of influence.

In summary, both the individual differences model and the social psychological model have limitations that prevent us from settling the question of whether there are socially significant sex differences. It is important to consider why we expend so much energy on this question. For those interested in research as a vehicle for social change, I think that continuing to focus our efforts on the question of whether there are sex differences in abilities or personality traits is a mistake. Feminist pioneers

in psychology, including Helen Thompson (Woolley), used traditional scientific methods at the start of the twentieth century to counter the social myths about women; yet Thompson's insights have had to be repeatedly rediscovered, and still the myths persist. Scientific research itself rarely seems to create the shift in attitudes that we desire, although the interpretation of our research to the public may have an impact. Repeated demonstrations that sex differences are mostly small and contextually determined will not in itself bring about equality for women. The pervasive belief in individualism, at least in Western industrialized countries, will make it difficult for those findings to be heard.

Women's place in society is different in many ways—for many women—from that of men; we need only look at the continuing wage discrepancies between male and female workers to be reminded of that fact. Accordingly, it is no surprise that, being differently situated, women and men may act differently. This does not mean that women are not capable of acting in the same ways—both good and bad—as men. Nor does it mean that intrinsic differences in abilities necessarily determine men's and women's places in society.

Equality of opportunity does not require that women and men be identical—or rather that women be identical to men, which is the subtext of many discussions of sex differences. Scott urges us to discard the belief that if we accept difference, we reject the idea of equality. She points out that equality is not needed when people are identical. Demands for equality are necessary only when groups differ. "Equality," she asserts, "might well be defined as deliberate indifference to specified differences." Conversely, inequality does not necessarily stem from differences in skills and abilities.

Moreover, those who want to deny women equal opportunity will do so whether research identifies sex sameness or difference. Research may be used to justify opinions (our own as well as others) rather than to change them. Newt Gingrich, then the Speaker of the U.S. House of Representatives, did not base his curious public statement about women being unfit for hand-to-hand military combat because they get infections, and men being biologically programmed to hunt giraffes, on scientific research. I think he was trying to say he believes that sex differences are innate; that social structure is the result, not the cause of difference; and that it behooves us to make sure that social structure does not contradict those innate differences. I do not think that any number of carefully crafted research studies finding otherwise would change his mind. If we want equal opportunity for women, we should work for equal opportunity, not assume that our research findings—or perhaps more important, that our interpretations of our findings—are going to convince others that social change is needed. As academics, we place great faith in reason, argumentation, and evidence, but these tools may not be the only—or even the most effective—means of bringing about political or social change. Research demonstrating equal abilities of women and men, or even demonstrating the variability among one sex, may be useful but not sufficient to bring about social equality. But research can docu-ment precisely how society is "gendered" or unequal in expectations and opportunities (thereby identifying targets for change); research can also examine how women and others who are disenfranchised cope with inequality (bringing to light strategies for survival).

Such research would have two goals:

1. First, it would make explicit the underlying gender coding—much of it gratuitous—of social structures and situations. That is, it would identify differences based on sex in expectations, opportunities, networks, and power. As Epstein has cogently put it, "No aspect of social life—whether the gathering of crops, the ritual of religion, the formal dinner party, or the organization of government—is free from the dichotomous thinking that casts the world in categories of 'male' and 'female' ". The transsexual British journalist Jan Morris discovered this firsthand after her surgical change from male to "female":

> We are told that the social gap between the sexes is narrowing, but I can only report that in the second half of the twentieth century, having experienced life in both roles [male and female], there seems to me no aspect of existence, no moment of the day, no contact, no arrangement, no response, which is not different for men and for women. The very tone of voice in which I was addressed, the very posture of the person next in [line], the very feel in the air when I entered a room or sat at a restaurant table, constantly emphasized my change of status.

Our research can particularize this observation by identifying how specific situations and social structures treat women and men differently.

2. Once we have identified gender-coding in social systems, we can look at how women negotiate these situations

and social structures—that is, accept them or engage in varying degrees of resistance against them. I assume here that women have a degree of agency, but that their ability to act is constrained in certain ways. That is, women both create and are shaped by social structures; research can document how these processes occur.

To do this research, to tell these stories, to understand women's experience at multiple levels of social organization, we need new research methods that neither considers women as sole determiners of their fate, ignoring situation constraints, nor consider them as mere pawns of larger social forces. Videotape is a useful metaphor for discovering such new research techniques. The assumptions underlying "videotape epistemology" differ radically from those of the snapshot-type research used by Galton and others.

First, the metaphor of videotape suggests that we consider people's behavior over time, enabling us to examine how people negotiate situations in light of particular constraints and opportunities. Thorne's research on school-children is a good example of this; she identifies times in children's lives when gender is salient and other times when its importance is muted. She advocates conceptualizing gender as fluid and situated rather than dichotomous and oppositional.

Second, videotape technology permits viewers to zoom in—that is, fill our field of vision with the person— and zoom out to include context and, over time, patterns of behavior in that context. In other words, the metaphor of videotape suggests that we adopt techniques that allow us to consider both micro-level and macro-level factors in understanding behavior.

Third, videotape enables us to hear the views of multiple participants. It suggests that we recognize the importance of individuals' interpretations, of the stories that people tell themselves, as determinants of behavior. We should not, however, deny the role of the camera operator (that is, the researcher) in choosing the object of focus, the length of time to focus on an event, and so on. By advocating videotape as a metaphor, I do not mean to imply that the camera operator is simply a technician, recording but not framing a scene.

Fourth, videotape enables us to splice and edit, thereby comparing multiple perspectives. It enables us to capture much of the complexity of a phenomenon, so that, for example, we do not consider race, sex, and social class as isolated variables.

Let me give two examples of research that capture some of these qualities. The first is Fine's study of why a rape victim would choose not to prosecute a rapist. Psychologists generally think of prosecuting as taking control of the situation, and therefore part of the process of successfully coping with rape. Fine questions the assumption that asserting individual control is the optimal form of coping. She argues that this model is appropriate only for a "small and privileged sector of society" with the social power and resources to assure that exerting control is likely to lead to successful outcomes. For those with few resources, exerting control in this manner can be delusory or even self-destructive. In the case she describes, a poor black woman on welfare chose not to prosecute her rapist, having little faith in the criminal justice system and a great fear that the rapist would harm those she loved. Fine concludes that the "systematic neglect of power relations" causes us to disregard the fact that our conceptions of taking control are not always applicable across class, race and ethnic lines.

A second example is Wittner's study of why battered women often drop charges against those who have beaten them. The professionals in the court system—the judges, lawyers, and so forth—see completed cases as the measure of success of Chicago's new Domestic Violence Court. They attribute the high rate of dropped cases to battered women's weakness, passivity, dependency, fear, and low self-esteem. But from the battered women's point of view, the choice to drop a case is anything but passive. Some women had the goal of getting the man to stop beating them or to leave, and merely bringing charges against him had accomplished that goal. Once they had obtained what they wanted, they saw no need to go through the tedious and time-consuming legal process. Others saw the inevitable delays and frustrations of the criminal justice system as attempts to discourage them from prosecuting. Perhaps most imposing, the state's attorney's office is in control of the course of a case, treating the battered woman as a witness for the state. Ironically, this loss of control may produce some of those feelings of dependency and helplessness among battered women that court personnel blame for dropped cases.

Wittner concludes that the Domestic Violence Court is a major resource for poor and working-class women (the majority of the complainants), enabling these women to hold men accountable. But the way the women use the court did not always accord with the way that court personnel had decided was appropriate, that is, by following complaints through to their legal conclusion. Rather, these women used the court as one among many resources—including other family members, both their own and the batterers'—in a complex series of negotiations that ensured their survival. Wittner links women's use of the court to large-scale economic changes, in particular, men's loss of high-paying manufacturing jobs. The decline in women's economic dependence on men has shifted the balance of power in relationships; women's use of Domestic Violence Court is part of a process of reconfiguring those relationships.

Both of these examples contrast the view of professionals in a social system with that of women affected by that system; both attempt to relate individual women's experiences to larger social and economic forces. Both examples use qualitative methods, although I do not believe that qualitative methods are the only approaches able to capture needed distinctions. A provocative model of quantitative methods comes from evaluation research. Stakeholder-based evaluation research attempts to incorporate into the evaluation process questions formulated by the different constituencies that have an interest in the results of an evaluation, especially those who are the least powerful. In doing so, it implicitly views organizations as political entities, composed of shifting groups with different interests, that compete for scarce resources. Therefore, many situations in which men and women interact or fail to interact can also be seen as political entities, forming and reforming on the basis of changing power dynamics. The metaphor of videotape rather than snapshot methods best capture this process.

CONCLUSION

There were numerous attempts in the 1980s and 1990s to use research to settle the question of whether there are sex differences. Yet one can still pick up a prestigious social science journal like *American Psychologist* and find one author who writes that sex differences are large and socially meaningful while another author concludes that many if not most differences are small and have a trivial impact. One subtext of this conflict is whether immutable, biologically determined differences in abilities and personality traits exist that justify limiting the potential opportunities and achievements of one sex or another. This wrongly conflates biology with biological determinism and ignores social forces that affect women's and men's roles. Understanding that different findings emerge depending on the methods used, the variables under scrutiny, the assumptions about causality, and whether the presentation of the findings chooses to highlight difference or similarities may help make sense of why the conclusions of researchers in this field are so diverse.

Continuing the debate about whether there are "truly" sex differences in personality and abilities is no longer a useful enterprise. It is time to imagine new directions for research on women and gender. Let us unpack the black box of the variable entity "sex" by taking into account specific biological, psychological, social, structural, and cultural dimensions that are linked in a given context to being female or male and examine the specific ways in which gender is created through social relations. Cross-level research that acknowledges the reciprocal influence between individuals and social systems promises the deepest understanding of behavior, although examination of phenomena within each dimension is also of value. Furthermore, similarities between males and females, or differences based on factors other than sex classification—such as variations within each sex category or among myriad social groups—may be as important or more important than gender differences.

Research that spans multiple levels of social organization goes against the grain of much of our training, in which each of these levels of analysis becomes the property of a particular discipline or a subfield within a discipline. Indeed, the thought of spanning all these levels is daunting. Level-spanning research might be less intimidating if we consider working in cross-disciplinary teams of researchers. One of the exciting possibilities of women's studies is that it brings together people from various disciplines who focus on the same question, making this sort of level-spanning possible. But working with those from other disciplines also sometimes makes apparent that the disciplines use different language, sources of evidence, argumentation styles, and research methods. We need to develop new ways of working that allow us to cross these disciplinary boundaries. Using videotape as a metaphor to guide our search for new methods can change the way we do research—and produce new stories to tell.

Business/Management Studies

Scholars in the field of business and management studies explore such areas as organizational theory, behavior, and effectiveness and strategic and human resources management. What do women and feminist perspectives have to offer business and the academic study of business? Fundamental to this question is the debate over gender differences—their existence, their significance, and their implications. Feminists who argue that gender makes a difference in the work arena explore the particular contributions women can bring and the ways corporate restructuring could facilitate taking advantage of those contributions. In the first selection, Gary N. Powell examines the research on gender differences in management and comes to the conclusion that these differences are minimal and ultimately unimportant. He advocates gender blind hiring, training, and promotion practices, which he believes will lead to the most effective managers and successful businesses. Jennifer S. Macleod is interested in examining the underlying causes of the lag in women's success in the business world. Unlike Powell, who offers an optimistic and easily remedied view of the situation, Macleod posits that underlying assumptions and structures would need to be altered in order to make way for women's advancement. Lastly, Joyce K. Fletcher uses an innovative feminist poststructuralist perspective to uncover dynamics in the workplace that put women at a disadvantage. In her study of women's "relational practices" at work, she argues that women bring something decidedly different and positive to the workforce that should be recognized and rewarded. Their contributions, however, often go unnoticed as they are "disappeared" not categorized as part of "real work."

Critical Thinking Questions

1. Does Powell make a strong case for the "no differences" point of view? What evidence supports his case and what evidence detracts from it?
2. Based on your readings in other fields (psychology, economics, sociology), do you think Powell's conclusion to create gender blind practices in the business world would be fair, desirable, or possible?
3. Macleod offers ten examples of "new requirements for effective organizations." Of these examples, which have already begun to be incorporated

in business practices, which seem especially significant to advance the cause of women and which seem less important or impractical?

4. Compare and contrast the conclusions reached by Powell and Macleod about how to achieve fairness and equity in corporate America. Which path seems more likely to be pursued, which more likely to be effective?

5. To what degree does Fletcher's work reflect stereotypes about women and gender differences? Does this undermine her argument?

6. Do you recognize the relational practices that Fletcher outlines? To what degree do you engage or have you experienced coworkers engaged in preserving, mutual empowering, achieving, or creating team? Should these activities count as "work," and are they appropriate in the public sphere?

40

Leadership and Gender
Vive la Différence?
(1996)

Gary N. Powell

There has been a dramatic change in the face of management over the past two decades. That face is now female more than one-third of the time. What are the implications for the practice of management? Most of us are aware of traditional stereotypes about male-female differences, but how well do these stereotypes apply to the managerial ranks? Do female and male managers differ in their basic responses to work situations and in their overall effectiveness (and if so, in what ways?), or are they really quite similar?

If you believe recent books and articles in business magazines, female and male managers bring different personal qualities to their jobs. For example, Jan Grant, in an *Organizational Dynamics* article entitled "Women as Managers: What They Can Offer to Organizations," argues that women have unique qualities that make them particularly well suited to be managers. She says that instead of forcing women to fit the male model of managerial success, which stresses such qualities as independence, competitiveness, forcefulness, and analytical thinking, organizations should place greater emphasis on such female qualities as affiliation and attachment, cooperativeness, nurturance, and emotionality.

Felice Schwartz's *Harvard Business Review* article, "Management Women and the New Facts of Life," triggered a national debate over the merits of "mommy tracks" (although she did not use the term herself). She proposed that corporations (1) distinguish between "career-primary women," who put their careers first, and "career-and-family" women, who seek a balance between career and family; (2) nurture the careers of the former group as potential top executives; and (3) offer flexible work arrangements and family supports to the latter group in exchange for lower opportunities for career advancement. Women were assumed to be more interested in such arrangements than men and were therefore less likely to be suitable top executives; there has

Powell, Gary N., "Leadership & Gender: Vive la Difference?" In *Women, Men and Gender*. New Haven, CT: Yale University Press, 1997.

been less discussion over the merits of "daddy tracks."

Judy Rosener, in her book *America's Competitive Secret: Utilizing Women as a Management Strategy*, distinguishes between male and female leadership styles. In contrast to the "command-and-control" model more associated with males, she finds that women prefer an "interactive" style, which is shaped by their life experiences and involves "managing in a collaborative rather than top-down fashion." Marilyn Loden, in a book entitled *Feminine Leadership, or How to Succeed in Business Without Being One of the Boys*, similarly concludes that female managers are more capable than male managers of exhibiting "feminine leadership," which she sees organizations as needing more than ever. She summarizes her view about male-female differences in the managerial ranks in three words: "Vive la différence!"

Women and men certainly differ in their success within the ranks of management. Although women have made great strides in entering management since 1970, with the overall proportion of women managers rising from 16 percent to 42 percent, the proportion of women who hold *top* management positions is less than 5 percent. This may simply be because the average male manager is older and more experienced than the average female manager. After all, managerial careers invariably start at the bottom. If there were no basic differences between male and female managers, it would be just a matter of time until the proportion of women was about the same at all managerial levels.

But *are* there basic differences between male and female managers? According to traditional gender stereotypes, males are more masculine (e.g., self-reliant, aggressive, competitive, decisive) and females more feminine (e.g., sympathetic, gentle, shy, sensitive to the needs of others). Grant's, Rosener's, and Loden's views of male-female differences mirror these stereotypes. But the applicability of these stereotypes to managers is debated. Four distinct points of view have emerged:

1. **No differences.** Women who pursue the nontraditional career of manager reject the feminine stereotype and have goals, motives, personalities, and behaviors that are similar to those of men who pursue managerial careers.

2. **Stereotypical differences favoring men.** Female and male managers differ in ways predicted by gender stereotypes as a result of early socialization experiences that leave men better suited to be managers.

3. **Stereotypical differences favoring women.** Female and male managers differ in accordance with gender stereotypes owing to early socialization experiences, but managers in today's work world need feminine traits in particular.

4. **Nonstereotypical differences.** Female and male managers differ in ways opposite to gender stereotypes because women managers have had to be exceptional to compensate for early socialization experiences that are different from those of men.

In this chapter, I briefly review the evidence on gender differences in management that has been gathered since women managers were first noticed by researchers in the mid-1970s to determine the level of support for each of these points of view. Possible differences in personal traits, behavior, effectiveness, values, commitment, and subordinates' responses are considered, then implications of the review are discussed.

DO FEMALE AND MALE MANAGERS DIFFER?

One of the most extensive research studies ever conducted of managers and their personal characteristics took place in the Bell System through its parent, the American Telephone and Telegraph Company (AT&T). Prior to the court-ordered 1984 divestiture of its regional operating companies, the Bell System was the nation's largest business enterprise. In the late 1970s and early 1980s AT&T initiated a study of 344 lower-level managers who were considered to be representative of those managers from whom Bell's future middle-and upper-level managers would come. Nearly half of those studied were women.

These managers went through three days of assessment exercises. Extensive comparisons were made in terms of background, work interests, personality, motivation, abilities, and overall managerial potential. Women had advantages in administrative ability, interpersonal skills and sensitivity, written communication skills, energy, and inner work standards. Men had advantages in company loyalty, motivation to advance within the company, and attentiveness to power structures. The greatest gender difference was masculinity/femininity: men were more likely to have traditionally masculine interests, whereas women were more likely to have traditionally feminine interests. There were no gender differences in intellectual ability, leadership ability, oral communication skills, or stability of performance. When the assessors took these tradeoffs into account, they judged women and men to have similar managerial potential. Forty-five percent of the women and 39 percent

of the men were judged to have the potential to attain middle management in the Bell System within ten years. Douglas Bray, who directed the AT&T studies until he was succeeded by Ann Howard, concluded: "Vive la no différence!"

Other research on the personality and motivation of managers generally has found few gender differences. Both male and female managers are high in their motivation to manage. Many researchers have found that women and men managers score essentially the same on psychological tests of needs and motives that are supposed to predict managerial success. When differences have been found in the relative strength of motives possessed by female and male managers, they have generally favored women and been contrary to gender stereotypes. In a study of nearly 2,000 managers that was similar to the AT&T study in scope but examined managers from different organizations, Susan Donnell and Jay Hall found that women managers reported lower basic needs and higher needs for self-actualization. Women were seen as exhibiting a "more mature and higher-achieving motivational profile" than their male counterparts, being more concerned with opportunities for growth, autonomy, and challenge and less concerned with work environment and pay.

Most studies of gender differences in managerial or leader behavior have examined two aspects of leadership style. The first, called *task style*, refers to the extent to which the manager initiates work activity, organizes it, and defines the way work is to be done. The second, called *interpersonal style*, refers to the extent to which the manager engages in activities that tend to the morale and welfare of people in the work setting. Task and interpersonal styles of leadership are typically regarded as independent dimensions. That is, a manager may be high in both task and interpersonal styles, low in both, or high in one but not the other. A third aspect of leadership style that has been frequently studied is the extent to which the leader exhibits *democratic leadership*, which allows subordinates to participate in decision making, versus *autocratic leadership*, which discourages such participation: these are considered to be opposites.

Although a "meta-analysis" of research studies found gender differences in each of these three dimensions of leadership style, the size of the difference varied, as did the circumstances under which it appeared. Small gender differences were found in task style and interpersonal style; however, these differences appeared only for subjects in laboratory experiments and for nonleaders who were assessed on how they would behave if they were actually leaders. There were no gender differences in the task and interpersonal styles of actual managers. In contrast, a more pronounced gender difference was found in democratic versus autocratic leadership. Women tended to be more democratic, less autocratic leaders than men, a difference that appeared for individuals in all settings—actual managers, nonmanagers, and subjects in laboratory experiments. These results offer support for both the no-differences and the stereotypical-differences views.

A separate meta-analysis found no sex difference in overall leader effectiveness. Still, men fared better in such male-dominated work environments as the military, whereas women fared better in such female-dominated work settings as schools. These results support a no-differences view overall, but a stereotypical-differences view within work environments dominated by either sex.

The values of managers, especially top executives, usually receive attention only when a corporate scandal takes place. Personal values have considerable influence on how managers handle the responsibilities of their jobs. Values may influence perceptions of others, solutions to problems, and the sense of what constitutes individual and organizational success. Values also influence what managers believe to be ethical and unethical behavior and whether they accept or resist organizational pressures and goals. Most evidence suggests that similarities outweigh differences in the value systems of male and female managers. With few exceptions, gender differences have not been found in the work values and personal business ethics of managers.

The sense of commitment that managers bring to their work is also important, at least as far as their organizations are concerned. More committed managers might be expected to work longer hours when the need arises, to relocate when the organization wishes, and to place a greater importance on the interests of the organization than on personal interests when the two are in conflict. Managers who are less committed are more likely to believe that "a job is a job" and to balk when they are asked to do anything that is outside their normal routines. Gender stereotypes suggest that women lack the high level of commitment essential for a successful managerial career, but a meta-analysis found no gender difference in commitment to either professional or nonprofessional jobs. Instead, commitment is better explained by other factors. Age and education are positively linked to commitment, for example. Greater job satisfaction, more meaningful work, and greater utilization of skills are also associated with stronger commitment.

Even if male and female managers did not differ in any respect, subordinates could still have different preferences for working with them or respond to them differently. A tendency to prefer male managers to female managers is present in many workers. A survey of employed adult Americans found that almost half preferred a boss of a specific sex. Among those workers who expressed a preference, 85 percent of men and 65 percent of women said they would rather work for a male boss. In contrast, studies of actual managers and their subordinates have typically found that subordinates express similar satisfaction with male and female managers. Overall, subordinates do not appear to respond differently to male and female leaders for whom they have actually worked. Once subordinates have experienced both female and male managers, the effects of gender stereotypes tend to disappear, and managers are treated more as individuals than as representatives of their sex.

In summary, the title of this section of the chapter posed the question "Do female and male managers differ?" The research evidence suggests the answer: "They differ in some ways and at some times, but, for the most part, they do not differ."

Although the AT&T study found several gender differences in managerial traits, these differences offset each other in the determination of overall management potential. In motivational profiles found in other studies, female managers tend to have the preferred managerial traits. Women and men do not differ in their effectiveness as leaders, although some situations favor women and others favor men. A stereotypical difference is present in the tendency to exhibit democratic versus autocratic leadership. In contrast, gender differences in task and interpersonal styles are confined to laboratory studies and are not present in the leadership styles of actual managers. Results outside the laboratory suggest an absence of gender differences in values and commitment. Actual male and female managers provoke similar responses in subordinates. Thus, few gender differences favoring either men or women have been found.

Overall, this review supports the no-differences view of gender differences in management. This does not necessarily mean that female and male managers are completely interchangeable, however. The leadership roles that women and men hold in organizations typically provide clear guidelines for acceptable behavior. Managers become socialized into their roles early in their careers. In addition, they are selected by their organizations to fill leadership roles because they are seen as meeting a specific set of attitudinal and behavioral criteria. These factors decrease the likelihood that female and male managers will differ substantially in the personal qualities they exhibit on their jobs, even if they are initially inclined to act differently. Because women remain in the minority in the managerial ranks, especially in the upper levels, they experience strong pressures to conform to standards based on a stereotypically masculine view of managerial effectiveness.

IMPLICATIONS FOR ORGANIZATIONS

The implications of this review are clear: *If there are no differences between male and female managers, organizations should not act as if there are.* Instead, they should follow two principles in their actions:

1. To be gender blind in how they fill managerial positions, except when consciously trying to offset the effects of past discrimination.
2. To minimize differences in the job experiences of equally qualified male and female managers, so that artificial gender differences in career patterns and success do not arise.

Organizations should do whatever they can to equalize the job experiences of equally qualified female and male managers. This means abandoning the model of a successful career as an uninterrupted sequence of promotions to positions of greater responsibility heading toward the top ranks. All too often, any request to take time out from a career for family reasons, by either a woman or a man, is seen as evidence of lack of career commitment.

Grant, Rosener, and Loden based their recommendations on a stereotypical-differences-favoring-women view. Although this view receives some support in my review, especially in women's greater tendency to exhibit democratic versus autocratic leadership, it is not supported by the bulk of the research evidence. Nevertheless, it has been used as the basis for sweeping assertions. Grant argues, for example, that organizations will benefit from placing greater value on women's special qualities.

These "human resources" skills are critical in helping to stop the tide of alienation, apathy, cynicism, and low morale in organizations. ... If organizations are to become more humane, less alienating, and more responsive to the individuals who work for them, they will probably need to learn to value process as well as product. Women have an extensive involvement in the processes of our society—an involvement that derives from their greater participation in the reproductive process and their early experience of family life. ... Thus women may indeed be the most radical force available in bringing about organizational change.

Human resources skills are certainly essential to today's organizations. Corporations that are concerned only with getting a product out and pay little attention to their employees' needs are unlikely to have a committed workforce or to be effective in the long run. But women are at risk when corporations assume that women have a monopoly on human resources skills. The risk is that they will be placed exclusively in managerial jobs that call for social sensitivity and interpersonal skills—for example, jobs in public relations, human resources management, consumer affairs, and corporate social responsibility. These jobs are typically staff functions, peripheral to the more powerful line functions of finance, sales, and production, and are seldom regarded in exalted terms by line personnel. Women managers are found disproportionately in such jobs, outside the career paths that most frequently lead to top management jobs. Corporations that rely on Grant's assertions about women's special abilities could very well perpetuate this trend.

Thus it is very important that the facts about gender differences in management be disseminated to key decision makers. When individuals hold onto stereotypical views about gender differences that are not supported by the research evidence, either of two approaches may be tried.

1. Send them to programs like cultural diversity workshops to make them aware of the ways in which biases related to gender (as well as race, age, etc.) can affect their decisions, and to learn how to keep these biases from occurring. For example, Levi Strauss put all of its executives, including the president, through an intense three-day program designed to make them examine their attitudes toward women and minorities on the job. In Ortho Pharmaceuticals, Avon, and Citizens Insurance, every *employee* receives diversity awareness training.

2. Recognize that beliefs and attitudes are difficult to change, and focus on changing behavior instead. If people are motivated by an effective performance appraisal and reward system backed by the CEO to be gender blind in their decision making, they often come to believe in what they are doing.

Schwartz based her recommendations on a real gender difference: more women than men leave work for family reasons owing to the demands of maternity and the differing traditions and expectations of the sexes. But her solution substitutes a different type of gender difference: that such women remain at work with permanently reduced career opportunities. It does not recognize that women's career orientation may change during their careers. Women could temporarily leave the fast track for the mommy track but be ready and able to resume the fast track later. Once classified as career-and-family, however, they would find it

difficult to be reclassified as career-primary, even if their career commitment returned to its original level.

More women and men are adopting a holistic approach to their careers and lives. By providing the opportunity for alternative work schedules and family supports for all employees, not just career-and-family women, as Schwartz recommended, organizations can help women and men achieve their full potential for success. Firms that offer flexible work arrangements not only are more likely to retain their employees. They may also attract more qualified employees (even for less pay) who view the opportunity to take advantage of a flexible work arrangement as a worthwhile substitute for higher pay at another firm.

Corporations could offer "parent tracks" rather than mommy tracks and accurately believe that they were treating their female and male employees alike. However, if women opted for such programs more than men did (as is often the case) and if anyone who opted for one was held back in pursuing a future managerial career, the programs would contribute to a gender difference in access to top management positions. Automatic restrictions should not be placed on the later career prospects of individuals who choose alternative work arrangements. Those who wish to return to the fast track should be allowed to do so once they demonstrate the necessary skills and commitment.

Organizations need to create both standard and flexible career paths so *all* the needs of *all* their employees may be fully met. A firm that develops a flexible as well as a core workforce may find considerable advantages during downturns in the business cycle, for layoffs may be avoided in favor of sabbaticals for those who prefer a flexible career pattern. Organizations need to reorganize their workforces in this manner to better meet the needs of employees and the pressures of business cycles.

There are other ways by which organizations can minimize gender differences in managers' job experiences. The majority of top male and female executives have had one or more mentors, and mentorship has been critical to their advancement and success. But lower-level female managers have greater difficulty in finding mentors than male managers at equivalent levels, because of the smaller number of female top executives and the preference people have for mentoring people like themselves. This gives lower-level male managers an advantage in achieving career success.

Some companies try to overcome barriers of gender by assigning highly placed mentors to promising lower-level managers. At the Bank of America, senior executives are asked to serve as mentors for three or four junior managers for a year at a time. Formal mentoring programs have also been implemented at Jewel Companies, Aetna, Bell Labs, Merrill Lynch, Federal Express, and the U.S. General Accounting Office. Good mentoring relationships cannot be engineered, however. They must emerge from the spontaneous and mutual involvement of two people who see value in relating to each other. If people feel coerced into or mismatched in mentoring relationships, the relationships are likely to flounder. Instead, a better approach for organizations is to offer educational programs about mentoring and its role in career development,

then to identify who is doing good mentoring and reward them for it.

Companies also influence job experiences through the training and development programs that they encourage or require their managers to take. These programs contribute to a gender difference in job experiences if (1) men and women are systematically diagnosed to have different developmental needs and thereby go through different programs, or (2) men and women are deliberately segregated in such programs. Female managers do not need to be sent off by themselves for assertiveness training, as they were in the past. They need access to advanced training and development activities, such as executive MBAs or executive leadership workshops, just the way male managers do.

The Executive Women Workshop offered by the Center for Creative Leadership (CCL) and similar programs are open only to women. In addition, some firms, such as Northwestern Bell, have their own executive leadership programs for women only. These programs are intended "to give female managers the unique opportunity to understand their individual developmental needs and establish personal and career objectives," as the CCL catalog puts it. In general, however, women and men should be recommended for training and development programs according to their individual needs, not their sex. Almost half of the companies regarded as "the best companies for women" rely on training and workshops to develop their high-potential managerial talent. Many of these companies, including Bidermann Industries, General Mills, Hewitt Associates, Neiman-Marcus, and PepsiCo, have no special programs for women; they simply enroll the best and brightest people, regardless of sex.

Organizations should not assume that male and female managers differ in personal qualities. They should also make sure that their policies, practices, and programs minimize the creation of gender differences in managers' experiences on the job. There is little reason to believe that either women or men make superior managers. Instead, there are likely to be excellent, average, and poor managers within each sex. Success in today's highly competitive marketplace requires organizations to make the best use of the talent available to them. They need to identify, develop, encourage, and promote the most effective managers, whether men or women. If they do so, what expression will best capture the difference between them and their less successful competitors? *Vive la différence!*

41

Women in Management

What It Will Take to Attain Truly Equal Opportunity

(1994)

Jennifer S. Macleod

It was the 1950s. Shortly before the young woman was to receive her advanced degree in a social science from an Ivy League university, she climbed the wide staircase to the university's placement office in search of a career-starting position that would utilize her considerable skills. At the landing, a sign directed students to the men's placement office on the right, and the women's placement office on the left. Just outside each office was a large bulletin board, with announcements of openings for the specified sex of applicant.

The offerings for women were sparse. In the young woman's field, the only opportunities were as a low-paid research assistant with no advancement opportunities mentioned, or as an "administrative assistant" with secretarial skills explicitly required. On the men's bulletin board, in the same field, promising professional positions were described, with attractive salaries and specified advancement opportunities—and with no requirement for clerical skills. Although the young woman was assertive in attempting to submit applications for those positions, she was not permitted to do so.

That was the usual picture for well-educated young women in the 1950s. It took that woman five years of "assistant" jobs, and great assertiveness, before she could manage to move into the kind of positions her male classmates had been given immediately. And even when she did move up, she was routinely paid less than 60 percent of the male salaries, and promotions continued to be far harder to obtain.

Since then, the situation has changed dramatically for the better.

DECADES OF CHANGE

By the end of the 1960s, as a result of growing feminist activism (and an economic need for women's greater participation in the work force), legislation eliminated the practice of

MacLeod, Jennifer, "Women in Management: What Will It Take to Attain Truly Equal Opportunity?" In *Hutner: Our Vision and Values*. Westport, CT: Praeger Publishers, 1994.

separate male and female help-wanted advertising, and gave women some legal recourse if denied opportunities because of their sex. And over the decades following the 1950s, one of the most striking changes in the world of employment was the influx of women into entry-level and even middle-level management positions, and professional positions with middle management status.

It may sometimes seem that truly equal opportunity for women in management is rapidly approaching. It generally takes two incomes to support a family adequately by today's standards, and the proportion of adult women who work outside the home is rapidly approaching that of men. In 1988, according to the U.S. Department of Labor,[1] 73 percent of women in the twenty-five to fifty-four age range were in the labor force, compared with 94 percent of men. The Department's projections for the year 2000 are that while the figure for men in that age range will stay about the same, the equivalent figure for women will rise to 81 percent. Thus the vast majority of women, like men, will spend almost all of their active adult years in the work force.

Graduate schools of business have admitted female students for quite some time, and in 1990 over a third of their graduating students were women.[2] And active discrimination against women in managerial jobs is surely a tiny fraction of what it once was.

There are those who look at the progress and conclude that women are fully "on their way"; that as current female managers gain experience, they will move to the top at a rate equivalent to their male counterparts; that the continuing evolution will soon all but eliminate the remaining pockets of discrimination.

There are others who despair, pointing out that after a quarter-century of the new feminism, of equal employment legislation, and of women entering the pipeline in managerial positions, there are still only a few female middle managers, and hardly any in top management. A 1990 study of the top *Fortune* 500 companies,[3] for example, showed that women were only 2.6 percent of corporate officers (the vice-presidential level and up). To many observers, these figures suggest that greatly increased legal, legislative, economic, and social pressure will be required if the evolutionary process is to be accelerated.

Whether people are optimistic or despairing, the remedies they propose mainly address the *symptoms* and often neglect the underlying *causes* of the situation. Unfortunately, the causes of the difficulties in attaining equity are deep, have their roots long in the past, and are built into the basic underlying structure of the work world and its institutions. Focusing only on the symptoms—even though they do indeed need to be addressed—is likely to improve the situation only in slow, agonizing steps, with many plateaus and setbacks along the way, and with almost the entire burden and cost borne by the aspiring women themselves. And that improvement may even cease entirely quite soon, if it hasn't done so already.

The remainder of this chapter describes, analyzes, and discusses those root causes. It then moves on to ways those causes, not just the symptoms, can be addressed so that truly equal opportunity for women in management can be attained.

THE MEANING OF EQUAL OPPORTUNITY: BASIC PREMISES

Let us start with the premise that equal opportunity for women in management positions, at all organizational levels including the top, is a desirable goal. This does not necessarily mean, however, that the goal must be equal *numbers* of male and female managers and executives.

Some argue that women will always be less interested than men in high-level management positions. Others believe that the abilities required of a good manager are more common in the female than in the male half of the population, so that given truly equal opportunity, managerial positions will be dominated by women rather than the other way around.

We will have a better handle on those questions if and when equal opportunities and rewards are achieved. Then, the proportions of women and men in managerial positions, at all levels in organizations, will seek their own level based on individuals' abilities and preferences. This may or may not be close to 50 percent. Be that as it may, equal opportunities and rewards have *not* yet been achieved. So the history and root causes of the inequity need to be examined and addressed.

A PERSISTENT LEGACY FROM THE PAST: THE WAY ORGANIZATIONS AND WORK ARE STRUCTURED

The basic structure of corporations was shaped many years ago, at a time when the predominant societal pattern was one in which the nuclear family was the central economic unit, with husbands/fathers the long-term full-time breadwinners. Single women (at least among the white population) might work for a short time, but as soon as they married (and most married young), they quit paid employment and spent the rest of their lives caring for home and husband, and bearing and raising numerous children.

Given those societal patterns, it was entirely sensible (fairness to women was not a consideration in those days) to structure employing organizations in such a way that only men were hired for managerial positions, or for jobs that provided opportunities to progress to management. And in office environments, it made good practical sense to place women mainly in short-term clerical positions.

There were large numbers of literate young women who needed to support themselves until marriage. They sought office jobs, where working conditions were reasonably good and they could meet potential husbands. By living with their parents or other relatives, or in shared apartments, they could manage on low income and, in fact, had little choice about it (unless they could qualify for the only somewhat better pay of nurses or teachers). Thus, employers could peg their wages very low indeed—far lower than any man would have to accept—and still easily obtain the office workers they needed.

Quite reasonably, employers did not provide these female employees with significant training or development, because they rarely stayed in the work force long enough to justify the investment. And the low pay and lack of advancement opportunity, in turn, tended to hasten young women into marriage—which must have seemed about the only way to escape permanent poverty.

Thus the office workplace was almost entirely segregated by sex. Women employees were almost all young and single. There were almost no female managers, with the exception of the occasional middle-aged single woman who might become a first-line supervisor of a group of women workers. And there were almost no male clerical workers, because men could obtain much higher pay and better advancement opportunities elsewhere.

As time went by, some women stayed in the office work force longer than a couple of years, because of later marriages or because financial need kept them in the work force until they had their first babies. Some returned to the work force after their children were grown. However, the pattern of job segregation by sex persisted because it was built into the organizational structure so thoroughly—and because employers found it economically advantageous. They could afford to pay loyal male managers and future managers enough to support a family, because they could fill essential support positions with women who had little choice but to accept what continued to be barely subsistence-level pay, with almost no advancement opportunities.

As the societal trends continued, there were increasing numbers of women who remained in the work force for extended periods or even their entire active lives. There came to be, theoretically at least, time and incentive for the employer to invest in their training and development, time for advancement and possible promotions into management.

However, male employers liked having bright and capable women as their personal assistants, and could keep them there for their entire careers by modestly increasing their salaries and status (the "executive secretary" syndrome), and continuing to deny them managerial opportunities. So change was slow, in spite of growing pressure by well-educated women with higher aspirations, most of whom nevertheless lacked economic or political clout.

The Situation for Women in Office Settings Today

The insistence that underpaid women secretaries and clerks were absolutely essential for an office to work has persisted until very recently. Now, however, ways of working are in major upheaval. Computerized word processing, electronic record-keeping and data bases, special telephone services such as call-waiting and call-forwarding, remote-controlled answering machines, fax machines, "smart" copying machines, and all the other electronic marvels are revolutionizing office work. The traditional secretary who typed, took shorthand and telephone messages, coordinated the manager's calendar, and "minded the store" when he was away is no longer nearly as necessary. Many of the traditional tasks of secretaries and clerks are now partially or entirely accomplished mechanically or electronically.

This is just as well, because the capable women who used to fill those jobs now educate themselves for, and have access to, much more varied and attractive careers. Even with increased salaries, employers find themselves extremely hard-pressed to fill secretarial jobs except with women with much lower abilities and skills than was the case in the past.

The capable, well-educated women still face significant and persistent discrimination in hiring and, especially, in promotions into and within management; and the many manifestations of that discrimination still need to be addressed. But there is a much more severely limiting barrier, that is only now *beginning* to be addressed. And it will require major structural changes to keep it from persisting and severely limiting the progress of women in management for a great many years to come.

The Great Remaining Barrier to Women's Progress as Managers

One way to describe and understand this remaining barrier to women's progress in management positions is by means of an experiential exercise that this chapter's author developed and entitled "The Short-Tall Scenario." While it was designed for administration in workshops, its essence is captured in the following:

> Imagine that you live in a society very much like the United States, except that there are two categories of people, the SHORTS and the TALLS.
> Imagine that you are a member of the TALL group. You, like all TALLS, are six feet tall or even taller. The TALLS constitute about half of the country's population.
> The other half of the population are SHORTS. All of them are well *under* five feet tall.
> The SHORTS have somewhat different physiological requirements from yours: They need to eat only two meals a day, and use a bathroom only twice a day, in both cases early in the morning and late in the evening.

For historical reasons, unrelated to innate abilities or talents, SHORTS are the people who currently dominate society, government, education, and business. The executive offices of corporations have therefore until recently been almost totally inhabited by SHORTS.

As a consequence, the doors to their offices are only five feet high. Ceilings are just seven feet high, and there are numerous lighting fixtures and ceiling-mounted storage units that hang down below the six-foot level. Chairs are low, with shallow seats and low backs; desks, too, are low.

There are no restrooms in the executive areas, and no eating facilities. Executives, once they arrive in the morning, are expected not to take any work breaks, nor eat, nor leave the area. To do so is considered a sign of insufficient dedication to work.

There is also a cultural standard that requires executives always to hold their heads high. It is considered highly undignified, and even disqualifying, to stoop or to lower their heads at any time.

Recently, there have been major societal and economic changes, and TALLS, such as you, have been acquiring all the needed education and business training and experience to be fully qualified to become executives.

SHORTS no longer automatically bar you from the executive ranks. The business leaders among the SHORTS have analyzed the situation and come to a major conclusion, with which some of the TALLS concur. They say that TALLS like you have two basic options in the corporate world:

1. You can adapt to the requirements of the executive positions and offices. To get through the doors and under the lighting fixtures and storage units, you can do so and still hold your head high (as required) by moving around on your knees rather than your feet. You can blend in as best you can—for example, by never calling at-

tention to your height or to any of height's advantages (such as a high or long reach, or the better vantage point for vision). You can somehow manage your eating habits and train your digestive system so that you can get through every working day without either eating or using a restroom. And you can, with willpower (and by tolerating or treating backaches), adapt yourself to the office furniture and equipment ill-suited to your body's dimensions.

While this may be uncomfortable and limiting to you—and may make for much more taxing conditions than SHORTS experience—it is, after all, up to you to decide whether you care enough about the substantial rewards of success to do what it takes. Or,

2. You can decide that you do not want to do that, and instead satisfy yourself with jobs well below the executive level in content, advancement opportunities, and compensation. If you make this choice, you work in other areas of the building, where the physical environment and furniture are more suited to your needs. There is enough headroom for you to move around on your feet instead of your knees. Restroom facilities and eating facilities are usually available (though often inconvenient and of poor quality); you are permitted to use them if and when you must, although of course your pay is docked for the missed work time.

While your career will be a relatively modest one, it can be generally pleasant, and you will be congenially surrounded by other TALLS like yourself. And you will have the satisfaction of knowing that you are contributing essential support services; executives often smile and tell you, "We couldn't do it without you!"

Given these realities, which of the two options would *you* choose?

Meanings and Implications

The absurdity of forcing TALLS to choose between two such undesir-able options, just because of organizational patterns that no longer suit reality, is obvious to anyone reading the above scenario. Most workshop participants who have experienced the exercise cry out that it is the *system*—the *organizational structure, physical environment, and rules*—that must change, rather than the people having to twist themselves into existing confines; that even though TALLS are now permitted in executive jobs, their access and opportunities are still vastly inferior to those of the SHORTS, for whose characteristics and needs the system was structured.

The situation in the scenario would be laughable if it were not so close to actuality, with direct parallels to current real-life situations for women managers and aspiring managers.

Today's corporations still follow the basic structure of organization and work that was formed in the old sex-segregated society in which women were only peripheral and temporary workers in corporate offices. The resulting structure is no better suited to the equal participation of women in managerial and executive jobs than the above-described organization is suited to similar participation by TALLS.

Women who aspire to managerial or executive positions are expected to deny or twist in totally unnatural ways their biological functions of pregnancy, birth, and breast-feeding, just as the TALLS who become executives are expected to go all day without eating or going to a restroom. TALL executives need to avoid leaving the executive floor to get a bite to eat, lest that be interpreted as a sign of insufficient dedication to career; similarly, it is hazardous to the career of the female executive if she takes a leave to give birth or breast-feed her infant.

Just as TALLS are expected to move around on their knees and hide the potential advantages of their height, women are expected to subordinate their inborn or culturally developed strengths—often including superior human relations skills—and to limit their behavior to that which is typical of men.

TALLS who choose the less-demanding jobs where restroom and cafeteria facilities are available are still expected to keep their use of those facilities to the barest minimum, and forfeit pay, job security, and advancement opportunities when they do use them. Similarly, those women who choose less demanding jobs in order to suit their needs and characteristics better are permitted to take only brief and often inadequate leaves, and are penalized for anything more.

In summary, it is ludicrous to insist that women, just because they happen to be latecomers to corporate management, contort themselves into the patterns designed to suit men's lives (or, to be more accurate, the lives of male executives in the days when they had full-time homemaker wives taking care of the home front), or instead accept permanently inferior status, pay, and opportunities.

However, there is surprisingly little understanding of this. Felice Schwartz, in her 1989 *Harvard Business Review* article, "Management Women and the New Facts of Life,"[4] set forth and argued in favor of the viewpoint that women should face realities and choose between those same two options, and then accept the consequences. She also argued that it may well be both reasonable and desirable for corporations to come to their own conclusions as to which pattern a particular woman fits into—and then

purposefully (and not necessarily with her knowledge or approval) shape her job and development opportunities accordingly.

While there was a torrent of well-articulated protest regarding what came to be called the "Mommy Track" concept,[5] Ms. Schwartz' thesis was accepted and warmly supported by many (including some women), who considered her one of the few women who were facing reality and talking practical sense. Since then, little if anything has been done to address what is surely the greatest remaining barrier to true equal opportunity for women in management.

The Current Situation: Still Stuck in Nonfunctional Patterns

The situation, as described above, is absurd. Therefore these questions loom: Whose problem is it? Is there anything that can be done about it, and if so, what, and by whom?

Most think of it as the *women's* problem. However, it is clear that it is a problem of society in general, definitely including men. While the existing system is most markedly ill-suited to women, it is also ill-suited to current *male* life-styles.

In an era in which both husband and wife typically work outside the home, men do not have the back-up household services the wife used to provide, and men are increasingly hard-pressed by the competing pressures from their employers and their family and home lives. Many men are also becoming aware of how much they—and their children—are missing because of the employment-shaped lack of time and involvement with their children, especially since "Mom" is no longer at home either. And divorce, increasingly common, exacerbates the situation for many fathers. So the problem is men's as well as women's.

The problem is also one of corporations and other employing organizations. Under the current organizational structure, companies find it increasingly difficult to attract and retain needed employees. Able, hard-working, low-paid, compliant female clerks and secretaries are difficult or impossible to find; increasing pay levels helps somewhat, but both the quantity and *quality* of the supply continues to decline. And many of the most talented men are no longer willing to sacrifice their personal and family lives for their employers.

There is another, closely related problem faced by employers. The competitiveness of the national—and global—marketplace is continually increasing, and companies need to be *enormously flexible* to be successful. The old rigid authoritarian hierarchical organizational structure, in which carefully selected young white men, formal education complete, are anointed to move up through the hierarchy, over decades in which they compete with one another but with no-one else, lacks that flexibility.

The traditional structure also lacks the ability to draw fully on the talents of its employees. When employees (other than the top executives) are expected to perform but not to think, to respond to communications and orders from above but not to contribute their own ideas or help solve problems, all the thinking and innovating and problem solving must come from a small homogeneous group of grey-haired white men at the top of the pyramid. And one of the time-consuming priorities of that small group has to be keeping control of an underutilized and frustrated work force.

Employers, society, and government—still dominated by men and male values—are nevertheless bound to resist change unless and until they see it in their individual and collective interest to do so. Most men, and most employers, will inevitably resist pressure to make change just to "be nice to the ladies"—which is not to say that pressure should not be continually exerted.

THE TRANSFORMATION THAT IS NEEDED

A totally different, much more radical approach to the situation is needed if change is to be sufficiently rapid to meet the needs of both society and business. Instead of asking, "What modifications do we need to make in the organizational structure we now have?" we should be examining the problem in a two-step fashion. We should ask, first:

If we were starting, today, entirely afresh, to design organizations to suit today's needs, today's society, what would they be like—what assumptions would they operate from, what organizational patterns would they have?

And only after that examination and design process is under way should we move onto the practicalities of answering this question:

OK. Now, given the organizational structure and patterns that we *now* have—which are far from those that we need—how can we best get from here to there?

The New Requirements for Effective Organizations

It would be foolish to think that one can sit down and instantly develop a detailed blueprint of the structure and operating patterns of an organization well-suited to today's realities. However, one can start the process by developing, examining, and analyzing the givens, the assumptions, on which the design should be based. Here are just a few examples:

- People who are educated, qualified, experienced, and eager to work—as managers as well as in all other occupational fields—come from both sexes, all ages, and every ethnic group. Recruiting, selection, training, and advancement opportunities should be provided without regard to stereotypes based on those characteristics. This means a revolution in selection criteria and methods.

- The generally accepted principles, styles, and methods of managing based on male values and the patriarchal model cannot automatically be assumed to be applicable or effective under the dramatically new conditions and demands. A totally fresh examination must be initiated, looking at many alternatives. Sally Helgesen, for example, in her book *The Female Advantage*,[6] persuasively describes the non-hierarchical but extremely effective managerial styles of four women leaders of major organizations.

- Rapidly growing numbers of women are starting and heading their own businesses,[7] and thus having the opportunity to structure them to suit their own needs and their own managerial styles. They are often handicapped by regulations and business and banking practices based on assumptions built up when almost all entrepreneurs were male. Regulations and practices need to be rethought and restructured in the light of the changed needs.

- Education and learning are lifelong, and both women and men need to have the time, energy, and resources for continuing education and training if they are to be flexible and optimally productive. Employers must accommodate those needs.

- People live in a wide variety of personal and family situations: The U.S. Census Bureau reports that in 1990, the prototypical nuclear family of husband, wife, and one or more minor children comprised only 26 percent of all U.S. households (down from 40 percent in 1970).[8] The demands of personal and family life therefore vary enormously. Work demands and schedules, benefits, housing, education for children and adults, and types and sources of assistance must take into consideration the widely varying needs of women and men, single and divorced people, parents and nonparents, working couples as well as those in which one partner stays home, people living alone, same-sex couples, and group living arrangements of various kinds.

- Pregnancy, childbirth, and breast-feeding are natural biological processes that require accommodation from employers for several or a few years in the lives of most women. Parental leave for parents of both sexes must also be a given, at the time of birth or adoption, and if and when children are ill or hurt.

- Even when children reach school age, they are typically in school only half of the days of the year—and only until mid-afternoon. Recognizing that, employers can appropriately provide or help support child care facilities for after-school time, school vacations and holidays, and when a child is too ill to go to school but not sufficiently sick to be hospitalized.

- Many adults have responsibility for aging parents or other family members who are infirm or disabled. "Sick leave" should be expanded in definition to include care for ill family members. Large employers might provide elder-care facilities, or support such facilities in the community.

- Work schedules based on outdated assumptions and fixed to suit the convenience of the employer (e.g., 9 to 5, Monday through Friday) are often highly inconvenient for some people, particularly women—or even prevent them from working at all at various times in their lives. Flexible hours, part-time and shared positions, options of working at home temporarily or permanently, full-time or part-time, can greatly increase the pool of talent from which employers can draw and the flexibility with which they can operate.
- Vacations and holidays must be sufficient, and supplementable when needed by personal time and personal leave, for working couples and single parents to meet their personal and family responsibilities adequately and without damaging stress and conflict.

How Do We Get There from Here?

Although we are only in the early stages of examining, analyzing, and understanding the structural problems, we can nevertheless begin to shape the ways in which we can move from "here" to "there." For example, there are many possible ways to increase the number of people, particularly those in positions with the power to initiate and implement change, who understand the need to restructure the way employment is organized in order to achieve the flexibility, productivity, and quality of products and services that are rapidly becoming essential to success.

Much can be done to "spread the word" through books, articles and oped pieces, speeches, television news and other programs, and through changes in business education, education for public administration and the law, and workshops and seminars for adults in business and government. The analysis can be presented in such a way as to show that the restructuring will benefit men as well as women and minorities; adults as well as children; corporations as well as families and society; executives and stockholders as well as employees; the rest of the world as well as the United States.

As understanding grows, it will become easier to change the corporate policies and practices, and laws and regulations, that now get in the way. And it will become easier to exert pressure for, and create and implement *new* policies and practices, and laws and regulations, to ease, encourage, and (when necessary) force the needed changes.

As the workplace becomes more flexible and laws better structured, women's strengths, talents, and abilities will be better utilized—and their different approaches to management allowed to blossom. It will become easier for women and men to take leaves for the care of their children, particularly in the crucial first several years; day care and child care facilities will become more available, more convenient, and higher quality; women will no longer be placed on the dead-end "mommy track" just because of the biological fact that they are the ones who bear the children; women will no longer be forced to deny their own values and abilities in order to fit into the traditional "male" mode that is not even appropriate for today's men, either.

People will no longer be evaluated by their sex or age in determining their fitness for a position or a promotion, since it will be recognized that the old rules of thumb no longer apply. Companies that stick to the lock-step white male graduation-to-retirement progression up the organizational pyramid will find themselves hopelessly handicapped and unable to compete for productive employees, and unable to be sufficiently flexible in the marketplace.

It will become not only possible, but considered the norm, for both women and men to move from "full-time" to "part-time" to "temporary" to "non-employed" status, and back, perhaps several times, over their working life-times, in order to meet the needs of their changing circumstances and priorities.

Workplaces will become vibrant, ever-changing kaleidoscopic mixtures of women and men who participate in different ways at different times of their lives, but always as *full* participants, contributing their skills, their ideas, and their problem-solving abilities wherever they are in the structure at that moment.

NOTES

1. U.S. Department of Labor, Bureau of Labor Statistics, "New Labor Force Projections, Spanning 1988 to 2000," *Monthly Labor Review*, November 1989, p. 5, Table 2.

2. Data provided by The American Assembly of Collegiate Schools of Business, St. Louis. Also cited in *Empowering Women in Business*. The Empowering Women Series, No. 1 (Washington, DC: The Feminist Majority Foundation, 1991), p. 2.

3. Mary Ann Von Glinow and Anna Krzyczkowska, "The Fortune 500: A Cast of Thousands," University of Southern California, 1988. Data updated by Von Glinow, 1990.

4. Felice N. Schwartz, "Management Women and the New Facts of Life," *Harvard Business Review*, No. 1 (January–February 1989).

5. For example, see the lead editorial, "Why Not Many Mommy Tracks?" in the March 13, 1989, issue of the *New York Times*, and some of the letters to the editor published in the *Harvard Business Review*, May–June 1989, no. 3, in a special section entitled "Management Women: Debating the Facts of Life."

6. Sally Helgesen, *The Female Advantage: Women's Ways of Leadership* (New York: Doubleday, 1990).

7. The 1987 U.S. Census reports 4.1 million women business owners, up 57 percent from 1982.

8. From Associated Press, Washington, DC, January 29, 1991; appeared in January 30, 1991, issue of the *New York Times*, under the headline "Only One U.S. Family in Four is 'Traditional.'"

42

Radically Transforming Work for the 21st Century

A Feminist Reconstruction of "Real" Work

(1995)

Joyce K. Fletcher

Abstract

A study uses a feminist poststructuralist perspective to reconceptualize the notion of "real" work to include a way of working that springs from a relational belief system–relational practice. Four themes of relational practice are identified. A poststructuralist analysis details the mechanisms and the organizational implications of the process through which this practice "gets disappeared" in organizational discourse. Detailing relational practice as intentional action to achieve goals of achievement, growth and development momentarily reconstructs the definition of real work by calling attention to the potential benefits to organizations of valuing relational practice and the skills needed to enact it.

INTRODUCTION

The findings from this exploratory fieldwork are presented here in the context of organizational calls to transform work and the workplace.

They are used to support the argument that the disconnect between the kind of work organizations and organizational theorists say they need for the 21st century and the kind of work that currently pets rewarded in organizations is a gendered phenomenon, one unlikely to be resolved by mere calls for transformation. More specifically, the findings suggest that despite organizational rhetoric about flatter, non-hierarchical structures and relational, holistic, empowered workers, when faced with specific behaviors that exemplify this approach, organizations routinely "disappear" these practices and the people who do them (primarily females) from the organizational screen.

THEORETICAL CONTEXT

The theoretical framing of this study occurs at the intersection of three different streams of thought. The first is feminist poststructuralism which is a form of postmodern philosophy. This literature establishes the context of the study in that it explores the relationship among discourse, knowledge and power (Clegg, 1989; Flax, 1990; Foucault, 1980; Mumby, 1988; Weedon, 1987). It is used to support the hypothesis that there are certain activities, broadly labeled relational activities, that are an important element of the experience of work for some (primarily female) people in organizations but that are marginalized in current organizational definitions of work. Furthermore, it is used to support the argument that the marginalization of these activities in the organizational discourse on work is an unobtrusive exercise of power that results in the devaluation and discounting of these activities, such that they are not considered "real" and their impact on organizational effectiveness is invisible. The second literature, on the sociology of work, is used to explore the current definition of work in organizational discourse as an artifact of the social construction of the public/private dichotomy along gender lines (Bellah et al., 1985; Ferguson, 1984; Game & Pringle, 1983; Harding, 1986; Nicholoson, 1990; Parson & Bales, 1955; Wadel, 1979). This feminist reading of the literature is used to support the hypothesis that organizational activities, language and practices that are congruent with the public, instrumental sphere and the subject position "man" will be considered "real" work, while activities associated with the private, relational sphere and the subject position "woman" will either disappear from view, or if visible, will be trivialized or considered marginal to work in the public domain. Lastly, feminist standpoint research, including the psychology of gender differences, the sociology

of "women's work" and the social construction of gender, is used to surface the types of activities, skills and experiences that are likely to be invisible in the current definition of work (Acker, 1992; Chodorow, 1974; Miller, 1986a; Mills & Tancred, 1992; West & Zimmerman, 1991), and the way in which this invisibility maintains, reinforces and recreates current power structures.

RESEARCH QUESTIONS

Feminist standpoint literature suggests that although the prevailing models of growth and achievement are based on public sphere characteristics such as separation, individuation and independence, there exists an alternative model, called growth-in-connection, that is rooted in private sphere characteristics of connection, interdependence and collectivity (Jordan et al., 1991; Miller, 1986a). Theories of the origin of gender difference indicate that there are strong forces operating to predispose women to enact this relational model of growth even within instrumental settings. These forces are both internal—based on women's early development in a context of communion (Chodorow, 1974; Gilligan, 1982) and external—based on socialization and societal expectations of gender appropriate behavior (Miller, 1986; West & Zimmerman, 1991). The first research question will explore the extent to which Relational Practice exists in organizational settings, the patterns of behavior that characterize it and the belief system these patterns reflect.

The second research question explores how the activities identified in the first level of inquiry as Relational Practice are made sense of when subjected to the sensemaking "truth rules" of the dominant discourse.

The third research question deals with the power dynamic inherent in the current definition of real work and explores three hypotheses. The first is that workplace interactions are sites of "doing gender." The second is that the process of enacting relational activities is one way of doing gender in the workplace. And the third is that by using these relational activities to enact the subject position "woman," females are shouldering activities which devalue them, contributing to the forces which keep these activities invisible and thereby becoming active participants in creating, maintaining and reinforcing a system of patriarchy and gender inequity.

METHOD

The research design reflects the exploratory nature of the research questions. It is a qualitative "direct research" (Mintzberg, 1979) design in which six female engineers were shadowed, each for one day. This was followed up by a debriefing interview in which the previous day's activities were reviewed and contextualized. These data were used to induce a set of categories of specific behaviors associated with relational activity as a way of working. Mid-way in the analysis a roundtable discussion with participants was held in which the preliminary categories and themes were shared and reactions invited. These data were used to further refine the categories and record the sensemaking frameworks underlying these ways of working. The first analysis of the shadowing, interview and roundtable data addressed the first research question. It yielded four themes of Relational Practice and a detailing of the specific activities and the belief system associated with each theme.

The second stage of the analysis entailed a poststructuralism re-reading of the data as "enacted text" (Jacques, 1992) in order to detail the power-knowledge structures underlying Relational Practice, thereby addressing the second and third research questions. This analysis yielded a detailed description of the "disappearing dynamic," an identification of three specific mechanisms through which Relational Practice "gets disappeared" when brought into the organizational discourse on work, and the organizational implications of this process.

FINDINGS

Relational Practice: The findings suggest that workers operating from a relational belief system look to relational interactions in the workplace not so much to enhance their affective personal relationships with others but rather to enhance their own and others' achievement and work effectiveness. Relational Practice appears to be motivated by a belief that relational interactions are sites of growth, development and professional achievement for both parties involved. It is characterized by work practices and strategies that differ in significant ways from conventional "strategies for success" and uses a set of skills not commonly associated with organizational effectiveness.

The data indicate that there are four types of Relational Practice. The first, Preserving, includes shouldering, connecting and rescuing activities. Shouldering refers to picking up activities that are outside the technical definition of the job. This included things such as using informal channels to pass on key information to other groups, working behind the scenes to create relational bridges between people who needed to be connected for the sake of the project, or picking up the slack and doing whatever it took to get the job done, even if it meant doing something that would be considered "low status" work. Connecting activities focused on keeping the project connected to critical resources in order to prevent potential problems from arising. This included such things as sending thank you notes to people in other subsystems who were providing valuable, but unrequired, resources to the project, "translating" one party to another or acting as a go-between when there was a breakdown in communication. Rescuing refers to the practice of picking up on problems and situations that might be overlooked by standard operating procedures and making sure that resources were diverted to address them.

Engaging in Preserving activities required relational skills in connecting with people, an ability to assess and pay attention to emotional data by, for example, noting when there was tension between people and taking steps to relieve it, an ability and willingness to do low status work without any loss to self-esteem, and an ability to think holistically and anticipate consequences. The willingness to engage in these activities appeared to be rooted in a certain set of relational beliefs: a belief that "good" workers have relational skills and will be able to operate in a context of implications and consequences as opposed to a context of separation and specialization, a belief that indirectness— doing these things without calling attention to them—adds value, and a belief that keeping relationships in good working order is important to the life and well-being of the project.

The second practice, Mutual Empowering, refers to activities that are undertaken to enable others to achieve. This included things such as "empathic teaching," a certain type of knowledge transfer in which the needs of the learner were paramount and the focus was on the other (what does s/he need to hear?) rather than on the self (what would I like to say?). Teaching empathically sometimes meant modifying the information according to the intellectual context, such as searching for an everyday example to illustrate an abstract principle and sometimes it meant modifying the information to respond to the emotional context, such as sitting down next to learners rather than standing over them. The chief characteristics of this practice were the intentional use of strategies that minimized the status difference inherent in a teacher-student interaction and a belief that being a teacher meant being open to learning from the "student." Engaging in this practice required skills in contexualizing and responding to the emotional as well as the intellectual context of teaching interactions. It also required an ability to take on another's perspective and strategize an appropriate response.

The second practice associated with empowering is protective connecting. This entailed using one's relational skills to smooth potentially explosive situations or potential rifts in other's relationships that could damage one or both party's ability to achieve results or be effective. Often it meant stepping in and "handling" difficult people who were causing others—like the boss—difficulty or stepping in to protect people from the consequences of their own lack of relational skill or effort.

A third category of empowering activity had to do with taking action aimed at eliminating barriers—both emotional and practical—that might hinder others' ability to achieve or be effective. Often this just meant sensing the emotional context of situations and cutting people some slack. At other times, it meant eliminating practical barriers, like offering to call to get information rather than just giving the number, or getting up from her chair to get a pad of paper rather than just point out where it was.

When the engineers talked about these activities it was clear that their willingness to help others in this way came from a mindset that sees needing help as part of the human condition, not as evidence of individual deficiency. The expectation of reciprocity was implicit and some engineers expressed disappointment that some people just didn't "get it". What they didn't get was that help is a two way street and should be given respectfully, without "lording it over" others and that teacher and learner are both natural—but temporary—states.

The third type of activity associated with Relational Practice is Achieving, a practice that uses relational skills to create conditions that enable not others, but one's own growth and achievement. It was characterized by a type of reflective activity that required an ability to be in touch with one's own feelings as a source of data, as well as an ability to understand the emotional context of situations in order to strategize one's response. For example, one of the activities in this category was asking for help in a way that called forth responsiveness in others. This relational asking included things such as freely granting expert status to another by, for example, being willing to reveal the full extent of one's own need, or communicating in the asking, a willingness to pass on to others whatever help or information might be received. Again, this type of asking seemed to stem from a belief in the essential nature of interdependence. The engineers clearly differentiated this type of value-added asking from more exploitive requests that were characterized as asking someone to do your job for you. Other types of Achieving activities entailed using one's relational skills to keep working relationships on an even keel by, for example, recognizing one's responsibility for breaks in relationships with others and taking steps to reconnect—such as going out of one's way to follow-up with someone after a disagreement in a meeting.

The final category of Relational Practice is Creating Team, a set of activities intended to promote group life and the experience of team. These activities entailed creating the background conditions in which group life could flourish and outcomes such as trust, affection, cooperation, collaboration and collective achievement could occur. It included things such as sending verbal and non-verbal messages of affirmation when listening to others by, for example, maintaining eye contact or nodding, smiling and making encouraging comments. It also included responding empathically to other's feelings or unique circumstances by, for example, taking on a minor aspect of a job someone else disliked or offering to work at a time that would allow someone else to make it to daycare on time. The willingness to undertake these activities appeared to stem from an expectation of mutuality and reciprocity—those who engaged in this activity expected to be treated the same way—and a belief that individual and collective achievement occurs best in a context of connection. More specifically, it appeared to depend on a belief in and a willingness to work for what Cato Wadel (1979) calls "embedded outcomes." These are outcomes that are embedded in people and in social situations and typically are invisible and rarely seen as evidence that "work" has been done. The willingness and motivation to engage in relational interactions that contribute to the development of others and the development of group life appeared to spring from a belief that the outcomes of this activity are achievements in their own right and are signs of competence and effectiveness that are worthy of effort and should be recognized as such.

Disappearing, Power and Resistance: The practice summarized in the findings above details a way of working that springs from a relational belief system, one that stands in sharp contrast to the instrumental belief system underlying the organizational discourse on work. The second stage of the analysis addresses the question of what happens to Relational Practice when it is lifted from its own belief system and brought into the organizational discourse on work in this engineering environment. That is, it explores the gap between the two discourses in order to identify the mechanisms by which Relational Practice "gets disappeared" as real work in organizational discourse and get constructed as something other than work.

The poststructuralist framing of this study argues that all public sphere activity is implicitly subjected to general "truth rules" about the characteristics of real work and that these truth rules are a reflection of Enlightenment thinking and its underlying values of rationality, abstraction, linearity and instrumentality. Within this general framework in which all organizations reflect the instrumental values of Enlightenment thinking, an engineering environment was intentionally selected as the research site (as opposed to, for example, a hospital, school or social service agency) because it was assumed to be an exemplar of this type of instrumental power-knowledge structure. The cultural diagnosis conducted prior to the shadowing indicated that this was indeed the case. The work environment in this unit was characterized by autonomy, self-promotion and individual heroics, where time was a surrogate for commitment, competence was measured by short term results and output was defined in terms of tangible, concrete "metrics."

When behavior motivated by a relational belief system (model of growth-in-connection) is brought into this organizational discourse it gets disappeared as real work because by its very nature it violates many of the "truth rules" underlying this culture, truth rules that express a different model of growth, development and achievement (growth-through individuation).

Thus, behavior undertaken to enact a relational belief system, Relational Practice, is destined to be labeled as inappropriate. For example, Preserving activities are rooted in a belief system that privileges context and connection. This leads to behavior rooted in an assumed responsibility for the whole, and results in such things as sending thank-you notes or doing work that is technically beneath the duties of an engineer. However, in a culture based on individuation and autonomy, in which technical competence and specialization are privileged, these types of activity lie outside the job description. In a culture where competence is measured by one's ability to self-promote, talk technical and associate oneself with high profile solutions, being quietly competent is an oxymoron. And in a culture where differential reward is based on hierarchy and status, doing work that is beneath you is career suicide and inexplicable in one who wants to get ahead. Thus, the payback on these preservative activities is likely to be invisible and the willingness to do them is likely to mystify others, who are operating from a different belief system. Certainly, conventional wisdom warns women away from exactly this kind of behavior. Rather than being seen as evidence of taking responsibility for the whole, this type of activity is commonly constructed as just the opposite, i.e. as a tendency to focus on minutiae, to exhibit an "excessive devotion to duty" and an inability to prioritize and see the big picture (Harragan, 1977; Hennig & Jardim, 1978). Others, more sophisticated in their awareness of gender dynamics might see some aspects of this preserving behavior, like sending thank you notes, as "wives' work" and

attribute it to women's desire to humanize the workplace (Huff, 1990). The important point, however, is that each of these "commonsense" analyses is fundamentally different from viewing the behavior as work, i.e. an intentional strategy to enhance project effectiveness.

Each of the other types of Relational Practice gets disappeared in similar fashion. For example, in a culture of individualism and heroics, behavior that springs from a belief in Mutual Empowerment doesn't make much sense. Indeed, in an environment where those who get paid to enable others, such as secretaries and other support staff, are lowest in the hierarchy and have little opportunity for advancement, it makes sense that those who voluntarily assume a support role are considered either incapable of achieving in their own right, or too naive to know better. As a result, support activity in any form routinely gets disappeared from the final product. As one engineer states, "If you get the answer it is assumed that YOU alone, got the answer."

The difficulty in describing an alternative environment—one in which support is acknowledged—is captured by one engineer who states "I know I am doing a good job when people think of me as someone who is 1) competent and 2) someone who will help. Most people around here only care about the first thing—competence—they don't care if they are seen as approachable. I do." Although she tries to describe what could be considered an expanded definition of competence, one that includes a willingness and an ability to share with and empower others, the limits of language in this discourse restrict her ability to describe this kind of outcome—an outcome that would be embedded in another person—as evidence of competence. So she settles on "approachability", a word that has a strong association with affect and likability, and leaves the definition of competence unchallenged. Poststructuralists would suggest that not only does she leave the current definition unchallenged, she actively reinforces it by constructing the ability and willingness to empower as something "other"—the other side of an assumed dichotomy.

The Relational Practice of Achieving gets disappeared in a similar fashion. Within organizational discourse, the world is divided into those with achievement needs and those with affiliation needs. In this framework, relational interactions are assumed to be motivated by strong affect and the desire, indeed the need to have those feelings reciprocated. The possibility of having achievement needs met through relational interactions isn't representable in this sensemaking schema—it is nonsense. Thus, individuals who seek relational interactions as sites of growth and achievement in the workplace are destined to be understood as seeking something other, such as affect, and operating out of a "need to be liked." In this engineering environment, a need to be liked is considered such a sign of personal deficiency that merely suggesting that certain people are motivated by this need is enough to taint them and their behavior as worthless, inappropriate, and a sign of incompetence.

Many of these same dynamics operate to disappear the Relational Practice of Creating Team. In an environment where a relational model of growth and development is non-sense, it is difficult to articulate or understand a motivation to engage in activity that socially constructs "team" and seeks to create conditions under which the outcomes of relational interactions can occur. For example, the use of collaborative language as an effective strategy gets disappeared because it violates one of the main truth rules of this culture. If there is only one best way to solve a problem and finding it defines you as the winner, then building on others' ideas is nonsense. So, if you operate from a relational belief system and use language that invites collaborative discussion, rather than being seen as effective, you are not seen at all. You and your ideas disappear. Interestingly, the language engineers used to describe the use of collaborative language—nice, polite, self-effacing—contributed to its near invisibility as a challenge to the dominant discourse on real work. Not having a language of competence readily available to describe it, engineers used words that constructed it as either a natural expression of gender (women are naturally more polite) or an expression of powerlessness (self-effacing). This belied their belief in it as a strategy that could make visible the reality of team, by, for example, creating a shared solution to a problem that transcended any one individual's ideas. This relational belief is articulated clearly by one engineer who says: "I see it as avoiding conflict. Because at least for me personally, I'm not somebody who feels very comfortable negotiating in an atmosphere of conflict. I like to talk about things, explain why I think something, hear about what the other person thinks about something (emphasis added).

The engineers' ability to more strongly articulate the belief system underlying these four types of Relational Practice and thereby give voice to an alternative way of working that would challenge the dominant discourse is constrained not simply by the limits of language or by the association of relational activity with the private sphere, but by a larger dynamic—the social construction of gender—that encompasses those two effects: they recognize that as females they do not really have the option of choosing what strategy to use. Because of gender dynamics, these engineers recognized that the option of using stereotypical masculine behavior was closed to them. This explanation invokes the dominant discourse sensemaking around such behavior—this is not a choice made because of all the options this is actually more effective, this is a choice made because there is no other option for her as a woman in this culture.

The pressure to "do gender" at work disappears what's new about Relational Practice in another subtle but very powerful way. For example, several of the engineers describe being asked routinely to do support tasks by male engineers, things like copying, delivering papers to another office or packing boxes. When they begin to feel they are being taken advantage of and try to set some boundary around how much or what kind of help they are willing to give, they are (jokingly) called things like "Tarantula Lady" or "Queen Bee." Getting called names for not being willing to help limitlessly makes visible the expectation that they, as women, should embrace this kind of helping behavior and do it willingly with no expectation of reciprocity. As a result, their belief in an alternative to current organizational norms gets overwhelmed by their experience and instead of articulating a new vision of

empowering, they end up cautioning each other not to do too much of it: "Although it might be good for the project, if you do it, you'll end up being a gopher your whole life."

THE DISAPPEARING DYNAMIC

The summary of the findings of the second stage of analysis suggests that when women enact Relational Practice in the workplace, it "gets disappeared" in three ways: through the attribution of "inappropriate," through the limits of language and through the social construction of gender. These three mechanisms operate in concert so that activity springing from a relational belief system gets disappeared as something new (an alternative way of working in the public sphere) and gets constructed as something familiar (private sphere activity, inappropriately applied to the public sphere). This construction of Relational Practice as private sphere activity sets in motion a patriarchal understanding of the motivation and intent underlying this activity. The important point is that once Relational Practice is brought into the dominant discourse as private sphere activity, the self-sealing loop in which private sphere activity is understood and re-created as the devalued side of the public/private dichotomy gets engaged. Thus, the work gets absorbed by the system but the challenge to assumptions about ways of working gets disappeared from that loop. This way of working is not considered an object for analysis or theorizing since, as the devalued side of the public/private dichotomy, it is assumed to be understood as non-essential to professional growth and achievement.

CONCLUSION

The significance of these findings lie in their potential use as an act of resistance to current organizational norms. Detailing Relational Practice as intentional action to achieve goals of achievement, growth and development momentarily reconstructs the definition of real work by calling attention to the potential benefits to organizations of valuing Relational Practice and the skills needed to enact it. This act of resistance opens up discursive space in which the possibility can be discussed that behavior enacting this belief system, if understood, theorized and explicated as "work" might challenge our common-sense understanding of ways of organizing. This study highlight the complex, interactive, gendered forces that are at play here, working to silence and suppress such transformative challenges to current organizational norms. What this means for organizations that are calling for team oriented, less hierarchical, empowered workers is that they are unlikely to get them from current practice, regardless of calls for transformation. Rather, it suggests that true transformation will require a feminist reconstruction of real work—one that makes visible a contradiction the power-knowledge system of patriarchy works to suppress: relational activity is not needed and women will provide it. Thus, the act of resistance in a feminist reconstruction of real work is not simply an act of resistance to hierarchy or other aspects of organizing. It is also, at a deeper level, an act of resistance to the way in which these ways of organizing create, re-create and maintain a gendered dichotomy between the public and private spheres, and to the power structure (patriarchy) that depends on this split.

REFERENCES

Acker, J. (1992). Gendering organizational theory. In A.J. Mills and P. Tancred (eds). Gendering organizational analysis. Newbury Park: Sage.

Bellah, R., Madsen, R., Sullivan, W., Swidler, A., Tipton, S. (1985). Habits of the heart. Berkeley: University of California Press.

Chodorow, N. (1974). Family structure and feminine personality. In M. Z. Rosaldo & L. Lamphere (eds.). Women, culture and society. Stanford, CA: Stanford University Press.

Clegg, S. (1989). Frameworks of power. Newbury Park, CA: Sage.

Ferguson, K.E. (1984). The feminist case against bureaucracy. Philadelphia: Temple University Press.

Flax, J. (1990). Thinking fragments. Berkeley: University of California Press.

Foucault, M. (1980). Truth and power. In C. Gordon (ed.). Power/knowledge: Selected interviews and other writings. 1972–1977, by Michel Foucault. New York: Pantheon

Game, A. & Pringle, R. (1983). Gender at work. Boston: George Allen & Unwin.

Gilligan, C. (1982). In a different voice. Cambridge, MA: Harvard University Press.

Harding, S. (1986). The science question in feminism. Ithaca, NY: Cornell University Press.

Political Science

Women's historical exclusion from formal politics and their continued underrepresentation in positions of power makes political science an especially intriguing field for feminist scholars. In these selections, feminist political scientists revisit traditional areas of research: the creation and implications of social policy, the process of politicization, and the field of human rights. Their work poses intriguing challenges to standard definitions and theories. Virginia Sapiro's essay helps us to "see the fault in analysis of social policy and in social policy itself." Her work shows that welfare policy has been construed to perpetuate gender roles and consequently women's dependency and poverty. Taking aim at standard or neutral examinations of the welfare state, she argues that recognizing how gender has operated in the creation of policy allows us to fully understand the impact of these policies on women, men, and American families. Carol Hardy-Fanta follows the path of many feminist scholars in testing standard disciplinary theories against the experience of previously ignored groups—in this case Latinas. Note how her research uses personal narratives to challenge traditional ideas about political socialization, consciousness, and activism. In this sense both her methodology and her subject matter reveal feminist sensibilities and concerns. Charlotte Bunch argues for a paradigm shift in the way we conceptualize human rights. She criticizes the Western conception of human rights for ignoring women's experiences with human rights abuses around the world and shows how inclusion forces changes in analysis and policy.

Critical Thinking Questions

1. How do Sapiro's historical examples illustrate her argument about the gender basis of American social policy?
2. Should mothers be compensated or supported by the state to care for their children? If so, which mothers and under what conditions or circumstances?
3. Can you imagine gender-neutral social welfare policies? Would they be feasible or desirable? How would they alter the social landscape?
4. Feminists of the second wave asserted that "the personal is political." In what ways does Hardy-Fanta's research support this idea?

475

5. Assess the level of your own political consciousness and consider the factors that contributed to its development. Can you devise a strategy for nurturing the political development of women?

6. Why have women's issues been omitted from discussions of and policies about human rights? Do any of these reasons seem justifiable to you?

7. Which of Bunch's four approaches to re-visioning women's rights as human rights would make the most difference for women and why?

8. Bunch states "sex discrimination kills women daily." Does this statement sound alarmist or counterproductive, or does it help clarify the significance of the task Bunch and others have set out to accomplish?

43

The Gender Basis of American Social Policy

(1986)

Virginia Sapiro

During the last quarter of the nineteenth century, women—thousands of them—became increasingly organized and active in the attempt to promote the general welfare, especially by helping the most vulnerable members of society. As individual leaders and as group participants they were instrumental in organizing and nationalizing movements for public health (mental and physical), poor relief, penal and other institutional reform, education for the previously uneducated, and child welfare. As the nineteenth century waned and the twentieth dawned, women were prominent among proponents of a principle that was hitherto nearly alien to American ideology but that has now, a century later, come to be an accepted part of our political views: the government and, they increasingly argued, the national government, have a responsibility to promote the general welfare actively by providing initiative and support where necessary. The degree and types of support remain, perhaps more now than then, matters of profound political contention, but in the late twentieth century even the most conservative ideologues tend to agree that government must provide a "safety net" for its people.

The late nineteenth and early twentieth centuries were also a time during which thousands of women, many of them the same as those involved in the general welfare movements, were agitating to promote women's welfare specifically.[1] The suffrage movement, aimed at providing women with what we now regard as the basic right of citizenship and the basic means of leverage within a democratic political system, is only the best-known facet of the women's movement of that era. As many historians have demonstrated, a large proportion of nineteenth-century feminists came to their concerns for women through their charitable and political efforts aimed at the needy.[2] Moreover, many nineteenth-century feminists conceived of their woman-directed activities as means to improve the lot not just of women but of women's families and communities.[3]

Sapiro, Virginia, "The Gendered Basis of American Social Policy." *Political Science Quarterly* 101, no. 2 (1986): 221–238.

The development of American social welfare policy was heavily influenced by women, who often saw themselves acting on behalf of women. These women—many of them feminists—were instrumental in the development of the American social welfare state, such as it is: the efforts in the 1840s of Dorothea Dix to get Congress to provide money and land for the construction of mental institutions (the bill passed but President Franklin Pierce's veto was sustained); the establishment of the United States Sanitary Commission: Josephine Shaw Lowell's New York Charity Organization Society and its counterparts; the settlement movement; Florence Kelley's National Consumers' League; many Progressive leaders; the instigators of the Children's Bureau; and the authors and primary promoters of the 1921 Infancy and Maternity (Sheppard-Towner) Bill.

The history of movements for women's welfare and for the general welfare are virtually inseparable. But we can go further and argue that it is not possible to understand the underlying principles, structure, and effects of our social welfare system and policies without understanding their relationship to gender roles and gender ideology. Three examples suggest how important understanding this relationship is: widows' or mothers' pensions, protective labor legislation, and the Sheppard-Towner Act of 1921.

In 1911, Missouri became the first state to provide for cash assistance to widows with dependent children. By 1935, the date of the nationalization of this policy through Title IV (Aid to Dependent Children) of the Social Security Act, all states except South Carolina and Georgia had acted similarly. As Walter Trattner argues, "Widow's pension laws marked a definite turning point in the welfare policies of many states. In theory at least, they removed the stigma of charity for a large number of welfare recipients. They also broke down the nineteenth-century tradition against public home relief."[4] Before the advent of widows' pensions, public pensions were limited to military personnel or civil servants, people whose willingness to work for limited public salaries would be rewarded with security.[5] Widows' pensions were different in that they provided for needy private persons. The Social Security Act, through Aid to Dependent Children (ADC), did the same at the federal level.

Protective labor legislation offers another example of the role that gender differentiation played in promoting social welfare ideas within the United States. At the turn of the century, efforts to provide for public regulation of working conditions advocated by both trade unions and groups such as the National Consumers' League were turned back consistently on the grounds that they would conflict with the right of employers and employees to make contracts freely and unimpeded by forces outside the market. The major turning point in employment and workplace policy came in 1908 when the Supreme Court, in *Muller v. Oregon*, upheld the right of a state to limit the working hours of women.[6] Although protective labor legislation has been highly contentious among feminists from the first for reasons that will be discussed, the "thin edge of the wedge" for regulation of the workplace was provided by policies based on a particular construction of gender ideology.

A third example of the importance of gender in the expansion of American social policy is the Sheppard-Towner Bill, enacted in 1921 and in force until Herbert Hoover assured its demise in 1929. Sheppard-Towner provided for the first time for matching federal grants-in-aid to states for the purpose of promoting child and maternal health services. This was the first time the federal government provided grants for state welfare programs other than education,[7] and it provided the precedent for later efforts. The program was widely attacked as the first incursion of "bolshevism" into the United States and was the subject of the first major—but certainly not the last—campaign against "state medicine."[8] Anxiety over socialism was one of the major reasons for the demise of the pure laissez-faire system of labor contract in the marketplace. Sheppard-Towner put government, notably the federal government, in the business of providing the public with social services other than protective services and education.

These cases mark turning points in American political ideology. The notion that "that government governs best that governs least" was transformed, at least to the degree that the standard of what constitutes "least" was questioned. To the belief that people should be self-reliant, which meant providing for themselves and their families, was added the idea that it was good for private individuals to engage in charitable acts (although it was not good for individuals to expect to depend upon these acts), and also that government had some responsibility to provide. Government was now to promote the general welfare not just by assuring civil order but by providing for that welfare directly.

Of crucial importance here, women were the apparent beneficiaries of these policies. When these policies were first set in place, there was no intention on the part of most policy makers to set any precedents for other parallel reforms or, certainly, for more widespread changes in the structure or theoretical basis of political economy. Indeed, there was considerable opposition to these changes, specifically because they might turn out to be turning points and precedents, as some interest groups such as the labor and the Progressive movements hoped they might be. Why were women so central to these changes? What does this "coincidence" tell us about the development of gender ideology, political ideology, and social policy in the United States?

Unfortunately, the standard treatments of social policy offer little assistance in answering these questions because the relationships among gender, feminism, and the development of social welfare policy has generally been neglected outside of feminist scholarship. Marxists and non-Marxists alike have identified the development of the welfare state as a part of the political process of the development of capitalist industrialism; to the non-Marxist especially it is a part of the political transformation of societies into mass democracies. Within the standard view of the history of welfare states, as Peter Flora and Arnold J. Heidenheimer write, "one may interpret the welfare state as an answer to increasing demands for socioeconomic equality or as the institutionalization of social rights relative to the development of civil and political rights."[9] Just so; but academic analyses tend to focus on demands and rights specifically relevant to class conflicts within society, thus obscuring the roles of women and gender. This, interestingly, is the case as much for non-Marxists as for Marxists. A woman's economic interests are generally assumed to follow from a husband when the woman is married, and especially a homemaker, and to be defined adequately by standard class definitions in cases where women are employed. The problem is that standard views of economic interest and organization are defined primarily through male history and experience, and feminist activists have often been aware of these differences.[10]

Analysis of the theory and practice of social policy has rarely taken full account of the relevance of gender, and it often implicitly accepts without examination certain paternalistic and patriarchal assumptions about the nature of gender that are also embedded in the policies themselves. As a result, there is little understanding of how social policy affects women in particular and, more generally, how women's welfare is linked to general welfare.

The remainder of this article examines the relationship between women's welfare and the general welfare within the framework of American social policy, especially as it treats economic dependency. Women have been defined primarily as dependents, *because* others depend upon their dependency. American social policy, it shall be argued, not only assumes but helps to maintain this state of affairs. Further, many social policies that most affect women are not, in fact, aimed primarily *at* them but rather, in many sense, *through* them. Finally, analysis of the relationship between women and social policy does not teach us "only" about women and social policy but about our construction and understanding of social policy and the general welfare more broadly.

AMERICAN SOCIAL POLICY: THE STANDARD VERSION

Social policy is, as Albert Weale has written, "a deliberate attempt by governments to promote individual and social welfare in certain specific dimensions using any suitable policy instruments."[11] This definition is useful because it underscores the point that social policy is not a matter simply of social services or even more narrowly (and perhaps more commonly believed) social services for the poor. Social policy, in other words, is not always what it seems to be to the untrained eye. Some of the most important social services are not aimed at the poor (e.g., public universities), and many of the social policies that might do the most to promote individual and social welfare are not services (e.g., occupational safety and health regulations or benefits policies and nondiscrimination policies). Indeed it has been argued repeatedly that it is not easy and not always worthwhile to draw definite boundaries among social policy and fiscal or civil rights policies.[12]

For the first century and more of American history, social policy basically rested on the belief that the welfare of the society and its component parts could best be assured by allowing—encouraging—individuals to pursue their own interests freely. This notion was as much a moral as an economic belief. What came to be known as the "protestant work ethic" supported moral and policy distinctions made among the "just" desserts earned by the diligent well-off and the shiftless poor and the unfortunate "deserving" poor. As Robert Goodin has pointed out, the emphasis on self-reliance was, at its heart, a concern about the moral character of individuals. Conservatives continue to maintain, despite empirical evidence to the contrary,[13] that provision of welfare benefits makes individuals psychologically dependent and removes their motivation to pursue their interests in the marketplace and, therefore, short circuits the entire system. In other words, provision of welfare changes the character of individuals so as to make them bad and unproductive members of society.

In practical terms, therefore, the nation was to be composed of diligent hardworking individuals who competed in the marketplace (or, for the agrarian ideal of self-sufficiency, worked their land) to make something of themselves and to provide for themselves. With the growth of industrialism and the ascendency of a middle class, the principle of individualistic competition in a free market to assure self-sufficiency became a moral, social, political, and economic ideal. The implications of this set of beliefs for social welfare have been well summarized by Ramesh Mishra: "Paternalism—of the state but also of the employer—is frowned upon."

Not the bonds of status but those of contract between "free" men typifies the basic model of social relationship

outside the family. Translating these generalities into patterns of welfare, we might say that the middle-class society is likely to develop a "residual" system of welfare. In the early states of industrialization neither state nor enterprise welfare is favored. Instead, friendly societies, voluntary organizations, charities, and market responses to the various problems and needs are encouraged.[14]

This is precisely what happened during the second half of the nineteenth century in the United States. There was an impressive growth of charity and social action (a growth especially among women) as the more negative by-products of industrialism became more obvious, but this "social action was largely a voluntary do-it-yourself arrangement among individuals with a common interest."[15]

Should individuals be in need of assistance or cooperation, such arrangements were to be made on a voluntary basis. There were clear hierarchies of responsibility or, as Michael Walzer puts it, spheres of justice.[16] The core in which assistance could be freely sought and in which others had the most responsibility to provide was the immediate family followed by more distant relatives. At the next stage were neighbors and others in the local community. As the public domain began to share in provision, the state was seen as more obliged than the federal government. Above all, aid and cooperation were to come from the private world rather than from government. As James Leiby notes, only in the twentieth century was "social welfare" rather than "charity and correction" widely used to label assistance. "Social welfare," he argues, connotes "a recognition of human interdependence . . . , a sense of mutual responsibilities and goals among [society's] classes and parts, and of the need for common policies to realize them."[17]

The earliest social policies fall into two general categories. The first, into which we might put social insurance (originally called "workingman's insurance") and pensions, were aimed at helping or providing some added security to those who were working to help themselves and their society. The second was assistance aimed at those who seemed most inevitably dependent: paupers without relatives to help, children and especially orphans, and "defectives" such as the insane and criminally inclined. Later a third type of social policy developed but did not really flower until the post–World War II era: social regulation or government intervention in the rules and procedures of the market. Above all, American social policy was developed with a continuing distaste for paternalism and an emphasis on allowing individuals, and by later policies helping individuals, compete as individuals in an open market in order to achieve self-sufficiency and self-reliance.

The previous paragraphs offer little more than a standard, albeit boiled down, rendition of American social policy thinking and practice. Turning our attention to the place of women in this story we find that this rendition is seriously flawed. It is written in apparently generic gender-neutral terms and, therefore, masks an extremely gender-based story.

THE REVISED VERSION: BEYOND GENDER NEUTRALITY

In order to see the fault in analysis of social policy and in social policy it-

self, let us look again at the main themes: dependence and self-reliance, individualism and paternalism. In fact, if we consider the subjects of policy not in the apparently gender-neutral terms (such as individual, worker, family) usually used but in the explicit terms of male and female, we find that the dominant ideology underlying social policy thinking and action has never stressed individualism pure and simple. It has never been uniformly opposed to either dependency or paternalism, and it has never supported a universal value of self-reliance, especially in economic terms. Instead, it has supported individualism, independence, and self-reliance for some people (primarily men) and dependence and reliance on paternalism for others (primarily women). This is largely because individuals have been viewed in terms of functional roles depending upon gender. Men are regarded as bread-winners for themselves and their families, and women are regarded as wives and mothers who are and should be economically dependent upon those breadwinners.

In order to understand the relationship of women to social policy, it is necessary to consider policy directly regarding the ability of women to provide for themselves. As we have seen, the primary purpose of most American social policy is supposed to be to allow "individuals" to provide for themselves, to reward those who have done so, and to provide a backup for those who have not been able to do so because of circumstances beyond their own control. If, however, this really was "the" American approach to social policy, it should apply in a gender-neutral way. In fact, this view did not apply to women; indeed, throughout most of American history it has been contradictory to the predominant prescription for women.

Until the enactment of the Married Women's Property Acts in the 1840s, women could not own property, including that which they inherited or earned through their own labor, and they could not make contacts without their husband's consent. In other words, women were barred by law from engaging in the activities that were supposed to be the primary principle of political economy and the civil right most fiercely protected by American law up to the twentieth century—the right to contract freely to pursue one's economic interest. The reason was the common-law principle of *femme couverte*. Women's economic and political identities and interests were incorporated into (not with) those of their husbands. Women's only voluntary contract was the marriage contract, by which they were thought to be giving blanket tacit consent to most future decisions made by their husbands.

Even when free women gained the right to own and manage property and to make contracts, they did not gain the right to provide for themselves. If employers wanted to bar women as a class from employment, their right to do so was protected by the principle of governmental noninterference in private contracts. Moreover, as women began to seek training and jobs outside the women's sphere of employment (domestic labor and sewing) states stepped in to help bar women's further progress.

The first Supreme Court case concerning women's economic rights was *Bradwell v. Illinois*, which in 1874 upheld a state's right to prohibit women's admission to the bar. Although the main reason offered by the Court was the principle of state's rights, the concurring opinion expressed the paternalistic view that has been repeated in law and political argument numerous times: "Man is, or should be, woman's protector and defender," and, therefore, must protect her from the world of work and individualistic competition. Further, "the harmony, not to say identity, of interests and views which belong, or should belong, to the family institution is repugnant to the idea of a woman adopting a distinct and independent career from that of her husband." Most telling of all, the prohibition covered not just married but all women, because women are defined by their actual or potential statuses as wives and mothers. "The paramount destiny and mission of women are to fulfill the noble and benign offices of wife and mother. This is the law of the Creator. And the rules of society must be adapted to the general constitution of things and cannot be based upon exceptional cases." Whereas the Protestant work ethic as applied to income-producing work was a moral and economic principle for men, economic dependency was a moral, God-given principle for women.

Government became increasingly involved in restricting women's abilities to provide for themselves and their families and even in denying women their own rights of citizenship separate from those of their husbands. Public institutions of higher education, including the land grant colleges, were generally sex segregated and, therefore, kept women from the programs that might lead them to professional careers. Women were barred from certain job classifications and in some jobs such as teaching, they were refused employment if they were married or certainly, if they were pregnant. Female employees were fired if they got married or if they became pregnant. Government discriminated against women in pay. Even the National Industrial Recovery Act (NIRA) signed by Franklin Delano Roosevelt in 1933 provided for sex differences in pay despite intensive lobbying by women's groups and assurances by Eleanor Roosevelt and Labor Secretary Frances Perkins. Moreover, women's jobs were especially likely to be excluded from minimum wage regulations, and the Public Works Administration and Federal Emergency Relief Administration tended to emphasize projects that involved male jobs.

Not until nearly a century after *Bradwell*, in Title VII of the 1964 Civil Rights Act, did the federal government take a stand against sex discrimination in hiring; only in 1971 did the Supreme Court, in *Phillips v. Martin Marietta*, argue that employers may not discriminate against women, in this case women with children. Following a case in which the Supreme Court upheld the right of an employer to discriminate against pregnant women in occupational benefits. Congress passed the 1978 Pregnancy Discrimination Act, which incorporated into Title VII the principle of nondiscrimination against pregnant women.

Because social policy tends to be analyzed as a class issue, we tend to look to labor movements and unions as some of the primary instigators of progressive social policy insofar as their role is to pursue the interests of workers. Although women have benefited from labor organization in gender-specific ways (e.g., gender differentials in pay are lower among unionized than nonunionized workers), the early history of the labor movement shows considerable support for paternalistic and exclusionary treatment of women in the job market. Although women constituted about 30 percent of printers by 1831 and 16 percent of newspaper compositors by 1850, for example, print unions would not accept women to full membership until 1873. Other unions continued to bar women. Samuel Gompers, among other union activists, was opposed to women workers on the grounds that they took wages from men and destroyed the family. In 1898 he urged the government to prohibit women from federal employment.

The perspective of labor unions leads us back to specific consideration of social policy. The labor movement and its leaders such as Gompers were among the most committed supporters of protective labor legislation for women. Their reasons varied. Certainly some of the motivation was the desire to assist those in a relatively weak position in the labor market. As suggested earlier, unions saw woman-directed policies as the "thin edge of the wedge" of more widespread protections for all workers. But another major motivation in the United States as in other countries was to use legislation directed at women to protect male jobs and wages. Protective labor legislation for women could directly and indirectly keep women out of competition for "male" jobs and make them less desirable to employers. Indeed, "protection" has generally been applied less strenuously to "female" than to "male" jobs. Hours and weightlifting limits, for example, were never applied to domestic labor, paid or unpaid. Protective labor legislation made women more expensive to hire than they had been. As feminist observers have often remarked, this type of policy has served at least as much to keep women out of higher paying jobs as it has to improve their working conditions. This has been true of later types of protective legislation as well.

Another early proposal of the labor and other movements concerned with workers was not just the provision of a *living* wage but of a family wage; that is, a wage that would give the (male) breadwinner the ability to support his family without needing to depend on a wage-earning wife. Again, the thinking did not simply concern the economic situation of a family but the character of those in the family. Women, it was thought, should not have to seek employment because their jobs were to care for the other members of the family. Men should not have to compete with women for jobs; after all, men need to support their families. Most important, "manhood" was defined in part by the ability of a man to support his family. Men were—and still to some degree are—taught to feel emasculated when they depend on women's wages. The goodness or badness of dependency depends on who is depending on whom. Husbands' economic dependence upon wives is bad. Wives' economic dependence upon husbands is good, in part because it is often thought to allow men to be more independent.

Most social policy aimed at women has been designed explicitly to benefit them in their capacity as wives and mothers and more particularly, to benefit those who depend upon them for nurturance and domestic service: husbands, children, and elderly relatives. The widows' pensions and Sheppard-Towner Act mentioned previously are early examples. In an important sense, women have not been the main targets of these policies but rather, they were the main conduit of these policies, which were aimed at providing for children. The original construction of ADC provided for support of the children in one-parent families. Only later was support extended to the care giver.

Social policy aimed at women has been designed to benefit them in their capacity as wives and mothers only in a limited sense. Its intention has been to enable them to *care* for their families and not, by and large, to *provide* for them in the sense that is expected of a breadwinner. Often, as in the case of ADC (and its later incarnation as AFDC (Aid to Families with Dependent Children)), it has been aimed at relieving mothers of the "need to work." Women were expected to remain economically dependent because of domestic responsibilities assigned to them. In contrast, the "man in the house" provisions, which allowed administrators to withhold funds if any evidence was found to indicate a man (related or not) was living in, or even a frequent visitor to the house, underscore the degree to which men were still regarded as responsible for economic support.

Only in the late 1960s and especially the 1970s were any serious efforts made to enable women to be economic providers for themselves and their families. Title VII of the Civil Rights Act was given some force in 1971 when the Equal Employment Opportunities Commission (EEOC) gained power to litigate. The growth of affirmative action programs signaled governmental support for improving the employment prospects of women, even if no employers were actually punished for failing to achieve hiring goals. The Work Incentive (WIN) Program established at the end of the 1960s began to suggest that even for women, "work goes with welfare." At first, however, men were given priority in WIN funding, followed by women on a first-come-first-served basis. In 1971, AFDC regulation required for the first time that female recipients of AFDC funds with children over six years old should seek employment. Even the relatively meager efforts to provide women with the means and incentive to seek employment have remained controversial and, during the Reagan administration, were attacked and reduced.

Even if there is more widespread support for the breakdown of familial gender roles in the marketplace, support for traditional gender roles within the home remain firm even, in a sense, with regard to families in which there is no adult male. Programs of employment incentives and supports for women have not included provision of child-care services, which remain the responsibility of mothers. A bill passed through Congress that would have provided federal funds for day-care centers was vetoed by Richard Nixon on the grounds that such services would break up "the family." Despite the pronationalist claims of recent administrations, the United States remains one of the few Organization for Economic Cooperation and Development (OECD) nations that lacks a maternity leave policy. It lags in other supports for pregnant women and families with children as well.

It is important to note that although women and children are supposed to depend upon a male breadwinner for financial support, public policy has not been vigorous in enforcing this goal. Marital law still assumes that husbands are responsible for financial support, but court cases continue to conclude that if a woman is actually residing with her husband that is proof enough that he is supporting her adequately regardless of what he provides or what he is capable of providing. This is an unwarranted assumption either that husbands provide adequate allowances to their wives or that married couples pool their resources in such a way as to allow each individual to draw on them freely. One of the major causes of poverty among women and children in recent decades has been the refusal of divorced husbands to comply with court orders for support payments. Only when the Reagan administration realized that considerable sums of AFDC money could be saved was a serious policy of enforcement initiated, but it was originally designed to encompass only women who were eligible for AFDC funding. The implication was that support of women by their husbands is a private matter of no concern to government unless or until women became public charges because of lack of spousal support. If for much of our history women's welfare was supposedly safeguarded by a husband, we are led to the deduction that for most of our history women's welfare has been of little concern to government, except insofar as it served instrumental purposes in providing care and services for others.

Women's primary relationship to the structure of the general welfare is to provide essential services that might otherwise cost money either to the private or public sector. As many feminist observers have pointed out, when it is said that families have the primary responsibility to care for themselves, what one really means is that women have the primary responsibility to care for others in the family. Given the continuing gender division of labor in the family, it is not the family as a unit but rather women in families who care for children, the elderly, and other dependents, including breadwinners, who are dependent upon these services for their own day-to-day maintenance. Of course, given gender divisions of labor in the marketplace, when people are employed to replace what has previously been women's domestic labor, these services continue to be rendered by women. A major and generally hidden question in social policy, therefore, is whether women should be required to provide for the general welfare in a way that often necessitates that they remain economically dependent and ultimately perhaps in need of social welfare provisions themselves. Or can women and others provide for the general welfare in a way that allows women to provide for themselves as well?

Women's contribution to the general welfare goes beyond the provision of services that need to be done.

Even in the minority of cases in which women do not contribute wages to a household, they help determine the worth of the wages that are contributed by others. Again, because of the continuing gender division of domestic labor, women's efforts in shopping, cooking, and other household tasks affect the value of each dollar brought in. Although public pronouncements have often acknowledged the importance of women's contribution to the home, there has been little effort to give women a return. Only in this decade, for example, have courts begun to recognize women's investment in domestic labor as an economic contribution to be considered in dividing household assets following divorce. Homemakers do not receive their own Social Security benefits but rather are supposed to benefit through their husbands' contributions. In fact, only 54 percent of women receiving Social Security benefits make their claims on the basis of their own work records; the other 46 percent claim as wives. In the case of divorced women, however, only those who qualify under very stringent conditions find that their years of contributing to their husband's maintenance and worth results in payment.

It is women's provision of care and the expectation that they should do so that does the most to make women dependent. Those who are most economically vulnerable are the women who do the most to fulfill a paternalistic and patriarchal gender ideology: they devote themselves full time to caring for their families. Any human capital investment they made in earlier years through education, training, or employment becomes devalued with each year they are homemakers, and they lack the further benefits afforded by continuing job experience. They foresake both the independent security of employment and employment-related benefits including pensions, and they foresake a considerable amount of ability to provide for themselves should the need arise. Women's economic activities, however, cannot be regarded as choices in the full sense of the word. Our social policies assume that women are the primary caregivers, which means there is little assistance to be offered to women who are, in addition, breadwinners. Our social welfare system depends on women either being dependent or taking on what has become to be known as the "double burden." Even when women attempt to seek employment, they continue to face job discrimination based on this gender ideology. Although it is illegal for employers to take marital or maternal status into account, they continue to devalue women as employees because of the assumption that women's primary focus of attention is the home.

Reality contradicts the persistent view that women are not providers. The majority of women are now in the labor force, including the majority of women with children as young as two. They now spend relatively few years out of the labor force. Women make important financial contributions to their households. Many people have noted that women who do not have a husband to help support themselves and their families are particularly likely to suffer from poverty. In 1983, more than one-quarter of all divorced and separated women were on welfare. Thirty-seven percent of single mothers with one child were poor, as were 85 percent of single mothers with four children. But married men are also poorer if they do not have a wife who makes financial contributions to the home. Among married white couples, 9 percent of the families in which the husband was the only earner were poor compared with 3 percent in which both spouses worked. The difference is even more stark among black families, where we find 24 percent were poor if only the husband was a wage earner compared with 4 percent if both were.

BEYOND GENDER-BIASED SOCIAL POLICY

Women constitute a majority of the beneficiaries of most major social welfare programs in existence today—with the exception of unemployment insurance. Among adults receiving AFDC, the largest single item in what is regarded as the welfare budget, over 80 percent of the beneficiaries are women. As Barbara Nelson reports, women constitute 70 percent of the housing beneficiaries, 65 percent of Medicare users, 62 percent of beneficiaries of Social Security (Old Age, Survivors and Disability Insurance or OASDI), 57 percent of food stamp recipients, and 56 percent of Medicaid users. It is no wonder. These programs are intended primarily for the poor and aged, and women are a majority of both. Indeed, they are an increasing proportion of the poor (now roughly two thirds), a phenomenon known as the "feminization of poverty."

American social policies, including those targeted particularly at helping the economically vulnerable, are not simply part of the solution, they are part of the problem. They have helped women primarily in their capacity as wives or, especially, as mothers and not because any positive value has been placed on removing women from a dependent state. As Barbara Nelson observes, "The poorer a woman, the greater the likelihood that she makes a claim for benefits on the basis of her position as a wife or mother." One of the reasons is that women's poverty is increased substantially by their economic dependence brought on by the dependence for care that others place on them. Here it must be reemphasized that those who depend on women's care include not just children and elderly relatives but able-bodied working husbands. Moreover, whereas the more obviously vulnerable such as children and elderly relatives depend on women's care and caring, husbands have also depended psychologically on women's dependency itself, a point made as long as a century ago by John Stuart Mill in his "Subjection of Women." Although this point might suggest that gender divisions of labor make women and men mutually and, therefore, acceptably dependent upon each other, the dependency of men on women's dependency and the particular vulnerabilities of women created by others' dependence on them means we cannot properly say that the women and men in this relationship are truly interdependent, a term that would suggest more symmetry of power.

Because of gender-role assumptions, the family presumption in caring—that those outside the family, and especially government, have only a residual role to play—is really a presumption that women should have the primary role in caring or offering personal services and only a secondary role in financial provision. Conversely, this outlook defines men's primary role as provision and their secondary role as caring. Contrary to the standard rendition of social policy, we do not assume a single line of responsibility for caring that runs from family to other private individuals and organizations to government. Predominant beliefs and attitudes encompass a dual hierarchy of responsibility, one for provision and one for caring. For provision the line extends from the male "head of the family" outward, in ideological terms skipping over the female adult on the grounds that it is less demoralizing for a man to be supported by outside males (or agencies) than to be supported by a woman. For caring, the line extends from the wife and mother outward, in ideological terms skipping over the male adult on the grounds that men are not competent at caring or that their primary role is provision. Here lies another interesting assumption: a man cannot provide *and* care, a combination of efforts faced by most married women today. The reality contradicts the belief; women do indeed provide. There has been somewhat less change in familial patterns of caring men; their assumption of the caring role has not increased as dramatically as has women's assumption of the provision role.

In order for our policies to cease supporting the dependency of women, it is necessary for society to cease depending on women as women; that is, it is necessary that we do not define women in terms of what have up to now been considered women's unique roles and propensities toward caring. This also requires that we no longer depend on men as men or, in other words, on the man's exclusive roles as provider.

The pressing policy question that arises from this discussion is: If we abandon the gender division of responsibility in the family, who will provide and, especially, who will care? Do we place the primary responsibility on governmental institutions? This is certainly the view taken by conservative critics of feminist arguments, who see women's apparent abandonment of exclusive domestic roles as both the cause of the need for social services and as a force that will weaken men's incentives to be providers. It has also been the suggestion of some early Marxist theorists, who called for the "socialization" of domestic labor, and of the influential Progressive Charlotte Perkins Gilman, who at the turn of the century offered a slightly different picture of taking domestic labor out of the home and out of the realm of women's familial responsibility.

It would be a sad commentary on the human state if our acceptance of responsibility to help others is based only on a structure of gender inequality and power hierarchies. As Robert Goodin has argued, our fundamental moral responsibilities spring from the situation of being able to help those who are vulnerable and dependent, and especially those who are vulnerable to us. We have these responsibilities regardless of gender. One cannot shirk moral responsibilities on the basis of a functionalism of gender.

Goodin's theory of responsibility and vulnerability is important, because it provides a way of analyzing and assessing our hierarchies of responsibility for others. It is in the intimacy of the family that we are most likely to find both vulnerability and ability to help that is linked to specific individuals, especially with respect to the kind of necessary caring that has been defined as women's responsibility. Responsibility does move outward to family, friends, community, and others most likely to be aware of the situation and have individual and mutual ties to those who need help. By emphasizing the notion of those who are next most responsible, Goodin draws the line of caring to the community as a whole and its administrative voice, government, which, he argues, has responsibility under three circumstances: "When no one has been assigned primary responsibility," when "those with primary responsibilities . . . prove unable to discharge them," and when "the persons with primary responsibilities prove unwilling to discharge them."

This construction of the residual responsibility of government does not leave us where we started, with government providing only the barest of safety nets for those who have already fallen. We know, for example, that parents are unable to work at full-time jobs with inflexible schedules (as most have) and take care of dependent children at the same time. If we, as a community, know this to be a pattern in a significant proportion of economically active members of our society, we could argue that we as a community, through government, have a responsibility to help. Alternative means of assistance include workplace policies that mandate more flexible job schedules; parental leave policies that allow parents leave time without making them and their families more vulnerable through loss of pay, benefits, or career opportunities; and direct or indirect provision of child-care services. Goodin argues that the purpose of social policy is to protect the vulnerable and dependent. Protecting the vulnerable implies protecting those at particular risk, not just those who are already in trouble. It follows that social policy, in seeking to protect the vulnerable and dependent, should not at the same time create vulnerability and dependency. Our minimalist social policies up to this point have done just that.

Women have suffered, in a sense, from the tendency to make relatively rigid distinctions between *social* policies and *rights* policies. There is not a space here to repeat in full the arguments that claim that the distinctions are not great and that some social policies, including the provision of certain services, constitute rights. Let us, rather, briefly consider one example that has served as a theme throughout this discussion. For most of our history, Americans have accepted the idea that women should be dependent upon their husbands and that they should not, if possible, provide for themselves through gainful employment. Following from this idea, men have been accorded higher priority in training and jobs, even when there were more qualified women available. In public debate today, policies aimed at securing education and jobs for women are labeled rights policies. If we also thought of them in terms of social policy, we would be more likely to define the goals of these policies as providing for the general welfare—that

is, of providing the means whereby a significant portion of the society could become more economically secure and less dependent and vulnerable. We would then not only allow women to become self-reliant, we would encourage it.

This is a call for collective as well as individual responsibility and it is a criticism of crass individualism, even if that individualism is softened with an overlay of voluntaristic altruism. Advocacy of collective responsibility does not, as some critics would argue, mean the demise of the individual as an agent in society. To the contrary, it is entirely consistent with Albert Weale's argument that "there is one overriding imperative to which government action ought to be subject to its authority. This principle of autonomy asserts that all persons are entitled to respect as deliberative and purposive agents capable of formulating their own projects, and that as part of this respect there is a governmental obligation to bring into being or preserve the conditions in which this autonomy can be realized."

This is precisely what has been missing in social policy as it concerns women: the preservation of conditions of autonomy. In a sense this is true for men as well, because their roles also have been dictated by prescriptions that are made on the basis of sex. But for women the prescription is dependency including dependency of identity itself. Social policy has assumed that women are not autonomous individuals and moral agents, but that they live contingent lives. With specific regard to their economic lives, their ability to provide for themselves and others is supposed to be contingent upon whether others around them need their caring services. Choice as a moral agent is missing. Women are defined as individuals who place themselves second. The irony is that this "altruism" often keeps them from helping not only themselves but others they would wish and feel obligated to help.

We are in great need of constructing more humane social policy for the future and also of reinterpreting what has gone before. Historically, for vast numbers of men the individualistic ideology of self-reliance has not worked. For women it never existed.

NOTES

1. On women's movements of this period see Barbara Berg, *The Remembered Gate: Origins of American Feminism: Women and the City, 1800–60* (New York: Oxford University Press, 1978); Ellen DuBois, *Feminism and Suffrage: The Emergence of An Independent Women's Movement in America, 1848–69* (Ithaca, N. Y.: Cornell University Press, 1978); Eleanor Flexner, *Century of Struggle: The Women's Rights Movement in the United States* (Cambridge, Mass.: Harvard University Press, 1975); Stanley Lemons, *The Woman Citizen: Social Feminism in the 1920s* (Urbana: University of Illinois Press, 1972).

2. For example, Berg, *Remembered Gate;* and DuBois, *Feminism and Suffrage.*

3. For example, Linda Gordon, *Woman's Body, Woman's Right: A Social History of Birth Control in America* (New York: Viking Press, 1976).

4. Walter I. Trattner, *From Poor Law to Welfare State: A History of Social Welfare in America* (New York: Free Press, 1974), 190.

5. James Leiby, *A History of Social Welfare and Social Work in the United*

States (New York: Columbia University Press, 1978), 212.

6. *Muller v. Oregon*, 208 U.S. 412, (1908).

7. Trattner, *From Poor Law to Welfare State*, 187.

8. Lemons, *Woman Citizen.*

9. Peter Flora and Arnold J. Heidenheimer, "The Historical Core and Changing Boundaries of the Welfare State," in *The Development of Welfare States in Europe and America* ed. Peter Flora and Arnold J. Heidenheimer (New Brunswick, N.J.: Transaction Books, 1981), 22.

10. For further discussion, see Christine Delphy, *Closer to Home: A Materialist Analysis of Women's Oppression* (Amherst: University of Massachusetts Press, 1984); Lydia Sargent, ed., *Women and Revolution: A Discussion of the Unhappy Marriage of Marxism and Feminism* (Boston: South End Press, 1981).

11. Albert Weale, *Political Theory and Social Policy* (London: Macmillan, 1983), 5.

12. Weale, *Political Theory and Social Policy;* Richard M. Titmuss, "The Social Division of Welfare: Some Reflections on the Search for Equity," in *Essays on the Welfare State*, ed. Richard M. Titmuss (London: Allen and Unwin, 1958), 34–55.

13. Robert E. Goodin, "Self-Reliance versus The Welfare State," *Journal of Social Policy* 14 (January 1985): 25–47.

14. Ramesh Mishra, *Society and Social Policy: Theories and Practice of Welfare* (London: Macmillan, 1981), 41.

15. Leiby, *A History of Social Welfare*, 33.

16. Michael Walzer, *Spheres of Justice* (New York: Basic Books, 1983).

17. Leiby, *A History of Social Welfare*, 2. For a parallel discussion of charity versus justice, see Robert E. Goodin, *Protecting the Vulnerable* (Chicago: University of Chicago Press, 1985), chap. 2.

44

Latina Women and Political Consciousness

La Chispa Que Prende

(1997)

Carol Hardy-Fanta

Es como una chispa que prende ¿verdad? y, que el espíritu de la persona en ese momento está listo. [It's like a spark that ignites, right? and, at that moment, the spirit of the person is ready.]

–Aracelis Guzmán

Central to the study of gender, culture, and Latina politics are questions about the ways political socialization occurs: How do women of color, specifically Latinas, become active in politics? What is the impact of cultural background on their political development? How do experiences gained in adulthood shape their sense of themselves as political actors? How does gender affect the political development of Latina women? Embedded in all these questions is one central issue: What role does political consciousness play in the development of a "political self"?

In the literature on Latino politics there has been remarkably little research on the political development of Latina women. The bulk of research on *Latino* political consciousness centers on the effects of the Chicano movement on political participation and access to political power (Garcia and de la Garza 1977; Guzmán 1976) or on the development of *ethnic* consciousness in multiethnic Latino communities (Padilla 1985; Uriarte Gaston 1988)—and thus misses or downplays the experiences of Latina women. Specific research on Latino political socialization also has tended to study Mexican American children (Garcia 1971; Howell-Martinez 1982), and the literature on Latina political consciousness is, with few exceptions, limited to Chicanas/Mexican Americans (Campos Carr 1989; Mota 1976).

In general, most writings on Latina women focus on women in their reproductive, social, or labor market roles. Latina women are portrayed in this literature as "three

Hardy-Fanta, Carol, "Latina Women and Political Consciousness: La Chispa Que Prende." In *Women Transforming Politics*, edited by Cohen et. al. (1997): 223–237.

493

times oppressed"—by racism, sexism, and cultural traditions (Mirandé and Enríquez 1979; Barragán 1980; Melville 1980). The stereotype of Puerto Rican and Mexican women, in particular, is that of passivity and submissiveness. *Marianismo*, the feminine correlate to and opposite of *machismo*, derives from the image of the Virgin Mary—meek, mild, and supportive of men. Assertiveness in social, public, and political arenas by Latina women supposedly runs counter to these cultural traditions. Garcia and de la Garza (1977) refer to a Latino tradition of "strong women," but these women are mythical figures; from these examples one would have to conclude that mainstream social and political science is comfortable with women only in their reproductive roles—or as goddesses.

In this chapter I propose to challenge these traditional political theories that view Latina women as "passive" and "apolitical." While Latina women do indeed face barriers to political participation that stem from sexism and cultural traditions, empirical research suggests that, for Latina women, political participation is inextricably linked with the development of the political self. At the same time, the political self evolves in conjunction with *personal* self-development. In a reciprocal fashion, political consciousness—a sense of "becoming political"—contributes to and emerges from personal and political self-development.

LATINA WOMEN IN BOSTON

This chapter is based on a study of the Latino community in Boston, Massachusetts. The community is a rela-
tively small one: Latinos now make up 11 percent of the city's population (1990 census). The community is also characterized by considerable diversity. Forty-two percent of the Latinos in Boston are Puerto Rican; the rest of the community is made up of Central and South Americans (approximately 30 percent), a rapidly increasing Dominican population (13.1 percent), Cubans (3.5 percent), and Mexican Americans (3.5 percent).

In this study I conducted in-depth interviews with twenty-nine Latina women and twenty-four Latino men—community activists, influential Latinos, and *la gente del pueblo*. I also participated in numerous community events: protest marches, election campaigns, voter registration, community forums, workshops, and conferences, and formal and informal discussions throughout the community. In all the observations and interviews conducted over the two-year research period, a recurrent theme emerged: Latina women are political actors and play crucial roles in Latino community mobilization. Of particular interest to the study of political development is the way Latina women revealed the interaction of personal development, political consciousness, and political and social change.

While in the overall study, interviews were conducted with men as well as women, specific gender differences will not be discussed here; the focus of the chapter will be on the experiences of Puerto Rican, Dominican, Mexican American, and Central and South American women. For a complete discussion of gender differences, see chapter 5 in Hardy-Fanta 1993. Of primary importance for the current discussion is that virtually all the Latina women in

Boston identified personal develop-ment with political consciousness and political change, while the men who were interviewed had little or nothing to say on political conscious-ness or the development of the polit-ical self.

As I sorted out the threads of many different life experiences, it became clear that all the women's stories had in common a theme: "becoming po-litical." There is a *process*, for many a contemplative process, of political development. For some, this process is quick—a sudden ¡*chispa*! of recog-nition that a change is needed. For others, there is a slow emergence of political consciousness, a question-ing of the conditions of life, and a searching for alternatives within themselves and with others.

"BECOMING POLITICAL"

The women I interviewed formally and talked with during community observations offered many perspec-tives on how they became politi-cized. For some Puerto Ricans, the status options for Puerto Rico—statehood, independence, socialism—created a political issue that formed their political identity and molded their activism. For others, and for those of other Latino groups, it was *la necesidad*, being confronted by the needs of the community, crush-ing problems such as a lack of de-cent housing, AIDS, and a high dropout rate for Latino public school children. A few *decided* to be-come political, others would have liked to be allowed into politics but felt shut out, and still more felt they emerged gradually despite personal and structural barriers.

Questions about the development of the political self (Dawson and Pre-witt 1969, 15–24) and the sources of politicization have concerned politi-cal scientists for decades. Traditional theories of political socialization generally focus on (1) childhood so-cialization, (2) adult resocialization and countersocialization (especially through structural changes such as the civil rights movement and the women's movement), and (3) politi-cal consciousness. Unfortunately, these theories have paid scant atten-tion to the political development of Latina women. However, as in the traditional literature, the role of the family in the political socialization process emerges in the stories of some Latinas.

CHILDHOOD SOCIALIZATION: THE ROLE OF THE FAMILY

Family background is frequently cited as one of the most influential factors in political development (Dawson and Prewitt 1969). "*Political socialization* assumes that the political habits of people are formed primarily before adulthood" (Orum et al. 1974, 198; emphasis in original). Political learn-ing in the family supposedly develops partisan attachment, ideology, na-tional loyalty, orientations toward au-thority, sense of regime legitimacy, and recruitment to bureaucratic and governmental roles (Hirsch 1971, 4). The family, according to theories of childhood socialization, affects the ac-quisition of participant values; these values then determine subsequent lev-els of political activism, party identifi-cation, political knowledge, and sense of political efficacy. Exposure in the home to political talk and activism thus is linked to future political behavior. Gender differences in adult women's (supposedly lower) levels of political participation are attributed to sex-linked restrictions, male dominance of the political domain (Campbell et al. 1960; Lane 1959), and feminine characteristics learned as children.

Family traditions of "being political" *do* affect some Latinas in the predicted way. Josefina Ortega, for example, agrees with earlier researchers that family background is an important component to political socialization. *"Vengo de una familia muy política"* [I come from a very political family], she says. Josefina Ortega locates the roots of her "becoming political" in her family of origin: *"Está en la sangre"* [It's in the blood].

Becoming political also may come from following a long tradition of activism in the family. Dalia Ruiz, for example, is a Puerto Rican woman of very humble background. She attributes her enjoyment of politics to her family: *"A mi mamá le gusta muchísimo la política. Porque ella se vuelve loca con las elecciones. ¡Ella se vuelve loca! A ella le encantaba la política."* [My mother likes politics a lot. She goes nuts about the elections, she just goes nuts! She adored politics.]

GENDER, POLITICAL SOCIALIZATION, AND THE "ETHICS OF CARE"

The stories of many Latina women from a variety of backgrounds and countries of origin revealed a vision of politics that is different from that of traditional political theorists, Latino and non-Latino alike. They seemed to emerge from their families with a view of politics imbued with what feminist theorists call an "ethics of care" (Flanagan and Jackson 1990). Politics, for them, consists of "helping others," "fulfilling an obligation," "sharing and giving," and "providing support." The women stated that this view of politics derived from values taught by their families.

For example, Marta Correa is a woman from Ecuador who sees politics as a way of helping members of her community get jobs and improve neighborhood services. The value Marta Correa places on political participation clearly comes from her family. As can be seen in the following quote, her family is the source of her political interest and her desire to help others:

> Es la forma en que nos han criado—así me criaron a mí. Yo soy de Ecuador; nos criaron con un respeto; nos criaron muy diferente. . . . Mi abuela me decía siempre, "Respeta para que te respeten.". . . O sea, tu cooperas con las personas siempre que te necesiten. Porque en el futuro—esa persona no te va a ayudar a tí pero otra persona te puede dar ayuda. Entonces, a mí me criaron en esa forma—ese respeto— esa ayuda. [It's the way that we were raised—that's the way they raised me. I am from Ecuador; we were raised with the value of respecting others; we were raised very different. . . . My grandmother always told me, "Respect others so they'll respect you.". . . In other words, you help others whenever they need you. Because, in the future, that person is not going to help you, but another person may give you help. So, that's the way I was raised—with that kind of respect—that kind of help.]

For many Latinas, a sense of family tradition had a major impact on the politicization process. The women recalled an ethos of sharing and giving in their families. For example, Latinas who come from political or politically supportive families describe the impetus to *compartir*—to share—as the basis of working with people. Josefina Ortega talks about how her family communicated the idea that, if they had only one piece of bread, they would share it with others. Catalina Torres, a Mexican American woman who moved to Boston from the West, is now in a position relatively high up in the city power structure. She says,

> My parents had been migrants—we call them *braceros*. My parents, both of them—although we were very poor—whatever we grew, you could always count on us to get you a hundred pounds of potatoes, a hundred pounds of beans, a hundred pounds of flour, what you needed—staples—to get you through the winter if you didn't have anything, because my dad had a year-round job and it wasn't seasonal, and he always would help somebody else, always. I would always say, "Why do you do that? You don't know those people, we need it too." That was my thing, and I was always told, *"Favores no se cobran"*—don't ever look at a favor and expect that favor to be repaid. Someone else will pay you back and it's a *sin* to ask to be paid back! So, all right, I grew up like that.

Jovita Fonseca, a longtime activist who, at the time of the study, worked in the Elections Division at Boston City Hall, states, "I could always remember somehow, somebody always saying things like—my family—we had an obligation." She recalls the network of Central American women who circulated through her house, helping each other become adjusted to this country, and providing both a source of inspiration to her and training in politics. Her first exposure to government institutions came when she served as a translator for these women. Another woman traces her interest in influencing political decisions at the governmental level to her anger at injustice—and to the fact that she comes from a family of social workers.

In these examples, Latinas did not say that their political activism derived from cultural or family traditions but that they drew on certain family traditions and values once they became active politically. The sense of politics as caring, giving, and helping was, at least among the men and women interviewed in Boston, uniquely expressed in the interviews of Latina women.

The role of family has another, equally gendered, impact on Latina political development: families often provide support to women as they move into the more formal political arenas. Marta Rosa, for example, is a Puerto Rican woman who was first elected to the school committee of a town across the river from Boston in 1989; she was reelected in 1991 and 1993. In 1994 she ran for city council in that town; she narrowly made it into office. She felt that the supportiveness of her family gave her the practical means and the emotional strength to weather the demands of her election campaigns: "My mother lives in the basement apartment I built for her and my sister lives on the first floor. I've always had babysitters, . . . It's always been my mother, my husband, my sisters—and they're *really* supportive of what I do, the work that I do. They know it's for a good cause" (emphasis in original). Her family, including her husband and her children, worked on her campaign.

Despite these testimonies in support of the family as the primary source of participatory political orientations, there are many examples of Latinas who illustrate how politicization can occur without a family tradition of political involvement and *despite* inactive and oppressive family conditions. Latina women in Boston, in particular, describe many experiences of adult resocialization—"a fundamental reorientation of an *adult* woman's political self" (Rinehart 1986, 13; emphasis in original). These women who, as adults, participate in experiences that run counter to female or cultural role expectations emerge from these experiences as political activists.

RISING FROM OPPRESSION: LATINA WOMEN AND ADULT RESOCIALIZATION

One of the barriers to political participation discussed in much of the literature on politics, and in the interviews conducted for this study, is the grinding down effects of poverty. Virtually all the Latina women talked about how difficult it is to think of going to a meeting, challenging a landlord, protesting, or even voting when just trying to survive consumes all your energy. The participation of poor people—poor Latinos in Boston—hinges on having a reason to participate, whether through personal relationships, the personal appeal of a Latino candidate or friend, or some combination of factors that pulls one into taking action on one's own behalf. For Latina women, "the triple oppression suffered by many women of color has fostered innovative methods and approaches to political organizing" (Morgen and Bookman 1988, 11). To discover how people who are poor, who are oppressed by life and larger socioeconomic structures, become political, one must examine the life experiences of people who have been there themselves.

María Luisa Soto is a housing activist in a Latino neighborhood in Boston. She is a woman who makes a clear connection between her personal development, her political consciousness, and her emergence into the arena of political activism. Her early life in Puerto Rico and New York City was lived within a very "traditional" Latina woman's role, restricted to the home under the watchful eye of first her father, then her husband. When asked about the roots of her community-based politics, María Luisa Soto focused on social and affiliative needs. Being a political person dates to her arrival in Boston. She recalls that, after hearing about a meeting on the problem of housing, "I went and I said to myself, 'This seems interesting.' " Meeting people and expanding her horizons outside the home created new thoughts and provided new opportunities for María Luisa Soto. As she connected with other women, she began to see the vacuum in leadership, and began to take action.

María Luisa Soto is eager to point out that she did all this while raising her two children in the projects, going to college, and working full-time—her pride in her personal development permeates her story. Her story also reveals that her politicization ran counter to her upbringing. Leaving her husband seems to have been a beginning marker for branching out into a broader lifestyle. While male researchers like Lane pay scant attention to the need for affiliation in political development, the fulfillment of social, affiliative needs—meeting other people—contributed substantially to the politicization of María Luisa Soto. She ended her interview by making a connection between her personal and political self-development. With great force and feeling she said that it was *"parte de mi desarrollo como una mujer"* [part of my development as a woman]. What is important about the story of María Luisa Soto is the way her childhood socialization was challenged in adulthood; she moved from a noninvolved, traditional woman's role to become one of the most politically active and influential people in Boston.

This process of adult resocialization is somewhat different, although the result may be the same, from childhood experiences that challenge female and cultural role expectations (countersocialization). For example, when, as a child, Jovita Fonseca acted as a translator for adult Central American women, her exposure to governmental institutions, the proactive role involved, and a sense of competence in the outside world created a socialization experience *during her childhood* that ran counter to the more traditional childhoods of many Latina girls. María Luisa Soto, on the other hand, had a very traditional childhood and was kept at home; she was challenged to become political only when adult circumstances opened up opportunities beyond those of her childhood and cultural expectations. The dynamics of adult resocialization (separate from childhood countersocialization) raise an important question: What is the *process* by which poor women of color become politicized as adults?

Whereas many influential, activist Latinas describe the impact of family background, opportunities for activism, and issues such as the status of Puerto Rico as stimulators of their political involvement, non-activists, *la gente del pueblo*, describe a more personal struggle against oppression. For Aracelis Guzmán, the politicization process began when she started working for the Department of Public Health as a nursing outreach worker. She described the debilitating effects of the poverty she saw when she went into the homes of poor Latina women:

> Creo que lo que yo estaba aprendiendo era que . . . cuando tu no tienes suficiente dinero para tu renta, para alimentar a tus hijos, cuando no tienes dinero para salir ni a un cine o ir a un baile, que estás todo el día encerrada en la casa, cuando tu no estás consciente de que hay otras alternativas en la vida aparte de ser mamá, que puedes ir a la escuela, que puedes sacar un inglés ¿verdad? es muy difícil dar educación preventiva. Que la mente no está abierta para recibir ese conocimiento, está uno embotado— unos lloran, unos tienen diarrea—si están en una relación abusiva con el marido o con el novio, es que . . . son demasiadas presiones. [I believe that what I was learning was that . . . when you don't have enough money for rent, to feed your children, when you don't have money to even go out to a movie or go to a dance, when you are locked in the house all day long, when you aren't conscious of having other alternatives in life other than being a mother, that you can go to school, that you can learn English, right? it's very difficult to do preventive education.

Because the mind isn't open to receiving that knowledge—one is dulled (enervated)—some cry, some have diarrhea—if they are in an abusive relationship with a husband or boyfriend . . . there are too many pressures.]

Aracelis Guzmán goes on to describe how the spark of political awareness transforms poverty and a sense of debilitating oppression into a potential for political participation:

> Entonces yo creo que para uno poder envolverse políticamente—¿verdad?— tiene que en primer lugar sentir esa necesidad de decir, "Bueno, ¿por qué es que yo estoy así? ¿cómo es que yo puedo cambiar esto? . . . Yo tengo que hacer algo," y entonces uno empieza a preguntar, ¿verdad? o a la vecina, o si hay una agencia dos cuadras acerca de mi casa. . . . Es como una *chispa que prende* ¿verdad? y que el espíritu de la persona en ese momento está listo. (Emphasis added.) [So I believe that, for one to get involved politically—right?—one has to first feel that need to say to oneself, "Well, why is it that I'm like this? What can I do to change this? I have to do something," and then one begins to ask, right? your neighbor, or if there's an agency two blocks away from my house. . . . It's like *a spark that ignites*, right? and, at that moment, the spirit of the person is ready. (Emphasis added.)]

For Aracelis Guzmán, making the initial connection between one's daily problems and larger political issues is the beginning step toward participation.

The feminist theme of the idea that the personal is political cannot have a stronger argument than this. Aracelis Guzmán describes this moment as a spark—*una chispa*—a critical moment in which one begins to question the nature of one's existence. Crucial to the present study of political con-sciousness is that the spark drives one to venture outward—to other people, other places, first for help, later with others in action for change. This spark can come from a *charla* ("chat"—a type of discussion group) for women at local community organizations, from interaction with a new friend, or from a slow process of questioning within the self, as the following example demonstrates. The story of Julia Santiago shows how, after the spark, there is a slower emergence of increasingly politicized consciousness and behavior.

JULIA SANTIAGO: FROM OPPRESSION TO "BEING POLITICAL"

I first met Julia Santiago at the National Puerto Rican Congress Convention, Memorial Day weekend, 1989. She was one of a panel of women in a workshop called "The Vision of the Woman: Head of the Family, Administrative Tasks of the Household—The Socio-political Struggle." At this workshop I heard Julia Santiago tell the story of her development from *una jibarita* to a political activist.

A *jíbaro* is one of the country folk of Puerto Rico, a "worker of the cane," a peasant. Julia Santiago uses the term *jibarita* in its (affectionate) diminutive and feminine form to describe her naïveté, her youth, and her oppressive, traditional family. It is important to keep in mind that this is not a woman who comes from the middle class or even the working class. She very much typifies the poor women who make up much of the Latino community. In her language and demeanor, she has not changed into a professional or middle-class person, despite the fact that she now works in an organization for women and has studied theories of oppression. There, as an adult, she has been able to reevaluate her life and conclude, "*Yo siempre he estado cuestionando la situación patriarcal*" [I have always been challenging the patriarchal system].

What is striking about the story of Julia Santiago is how similar her early life is to that of many Latino people who are the least active politically. In many ways her experiences as a child and young adult sound similar to the description given by Aracelis Guzmán in the previous example—someone too enervated to think beyond surviving day by day. Julia Santiago came from a family with a rigid, authoritarian father. She left Puerto Rico to "*salir de la dictadura de mi padre*" [leave the dictatorship of my father], but "like many young women, came to live in a house very similar to that of my father." Her husband made her lie to get welfare; Julia said, "You have to lie so that they'll serve you." She recalls how alienating and intimidating the experience of "seeking help" was; she describes the welfare workers as "*majadores*," real bruisers. After ten months she went to work in a factory and went from *mal en peor* (from bad to worse). She finally decided to put an end to her marriage because "*mejor ir sola, que mal acompañada*" [better to go it alone than in bad company].

With the decision to leave her husband began a new period in her life. She moved to Boston with her children and got a job as a hospital aide. At first she enjoyed the job so much that she believed she would stay as long as they would keep her. After a while, however, she began to be aware of discrimination and was the brunt of demeaning jokes against Latinos. At the same time, problems with her landlord and her children led her to seek solutions in ways she had not thought of before.

During the workshop Julia Santiago passed quickly over how she changed from a woman suffering quietly—alone—to one leading a tenant action, attending college classes, and "*haciendo trabajo político*" [doing political work]. Only in a later interview were we able to explore the process of her politicization.

Julia Santiago confirms, in many ways, the route to becoming political discussed in Aviel (1981)—through her daily life and the needs of her children:

> Es bien curioso, precisamente es que todo de momento te encuentras que los hijos te lleguen a tener problemas y tu no sabes que hacer. Porque no importa que tu estás trabajando, cuan honesta tu eres, no se te—no es lo mismo. Tu, como los niños no entienden y lo único que te queda por él es tirarte por la calle buscar información—de momento. [It's really curious, it's just like, all at once you find that your children begin to have problems and you don't know what to do. Because it doesn't matter that you're working, how honest you are, it doesn't—it's not the same. Your children don't understand, and the only thing left to you is to throw yourself out into the street looking for help—all of a sudden.]

In the process of seeking help for her children, Julia Santiago developed relationships that brought her out of the social isolation common to many Latina women and created social connections and opportunities to go beyond her personal experience into questioning why things had to be the way they were. She says, *"De momento me encuentro con gente que sabían tanto más que yo, de momento, digo, 'Pero, ¡¿qué es lo que pasa conmigo?!'"* [All of a sudden I find myself with people who knew so much more than me, all of a sudden, I say, "But what's going on with me?!"]. Like Aracelis Guzmán, Julia Santiago experienced the *spark*, the moment of being conscious of the need for change. This consciousness, together with greater social connectedness, is the crucial ingredient in the politicization process of Latina women who move from oppressed backgrounds to political involvement.

Later in the interview Julia Santiago discussed her tenant organizing experiences; how her new role evolved reveals much about the theme of "becoming political." She is able to describe the fine line between the "not-conscious" to the "consciously political" as she describes her early days in New York:

> Es que *tu misma* no lo sabes que es algo político. Por ejemplo, . . . yo vivía en New York, yo siempre ayudaba la gente. Yo estaba en welfare y las mujeres, muchas veces me decían: ¿qué yo podría hacer en tal y cual situación? y siempre yo estaba aclarandoles a ellas, cómo era una manera de saber defenderse—y a la misma vez luchar por lo que *ellas* querían. [It's that *you yourself* don't know that it's political. For example, . . . I lived in New York, I was always helping people. I was on welfare, and the women would often come to me asking what I could do to help them with this and that situation, and I was always explaining things to them how there was a way to stick up for oneself— and at the same time fight for what *they* wanted (emphasis in original).]

Julia Santiago then goes on to link this experience to a point she made at the workshop:

Parte de lo que yo dije en mi presentación—que en mi trabajo ahora yo siempre me considero político; yo lo veo como el mismo—de eso de sobrevivir—y no, tu sabes—tu siempre estás haciendo trabajo político y tu no lo sabes. [Part of what I was saying in my presentation (at the workshop)—that in the work I do now I always consider myself political; I see them as the same thing—that of surviving—and not, you know—you're always working politically and you don't (even) know it.

Julia Santiago's life illustrates that adult resocializing experiences are as important as childhood socialization in the development of the political self. Julia Santiago became political as an adult through a network of personal relationships in her daily life. Her radical feminist ideology is thoroughly entrenched in her worldview but is an ideology clearly learned in adulthood. Her family was part of her oppression, not a source of political strength.

Julia Santiago sees the fine line between political unawareness and political consciousness; she also connects daily survival with politics. Political development is not a fixed characteristic, handed down through the family; it is a process that occurs in interaction with others. In addition, being political and becoming political may develop out of actions begun within women's traditional roles. Latina women's decisions to protest or take other forms of political action may first be stimulated by concerns for children and family needs. However, the internal and collective process that occurs by participating in such activities can itself be politicizing.

Pardo, for example, describes a similar "transformation" process for Mexican American women in East

Los Angeles. She states that "women have transformed organizing experiences and social networks arising from gender-related responsibilities into political resources"; she traces this political development to women's concerns (Pardo 1990, 2). "In these processes, women meet other mothers and begin developing a network of acquaintanceships and friendships based on mutual concern for the welfare of their children." This concept of transformation suggests that, in contrast to earlier theories that saw motherhood as a constraint on participation, many poor women are motivated to action precisely out of concern for their children. In other words, political development begins with concerns rooted in their roles as mothers, but personal empowerment leads to political action with wide-reaching impact. Marisela Pena, a teacher at a local community organization, for example, sees the political education of Latina women as having a greater impact than the education of men because of women's socializing effect on children. She quoted a Latino saying: *"Educar un hombre es educar una persona; educar una mujer es educar una familia"* [To educate a man is to educate one person; to educate a woman is to educate a family].

LATINA WOMEN, MARRIAGE, AND THE POLITICIZATION PROCESS

Julia Santiago is one of several Latina women who marked her entrance into a political life with the decision to leave her husband. María Luisa Soto, an activist discussed earlier, is another woman who became in-

volved in politics only after she moved away from her husband. I did not specifically collect marital status information on the people interviewed. However, only nine (37 percent) of the twenty-four women for whom I had marital status information were married. The rest were divorced or separated. Three of the nine married women portrayed their husbands as supportive of their political activism; these three were women with higher educational levels and income. For the poorer women, not having a husband seemed associated with a higher degree of politicization that began after separation from their husbands. The Latino men interviewed as part of the study did not mention marriage as having an impact on their degree of political participation or their path to becoming political.

Why poorer Latina women may become more political after separation is a tantalizing question that deserves future research. There is a wide-ranging debate about whether child-rearing and homemaking responsibilities limit the time or energy women have available for political participation (Jaros 1973; Lipset 1963; Pomper 1975; for a feminist perspective, see Randall 1987, 85–88). Since the Latina women who were poor but who had become politicized as adults all had children, worked, and often went back to school as adults, it may be marriage, not child and home responsibilities per se, that constrains certain groups of women.

GENDER, CONSCIOUSNESS, AND POLITICAL PARTICIPATION

The political development of Latina women in Boston demonstrates that political consciousness emerges within the social context—in connection with others. The image of political socialization and political consciousness that exists in mainstream literature is revealed to reflect male concerns for power and autonomy, the assertion of the self, and competition—concerns that overshadow what feminists suggest are equally valid political needs: the needs for affiliation, caring, connection, and community.

The process of coming to political consciousness seems to be a process of making connections—between their own lives and those of others, between issues that affect them and their families in the neighborhood or community and those that affect them in the workplace. Latina women who become politicized do so, therefore, by making connections between the so-called differing spheres of their lives, between the apparently private sphere of family and home and the supposedly public sphere of formal politics. Rather than the "fragmented consciousness" that, in Katznelson's view, constrains political action in the United States (Ackelsberg 1988, 305), Latina women's political consciousness is made up of a seamless cloth in which their personal development as women is intertwined with their roles as mothers and their emergence as political activists.

45

Women's Rights as Human Rights
Toward a Re-Vision of Human Rights
(1990)

Charlotte Bunch

Significant numbers of the world's population are routinely subject to torture, starvation, terrorism, humiliation, mutilation and even murder simply because they are female. Crimes such as these against any group other than women would be recognized as a civil and political emergency as well as a gross violation of the victims' humanity. Yet, despite a clear record of deaths and demonstrable abuse, women's rights are not commonly classified as human rights. This is problematic both theoretically and practically, because it has grave consequences for the way society views and treats the fundamental issues of women's lives. This paper questions why women's rights and human rights are viewed as distinct, looks at the policy implications of this schism, and discusses different approaches to changing it.

Women's human rights are violated in a variety of ways. Of course, women sometimes suffer abuses such as political repression that are similar to abuses suffered by men. In these situations, female victims are often invisible, because the dominant image of the political actor in our world is male. However, many violations of women's human rights are distinctly connected to being female—that is, women are discriminated against and abused on the basis of gender. Women also experience sexual abuse in situations where their other human rights are being violated, as political prisoners or members of persecuted ethnic groups, for example. In this paper I address those abuses in which gender is a primary or related factor because gender-related abuse has been most neglected and offers the greatest challenge to the field of human rights today.

The concept of human rights is one of the few moral visions ascribed to internationally. Although its scope is not universally agreed upon, it strikes deep chords of response among many. Promotion of human rights is a widely accepted goal and thus provides a useful framework for seeking redress of gender abuse. Further it is one of the few concepts that speaks to the need for transnational activism and concern about the lives of people globally. The Universal Declaration of Human Rights, adopted in 1948, symbolizes this world vision and defines human rights broadly. While not much is said about women, Article 2 entitles all to "the rights and freedoms set forth in this Declaration, without distinction of any kind, such as race, colour, sex, language, religion, political or other opinion, national or social origin, property, birth or other status." Eleanor Roosevelt and the Latin American women who fought for the inclusion of sex in the Declaration and for its passage clearly intended that it would address the problem of women's subordination.

Since 1948 the world community has continuously debated varying interpretations of human rights in response to global developments. Little of this discussion, however, has addressed questions of gender, and only recently have significant challenges been made to a vision of human rights which excludes much of women's experiences. The concept of human rights, like all vibrant visions, is not static or the property of any one group; rather, its meaning expands as people reconceive of their needs and hopes in relation to it. In this spirit, feminists redefine human rights abuses to include the degradation and violation of women. The specific experiences of women must be added to traditional approaches to human rights in order to make women more visible

and to transform the concept and practice of human rights in our culture so that it takes better account of women's lives.

In the next part of this article, I will explore both the importance and the difficulty of connecting women's rights to human rights, and then I will outline four basic approaches that have been used in the effort to make this connection.

BEYOND RHETORIC: POLITICAL IMPLICATIONS

Few governments exhibit more than token commitment to women's equality as a basic human right in domestic or foreign policy. No government determines its policies toward other countries on the basis of their treatment of women, even when some aid and trade decisions are said to be based on a country's human rights record. Among nongovernmental organizations, women are rarely a priority, and Human Rights Day programs on 10 December seldom include discussion of issues like violence against women or reproductive rights. When it is suggested that governments and human rights organizations should respond to women's rights as concerns that deserve such attention, a number of excuses are offered for why this cannot be done. The responses tend to follow one or more of these lines: (1) sex discrimination is too trivial, or not as important, or will come after larger issues of survival that require more serious attention; (2) abuse of women, while regrettable, is a cultural, private, or individual issue and not a political matter requiring state action; (3) while appropriate for other action, women's rights are not human rights per se; or (4) when the abuse of women is recognized, it is considered inevitable or so pervasive that any consideration of it is futile or will overwhelm other human rights questions. It is important to challenge these responses.

The narrow definition of human rights, recognized by many in the West as solely a matter of state violation of civil and political liberties, impedes consideration of women's rights. In the United States the concept has been further limited by some who have used it as a weapon in the cold war almost exclusively to challenge human rights abuses perpetrated in communist countries. Even then, many abuses that affected women, such as forced pregnancy in Romania, were ignored.

Some important aspects of women's rights do fit into a civil liberties framework, but much of the abuse against women is part of a larger socioeconomic web that entraps women, making them vulnerable to abuses which cannot be delineated as exclusively political or solely caused by states. The inclusion of "second generation" or socioeconomic human rights to food, shelter, and work—which are clearly delineated as part of the Universal Declaration of Human Rights—is vital to addressing women's concerns fully. Further, the assumption that states are not responsible for most violations of women's rights ignores the fact that such abuses, although committed perhaps by private citizens, are often condoned or even sanctioned by states. I will return to the question of state responsibility after responding to other instances of resistance to women's rights as human rights.

The most insidious myth about women's rights is that they are trivial or secondary to the concerns of life and death. Nothing could be farther from the truth: sexism kills. There is increasing documentation of the many ways in which being female is life-threatening. The following are a few examples:

- Before birth: Amniocentesis is used for sex selection leading to the abortion of more female fetuses at rates as high as 99 percent in Bombay, India; in China and India, the two most populous nations, more males than females are born even though natural birth ratios would produce more females.
- During childhood: The World Health Organization reports that in many countries, girls are fed less, breast fed for shorter periods of time, taken to doctors less frequently, and die or are physically and mentally maimed by malnutrition at higher rates than boys.
- In adulthood: the denial of women's rights to control their bodies in reproduction threatens women's lives, especially where this is combined with poverty and poor health services. In Latin America, complications from illegal abortions are the leading cause of death for women between the ages of fifteen and thirty-nine.

Sex discrimination kills women daily. When combined with race, class, and other forms of oppression, it constitutes a deadly denial of women's right to life and liberty on a large scale throughout the world. The most pervasive violation of females is violence against women in all its manifestations, from wife battery, incest, and rape, to dowry deaths, genital mutilation, and female sexual slavery. These abuses occur in every country and are found in the home and in the workplace, on streets, on campuses, and in prisons and refugee camps. They cross class, race, age, and national lines; and at the same time, the forms this violence takes often reinforce other oppressions such as racism, "able-bodyism," and imperialism. Case in point: in order to feed their families, poor women in brothels around U.S. military bases in places like the Philippines bear the burden of sexual, racial, and national imperialism in repeated and often brutal violation of their bodies.

Even a short review of random statistics reveals that the extent of violence against women globally is staggering:

- In the United States, battery is the leading cause of injury to adult women, and a rape is committed every six minutes.
- In Peru, 70 percent of all crimes reported to police involve women who are beaten by their partners; and in Lima (a city of seven million people), 168,970 rapes were reported in 1987 alone.
- In India, eight out of ten wives are victims of violence, either domestic battery, dowry-related abuse, or among the least fortunate, murder.
- In France, 95 percent of the victims of violence are women; 51 percent at the hands of a spouse or lover. Similar statistics from places as diverse as Bangladesh, Canada, Kenya, and Thailand demonstrate that more than 50 percent of female homicides were committed by family members.

Where recorded, domestic battery figures range from 40 percent to 80 percent of women beaten, usually repeatedly, indicating that the home is the most dangerous place for women and frequently the site of cruelty and torture. As the Carol Stuart murder in Boston demonstrated, sexist and racist attitudes in the United States often cover up the real threat to women; a woman is murdered in Massachusetts by a husband or lover every 22 days.

Such numbers do not reflect the full extent of the problem of violence against women, much of which remains hidden. Yet rather than receiving recognition as a major world conflict, this violence is accepted as normal or even dismissed as an individual or cultural matter. Georgina Ashworth notes that:

> The greatest restriction of liberty, dignity and movement and at the same time, direct violation of the person is the threat and realization of violence. . . . However violence against the female sex, on a scale which far exceeds the list of Amnesty International victims, is tolerated publicly; indeed some acts of violation are not crimes in law, others are legitimized in custom or court opinion, and most are blamed on the victims themselves.

Violence against women is a touchstone that illustrates the limited concept of human rights and highlights the political nature of the abuse of women. As Lori Heise states: "This is not random violence. . . . [T]he risk factor is being female." Victims are chosen because of their gender. The message is domination: stay in your place or be afraid. Contrary to the argument that such violence is only personal or cultural, it is profoundly political. It results from the structural relationships of power, domination, and privilege between men and women in society. Violence against women is central to maintaining those political relations at home, at work, and in all public spheres.

Failure to see the oppression of women as political also results in the exclusion of sex discrimination and violence against women from the human rights agenda. Female subordination runs so deep that it is still viewed as inevitable or natural, rather than seen as a politically constructed reality maintained by patriarchal interests, ideology, and institutions. But I do not believe that male violation of women is inevitable or natural. Such a belief requires a narrow and pessimistic view of men. If violence and domination are understood as a politically constructed reality, it is possible to imagine deconstructing that system and building more just interactions between the sexes.

The physical territory of this political struggle over what constitutes women's human rights is women's bodies. The importance of control over women can be seen in the intensity of resistance to laws and social changes that put control of women's bodies in women's hands: reproductive rights, freedom of sexuality whether heterosexual or lesbian, laws that criminalize rape in marriage, etc. Denial of reproductive rights and homophobia are also political means of maintaining control over women and perpetuating sex roles and thus have human rights implications. The physical abuse of women is a reminder of this territorial domination and is sometimes accompanied by other forms of human rights abuse such as slavery (forced prostitution), sex-ual terrorism (rape), imprisonment (confinement to the home), and torture (systematic battery). Some cases are extreme, such as the women in Thailand who died in a brothel fire because they were chained to their beds. Most situations are more ordinary like denying women decent educations or jobs which leaves them prey to abusive marriages, exploitative work, and prostitution.

This raises once again the question of the state's responsibility for protecting women's human rights. Feminists have shown how the distinction between private and public abuse is a dichotomy often used to justify female subordination in the home. Governments regulate many matters in the family and individual spheres. For example, human rights activists pressure states to prevent slavery or racial discrimination and segregation even when these are conducted by nongovernmental forces in private or proclaimed as cultural traditions as they have been in both the southern United States and in South Africa. The real questions are: (1) who decides what are legitimate human rights; and (2) when should the state become involved and for what purposes. Riane Eisler argues that:

> the issue is what types of private acts are and are not protected by the right to privacy and/or the principle of family autonomy. Even more specifically, the issue is whether violations of human rights within the family such as genital mutilation, wife beating, and other forms of violence designed to maintain patriarchal control should be within the purview of human rights theory and action. . . . [T]he underlying problem for human rights theory, as for most

other fields of theory, is that the yard-stick that has been developed for defining and measuring human rights has been based on the male as the norm.

The human rights community must move beyond its male defined norms in order to respond to the brutal and systematic violation of women globally. This does not mean that every human rights group must alter the focus of its work. However it does require examining patriar-chal biases and acknowledging the rights of women as human rights. Governments must seek to end the politically and culturally con-structed war on women rather than continue to perpetuate it. Every state has the responsibility to inter-vene in the abuse of women's rights within its borders and to end its col-lusion with the forces that perpe-trate such violations in other countries.

TOWARD ACTION: PRACTICAL APPROACHES

The classification of human rights is more than just a semantics problem because it has practical policy conse-quences. Human rights are still con-sidered to be more important than women's rights. The distinction per-petuates the idea that the rights of women are of a lesser order than the "rights of man, " and, as Eisler de-scribes it, "serves to justify practices that do not accord women full and equal status." In the United Nations, the Human Rights Commission has more power to hear and investigate cases than the Commission on the Status of Women, more staff and budget, and better mechanisms for implementing its findings. Thus it makes a difference in what can be done if a case is deemed a violation of women's rights and not of human rights.

The determination of refugee status illustrates how the definition of hu-man rights affects people's lives. The Dutch Refugee Association, in its pio-neering efforts to convince other na-tions to recognize sexual persecution and violence against women as justifi-cations for granting refugee status, found that some European govern-ments would take sexual persecution into account as an aspect of other forms of political repression, but none would make it the grounds for refugee status per se. The implications of such a distinction are clear when examining a situation like that of the Bangladeshi women, who having been raped dur-ing the Pakistan–Bangladesh war, sub-sequently faced death at the hands of male relatives to preserve "family honor." Western powers professed out-rage but did not offer asylum to these victims of human rights abuse.

I have observed four basic ap-proaches to linking women's rights to human rights. These approaches are presented separately here in order to identify each more clearly. In prac-tice, these approaches often overlap, and while each raises questions about the others, I see them as com-plementary. These approaches can be applied to many issues, but I will il-lustrate them primarily in terms of how they address violence against women in order to show the implica-tions of their differences on a con-crete issue.

1. **Women's Rights as Political and Civil Rights.** Taking women's specific needs into consideration as part of the al-ready recognized "first generation" polit-

ical and civil liberties is the first approach. This involves both raising the visibility of women who suffer general human rights violations as well as calling attention to particular abuses women encounter because they are female. Thus, issues of violence against women are raised when they connect to other forms of violation such as the sexual torture of women political prisoners in South America. Groups like the Women's Task Force of Amnesty International have taken this approach in pushing for Amnesty to launch a campaign on behalf of women political prisoners which would address the sexual abuse and rape of women in custody, their lack of maternal care in detention, and the resulting human rights abuse of their children.

Documenting the problems of women refugees and developing responsive policies are other illustrations of this approach. Women and children make up more than 80 percent of those in refugee camps, yet few refugee policies are specifically shaped to meet the needs of these vulnerable populations who face considerable sexual abuse. For example, in one camp where men were allocated the community's rations, some gave food to women and their children in exchange for sex. Revealing this abuse led to new policies that allocated food directly to the women.

The political and civil rights approach is a useful starting point for many human rights groups; by considering women's experiences, these groups can expand their efforts in areas where they are already working. This approach also raises contradictions that reveal the limits of a narrow civil liberties view. One contradiction is to define rape as a human rights abuse only when it occurs in state custody but not on the streets or in the home. Another is to say that a violation of the right to free speech occurs when someone is jailed for defending gay rights, but not when someone is jailed or even tortured and killed for homosexuality. Thus while this approach of adding women and stirring them into existing first generation human rights categories is useful, it is not enough by itself.

2. **Women's Rights as Socioeconomic Rights.** The second approach includes the particular plight of women with regard to "second generation" human rights such as the rights to food, shelter, health care, and employment. This is an approach favored by those who see the dominant Western human rights tradition and international law as too individualistic and identify women's oppression as primarily economic.

This tendency has its origins among socialists and labor activists who have long argued that political human rights are meaningless to many without economic rights as well. It focuses on the primacy of the need to end women's economic subordination as the key to other issues including women's vulnerability to violence. This particular focus has led to work on issues like women's right to organize as workers and opposition to violence in the workplace, especially in situations like the free trade zones which have targeted women as cheap, nonorganized labor. Another focus of this approach has been highlighting the feminization of poverty or what might better be called the increasing impoverishment of females. Poverty has not become strictly female, but females now comprise a higher percentage of the poor.

Looking at women's rights in the context of socioeconomic development is another example of this approach. Third world peoples have called for an understanding of socioeconomic development as a human rights issue. Within this demand, some have sought to integrate women's rights into development and have examined women's specific needs in relation to areas like land ownership or access to credit. Among those working on women in development, there is growing interest in violence against women as both a health and development issue. If violence is seen as having negative consequences for social productivity, it may get more attention. This type of narrow economic measure, however, should not determine whether such violence is seen as a human rights concern. Violence as a development issue is linked to the need to understand development not just as an economic issue but also as a question of empowerment and human growth.

One of the limitations of this second approach has been its tendency to reduce women's needs to the economic sphere which implies that women's rights will follow automatically with third world development, which may involve socialism. This has not proven to be the case. Many working from this approach are no longer trying to add women into either the Western capitalist or socialist development models, but rather seek a transformative development process that links women's political, economic, and cultural empowerment.

3. **Women's Rights and the Law.** The creation of new legal mechanisms to counter sex discrimination characterizes the third approach to women's rights as human rights. These efforts seek to make existing legal and political institutions work for women and to expand the state's responsibility for the violation of women's human rights. National and local laws which address sex discrimination and violence against women are examples of this approach. These measures allow women to fight for their rights within the legal system. The primary international illustration is the Convention on the Elimination of All Forms of Discrimination Against Women.

The Convention has been described as "essentially an international bill of rights for women and a framework for women's participation in the development process ... [which] spells out internationally accepted principles and standards for achieving equality between women and men."

Adopted by the UN General Assembly in 1979, the Convention has been ratified or acceded to by 104 countries as of January 1990. In theory these countries are obligated to pursue policies in accordance with it and to report on their compliance to the Committee on the Elimination of Discrimination Against Women (CEDAW).

While the Convention addresses many issues of sex discrimination, one of its shortcomings is failure to directly address the question of violence against women. CEDAW passed a resolution at its eighth session in Vienna in 1989 expressing concern that this issue be on its agenda and instructing states to include in their periodic reports information about statistics, legislation, and support services in this area. The Commonwealth Secretariat in its manual on the reporting process for the Convention also interprets the issue of violence against women as "clearly fundamental to the spirit of the Convention," especially in Article 5 which calls for the modification of social and cultural patterns, sex roles, and stereotyping that are based on the idea of the inferiority or the superiority of either sex.

The Convention outlines a clear human rights agenda for women which, if accepted by governments, would mark an enormous step forward. It also carries the limitations of all such international documents in that there is little power to demand its implementation. Within the United Nations, it is not generally regarded as a convention with teeth, as illustrated by the difficulty that CEDAW has had in getting countries to report on compliance with its provisions. Further, it is still treated by governments and most non-governmental organizations as a document dealing with women's (read "secondary") rights, not human rights. Nevertheless, it is a useful statement of principles endorsed by the United Nations around which women can organize to achieve legal and political change in their regions.

4. Feminist Transformation of Human Rights. Transforming the human rights concept from a feminist perspective, so that it will take greater account of women's lives, is the fourth approach. This approach relates women's rights and human rights, looking first at the violations of women's lives and then asking how the human rights concept can change to be more responsive to women. For example, the GABRIELA women's coalition in the Philippines simply stated that "Women's Rights are Human Rights" in launching a campaign last year. As Ninotchka Rosca explained, coalition members saw that "human rights are not reducible to a question of legal and due process. . . . In the case of women, human rights are affected by the entire society's traditional perception of what is proper or not proper for women. Similarly, a panel at the 1990 International Women's Rights Action Watch conference asserted that "Violence Against Women is a Human Rights Issue." While work in the three previous approaches is often done from a feminist perspective, this last view is the most distinctly feminist with its woman-centered stance and its refusal to wait for permission from some authority to determine what is or is not a human rights issue.

This transformative approach can be taken toward any issue, but those working from this approach have tended to focus most on abuses that arise specifically out of gender, such as reproductive rights, female sexual slavery, violence against women, and "family crimes" like forced marriage, compulsory heterosexuality, and female mutilation. These are also the issues most often dismissed as not really human rights questions. This is therefore the most hotly contested area and requires that barriers be broken down between public and private, state and non-governmental responsibilities.

Those working to transform the human rights vision from this perspective can draw on the work of others who have expanded the understanding of human rights previously. For example, two decades ago there was no concept of "disappearances" as a human rights abuse. However, the women of the Plaza de Mayo in Argentina did not wait for an official declaration but stood up to demand state accountability for these crimes. In so doing, they helped to create a context for expanding the concept of responsibility for deaths at the hands of paramilitary or right-wing death squads which, even if not carried out by the state, were allowed by it to happen. Another example is the developing concept that civil rights violations include "hate crimes," violence that is racially motivated or directed against homosexuals, Jews or other minority groups. Many accept that states have an obligation to work to prevent such rights abuses, and getting violence against women seen as a hate crime is being pursued by some.

The practical applications of transforming the human rights concept from feminist perspectives need to be explored further. The danger in pursuing only this approach is the tendency to become isolated from and competitive with other human rights groups because they have been so reluctant to address gender violence and discrimination. Yet most women experience abuse on the grounds of sex, race, class, nation, age, sexual preference, and politics as interrelated, and little benefit comes from separating them as competing claims. The human rights community need not abandon other issues but should incorporate gender perspectives into them and see how these expand the terms of their work. By recognizing issues like violence against women as human rights concerns, human rights scholars and activists do not have to take these up as their primary tasks. However, they do have to stop gatekeeping and guarding their prerogative to determine what is considered a "legitimate" human rights issue.

As mentioned before, these four approaches are overlapping and many strategies for change involve elements of more than one. All of these approaches contain aspects of what is necessary to achieve women's rights. At a time when dualist ways of thinking and views of competing economic systems are in question, the creative task is to look for ways to connect these approaches and to see how we can go beyond exclusive views of what people need in their lives. In the words of an early feminist group, we need bread and roses, too. Women want food and liberty and the possibility of living lives of dignity free from domination and violence. In this struggle, the recognition of women's rights as human rights can play an important role.

Considerations/Critiques
of Women's Studies

Since the inception of Women's Studies in the late 1960s, the contributions of feminists to the academy have been varied and significant. Almost every field of study, the curriculum, institutional structures, and pedagogical practices have been influenced by attention to women and gender. Through this collection of readings, students have been invited to learn and assess the merits and flaws of a wide range of scholarship that falls under the rubric of Women's Studies. Despite the outpouring of work in this field, its worthiness, shape, fate, and future in the academy continue to be hotly debated. Women's Studies has its share of detractors and supporters, examples of which appear in this concluding section. Among the readings you will find careful considerations of the directions in which the field should be moving, assessments of the obstacles to its growth, celebrations of its potential, and searing critiques of its flaws. As you read these final pieces, think about how each author's opinion, assessment, or argument fits with the Women's Studies you have come to know through this text. Whose hopes or plans seem reasonable? Whose critique accurate?

Critical Thinking Questions

1. Name and explain the five "Games that Feminists Play," as described by Patai. How does your personal experience with Women's Studies compare?
2. Patai contends that "feminists today lack the power to impose their vision on society." Do you agree with this statement? What is your reasoning?
3. Stacey asks: "If feminists can no longer profess the primacy of gender as a category of analysis, does this leave us any disciplinary or discursive domain that we can claim to be distinctively feminist?" What is your response to this question?
4. How have the added considerations of race, class, and sexuality changed the landscape of Women's Studies? Is this a positive or negative change?
5. Do you think O'Barr's "master list for the millennium" provides constructive criticism for the future of feminism? How are her suggestions related

to the founding principles of Women's Studies? What differences do you see?

6. What suggestions do you have for the future of Women's Studies? What should be changed about the discipline and what is important to maintain? Are you hopeful or discouraged about the future of the field?

7. What do you think the reaction from academics and the general public would be if Men's Studies were added to the Women's Studies curriculum, as suggested by Brod? What consequences, both positive and negative, would this have on traditional academic feminism?

46

What's Wrong with Women's Studies

(1995)

Daphne Patai

Feminism, today, is the most utopian project around. That is, it demands the most radical and truly revolutionary transformation of society, and it is going on in an extraordinary variety of ways." Full of hope, energized by the rapid growth of women's studies programs in the United States (one of the great success stories—so it would seem—of second-wave feminism), I wrote that line in the early 1980s. It expressed the belief I then held that feminism's enormous reach made it the proper fulfillment of generations of utopian aspirations. At the time I had no experience with women's studies programs, but I had been writing about utopian fiction from a feminist perspective since my graduate school days in the early 1970s.

As a teacher, I initially saw no problem with the ubiquitous slogan, "Women's studies is the academic arm of feminism." In fact, I found it exhilarating and inspiring. But that was before I spent a dozen years involved with women's studies, nearly ten of those years with a joint appointment in women's studies and Spanish and Portuguese. Now that I am out of women's studies and can look back upon the experiences that made me want to sever my connections with it, I am shocked that I should have ever forgotten how routinely utopian dreams turn into dystopian nightmares, and that I should have failed to foresee how risky it is to institutionalize a politicized form of education in American universities. Sadly, I now realize, feminism is no different from other grand totalizing schemes that are far more problematic in the implementation than in the imagining.

In late 1994, with Noretta Koertge, a philosopher of science at Indiana University, Bloomington, I published a book titled *Professing Feminism: Cautionary Tales from the Strange World of Women's Studies*. This book details our critique of how badly awry feminism has gone in the academy. It was a painful book for us to contemplate, and we put off the writing of it

Patai, Daphne, "What's Wrong with Women's Studies?": Academe: *Bulletin of the American Association of University Professors*. July/August 1995 pp. 30–35. Reprinted by permission of the author.

for a long time. We first talked about such a project (tentatively titled "Ideological Policing in Contemporary Feminism") in the mid-1980s. But for years it remained just that, talk. Neither of us initially had the stomach to face up to the full consequences of the critique we found ourselves making to ourselves and to one another as we discovered that, coming from very different parts of the country and of academe, we had observed similar practices among feminists. But as we became increasingly sensitive to—and incensed by—the proliferating instances of intolerance, orthodoxy-sniffing, and general bad-mouthing of other women—as not-good-enough-feminists, or not-the-right-kind-of-feminists, or lacking the right credentials of race or class or sexual orientation—we decided that it was feminists themselves, not opponents of feminism, who needed to speak out about all this, and to do it now.

We knew, of course, that the book would cause us to be denounced as "enemies," especially by feminists in the academy—the very people we were hoping to reach. Susan Faludi's best-seller *Backlash* was providing a handy tag for dismissing any and every criticism of feminism, no matter how justified. But even before the vocabulary of "backlash" became current, we had observed feminist double standards at work: proclaiming the authority of *my* experience, while denouncing the authority of *yours*, asserting that *my* personal is political, while *yours* is delusional. The belligerent and intolerant self-promotion within contemporary feminism, allied to its anti-intellectualism, struck us as depressingly undifferent from traits we disliked in society at large, and

on reflection we came to see that feminism has behaved like other political movements and special interests. It pursues a the-worse-the-better strategy, making little of women's considerable progress in this country or even denying it altogether. It exaggerates to the point of absurdity the awfulness of men. And it indulges in "concept stretching" until terms such as rape or sexual harassment lose all definition and become mere signifiers of original patriarchal sin.

Judging from our own observations and from the stories Noretta and I heard from other disillusioned feminist faculty and students, we felt compelled to conclude that the propagandizing and scare tactics common in many women's studies classrooms have nothing to do with "education" in any meaningful academic sense. What students learn is that concept stretching, blame and accusation, self-righteous personal confrontations, so-called "political" criteria for deciding among different knowledge claims, and recrimination for "enemies" and pop-therapeutic group support for friends, are habits prized and flaunted in the name of feminism. What students do not often learn is that sound and unsound reasoning must be differentiated, and that methods exist, and can be taught, for doing so. Asking of a pair of propositions "Which is the more 'feminist of the two?" is not a good guide to that differentiation.

GAMES FEMINISTS PLAY

In an effort to make our case as vividly as possible, but also to keep our spirits up, my co-author and I presented the major excesses disfiguring many women's studies programs as a series of games. Games, of course, are utterly serious activities for those who play them. In women's studies, every game begins, naturally enough, with the very language in which the rules are laid down. WORDMAGIC—as we call women's studies' way with language—is always apt eventually to lead to the demand for censorship—which, if heeded, would make the United States the first democratic country to do voluntarily what until now only dictatorships have done effectively. But our main focus was on some of the more immediate threats to intellectual work now posed in the name of feminism. One of these is the game of TOTAL REJ—rejecting everything tainted by masculinism. TOTAL REJ is often justified as "throwing away the master's tools," which may sound lovely when first encountered. But it has become abundantly clear by now that this attitude leads to the cultivation of ignorance, resulting, for example, in student papers crediting contemporary feminist novelists with a born-yesterday originality that fragments time, space, and character, and (so students confidently assert) sets women's writing apart from the "linear" narratives of men.

GENDERAGENDA, another game, enables feminists who play it to reduce any and every question to gender alone, allowing them, for example, not only to criticize the traditional exclusion of women from science, but also to indict the scientific method itself as inherently masculine and thus inimical to women. As we contemplated the totalizing aspirations evident in these games, we were struck by the odd belief implicit in them that feminism itself would collapse if it were not able to formulate a critique of every single thing in the world.

TOTAL REJ also promotes the game of BIODENIAL, an extreme form of social constructionism often espoused in women's studies programs. Defenders are quick to retort that since there is still much essentialism in feminist thought today, the charge of BIODENIAL must be false. But, as we point out in *Professing Feminism*, women's studies seems to have little trouble opportunistically switching from one order of explanation to the other. I have repeatedly heard students argue that everything that might be criticized in women is due to social construction, while everything they admire is a mark of women's inherent nature. Men, of course, get the opposite treatment. And since logic can be dismissed handily as just one more male tool of oppression, the inconsistency need never be faced.

A good example of the confusions to which BIODENIAL leads students surfaced recently in an essay in which a student declared that she was a white, upper-middle-class, bisexual woman because she had chosen these identities at this moment in her life. I invited her to discuss with me the meaning of "social constructionism." She did not take me up on the offer, perhaps because she had already identified me as not a proper feminist teacher.

The most pernicious game of all, which has contributed most to the unpleasant atmosphere found in many feminist circles, is one we call IDPOL. This is a particularly apt abbreviation because it can stand for both "identity politics" and "ideological policing." A recent example from my own local scene illustrates how it works in these two ways. I live in Amherst, which is part of a very lively academic community that, within a ten-mile radius, comprises the University of Massachusetts and four private colleges: Amherst, Hampshire, Smith, and Mt. Holyoke. About a year ago, feminist faculty from all five campuses met to discuss the possibility of establishing a five-college graduate program in women's studies. The minutes of this meeting record the request, made by an African-American faculty member, "that the white women present answer the question of what [they] personally were doing to dismantle [the] racial privilege in [their] outlook, teaching, and research in women's studies." IDPOL thus serves some as a badge and bludgeon, and others as an occasion to feel guilt and shame. I have observed such tactics repeatedly over the years, and only rarely have I seen them challenged.

Some may say that my example is merely one more anecdote and has no general validity. And indeed that has been a main line of defense against the portrait of women's studies my co-author and I present. All over the country women are no doubt declaring that, in *their* programs, no such problems exist. It would, in fact, be of immense value to have a comprehensive empirical analysis of women's studies programs. But given many feminists' notorious disparagement of quantitative methods as "masculinist" (whenever it suits immediate feminist purposes), and in light of their hostility to serious discussion of problems in women's studies, few programs are likely to participate forthrightly in an appraisal of their activities and practices. Moreover,

such an appraisal would be worth little if a program's success or failure were measured by internal feminist criteria, for these are quite unlike the indices of evaluation adopted elsewhere in the university.

CRITICIZING THE CRITICS

In *Professing Feminism* we analyze some well-known writings produced by supporters of women's studies programs, writings that provide confirmation of the personal testimony we cite in our book. But this corroborating evidence from widely used feminist sources has been largely ignored by hostile commentators—foolishly so, for what these texts demonstrate is that the flaws criticized by us, and the virtues applauded by True Believers, are often the very same things.

A review of *Professing Feminism* underscored this point. The feminist scholar Carol Sternhell, writing in *The Women's Review of Book*, December 1994, noted the congruence between our book and another volume published at about the same time, which dismayed her even more than ours because of its heady celebration of a feminist pedagogy all but devoid of intellectual substance. Sternhell tried to distance herself from both books by assuring her readers that none of these things went on at her university and that her faith in women's studies continued. But what she noted is very revealing. It is that we, the critics, and the celebrants write about the very same phenomena, viewing them from different vantage points. Where many women's studies faculty see "politics" as what *should* be going on in institutions of higher learning, we see it as a danger to the process of learning itself. Where they see IDPOL as an appropriate atonement for past discrimination, we see it as the seed of ever more conflicts. Where they see the therapeutic and supposedly "safe" classroom as a high achievement of feminist pedagogy, we see it as a mark of a debased education.

We said all this in our book, but most critics seem not to have noticed. Nor have they commented on our discussion of women's studies' habit of carefully screening courses proposed for cross-listing, a habit prompted by the desire to ensure the ideological suitability of course contents and instructors. On this point, too, our arguments continue to receive up-to-the-minute confirmation: in a recent posting on the Women's Studies E-mail List (WMST-List), a professor took the familiar line that it is not enough for a course to be "on women"; it must also incorporate a feminist perspective. At her college, a course on the psychology of women was not cross-listed because its instructor said she was not a feminist. The same e-mail message also had troubling things to say about the limited roles men might safely be allowed to play in women's studies. Perhaps my co-author and I are among the few who find something wrong with all this. Indeed, as the evidence cited in our book and the recent WMST-List message make clear, there are feminist faculty who count such restrictions as a credit to their programs.

Another recent posting on the WMST-List nicely conveys the discomfort some feminists evidently feel in academe. In the course of a discussion of "intellectuals and elitism," a professor of philosophy saw fit to declare: "I have eliminated the term 'intellectual' from my vocabulary because it seems to me to suggest that some women are (not just different from others in a particular way but) superior to others." She went on to say, "To speak of intellectuals, I believe, tends to exclude and depreciate some women, to foster envy and competition, and to encourage conventional achievement within the mainstream." These sentiments make it hard to imagine how she could in good conscience keep her position at a university. In *Professing Feminism*, we commented on the problems created in women's studies programs by such efforts at "levelling," which display profound ignorance of the outcomes of some of the more damaging social and political experiments of the 20th century. Feminists, above all, if they are serious about what they say, should be aware of the experiences of reforms and reformers in the past. But their passion for TOTAL REJ helps them economize on their efforts to inform themselves.

Reviews of *Professing Feminism* have ranged from nasty attacks in *In These Times and Democratic Culture* to praise from feminist scholars such as Elizabeth Fox-Genovese and Joan Mandle (both of whom have served as directors of women's studies programs), who affirm that feminists need to deal with the issues the book raises. Of particular interest to me were the responses that appeared on the Internet, where a brief discussion of the book took place on the WMST-List. Here there was little engagement with our critique; instead, several objections to the book were reiterated: the book was published by a trade publisher rather than a university press—evidence, it was implied, of the authors having sold out and showing contempt for the feminist academic community; the book used personal testimony, i.e., a limited and allegedly biased sample (an interesting criticism, by the way, coming from feminists who, in other circumstances, place great store in the "authority of experience" and listening to women's own voices); the feminist excesses critiqued in the book may happen once in a while, but "not at my university" and even if these things do go on, Patai and Koertge shouldn't be airing them in public because doing so harms feminism.

We did, however, have a few defenders on the WMST-List, though their comments never seemed to elicit much of a reply initiate a "thread." One scientist wrote that her interviews with other women scientists confirmed our criticisms of feminist hostility to science and even to women scientists. Another wrote:

> The part of the book that I can vouch for is a persistent lack of tolerance in women's studies. I wouldn't generalize to say there's intolerance everywhere, but I haven't been to a women's studies function yet where there was not someone speaking for the group as though the group agreed on everything, or someone being criticized for daring to criticize another. Even on this list, there have been several times when views I agreed with were automatically labeled *backlash*, which has the tendency to stifle discussion.

In another comment, a professor wrote:

> My experience through much of my undergraduate and graduate work was that other self-proclaimed "feminists" were outright hostile to everyone. I, and others, felt that there was a private club where if you said the right thing and agreed and were liked, you could join, and if you said the wrong thing, you were ignored.... Sometimes I said the right things and was liked and accepted, other times I was not; either way it was a system I did not want to play in, so silently I avoided it. As a result, I also avoided the term feminist because I did not want to be associated with people I viewed as petty and closed-minded, even if we did share a view of how the world operated.

ASKING THE TOUGH QUESTIONS

But, some feminists will object, aren't these merely more reports of isolated incidents? To which I would reply with further questions: How many of these "incidents" need to take place before feminists begin to take them seriously? If they characterize only 25 percent of women's studies programs, is that too erable? Will 51 percent arouse something other than denial? If only one of our "games" predominates in a given classroom, is that an acceptable situation? And can feminists afford to keep denying and trivializing the problems instead of admitting and confronting them? Is the avoidance of women's studies by so many women on college faculties—not to mention the vast majority of women students—merely the result of "backlash?"

When feminist faculty who have devoted years to women's studies are sufficiently discouraged to want to take "inner flight" or move full-time to other departments (as I and some of the women we interviewed have done), when programs are in danger of collapse from internal dissension and more-feminist-than-thou bickering, when proper search procedures are subverted in the name of feminism, when criticisms of a candidate's scholarship invariably lead to reductionist attacks on the very notion of scholarship and scholarly achievement, when programs and individuals committed to maintaining high intellectual standards are denounced as "elitist" or "careerist" (and all these are practices I have witnessed repeatedly), we are clearly in trouble.

When feminist students hand in doctrinaire manifestos (as many feminist faculty report, although some seem to approve the practice) that repeat patently false or simple-minded assertions, utterly confident that they arise from fundamental feminist truths—when, for example, they insist that we live in a society in which women have no rights and are "forced" by men to conceive and bear children, when they affirm that nothing has really changed for the better in the last 100 or 200 or 300 years, when they announce that childbirth would be painless were it not for patriarchy and that infant mortality was low before "men medicalized childbirth" (and all these are assertions made in my classes by women's studies majors in the past few years)—it is clear that what these students have picked up from their mentors is not education but indoctrination. When they are quick to point out which oppressed group is underrepresented on their imperfectly feminist professor's syllabus, when they indulge in breast-beating over their own "white privilege" or in name-calling over the privilege they detect in others, when they readily believe the wildest statistics (doesn't

it say on the toilet stall right outside my classroom that one out of two women will be raped in her lifetime?) and show themselves incapable of establishing facts and exercising independent judgment on them, when any criticism of feminism is rejected out of hand as "backlash," how can I fail to conclude that feminism has lost its way? And that what is happening now in academe, which should have been one of feminism's most promising testing grounds, hardly gives cause for optimism?

When students with no knowledge of either geography or history parrot the current insistence on a "multicultural" perspective in their feminism while rarely learning a foreign language, when their curiosity about foreign cultures is satisfied by a course on "indigenous women in resistance," when to them Brazil and Bolivia are the same and they can't quite remember what country the inspiring "Third World" feminist autobiography they're reading comes from, when they're hostile to theory because it is "abstract" and not "political" enough, when they want their lives to be a seamless and coherent demonstration of their Proper Feminist Consciousness, when they know the answers without even hearing the questions, it is clear they have absorbed attitudes and learned phrases but have not developed the ability—because it is not demanded of them—to analyze what they think and say.

As my co-author and I wrote, we are convinced that all these things are happening because feminists have undertaken to turn the academy into a political staging ground. The facile retort that "education is always political" is a disingenuous response. Intended to shut down discussion, it tries to

What's Wrong with Women's Studies **523**

ward off the important questions: Political in what way? With what aims? Leading to what results? At what cost? Bearing what relationship to other historical efforts to use education for purposes of indoctrination?

Feminists should remember the categorical imperative and ought not to claim privileges in the university that they would in no way be willing to allow to other political groups. And because feminists have made so many mistakes, it is fatuous to argue that feminist politics alone deserve representation in academic forums and that it is feminists alone who possess The Truth.

Of course, feminists today largely lack the power to impose their vision on society (though in certain areas—such as extending discussion of sexual harassment down through the school system into the playground—they have been remarkably successful). But this should not lull us into complacence about the substance of that vision and the steps that some, in the name of feminism, are prepared to take to implement it. A feminism pious and narrow, scornful and smug, dismissiv of the past and derisive of those who dare to disagree—is this really a feminism with a future?

47

Is Academic Feminism an Oxymoron?

(2000)

Judith Stacey

academic: scholarly to the point of being unaware of the outside world. . . . Formalistic or conventional . . . Theoretical or speculative without a practical purpose or intention. Having no practical purpose or use.

feminism: Belief in the social, political and economic equality of the sexes. The movement organized around this belief.

Readers, please put away your books and take out a pen and paper. This is a pop quiz. Select from the following three statements about contemporary academic feminism the only one that was not written by a feminist:

1. "The institutionalization of women's studies at some visible colleges and universities has made scholars forget the founding tenets of women's studies as they slavishly attempt to recreate it in the image of the traditional disciplines."
2. "We should be yoking together Women's Studies, Ethnic Studies, Jewish Studies and Queer Studies under the rubric of Liberation Studies."
3. "Feminism is more threatening than Marxism, and therefore more resolutely repressed but ultimately all the more irrepressible than Marxism . . . "

The correct answer, paradoxically enough, is the laudatory view of feminist thought in the last statement. Michael Burawoy, a prominent Marxist sociologist, offered this affirmation of the enduringly radical promise of feminist sociology in his response to a retrospective assessment (Stacey and Thorne 1996) that Barrie Thorne and I provided of "The Missing Feminist Revolution in Sociology" (1985), an essay we had coauthored more than a decade earlier. Burawoy offered "no apologies for romanticizing feminism since my intention is to counter the jaded disquisition of Stacey and Thorne" (1996, 5). Compounding the paradox, in the same symposium, feminist theorist Dorothy Smith gently took us to task for erring in the opposite direction: she believed that we

Stacey, Judith, "Is Academic Feminism an Oxymoron?" SIGNS 25:4 (2000), pp. 1189–94. Used with permission of the University of Chicago Press.

had mistakenly indulged in feminist self congratulation despite the appalling conditions of political backlash, co-optation, and free market intellectual triumphalism that now confront feminist scholars. As the century and millennium turn, is the academic feminist glass half full or half empty? Half and half? All or none of the above? Opinions differ widely and fluctuate wildly, not only among diverse feminist scholars but within most of us internally as well.

The question that my title poses is intentionally provocative, of course, and somewhat Jesuitical. By literal dictionary standards, academic feminism is by definition oxymoronic. If an academic is someone "scholarly to the point of being unaware of the outside world" who pursues knowledge that is "theoretical or speculative without a practical purpose or intention" and produces work "having no practical purpose or use," such an intellectual should find herself categorically at odds with the fundamentally political character of the "F" word. Readers of this journal don't need to be reminded of the profoundly worldly origins and ambitions of academic feminism—this very wanted, nurtured child of the grassroots activism of the "second wave." Original subscribers to *Signs*, like me, probably stockpile memories of sit-ins, demonstrations, petition drives, and vigorous direct—action efforts through which we struggled to introduce women's studies courses, programs, faculty, and ideals into our universities. And yet I doubt that many readers will be shocked by the discouraged sentiments expressed in the first of the choice statements above or surprised to learn that they represent the views of Joan Catapano

and Marlie Wasserman, two feminist editors at major university presses who have been publishing our books for more than two decades.

However oxymoronic the concept may be in theory, in practice academic feminism has become a social fact. Few of us "women of a certain age" who have reaped a disproportionate share of the professional privileges and burdens of its remarkable growth can be strangers to recurrent angst-ridden exchanges in corridors, seminars, or kitchen table conferences over this uncomfortable theme. For what was once the subversive, intellectual arm of a thriving grassroots movement has been institutionalized and professionalized, while the movement that launched our enterprise is far less activist, confident, or popular. Today more than six hundred women's studies programs in the United States alone, some with departmental status, grant degrees at the bachelor's, master's, and even doctoral levels, and women's studies programs, courses, and projects continue to spread globally. Feminist professional associations, conferences, journals, presses, book series, prizes, fellowships, conferences, archives, institutes, list serves, foundations, and the like abound. Feminists occupy senior faculty and administrative positions, including endowed chairs for feminist scholarship, throughout most disciplines and professional schools, even at the nation's most elite universities. Indeed, numerous feminists actively participate in the global jet set of an academic commodity market whose excesses compete with those parodied in the novels of David Lodge (1975, 1985). Boasting our own celebrity system replete with agents, speaking tours, publicists, photo shoots, and even fanzines, many feminist scholars too often do produce works that are quite literally "academic"—that is, "theoretical or speculative without a practical purpose or intention"—as Catapano and Wasserman lament, composed in ungainly prose infused with gratuitous displays of arcane jargon. How sobering to note that academic feminist "sisterhood" has proven powerful enough to replicate many of the less endearing status hierarchies, anxieties, affectations, and schisms of "normal science."

Signs is not a dictionary, however, and neither this symposium nor my title invites such a literalist response to the question my title poses. Otherwise, I could end my essay on this depressingly affirmative; but unconstructive, note. Instead, I want to identify a few of the paradoxical challenges, both external and internal, to the future of feminism in the academy that our professional success has produced. The external threats are the most obvious and perhaps the most serious. Dorothy Smith is unequivocally correct that in "a surrounding climate becoming more deeply conservative and more deeply committed to sustaining the power of the wealthy over the people, it is difficult for the academy to sustain the independence on which feminist sociology [and feminist scholarship generally] has relied" (1996, 4). Like Smith, I too worry that "present technological and managerial transformations of the academy may subdue altogether the values of enlightenment and freedom in the academy which enabled feminism to struggle to the level of success" we have achieved (4). This clear and present danger threatens

the ultimate survival of academic feminism and other progressive knowledge projects, as well as most of the worldly dreams of the social movements that spawned them.

I lack space or spirit to rehearse here the ubiquitous consequences of these unfavorable winds-the chilling effects of university retrenchment and of the backlash against affirmative action and "political correctness," which include not only broad assaults on the humanities and on the tenure system itself, but also increasingly direct attacks on feminist scholarship and teaching. Particularly dispiriting to those of us old and confessional enough to admit that we once naively endorsed the slogan "sisterhood is powerful" is the fact that these days an almost unimaginable oxymoron spearheads many of these attacks—a highly vocal, articulate cadre of antifeminist academic "feminists" such as Christina Hoff Sommers, Jean Bethke Elshtain, Elizabeth Fox-Genovese, and Camille Paglia, to name but a few it should not surprise us therefore, that state and local legislators have begun to take direct aim at women's studies programs. The week I began to compose these reflections in February 1999, for example, I received an e-mail alert that some Arizona legislators were attempting to eliminate funding for women's studies programs at their state's public universities. Likewise, following the successful repeal of affirmative action admissions policies at the University of California, some conservative legislators began to challenge the educational legitimacy of women's studies and ethnic studies programs in my home state. While feminists can read such threats as testimonies to our success, they should also remind us that, however ambivalent we may feel about the oxymoronic character of academic feminism, by no means can we take for granted its institutional survival.

Moreover, two major intellectual developments internal to academic feminism also threaten its future as an autonomous enterprise. Paradoxically, the staggering transdisciplinary growth of feminist scholarship has propelled an increasing level of disciplinary specialization. It was not immodest for those of us who began to study and teach women's studies in the early 1970s to aspire to comprehensive, cross-disciplinary expertise in feminist theory and scholarship. The literature was so limited that reading across the disciplines was not daring; it was both feasible and necessary. We debated the pros and cons of building an autonomous new "discipline" that would draw from and transcend traditional boundaries of knowledge. However, one of the ironic by-products of the staggering proliferation of feminist scholarship has been a sharp decline in interdisciplinarity. In academia today, feminist typically functions as an adjectival modifier to the established disciplines. Few scholars can achieve comprehensive knowledge of the feminist literature even in their own disciplinary subfields, let alone indulge in the "dream of a common language" in which feminist scholars might write and speak fluently in an intellectual world without disciplinary borders.

Of course, potent political and intellectual developments have compelled most white, Western, heterosexual feminists to renounce universalistic longings for sisterhood, identity, and transparency, and in my view these pose the most challenging questions about the institutional future of academic feminism. Indeed, they threaten to pull the intellectual rug out from under the autonomous status of women's studies or gender studies programs. I now title my (doggedly interdisciplinary) graduate seminar in contemporary feminist theory "The Decentering of Gender in Feminist Theory: Different Differences and Significant Others." The seminar focuses on twin deconstructive challenges to universalistic theories of gender posed by critiques derived from identity politics and from the post-Enlightenment "theory revolution." Since the early 1980s, lesbians, feminists of color, postcolonial critics, and queer theorists, as well as postfeminists and antifeminist women, have exposed the ethnocentric conceits and consequences of the foundational categories of Western feminist thought—women, gender, and sex Meanwhile, post-Marxist critical theories have been relentlessly deconstructing the illusory grounding of all foundational categories. Consequently, feminist theory now proceeds from the premise that gender never operates uniformly or in isolation from race, nationality, sexuality, class, or any other powerful axis of identity and power. But this admirable principle presents a dilemma: if feminists can no longer profess the primacy of gender as a category of analysis, does this leave us any disciplinary or discursive domain that we can claim to be distinctively feminist? As my course description asks, "What constitutes feminist theory after gender has been radically decentered? Can there be a feminism without woman? Without women? Without illusions?"

These are not merely "academic" questions. Nettlesome, decidedly practical matters governing curriculum, departmental structure, and staffing hinge on our answers. How can we prevent feminist studies from condensing de facto into straight white feminist studies? Must (or rather, can) feminist scholarship always devote "equal time" to gender, race, class, sexuality, and other major categories of cultural difference and social domination? Consider just the question of selection criteria for required course readings: Does The Alchemy of Race and Rights (1991) by critical legal theorist Patricia Williams qualify as a specifically feminist work? What about The Epistemology of the Closet (1990), Eve Sedgwick's canonical contribution to queer theory, or Ghostly Matters (1997), a stunningly original contribution to cultural studies by Avery Gordon? Or Anne McClintock's postcolonial theory opus, Imperial Leather (1995)? None of these works makes gender the central category of analysis; all four have appeared on my recent feminist theory syllabi.

Analogously, how can or should we identify, recruit, and hire feminist faculty whose work does not center on women or gender? What institutional relationships should we promote between gender studies and academic programs in ethnic studies, gay and lesbian and queer studies, cultural studies, and their progressive kin? Is the feminist author of the second multiple-choice statement above correct that "we should be yoking together Women's Studies, Ethnic Studies, Jewish Studies and Queer Studies under the rubric of Liberation Studies"? If so, can we evade the snares of being identified as "grievance studies" by friends and foes alike, thereby intensifying the likelihood of debilitating ideological battles within and political assaults from without? And how could we protect our intellectual progeny from a traditional "unhappy marriage" that once again consigned feminist theory to a subordinate helpmeet status? These are but a few of the very real conundrums that academic feminists now confront in our institutions, classrooms, and scholarship.

If I go back to my dictionary, I must conclude that academic feminism is indeed an oxymoron, "a rhetorical figure in which incongruous or contradictory terms are combined, as in a deafening silence or a mournful optimist." Conceding this enables us to take justifiable pride in our collective accomplishments, even as we feel threatened by enemies without and fissures and ambivalence within. Mournful optimism seems a fitting sensibility to adopt as we observe the rituals of Y2K reflections. In that spirit, let us raise our half full, half empty glasses in a toast to the irrepressible ghosts of academic feminism—past, present, and future.

48

My Master List for the Millennium

(2000)

Jean F. O'Barr

Like many who will read this essay, I am a list maker. What do I plan to do and when do I need to do it? And every once in a while, I enter the major leagues and make a list of my lists. What have I committed myself to do and how will I prioritize those commitments? And, like some who will read this essay, I do not quarrel with using events such as the millennium to encourage reflection. I find such events an ideal time to make lists, for they focus me both backward and forward simultaneously.

My colleague Mary Armstrong, who read this essay in draft form, suggested that list making is indeed a feminist practice. Feminism, she observed, is constantly in the process of thinking of, and consistently and repeatedly fighting for the recognition of, its own history and the history of women. Feminism envisions the future with an ongoing consciousness. In short, the work of feminism is the work of always having the master lists in mind. The millennium may help us acknowledge the very special

consciousness we try to cultivate and maintain as feminists.

In rethinking my personal habit in light of her comments about our collective tendencies, I plunged ahead to compile a list of the commitments I believe feminism needs to pursue, with some notes on how to get going. And like all lists, some items will be scratched off over time and others will reappear under various headings for decades.

CHALLENGES THAT CONFOUND ME

1. Negotiating the many languages of feminism. Figure out how to talk to feminist colleagues in our own specialized and theoretical language at one moment and in the next moment discuss feminist issues with my campus and community colleagues in terms that are meaningful for them.
2. Pursue the tough research questions interdisciplinarily in a climate that pretends there are few if any left to pursue. Seek outlets to publish inter-

O'Barr, Jean F., "My Master List for the Millennium." SIGNS 25:4 (2000), pp. 1205–8. Used with permission of the University of Chicago Press.

disciplinary analyses and then build a curriculum vitae of works that meets the measure of senior colleagues who bring disciplinary judgments to bear in campus decision making.

3. Keep political commitments at the core of all these endeavors. When colleagues say that feminist scholarship is political, remember that theirs was too—at some point every discipline arose in response to a social problem. When colleagues resist a feminist proposal on political grounds (but never saying so), remember that according women and gender center stage always causes discomfort since it means a rearrangement of power. And when colleagues worry that feminists disagree, agree with them—healthy disagreement is a key marker of vigorous intellectual inquiry, so celebrate it.

4. Work with the folks who have more power and different politics. To achieve institutional compromise, to choose the battle that might be won at the moment (and, hopefully, will not backfire later), is to maintain the long view while surviving in the short run. Be around, and active, for the long haul.

5. Learn to talk to the next generations, whose experiences are different from my own. Repeat to myself that their issues show a difference on the surface but that underneath there is a substantial similarity. And remember not to tell them to be grateful for all that we have done.

6. Find the balance between arrogance and apathy (a Charlotte Bunch phrase) when it comes to women from backgrounds and cultures other than my own. Acknowledge that (a) they have many of the keys to understanding their own needs, (b) some of the strategies people like me have developed might aid their success, and (c) they have much to teach and we have much to learn in the exchange.

7. Turn jokes about women and feminism around, driving a point home but leaving out the egregious insults.

IDEAS ABOUT WHAT TO DO

1. Develop a complex agenda. Get out of the either-or mentality when thinking about what to do and go for the both-and strategy (although maybe not in the same day). Remember that, along with most women who have assumed multiple tasks and roles in family, work, and community, I am accomplished at doing several things at once.

2. Get space. Space of all kinds, so that we can come together across the lines that demarcate us now: campus space in offices, classrooms, hallways, parking lots, mailrooms, and toilets; community space where women from many locations find common ground; public space at national and regional conferences on disciplinary and topical issues; intellectual space at research conferences of our own that are genuinely interdisciplinary; organizational space in an association that speaks for feminists, with us, about us as a field of inquiry; space in print and on electronic media that spreads the ideas and options we are developing about women, gender, and feminism.

3. Foster coalitions. Individuals and groups always have agendas. Their agendas will not be identical to ours, but our agendas will overlap. Think about ways to come together at those intersections. This applies to community-campus interfaces, to the relationships between various theories in the academy, and to the myriad policy decisions in institutions of higher education. Note that coalition building will be helped by a multitask agenda and some spaces to pursue it.

4. Do not get stuck. Think of the feminist toolbox as having everything—

master's tools, new tools, and old tools that can be deployed for new purposes. Use the toolbox: spend energy on deciding which tools to use, not only on how to equip the toolbox. I will know what I need when I try using the tools that I have—then I can search out others.

5. Write, speak, think, argue, reinforce. Be conscious of our history and develop a sense of responsibility to communicate it. Do whatever it takes to leave a richer legacy than the one inherited. That includes leaving private papers to a library and telling children and younger friends what all this fuss about women has meant.

6. Change structures. (This is the hardest one.) Begin by changing women and the circumstances in which they sometimes find themselves and the ways many present themselves and are represented. Do not stop with changing people: get people to change structures. Remember: only when there is a shift in institutional patterns of power can people sustain the changes they have initiated.

7. Persist, persist, persist and then take a few days off. (No, this is the hardest one.) There is no way to battle sexism constantly and stay balanced. Feed the spirit and tend the body so that the mind can soar. Be passionate in commitment and use the power of that passion, knowing that the glass is better imagined as half full than as half empty.

49

Scholarly Studies of Men

The New Field is an Essential Complement to Women's Studies

(1990)

Harry Brod

In something of a turn of the tables, scholars in women's studies are having to decide what to do about a new field that is emerging in academe. The new kid asking to enter the club is "men's studies."

For some feminist scholars, the phenomenon seems either preposterous or dangerous, or more likely both. After all, the traditional curriculum that women's studies sought to reform was, in essence, men's studies. Other feminists, however, believe that the new field of men's studies is really a welcome extension of feminism's intellectual insights into hitherto male terrain. I believe that the field of men's studies is not only compatible with women's studies, but also an essential complement.

Men's studies begin by accepting as valid feminism's critique of traditional scholarship for its androcentric bias in generalizing from men to all human beings. The field adds the perspective that this bias not only excludes women and/or judges them to be deficient, but also ignores whatever may be specific to men *as men*, rather than as generic humans. The field also invokes feminist concepts that "gender" is not natural difference, but constructed power, to argue that the multiple forms of masculinities and femininities need to be reexamined.

The field of men's studies, for most of us anyway, thus is rooted in a feminist commitment to challenge existing concepts of gender. The debate within our still-nascent field over that commitment, however, has made some feminists skeptical about our entire enterprise. They see in the call for a new "gender studies" focused on both men and women the possibility that women's priorities and standpoints will again be subsumed and ignored under generic labels. Other feminists, though, find that the idea of a broadly conceived "gender studies," in which "gender" describes power and not just difference, does reflect the underlying conceptualization of their field. We

Brod, Harry, "Scholarly Studies of Men: The New Field Is An Essential Complement to Women's Studies." Chronicle of Higher Education (1990). Reprinted by permission of the author.

should recognize, however, that the meaning of terms is still in flux. At my own institution, for example, our current solution is to develop a program in "Women's and Gender Studies."

Feminists' legitimate fear of once again having women's discourse subordinated to men's should not blind us to the very real and much-needed intellectual project that the field of men's studies is undertaking. To simplify a more extended argument, I believe the field is an essential complement to women's studies because neither gender ultimately can be studied in isolation. Gender is, itself, a relational concept: Masculinities and femininities are not isolated "roles," but contested relationships.

But it does not follow from my argument for men's studies as an intellectual enterprise that the field must be established in any particular form in academic institutions. Such decisions should be made by women in women's studies. And any efforts to divert resources from women's studies to men's studies must be resisted; funds for the new men's studies must come from the old.

The new field has important implications for scholarship. For example, many explanations of the "gender gap" in political voting patterns have failed to see that it takes two to make a gap. Having noted the appearance of a "gap," social scientists have rushed to explain the changes in women that have produced it. Yet some of the evidence shows that the gap was produced more by a shift in men's than in women's political identification and voting patterns. By trying to understand the mutability and diversity of masculinities, men's studies avoid the pitfall of associating change only with

women while assuming male constancy—a sexist bias.

By pointedly taking up the question of power relations among men in addition to those between the sexes, the new field also allows for a more differentiated conception of patriarchy. For the power of the real and symbolic father is not simply that of male over female, but also that of heterosexual over homosexual, one generation over another, and other constellations of authority. The field forces us to ask, Why does society privilege some men over others, even as it gives all men power over women? Why do so many of our founding myths contain fathers willing to kill their sons—the violence committed and permitted by Abraham against Isaac, Laius against Oedipus, the Christian God the Father against Jesus?

Further, the field of men's studies is not simply calling for sensitivity to diversity, though it surely does that, but also tries to apply an understanding of difference gained from radical feminism to men, arguing that sexuality is as socially constructed as identity. The field therefore is also forging special links to gay studies.

Two current phenomena show the need for men's studies to transcend a white, middle-class origin and orientation: the large number of suicides among Vietnam-era veterans and the huge number of college-age black men in prison rather than in college. When we speak of men's issues, there really is more to consider than the existential anxieties of middle-aged, middle-class executives and fathers, popular media treatments notwithstanding.

A final example from my own experience highlights the way feminism has helped me to ask new questions about men. I have noticed in recent years that many of the female political activists I know have devoted increasing attention to women's issues, for example moving from the peace movement to the women's peace movement or from environmentalism to the fusion of ecological and feminist concerns called ecofeminism.

At first, I simply contrasted this to the conventional wisdom that people become more conservative, *i.e.*, more "mature," with age. But I also recalled that the women's movement has been said to differ from others precisely because its members tend to become more radical as they age; it took only brief reflection to identify the conventional dictum as a male norm. Accordingly, I then asked myself what it was about women's lives that made them different. As I was coming up with various plausible answers I suddenly caught myself. I realized that I was committing the usual error of looking only to women to explain difference. In fact, as I started to see, if one believes as I do that there is validity in various radical social critiques, then the women's pattern should be the norm, as life experiences increasingly validate early perceptions of biased treat-ment of certain groups. Thus the question should not be, "What happens to women to radicalize them?" but rather "What happens to men to deradicalize them?" That question, more for men's studies than for women's studies, can open up fruitful areas of inquiry.

Indeed, I believe that any strategy for fundamental feminist transformation requires a more informed understanding of men. By exposing and demystifying the culture of male dominance from the inside out, the field of men's studies offers both women and subordinated men the empowerment such knowledge brings.

By elucidating the many and varied prices of male power—the drawbacks and limitations of traditional roles—the field helps motivate men to make common cause with feminist struggles, though not, it must be said, on the basis of any simple cost-benefit analysis, since the price men pay still purchases more than it pays for.

The field of men's studies, then, emerges not as some counterweight or corrective to women's studies, but as the extension and radicalization of women's studies. For it is the adoption of thoroughly women-centered perspectives, taking women as norm rather than "other," that helps us ask new questions about men.